5

Annotated Teacher's

Grammar Connection

STRUCTURE THROUGH CONTENT

SERIES EDITORS

Marianne Celce-Murcia

M. E. Sokolik

Jill Ortman

HEINLE
CENGAGE Learning™

Australia • Canada • Mexico • Singapore • United Kingdom • United States

HEINLE
CENGAGE Learning™

Grammar Connection 5:
Structure Through Content
Annotated Teacher's Edition
Jill Ortman

Series Editors: Marianne Celce-Murcia,
M. E. Sokolik

Publisher: Sherrise Roehr

Acquisitions Editor, Academic ESL: Tom Jefferies

Senior Development Editor: Michael Ryall

Executive Assistant: Lauren Stephenson

Product Marketing Manager: Katie Kelley

Senior Content Project Manager:

Maryellen Eschmann-Killeen

Manufacturing Buyer: Betsy Donaghey

Production Project Manager: Chrystie Hopkins

Composition Services: Parkwood

Cover and Interior Design: Linda Beaupre

Cover Image: Cristiano Mascaro/SambaPhoto/
Getty Images

Library of Congress Control Number: 2008920430

ISBN 13: 978-1-4240-0222-1

ISBN 10: 1-4240-0222-2

Heinle
20 Channel Center Street
Boston, Massachusetts 02210
USA

Cengage Learning products are represented in Canada by Nelson Education, Ltd.

Visit Heinle online at **elt.heinle.com**

Visit our corporate website at **www.cengage.com**

Printed in the United States of America.
1 2 3 4 5 6 7 8 9 10 — 12 11 10 09 08

Contents

Using language grammatically and being able to communicate authentically are important goals for students. My grammar research suggests that students' mastery of grammar improves when they interpret and produce grammar in meaningful contexts at the discourse level. *Grammar Connection* connects learners to academic success, allowing them to reach their goals and master the grammar.

— Marianne Celce-Murcia

"Connections" is probably the most useful concept in any instructor's vocabulary. To help students connect what they are learning to the rest of their lives is the most important task I fulfill as an instructor. *Grammar Connection* lets instructors and students find those connections. The series connects grammar to reading, writing, and speaking. It also connects students with the ability to function academically, to use the Internet for interesting research, and to collaborate with others on projects and presentations. — M. E. Sokolik

Dear Instructor,

With experience in language teaching, teacher training, and research, we created *Grammar Connection* to be uniquely relevant for academically and professionally oriented courses and students. Every lesson in the series deals with academic content to help students become familiar with the language of college and the university and to feel more comfortable in all of their courses, not just English.

While academic content provides the context for this series, our goal is for the learner to go well beyond sentence-level exercises in order to use grammar as a resource for comprehending and producing academic discourse. Students move from shorter, more controlled exercises to longer, more self-directed, authentic ones. Taking a multi-skills approach, *Grammar Connection* includes essential grammar that students need to know at each level. Concise lessons allow instructors to use the material easily in any classroom situation.

We hope that you and your students find our approach to the teaching and learning of grammar for academic and professional purposes in *Grammar Connection* effective and innovative.

Marianne Celce-Murcia
Series Editor

M. E. Sokolik
Series Editor

Welcome to
Grammar Connection

■ What is *Grammar Connection?*

Grammar Connection is a five-level grammar series that integrates content with grammar instruction in an engaging format to prepare students for future academic and professional success.

■ What is the content?

The content in *Grammar Connection* is drawn from various academic disciplines: sociology, psychology, medical sciences, computer science, communications, biology, engineering, business, and the social sciences.

■ Why does *Grammar Connection* incorporate content into the lessons?

The content is used to provide high-interest contexts for exploring the grammar. The charts and exercises are contextualized with the content in each lesson. Learning content is not the focus of *Grammar Connection*—it sets the scene for learning grammar.

■ Is *Grammar Connection* "discourse-based"?

Yes. With *Grammar Connection,* learners go beyond sentence-level exercises in order to use grammar as a resource for comprehending and producing academic discourse. These discourses include conversations, narratives, and exposition.

■ Does *Grammar Connection* include communicative practice?

Yes. *Grammar Connection* takes a multi-skills approach. The series includes listening activities as well as texts for reading, and the production tasks elicit both spoken and written output via pair or group work tasks.

■ Why are the lessons shorter than in other books?

Concise lessons allow instructors to use the material easily in any classroom situation. For example, one part of a lesson could be covered in a 50-minute period, allowing instructors with shorter class times to feel a sense of completion. Alternatively, a single lesson could fit into a longer, multi-skills class period. For longer, grammar-focused classes, more than one lesson could be covered.

■ Does *Grammar Connection* include opportunities for students to review the grammar?

Yes. A Review section is included after every five lessons. These tests can also be used by instructors to measure student understanding of the grammar taught. In addition, there are practice exercises in the Workbook and on the website (elt.thomson.com/grammarconnection).

■ Does *Grammar Connection* assist students in learning new vocabulary?

Yes. The Content Vocabulary section in each lesson of *Grammar Connection* incorporates academic vocabulary building and journaling. In Book 1 this takes a picture dictionary approach. In later books words from the Academic Word List are used. This, along with the content focus, ensures that students expand their vocabulary along with their grammatical capability.

A **picture-based vocabulary** section in lower levels familiarizes students with the content-based academic vocabulary that is used in the lesson. At higher levels, students are introduced to words from the **Academic Word List**.

Thought-provoking **discussion questions** activate students' knowledge of the content area. The questions can also be used as **diagnostic tests** to assess students' mastery of the grammar before it is taught.

An integrated **audio program** allows students to listen to the content readings and dialogues.

Content readings and dialogues present the grammar in a meaningful and interesting way.

Grammar Connection is organized into thirty concise lessons, each containing two or three parts of connected grammar points. Every lesson follows a unique pedagogical approach.

The grammar in each lesson is **contextualized** with topics from different **academic disciplines**.

Contextualized grammar charts provide **easy-to-understand** clear explanations of grammar form as well as notes on usage.

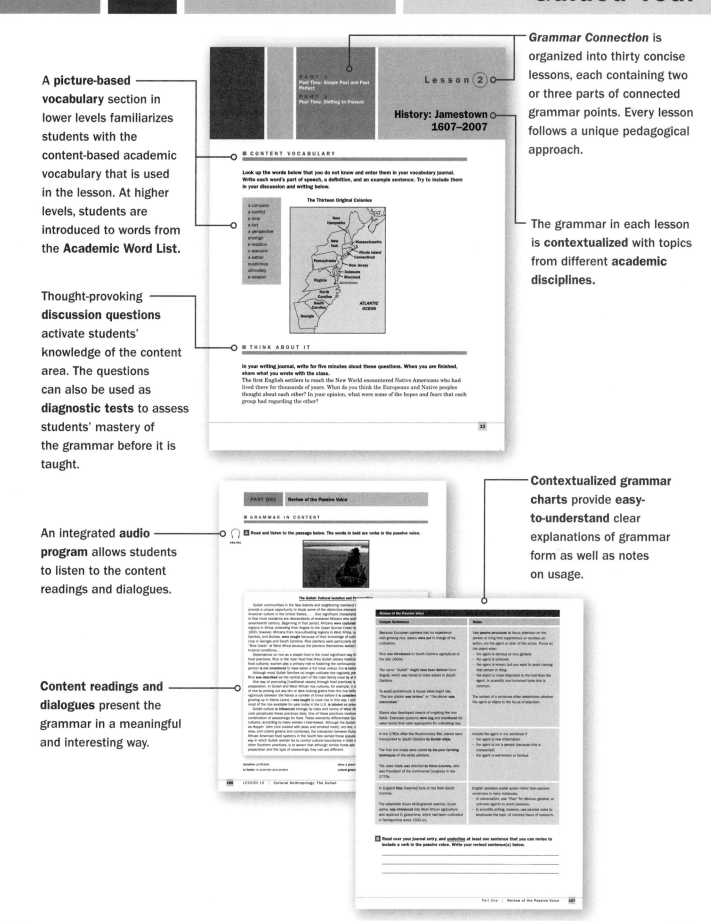

Students move from a **variety** of controlled exercises to more self-directed ones enabling students to become comfortable using the grammar.

B Change the sentences below to reported speech or thought, disregarding the source of the idea. Use the passive voice, begin each sentence with *It*, and choose the main verb according to the level of certainty of the information.

1. According to experts, animals in European cave art from the Paleolithic Age (32,000 to 11,000 years ago) may have lived in that area.

   It has been suggested that animals in European cave art lived in that area.

2. Researchers are fairly sure that the art also includes imaginary animals like unicorns.

3. There has been some discussion as to whether ambiguous symbols in the caves also represent animals.

4. According to one theory in the 1950s, the large number of paintings of horses and bison must have meant that these animals represented the duality of male and female.

5. According to anthropologists, the red pigment found in Paleolithic cave art has been found in art from the same period around the world.

6. According to one article, cave artists often redrew pictures on top of the old ones in order to guarantee that the animals returned the next year.

7. One researcher wondered if cave artists used red pigment in the paintings because it is aesthetically pleasing.

Guernica symbolizes the chaos and terror of the Spanish Civil War.

C Edit one of the sentences in each of the texts below, focusing on the information rather than the source of the information. Select main verbs that express the level of certainty of the information.

1. In addition to images, colors have various connotations. In all cultures people have words for at least three colors: black, white, and red. ~~The assumption of researchers is~~ Humans are thought to have ~~that all humans have~~ an emotional reaction to red since it is the color of blood. It may represent life, or as the color of sunrise and sunset it may connote the East or the West.

2. Images of imaginary or mythological creatures can be found in art throughout the world. Although a creature may be frightening to people in one culture, it may be very positive in another cultural context. For example, people interpret the bat as a sign of happiness in China whereas in the European tradition it is connected with darkness and black magic.

3. Groups of images and figures in some works of art may be allegories, or representations of abstract ideas. For instance, artists have often depicted "the four seasons" with four different flowers or other types of plants. Likewise, viewers realized that human or mythological figures represented the four seasons when they were shown doing seasonal tasks.

4. Pablo Picasso's black and white painting *Guernica* (1937) is a modern allegory protesting war. One can see that the work expresses Picasso's outrage at the Nazi's destruction of this Spanish town in 1937. As in a nightmare, the scene contains many images of panic and claustrophobia.

C Listen to each conversation, and then (circle) the letter of the correct interpretation.

CD2,TR4
1. a. Sam persuaded Kirk to photograph the team.
   b. Kirk persuaded Sam to be photographed.
2. a. The coach allowed Kirk to interview Jeff.
   b. Jeff was allowed to be interviewed.
3. a. Kirk encouraged Sam to help Jeff with his equipment.
   b. Kirk was encouraged to help Jeff.
4. a. The coach prompted Sam to introduce Jeff to the others.
   b. Sam was prompted to be introduced to Jeff.
5. a. Sam expected Kirk to pass him the first ball of the game.
   b. Sam was expected to pass Kirk the first ball of the game.
6. a. Sam doesn't permit Kirk to check his wheelchair.
   b. Sam isn't permitted to check Kirk's wheelchair.
7. a. Only the coach is authorized to load the wheelchairs in the van.
   b. The coach has authorized only one person to load the wheelchairs in the van.
8. a. This season the coach made Kirk captain of the team.
   b. Next season Sam will be made captain.

■ **COMMUNICATE**

D **GROUP WORK** What devices have been invented or refined to increase our mobility? Discuss the design, purpose, and benefits of these inventions. Use gerunds and infinitives with passive constructions whenever possible.

> Elevators **were invented** to help people get to the top of a high building.

> What about escalators? They **are used** for going up just one or two levels.

> Nowadays there are even moving sidewalks, especially at airports. They **might have been invented** for people who can't walk, but lots of people use them because they're tired or want to move more quickly.

Communicate sections allow students to speak or write about their thoughts and experiences.

At the end of each lesson, students are encouraged to put together the **grammar and vocabulary** from the lesson in a productive way.

Interesting projects allow students to put newly learned grammatical forms and vocabulary to use in ways that encourage additional independent reading, **research**, and/or communication. Many of these activities are group activities, further requiring students to put their language skills to work.

Internet activities encourage students to connect the grammar with online resources.

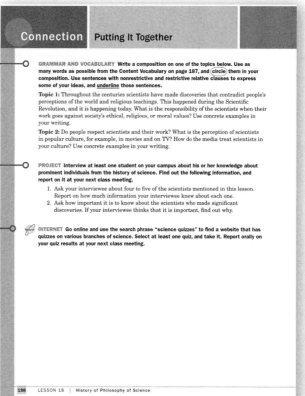

Connection   Putting It Together

GRAMMAR AND VOCABULARY Write a composition on one of the topics below. Use as many words as possible from the Content Vocabulary on page 187, and (circle) them in your composition. Use sentences with nonrestrictive and restrictive relative clauses to express some of your ideas, and underline those sentences.

Topic 1: Throughout the centuries scientists have made discoveries that contradict people's perceptions of the world and religious teachings. This happened during the Scientific Revolution, and it is happening today. What is the responsibility of the scientists when their work goes against society's ethical, religious, or moral values? Use concrete examples in your writing.

Topic 2: Do people respect scientists and their work? What is the perception of scientists in popular culture, for example, in movies and on TV? How do the media treat scientists in your culture? Use concrete examples in your writing.

PROJECT Interview at least one student on your campus about his or her knowledge about prominent individuals from the history of science. Find out the following information, and report on it at your next class meeting.

    1. Ask your interviewee about four to five of the scientists mentioned in this lesson. Report on how much information your interviewee knew about each one.

    2. Ask how important it is to know about the scientists who made significant discoveries. If your interviewee thinks that it is important, find out why.

INTERNET Go online and use the search phrase "science quizzes" to find a website that has quizzes on various branches of science. Select at least one quiz, and take it. Report orally on your quiz results at your next class meeting.

A **Review** section after every five lessons helps assess and reinforce language learning.

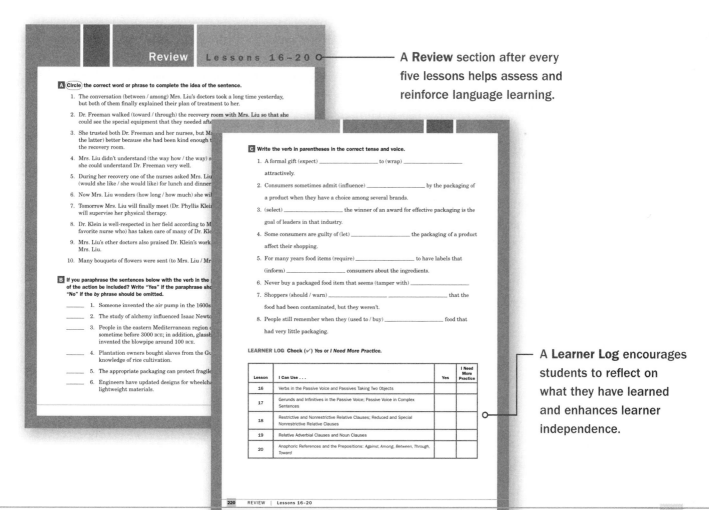

Review   Lessons 16–20

A (Circle) the correct word or phrase to complete the idea of the sentence.

    1. The conversation (between / among) Mrs. Liu's doctors took a long time yesterday, but both of them finally explained their plan of treatment to her.

    2. Dr. Freeman walked (toward / through) the recovery room with Mrs. Liu so that she could see the special equipment that they needed after

    3. She trusted both Dr. Freeman and her nurses, but M the latter) better because she had been kind enough t the recovery room.

    4. Mrs. Liu didn't understand (the way how / the way) s she could understand Dr. Freeman very well.

    5. During her recovery one of the nurses asked Mrs. Liu (would she like / she would like) for lunch and dinner

    6. Now Mrs. Liu wonders (how long / how much) she wil

    7. Tomorrow Mrs. Liu will finally meet (Dr. Phyllis Klein will supervise her physical therapy.

    8. Dr. Klein is well-respected in her field according to M favorite nurse who) has taken care of many of Dr. Kle

    9. Mrs. Liu's other doctors also praised Dr. Klein's work Mrs. Liu.

    10. Many bouquets of flowers were sent (to Mrs. Liu / Mr

B If you paraphrase the sentences below with the verb in the of the action be included? Write "Yes" if the paraphrase sho "No" if the by phrase should be omitted.

    _____ 1. Someone invented the air pump in the 1600s

    _____ 2. The study of alchemy influenced Isaac Newto

    _____ 3. People in the eastern Mediterranean region sometime before 3000 BCE; in addition, glassb invented the blowpipe around 100 BCE.

    _____ 4. Plantation owners bought slaves from the Gu knowledge of rice cultivation.

    _____ 5. The appropriate packaging can protect fragile

    _____ 6. Engineers have updated designs for wheelcha lightweight materials.

C Write the verb in parentheses in the correct tense and voice.

    1. A formal gift (expect) _____ to (wrap) _____ attractively.

    2. Consumers sometimes admit (influence) _____ by the packaging of a product when they have a choice among several brands.

    3. (select) _____ the winner of an award for effective packaging is the goal of leaders in that industry.

    4. Some consumers are guilty of (let) _____ the packaging of a product affect their shopping.

    5. For many years food items (require) _____ to have labels that (inform) _____ consumers about the ingredients.

    6. Never buy a packaged food item that seems (tamper with) _____

    7. Shoppers (should / warn) _____ _____ that the food had been contaminated, but they weren't.

    8. People still remember when they (used to / buy) _____ food that had very little packaging.

LEARNER LOG Check (✔) Yes or I Need More Practice.

Lesson	I Can Use . . .	Yes	I Need More Practice
16	Verbs in the Passive Voice and Passives Taking Two Objects		
17	Gerunds and Infinitives in the Passive Voice; Passive Voice in Complex Sentences		
18	Restrictive and Nonrestrictive Relative Clauses; Reduced and Special Nonrestrictive Relative Clauses		
19	Relative Adverbial Clauses and Noun Clauses		
20	Anaphoric References and the Prepositions: Against, Among, Between, Through, Toward		

A **Learner Log** encourages students to reflect on what they have learned and enhances learner independence.

Supplements

■ Audio Program

Audio CDs and Audio Tapes allow students to listen to every reading in the book to build listening skills and fluency.

■ Workbook

The Workbooks review and practice all the grammar points in the Student Book. In addition each workbook includes six Writing Tutorials and vocabulary expansion exercises.

■ Website

Features additional grammar practice activities, vocabulary test items, and other resources: elt.heinle.com/grammarconnection.

■ Annotated Teacher's Edition with Presentation Tool CD-ROM

Offers comprehensive lesson planning advice and teaching tips, as well as a full answer key. The Presentation Tool CD-ROM includes a PowerPoint presentation for selected lessons and includes all the grammar charts from the book.

■ Assessment CD-ROM with ExamView® Test Generator

The customizable generator features lesson, review, mid-term, and term-end assessment items to monitor student progress.

Grammar Connection is based on scientific research on the most effective means of teaching grammar to adult learners of English.

■ Discourse-based Grammar

Research by Celce-Murcia and Olshtain (2000) suggests that learners should go beyond sentence-level exercises in order to use grammar as a resource for comprehending and producing academic discourse. *Grammar Connection* lets students move from controlled exercises to more self-expressive and self-directed ones.

■ Communicative Grammar

Research shows that communicative exercises should complement traditional exercises (Comeau, 1987; Herschensohn, 1988). *Grammar Connection* balances effective controlled activities, such as fill-in-the-blanks, with meaningful interactive exercises.

■ Learner-centered Content

Van Duzer (1999) emphasizes that research on adult English language learners shows that "learners should read texts that meet their needs and are interesting." In *Grammar Connection* the content readings are carefully selected and adapted to be both high-interest and relevant to the needs of learners.

■ Vocabulary Development

A number of recent studies have shown the effectiveness of helping English language learners develop independent skills in vocabulary development (Nation, 1990, 2001; Nist & Simpson, 2001; Schmitt, 2000). In *Grammar Connection,* care has been taken to introduce useful academic vocabulary, based in part on Coxhead's (2000) work.

■ Using Background Knowledge

Because research shows that background knowledge facilitates comprehension (Eskey, 1997), each lesson of *Grammar Connection* opens with a "Think About It" section related to the lesson theme.

■ Student Interaction

Learning is enhanced when students work with each other to co-construct knowledge (Grennon-Brooks & Brooks, 1993; Sutherland & Bonwell, 1996). *Grammar Connection* includes many pair and group work exercises as well as interactive projects.

■ References

Celce-Murcia, M., & Olshtain, E. (2000). *Discourse and Context in Language Teaching.* New York: Cambridge University Press.

Comeau, R. Interactive Oral Grammar Exercises. In W. M. Rivers (Ed.), *Interactive Language Teaching* (57–69). Cambridge: Cambridge University Press, 1987.

Coxhead, A. (2000). "A New Academic Word List." *TESOL Quarterly,* **34** (2), **213–238.**

Eskey, D. (1997). "Models of Reading and the ESOL Student." *Focus on Basics 1 (B),* **9–11.**

Grennon Brooks, J., & Brooks, M. G. (1993). *In Search of Understanding: The Case for Constructivist Classrooms.* Alexandria, VA: Association for Supervision and Curriculum Development.

Herschensohn, J. (1988). "Linguistic Accuracy of Textbook Grammar." *Modern Language Journal 72(4),* **409–414.**

Nation, I. S. P. (2001). *Learning Vocabulary in Another Language.* New York: Cambridge University Press.

Nation, I. S. P. (1990). *Teaching and Learning Vocabulary.* Boston: Thomson Heinle.

Nist, S. L., & Simpson, M. L. (2001). *Developing Vocabulary for College Thinking.* Boston: Allyn & Bacon.

Schmitt, N. (2000). *Vocabulary in Language Teaching.* New York: Cambridge University Press.

Sutherland, T. E., & Bonwell, C. C. (Eds.). (1996). "Using Active Learning in College Classes: A Range of Options for Faculty." *New Directions for Teaching and Learning, Number 67,* **Fall 1996.** San Francisco, CA: Jossey-Bass Publishers.

VanDuzer, C. (1999). "Reading and the Adult Language Learner." *ERIC Digest.* Washington, D.C.: National Center for ESL Literacy Education.

Acknowledgments

Special thanks to my family, friends, and colleagues who made it possible for me to devote my time to writing this book in the aftermath of Hurricane Katrina.

— *Cathleen D. Cake*

The author, series editors, and publisher wish to thank the following people for their contributions:

Susan Alexandre
Trimble Technical High School
Fort Worth, TX

Joan Amore
Triton College
River Grove, IL

Cally Andriotis-Williams
Newcomers High School
Long Island City, NY

Ana Maria Cepero
Miami Dade College
Miami, FL

Jacqueline Cunningham
Harold Washington College
Chicago, IL

Kathleen Flynn
Glendale Community College
Glendale, CA

Sally Gearhart
Santa Rosa Junior College
Santa Rosa, CA

Janet Harclerode
Santa Monica College
Santa Monica, CA

Carolyn Ho
North Harris College
Houston, TX

Eugenia Krimmel
Lititz, PA

Dana Liebowitz
Palm Beach Central
  High School
Wellington, FL

Shirley Lundblade
Mt. San Antonio College
Walnut, CA

Craig Machado
Norwalk Community College
Norwalk, CT

Myo Myint
Mission College
Santa Clara, CA

Myra Redman
Miami Dade College
Miami, FL

Eric Rosenbaum
BEGIN Managed Programs
New York, NY

Marilyn Santos
Valencia Community College
Valencia, FL

Laura Sicola
University of Pennsylvania
Philadelphia, PA

Barbara Smith-Palinkas
University of South Florida
Tampa, FL

Kathy Sucher
Santa Monica College
Santa Monica, CA

Patricia Turner
San Diego City College
San Diego, CA

America Vasquez
Miami Dade College,
  Inter-American Campus
Miami, FL

Tracy von Mulaski
El Paso Community College
El Paso, TX

Jane Wang
Mt. San Antonio College
Walnut, CA

Lucy Watel
City College of Chicago -
  Harry S. Truman College
Chicago, IL

Donald Weasenforth
Collin County Community
  College
Plano, TX

Lesson 1

Business Administration: Developing a Business Plan

■ CONTENT VOCABULARY

Look up any words below that you do not know and enter them in your vocabulary journal. Write each word's part of speech, a definition, and an example sentence. Try to include them in your discussion and writing below.

bankrupt	an entrepreneur	initiative	to persevere	to undermine
a commitment	a franchise	innovative	to signal	to undertake
crucial	inadequate	a line of credit		

■ THINK ABOUT IT

More and more people are starting small businesses. What ideas do you have for starting a new business? What type of business appeals to you? Do you see yourself as an owner of a small business? Discuss your ideas with a classmate.

In your writing journal, write for five minutes about the questions below. When you are finished, share what you wrote with the class.
What kinds of small businesses are there in your community? Which ones succeed and which don't? What is the key to running a successful small business?

1

Lesson 1

Overview

1. Ask students to raise their hands if they are going to study business in college.
2. Call on a few individuals to tell the class what kind of business major they are interested in pursuing (for example, marketing, finance, consulting, and so on).

■ CONTENT VOCABULARY

Ask students to review the words in the box. Tell them to look up any unfamiliar words.

■ VOCABULARY JOURNAL

Have students add new words to their vocabulary journals and write down the parts of speech, definitions, and example sentences for each.

■ THINK ABOUT IT

1. Read the instructions with the class.
2. Divide the class into pairs. Have students discuss the questions posed in the activity.
3. Give students five minutes to write in their journals.

■ CONTENT NOTES

The topic of this lesson is Business Administration: Developing a Business Plan. Students will learn about some basic strategies for opening a business and applying for loans. Use this opportunity to remind students that they can visit the campus career center to find information about jobs and internships.

PART ONE

Present Time: Contrasting Present and Past

■ GRAMMAR IN CONTENT

■ EXERCISE A 🎧 CD 1, Track 1

1. Ask students to look at the picture and read the title.
2. Call on a volunteer to describe the picture.
3. Write *business plan* on the board and elicit a definition from a class member if possible.
4. Play the audio and have students follow along in their books as they listen. Ask students to circle any words or phrases that they don't understand.
5. Call on students to read any words or phrases they circled. Elicit definitions for them from the class if possible.
6. Ask a few comprehension questions, such as: *What are some of the reasons that businesses close? What are some of the benefits of having a well-prepared business plan? Give a few of the reasons that Pat Newton's business has been successful. What percent of small business in the United States fail within four years?*

■ GRAMMAR IN CONTENT

🎧 **A** Read and listen to the passage below. The words in bold in the text are present perfect verb forms.

CD1,TR1

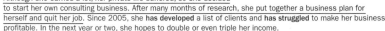

Plan Your Work—And Then Work Your Plan!

Every year, thousands of Americans decide to go into business for themselves. Every year, thousands of small firms go out of business. Why? The reasons range from too much debt to too much stress. How do some entrepreneurs persevere and become successful? According to many business experts, the answer lies with a business plan.

Experts see the business plan as a crucial tool. On the basis of a well-prepared plan, an entrepreneur can convince a bank or other source of investment funds that he or she is the right person to undertake the hard work of starting up a new business. Also, the plan provides the prospective owner with a road map for assembling the key pieces of the business, including financing, personnel, and marketing.

Take Pat Newton, for example. She **has joined** more than 10 million women who run their own businesses in the United States. Until 2004, she worked for a large corporation in the wireless technology sector. Although she earned a lot, her private life suffered, so she decided to start her own consulting business. After many months of research, she put together a business plan for herself and quit her job. Since 2005, she **has developed** a list of clients and **has struggled** to make her business profitable. In the next year or two, she hopes to double or even triple her income.

Pat Newton's business plan **has played** an important part in her growing success. First, she has a clear idea of her business service since she **has worked** in the field for many years. Naturally, she **has had** business dealings with her competition, so she knows their strengths and weaknesses as well as her own. As a result, she **has found** a special niche for herself within the wireless industry. Second, as a self-employed person, she depends completely on her own skills and talents. She **has been** able to get advice and some financial assistance based on her track record with her previous employer. Third, her target market is essentially the same as the market she served before she quit her former job. Her previous clients **have continued** to give her projects or **have referred** her to potential clients in the field.

Will Pat Newton still be in business four years from now? According to statistics from the U.S. Small Business Administration, more than 50% of new small businesses fail within that amount of time. If Pat is going to be successful, she will need to pursue her dream with passion and persistence. Not everyone is willing to take such risks. Only those who thoroughly analyze their product or service, their management team, their target market, and their financial resources stand a fighting chance.

a niche: a special area or division of a market for a particular product or service

a track record: a record of successes or accomplishments

a target market: a specific market or group of consumers for a product

persistence: pursuing a goal in spite of difficulties and disappointments

a fighting chance: a possibility of succeeding

■ EXPANSION IDEA

Exercise A

Divide the class into small groups. Have students discuss the first steps that they would take when making a business plan. Ask them to consider the product, how they would finance their project, their location, and how many employees they would want to hire.

Sample Sentences	Notes
Experts **recommend** a detailed business plan for new business owners. Many promising small businesses **have gone** bankrupt as a result of poor planning. The owners of such firms **have believed** in their own effort, but **have not anticipated** unexpected circumstances that can seriously undermine a new business.	Use the **simple present** and the **present perfect** to express an idea or an action that has relevance in the present.
The U.S. Small Business Administration **has encouraged** an increase in the number of small businesses for years. It **offers** special loans at lower interest rates. Experts from this office also **advise** potential owners on strategies for growth.	Use the **present perfect** to express a time contrast within the present time. This choice of tense signals that the action or idea is still important to you or to the current situation. In the sample sentence, the **present perfect** introduces the topic, and the **present** gives more detailed information about that topic.
Mr. Peters: Advertising costs a lot at the beginning. You need to contact the bank for a line of credit to cover your advertising costs. **Have you had** any experience with that? Ms. Owens: **I've taken** out loans before but **I've never applied** for a line of credit. How does it work?	Use the present perfect in conversational questions. It "softens" the impact of personal questions while emphasizing the relevance of the topic to the present time. The answers to such questions are usually in the present perfect as well.
A business plan that includes a home office benefits stay-at-home mothers. **A few decades ago**, such a plan was quite unusual. **Now**, however, many people have realized the advantages of working from their homes.	Use an **explicit time expression** to signal a change from the present to past completed actions that are not relevant to the present situation. Also, use an explicit time expression to signal a switch from past time to present time.

B Read the text on page 2 again, and <u>underline</u> sentences in the past tense. (Circle) the time expressions that signal a change from the present to the past time. Then, compare your answers with a partner's.

1. Write on the board *We know that many women have opened their own businesses.* Ask students to identify the verb forms used in this sentence.
2. Call on students to read the sample paragraphs and dialog.
3. Have students go over the Notes. Answer any questions that they have about when to use each of the two verb forms.

■ **EXERCISE B**

Have students complete the exercise and then check their work with a partner.

■ **EXPANSION IDEA**

Grammar

1. Divide the class into pairs and have them expand the conversation between Mr. Peters and Ms. Owens.
2. Have students practice role-playing their dialogs.
3. Call on a few pairs of volunteers to role-play their dialogs for the class. For example:

Student 1: *I can help you with that. You need to get all of your financial information together and we can go online to see what is available.*

Student 2: *I'm afraid of getting too far into debt. Can I get by with just a small personal loan?*

■ EXERCISE C

1. Ask students to read the instructions.
2. Call on a student to read the example aloud.
3. Ask students to complete the activity.

■ EXERCISE D

1. Ask students to raise their hands if they have ever prepared a résumé. Have them tell the class what they included in their résumés.
2. Have students read the instructions.
3. Call on a student to read the first sentences of the business plan. If this activity is too challenging for your class, have students work in pairs.

C Using the present perfect, write five sentences about past experiences that have been relevant to your success in a job or business. If you do not have such work experience, write about another person you know. Answers will vary.

1. *I have always been good in math, so I've done well in my summer jobs as a cashier.*
2. Sandra has seen a lot of success in retail.
3. We've had a lot of opportunities to expand.
4. I have always suggested business school to others.
5. They've used networking as a valuable tool.
6. Gill has always carefully evaluated his assets.

D Jim Kerr plans to start a smoothie franchise next year. (Note: A smoothie is a cold beverage made of different ingredients mixed in a blender.) Read Jim's résumé, and then, in the space provided, write the section of his business plan that describes his management and work experience. Share your first draft with a partner, then work together to create a final version.

Education
| 1998 | B.A., University of Arizona, Majors: Political Science, Spanish |
| 2005– | Student, Evening M.B.A. Program, Arizona State University |

Work Experience
2006–	Assistant Director, Marketing Dept., Ideal Printing Company, Tempe, AZ
2001–06	Project Coordinator, Marketing Dept., Ideal Printing Company, Tempe, AZ
2000–04	Evening Manager, Stop-N-Go Convenience Store, Tempe, AZ
1998–2001	Assistant Manager, Barnes & Noble Books, Tempe, AZ
1995–98	Part-time Manager, Coffee Stop, University of Arizona

Volunteer Experience
| 1996–98 | tutored children of Spanish-speaking migrant workers |

I have gained the pertinent education and supervisory experience needed to manage my own Slush-E-Treat franchise in Tempe. My first management position began back in 1995 when I was part-time manager at the Coffee Stop at U of A. I gained more experience later as the Assistant Manager of Barnes & Noble in Tempe, AZ. Since 2001, I've been working at the Ideal Printing Co., first as a Marketing Project Coordinator then, starting in 2006 as the Assistant Director of the Marketing Dept.

■ EXPANSION IDEA

Exercise D

1. Ask students to write their own résumés. Have the students model their résumés on the one in Exercise D.

2. Divide the class into pairs and have students help each other strengthen their résumés.

E Read each conversation below, and <u>underline</u> the verbs that show time changes. Then, look at the verbs you underlined and select the reason for the time change from the choices below. Follow the examples.

A = a time contrast within the present time. The action is still relevant.
B = a time contrast. The action is no longer relevant to the present time.
C = the introduction of a different topic relevant to the present time.
D = a question to confirm that the listener is following the conversation.

1.   **Jim:**   Thanks for meeting with me. I appreciate your time.

    Loan Officer: No problem. I have your loan application papers right here. <u>Have</u>

                   you <u>applied</u> for a business loan with our bank before? | A |

         Jim: No, I've only had a car loan. I <u>paid</u> that off about 2 years ago. | B |

    Loan Officer: I see that in your records. How about a line of credit?

         Jim: I don't think so. I don't own a house and <u>have</u> always <u>worked</u> for

                   someone else. I've never needed a large amount of money. | A |

2.   **Jim:**   I need to decide on the site for my business. What do you think of

                   the building down on Fifth Street?

         Rita: It's OK, but the neighborhood isn't too great. I like the one over on

                   Howard Street better. <u>Have</u> you <u>seen</u> that one? | A |

         Jim: No, I haven't.

3.   **Jim:**   Ms. Roberts, I'd like to make an appointment to see the shop on

                   Howard Street. I <u>drove</u> by it yesterday, and I want to take a closer

                   look. | B |

    Ms. Roberts: What time is convenient for you? I <u>haven't made</u> any other

                   appointments for tomorrow, so I'm flexible. | A |

         Jim: Let's say 10 o'clock tomorrow morning.

    Ms. Roberts: Sounds good. The owner is eager to rent. He <u>hasn't had</u> a tenant in

                   there for over a year. | A |

         Jim: At this point I have to wait until the bank approves my loan.

                   I <u>haven't heard</u> from them in a few weeks, but I guess that

                   everything is OK. | A |

■ **EXERCISE E**

1. Ask students to read the instructions and the time change choices. Ask volunteers to give an example of each of the types of time changes.
2. Call on two students to read the example (number one).
3. Answer any questions that students have about the exercise.
4. Have students complete the activity and then check their answers with a partner.
5. Go over the answers together. If necessary, review the Grammar Chart again.

■ **EXPANSION IDEA**

Exercise E
1. Divide the class into pairs and have them practice role-playing the three dialogs.
2. Ask students to discuss the steps that Jim is taking in order to start his business. Ask them to think about what he will have to do next.
3. Have students talk about the steps needed to open a new business in their home countries.

1. Ask students to read the instructions.
2. Call on students to read the questionnaire.
3. Have students complete the questionnaire and then write their sentences.
4. Divide the class into pairs and have them discuss their answers.
5. Call on volunteers to read their answers to the class.

F Respond to the questionnaire below, (circling) "Yes" or "No" to show which traits apply to you. Then, elaborate on each response, writing one or two sentences. Use the past, present, and present perfect in your responses. When you are finished, share your examples with classmates.   Answers will vary.

Are you a budding entrepreneur?
How many personality traits do you share with successful business owners?

Yes	No	possessing a strong desire to achieve
Yes	No	creativity
Yes	No	having strong personal initiative
Yes	No	having a demanding nature
Yes	No	adaptability
Yes	No	trustworthiness

1. *I have always had a strong desire to achieve. I've always tried my best, and I usually reach the goals I set for myself.*

OR: *I have never cared if my work was perfect. I'm satisfied with a passing grade.*

2. I have never been creative artistically, but I like to think of new ways to do things.

3. I haven't taken much initiative in my studies but I put a lot of energy in sports.

4. I have always expected a lot of myself, but I haven't demanded much of my friends.

5. I haven't had much opportunity to find out if I'm adaptable.

6. I have always been trustworthy and honest.

■ **EXPANSION IDEA**

Exercise F

1. Have students use their sentences from Exercise F to write a cover letter for their resumes.
2. Have students exchange work with a partner. Ask them to correct errors and help each other strengthen their letters.

Example:
I am anxious to pursue a career in business. I am a creative person who has a strong desire to achieve.

G **PAIR WORK** Look at the pie chart below. Explain the data to your partner. Use the past, present, and present perfect as appropriate.

**Ownership of Companies
by Race and Ethnicity**

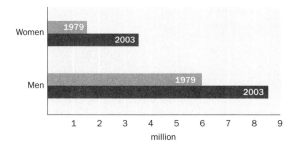

5% African American
7% Hispanic
5% Asian American
1% American Indian/
Alaska Native
87%
White

According to the pie chart, Asian Americans and African Americans own the same percentage of small businesses.

Self–Employment by Gender, 1979–2003

Women
1979
2003

Men
1979
2003

1 2 3 4 5 6 7 8 9
million

H **PAIR WORK** With a partner, discuss how graduates from your college or university get jobs. As you discuss the system, ask your partner some questions to be sure that he or she understands what you're saying.

We usually register with an employment agency that specializes in jobs for recent graduates. **Have you heard** of this kind of agency?

Yes, I have. We've got the same kind of agencies at my school, too.

■ **COMMUNICATE**

■ **EXERCISE G**

1. Go over the instructions. Have students look at the two charts and answer any questions that they have about them.
2. Divide the class into pairs. Have students discuss the charts.
3. Circulate as students work, assisting as needed and encouraging students to use all three tenses as appropriate.

■ **EXERCISE H**

1. Ask students to read the instructions.
2. Call on a pair of volunteers to read the text in the speech balloons.
3. Divide the class into new pairs and have students discuss how university graduates get jobs.
4. Remind them to use all three tenses as appropriate.

■ **EXPANSION IDEA**

Exercise H
Have students write a brief essay about how graduates in their partners' countries get jobs.

■ GRAMMAR IN CONTENT

■ EXERCISE A

Have students complete the exercise and then check their work with a partner.

■ GRAMMAR CHART
Future

1. Call on volunteers to talk about the future. As they speak, write *will* and *going to* on the board.
2. Call on students to read the sample sentences aloud.
3. Ask the class which sentence sounds more formal.

■ EXERCISE B

1. Go over the instructions with the class.
2. Ask students to identify any unfamiliar terms in the box, eliciting definitions from other class members, if possible.
3. Call on a student to read the example.
4. Give students time to complete the activity.
5. Have students check their work with a partner.
6. Call on volunteers to read their answers to the class.

■ GRAMMAR IN CONTENT

A Reread the text at the beginning of this lesson, and put an "X" by every sentence that expresses future time. Which verb form(s) signal the future?

Future	
Sample Sentences	**Notes**
Mr. Lewis has almost completed his marketing program and **is going to meet** with his advisor next week. Once the advisor gives his approval, Lewis **will present** the plan to his investors.	Use an **explicit time expression** to signal a change from the present time to the future.
According to the latest issue of *Business Quarterly*, the website MySpace has experienced double-digit growth since January and **will continue** at this rate well into the next quarter.	Use *will* in more formal contexts.

B Select seven characteristics of successful entrepreneurs from the box below. For each characteristic, write 2–3 connected sentences explaining why that characteristic is important for the success of a small business. Answers will vary. Sample answers below.

persistence	curiosity	~~high energy level~~
self-confidence	vision	reliability
tolerance for failure	problem-solving skills	independence
commitment	competitiveness	innovation

1. Small business owners need a high energy level because they will handle all of the problems and complaints in their businesses as well as the daily routine. They will have to work from morning to night and maybe on the weekends, too.

2. They need to be self-confident since they will have to convince someone to give them financial help. They will also need to convince customers that their products are worth buying.

3. They should have vision. They will have to write a business plan that describes how the business will grow.

4. They should be competitive because they will have to attract customers away from other businesses. One way business owners can be competitive is by offering unique, contemporary goods. If they are competitive, they will earn more customers.

■ EXPANSION IDEA

Exercise B
Divide the class into pairs. Have students role-play two entrepreneurs who are going to start their own small businesses. Ask them to use the future tense to talk about what they are going to/will do to get started.

5. Their tolerance for failure must be high. The first years will be very hard and maybe

disappointing for them.

6. Problem-solving skills are a priority because they will not anticipate everything that will face them as they begin their businesses. They should also hire employees that have good problem-solving skills so that those employees can address problems that arise in the store when the owner is not present.

7. If they aren't innovative, they will never attract customers. Business owners need to be innovative so that customers remember the store and its products and can recommend both to other shoppers.

8. They will need persistence because success is unlikely to come right away. Persistence is important because it can take a business a few years before it breaks even or makes a profit.

CD1,TR2

C Read while you listen to Jim Kerr's conversation with Helen, a new part-time employee at the Slush-E-Treat shop. Jim needs to plan Helen's training at his shop, so he has to find out her job skills. In the chart on the next page, take notes on Helen's skills.

Jim:	OK, Helen, we need to figure out your training plan. I'm going to give the information to Sara and she'll actually do the training in the next few days.
Helen:	OK.
Jim:	I remember from your interview that you used a cash register in your last job. How often did you ring up sales?
Helen:	Not very often—only when the other salespeople were on lunch break.
Jim:	You know that you will have to do it all the time for us, right?
Helen:	No problem.
Jim:	How about processing credit card payments?
Helen:	Not many customers paid by credit card, and I never had to do that. They showed me how, but I never practiced.
Jim:	OK, then Sara will work with you on that. Another important part of the job here is making sure that the customers have a positive impression, not just a good Slush-E-Treat. Whether they call or come into the store, I want each person to receive great service.
Helen:	I think that I'm pretty good at that. I love to talk on the phone, so that part's no problem.
Jim:	As long as you don't talk on the phone too much!
Helen:	Don't worry. You know, I think I'm pretty good at talking with customers. My previous boss always complimented me. All of my friends say that I'm easy to talk to. I think that I can handle it.
Jim:	But what about people who complain? How do you handle those customers?
Helen:	I don't. I just call the manager, or I ask one of the other workers.
Jim:	Around here, you might be alone sometimes. I don't want you to ask other people to handle your problems. I want to be sure that you know what to say. OK, last thing—the equipment. I don't expect you to know how to operate the machines now, but I need to know how comfortable you are with equipment like this.
Helen:	As far as I can see, they don't look too complicated. If Sara shows me, I'll take notes on how to do it.
Jim:	Sounds good. I'll have Sara contact you after we decide on the training schedule.
Helen:	Thank you.

■ **EXERCISE C** CD 1, Track 2

1. Read the instructions with the class. Ask them to look at the chart on page 10, where they should take notes on Helen's skills.
2. Play the audio and have students listen and follow along in their books.
3. Play the audio again and have students take notes on the chart.

■ **EXPANSION IDEA**

Exercise C
Divide the class into pairs. Tell students that they will create a dialog in which one of them will role-play Jim and the other will role-play the part of Jim's partner. They should discuss Helen's strengths and weaknesses and what they will need to teach her to do. Have each group act out their dialog for the class.

■ EXERCISE D

1. Go over the instructions with the class.
2. Call on a student to read the example.
3. Have students write their memos, modeling them on the format of the example.

Skills	OK → Good	Inadequate
cash register		*training, but didn't use much*
phone etiquette	adequate on phones	
credit card payments		training, but minimal experience
customer relations	can deal appropriately	
operating equipment		will require some training
teamwork	will work well with others	

D Now write a memo from Jim to Sara, the employee who will train Helen. In the memo tell Sara about areas where Helen's skills are inadequate and Jim's instructions for her training. The first sentence has already been written.

> **TO:** Sara
> **FROM:** Jim
> **DATE:** June 10
> **RE:** Training plan for Helen
>
> Helen has had some retail experience with customer contact, so you will spend most of your time on the more technical aspects of her job.

She has only used a cash register while other employees had lunch break. You will need

to show her how ours works and watch her the first days as she takes payments. Her

experience with the credit card payments is about the same. The first week you'll process

the payments and Helen will watch. After that, she'll have to take care of those, too.

■ EXPANSION IDEA

Exercise D

1. Divide the class into pairs and have them compare their memos.
2. Ask students to write a new memo together, incorporating the best of each of their memos.
3. Call on volunteers to read their memos to the class.

E There are five errors in the e-mail message below. The first error has been corrected. Find and correct the remaining four errors.

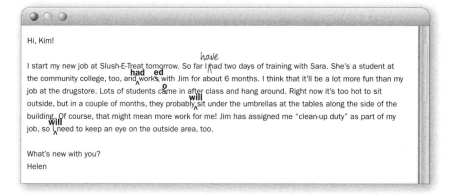

Hi, Kim!

I start my new job at Slush-E-Treat tomorrow. So far I ~~had~~ *have* two days of training with Sara. She's a student at the community college, too, and works with Jim for about 6 months. I think that it'll be a lot more fun than my job at the drugstore. Lots of students came in after class and hang around. Right now it's too hot to sit outside, but in a couple of months, they probably *will* sit under the umbrellas at the tables along the side of the building. Of course, that might mean more work for me! Jim has assigned me "clean-up duty" as part of my job, so I *will* need to keep an eye on the outside area, too.

What's new with you?
Helen

■ COMMUNICATE

F **PAIR WORK** Choose a business from the list below, and then compile a list of 6–8 questions to ask applicants for a job in that field. Role-play interviews for the job with a classmate.

Types of Businesses:
- retail
- hotel/restaurant
- medical/dental
- security
- publishing
- teaching
- computer programming

Have you operated a cash register before?

Yes, I used a cash register at my last job.

G **SMALL GROUP** Discuss customer service with your group and include the topics below in your discussion. Be ready to share your group's ideas with the class.

- In the U.S., there is the saying: "The customer is always right." Do you know any other proverbs related to business?
- What are some examples of good customer service? What do companies and employees do to provide their clients and customers with excellent service?
- Have you noticed good customer service in the shops and businesses in the town or city where you live? Have you been satisfied with the employees' behavior in the places where you shop? Why or why not?

---

1. Ask students to read the instructions and the first correction.
2. Have them find the rest of the errors and then check their work with a partner.
3. Call on students to read the e-mail aloud.
4. Ask for corrections as needed.

■ **COMMUNICATE**

■ **EXERCISE F**

1. Review the instructions and call on two students to read the text in the speech balloons.
2. Divide the class into pairs and have students complete the activity.
3. Circulate as students work, encouraging them to use the vocabulary and grammar targeted in the lesson.

■ **EXERCISE G**

1. Call on a student to read the instructions.
2. Call on students to read the bulleted questions. Clarify the questions as needed.
3. Divide the class into small groups and have them discuss customer service in the United States and in their home countries.
4. Have groups share their ideas with the rest of the class.

■ **EXPANSION IDEA**

Exercise G

Have students write a brief essay on how customer service varies from country to country.

Connection

Putting It Together

▉ GRAMMAR AND VOCABULARY

1. Ask students to read the instructions.
2. Call on two students to read the topics. Answer any questions students have about them.
3. Give students time to write their compositions.

▉ PROJECT

Review the instructions and have students complete the activity.

▉ INTERNET

Have students conduct their searches and then share their findings with the class.

GRAMMAR AND VOCABULARY Write a composition on one of the topics below. Use as many words as possible from the Content Vocabulary on page 1. Use verbs in the present time to express your ideas, and <u>underline</u> those verbs.   Answers will vary.

Topic 1: Every community has particular types of small businesses. What kind of business do you think is missing from your campus or in the place where you live now? Describe that business, and explain why it is a good idea to have that type of business where you are now.

Topic 2: Some business owners make a lot of money, but many self-employed people don't. In fact, many people start their businesses to gain independence and respect or to use their creativity, not to become rich. How have you balanced the need for money with your values, talents, and skills in thinking about your career choices?

PROJECT Interview at least one student who has a part-time job off-campus. Find out the following information and report on it at your next class meeting: Answers will vary.

    a. What kind of business? How many employees work there? How does the business treat the employees?
    b. What is the target market for the business? How does the business advertise?
    c. Has the student met the owner? What kind of business person is he/she? Does he/she manage the business effectively?

 INTERNET Go online, and use the search phrase "sample business plans" to find examples of business plans and executive summaries. Go to one of the websites and choose a business plan that interests you. In class, present an oral report on the product or service.
Answers will vary.

▉ EXPANSION IDEA

Grammar and Vocabulary

1. Divide the class into pairs and have them edit each other's compositions, checking the grammar and spelling. Ask students to discuss the strengths and weaknesses of their partner's essay.

2. Give students time to revise their essays.
3. Call on volunteers to read their essays to the class.
4. Discuss the topics as a class.

History: Jamestown 1607–2007

■ CONTENT VOCABULARY

Look up the words below that you do not know and enter them in your vocabulary journal. Write each word's part of speech, a definition, and an example sentence. Try to include them in your discussion and writing below.   Answers will vary.

a compass
a conflict
a crop
a fort
a perspective
prestige
a reaction
a scenario
a settler
suspicious
ultimately
a weapon

The Thirteen Original Colonies

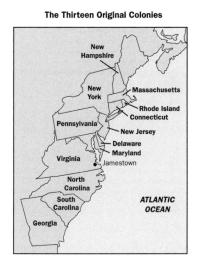

■ THINK ABOUT IT

In your writing journal, write for five minutes about these questions. When you are finished, share what you wrote with the class.   Answers will vary.

The first English settlers to reach the New World encountered Native Americans who had lived there for thousands of years. What do you think the Europeans and Native peoples thought about each other? In your opinion, what were some of the hopes and fears that each group had regarding the other?

13

Overview

1. Ask students to raise their hands if they have ever studied U.S. history.
2. Write *Jamestown* on the board and elicit information about the settlement, if possible.

■ CONTENT VOCABULARY

Ask students to review the words in the box. Tell them to look up any unfamiliar words.

■ VOCABULARY JOURNAL

Have students add new words to their vocabulary journals and write definitions and sentences for each.

■ THINK ABOUT IT

1. Read the instructions with the class.
2. Give students five minutes to write in their journals.
3. Have students share their journal entries with the class.

■ CONTENT NOTES

The topic of this lesson is History: Jamestown 1607–2007. Students will learn about the first English settlements in the New World and settlers' relationships with the Native Americans who already lived there.

PART ONE

Past Time: Simple Past and Past Perfect

■ GRAMMAR IN CONTENT

■ EXERCISE A CD 1, Track 3

1. Ask students to look at the pictures and read the title.

2. Ask students if they have seen the movie *Pocahontas*. Call on a volunteer to give a brief account of the story.

3. Play the audio and have students follow along in their books as they listen. Ask students to circle any words or phrases that they don't understand. As this is a difficult passage, you might want to stop the audio periodically to check for comprehension.

4. Ask students how this text differs from others they have read. Elicit that the language is formal and antiquated.

5. Call on students to read any words or phrases they circled. Elicit definitions for them from the class if possible.

6. Call on a volunteer to summarize the passage.

■ GRAMMAR IN CONTENT

John Rolfe

Pocahontas

A Read and listen to the passage below. The words in bold signal a time contrast.

CD1,TR3

Survival in Virginia

From the very outset, the officers of the Virginia Company intended that the settlers in their proposed colony should produce their own food, trade with the natives, and send back home a variety of vendible commodities, some exotic, others of their own manufacture. Virginia was a country where fruits, berries, game, and fish existed in profusion, and to the organizers of the colony their expectations did not seem unreasonable . . .

The first colonist to succeed in growing marketable West Indian tobacco was John Rolfe, formerly of Norfolk in East Anglia, who **had reached** Virginia from the Bermudas in 1610. His ship, *Sea Venture,* was blown aground there in a storm on the voyage out to Virginia, and several months passed before the survivors could build two pinnaces from the timbers of the wrecked vessel and proceed to the Chesapeake. During this delay, Mrs. Rolfe gave birth to a daughter, christened Bermuda, who soon died; the mother died shortly after they reached the colony. No man among the early English colonists of Virginia, not even Captain John Smith, contributed more, ultimately, to making the plantation a going concern or was so influential in giving direction to its destiny than the young widower.

On April 13, 1613, at the very time John Rolfe was raising his first good crop of tobacco, Captain Samuel Argall brought Pocahontas, the favorite daughter of Powhatan and niece of Opechancanough, to Jamestown as a prisoner and hostage. This "well featured but wanton [lively]" friend of Captain John Smith, called Matoaka by her own people, **had not visited** her English acquaintance since she saved the soldier's life five years before. Now she **had matured** and **blossomed** into an attractive young woman of eighteen or nineteen years of age. According to a report written two years before her death by Ralph Hamor, an intimate of Rolfe, the young planter **had fallen** in love with Pocahontas within a few months of her arrival in the English village, "and she with him."

Jamestown 1544-1699 © 1980, Carl Bridenbaugh, pg 34-35. By permission of Oxford University Press, Inc.

the Virginia Company: the British company that financed the Virginia colony

vendible: marketable, capable of being sold

aground: onto the shore

a vessel: a ship

a pinnace: a small sailing ship

christened: named

Captain John Smith: leader of the Virginia Colony from 1607–1609

a widower: a man whose wife has died

profusion: abundance

an intimate: a close friend

a going concern: a successful business

■ EXPANSION IDEA

Exercise A

1. Divide the class into pairs and have them discuss the reading, one paragraph at a time. Because students will have a hard time completing the activities in this lesson if they do not understand the text, it is important for them to decipher all of the details. Circulate as students work, helping them as needed.

2. Tell students to take turns asking and answering questions about the passage.

Sample Sentences	Notes
When English colonists **landed** at Jamestown, Virginia, they **built** a fort and **prepared** to plant corn. The Pasbehay Indians **had lived** in that area for centuries, and a major village of theirs was located nearby. Like other Native American tribes in this area, they **spoke** the Algonquian language and **had accepted** the Powhatans as chiefs years before the English arrived.	Use the **simple past** to tell about past events, situations, and conditions that are completed and remote to you now. Use the **past perfect** to tell about a situation or event that happened at an even earlier point in the past.
In the first year of the Jamestown settlement, the Powhatans and other tribes **cooperated** with the Englishmen. The settlers **learned** about native crops from them, and everyone **shared** local hunting and fishing grounds. The first permanent British colony **had finally taken** root in 1607, thanks to the efforts of these native people.	Use the **past perfect** in informal writing to express the purpose or climax of an event or situation in the **past.** In this context, past perfect does not express a time contrast. It signals the result or resolution of a situation.

B Read over your journal entry on page 13, and <u>underline</u> at least one sentence that you can revise to include a time contrast in the past. Write your revised sentence(s) below.

Answers will vary.

C Imagine you are a colonist in Jamestown, and that you have to write a report to the Virginia Company in England. Use the words in parentheses to describe what happened, including time shifts whenever possible.

1. (row ashore; return from trip up James River)

   May 14: *About noon the first group of men began to row ashore. We had returned earlier from our trip up the James River and decided that this area looked the best.*

2. (gather wood for campfires; shoot some rabbits and birds)

   May 14: Two men spent several hours in the forest and gathered wood for campfires. They also shot some rabbits and birds for food.

3. (cut down trees for fort; bring tools and supplies from the ships)

   May 15: About 15 sailors had cut down 20 trees yesterday to build a fort, and we were able to begin our labor once some crew members brought tools and supplies from the ship.

■ **GRAMMAR CHART**
Simple Past and Past Perfect

1. Call on students to read the sample sentences.
2. Call on volunteers to point out time contrasts in the two examples.
3. Ask students to review the Notes and answer any questions they have about how and when to use each of the two tenses.

■ **EXERCISE B**

Go over the instructions and give students time to rewrite their sentences.

■ **EXERCISE C**

1. Read the instructions with the class.
2. Call on a student to read the example.
3. Have students complete the activity.
4. Circulate as they work and assist as needed.

■ **EXPANSION IDEA**

Exercise C
1. Divide the class into pairs and have students discuss their answers.
2. Call on volunteers to read their answers to the class. After each sentence is read, ask the students if they have any comments. Discuss use of verb tenses to show time contrasts.

■ EXERCISE D

1. Ask students to read the example. Point out that the final sentence expresses a result or resolution.

2. Ask students to complete the activity, adding a result or resolution to each of the paragraphs.

3. Divide the class into pairs and have students compare their answers.

4. Call on volunteers to read their answers to the class.

---

4. (see a group of Indians in canoes; prepare gifts for the Indians)

May 15: **A group of men saw a group of Indians in canoes today. We prepared gifts for them to befriend them.**

5. (unload other supplies from the ships; hunt for deer and other larger game)

May 16: **We unloaded the other supplies from the ships to continue construction. Then we hunted deer and other large game.**

6. (meet with Powhatan chiefs; travel to nearby Indian village)

May 17: **We travelled to a nearby Indian village to introduce ourselves and meet with the Powhatan chiefs.**

D Complete the final sentence in the passages below to express the results or resolution of the situation. The first exercise has been completed as an example.

1. The English settled Roanoke Island in 1585, but all of those colonists died sometime between 1587 and 1590. They didn't have enough food, clothing, or tools. When the ships left England in 1607, *the colonists had planned better and had loaded the necessary supplies and equipment.*

2. The crews of the *Discovery,* the *Susan Constant,* and the *Godspeed* rowed ashore on May 14, 1607, with their weapons and basic tools. Each of the colonists was responsible for getting his personal items from the ship. By the night of May 17, **they had emptied the ship of all their possessions and equipment.**

3. When the Powhatans saw the three English ships on the Powhatan River, they became worried. When the Englishmen started to build a fort, the Indians suspected that the Englishmen planned to stay in the Powhatans' territory. Within a month, **the Englishmen had established a settlement that served as the foundation of the colony.**

4. Opechancanough, who was the older brother of the Powhatan chief, went to Spain in 1561 with a group of Spanish sailors who were returning home from Cuba. There the young Indian man learned Spanish and had lessons about Christianity. By the time he returned to America in 1570, **he had learned the values of the European colonists.**

■ EXPANSION IDEA

Exercise D

Divide the class into pairs. Have students take turns summarizing the paragraphs.

E (Circle) the correct paraphrase of the sentences. The first one has been done as an example.

1. Indians in Virginia met the English with feelings of suspicion. They had already learned about European ways from the Spanish.
   a. Their suspicion of the English was based on their previous experiences with the Spanish.
   b. They felt suspicious of the English, so they felt that way about the Spanish, too.

2. When the Powhatan chief first met the English settlers, many Indians hid nearby with bows and arrows. They had observed that some of the Europeans carried guns.
   a. The Indians saw the Europeans' guns and then hid near the village.
   b. The Indians hid nearby, and as a result they saw the guns.

3. During the winter of 1609–1610, the settlers didn't have enough to eat because they hadn't grown enough food. Many of them lived with the Indians, who shared their food.
   a. Many of the settlers had lived with the Indians so they didn't grow enough food for the winter.
   b. Many of the settlers did not grow enough food to prepare for the winter, so they lived with the Indians who had enough food.

4. The bad relationship between the English settlers and Indians got worse, especially after the English had kidnapped Pocahontas.
   a. The relationship worsened, so the Englishmen kidnapped Pocahontas.
   b. The Englishmen kidnapped Pocahontas, and then the relationship worsened.

5. John Rolfe and Pocahontas had fallen in love, and then they married in 1614. The relationship between the Indians and the English improved after that.
   a. The relationship between the Indians and the English improved, so Rolfe married Pocahontas.
   b. Rolfe married Pocahontas, and then the relationship between the Indians and the English improved.

6. Tobacco from Virginia became very popular after Rolfe had sent his first crop to England. By 1617, tobacco was the only crop that people raised in the area.
   a. Rolfe's tobacco had grown very popular in England, so everyone planted this crop.
   b. Because Virginia tobacco had become popular in England, Rolfe planted this crop.

■ **EXERCISE E**

1. Go over the instructions with the class.
2. Call on a student to read the example. Ask a volunteer to paraphrase the sentences before students check the answer options. Tell students that their answer choice should be the one that is closest to their own paraphrased sentence.
3. Have students complete the activity individually and then check their work with a partner.
4. Call on volunteers to read their answers to the class. If there is any disagreement, ask a volunteer to paraphrase the sentence in his or her own words so that the correct answer is clear.

■ **EXPANSION IDEA**

Exercise E

Have students work in pairs and look at the passage in Exercise A on page 14. Have each student choose three sentences and paraphrase them. Each student should then compare their answers with their partner.

■ EXERCISE F

1. Call on a student to read the instructions aloud.
2. Call on another student to read the text in the speech balloon.
3. Divide the class into pairs and have students discuss their experiences with people from different cultures.

Past Time: Shifting to Present

■ GRAMMAR IN CONTENT

■ EXERCISE A CD 1, Track 4

1. Have students read the instructions.
2. Play the audio once, asking students to listen carefully for comprehension only.
3. Play the audio again and have students underline verbs that show a tense shift.
4. Call on students to read the paragraph aloud, stopping to point out tense shifts. Ask them why they think the speaker chose to shift tenses.

F **PAIR WORK** Talk about a time you first met someone from a different culture. What assumptions did you have about that person's country or culture? Were those assumptions confirmed, or did you change them as a result of getting to know that person? Use the simple past and past perfect as appropriate.

> My friend Amos is from Nigeria. Before I **met** him, I **had never known** anybody else from Africa. Amos **told** me that the British **had colonized** Nigeria, and that's why English is an official language there.

| PART TWO | Past Time: Shifting to Present |

■ GRAMMAR IN CONTENT

A Listen as a Virginia Indian tells about his experience as a member of the 54-member delegation that went to England during the week of July 12, 2006. Underline the verbs that show a tense shift. Why do you think the speaker chose to shift tenses?

CD1,TR4

The Gravesend Festival

"After we arrived in Gravesend—you know it's a few miles southeast of London—we met all of the local officials in the town hall. It was incredible. They were wearing these long robes—just like in the movies. I guess that you can say the same about us with all of our feather headbands, leather clothes, and moccasins. Anyway, we presented our gifts, and the chiefs of the eight tribes danced the welcome dance and sprinkled tobacco on the ground according to our custom. After all of these centuries, it's amazing to think that we can meet together with the descendants of the men who changed the lives of all the native people of Virginia.

The next day we were all guests at the Gravesend annual multicultural festival. Some of the Virginians played music and others performed ceremonial dances for the crowds. This was the first time that any Native Americans had participated in their festival. It was a great event, but later in the day, they took us to see Pocahontas's grave at St. George's Church. We get out of the bus and walk around the church to the little cemetery—and there it is. Everyone just stands around the tomb silently. It was quite a spiritual moment.

On our last day we went to a seminar at the University of Kent. The professors there had organized a program for all of us to discuss the history and culture of the Virginia Native Americans in the last 400 years. A lot of people don't even know that there are any native people left in Virginia! We appreciated their interest and tried our best to present our perspective on colonial times and our opinions about the issues that face Native Americans who live in Virginia today."

■ EXPANSION IDEA

Exercise A

Divide the class into small groups. Have students role-play a discussion among Virginia Indians using the information from Exercise A.

For example:

Student 1: *Wasn't it an amazing experience meeting all those local officials in the town hall?*

Student 2: *It was incredible. I wonder what they thought when they saw us in our feathers and leather clothing.*

Student 3: *They probably thought we looked like something straight out of the movies!*

Shifting from Past to Present

Sample Sentences	Notes
"We **started** rowing down the James River, but at the bend we **saw** a Powhatan canoe. John **takes** his oars out of the water and **gets** his gun. Meanwhile, Joseph and I **turn** the boat toward the tall grass along the south shore."	English-speakers often start a story in the **past** tense, but then switch to the **present** when telling the main part of the story. In such contexts, speakers do not tend to use explicit time expressions to signal a shift in verb tense.
"After they **shot** Joseph with an arrow, John and I **hid** behind the trees and **waited** for them to come ashore. **It's** amazing what **flashes** through your mind at a time like that. It **seems** like time stands still."	Switching from the **past** to the **present** can make a story more vivid or lively. It also provides a way to comment on the situation or to give background information.
The Powhatans **were** suspicious of the settlers' expansion along the James River. By 1609, many families **had arrived** in Virginia, and the colonists **pushed** the Indians farther inland. The same scenario **repeats** itself throughout U.S. history as Europeans **take** possession of land that the Native Americans **view** as open for all to use.	In some academic writing, authors use a combination of **present** and **past** tenses. Typically, the past tense is used for real-life examples, and the present tense is used for comments or generalizations about the example.

B (Circle) the choice that tells why the speaker changes from the past tense to the present tense in each conversation. The first one has been done for you.

1. A: How was your trip to Hong Kong?
   B: I had never been to Asia before, so it was really interesting. It's the most interesting trip I have ever taken. I met so many friendly people who showed me around.
   - (a.) shift from an example to a generalization
   - b. shift from the story to a comment about the story
   - c. shift to a lively style of telling the story

2. A: I had read about a church on the top of the mountain above Hong Kong, so I went to the tram stop at the bottom of the mountain. I'm standing there, looking at the ticket machine. An older Chinese gentleman comes up to me and helps me buy the ticket that I need. Then, he shows me where to get on the right tram. He actually ended up going with me and showed me the church and the other sights at the top of the mountain.
   - a. shift from an example to a generalization
   - b. shift from the story to a comment about the story
   - (c.) shift to a lively style of telling the story

■ GRAMMAR CHART
Shifting from Past to Present

1. Call on students to read the sample sentences aloud.
2. Ask volunteers to point out tense shifts and say why the speaker uses them.
3. Have students review the Notes. Answer any questions they have about tense shifting.

■ EXERCISE B

1. Read the instructions with the class.
2. Ask students to cover the answer options as they look at the example.
3. Call on a few volunteers to suggest why the speaker changes from the past tense to the present tense.
4. Ask students to complete the activity.
5. Go over the answers together as a class.

■ EXPANSION IDEA

Exercise B

1. Ask students to discuss an experience using tense shifts in their conversations.
2. Circulate as students work to assist them as needed.

For example:

Student 1: *Disneyland was awesome. The nights are amazing. The lights come on and you feel like you're on a movie set.*

Student 2: *I felt the same way when I saw snow for the first time. It's something you can't describe. You wake up in the morning and the whole world is white.*

3. A: How did you like the food in Hong Kong?
   B: Luckily, one of the people that I'd met took me to a local restaurant. The food was great, but it was the first time that I'd ever eaten with chopsticks. It's a lot harder to eat with them than you might expect. It took me much longer to eat than it usually does.

   a. shift from an example to a generalization
   (b.) shift from the story to a comment about the story
   c. shift to a lively style of telling the story

4. A: Pocahontas went to London with John Rolfe and lived there for only one year. She died, probably of tuberculosis, in 1618. She is a famous example of how diseases that are common in one region can affect people who have had no contact with them before.

   a. shift from an example to a generalization
   (b.) shift from the story to a comment about the story
   c. shift to a lively style of telling the story

5. A: The colonists in Jamestown had few supplies from England, so they depended on hunting and gathering local fruits and vegetables until they could grow their own food. The Indians showed them how to plant native vegetables and gave them gifts of food so that they were able to survive. Regardless of language or culture, this kind of hospitality often saves the lives of newcomers.

   (a.) shift from an example to a generalization
   b. shift from the story to a comment about the story
   c. shift to a lively style of telling the story

6. A: My men and I were out hunting deer when a group of Indians captured us and took us to the Powhatan village. The chief himself comes out to see what's happening. I'm thinking that we're in very bad trouble when I remember that I have my compass in my pocket. I take it out and show it to the chief.

   a. shift from an example to a generalization
   b. shift from the story to a comment about the story
   (c.) shift to a lively style of telling the story

7. A: How did you escape from there alive?
   B: I thought that the compass was probably something new for the Indians. The chief looked at it and passed it around so that everyone could take a look at it. Thank goodness, I can speak some of their language. I told the chief how it worked and showed them how to use it. After that, he decided to let us go.

   a. shift from an example to a generalization
   (b.) shift from the story to a comment about the story
   c. shift to a lively style of telling the story

C Write the beginning of a story about one of the topics below. After you set the stage for your story, continue in a livelier style. Write only the beginning of the story (4–5 sentences) and stop at a suspenseful moment. **Answers will vary.**

Topics:
- **your arrival in a new place**
- **your first day at a new school or job**
- **the first time you ate something very strange**

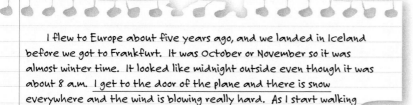

I flew to Europe about five years ago, and we landed in Iceland before we got to Frankfurt. It was October or November so it was almost winter time. It looked like midnight outside even though it was about 8 a.m. <u>I get to the door of the plane and there is snow everywhere and the wind is blowing really hard.</u> As I start walking

D There are five errors in the e-mail below. The first error has already been corrected. Find and correct the four errors that remain.

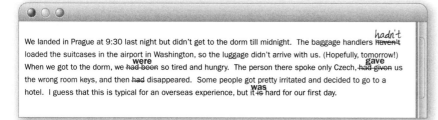

We landed in Prague at 9:30 last night but didn't get to the dorm till midnight. The baggage handlers ~~haven't~~ *hadn't* loaded the suitcases in the airport in Washington, so the luggage didn't arrive with us. (Hopefully, tomorrow!) When we got to the dorm, we ~~had been~~ *were* so tired and hungry. The person there spoke only Czech, ~~had given~~ *gave* us the wrong room keys, and then ~~had~~ disappeared. Some people got pretty irritated and decided to go to a hotel. I guess that this is typical for an overseas experience, but it ~~is~~ *was* hard for our first day.

■ C O M M U N I C A T E

E **PAIR WORK** Choose one of the statements below. Brainstorm some real-life examples of the statement and choose one. Prepare your example with as much detail as you can. Then, present it to your classmates. They will then decide which of the statements below is the appropriate generalization for your example. **Answers will vary.**

a. Different beliefs or values can create misunderstandings or cause conflict between people of different cultures.
b. People who know the language of the other group gain power or prestige.
c. Body language can cause serious misunderstandings between people of different cultures.
d. People from different cultures may avoid contact with each other as a result of cultural misunderstandings.

■ **EXERCISE C**

1. Go over the instructions with the class and review the topics.
2. Ask students to read the example, underlining the point at which the tone of the description becomes livelier.
3. Call on volunteers to explain where the tone changes and why.

■ **EXERCISE D**

1. Have students find the five errors in the e-mail.
2. Ask students to check their work with a partner.
3. Call on students to read the corrected e-mail aloud.

■ **COMMUNICATE**

■ **EXERCISE E**

1. Go over the instructions with the class and answer any questions they have about the activity.
2. Divide the class into pairs and have students prepare their examples.
3. Call on students to present their examples to the class.

■ **EXPANSION IDEA**

Exercise D

1. Ask students to write an e-mail, modeling it on the example in Exercise D.

2. Call on volunteers to read their e-mails to the class.

Connection

Putting It Together

■ GRAMMAR AND VOCABULARY

1. Go over the instructions with the class.
2. Call on two students to read the topics. Answer any questions students have about the topics or the activities.
3. Give students time to complete the activity.

■ PROJECT

1. Go over the instructions.
2. Have students complete the activity and report on their interviews at the next class meeting.

■ INTERNET

Have students complete their searches and discuss their expectations and reactions in class.

GRAMMAR AND VOCABULARY Write a composition on one of the topics below, using specific examples. Use as many words as possible from the Content Vocabulary on page 13. Use verbs in the past time to express your ideas where appropriate, and underline those verbs.

Topic 1: Mark Twain, an American humorist and writer, said, "Travel is fatal to prejudice, bigotry and narrow-mindedness." Explain what this quotation means. Do you agree or disagree? Use specific examples from your past experience to support your opinion.

Topic 2: Write about the contact between two cultural or ethnic groups in the history of a country that interests you. How or why did they make contact? How did they live and work together? Were there conflicts between the groups? What caused misunderstandings and conflicts? Use specific examples. **Answers will vary.**

PROJECT Interview a student on your campus who has studied abroad.

Find out: **Answers will vary.**

    a. the student's first impressions of the place where he/she stayed
    b. the student's experience with local people in the market or supermarket
    c. an example of the student's opinion about the local people's customs or behavior

Be prepared to report on your interview at your next class meeting.

 INTERNET Go online, and use the search term "Powhatan clothing." Find and read information about clothing that Powhatan Indians wore at the time that the English arrived in Virginia. Are you surprised by this information? What were your assumptions before reading this information? How had you learned about Native American clothing and lifestyle before you looked at this material? Be prepared to talk about your expectations and your reactions in class.   **Answers will vary.**

■ EXPANSION IDEA

Internet
Have students research a South American indigenous group and report back on what its members wear today.

Food Sciences: Biotech Crops

■ CONTENT VOCABULARY

Look up the words below that you do not know and enter them in your vocabulary journal. Write each word's part of speech, a definition, and an example sentence. Try to include them in your discussion and writing below.   Answers will vary.

an acid/a base	ethical	to germinate	to reap
an allergic reaction	to field test	manipulation	resistant
aware	genetic engineering	ongoing	unforeseen

■ THINK ABOUT IT

How are organic products different from conventional food products? What are the advantages of organic food? Can you think of any disadvantages?

In your writing journal, write for five minutes about the questions below. When you are finished, share what you wrote with the class.   Answers will vary.
Does your local grocery store sell organic products? What does "organic" mean in this context? Do you ever buy organic food products? Why or why not? Discuss your ideas with a classmate.

23

Overview

1. Write *genetic engineering* on the board and ask students to raise their hands if they are familiar with the term.
2. Elicit prior knowledge by calling on volunteers to relate what they know about genetic engineering.

■ CONTENT VOCABULARY

Ask students to review the words in the box. Tell them to look up any unfamiliar words.

■ VOCABULARY JOURNAL

Have students add new words to their vocabulary journals, and write down the parts of speech, definitions, and example sentences for each.

■ THINK ABOUT IT

1. Ask students to read the questions.
2. Give students five minutes to write in their journals.
3. Divide the class into pairs and have students discuss the questions.

■ CONTENT NOTES

The topic of this lesson is Food Sciences: Biotech Crops. Students will learn the vocabulary necessary to discuss the ethics, benefits, and drawbacks involved in genetically engineered foods. Encourage students to consider the effects that genetic engineering might have on the economies of their countries.

■ GRAMMAR IN CONTENT

■ EXERCISE A *CD 1, Track 5*

1. Ask students to look at the pictures and read the title.

2. Write *organic* on the board and elicit a definition from a class member.

3. Ask students to raise their hands if they buy organic foods. Ask students to discuss the pros and cons of buying organic products.

4. Play the audio and have students follow along in their books as they listen.

5. Check comprehension by asking questions such as the following: *What does "replacement level" mean? How do people's diets change as they move into urban areas? What do scientists hope genetic engineering will achieve?*

■ GRAMMAR IN CONTENT

CD1,TR5

A Read and listen to the passage below. The words in bold are verb forms expressing future time.

Food Options in Our Future

McDonald's, Starbucks, and similar companies are rising to meet the demand for food that is quick and convenient. Could there be any negative consequences of this trend? The world's population is becoming more urban, and experts worry that our eating habits **won't match** the availability of the food that farmers produce. What solutions **will** researchers **find** in order to deal with the demand for more nutritious food for more people on Earth?

Predictions about population growth are rather gloomy. According to the United Nations Population Division, the world's population **will continue** to grow until about 2050 when it **will reach** 10.5 billion. By that point, experts predict that life expectancy rates around the world **will have improved** and fertility rates **will have declined**. If those expectations bear out, the world's population **will have achieved** a replacement level; in other words, there **will be** no more net growth. What **will happen** to the percentage of Earth's land used for crops and pastureland as the population grows and then levels off?

Specialists in the fields of biotech engineering and agriculture are working on ways to increase the productivity of the land available for raising food. Researchers have observed that as people move into urban areas, their diets change to include a larger variety of fruit and vegetables and more protein from meat. Currently, farmers cultivate approximately 300 plants for human and animal consumption, but only 24 of those plants provide us with nearly all of our food. Farmers are changing their crops to match the demand for animal feed and are devoting more acreage to pasture. Given the increased land resources needed to support such food preferences, scientists are hoping that genetic engineering **will prove** to be a powerful tool to solve this global problem.

Researchers and advocates of genetic engineering **will persevere** in their efforts to increase agricultural productivity. So far, genetically engineered crops have developed many desirable characteristics. These transgenic plants **will yield** more crops per acre because they are resistant to disease, tolerant of extreme weather and of various soil conditions, and uniform in size and shape and, therefore, easier to harvest. Despite these improvements, many consumers and consumer organizations are highly critical of "genetically manipulated" food. They fear that such products **will have** unpredictable, long-term harmful effects on the environment and on people.

an acre: a measure of land (one hectare = 2.47 acres)
to bear out: to confirm
fertility rates: rate of births in a population

life expectancy: the average age of death according to population statistics
a pasture: grassland for domestic animals

■ EXPANSION IDEA

Exercise A
Divide the class into pairs and have them take turns asking and answering questions about the food options in our future.

Sample Sentences	Notes
Fewer people **will go** hungry in the next decades. **I'm going to contribute** to UNICEF to help feed children around the world.	Use *will* or *be going to* + verb to tell about an action, event, or situation in the future.
Researchers **will have field-tested** the new tomato crop for better texture by the time government officials review the research for approval next year.	Like the present perfect in a present context and the past perfect in a past context, use the future perfect (*will* + *have* + past participle) to express a prior time within a future context.
According to the United Nations, the percentage of hungry people in developing countries **will have fallen** to 10% by 2015.	Use the preposition *by* with the future perfect to express a deadline or point of completion for a future action.
Our Biology Department **is going to offer** a lecture series about ethics in biotech research. They'll **invite** some researchers from other universities. A representative from Greenpeace **will be included** in the series, too. I'll save you a seat at the lecture tomorrow.	Like the present perfect tense, the future form (*be going to* + verb) is often used to introduce a topic or to set the scene. In a narrative about the future, English speakers may use *will* or its contracted form ('ll) in the rest of the narrative in the future context.
This lecture series **will be** extremely interesting.	*Will* is used to make offers and promises and to make predictions about formal occasions in the future.
I'm going to attend all of the sessions—they're already on my calendar. The campus newspaper **is going to announce** each lecture two days in advance. Our speaker **arrives** around 10:00 A.M., so someone will have to pick her up at the airport and bring her to the meeting. At 11:00 A.M. **she's speaking** about biotech projects across our state.	*Be going to* shows more personal involvement or interaction. Use it for · predictions · plans · scheduled events The present and present progressive verb forms can sometimes express the future time. Use the **present** for scheduled events and the **present progressive** for scheduled activities that are a bit longer in duration.

B Read over your journal entry, and <u>underline</u> at least one sentence that you can revise to include a verb in future time. Write your revised sentence(s) below.

Answers will vary.

_____

_____

_____

Future Time

1. Ask students to make statements about the future, eliciting the use of *will*, *going to* and *will have* + past participle.
2. Have students review the sample sentences and Notes.
3. Ask students which form they would use on formal occasions.

■ **EXERCISE B**

Have students complete the activity and read their sentences aloud to the class.

■ **EXPANSION IDEA**

Grammar
Divide the class into pairs and have students discuss an upcoming school event using *will*, *going to*, and *will have* + past participle.

EXERCISE C

1. Have students review the instructions and read the conference schedule.
2. Answer any questions students have about the activity. Remind them that they are writing a newspaper article and should use an expositional, informative style.

EXERCISE D

1. Have students read the instructions and example. Answer any questions they have about the exercise.
2. Ask students to complete the activity on their own. Then have students check their work with a partner.
3. Call on volunteers to read their answers to the class.

C Imagine you write for your campus or local newspaper. Prepare a short article for the newspaper about an upcoming conference on biotech ethics. Use the information below. **Answers will vary.**

Date/Time: Tuesday, 9:00 a.m.–12:00 noon
Location: Williamson Auditorium
Admission: Free with student ID card
Sessions/Topics:
9:00 Professor James Leonard, "The Dangers of Biotech Crops in the Third World"
10:00 Professor Michael Barnes, "Appropriate Labels on Genetically Engineered Foods in the Grocery Store"
11:00 Professor Julie Reagan, "Proper Testing of Genetically Engineered Crops"

D Complete the sentences below, predicting the outcomes of various types of transgenic food items. **Answers will vary. Sample answers below.**

1. When farmers raise tomatoes that all become ripe at the same time, _they won't need to hire tomato-pickers more than once._

2. When Hawaiian farmers plant papaya seeds that are virus-resistant, **they will have a better harvest.**

3. When cotton farmers decide to plant varieties of cotton that produce their own natural pest-killing proteins, **they won't need to use any pesticides any more.**

4. When farmers plant soybeans with a higher protein content, **more people will have a better diet.**

5. When farmers in developing countries raise crops of "golden rice" that should meet daily vitamin A requirements for rice-based diets, **children will grow up healthier.**

6. When Mexican farmers raise drought-resistant maize, **they won't be so dependent on the weather for good crops.**

7. When Colombian farmers plant maize that has been adapted to acidic soils, **they'll grow corn in many more areas of the country.**

■ EXPANSION IDEA

Exercise C

1. Divide the class into pairs. Tell students to imagine that one of them is a journalist and the other a professor who will present a lecture at the conference.
2. Have students role-play a short interview.

For example:

Student 1 (journalist): *Dr. Leonard, do you serve genetically engineered food to your children?*

Student 2 (professor): *No, I don't. Based on recent research, I feel the dangers of these foods outweigh their benefits.*

E Select 3–4 criticisms of genetically modified (GM) crops in the notes below. Complete the paragraph below about future predictions.   Answers will vary.

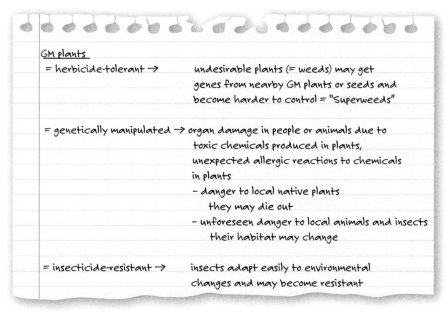

GM plants
= herbicide-tolerant →   undesirable plants (= weeds) may get
                             genes from nearby GM plants or seeds and
                             become harder to control = "superweeds"

= genetically manipulated → organ damage in people or animals due to
                             toxic chemicals produced in plants,
                             unexpected allergic reactions to chemicals
                             in plants
                             – danger to local native plants
                                they may die out
                             – unforeseen danger to local animals and insects
                                their habitat may change

= insecticide-resistant →   insects adapt easily to environmental
                             changes and may become resistant

According to critics of genetically modified foods, our world will probably change in many unforeseen ways if farmers continue to plant GM crops.

Critics say that weeds may get genes from nearby biotech crops and become herbicide

intolerable. If that happens, these new "superweeds" will be almost impossible to kill. Also,

when scientists genetically manipulate plants . . . .

_____

■ COMMUNICATE

F GROUP WORK Discuss the typical grocery store that you imagine you might find ten years from now. In this age of the global economy and world travel, what kinds of food items will we see in a typical grocery store? What will consumers expect? Will an urban store be considerably different from a rural one?   Answers will vary.

I think consumers are going to expect more choices.   They already have lots of choices. In the future, I think they'll expect more quality.

---

1. Ask students to read the notes that appear on the lined paper.
2. Give students time to complete their paragraphs.
3. Divide the class into pairs and have students exchange their work. Ask them to edit each other's writing, paying particular attention to targeted grammatical structures and vocabulary.

■ COMMUNICATE

■ EXERCISE F
1. Ask students to read the instructions.
2. Call on two students to read the text in the speech balloons.
3. Divide the class into small groups and have students discuss the questions.
4. Call on a member of each group to summarize his/her group's conclusions.

■ EXPANSION IDEA

Exercise F
1. Divide the class into pairs. Tell pairs to invent an exotic recipe using ingredients from a variety of countries, including some organic and some genetically engineered products.

2. Have students write a shopping list for their recipes.
3. Call on volunteers to read their shopping lists to the class.

PART TWO

Review of Progressive Aspect

■ GRAMMAR IN CONTENT

■ EXERCISE A

1. Write *progressive aspect* on the board and elicit a definition from a class member if possible. If necessary, explain that "progressive aspect" refers to actions that are ongoing or temporary.

2. Ask students to complete the activity on their own and then check their work with a partner.

■ GRAMMAR CHART

Review of Progressive Aspect

1. Ask students to review the Notes and examples. Be sure that they are able to distinguish between an action that is continuous and one that is habitual.

2. Answer any questions that students have about how and when to use the progressive aspect.

■ EXERCISE B

1. Ask students to read the instructions.

2. Call on volunteers to explain the differences among the three interpretations.

3. Have students complete the activity and then check their work with a partner.

4. Call on volunteers to read their answers to the class.

■ GRAMMAR IN CONTENT

A Reread the text at the beginning of this lesson, and (circle) the examples of verbs in the progressive aspect. Compare your results with a partner.

Review of Progressive Aspect

Examples	Notes
Farmers have been testing tomato seeds that should produce tomatoes of a uniform size. Local farmers are raising the transgenic tomatoes in fields next to their regular crops. Volunteers have been tasting the new crops of transgenic tomatoes to be sure that the tomatoes haven't lost any flavor.	Choose a progressive form of the verb to emphasize that an action is not yet complete or can still change. Progressive forms signal an activity still in progress or a temporary situation. Remember, stative verbs are rarely used in progressive aspect.
A good tomato tastes tangy and slightly sweet. Some gardeners raise tomatoes in big pots.	Use simple verb tenses to tell about a generalization, habit, fact, or situation that will not change or is complete.
My father was forever tending his tomatoes. He's always looking at seed catalogs and ordering new seeds for his big flowerpots.	In conversation, use present or past progressive to comment on behavior or actions.

B Read the statements below and label each with the correct interpretation of the verb in progressive aspect:

a. the action or activity is happening right now or was happening right then
b. the action extends over a period of time
c. the situation is temporary and can change

1. ___*a*___ Dr. Cho is checking some rice seedlings while Mark takes notes.
2. ___*b*___ Mark has been working in Dr. Cho's lab since he started graduate school.
3. ___*c*___ The seeds that Mark planted last week are starting to germinate.
4. ___*b*___ Dr. Cho has been researching several varieties of rice.
5. ___*c*___ She is now conducting a study on the effects of quicker germination in rice.
6. ___*a*___ When she came into the lab earlier, Mark was monitoring the seedlings.
7. ___*c*___ Since then, she has been supervising Mark's work but has to leave soon.
8. ___*b*___ Mark is working as a lab assistant to earn money during his studies.

■ EXPANSION IDEA

Exercise B

1. Ask students to write an example of each of the three uses of the progressive aspect.

2. Divide the class into pairs. Have students exchange sentences and assign the correct interpretation to each.

C Complete each sentence with a verb from the box below. More than one correct form of the verb may be possible.

mention	~~practice~~	perform	examine
test	maintain	determine	develop

Since she hasn't done lab work in a long time, Dr. Petersen's new lab assistant Pat Furey __has been practicing__ (1) her lab techniques so that she doesn't skew the results of Dr. Petersen's new experiments on maize. Last week she __examined__ (2) the equipment in the lab and the notes on various ongoing experiments while Mark was preparing some new maize seeds for the experiments. She __was testing__ (3) some new equipment when Mark knocked it over with a seed tray and broke it. Tomorrow when she meets with Dr. Petersen, she __is going to mention__ (4) the incident because she is afraid that she'll be blamed for Mark's carelessness.

At Pat's meeting with Dr. Petersen, they discussed the new maize research at great length. In the course of the research, they __will perform__ (5) a series of experiments to identify a gene that will make the maize more tolerant of poor soil conditions. Dr. Petersen __is developing__ (6) a new hypothesis, and she needs to have meticulous records of each experiment. Pat __will maintain__ (7) records for each set of maize seeds. On the basis of Pat's records, Dr. Petersen __will identify__ (8) the seeds that have low tolerance and will proceed with new experiments on the seeds with higher tolerance.

CD1,TR6

D Listen to an interview with two students at Yale who support their university's efforts to provide sustainable food in the campus cafeteria. As you listen, take notes on the various campus activities they describe. Then, summarize the ongoing activities by continuing the summary that starts below.   Answers will vary.

> Yale students have been working together with campus staff to broaden the cafeteria choices to include dishes made with "sustainable" food.

■ EXERCISE C

1. Have students read the instructions and the words in the box.
2. Tell students to read the example and answer any questions they may have about the activity.
3. Ask students to complete the activity individually and then check their work with a partner.
4. Call on volunteers to read the passage aloud to the class. Call for corrections as needed.

■ EXERCISE D   *CD 1, Track 6*

1. Ask students to read the instructions and the note on the lined paper.
2. Tell students that they will hear the audio twice. The first time they should listen for comprehension only.
3. Play the audio again and have students take notes on the campus activities that are described.

■ EXPANSION IDEA

Exercise D
Put students into pairs. Have students write a paragraph together, using the progressive aspect, on any topic of their choice. Have each group read their paragraph to the class.

■ COMMUNICATE

■ EXERCISE E

1. Have students read the instructions. Write an example of sustainability that the school or community is doing.
2. Put students into groups of three or four and have them create their lists.
3. Have groups share their lists with the class.

Connection

Putting It Together

■ GRAMMAR AND VOCABULARY

1. Read the instructions aloud to the class. Have two students read the topics aloud.
2. Give students time to write their compositions, reminding them to use verbs for events in the future where appropriate.

■ PROJECT

1. Read the instructions aloud. Have students interview a student outside of the class.
2. Have students report their findings to the class.

■ INTERNET

Have students research their personal diets and present their findings to the class.

E PAIR WORK Make a list of things that your school or community is doing to encourage sustainability. Sustainability includes not only food, but also all other actions to conserve Earth's resources and to act responsibly toward our environment. When you are finished, compare your list with the lists of your classmates. Answers will vary.

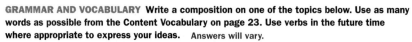

Connection | Putting It Together

 GRAMMAR AND VOCABULARY Write a composition on one of the topics below. Use as many words as possible from the Content Vocabulary on page 23. Use verbs in the future time where appropriate to express your ideas. Answers will vary.

Topic 1: Many people fear a future in which scientists will manipulate genetic material in all kinds of organisms and thereby change our lives in unforeseen ways. How will we protect ourselves and our planet while also reaping the benefits of such groundbreaking research? Give concrete examples.

Topic 2: Many supporters of genetically engineered plants consider the natural world to be imperfect. Consequently, they see this kind of technology as a way to use their creativity to overcome problems and make the world better for future generations. Critics of transgenic plants often see nature quite differently—as a complete system that works perfectly well without human interference. How will we resolve these differences as we secure the food supply for the future? Give concrete reasons to support your position.

 PROJECT Interview at least one student on your campus about the food available in the cafeterias or dining halls. Find out the following information and report on it at your next class meeting: Answers will vary.

1. Does the student think that the campus food service offers enough healthy foods?
2. Is there any organic food available in campus cafeterias?
3. What does the student know about sustainable food?
4. Does your school offer advice on smart food choices and a balanced diet?
5. Is the student satisfied with his/her diet? What should be changed?

INTERNET Go online, and use the search term "food pyramid" to find a website that is sponsored by the U.S. Department of Agriculture. Here you can evaluate your eating habits when you click on the box to "track" your diet. Create a profile of your diet for the last 24 hours. After you complete the list of food that you ate, the website will evaluate your diet. In class, report on the website's evaluation of your eating habits. Answers will vary.

30 | LESSON 3 | Food Sciences: Biotech Crops

■ EXPANSION IDEA

Grammar and Vocabulary
Have students edit each other's compositions, noting where more verbs for events in the future could be used.

PART 1
Verb Review: Transitive,
Intransitive, and Middle Voice

PART 2
Verbs with Indirect Objects

Lesson (4)

Journalism: Sources of the News

■ CONTENT VOCABULARY

Look up the words below that you do not know and enter them in your vocabulary journal.
Write each word's part of speech, a definition, and an example sentence. Try to include them
in your discussion and writing below.

a briefing	to decline	to fare	an overview
to broadcast	to detach	a figure	a shelter
a deal	an evacuee	a news anchor	vis-à-vis

■ THINK ABOUT IT

How are news broadcasts on TV different from news broadcasts on the radio? How do they
differ from newspapers? In your writing journal, write for five minutes about the questions
below. When you are finished, share what you wrote with the class.

What sources of news do people use regularly? What is your favorite source of news? What
kinds of reports do you read or listen to? What are the advantages and disadvantages of
each source?   Answers will vary.

31

Lesson (4)

Overview
1. Ask students to name different ways of getting the news. Write their suggestions on the board.
2. Ask students who follow the news on a daily basis to raise their hands.
3. Call on a few students and ask them if they follow the news in their countries, the United States, or both.

■ CONTENT VOCABULARY
Ask students to review the words in the box. Tell them to look up any unfamiliar words.

■ VOCABULARY JOURNAL
Have students add new words to their vocabulary journals and write down the parts of speech, definitions, and example sentences for each.

■ THINK ABOUT IT
1. Read the instructions with the class.
2. Give students five minutes to write in their journals.
3. Divide the class into small groups and have students discuss their answers.

■ CONTENT NOTES

The topic of this lesson is Journalism: Sources of the News. Students will acquire vocabulary associated with news and journalism. Use this lesson to encourage students to listen to, watch, and read the news on a daily basis. This is an excellent way for them to increase their vocabulary and become more familiar with life and politics in the United States.

PART ONE

Verb Review: Transitive, Intransitive, and Middle Voice

■ **GRAMMAR IN CONTENT**

■ **EXERCISE A** *CD 1, Track 7*

1. Ask students to look at the picture and read the title of the article. Have them predict what the interview will be about.

2. Write *blog* on the board. Ask students to raise their hands if they read blogs on the Internet. Have them name some of the kinds of blogs they read on a regular basis.

3. Play the audio and have students follow along in their books as they listen.

4. Check for comprehension by asking questions such as the following: *What does Mr. Cotter call "traditional" sources of the news? How much time do Americans over age 25 spend listening to, reading, or watching the news? Which kind of news in particular do people over age 25 log onto Internet news sites to find? What do most major newspapers offer readers? Why do they do this?*

■ **GRAMMAR IN CONTENT**

A Read and listen to the panel discussion among journalists. The words in bold are verbs used intransitively.

CD1,TR7

Getting the Latest News

Moderator: Last week the Pew Research Center released its survey on the audience for Internet news and trends in newspaper readership. Richard, can you give <u>us</u> an overview?

R. Cotter: I think that most journalists were pleasantly surprised to learn that the amount of time Americans spend on the news **hasn't decreased** since 1996. The report indicates that Internet news has taken some of the audience away from traditional sources of the news—newspapers, TV, and radio. Americans over 25 still spend about 1 hour per day on the news.

Moderator: Henry Atkins, let's examine that demographic in more detail.

H. Atkins: Mike, Internet use among adults in the 25–64 age group **has grown** substantially in the last 10 years, vis-à-vis getting the news. It used to be that 18–25-year-olds made up a major part of the audience of Internet news sites. Now many more people over 25 appreciate the convenience of online news sites and log on to the Internet for business and international news in particular.

Moderator: How **have** news blogs **fared?**

H. Atkins: The percentage of young people who read news blogs **has risen**, but most online news consumers have never even read a news blog. Older Americans still prefer radio programs or the editorial page for opinions or commentary on the news.

Moderator: Richard, according to the report, fewer people get their news from newspapers and news broadcasts. How much **have** the numbers actually **declined?**

R. Cotter: The country's major newspapers and broadcast news outlets **have stabilized**. As you may **recall**, in the 90s the market for all of the traditional news outlets **dropped** alarmingly. Now, for example, newspaper readership has **leveled off**. This is primarily due to online newspapers. Most major newspapers offer <u>readers</u> an online version, hoping to attract new customers.

Moderator: So the figures for newspaper readership include online readers, too?

R. Cotter: That's right. And, I need to point out that the people who read online newspapers are a much smaller number than those who check the headlines out at CNN or MSNBC.

Moderator: Thank you, gentlemen. For those of you who want to read over the full report, you can go to our website.

a demographic: a portion of a population
substantially: to a great extent, significantly

an editorial page: the page of a newspaper with articles that express opinions
to level off: to become stable; to no longer change

32 LESSON 4 | Journalism: Sources of the News

■ **EXPANSION IDEA**

Exercise A

1. Divide the class into pairs and have students take turns reading each of the parts of the dialog.

2. Call on volunteers to role-play the dialog for the class. Tell them to pay attention to pronunciation and intonation as they speak.

Verb Review: Transitive, Intransitive, and Middle Voice

Sample Sentences	Notes
A good editor **demands** accuracy from every reporter.	Transitive verbs are verbs with direct objects (*demand, cause, get, need, think through, look up, create*).
When a serious traffic accident **occurs**, a local TV reporter usually broadcasts from the scene. When TV reporters **set out** from the studio, they never know what might happen.	Intransitive verbs are verbs without direct objects (*seem, die, happen, set out, come back, stand out*).
The news anchor usually **opens** the broadcast with an overview of the stories. Our local TV news **opened** with a story about a local case of arson. Some vandals **burned down** an old barn. The weather has been so hot and dry that the barn **burned down** in 30 minutes.	Some verbs can be both transitive and intransitive (*end, change, drop, close; burn down, blow up, light up*). When intransitive, these verbs express a **middle voice** between active and passive structures. In such sentences, grammatical subjects do not take the role of the agent or "doer" despite the active form of the verb.
1. Porter **brought the weapon up** because he was curious about the lack of evidence in the case. 2. During the news conference, the reporter Ned Porter **brought up the missing weapon**. 3. The police chief was angry that Porter **had brought it up**. Porter **ran into** Chief Walker later and asked him again.	Many transitive phrasal verbs follow special rules for the order of the particle and direct object. If the direct object is a noun, use: 1. verb + noun + particle **OR** 2. verb + particle + noun. But if the direct object is a pronoun, use: 3. verb + pronoun + particle. NOTE: A small group of transitive phrasal verbs are not separable, such as *come across, get over, run into*.

Useful Transitive Phrasal Verbs That Are Separable

bring up	figure out	put/set forth	sum up
carry out	get/put across	read up on	work out
clear up	point out	rule out	write up

B Read over your journal entry, and <u>underline</u> at least one sentence that you can revise to include a verb that is used intransitively. Write your revised sentence(s) below.

Answers will vary.

_____

_____

_____

Verb Review: Transitive, Intransitive, and Middle Voice

1. Write *transitive* on the board and elicit a definition from a class member.
2. Write *A good reporter gets the facts* on the board. Call on a volunteer to underline the subject, circle the verb, and put two lines under the direct object of the sentence. Ask a volunteer to explain why *get* is a transitive verb.
3. Have students review the sample sentences and the Notes.
4. Call on volunteers to point out the subjects, verbs, and direct objects of each of the sample sentences whenever possible. All class members should be comfortable doing this before you move on.

■ **EXERCISE B**

Have students complete the activity and compare their sentences with a partner.

■ **EXPANSION IDEA**

Grammar

1. Divide the class into pairs. Have them go through the dialog in Exercise A and identify subjects, transitive verbs, and direct objects.

2. Circulate as students work and assist as needed.

EXERCISE C

1. Ask students to name some verbs that can be both transitive and intransitive and write them on the board.
2. Call on volunteers to give examples of sentences using the verbs on the board.
3. Have students complete the activity and the check their work with a partner.
4. Call on volunteers to read their answers to the class. If any errors or disagreements about answers occur, go over the question explaining why the verb can or cannot be used both transitively and intransitively.

EXERCISE D

1. Have students complete the activity individually and then check their answers in pairs.
2. Go over the answers as a class.

EXERCISE E

1. Ask students to read the instructions and the words in the box.
2. Have students edit the excerpt.
3. Call on volunteers to read the paragraph aloud. If any transitive verbs are used, ask other class members to suggest ways to change the focus of the sentence from the agent of the action to the object.

C Write "X" by each sentence with at least one verb that can be used both transitively and intransitively. (Circle) the verb. Follow the example.

  X   1. My Jetta (drives) really well, but I rarely drive it any more.

  X   2. Fifty journalists were waiting when Air Force One (landed) at the Air Force base in Nebraska.

       3. All of the journalists rose when the President entered the briefing room.

  X   4. The news conference (finished) early.

       5. Several of the reporters left even earlier.

  X   6. Air Force One (refuels) after every flight as a security precaution.

       7. After the news conference, the President immediately turned and walked out.

       8. Back at the Air Force base, he boarded the plane and waved to the crowd.

  X   9. Air Force One taxied down the runway and (took) off.

D Underline the verbs used intransitively in the news item below. Then, (circle) the verbs that can also be used transitively.

> Houston—According to NASA scientists, communications with a Mars probe broke down late last week. Earlier an antenna (had detached,) and the signal from the probe (weakened) considerably. The probe was operating on energy from its solar packs, which have also partially (shut down.) Researchers had anticipated such problems if any part of the probe deteriorated or fell off.

E Edit the following article. Change the focus in each sentence from the agent of the action to the objects. Use intransitive verbs from the list below. You will not use all of the verbs.

start	increase	burn	burn down
die	light up	end	~~survive~~

>   **fifty houses survived**
> Griffin, OR—~~Firefighters saved 50 houses~~ in the eastern part of Griffin, Oregon, as ~~fires burned~~ another
>   **burned**   **25 homes burned.**
> 500 acres of grassland outside town. In the past 2 weeks, ~~fires have destroyed 25 homes in the area.~~
>   **the fires started**
> According to local fire officials, ~~careless campers may have started the fires~~ in a campground about 5
>   **no one has died.**
> miles from Griffin. So far ~~the fires have not killed anyone.~~

■ EXPANSION IDEA

Exercise E

1. Ask students to think of a news item that they read about recently. Have them write an introductory paragraph to a news article on the subject. Tell them to use as many intransitive verbs as possible.

2. Have students exchange work with a partner. Ask partners to edit each other's work, making active sentences passive when appropriate.

3. Call on a few volunteers to read their paragraphs to the class.

F **SMALL GROUP WORK** Imagine you work at a newspaper. Explain to your editor why you need an extension for your group project. Use all the phrasal verbs in the box for each excuse. An example has been provided. **Answers will vary.**

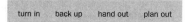

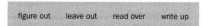
turn in   back up   hand out   plan out

1. *I'm sorry, but we won't be able to (turn our article in) tomorrow. When you (handed out) the assignment, our team met right away and (planned it out) very carefully. Unfortunately, Suzie's computer crashed, and she forgot to (back her interviews up.)*

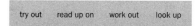
figure out   leave out   read over   write up

2. I'm sorry, we won't be able to finish the assignment on time. We need time to (read over) what information we've gathered and (figure out) what we've (left out.) Then we'll (write the report up.)

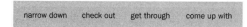
narrow down   check out   get through   come up with

3. Sorry, we need more time to (come up with) a list of interviews for the article. Once we (get through) to everyone, we'll (narrow down) the list and (check out) the leads.

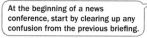
try out   read up on   work out   look up

4. I'm sorry, the group won't be able to turn the project in on time. My computer broke and I need to (look up) what the problem is. After I (read up) on it, I'll (try it out,) I'll (work out) what to do then with the rest of the group.

G **PAIR WORK** Using as many phrasal verbs as possible, make a short, informal presentation on tips for a successful news conference. **Answers will vary.**

At the beginning of a news conference, start by clearing up any confusion from the previous briefing.

■ **COMMUNICATE**

■ **EXERCISE F**

1. Ask students to read the instructions and the example.
2. Divide the class into small groups and have students write their excuses.
3. Circulate as students work; assist as needed.
4. Call on volunteers to read their excuses to the class.
5. Vote informally on which group has the best excuses.

■ **EXERCISE G**

1. Review the instructions with the class.
2. Call on a student to read the text in the speech balloon.
3. Divide the class into pairs. Have students brainstorm ideas for their presentations and write them down.
4. Have pairs present their presentations to the class.

■ **EXPANSION IDEA**

Exercise G

Divide the class into pairs. Have students role-play a prep session for a news conference, with one student playing the role of a consultant and the other person about to give the conference.

For example:

Student 1: *Have you confirmed all of your facts? You don't want to say something accidentally that can be proven to be false.*
Student 2: *That's not a problem. My facts are all confirmed. What I'm nervous about is having the question session last too long.*

PART TWO

Verbs with Indirect Objects

■ GRAMMAR IN CONTENT

■ EXERCISE A

1. Write *indirect object* on the board. Call on a volunteer to write on the board a sentence that includes an indirect object.
2. Have students complete the activity on their own.
3. Go over the answers together, explaining how to identify indirect objects if necessary.

■ GRAMMAR CHART

Verbs with Direct and Indirect Objects

1. Call on students to read the sample sentences one sentence at a time. After each sentence has been read, ask students to identify the subject, verb, object, and indirect object. Then read the accompanying Note.
2. Review the list of verbs that use the preposition *for*.

■ GRAMMAR IN CONTENT

A Reread the text of the panel discussion on page 32, and <u>underline</u> examples of indirect objects. Compare your answers with a classmate's.

Verbs with Direct and Indirect Objects	
Sample Sentences	**Notes**

Diana and her friends Irene and Owen follow the news, and Diana often sends Owen^{I.O.} e-mail messages with commentaries from news blogs.^{D.O.} She sent one ^{D.O.} to Owen^{I.O.} last night.
 	
She e-mailed some other people^{I.O.} the same information,^{D.O.} but they didn't respond.
 	
She doesn't e-mail the blogs ^{D.O.} to other friends^{I.O.} because they don't care very much about bloggers' opinions.
	Some transitive verbs have two objects: a direct and an indirect object. For many verbs, for example *give, send, lend, bring, pay,* the order of objects depends on the information the speaker wants to highlight.
	
	1. **Verb + Indirect Object (I.O.) + Direct Object (D.O.)** shows that:
	  · the indirect object is already known or of less importance to the context.
	  · the direct object is the focus of attention in the context.
	
	2. **Verb + Direct Object +** *to* **+ Indirect Object** shows that:
	  · the direct object is already known or of less importance.
	  · the indirect object is the highlight of the communication.

She promised him^{I.O.} a list of her favorite blogs.^{D.O.} She'll probably send it ^{D.O.} to anyone who is interested.^{I.O.} She'll send it ^{D.O.} to us^{I.O.} if you ask for a copy, too.	If either object is a pronoun, put the pronoun after the verb. Then, follow the rules above.
She explained her interest in the blogs ^{D.O.} to her friends,^{I.O.} but they weren't interested. Did she mention the purpose of the blog ^{D.O.} to them?^{I.O.}	For other verbs, such as *explain, mention, describe, say, announce,* only pattern 2. above is correct.
A friend of Diana's had found her^{I.O.} a whole list of news blogs,^{D.O.} so Diana made a copy of the list ^{D.O.} for Owen.^{I.O.} She left it ^{D.O.} for him^{I.O.} with a note on it. She saved it ^{D.O.} for some other friends,^{I.O.} too.	Some verbs with two objects express an action done for somebody's benefit. (See the list of verbs below.) Use one of these two patterns: 3. **Verb + Indirect Object + Direct Object** 4. (Verbs that use *for* include *buy, cook, draw, find, get, leave, make, order, save, sew, spare.*) **Verb + Direct Object +** *for* **+ Indirect Object**

■ EXPANSION IDEA

Grammar Chart

1. Have students write four sentences that use indirect objects. Tell them to scramble their sentences.
2. Have students exchange scrambled sentences with a partner. See how quickly they can unscramble each other's work.

For example:
promised/a/she/him/box/his/of/candy/favorite
She promised him a box of his favorite candy.

B Each of these editorials has three errors in usage. Edit the awkward phrases, rewriting them to correct or improve the usage of indirect objects. Follow the example.

> ... according to recent reports, the Prime Minister approved the purchase of ten fighter planes. He shouldn't
>
> *order them for the military*
> ~~order the military them~~ just as peace negotiations are beginning among the countries in that region. It sends ~~the~~
>
> **their allies the wrong message.**
> ~~wrong message to their allies.~~ Instead the Prime Minister should promise a postponement of the airplane deal

> ...announced the creation of a new national monument around a chain of Hawaiian islands. We applaud this
>
> decision, which sets aside 1,200 nautical miles of the Pacific Ocean to protect the fragile coral reef there. The
>
> **for**
> law saves the extensive reef ~~to~~ the native fish and sea mammals. Since the area is so remote, only a limited
>
> **visitors access to the monument**
> number of tour operators will offer ~~to visitors access to the monument.~~ We urge all citizens to contact their
>
> **them positive feedback on the measure**
> representatives and give ~~positive feedback on the measure to them.~~...

C Listen to each statement and (circle) the letter of the correct interpretation. The first one has been done as an example.

CD1,TR8

1. (a.) Jay didn't mention his children.
   b. Jay didn't mention his daughter.
2. (a.) The bookstore placed a textbook order for us.
   b. The bookstore told us that we had to buy copies of the textbook.
3. (a.) His supervisor found the mistake for him.
   b. His supervisor pointed at the mistake with her finger.
4. a. George took the newspaper out of the mailbox when he came in the house.
   (b.) George bought a newspaper for me when he came home from work.
5. (a.) I'll e-mail him about the new deadline.
   b. I'll e-mail her about the new deadline.
6. a. My editor read over the article and then approved it.
   (b.) My editor read the articles over and then approved them.
7. a. A colleague left the office and now I can't find his message.
   (b.) A colleague wrote a message to me and put it in my office, but it's lost.
8. a. I need to ask them more questions to finish the interview.
   (b.) I need to ask him more questions to finish the interview.

■ **EXERCISE B**

1. Ask students to read the instructions and the example.
2. Answer any questions students have and then have them complete the activity individually.
3. Ask students to check their work with a partner.
4. Call on volunteers to identify the errors and read their corrections to the class.

■ **EXERCISE C** 🎧 *CD 1, Track 8*

1. Tell students that they will hear a series of statements. They will be asked to choose the correct interpretation. Play the first problem and pause the audio so that students can check the example.
2. Play the audio, pausing after each statement so that students can mark their answers.
3. Play the audio through once more so that students can check their answers.
4. Go over the answers together. If students disagree about an answer, play the audio again so that they can identify the correct interpretation.

■ **EXPANSION IDEA**

Exercise B

Have students choose an article from a local newspaper (print or online) and have them examine the article for any awkward phrases. Have them rewrite those sentences and share their changes with the class.

1. Read the instructions aloud to the class. Tell students that they should make up details as they write their reports.
2. Have students exchange work with a partner. Ask students to edit each other's work, concentrating on target grammar and vocabulary from the lesson.

■ EXERCISE E

1. Read the instructions aloud to the class.
2. Put students into seven groups.
3. Assign each group one of the verbs in the box.
4. Have each group write a sentence for the briefing script using their assigned verb. Groups will have to collaborate so that the briefing has a logical order.
5. Circulate and assist groups as needed.

D On a separate piece of paper, write a 5–6 sentence report about relief efforts for evacuees of a recent typhoon on the island of Macao (off China). Focus on the efforts of local volunteers to assist the evacuees, who arrived with few possessions and must live in shelters for at least 2–3 weeks.

E Use the notes below to prepare a briefing for the press about the President's agenda for an upcoming trip. Complete the script for the briefing below, using verbs in the box.
Answers will vary. Sample answers below.

promise	give	teach	show
offer	grant	assign	award

Monday:
10:00 meeting with Gov. Ortiz: $15 million in federal funds for school construction
$300 million increase in scholarships for minority students
12:00 Lunch Gov. & mayors: "Most Improved School System" prize to Mayor Scott of Springfield
2:30 Central H.S.: donation of 500 books to school library
meeting with junior class and demonstration of software for scholarship applications

Ladies and gentlemen, on Monday, President Ryan will offer $15 million to Governor Ortiz for school construction.   In addition, Ryan has promised minority students $300 million in scholarships. After lunch, the President will award Mayor Scott the "Most Improved School System Prize." From there, President Ryan will go to Central High School. He plans to give the school 500 books for their library. Also, at a meeting with the junior class, he will show them the software that they can use for scholarship applications.

■ EXPANSION IDEA

Exercise D
1. Ask students to find an article in a newspaper or online about an accident or natural disaster. Have them circle examples of the use of verbs with direct and indirect objects.

Ask them to note how much of the article is written in the passive voice.
2. Divide the class into pairs and have students compare their articles. Ask them to discuss how journalists' writing differs from academic writing.

F Use the notes and the verbs in the box to prepare another briefing for the press about the President's trip. Look at the example to see how one student got started. **Answers will vary.**

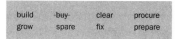

build	~~buy~~	clear	procure
grow	spare	fix	prepare

Tuesday:

Meeting with Mayor Nguyen about emergency planning
· promise to purchase emergency supplies for shelters at schools
· up to $200 million in federal funds available for school safety/construction
· models of "safe school" available from Corps of Engineers
· 10-year program: $10 million available annually for school infrastructure

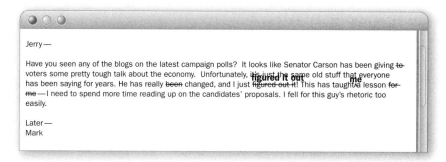

The government will buy supplies for schools that operate as emergency shelters.

G Find and correct the four errors in the informal e-mail message below.

Jerry—

Have you seen any of the blogs on the latest campaign polls? It looks like Senator Carson has been giving ~~to~~ voters some pretty tough talk about the economy. Unfortunately, **figured it out** same old stuff that everyone has been saying for years. He has really ~~been~~ changed, and I just ~~figured out~~ it! This has taught **me** a lesson ~~for me~~—I need to spend more time reading up on the candidates' proposals. I fell for this guy's rhetoric too easily.

Later—
Mark

■ **COMMUNICATE**

H **SMALL GROUP/CLASS WORK** Write a story to be included in a newsletter about the people in your English class. Before you begin, decide about the items for the newsletter with your classmates, and choose a topic with your partner. Together, draft a short article (5–7 sentences) about the latest news in your class. Once you have finished your draft, give it to another team so that they can edit it. After all of the articles have been edited, compile them as a newsletter. **Answers will vary.**

■ **EXERCISE F**

Have students complete the activity, preparing another press briefing using the notes provided.

■ **EXERCISE G**

1. Have students complete the activity individually and then check their answers with a partner.
2. Call on volunteers to read the corrected e-mail aloud.

■ **COMMUNICATE**

■ **EXERCISE H**

1. Go over the instructions with the class.
2. Discuss possible topics for your class newsletter and write them on the board.
3. Divide the class into pairs and have the class decide the topic each group will write about.
4. Give students time to write their articles. Then have groups exchange work for editing.
5. Compile the class newspaper.

■ **EXPANSION IDEA**

Exercise H

Ask students to find an editorial in a local newspaper. Have them compare articles with a partner and discuss how an editorial is different from a news item.

Connection

Putting It Together

■ GRAMMAR AND VOCABULARY

1. Ask students to read the instructions.
2. Call on two students to read the topics aloud.
3. Give students time to write their compositions.
4. Circulate as students work; assist as needed. Remind them to use the vocabulary and structures from the lesson.

■ PROJECT

1. Go over the instructions with the class and have students conduct their interview.
2. Have students report the results of their interviews to the class.
3. Discuss the results, asking students to compare U.S. student interest in the news with that of students in their home countries.

■ INTERNET

Review the instructions. Have students conduct their searches and report their findings to the class.

GRAMMAR AND VOCABULARY Write a composition on one of the topics below. Use as many words as possible from the Content Vocabulary on page 31. Use structures that you practiced in this lesson to express your ideas.   Answers will vary.

Topic 1: Does recent news have any personal relevance or importance for you? Explain why or why not and give concrete examples.

Topic 2: Statistics show that local news is especially popular among people who read newspapers and watch or listen to TV and radio news broadcasts. Why do people take an interest in this kind of news and pay less attention to national or international news stories? Explain and give concrete examples.

PROJECT Interview a student.

Interview at least one student on your campus and find out the following information:

1. Does the student follow the news?
2. How much time does the student spend every day on the news?
3. What is the main source of the news for that person?
4. Does the student talk about the news with friends or classmates?

Then, report on the student's responses in your class.   Answers will vary.

 INTERNET Compare Sources

Go online or look at the print version of major newspapers available on your campus or in your town. Compare how the same story is reported in several different sources and report to your class on 2–3 similarities and/or differences. Choose one of these newspapers: *The New York Times* (www.nytimes.com), *USA Today* (www.usatoday.com), *The Washington Post* (www.washingtonpost.com), the *Los Angeles Times* (www.latimes.com), *The Wall Street Journal* (www.wallstreetjournal.com).
Answers will vary.

■ EXPANSION IDEA

Grammar and Vocabulary

1. Divide the class into groups of students who wrote about the same topic.
2. Have students discuss their ideas about the news.

Internet

Have students choose an article about international news in a U.S. newspaper. Then have them find an article on the same topic in a foreign language newspaper or website. Have them report to the class on how the information in and presentation of the story differed.

Lesson ⑤

History and Musicology: The Silk Road

■ CONTENT VOCABULARY

Look up the words below that you do not know and enter them in your vocabulary journal. Write each word's part of speech, a definition, and an example sentence. Try to include them in your discussion and writing below.

cast iron	a fabric	a repertoire	to originate
a commodity	a fiddle	a route	unique
a device	goods	a technique	widespread

■ THINK ABOUT IT

Look at the map on the following page of the trade route known as the Silk Road. With a partner, brainstorm a list of the modern countries that are located along the Silk Road. What goods did merchants probably transport over this route? Discuss your ideas with a classmate.

In your writing journal, write for five minutes about the questions below. When you are finished, share what you wrote with the class.   Answers will vary.

In ancient times, what countries were trading partners with your country? Did any trade routes cross through your country or include your harbors? Do you know what goods merchants transported over this route? What kinds of goods did people in your country consider precious in those times?

41

Lesson ⑤

Overview

1. Elicit prior knowledge about the Silk Road by asking students to name the countries that the route passed through. Write the countries on the board.
2. Ask the students if they can tell the class anything about the history of the Silk Road.

■ CONTENT VOCABULARY

Ask students to review the words in the box. Tell them to look up any unfamiliar words.

■ VOCABULARY JOURNAL

Have students add new words to their vocabulary journals and write down the parts of speech, definitions, and example sentences for each.

■ THINK ABOUT IT

1. Have students read the instructions.
2. Divide the class into pairs and have them discuss the questions posed in the exercise.
3. Circulate as students work and assist with vocabulary as needed.
4. Give students five minutes to write in their journals. Then call on volunteers to discuss the ancient trade routes, harbors, and goods traded in their countries.

■ CONTENT NOTES

The topic of this lesson is History and Musicology: The Silk Road. Students will have the opportunity to learn about early trade routes and how trade influenced different Asian cultures. Encourage students to discuss how trade affected dress and customs in their countries.

PART ONE

Articles to Express a Generic Reference

■ GRAMMAR IN CONTENT

■ EXERCISE A 🎧 CD 1, Track 9

1. Play the audio and have students follow along in their books as they listen.

2. Ask students to circle any words or phrases that they don't understand.

3. Call on students to read any words or phrases that they circled. Elicit definitions for these words or phrases from the class if possible.

4. Check comprehension by asking questions such as *Which product was exported from China before the Silk Road got its name? What was China's first important export product to the West? Who specifically bought it? What kinds of academics are interested in tracing the consequences of cultural contacts along the Silk Road?*

■ GRAMMAR IN CONTENT

🎧 **A** **Read and listen to the passage below. The words in bold express generic references.**

CD1,TR9

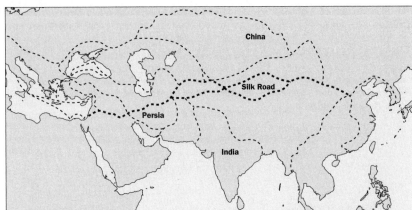

The Mystery and Romance of the Silk Road

Centuries before the Silk Road got its name in 1877 from German explorer Ferdinand von Richthofen, the trade in jade between the Chinese and the people in oasis towns of Central Asia was quite active. In this area the jade-carvers were famous, and their carvings were transported from China along the southern Silk Road for centuries. In contrast to the sale of jade, which stayed primarily within Asia, Chinese silk became the East's first important export to the West, specifically to the Romans. By the second century BCE, silk had reached the Mediterranean, but the people there had no clear idea of the source of this highly prized fabric.

Those who moved along the Silk Road generally traveled only part of the total distance, except for the great explorers like Marco Polo. Traders and pilgrims went from oasis to oasis, avoiding the harsh central desert. The two-humped camel was especially well suited to this environment, and stories of caravans of camels piled with exotic fabrics and jewels fueled the West's romantic view of the arduous trek toward China. However, other travelers went by foot or on horseback. The Buddhists, for example, usually walked between their holy sites and monasteries in China and India.

Today, anthropologists, ethnomusicologists, art historians, and even engineers in materials science have become interested in tracing the consequences of cultural contacts along the Silk Road. For example, extra-long sleeves are still seen today in Chinese opera and in some traditional Asian clothing, but that style of sleeve came from Western Asia, near modern-day Ukraine. In the eighth-century Shosoin collection of stringed musical instruments in Japan, the design on one lute (biwa in Japanese or pipa in Chinese) shows camels and another has an elephant. Clearly, these instruments did not originate in Japan, but somewhere else along the Silk Road. Chinese industrial texts from the seventeenth century include illustrations of blast furnaces and describe techniques that didn't become widespread until several centuries later in the West. Over time, as traders moved their goods from region to region, ideas, philosophies, arts, religions, and technologies accompanied them, found new homes, and developed in new directions.

a lute: a stringed instrument with a pear-shaped body   jade: a green gemstone that is often carved for decorations or jewelry

42   LESSON 5 | History and Musicology: The Silk Road

■ EXPANSION IDEA

Exercise A

Divide the class into small groups and have students discuss the following questions:

Imagine you are stranded on an island where people have been isolated for centuries. Which of your personal items do you think would interest them most? What do you think they could offer you that you would need to survive on their island?

Articles to Express a Generic Reference

Sample Sentences	Notes
Without **the camel**, transportation was very difficult along much of the Silk Road.	Some articles can signal generic meanings of the nouns they modify. In other words, an article and noun refer to **something general or abstract**, not concrete or specific. The choice of article depends on the formality of the context and the meaning of the noun.
The best filaments for making silk are produced by **the moth** *Bombyx mori.* **The mechanical clock** was in use in China by the eleventh century. **The mulberry tree** provides nourishment for caterpillars of the *Bombyx mori.*	In a formal context, you can use **the** and **a singular countable noun** from the following categories: · animate objects (animals, plants, body parts/organs). · musical instruments. · human inventions and devices (*the iPod*, *the engine*), but not everyday items that developed through history (*tables, pencils*).
Among the travelers, there were **pilgrims**, **traders**, and **adventurers.** A trader on the Silk Road might have transported **silk** toward the West and **furniture** toward the East to satisfy his customers.	Using Ø (no article) and **a plural noun** is common in informal contexts. You can also use Ø with **noncount nouns.**
A caravan was the most economical way to transport precious goods because **a trader** needed to carry enough merchandise to make the long trip profitable.	Use **a** or **an** and **a singular countable noun** when giving an example of a group, type, or category.
In contrast to **the Chinese**, **the Europeans** didn't have clocks until the fourteenth century.	Use *the* and **a plural noun** when referring to human groups for people of the same religion, nationality, language, social, or professional background.
Nowadays you can take **the plane** to Xi'an, which was the beginning of the Silk Road in China. In rural areas people use **the Internet** to sell their goods to the outside world. In central Asian towns and villages, most locally produced goods are available at **the bazaar.**	Use *the* and **a singular noun** when you mention the following in daily routine activities: · Public transportation: the bus, the train, the plane. · Mass communications: the phone, the radio, the Internet. · Common institutions and businesses: the store, the bank, the movies/cinema, the hairdresser, the dentist.

B Read over your journal entry, and <u>underline</u> at least one sentence that you can revise to include an article with a generic reference. Write your revised sentence(s) below.

Answers will vary.

_____

_____

_____

Articles to Express a Generic Reference

1. Write on the board *The horse was introduced to South America by the Spaniards.* Ask students whether *the horse* refers to a specific horse. Point out that as used in this sentence, *the* refers to a general category.
2. Call on students to read the sample sentences aloud. Ask them to read the corresponding Notes.
3. Answer any questions that students have about the use of articles to express generic references.

EXERCISE B

Have students read the instructions and complete the activity individually. Have students compare their sentence with a partner.

EXPANSION IDEA

Grammar

1. Divide the class into small groups. Have groups review the clothing they are wearing and the items they brought with them to class. Ask each group to make a list of the products and countries where these products were produced, using the correct articles.
2. Call on a member of each group to report back to the class.

EXERCISE C

1. Read the instructions and example with the class.
2. Have students complete the activity individually and then check their answers with a partner.
3. Call on volunteers to read their answers to the class.

EXERCISE D

1. Call on a volunteer to explain the difference between *generic* and *definite* nouns.
2. Call on a student to read the example. Ask a volunteer to explain why *the yak* is used generically.
3. Ask students to complete the activity individually. Then have students check their work with a partner.
4. Go over the answers together as a class. If students appear to be confused, have them refer to the Grammar Chart and give a few additional examples.

C Does the underlined noun phrase express a generic reference? Write "Yes" or "No" in the space provided. Follow the example.

1. *Yes* Many explorers wrote about a huge wild sheep in remote areas along the Silk Road.
2. **No** The zoo in Samarkand has a huge wild sheep in one of the exhibits.
3. **Yes** Buddhists were among the pilgrims that traveled on the Silk Road.
4. **Yes** Travelers on the Silk Road watched for palm trees in some regions because they knew that water was available nearby.
5. **Yes** The palm tree is native to this region.
6. **No** In one traveler's diary, he mentioned a Buddhist among the other travelers in the caravan.
7. **No** At the end of each day, Samir took the saddles off his camels after he unloaded his goods.
8. **No** A saddle lay by the side of the road, and members of the caravan wondered what had happened.
9. **No** Later, the caravan passed a Buddhist and a camel.
10. **No** At night one of the travelers entertained his fellow travelers by playing a flute.
11. **Yes** Musicologists have found the flute or a similar instrument in most cultures.
12. **Yes** The silk weaver was a valued member of Chinese society.

D Read the texts below, looking closely at the underlined articles and nouns. If the noun is used generically, write "G." If the noun is definite, write "D."

1. **G** Several types of animals were brought to China from western regions. Tibetans, for example, introduced the yak to China.
2. **D** The Chinese used dogs from Persia and Tibet as hunting dogs. The dog in Castiglione's painting of the Chinese court was known as a "Roman dog."
3. **G** Most eastern houses and palaces were designed for people to sit on mats, rugs, or cushions on the floor. When traders brought the chair to China, Chinese court architecture changed.
4. **G** Although Indians produced both silk and cotton, the cotton was more famous.
5. **D** The Chinese learned techniques to make iron from metal-workers in West Asia, but Chinese artisans were able to improve the techniques.
6. **G** By 1100 the Chinese were able to mold cast iron objects. The Europeans did not produce the cast iron cooking pot for another 300 years.
7. **G** Buddhism had a strong influence on Chinese culture over the centuries. This influence is even visible in silk designs, which included the elephant.

EXPANSION IDEA

Exercises C and D
Ask students to write a short essay about outside influences on Chinese culture and society using information introduced in the lesson. Tell them to circle *the* when it is used generically in their essays, and to underline it when it is used with a noun that is definite.

E **GROUP WORK** Choose five things (animate or inanimate) that visitors to your country may notice or want to see as they travel across your land. Give some background or an explanation about those five things in 1–2 sentences. Then, share the information with a group.

Answers will vary.

> Visitors may see buffaloes in many western states. Settlers nearly killed off the buffalo in the 1800s, but now there are big herds of them in reserves and other protected areas.

PART TWO	*The* for Unique Reference: Definite Reference

■ GRAMMAR IN CONTENT

A Reread the text about the Silk Road, and <u>underline</u> every example of *"the + noun"* that is not in bold print. Which phrases express something that is unique, not to be confused with anything else? Which phrases are definite or specific because of information that comes *after* the noun? Compare your answers with a classmate's.

The for Unique Reference

Sample Sentences	Notes
(at rehearsal) Could I move **the stand** a little closer, please? (at rehearsal) I saw your violin case in **the rehearsal room** before rehearsal started. (at the theater) Is **the ticket office** near **the stage door**? **The moon** rose directly over **the stage** at their first outdoor concert.	Use *the* to signal information is shared with your listener or reader and can be inferred from: • environment • context • general knowledge
The first selection on tonight's program is considered **the best** song in their repertoire. **The remaining** music will be performed by **the same** string players with a guest singer.	Use *the* before adjectives that uniquely identify nouns: *the first, second, third . . . last/final* *the same/identical* *the only/single* superlative forms: *the best, the highest . . .*

■ **EXPANSION IDEA**

Grammar

1. Ask students to review "Food Options in Our Future" in Lesson 3, on student book page 24. Have students look for examples of articles used for definite or unique reference.

2. Divide the class into pairs and have students compare and discuss answers.

■ EXERCISE E

1. Ask students to read the instructions.
2. Call on a student to read the example. Ask a volunteer to add an additional sentence to the text in the bubble. For example: *The American buffalo is no longer on the endangered species list.*
3. Have students complete the activity.
4. Call on volunteers to read their answers to the class.
5. Have students discuss each other's answers.

PART TWO

The for Unique Reference: Definite Reference

■ GRAMMAR IN CONTENT

■ EXERCISE A

1. Write *unique* on the board and call on a volunteer to give a synonym or definition for the word.
2. Have students complete the activity.
3. Have students check their answers with a partner.

■ GRAMMAR CHART
The for Unique Reference

1. Call on students to read the sample sentences and the corresponding Notes.
2. Answer any questions students have about the use of *the* for unique reference.

■ GRAMMAR CHART

Definite Reference

1. Call on students to read the sample sentences and corresponding Notes.
2. Call on a volunteer to explain how *definite reference* differs from *unique reference* in his or her own words.
3. Answer any questions that students have about the use of *the* for definite reference.

■ EXERCISE B

Have students complete the activity and then compare their answers with a classmate.

■ EXERCISE C

1. Ask students to read the instructions.
2. Have students complete the activity individually. Go over the answers as a class.

Definite Reference	
Sample Sentences	**Notes**
Our host played a folk song for us, and then his family sang the song again later.	Use *the* when previous information in the sentence or text identifies the noun.
I had never heard **the music of Azerbaijan** before. I have a DVD of **the performance that introduces several musicians from the Silk Road Project.** One segment of it was filmed in **the town square where the musicians often play.** The DVD included interviews with **the people there.**	Use *the* when a noun is followed by identifying information in: · prepositional phrases · relative clauses · adverbials

B For each of the contexts below, write five things that you expect to find there.

1. a concert hall: *the stage, the orchestra pit, the balcony, the coat room, the restrooms*
2. an airport: the baggage claim, the control tower, the check-in counter, the security check-point, the waiting area
3. a sports center: the locker room, the weight room, the basketball court, the equipment room, the pool
4. a hospital: the emergency room, the nurse's station, the intensive care unit, the maternity ward, the operating room
5. a college campus: the cafeteria, the admissions office, the sports center, the English department, the registrar's office
6. a typical house in your country or region: the front door, the garage, the refrigerator, the kitchen, the attic

C Edit the text below, inserting the definite article wherever necessary.

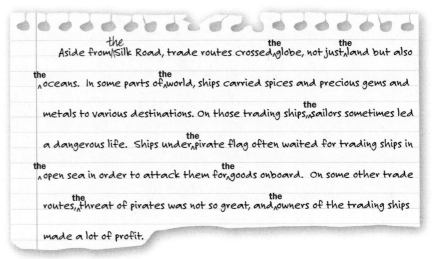

the
Aside from ⁁Silk Road, trade routes crossed ⁁*the* globe, not just ⁁*the* land but also

the
⁁oceans. In some parts of ⁁*the* world, ships carried spices and precious gems and

metals to various destinations. On those trading ships, ⁁*the* sailors sometimes led

the
a dangerous life. Ships under ⁁pirate flag often waited for trading ships in

the
⁁open sea in order to attack them for ⁁*the* goods onboard. On some other trade

the   *the*
routes, ⁁threat of pirates was not so great, and ⁁owners of the trading ships

made a lot of profit.

■ EXPANSION IDEA

Exercise C

1. Ask students to write a paragraph about a major route in their own countries, modeled on Exercise C.

   For example: *The Pan-American Highway stretches from Alaska to Ushuaia, in my home country, Argentina. The highway is nearly 30,000 miles long.*

2. Call on volunteers to read their paragraphs to the class.

D On a separate piece of paper, write a comparison/contrast of three types of fiddles found in countries along the Silk Road. Use *the* as appropriate.   Answers will vary.

Name of fiddle	*erhu* "foreign string instrument"	*kemancheh*	*morin khuur* "horse fiddle"
Countries	China	Iran, Azerbaijan	Mongolia
Strings	2		3, horsehair
Bow	horsehair on bamboo		horsehair
Body	wood: round, hexagonal, octagonal, or tubular	wood: small, round w/spike from the base	wood, or wood frame with camel, goat, or sheepskin covering
Face of body	snakeskin	animal skin	
Neck	long	cone-shaped	peg box in shape of horse's head; tuning pegs = "horse's ears"
Playing position	supported on left thigh with left hand	on player's knee or on ground; turned on spike	sound box on lap or between player's knees
Sound	fine, lyrical	elegant, warm, like human voice	like a horse neighing or a breeze
Use	solo instrument	solo or small groups	with folk singers
Cultural note		used in tradition of improvised music	horses are important to national identity

E Listen to part of Professor Taylor's musicology class. (Circle) your interpretation of each part of his presentation.

CD1,TR10

1. a.   He is defining the *kemancheh*.
   (b.) He is talking about a particular *kemancheh*.
2. (a.) He is defining the *ney*.
   b.   He is talking about a particular *ney*.
3. (a.) He is describing the general technique for playing the *ney*.
   b.   He is describing how a particular musician plays the *ney*.
4. a.   He is talking about the material used to make a particular *ney*.
   (b.) He is talking about the general construction of all *neys*.
5. (a.) He is describing the general techniques of playing the *shakuhachi*.
   b.   He is describing the way that a particular player performed on the *shakuhachi*.
6. (a.) He compares the general use of the *ney* and the *shakuhachi* in meditation.
   b.   He compares the use of both instruments in particular types of meditation.

■ EXERCISE D

1. Ask students to read the instructions and the example.
2. Have students complete the activity.
3. Call on volunteers to read their answers to the class.

■ EXERCISE E
CD 1, Track 10

1. Write *musicology* on the board. Elicit a definition from class members, if possible.
2. Tell students that they will hear a lecture from a musicology course. Ask them to listen for comprehension only.
3. Have students read through the questions. Play the audio again, pausing it frequently so that students can circle their answers.
4. Play the audio again so that students can verify their answers.
5. Go over the answers together. If necessary, play the audio again.

■ EXPANSION IDEA

Exercise D
Divide the class into pairs and have them compare their essays. Remind students to look for use of *the*.

■ EXERCISE F

1. Read the instructions with the class.
2. Divide the class into small groups and ask students to choose one of the themes. Have students compare their choice to a similar theme in their home country.
3. Circulate as students work and assist as needed.
4. Ask students to share their findings with the class.

Connection

Putting It Together

■ GRAMMAR AND VOCABULARY

1. Read the instructions aloud to the class and have two students read the topics.
2. Give students time to write their compositions.
3. Have students pair up and edit each other's essays, checking whether all articles are underlined.

■ PROJECT

1. Review the instructions with the class.
2. Have students conduct their interview and then report on it at the next class meeting.

■ INTERNET

1. Review the instructions and have students conduct their searches and prepare their comparisons.
2. Call on volunteers to present their findings to the class.

F GROUP WORK Ask classmates about the cuisine, traffic, music, fashion, or celebrations in a country that they have visited.

Are you familiar with the cuisine of Venezuela?

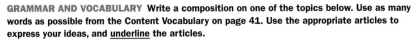

Connection Putting It Together

GRAMMAR AND VOCABULARY Write a composition on one of the topics below. Use as many words as possible from the Content Vocabulary on page 41. Use the appropriate articles to express your ideas, and <u>underline</u> the articles.

Topic 1: Around the world individuals learn and perform traditional songs and dances, often in costumes based on traditional clothing from their culture. These individuals may also learn the folk songs and dances of other cultures and perform them at festivals or ceremonies. In our high-tech world, why do these "old-fashioned" arts survive?

Topic 2: Since ancient times countries have had both cultural and economic connections. China was a "major player" in the world of the Silk Road, and the impact of Chinese culture and technology has been found in different corners of the world. Choose one cultural connection with the United States that has affected another country that you are familiar with in the last 50 years—either positively or negatively. Explain that connection or influence, and give examples.
Answers will vary.

 PROJECT Interview at least one student on your campus about traditional North American music. Find out the following information, and report on it at your next class meeting.

1. Which musical instruments do Americans typically use for playing folk songs or other traditional music?
2. What kinds of music do most people consider typical traditional American music?
3. Does the student enjoy folk music? Why, or why not?
Answers will vary.

INTERNET Go online, and use the search phrase "musical instruments from Middle East" or "musical instruments from Asia." Find an instrument that is similar to a traditional musical instrument in your culture. Then, prepare a comparison of the two instruments for class, and, if possible, print out pictures of the instruments for your classmates to see. (If you search for the name of your instrument, you will find many websites with pictures of musical instruments from around the world.)
Answers will vary.

■ EXPANSION IDEA

Grammar and Vocabulary
Ask students to sing a traditional folk song from their countries. Then play some North American folk music for the class.

A Complete each sentence, using a verb from the box in the appropriate verb tense and aspect. When appropriate, put an article (including Ø) or indirect object that completes the ideas.

observe	exceed	harvest	send	build	appear	strike
plant	germinate	burn down	develop	return	grow	

TO: Partners of the Virginia Company
FROM: John Rolfe
DATE: July 15, 1613
RE: Update on Tobacco Cultivation in Jamestown, Virginia

_____ **The** _____ tobacco crop this year _____ **has exceeded** _____
        (1)   (2)

our expectations. After we _____ **planted** _____ 20 more acres in early
                              (3)

spring, _____ **the** _____ seeds _____ **germinated** _____ and
           (4)   (5)

quickly matured. For the past three weeks my men _____ **have harvested** _____ the
                                             (6)

tobacco leaves. _____ **The** _____ tobacco _____ **appears to be** _____
                 (7)   (8)

well-suited to _____ **the** _____ climate and soil in Virginia. While
                   (9)

visiting Indian settlements last summer, I _____ **observed** _____ that
                                    (10)

_____ **the Ø** _____ corn, _____ **the Ø** _____ beans, and other
       (11)   (12)

vegetables also _____ **grow** _____ well in this region.
                     (13)

    This winter I _____ **am going to develop** _____ a 5-year plan for my plantation,
                       (14)

which I _____ **will send** _____ on _____ **the** _____ ship which
           (15)   (16)

is scheduled to leave here in April. Aside from agricultural products, I intend to raise

_____ **the Ø** _____ livestock. _____ **The** _____ first structure
       (17)   (18)

on my property for our few cattle _____ **burned down** _____ after lightning
                               (19)

_____ **struck** _____ it a few weeks ago. We _____ **are going to build** _____ a barn
       (20)   (21)

after the next ship _____ **returns** _____ from England.
                  (22)

Review Lessons 1-5

The purpose of this lesson is to help students review the language and concepts they have learned in the last five lessons. Encourage them to go back to the lessons and review the grammar charts to help them complete the review activities.

■ EXERCISE A

1. Ask students to read the instructions and the verbs in the box.
2. Ask students to complete the activity individually and then check their work in pairs.
3. Call on volunteers to read their answers aloud.
4. Discuss any differences of opinion among class members.

■ EXPANSION IDEA

Exercise A

1. Divide the class into pairs.
2. Have students take turns asking and answering questions about the information in Exercise A, using the verbs from the box in the correct tenses.

For example:

Student 1: *How many acres of tobacco were planted in early spring?*
Student 2: *According to Rolfe, 20 more acres were planted.*

1. Have students read the instructions.
2. Have students complete the activity individually and then check their work in pairs.
3. Call on volunteers to read their answers aloud.

■ **LEARNER LOG**

Have students complete the Learner Log. Suggest that they review the Grammar Charts for areas that need more practice.

B (Circle) the correct word(s) or phrase(s) in the second sentence of the text or conversation.

1. Many farmers are interested in transgenic crops because such crops can offer an alternative to herbicides and pesticides. These chemicals (had posed / (have posed)) potential health problems to farm workers and to consumers.

2. For several years farmers in the United States have been experimenting with drought-resistant corn. They ((plant) / planted) this type of corn in small quantities in isolated parts of their property.

3. **Fred Porter:** "What do you think of the insect-resistant plants that you've planted this year?"
   Luke Walker: "They seem to be doing well, but (the cotton / (cotton)) grows well this time of year anyway."

4. Some genetically manipulated crops are very nutritious. For example, biotech researchers have been able to raise the protein content of (a soybean / (the soybean)).

5. **Wilt Owens:** ". . . I was checking out the corn field yesterday afternoon and heard a strange buzzing sound. I ((walk) / walked) over to the section with the biotech corn and see this giant grasshopper, and then it flies . . ."

6. In order to survive, farmers in Jamestown had to increase their agricultural knowledge. They planted seeds that they (brought / (had brought)) from England and learned to harvest fruits and vegetables that ((grew) / had grown) wild in Virginia.

7. **Mary Carter:** "I wasn't familiar with some vegetables in Virginia, so at the beginning I followed the Powhatans' style of preparing them. Later, I cooked them ((for us) / to us) with different spices."

8. **Ned Baker:** "I have to be careful with the biotech crops because I want to keep them separate from everything else that I harvest. I store all of the biotech crops in (a barn / (the barn)) since I have space in there."

9. Many people fear the long-term effects of eating genetically engineered food. By 2020 researchers (will complete / (will have completed)) several studies that track the effects of such food on humans and animals.

10. Agricultural entrepreneurs pay attention to the research on biotech crops and to public response to such crops. Before they plan their planting schedule for the year, they ((have considered) / considered) the potential market for their products.

LEARNER LOG Check (✔) *Yes* or *I Need More Practice.*
Answers will vary.

Lesson	I Can Use . . .	Yes	I Need More Practice
1	Verbs in the Present, Past, and Future		
2	Verbs in Simple Past and Past Perfect; Shifts to the Present		
3	Verbs in the Future Time; Verbs in the Progressive Aspect		
4	Transitive Verbs, Intransitive Verbs, and Verbs in Middle Voice; Verbs with Indirect Objects		
5	Articles for Generic, Unique, and Definite Reference		

■ **EXPANSION IDEA**

Exercise B

1. Divide the class into pairs.
2. Tell students to discuss genetically engineered foods, basing their conversations on the information presented in the exercise.

For example:

Student 1: *I don't think you can judge the success of insect-resistant cotton if it was planted during a time of year when cotton grows well anyway.*

Student 2: *If the cotton crop were larger than usual, that would provide some proof.*

Lesson ⑥

Linguistics: Spelling, Codes, and Alphabets

Lesson ⑥

■ CONTENT VOCABULARY

Look up the words below that you do not know and enter them in your vocabulary journal. Write each word's part of speech, a definition, and an example sentence. Try to include them in your discussion and writing below.

a correspondence	literacy	a shortcut	to encode
cursive script	presumably	a syllable	to digitize
cyberspace	reasonable	to condone	to reform

■ THINK ABOUT IT

How much experience have you had with learning a different alphabet or another writing system? How long did it take you to become comfortable writing in a new way? What was the hardest part of learning to write the new language? Discuss your ideas with a classmate.

In your writing journal, write for five minutes about these questions. When you are finished, share your opinions with the class.
In your opinion, should students use the language and spelling of text messaging in school assignments and tests? Is it appropriate to e-mail your instructor with the same special e-mail symbols and spellings that you use with your friends and family? Why or why not?

51

■ CONTENT NOTES

The topic of this lesson is Linguistics: Spelling, Codes, and Alphabets. Students will discuss appropriate uses of "text-speak" and some of the difficulties associated with learning foreign languages. Use this opportunity to stress the fact that learning any new language is challenging and that students should not be discouraged if they encounter problems learning English.

Overview

1. Ask students who text message frequently if they use abbreviations when they write to their friends.
2. Call on a few volunteers to write a line or two on the board using text-message style abbreviations.
3. Ask students if they do this in their first languages as well.

■ CONTENT VOCABULARY

Ask students to review the words in the box. Tell them to look up any unfamiliar words.

■ VOCABULARY JOURNAL

Have students add new words to their vocabulary journals and write down the parts of speech, definitions, and example sentences for each.

■ THINK ABOUT IT

1. Have students read the instructions.
2. Ask students to raise their hands if they have ever studied a different alphabet or writing system. Call on a few volunteers to tell the class what the experience was like.
3. Divide the class into pairs and have students continue to discuss the topic. If students have no experience with learning a new alphabet or writing system, have them imagine what it would be like.
4. Give students five minutes to write in their journals about using the language of text-messaging.

■ GRAMMAR IN CONTENT

■ EXERCISE A
CD 1, Track 11

1. Write on the board *If u thnk text-spk is the deth o nglsh, thnk agin* and call on a student to read the sentence.

2. Play the audio and have students follow along in their books as they listen. Ask students to circle any unfamiliar words or phrases.

3. Check comprehension by asking questions such as the following: *What does the author believe is the "real threat to the English language"? What are some of the limitations of text-speak? What are some of the contexts in which text-speak will never be appropriate?*

■ GRAMMAR IN CONTENT

A Read and listen to the passage below. The words in bold are phrasal modals or modal-like verbs.

CD1,TR11

If u thnk txt-spk is the deth o nglsh, thnk agin

As a new academic semester begins, educators around the country are haunted by New Zealand's decision to allow text-speak—those shortcuts and abbreviations used in text messaging—on national exams.

What does the New Zealand Qualifications Authority's policy say about the future of our language? **Are we to condone** Suzi who <u>cant</u> use apostrophes? and what about chad, a student I know whos given up on capitals? Worse yet, what do we do about Johnny (u <u>wont</u> believe this 1) who drops vowels and uses acronyms?

Given the prevalence of such language abuses, why <u>would</u> New Zealand officially allow students to use abbreviations that most of us <u>would</u> like to see confined to the world of IM and text messaging? Surely, if we **are to believe** the media hype, those New Zealanders (must) have kiwi-size brains to degrade our language in such a deliberate manner.

The hype, however, is not the reality.

The real threat to the English language comes from bad writing and questionable literacy. Most of us <u>can</u> think of a U.S. president who abuses our language more than the average teenage blogger.

Text-speak does, of course, have significant limitations. The most commonly used acronyms are just that—common—and we**'re not going to win** any Pulitzer Prizes writing either "GMTA" or "great minds think alike." An acronym of a cliché is still a cliché.

Rather than view text-speak as a Hurricane Katrina of language, educators <u>should</u> recognize its appearance as that most valuable of pedagogical tools, the "teachable moment." Text-speak provides us with an opportunity to introduce students to some basics of English composition: tone, audience, style, and clarity.

Our mode of writing is always context-specific. A biology lab report (might) be written entirely in the passive voice, but a passive style will make that paper on *Great Expectations* a dud. Contractions (might) be acceptable in an editorial, but not a formal history essay. The first-person voice works in an opinion piece or job letter, but we**'d better** use the third-person when writing a biography of Harriet Tubman.

Text-speak requires similar <u>rules</u>. Only a fool <u>would</u> try to write in full Standard English using a cell-phone keypad. At the same time, we (should) recommend a cranial CAT scan for the student who writes a term paper using text-speak. The guidelines of the New Zealand Qualifications Authority make such distinctions clear—students <u>will</u> be penalized for using abbreviations in an exam that requires them to demonstrate language use.

In many academic contexts, text-speak <u>will</u> never be appropriate. Formal essays, which presumably always require a demonstration of sound language use, are not the place for shortcuts. Exams represent a different scenario. Students need to consider the subject matter and exam issues. In a timed psychology test, abbreviations such as "b/c" and "M/F ratio" (should) pose no problem. In a literature exam with tight time constraints, a student (might) be wise, after the first usage, to save time by abbreviating "point of view" and "Fyodor Dostoevsky" with POV and FD.

Whatever the exam guidelines, students need to show clearly their understanding of the subject. The student who writes "drng t g8 dprsn, pvrty wz, ttbomk, a bg prblm" (during the Great Depression, poverty was, to the best of my knowledge, a big problem) is being neither clear nor insightful, whether in the United States or New Zealand.

Two centuries ago, Jane Austen's Henry Tilney mocked female letter writers for having a "general deficiency of subject, a total inattention to stops, and a very frequent ignorance of grammar." Then, as now, language was in flux. However, if we approach current changes thoughtfully, as Austen did, language need not be in a state of decline.

IM: instant messaging, a form of interpersonal communication on the Internet

media hype: excessive media attention and publicity

a Pulitzer Prize: an annual American prize for journalism and literature

a cliché: a superficial or overused expression or saying

M/F ratio: the proportion of males to females

a dud: something that is unsuccessful or disappointing

a CAT scan: a 3-dimensional, computerized scan

Jane Austen: a British novelist (1775–1817)

Henry Tilney: a character in Austen's novel *Northanger Abbey*

to mock: to ridicule, to make fun of

in flux: in the process of changing

■ EXPANSION IDEA

Exercise A
Divide the class into pairs. Have students write two sentences each and translate the sentences into text speak. Have each student write one of their sentences onto the board for the class to translate.

Sample Sentences	Notes
Bill **was about to** text his friends when his teacher walked in the door.	*Be about to* signals that an action will occur in the near future, even immediately.
If you **are to** master English spelling, you need to learn all of the exceptional spellings.	*Be to* signals a future plan or intention. It represents formal usage.
Any ESL student **has to** spend a lot of time on spelling.	*Have to* signals both personal and external necessity. Americans prefer **have to** for this meaning and use *must* for inferences (see Part Two).
I've **got to** study this list of terms before class tomorrow.	*Have got to* expresses an urgent necessity, mostly in informal contexts.
Homework assignments **ought to** have correct spelling and punctuation.	*Ought to* signals an obligation to follow external social or moral rules.
Students **shouldn't** hand in assignments with spelling errors.	Use *should* instead of *ought to* in questions and negative sentences.
We're **supposed to** have a spelling test next week.	*Be supposed to* expresses the obligation to follow rules imposed by an impersonal outside authority or by a plan or schedule. In the past tense, the affirmative implies the action didn't happen, and the negative implies that the action did happen.
The teacher **wasn't supposed to** tell us the words on the next test (but she did).	
The test **was only supposed to** take 10 minutes (but it took 30 minutes).	
Were we **to** memorize all of the irregular spelling words for the /f/ sound?	*Be to* expresses an arrangement that implies external supervision or authority.
My advisor said I **am to** complete all my required courses by the end of the year.	

B Read over your journal entry, and <u>underline</u> at least one sentence that you can revise to include a phrasal modal. Write your revised sentence(s) below.

Answers will vary.

■ GRAMMAR CHART
Academic Phrasal Modals

1. Write *modal auxiliary* on the board and call on volunteers to give some examples, if possible. Write them on the board.
2. Write *phrasal modal* on the board and call on volunteers to give examples, if possible.
3. Call on students to read the sample sentences and accompanying Notes.
4. Answer any questions students have about using phrasal modals.

■ EXERCISE B

Have students complete the exercise and share their answers with a partner.

■ EXPANSION IDEA

Grammar

Write *Have you ever . . . ?* on the board. Divide the class into pairs and have students take turns finishing sentences that contain academic phrasal modals.

For example:

Student 1: *Have you ever jumped out of a plane?*
Student 2: *No, I haven't. I once was about to, but then I changed my mind.*

▪ EXERCISE C

1. Read the instructions and example.
2. Have students complete the activity.
3. Call on volunteers to read their answers to the class, explaining their choices if challenged by classmates.

C (Circle) the letter of the appropriate paraphrase for each statement below.

1. The Simplified Spelling Society (SSS) is to meet next Friday to elect its next president.
   a. The Simplified Spelling Society has a meeting scheduled for next Friday.
   b. The president of the Simplified Spelling Society has required that the members meet next Friday.

2. According to the SSS, English speakers have to reform English spelling.
   a. The SSS thinks that it is necessary for English speakers to reform the spelling of English words.
   b. The SSS thinks that English speakers have an obligation to reform the spelling of English words.

3. English spelling has got to change to make worldwide communication easier.
   a. Worldwide communication will only improve after certain spelling changes have been made.
   b. Certain changes have to happen before spelling can be improved.

4. For example, they say that extra, or surplus, letters like the final *-e* in the words *little, terrible,* or *resemble* ought to disappear from English spelling.
   a. The SSS recommends omitting surplus letters.
   b. The SSS claims that surplus letters have disappeared from English spelling.

5. Teachers aren't supposed to use any of the SSS's spelling reforms.
   a. People generally assume that teachers don't use the spelling reforms.
   b. Teachers shouldn't use the spelling reforms.

6. During their past meetings, SSS members were supposed to recommend five reforms for future application in computer software.
   a. The members recommended five reforms.
   b. The members didn't recommend five reforms.

7. During the last meeting, they were about to discuss using the letter *f* for all /f/ sounds when the president had to end the session.
   a. The members were ready to discuss the letter *f* just before the end of the meeting.
   b. The members discussed the letter *f* before the end of the meeting.

▪ EXPANSION IDEAS

Exercise C

Divide the class into small groups. Have groups discuss the topic of simplified spelling. How much easier do they think it would be to learn English with simplified spelling? What changes would they make?

Exercise C

1. Ask students to write a few sentences using simplified spelling.
2. Have students exchange work with a partner.
3. Call on volunteers to report on whether they were able to read their partner's sentences easily or if simplified spelling created new problems for them.

D What are the students' questions in each situation? Work with a partner and make questions, using different modals. Follow the example.

1. Mr. Atkins assigns his class a research paper on the history of English spelling.

   a. team work? ___*Do we have to work together? Who should we work with?*___

   b. due date? __When are we supposed to turn it in?__

2. Mr. Atkins gives his students a spelling exercise that introduces some new spelling rules of the Simplified Spelling Society.

   a. omit surplus letters? __Are we supposed to omit the surplus letters?__

   b. write by hand? __Are we to write it by hand?__

3. Mr. Atkins returns homework papers with his feedback on them.

   a. correct mistakes? __Am I supposed to correct the mistakes?__

   b. the way to find correct answers? __How am I supposed to find the correct answers?__

E Look at each question. Write an appropriate answer to each one, using the same phrasal verb in the question. Follow the example.

1. Do I have to dot the letter *j*?

   ___*You don't have to, but it may be easier to read that way.*___

2. Were they to use text-speak on this test?

   __They didn't have to, but it saved a lot of time.__

3. Should I write my class notes in text-speak?

   __It's probably a good idea since you can write it so fast.__

4. Aren't you supposed to omit all capital letters in text-speak?
   __There are no rules about capitalizing letters when using text-speak—you can do whatever you want.__

5. Did we have to use text-speak on the test?

   __We didn't have to but he said that we wouldn't get any extra time for the test.__

6. Were we to finish this lesson by Friday?

   __Yes, because we're on a tight schedule.__

■ EXERCISE D

1. Review the instructions.
2. Ask students to look at the example.
3. Have students complete the activity with a partner.
4. Call on volunteers to read their answers to the class, defending their answers if classmates disagree.

■ EXERCISE E

1. Ask students to review the instructions and examples.
2. Have students complete the activity.
3. Call on volunteers to read their answers to the class, defending them if classmates disagree.

■ EXPANSION IDEA

Exercise E

1. Ask students to write instructions for an exam. Tell them to use as many academic phrasal modals in their instructions as possible.

2. Have students exchange work with a partner. Tell students to ask and answer questions about their partner's instructions.

EXERCISE F

1. Ask students to read the instructions.
2. Call on a few students to read the notes for Mr. Atkins's presentation.
3. Ask a volunteer to summarize Mr. Atkins's proposal.
4. Call on a student to read the example.
5. Have students complete the activity individually.
6. Call on volunteers to read their answers to the class.

COMMUNICATE

EXERCISE G

Have students develop their codes in pairs, write their sentences, and then decode each other's messages.

F Use the class notes from Mr. Atkins's presentation about spelling reform to answer the questions. Use phrasal modals in your answers. Follow the example.

> Some Principles for International English Spelling
>
> Purpose: to make learning to read easier for children and for non-native speakers
>
> #1: Don't change irregular words that are very common (= 31 words of 100 most frequent words!!)
> examples: are, come, should, half, know, of, one, other, pull, what
>
> #2: Use vowel letters a, e, i, o, u for both long and short vowels with a grave accent for long vowels. In other words, omit final silent -e.
> examples: mat (= mat) / màt (= mate); bit (= bit) / bìt = bite)
>
> #3: Make consonant letters match the sounds in words:
> scent and cent → sent; pleasure → plezhur, little → litl

1. Why does the SSS propose various spelling reforms?
   So people who learn how to read don't have to struggle with spelling.

2. How does this system handle the most frequent words in English?
   They are left unchanged.

3. How will the grave accent help learners of English?
   They will understand pronunciations of confusing spellings.

4. How can someone tell the difference between a long and short vowel in a text?
   The grave accent indicates a long sound.

5. According to these principles, what are better spellings of *numb, leisure, gauge, leave,* and *enough?*
   num, lèzhur, gàj, lèv, ènuf

COMMUNICATE

G PAIR WORK Develop a secret code substituting letters with other letters, numbers, or symbols. (If the number 5 represents *h*, for example, and 2 represents *i*, then 52 spells "hi.") Then, convert this sentence into your code: *Some codes are easy to crack.* Exchange your encoded sentence with another pair. Can you figure out the other pair's code? When you finish, check each other's work.
Answers will vary.

EXPANSION IDEA

Exercise F

1. Ask students to try writing a sentence in their first language using a simplified spelling system.
2. Divide the class into small groups. Have them discuss spelling rules in their first languages and whether a simplified spelling system would be useful.

GRAMMAR IN CONTENT

A Reread the text at the beginning of the lesson, and underline all of the other modals. Circle the modals that express an inference, deduction, or prediction, and compare your answers with a partner.

Modals: Troubleshooting

Sample Sentences	Notes
Before alphabetic writing, people **used to** keep records in other kinds of writing systems. In Mesopotamia they **would** preserve information in signs, or pictographs. Later, the Egyptians **would** take this form of writing and develop it further into their hieroglyphics.	The following phrasal modals express past habitual actions: · *Used to* signals a past action or condition, including location and ownership. · *Would* signals past actions or events, often ones that happened regularly. NOTE: A story or text is often introduced with *used to* and continued with *would* or its contraction *'d*.
Did the Egyptians **used to** write in a cursive script, too?	
Children **used to** have fountain pens that they used for penmanship lessons.	
It **must** be hard to learn a totally new script.	To express a very strong logical inference or logical necessity, use *must* or (especially to express an emotional reaction) *have got to*.
Our teacher **has got to** be kidding! We can't learn 25 new Chinese characters by tomorrow!	
You **must not** understand the way to connect Arabic letters because you wrote the words all wrong.	Express a negative inference with *must not*.
We **should** finish learning the Russian alphabet soon because we've finished all of the consonants already.	Do not use *must* with references to the future. Use *should* instead: **Incorrect:** We ~~must~~ have a spelling quiz soon. **Correct:** We *should* have a spelling quiz soon.
It **shouldn't** take long to learn to read Russian because most of the letters are the same as the Latin alphabet.	*Should* expresses an inference of reasonable certainty or a prediction.

■ GRAMMAR IN CONTENT

■ EXERCISE A

1. Ask students to brainstorm modals and write them on the board.
2. Have students underline modals in the reading and then compare their answers with a partner.

■ GRAMMAR CHART
Modals: Troubleshooting

1. Call on students to read the sample sentences and corresponding Notes aloud.
2. Answer any questions students have about the use of *used to, would, have got to, must not, have to, should.*

■ EXPANSION IDEA

Grammar Chart

Have students write a sentence of their own for each modal used in the Grammar Chart.

EXERCISE B

1. Have students read the instructions and the example.
2. Ask students to complete the activity, using modals whenever possible in their answers.
3. Ask students to exchange answers with a partner. Ask partners to suggest where additional modals might be used.
4. Call on volunteers from as many different countries as possible to read their answers to the class.

EXERCISE C

1. Have students complete the activity and then check their work with a partner.
2. Call on volunteers to read their answers to the class. If more than one modal is possible, have them explain why.

B Using modals of past habitual actions, answer the questions about the history of literacy. You can write about the history of English or the history of your first language. The first item provides a sample answer.

1. In previous centuries, what kinds of people were able to read?

    Religious leaders and people in the upper class would learn to read.

2. In the old days, where did people learn to read and write?

    People used to learn to read and write from tutors.

3. In those days, how did illiterate people conduct business or learn about things?

    In those days, illiterate people would pay people to read or write letters for them.

4. In the old days, what other languages did people in your country learn? Why?

    In the old days, rich people used to learn French because it was a sign of sophistication.

5. When you were a child, how did you learn the writing system for your language?

    When I was a child, we would practice the alphabet and hand-writing.

6. How did your teacher motivate you to write clearly and legibly?

    My teacher would give us prizes for nice penmanship.

C Circle the appropriate modal(s) for each sentence. If more than one modal is possible, explain why on a separate piece of paper.

1. When you learn Arabic, you ___ train yourself to write from right to left.
   a. have to   b. must   c. have got to
   Reason: a & c mean necessity, and c is OK if the speaker is emphasizing the idea in an informal conversation.

2. Students of the Japanese or Chinese language ___ learn the proper order of brush strokes or pen strokes for each character. **Reason: a, b, & c mean necessity.**
   a. have to   b. must   c. have got to

3. Since Arabic letters have different forms at the beginning, in the middle, and at the end of a word, beginning students ___ have a hard time learning the forms.
   a. have to   b. must   c. have got to

4. Japanese and Chinese schoolchildren ___ take years to learn how to read their languages because there are so many characters.
   a. have to   b. must   c. have got to

5. It ___ be easier for a Korean student to learn English than for a Japanese student because the Korean writing system is partly alphabetic.
   a. has to   b. must   c. should

6. Students who first learn to write using an alphabet ___ have some difficulty when they begin to study a language with a system based on syllables as in Japanese.
   a. have to   b. must   c. should

7. When you write Arabic words, you ___ connect the letters.
   a. must   b. should   c. are supposed to

8. It ___ be easy for children to learn two different writing systems at the same time.
   a. doesn't have to   b. must not   c. shouldn't

EXPANSION IDEA

Exercise B

1. Divide the class into small groups, grouping students from different countries, if possible.
2. Ask students to discuss literacy in their own countries. What percentage of the people there know how to read and write?
3. Call on a member of each group to report on the group's findings.

D Make at least one inference and one prediction about each of the situations.

1. Twenty students enrolled in Hindi 101 this semester. It's the first time that the university has offered a course in Hindi.

   INFERENCE: The instructor must be happy that so many students want to learn Hindi.

   PREDICTION: They should offer another Hindi course next semester because the students will need two semesters of Hindi to fulfill their language requirements.

2. Alice Drake, a student in Hitoshi Sakakibara's Japanese 201 course, won the statewide Public Speaking contest. She will receive a plane ticket to Japan as her prize.

   INFERENCE: She must study her vocabulary very hard.

   PREDICTION: Her speaking skills should improve while she's in Japan.

3. This summer Dan Kowalski is spending a month in Honduras, where he will help on a construction project with local workers.

   INFERENCE: He must know a little Spanish.

   PREDICTION: He should have an interesting life experience.

4. Richford College is developing a summer study abroad program with a university in Lebanon.

   INFERENCE: Richford must have courses in the Arabic language.

   PREDICTION: The students should have a wonderful time in their home stays.

5. Jeannie Wu and her cousin Cindy Li have decided to spend one month at a language school in Taiwan and then go sightseeing there for another month this summer.

   INFERENCE: They must have a family connection to Taiwan.

   PREDICTION: They should enjoy all of the sights there.

6. LeMar Peters is a business major, and he hopes to spend one semester in Turkey during his junior year.

   INFERENCE: He must have some connections in Turkey.

   PREDICTION: He should make a lot of contacts for his future career in international trade.

■ **EXERCISE D**

1. Call on a volunteer to explain the difference between an *inference* and a *prediction*.
2. Have students read the instructions.
3. Call on students to read the statement, inference, and prediction in the first question.
4. Call on volunteers to give other inferences and predictions based on the first statement, such as:

Inference: *The university realized that students were interested in studying Hindi.*
Prediction: *Next semester, the school will open more Hindi 101 sections to accommodate demand.*

3. Have students complete the activity.
4. Call on volunteers to read their inferences and predictions to the class.

■ **EXPANSION IDEA**

Exercise D

1. Write on the board *The Earth's temperature is rising, causing heat waves and unusually warm weather. Associated with temperature changes are higher levels in oceans and the melting of glaciers.*

2. Divide the class into small groups and have them use the statement on the board to make inferences and predictions.
3. Circulate as students work. Encourage students to use modals as they discuss.

1. Tell students that they will hear a professor discuss a homework reading with his class.

2. Call on a student to read the text in the speech balloon.

3. Play the audio and have students listen for comprehension only.

4. Ask students to read through the questions. Then play the audio again, pausing to give students time to write their answers. If students request, play the audio again.

5. Have students compare their answers with a partner.

6. Call on volunteers to read their answers to the class. If there is any disagreement about answers, play the appropriate part of the audio again.

E Listen to Professor Wilkes and his class discuss a homework reading. Answer the questions below, using modals of inference.

CD1,TR12

Let's turn to the article by Dr. Bosworth about globalization and technology. What is the link to our class topic today?

1. What do you think the topic of today's class is?

   They must be talking about languages and computer systems.

2. What is the background of Bosworth, the author of their homework assignment?

   He must be a linguist or a computer scientist.

3. Why do they refer to Chinese characters as ideograms?

   Chinese characters are supposed to have a close relationship between image and meaning.

4. If ideograms really stimulate the right side of the brain, what does Bosworth predict?

   It should lead to a more creative and interactive relationship with computers.

5. How could this new operating system impact other Asian countries?

   It should be very attractive.

6. How is the growth of the Arabic immigrant population relevant to digitized Arabic in media technology?

   That should encourage even more use of the Arabic alphabet in computers.

7. What does Zhihua imply about the preference of Arabic-speaking readers?

   That they must prefer to read in their native language, like most people.

8. What does Bosworth seem to imply about the direction of globalization?

   Asia and the Middle East should continue to grow in importance.

■ **EXPANSION IDEA**

Exercise E

Have students write a summary of the discussion that took place in Professor Wilkes's class. Have them be sure to use modals of inference in their writing.

F Find and correct the four errors in the following letter.

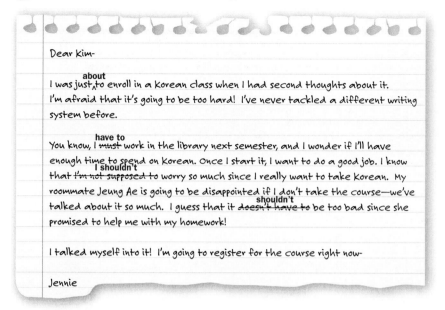

Dear Kim-

about
I was just ~~to~~ enroll in a Korean class when I had second thoughts about it. I'm afraid that it's going to be too hard! I've never tackled a different writing system before.

have to
You know, I ~~must~~ work in the library next semester, and I wonder if I'll have enough time to spend on Korean. Once I start it, I want to do a good job. I know
I shouldn't
that ~~I'm not supposed to~~ worry so much since I really want to take Korean. My roommate Jeung Ae is going to be disappointed if I don't take the course—we've talked about it so much. I guess that it
shouldn't
~~doesn't have to~~ be too bad since she promised to help me with my homework!

I talked myself into it! I'm going to register for the course right now-

Jennie

■ COMMUNICATE

G **PAIR WORK** Talk with your partner about your most effective methods of studying English (and any other language) before you entered this program.

When I first started learning English, I would make flash cards of new vocabulary.

I used to do that, too. But I'd also learn a lot of words by taking notes in class. I would look up any words I didn't know in the dictionary.

H **GROUP WORK** Design either (a) an English program or (b) a program for students of your native language. Write a short description, giving the basic philosophy or rationale for the course.   Answers will vary.

The students in our class are supposed to attend class five hours per day.

Yes, they are to spend most of their day speaking Russian.

■ **EXERCISE F**

1. Read the instructions to the class.
2. Have students read the letter silently, then put them into pairs.
3. Have each pair find the errors together.

■ **COMMUNICATE**

■ **EXERCISE G**

1. Read the instructions aloud to the class and have two students read the text in the speech bubbles.
2. Give students time to discuss.

■ **EXERCISE H**

1. Ask students to read the instructions.
2. Call on two students to read the text in the speech bubbles.
3. Divide the class into groups of three or four and have them design either an English program or a program for students learning the native language of one of the students in the group. Tell students to consider the challenges they faced when learning a foreign language for the first time.
4. Have groups present their descriptions for the program to the class.

■ **EXPANSION IDEA**

Exercise G

Have students discuss with their partners the aspects of English that they found most challenging when learning it. Have them think of remedies that helped them overcome these challenges.

Putting It Together

■ GRAMMAR AND VOCABULARY

1. Ask students to read the instructions. Call on a few volunteers to name phrasal modal verbs.

2. Call on students to read the two topics aloud. Ask if anyone in the class knows how to do calligraphy. If so, invite them to write a few words on the board and to tell students how they acquired this skill.

3. Have students write their compositions. Remind them to use as many modals and phrasal modal verbs as possible, and to underline them.

■ PROJECT

1. Ask students to review the instructions and answer any questions that they may have about the interviews.

2. Call on students at the next class meeting to report their findings.

■ INTERNET

Have students conduct their searches and then report back to the class on their findings.

GRAMMAR AND VOCABULARY Write a composition on one of the topics below. Use as many words as possible from the Content Vocabulary on page 51. Use modal verbs and phrasal modal verbs where appropriate to express your ideas, and <u>underline</u> those verbs.

Topic 1: In our modern world full of e-mails and text messages, is there still a place for calligraphy and nice handwriting? In many cultures, both the words of a text and the skill of writing the text have been highly prized. Do people still appreciate these handwriting and brush-stroke skills? Comment and give concrete examples.

Topic 2: For decades English has been the major world language. As Chinese and Arabic become more widespread in media technology, do you see English losing its place as the medium of international communication? Comment and give concrete examples.
Answers will vary.

PROJECT Interview at least one student on your campus about text messaging.
Find out the following information and report on it during your next class meeting:

1. What are the most important signs or abbreviations that you need to know to text message an American friend?
2. When does your interviewee use text-speak (aside from text messaging)?
3. Does your interviewee text message in class? How?

 INTERNET Go online, and use the search term "writing systems" to find a website with information about writing systems from around the world. Select one group, for example "syllabic alphabets," and then click on one of the languages to get more information. Report to the class on either one alphabet that is no longer used or one that is currently in use. Include brief information on

- who used to use it, or where the alphabet is in use today.
- how it is supposed to be written.
Answers will vary.

■ EXPANSION IDEA

Grammar and Vocabulary

1. Have students exchange their compositions with a partner.

2. Ask students to edit each other's work, checking for use of terms and grammar from the lesson, as well as concrete examples.

Social Psychology: Experiments

■ CONTENT VOCABULARY

Look up the words below that you do not know and enter them in your vocabulary journal. Write each word's part of speech, a definition, and an example sentence. Try to include them in your discussion and writing below.

to administer	deceptive	guidelines	to subject to
a bystander	an electric shock	a maze	a test subject
to conduct	groundbreaking	to postulate	willingness

■ THINK ABOUT IT

Have you ever been a test subject in an experiment? What kind of experiment was it? What did you have to do? How did you feel about participating as a test subject? Discuss your ideas with a classmate.

In your writing journal, write for five minutes about the questions below. When you are finished, share what you wrote with the class.

Have you ever read or heard about an experiment in which the participants had to do something that they didn't expect? Describe the experiment and then imagine how the participants felt about their experience. If you haven't read about such an experiment, think about a TV show or other type of entertainment in which members of the audience have to do something unexpected.   **Answers will vary.**

63

Lesson ⑦

Overview

1. Ask students to raise their hands if they have ever taken a psychology course.
2. Ask if any of them did experiments in their classes. If so, have them describe the experiments to the class.
3. Have the class brainstorm some types of experiments that psychology students might perform.

■ CONTENT VOCABULARY

Ask students to review the words in the box. Tell them to look up any unfamiliar words.

■ VOCABULARY JOURNAL

Have students add new words to their vocabulary journals and write down the parts of speech, definitions, and example sentences for each.

■ THINK ABOUT IT

1. Have students read the instructions.
2. Divide the class into pairs and have students discuss their ideas.
3. Ask students to review the journal assignment. Then give them five minutes to write in their journals.
4. Call on volunteers to share their journal entries with the class.

PART ONE

Modal Verbs:
Past Logical Scale

■ GRAMMAR IN CONTENT

■ EXERCISE A
CD 1, Track 13

1. Play the audio and have students follow along in their books as they listen.

2. Ask a few comprehension questions such as: *What did Milgram ask "teachers" to do? What did the actors do to put pressure on the "teachers"? Why did some people think that the experiment was unethical?*

3. Call on a volunteer to give a brief account of the experiment, in his or her own words.

■ GRAMMAR IN CONTENT

A Read and listen to the passage below. The words in bold are perfect modals.

CD1,TR13

A Lesson in Obedience

The famous Milgram experiment brought important information about human behavior to light, but the design of the experiment raises questions about ethical research methods. For his first experiments in 1963, Stanley Milgram recruited volunteers for a psychological experiment, but his advertisements did not give any specific information about the participants' role in the experiment. On arrival, each vounteer was introduced to another participant who was actually a paid actor that Milgram had hired. The volunteer was not told about this arrangement. The volunteer then played the role of "the teacher" in an experiment on memorization while the actor played "the student." The student sat in a separate room, and the two were able to communicate only by voice.

While the teachers were helping the students with the memorization task, they also had the job of punishing the students if they made mistakes. The teachers gave electric shocks to the students as punishment. The first shocks were at a very low intensity, but the intensity increased as the students continued to make mistakes. The actor/students made many mistakes on purpose, and the teachers gave shocks with higher and higher voltage. Meanwhile, the actors began complaining about the shocks and then screamed in pain after each shock. Milgram and his research team encouraged the teachers to continue with the punishment and told them that they had no choice. The teachers then continued, and their students received shocks until they became completely silent.

At the end of each experiment, Milgram met with the volunteer and explained the experiment. A full 65% of the participants, who were both men and women, had obeyed the experimenters and had administered electric shocks at the highest voltage. At this point, Milgram told them about the "learner's" true identity. Also, they learned that they hadn't actually given any electric shocks at all. Many of the participants had asked the researchers about the procedures during the experiment, but few had actually disobeyed. They <u>could have stopped</u> the shocks at any time and quit the experiment.

When people first hear about this experiment, they have similar responses. Most people think that a large majority of participants **must have disobeyed**. When they hear the statistics, they imagine that Milgram **must have been surprised**, too. People ask themselves how those volunteers could ignore the screams of the learners. Of course, the next step is the question **"Might I have done** the same thing?" The data shows that the answer to that question is probably "Yes." Finally, there are questions about the ethics of such an experiment and about the reactions of the participants. Many critics think that Milgram <u>shouldn't have subjected</u> the volunteers to such a stressful situation. There was concern that the volunteers **may have reacted** very negatively to their own willingness to cause severe pain to another person. However, according to Milgram, most of the volunteers felt that they had learned something valuable about themselves.

In response to the Milgram experiment and others, professional organizations and universities now monitor research designs. Modern guidelines for ethical research place a high value on the safety of participants—both mental and physical—regardless of the knowledge that could be gained from experiments.

to bring to light: to make public, to draw to public attention

an arrangement: an agreement, a plan

on purpose: intentionally

a professional organization: an association of people in a particular profession

■ EXPANSION IDEA

Exercise A
Ask students to discuss any other psychological experiments they have heard of. If they cannot offer any, tell them to research some experiments.

Examples are Pavlov's dogs, Asch conformity, and the Stanford Prison experiment. Note any ethical issues surrounding these experiments.

Modal Verbs: Past Logical Scale

Sample Sentences	Notes
The participants **might have reacted** negatively to the experimental results. Milgram **may not have expected** such results.	Use modals in their perfect form (**modal + have + past participle**) to express your interpretation of a past action or situation. Place *not* after the modal for negation: **modal + not have + past participle**
Some participants **must have regretted** their actions. Milgram **should have been** surprised by the results. Some of the actors **may have reacted** more strongly than others. The stressful experience **could have caused** psychological problems for the volunteers. The actors **might have screamed** more convincingly with practice.	Choose the modal below that expresses your opinion or feeling about the likeliness of a past event. Your choice signals your inference, expectation, or deduction about an action or situation that occurred previously. *must* *should* high probability *may* *could* low probability *might* NOTE: *Can* is not used at all for affirmative inferences or predictions.
The volunteers **might not have felt** comfortable about their actions. Milgram **may not have anticipated** the future criticisms of his experiments. The volunteers **must not have realized** that the experiment depended completely on their actions. Milgram **couldn't have predicted** the high rate of obedience among the volunteers. He **can't have known** the level of a regular person's obedience before he started the experiments.	The negative forms of perfect modals that express inferences and predictions do not all express the same levels of probability as the affirmative forms above. *might not* high negative probability *may not* *must not* *can't/couldn't* low negative probability You can use the contracted forms *can't* and *couldn't* in these cases, but don't contract *must/may/might + not*.

B Read over your journal entry, and <u>underline</u> at least one sentence that you can revise to include a perfect modal. Write your revised sentence(s) below.

Answers will vary.

_____

_____

_____

■ GRAMMAR CHART

Modal Verbs:
Past Logical Scale

1. Ask students to name modals and write them on the board. If possible, elicit *must, should, may, could, might.* Call on a volunteer to write the words on the board in order from highest to lowest probability. Ask classmates if they agree with the order chosen.
2. Call on students to read the first set of sample sentences and the corresponding Notes.
3. Ask volunteers to read the sentences in the second set of sample sentences. Discuss why *must have* indicates stronger conviction than *should have, may have,* and *might have.* Ask students to read the corresponding Notes.
4. Call on students to read the negative sentences and Notes.
5. Answer any questions students have about the use of modals in their perfect form.

■ EXERCISE B

Have students complete the activity and compare their answers with a partner.

■ EXPANSION IDEA

Grammar

1. Divide the class into small groups. Have students discuss what the participants in the experiment might have done and felt, using the perfect form.

2. Circulate as students work and encourage them to use the words and grammar from the lesson.

C Complete each sentence using a verb from the box and a perfect modal. Follow the example.

question	assume	approve	understand
misunderstand	respond	explain	cooperate

1. **Dr. Kern:** Your experimental design is excellent, so the ethics committee _____ *should have approved* _____ it by tomorrow afternoon when they meet.

2. **Prof. Walker:** The subjects ___ **must have misunderstood** ___ your directions because few of them filled out the questionnaire properly.

3. **Prof. Aikens:** Milgram _____ **must have assumed** _____ that some of his volunteers would obey an authority figure without question.

4. **Prof. Erwin:** Participants ___ **couldn't have understood** ___ the purpose of our research, and so there will be a margin of error in the results.

5. **Dr. Gunther:** The volunteers _____ **may not have responded** _____ in the same way without Milgram's deceptive experimental design.

6. **Prof. Nichol:** Don't worry about the experiment. Your research subject ___ **should have cooperated with** ___ the conditions because he signed a consent form.

7. **Prof. Rollin:** Participants _____ **might have questioned** _____ the researcher's authority. That's the only explanation for their submissive behavior.

8. **Dr. Clark:** My assistant _____ **must not have explained** _____ the purpose of our experiment because the subjects were asking me about it before we started.

■ **EXPANSION IDEA**

Exercise C

1. Divide the class into groups of three. Have students role-play a conversation between Milgram and two of his colleagues, one who agrees with his tactics and another who thinks that they were unethical.

2. Circulate as students work and assist as needed. Encourage them to use modals in their perfect form.

D Select the better modal for the situation and (circle) it. Be ready to explain your choice.

1. During an experiment on participant motivation, a researcher gave volunteers 2,000 sheets of paper. On each sheet there were 24 addition problems, which the volunteers were supposed to work on. The researcher said that he would return later and left the room. The volunteers were still working on the problems when he returned 5 hours later.

   a. The volunteers ((must) / may) have thought that the research was important.

      REASON: *The volunteers worked for a long time, so they thought it was important.*

   b. The researcher ((couldn't)/ may not) have expected them to work for 5 hours.

      REASON: It seems unreasonable that they expected people to work for 5 hours.

2. The researcher who designed the experiment in #1 wanted to give the volunteers a task that they would refuse.

   a. The experimenter (can't /(may not)) have started his research with this task.

      REASON: It's unlikely that he began with this task.

   b. The volunteers ((could)/ must) have been angry about the purpose of his research.

      REASON: It's possible that they were angry but the research doesn't show it.

3. The same researcher designed another experiment. He handed out the same sheets. This time the participants had to complete a sheet, tear it into at least 32 pieces, and then continue with the next sheet. Again, the volunteers worked on this task for many hours.

   a. The volunteers (may /(must)) have wondered about the purpose of this task.

      REASON: The task is so crazy, they surely wondered.

   b. Some volunteers ((may)/ might) have torn the sheets into fewer pieces.

      REASON: There is some likelihood that they did so.

■ EXERCISE D

1. Call on a student to read the instructions.
2. Ask students to read the example. Call on a volunteer to explain why *must* is a better answer than *may* in the first question.
3. Have students complete the activity individually.
4. Call on volunteers to read their answers to the class. Ask them to explain why they chose their answers, and poll classmates to see if they agree.

■ EXPANSION IDEAS

Exercise D

1. Divide the class into pairs.
2. Have students discuss their answers to Exercise D. Ask them to explain why they chose the different modals.
3. Call on volunteers to read their answers to the class.

■ EXERCISE E

1. Review the instructions with the class.
2. Call on a student to read the example.
3. Have students complete the activity individually.

1. The subjects in the motivation experiments above spent many hours doing an extremely boring task.

   a. _They might not have wanted to ruin the researcher's experiment by quitting._

   b. _The experiment may have seemed silly to them._

2. People who volunteered for both deceptive and nondeceptive experiments have said that they liked the deceptive experiments better.

   a. **They might have found the situation funny.**

   b. **They must not have minded being deceived.**

3. In one study, researchers stared at certain drivers who had stopped at an intersection. Those drivers left the intersection more quickly than other drivers.

   a. **The drivers might not have felt comfortable.**

   b. **The drivers must have wondered what the researchers were looking for.**

4. In a series of experiments, bystanders who were alone in a situation helped a stranger in an emergency; however, the same bystanders were much less likely to help a stranger if there were other people standing or sitting nearby.

   a. **The bystanders could have thought that they had no choice but to help.**

   b. **The bystanders may not have wanted to take responsibility in front of others.**

5. A researcher asked a group of 10 participants to identify lines of the same length on two sheets of paper. Participants gave their answers orally. Only one participant was a true volunteer, and the others were paid to give wrong answers. Only 25% of the real volunteers gave the correct answer, and the other 75% gave the same wrong answer as the paid actor/participants.

   a. **The real participants may have thought that they had misunderstood the directions.**

   b. **Some of the real participants must not have had any self-confidence.**

6. Researchers investigated the effect of noise on the willingness of subjects to help another person. A paid assistant dropped some books in front of a subject in two settings: a quiet one and a noisy one. The test subject helped to pick up the books more frequently in the quiet setting than in the noisy one. The results were the same in a laboratory situation or on the street.

   a. **The person on the busy street might not have noticed.**

   b. **The person in the quiet setting must have felt that the noise couldn't be overlooked.**

■ EXPANSION IDEA

Exercise E

1. Have students choose one of the experiments from Exercise E to write about. Tell them to write a paragraph and their interpretations of the results using modals in their perfect form.

2. Call on volunteers to read their paragraphs aloud.

F **PAIR WORK** Discuss and comment on the experiment that Stanley Milgram conducted.

A lot of people don't question authority. I bet the majority of volunteers **must have done** exactly what they were told.

But a few people **might have refused**—at least I hope so!

PART TWO	Modal Verbs: Other Perfect Meanings

■ GRAMMAR IN CONTENT

A Reread the text at the beginning of the lesson, and <u>underline</u> other examples of perfect modals. Compare your answers with a partner and discuss the meaning of the modals that you found.

Modal Verbs: Other Perfect Meanings

Sample Sentences	Notes
The researcher should **have gotten** a written consent form (but he didn't). The researcher **shouldn't have lied** to the participants (but he did).	Use the perfect form of *should* to express an obligation or piece of advice that someone did *not* fulfill or follow.
He **could have recruited** many more participants (but he didn't).	Use the perfect form of *could* to express an opportunity that someone missed.
"**Could** you explain the procedure again?" "**Can** I try again?" "**May** I leave now?" He **couldn't** see the participant in the other room during the experiment. They **could** communicate via the intercom system during the experiment.	Do not use modals in perfect form to express • permission or requests • physical ability • possibility/potentiality

---

■ **EXERCISE F**

1. Have students read the instructions.
2. Call on a pair of students to read the text in the speech balloons.
3. Divide the class into pairs and have them discuss and comment on Milgram's experiments.
4. Call on students to share their comments with the rest of the class.
5. Tell students the results of the experiments.
6. Ask students to comment on how well they predicted the results.

PART TWO

**Modal Verbs:
Other Perfect Meanings**

■ **GRAMMAR IN CONTENT**

■ **EXERCISE A**

1. Have students complete the activity individually and then check their answers with a partner.
2. Have partners discuss the meaning of the modals that they found.
3. Discuss the meaning of modals as a class.

■ **GRAMMAR CHART**
*Modal Verbs:
Other Perfect Meanings*

1. Call on students to read the sample sentences and corresponding Notes.
2. Answer any questions students have about how and when to use these modal verbs.

■ **EXPANSION IDEA**

Exercise F

1. Divide the class into small groups. Have them brainstorm additional ways in which Milgram could have expanded his experiment. Then have students decide which of these are ethical and which are not.

2. Call on members of each group to present their group's ideas to the class.

3. Hold a class discussion about the ideas.

■ EXERCISE B

1. Write on the board *Characteristics of Ethical Experimental Design.*

2. Ask the class to brainstorm characteristics of an ethical experiment. Write ideas on the board.

3. Have students read the notes on ethical design. Elicit answers or answer any questions they have about them.

4. Call on a student to read the instructions for the exercise.

5. Read the first example aloud to the class. Call on volunteers to suggest criticisms and missed opportunities. Then have them read the sample answer.

6. Have students complete the activity individually.

7. Call on volunteers to read their answers to the class.

B Comment on the mistakes that students made in their experiments, expressing a criticism or telling about a missed opportunity. Use the notes from your psychology lecture about ethical experiments below.

> **Characteristics of Ethical Experimental Design:**
> Goal = balance the right to do research / the rights of participants
>   (= no abuse)
> • identify physical risks: check equipment & medical procedures;
>   age & health
> • identify psychological risks: anxiety? depression? invading privacy? anger?
> • keep information confidential = reduces participants' anxiety
> • consult Human Subjects Review Committee = advice about ethical
>   treatment of subjects
> • obtain "informed consent" =
>   describe general purpose and procedure of the experiment
>   warn subjects of risks
>   inform subjects that they can quit at any time
>   get signatures
> • debrief subjects after experiment =
>   tell them about deception
>   help subjects with emotional reactions to experiment

1. Team One did not tell subjects anything about the experiment.

   They shouldn't have hidden the procedures of the experiment from the subjects.

2. Team Two conducted the Milgram experiment again with college students.

   They should have warned the participants about the risks.

3. Team Three investigated subjects' willingness to help a stranger. Before the experiment, the participants answered questions about their personal lives.

   They should have promised to keep the information confidential.

4. The test subjects for Team Four left the laboratory as soon as they had finished the experiment on visual perception.

   They should have debriefed them.

5. Team Five investigated the relationship between anger and high temperatures. An older subject became so upset that he fainted in the laboratory.

   They could have asked some simple health questions.

■ EXPANSION IDEA

Exercise B

1. Divide the class into small groups. Have them choose one of the experiments from Exercise B.

2. Tell them to identify one student who will play the role of the psychologist. The rest of the students will play the roles of members of the Human Subject Review Committee.

3. Ask students to role-play a conversation in which the psychologist tries to justify his experiment to the committee. Committee members should use the characteristics of ethical experimental design to critique the design.

C Rewrite each sentence, paraphrasing it to show the meaning of the sentence with the modal. Follow the example.

1. Many experimenters should have treated test animals more humanely.

   Many experimenters didn't treat animals humanely.

2. The test subjects could have refused to give electroshocks in the Milgram experiment.

   The test subjects did not refuse to give electroshocks in the Milgram experiment.

3. Participants in the experiment should have felt upset when they learned the truth.

   Participants in the experiment did not feel upset when they learned the truth.

4. Milgram could have felt uncomfortable about the behavior of the participants.

   Milgram was or wasn't uncomfortable about the behavior of the participants.

5. Milgram should have realized that his experiments were groundbreaking.

   Milgram did not realize that his experiments were groundbreaking.

6. Some of the participants could have been very angry at Milgram.

   Some of the participants were or were not angry at Milgram.

D Listen to the classroom discussion of a psychology experiment that a teacher conducted with her students. Then, answer the questions with your inferences.

CD1,TR14

1. Why did Elliott decide to do this exercise on that particular day?

   The death of Martin Luther King Jr. must/could have affected her.

2. Why did she think that children in Iowa needed a lesson on discrimination?

   She must have thought that they had no other way to learn about it.

3. What kind of special classroom rules did Elliott make for the blue-eyed children?

   She would not allow them the same privileges that brown-eyed students were given.

4. How did the brown-eyed children probably feel on the first day of the lesson?

   They could have felt superior to the other children.

5. How did the parents probably react when they heard about Elliott's lesson?

   They must have been very upset.

6. Why did people in Riceville feel so negatively about the media's attention to Elliott?

   They felt the teacher's experiment was unethical.

■ EXPANSION IDEA

Exercise D

Put students into groups of three and have them discuss how Elliott's experiment made them feel. Have them use modals whenever possible.

■ EXERCISE C

1. Have students read the instructions.
2. Call on a student to read the example aloud. Discuss the answer with the class.
3. Have students complete the activity on their own and then compare their answers with a partner.
4. Have volunteers read their answers aloud. Call on class members to discuss other possible answers for each.

■ EXERCISE D
CD 1, Track 14

1. Tell students that they will hear a discussion about a junior high school experiment. Inform students that junior high school students usually range from 11 to 14 years of age.
2. Play the audio, telling students to listen for comprehension only.
3. Have students read the questions and example.
4. Play the audio again, pausing it frequently so that students can answer the questions.
5. Play the audio again so that students can check their answers.
6. Call on volunteers to read their answers to the class.
7. Discuss any answers that class members disagree on.

■ COMMUNICATE

■ EXERCISE E

1. Ask students to read the instructions.
2. Divide the class into small groups and have them discuss the questions posed in the instructions.
3. Have group members report their findings to the class.

● Connection

Putting It Together

■ GRAMMAR AND VOCABULARY

1. Ask students to read the instructions and the topics.
2. Answer any questions that students have about the assignment or the topics.
3. Give students time to write their essays. Remind them to use vocabulary and grammar from the lesson whenever possible.

■ PROJECT

Have students conduct their interviews and report back to the class on their findings at the next class meeting.

■ INTERNET

Tell students to complete one of the psychological surveys on the BBC website. Note that the new website is: http://www.bbc.co.uk/science/humanbody/mind/index_surveys.shtml. Then have students report on their experience and survey results at the next class meeting.

E **SMALL GROUP WORK** Discuss Elliott's experiment from the viewpoint of a Human Subjects Review Committee. Did her exercise meet your ethical standards? What should she have done? What shouldn't she have done? What could she have done differently? Report your findings to the class.   Answers will vary.

Connection   Putting It Together

GRAMMAR AND VOCABULARY Write a composition on one of the topics below. Use as many words as possible from the Content Vocabulary on page 63. Use modal verb forms from this lesson where appropriate to express your ideas, and underline those verb forms.

Topic 1: People today criticize some researchers from previous decades for a lack of concern about the risks of their experiments to people or to animals. How can we justify the use of animals or people in research projects, especially if there is some physical or psychological danger to the test subjects? Give examples.

Topic 2: Given the lessons of the Milgram experiment, explain the following quotation from Oscar Wilde: "Disobedience, in the eyes of anyone who has read history, is man's main virtue. It is through disobedience that progress has been made, through disobedience and through rebellion." Give concrete historical examples.
Answers will vary.

PROJECT Interview at least two students on your campus about ethical research.

Find out the following information and report on it at your next class meeting.

   a. Do your interviewees think that research with animals is ethical?

   b. What kind of research is done with animals nowadays?

 INTERNET Go online to the website www.bbc.co.uk/science/humanbody. This website has several surveys that you can take. Choose and complete at least one psychological survey, which will take approximately 10 minutes. At the end of the survey, you will see your results and some explanations. Report on your experience and the survey results at your next class meeting.   Answers will vary.

■ EXPANSION IDEAS

Exercise E
Have students write a short essay about whether Elliott's experiment met ethical standards.

Internet
1. Have students research the Stanford Prison Experiment. Have them take notes on the experiment.
2. Divide the class into small groups and have students discuss the experiment.

Economics: Microfinance

Lesson 8

■ CONTENT VOCABULARY

Look up the words below that you do not know and enter them in your vocabulary journal. Write each word's part of speech, a definition, and an example sentence. Try to include them in your discussion and writing below.

to be liable for	considerable	to encounter	to guarantee
collateral	to default	an entrepreneur	to pay off
to comprise	eligible	funds	a stimulus

■ THINK ABOUT IT

What do you know about small businesses in developing countries? What kinds of businesses exist in a village? How do people start a business in this type of environment?

In your writing journal, write for five minutes about these questions. When you are finished, share what you wrote with the class.
In your opinion, should all adults have credit available to them? What qualifications are important for a person to receive credit, either for a credit card or for a bank loan?
Answers will vary.

73

Overview

1. Write *microfinance* on the board. Have volunteers define the term, if possible.
2. Ask students to brainstorm how small loans might play a significant role in helping individuals start businesses in developing countries.

■ CONTENT VOCABULARY

Ask students to review the words in the box. Tell them to look up any unfamiliar words.

■ VOCABULARY JOURNAL

Have students add new words to their vocabulary journals and write down the parts of speech, definitions, and sentences for each.

■ THINK ABOUT IT

1. Ask students to read the instructions.
2. Hold a brief class discussion about the kinds of businesses that exist in villages and how people usually start a business in this environment.
3. Have students read the journal assignment. Then give them five minutes to write in their journals.
4. Call on volunteers to share their journal entries with the class.

■ CONTENT NOTES

The topic of this lesson is Economics: Microfinance. Students will learn some of the vocabulary associated with credit and loans. They will also read about how the Grameen Bank has allowed poor people to pursue entrepreneurial projects as a result of the bank's microfinance projects.

■ GRAMMAR IN CONTENT

■ EXERCISE A

CD 1, Track 15

1. Call on a few volunteers to describe the usual process involved in applying for and receiving a bank loan in their home countries and who qualifies for loans.

2. Play the audio and have students follow along in their books as they listen.

3. Ask a few comprehension questions, such as: *How do the loans that Grameen Bank offers poor people differ from traditional bank loans? Which group in particular has benefited from the loans? What kinds of businesses do borrowers start?*

4. Call on a volunteer to summarize the loan process.

PART ONE	Quantifiers with *Of*

■ GRAMMAR IN CONTENT

CD1,TR15 **A** **Read and listen to the passage below. The words in bold are phrases with quantifiers.**

An Entrepreneurial Opportunity

Since 1976 the Grameen Bank has enabled **millions of poor people** to borrow money to pursue their own entrepreneurial projects. This bank started in villages in Bangladesh when Dr. Muhammed Yunus made credit available to the rural poor, a segment of the population that had never been considered "bankable" before. According to Dr. Yunus, providing bank services to such men and women results in the growth of small businesses, which can reduce unemployment in developing countries and serve as a stimulus for economic development.

The sort of loans that the Grameen Bank offers poor people differ from traditional bank loans. Typical bank loans require some kind of collateral; however, borrowers are eligible for these special loans if they apply as a group of five people. Each of the members has to have her own viable business project that the bank officials approve. Then, **two members of the group** receive loans, usually less than $200 each. The group supports those two members as they begin or expand a small business. If either borrower encounters difficulty, bankers supervise and give advice, and the group members may even assist in the business. However, **none of the group members** is liable for the loan payments of the others. Once the loans have been repaid, two more members of the group can borrow money, and then finally the fifth person. The bank pays 5% of the loans into a special group fund so that the five borrowers will also have earned some savings by the time the fifth person has repaid her loan. **The remainder of the loan repayments** (including interest) is used for loans to other groups of five entrepreneurs.

According to data from UNESCO, a considerable number of borrowers have already overcome extreme poverty. This system of credit has especially benefited rural women, who had never been eligible for their own loans before the Grameen Bank offered them. In fact, the vast majority of borrowers are women, who have repaid their loans at a rate above 90%. **Many of their businesses** involve simple processes related to agriculture like selling eggs or traditional skills such as pottery, weaving, and sewing. Research shows that **most of these women entrepreneurs** also reinvest their money in their business projects and in their families. Aside from **all the personal benefits** of this access to credit, women gain recognition for contributing to their communities.

viable: workable, capable of being successful

a fund: an amount of money that is reserved for a specific purpose

interest: a fee for a loan that is a percentage of the loan

UNESCO: United Nations Educational, Scientific, and Cultural Organization

to overcome: to succeed in spite of great obstacles

■ EXPANSION IDEA

Exercise A

1. Divide the class into pairs, pairing students from different countries, if possible.

2. Have students take turns asking and answering questions about the reading passage.

3. Ask students to discuss whether a loan program similar to the Grameen Bank's would be beneficial and possible in their countries.

Sample Sentences	Notes

Grameen Bank makes many loans to women. **Few** borrowers default on their loans. (= nonspecific borrowers)
 	
Few of the borrowers need assistance from their groups. (= a small number of a specific group of borrowers)
 	
In a few villages both men and women applied for loans. In **one of them**, the women received **much of the money**, but the men only got **a little of it.**
 	
Millions of women receive loans annually, and **hundreds of them** may hire other women in their villages.
	The two following patterns change the meaning of a noun phrase from **general** to more specific:
	1. Quantifier + *of the* + Plural Count Noun
	2. Quantifier + *of the* + Noncount Noun
	  • Apply this rule to numbers as well as to other quantifiers. Large numbers used in general estimates require only the word *of*.
	  • Use a plural pronoun in place of a plural count noun.
	  • Use a singular pronoun in place of a noncount noun.
	In this pattern, *no* becomes *none*
	(e.g., *no people* → *none of the people*).

All of the members repaid their loans early because they were able to sell **half of the** merchandise within three months. She sold **both of her** goats and **most of those** eggs on Saturday.	Choose either of the following patterns to express a specific noun phrase with *all*, *both*, and *half*: 3. *all/both/half of the* + noun 4. *all/both/half the* + noun Use a possessive determiner or a demonstrative instead of the word *the* to add more specific information.
The Grameen Bank works with **groups of** borrowers. **A team of** bankers advises each group. Most women use their profits to repay the loans and invest **the rest of the** money in their businesses and families.	Some patterns (e.g., count noun + *of*) express a collection of individuals or part of a whole. Follow the regular rules to choose the articles or determiners that precede the count noun following the word *of*.

B Read over your journal entry, and <u>underline</u> at least one sentence that you can revise to include a quantifier from the chart above. Write your revised sentence(s) below.

Answers will vary.

_____

_____

_____

1. Write *few*, *few of the*, and *in a few* on the board. Call on volunteers to make sentences using each word. Try to elicit an explanation of how the three usages differ.

2. Call on students to read the first group of sample sentences and corresponding Notes. Answer any questions that students have about how and when to use quantifiers with *of the* and count and noncount nouns.

3. Call on students to read the second group of sample sentences and corresponding Notes. Answer any questions students have about the use of *all*, *both*, and *half*.

4. Have students read the last set of sample sentences and Notes, and answer any questions that students have.

■ **EXERCISE B**

Have students complete the exercise and share their sentences with a partner.

■ **EXPANSION IDEA**

Grammar

Divide the class into pairs. Have students role-play a conversation between a loan applicant and a banker. Encourage them to use as many quantifiers with *of* as possible.

For example:

Student 1: *A few of the women in my village have already received loans. All of them are making money now. I would like to borrow money to start my own business.*

Student 2: *What kind of business are you thinking of starting? All of the people who borrow money from our bank must have a plan that is approved.*

■ EXERCISE C

1. Call on a student to read the instructions.
2. Call on another student to read the example.
3. Ask a volunteer to explain how the sample answer makes the text more specific.
4. Have students complete the activity individually. Then ask them to check their work with a partner.
5. Call on volunteers to read the answers aloud. If class members have different answers, call on them to read them aloud as well.

■ EXERCISE D

1. Ask students to read the instructions and review the chart.
2. Call on a volunteer to read the example aloud.
3. Have students complete the activity individually and then compare their answers with a partner.
4. Call on volunteers to read their answers aloud.

C Edit the noun phrases with quantifiers to make the text below more specific. Some of the phrases may have two correct forms.

When Dr. Yunus first proposed his Grameen Bank Project, many *of his* colleagues doubted that the poor would repay their loans. ~~No banks~~ *None of the banks* in his region gave credit to anyone below the poverty line, especially women. Dr. Yunus spoke with several *of the region's* bankers because he hoped that a few *of them* might support his project. Instead, ~~they~~ all *of the bankers* laughed at him. Then, he changed his strategy. All *of* the loans borrowed that year came from some *of the* funds that Dr. Yunus had borrowed from one bank. After all *of the* loans were repaid, he had more success with his microfinance projects.

D Look at the current records of Mr. Haq, a local banker with Grameen Bank. Make sentences about Mr. Haq's loan groups, using the data from the chart and the words in parentheses. Follow the example.

Group 1273	Mrs. S	Mrs. F	Mrs. T	Mrs. W	Mrs. T
Amount requested	200	175	175	200	250
Amount received	200	150	175	175	
Amount repaid	200	150	155	160	

Group 1733	Mrs. T	Mrs. G	Mrs. W	Mr. H	Mr. M
Amount requested	150	175	200	175	175
Amount received	150	175			
Amount repaid	0	25			

Group 1349	Mrs. H	Mrs. S	Mrs. T	Mrs. U	Mrs. S
Amount requested	175	150	75	175	100
Amount received	175	150	75	175	100
Amount repaid	175	150	75	175	50

(Note: Bangladeshi currency, the taka, has been converted to approximate U.S. dollar amounts in the chart.)

1. (most/woman in Group 1349) _Most of the women in group 1349 have already repaid their loans._
2. (hardly any/person in Group 1733) **Hardly any of the people in Group 1733 have repaid their loans.**
3. (all/loan in Group 1349) __All of the loans in Group 1349 have been paid to some extent.__

■ EXPANSION IDEA

Exercise C

Ask students to write short essays about how Dr. Yunus convinced his colleagues to support his project. Tell students to use as many quantifiers as possible in their writing.

4. (almost all/borrower) __Almost all of the borrowers are women.__

5. (quite a few/loan) __Quite a few of the loans were for $175 or less.__

6. (more than half/borrower) __More than half of the borrowers have completely repaid their loans.__

7. (none/payment from Group 1733) __None of the payments from 1733 have been fully repaid.__

8. (one/borrower in Group 1349) __One borrower in Group 1349 still has to repay her loan.__

E Read Mr. Haq's oral report to his supervisor. Mr. Haq is worried that his groups are not performing well, so he makes some misleading statements or mistakes to hide some of the problems in his groups. Find the mistakes by checking the information in the charts on page 76. On a separate piece of paper, write a short report with the correct information. Follow the example.

Supervisor: Mr. Haq, I understand that some of your groups aren't performing as well as we had expected.

Mr. Haq: No, sir, I wouldn't say that. I can report that all the groups are making progress on repayment.

Supervisor: I'd like to hear some specific information.

Mr. Haq: In the first group—Group 1273—the majority of the women requested $200 or more, and most of them have completed their repayments.

Supervisor: Excellent. How's your newest group handling their loans?

Mr. Haq: Group 1733? They had a rough start, but since the beginning of the month, I have received a couple of payments from each of the first two borrowers. Both of them requested smaller amounts, so I'm hoping that they will be more consistent now.

Supervisor: That's a relief. What about the third group?

Mr. Haq: All of the borrowers in this group requested less than $200, and we have received almost all of the money back. The fifth borrower should pay back the rest of the loan next week.

Supervisor: How much is that?

Mr. Haq: Five dollars.

Supervisor: Well done, Haq.

Mr. Haq: Thank you, sir.

> <u>Report on the Grameen Bank Project</u>
>
> Some of the groups are making good progress on repaying their loans, but not all of them.

■ **EXERCISE E**
1. Ask students to read the instructions and the example.
2. Have students correct the errors in Mr. Haq's oral report by checking the information on the chart on student book page 76. Then ask the students to write a short report with the correct information.

■ **EXPANSION IDEAS**

Exercise E
1. Divide the class into pairs. Have students practice reading the corrected dialog, taking turns reading the two parts.
2. Call on a pair of volunteers to role-play the dialog for the class. Encourage them to be expressive.

Exercise E
Divide the class into pairs and have them edit each other's essays. Ask them to look for places where their partners could have used additional quantifiers to make their sentences more specific.

■ EXERCISE F

1. Ask students to read the instructions. Answer any questions they have about the exercise.
2. Call on students to read the two case studies and example aloud.
3. Have students complete the activity individually.
4. Call on volunteers to read their answers to the class.

■ COMMUNICATE

■ EXERCISE G

1. Go over the instructions with the class.
2. Divide the class into groups representing as many different countries as possible. Have students discuss credit in their home countries.
3. Circulate as students work and assist with vocabulary as needed. Encourage them to use vocabulary and grammar from the lesson.

■ EXERCISE H

1. Review the instructions with the class.
2. Divide the class into pairs of students from different countries or areas. Have them discuss the questions posed in the instructions.

F Read the case studies of borrowers from the Grameen Bank below. Then, comment on the way that each borrower probably spends her loan money and her profit. Also, speculate on the way that each person spends her time. Use quantifiers from this lesson in your comments. Follow the example.   Answers will vary.

Case Study 1: Mrs. Jamirun Haq in Jolarpar
Mrs. Haq is a member of the Village Phone system, which is run by GrameenPhone. With her loan, she got a cellular phone with a 50% discount on airtime. She charges villagers in her region the market rate for calls—about 20 cents per minute for local calls and more for long-distance calls. When villagers receive a call at her home, she makes an appointment with the caller for a return call. Then, she or her children go to the villagers' homes to tell them when to come for the return call. With her profit, Mrs. Haq has been saving money for her daughters' education.

Case Study 2: Mrs. Sufia Begum in Jobra
Mrs. Begum weaves bamboo stools with bamboo that she buys from a local merchant. She sells her stools at local markets. She has helped to raise her family above the poverty line.

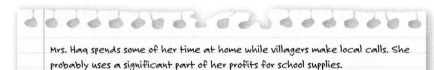

Mrs. Haq spends some of her time at home while villagers make local calls. She probably uses a significant part of her profits for school supplies.

■ COMMUNICATE

G **GROUP WORK** Talk with the members of your group about credit. Is credit readily available where you come from? Do you and your friends or coworkers have credit cards? Can you get a bank loan to buy a car or other major purchase? What are the attitudes of people where you come from about taking out a bank loan? Do you need collateral?

H **PAIR WORK** Talk with your partner about people who start small businesses in an area you're familiar with. Who are the owners or workers in these businesses? Are women encouraged to open their own businesses in that area? Do you have any idea how small business owners finance their businesses? Be prepared to tell your classmates about the information that you learned from your partner. Use quantifiers as you explain the information that you learned.

78   LESSON 8 | Economics: Microfinance

■ EXPANSION IDEAS

Exercise F
Have students develop their own case studies, modeling them on those in Exercise F. Their study can refer to a person who has or has not been successful. Tell them to include how much money the person received, what he or she has used it for, and how effective the person's plan has been. Also ask them to include the individual's repayment history.

Exercise H
Ask students to write what they learned about starting a small business in their partner's country.

■ GRAMMAR IN CONTENT

A Reread the text at the beginning of this lesson, and underline the rest of the grammatical subjects that include quantifiers. Look at the main verbs in those sentences. Can you explain why some subjects take singular verbs and others take plural verbs?

Subject-Verb Agreement

Sample Sentences	Notes
First, **a team** of bankers evaluates loan applications. **The team** then meets with loan applicants to get more information.	**Collective nouns** (see the list at the bottom of the chart) usually take the singular verb form in American English.
Later, **a committee** of advisors helps each borrower with her business plan.	
In one village, **a number of** borrowers have repaid their loans, but **the number of** payments hasn't reached 100 yet.	Learn the differences: · *A number of* (similar in meaning to *some* or *several*) takes a plural verb. · *The number of* refers to a sum or total and takes a singular verb.
Before 1976 **the vast majority** of poor people was not eligible for bank credit.	· *The majority (of)* and *the minority (of)* usually take singular verbs, but a plural verb signals an emphasis on individuals.
Since that time, Grameen Bank has shown that **a considerable majority of** poor Bangladeshis use their loans wisely.	· *A majority (of)* refers to a specific group of individuals and takes a plural verb.
Until 1976 **none of** the poor villagers in Jorba was/were able to receive a loan. Since then, **none of the Grameen Bank branches** has/have asked for collateral from any of the poor. **Each of the borrowers** is/are making weekly payments.	· *None of* takes a singular verb in formal English. · Use a plural verb with *none of* + *plural noun* in informal English. · The same is true for *each of* and *every one of*.
Two hundred dollars is the maximum for most loans.	· Use a singular verb when a unit of time, distance, or money is expressed as a unit.

Collective Nouns

audience	club	couple	family	jury
cast	committee	crew	group	staff
class	council	crowd	institute	team

■ GRAMMAR IN CONTENT

■ EXERCISE A

1. Ask students to complete the activity on their own and then check their work with a partner.
2. Go over the answers together.

■ GRAMMAR CHART
Subject-Verb Agreement

1. Call on students to read the sample sentences and corresponding Notes.
2. Answer questions that students have about subject-verb agreement.

■ EXPANSION IDEA

Grammar Chart

Have students pick five of the collective nouns in the chart and write a sentence with each. Remind them of subject-verb agreement.

EXERCISE B

1. Review the instructions and have students complete the activity. Encourage them to refer to the Grammar Chart if they are uncertain about whether to use a singular or plural verb.
2. Have students check their answers with a partner. Encourage them to discuss their choices.
3. Call on volunteers to read their answers and explain their choices to the class.

EXERCISE C

1. Have students read the instructions.
2. Call on a student to read the example. Ask a volunteer to explain why the verb is singular in this case.
3. Have students complete the activity individually and then check their work with a partner.
4. Call on volunteers to read their answers to the class, and explain their choices.
5. Have students review the Grammar Chart if they are confused about subject-verb agreement with collective nouns.

B **Circle** the correct verb. With a partner, discuss why you chose either the singular or plural form of the verb.

1. Everyone in the Vista Grande valley has to submit his or her loan application to a committee at the local microfinance institution (MFI). The committee (**is**/are) meeting
   (1)
   this Friday to discuss the applications on file and to revise the guidelines for next year. It is concerned about the loan balance that current borrowers (has/**have**) to pay
   (2)
   off. Six hundred dollars (**has**/have) been the average loan balance for a few years, but
   (3)
   a number of the committee members (has/**have**) mentioned that they would like to
   (4)
   see the loan balance decrease in the coming years.

2. Ms. Mendez is afraid that she will have to default on her loan of approximately $550. None of her chickens (has/**have**) laid as many eggs as she had anticipated. The
   (5)
   number of eggs (**has**/have) been so low that she had to consult with the advisory
   (6)
   team at the MFI. The team (**wasn't**/weren't) very sympathetic to her situation, but
   (7)
   agreed to take a look at her new hen house and make suggestions.

3. When a new MFI opened in the nearby town, many villagers in San Miguel made plans to apply for a loan to expand or create a small family business. In the first year, the majority of borrowers (was/**were**) able to see considerable improvements in family
   (8)
   income. Since then, the financial results haven't always been so visible, but gradually each of the borrowers (**has**/have) earned enough to change the lives of their families.
   (9)

C Complete the sentences using one of the verb phrases in the box in the appropriate form.

meet with the villagers	caution the committee	become disappointed
divide into smaller teams	schedule a meeting	criticize various policies

1. Last year all of the researchers at an economics institute decided to work together on a microfinance project with one village in El Salvador. Since then, the institute
   has met with the villagers several times to plan the project.

2. The villagers were extremely excited about the opportunity to work with the staff from the institute. Since then, none of the villagers **have become disappointed**
   with them.

EXPANSION IDEA

Exercise C
Divide the class into pairs. Have students role-play a discussion between a researcher from a local microfinance institution and a reporter, in which they discuss the project in the village in El Salvador.

For example:
Student 1: *So your team meets with villagers to help them with their project?*
Student 2: *Yes, we meet with the village committee regularly. They often have questions for us or problems they need help solving.*

3. The villagers decided to form a committee to assist anyone who runs into difficulty with a loan. In the future, the committee __is going to divide into smaller teams.__

4. Although the researchers at the institute support the villagers' decisions, a number of the economists __have cautioned the committee.__

5. In general, the members of the committee respect the advice of the researchers. However, a small minority of the committee members __have criticized various policies.__

6. The institute researchers anticipated some criticism as they worked with the village. Next week the institute staff __is going to schedule a meeting with them.__

D Look at the statistics on microfinance in Central America from 2004. Write three sentences about borrowers and loans based on this data.   Answers will vary.

Microfinance in Central America

Outreach Indicators	Central America	Costa Rica	El Salvador	Guatemala	Honduras	Nicaragua
# active borrowers	5,854	721	5,854	4,431	13,310	7,319
% female borrowers	65.7%	65.0%	61.0%	75.6%	81.3%	61.0%
Gross loan portfolio (US $)	3,008,127	651,862	4,903,319	989,743	3,780,661	3,935,179
Average loan balance/ Borrower	601	904	713	406	445	536

1. _According to this information, 406 is the lowest average proportion of loan balance to borrower in Central America._

2. __The greatest percentage of female borrowers lives in Honduras.__

3. __The majority of borrowers in Central America are women.__

4. __The highest number of active borrowers is 13,310 in Honduras.__

---

1. Ask students to review the chart.
2. Call on a student to read the example.
3. Have students write their sentences. Then have them compare their answers with a partner.
4. Call on volunteers to read their answers to the class.

■ **EXPANSION IDEA**

Exercise D

1. Divide the class into groups, including students from as many different countries as possible in each group.
2. Have students apply what they know about microfinance in developing countries to the chart in Exercise D. Ask them to discuss factors that might influence why the different countries have higher numbers of female borrowers, fewer or more active borrowers, larger loan portfolios, and so on.
3. Circulate as students discuss; assist as needed.

EXERCISE E
CD 1, Track 16

1. Tell students that they will hear a guest speaker at an Economics class discussing the Grameen Bank.
2. Play the audio for comprehension only.
3. Ask students to review the questions. Play the audio again, pausing frequently so that students can write their answers.
4. Have students compare their answers with a partner.
5. Call on volunteers to read their answers to the class. If there is any disagreement among class members, play the audio again.

EXERCISE F

1. Review the instructions and call on a student to read the example.
2. Have students complete the exercise on their own and then check their work with a partner. Encourage them to discuss their decisions.
3. Call on volunteers to read their answers to the class. Discuss differences of opinion about the answers, referring to the Grammar Chart when necessary.

CD1,TR16 **E** Answer the questions below about Dr. Richard Browning's comments on microfinance in Central America. Dr. Browning of Microfinance Information eXchange (MIX) is a guest speaker in an economics class that has been discussing the Grameen Bank.

1. What is an MFI?

   It's the acronym for microfinance institution.

2. How many MFIs are controlled by nongovernmental organizations?

   The majority is controlled by NGO's.

3. How many of the MFIs have as many borrowers or services as the MFIs in Asia?

   None of them has as many.

4. How many extremely poor borrowers are there in Central America?

   The number is very low.

5. What proportion of the borrowers in Central America are women?

   A high percentage are women.

6. In Honduras, how many of the MFIs work with village-level banks?

   The majority works with village-level banks.

F Read each statement and (circle) the letter of the correct interpretation. The first one has been done as an example.

1. The committee has to wait until its meeting next week to announce the loans.
   - (a.) The committee works as a unit.
   - b. The people on the committee are working as individuals.
2. None of the farmers were able to make payments after the terrible floods.
   - a. This is from a formal context.
   - (b.) This is from an informal context.
3. The crowd is protesting against the increase in bank rates.
   - (a.) The people in the crowd are acting as one unit.
   - b. The people in the crowd are behaving as individuals.
4. Generally, the minority support political candidates for strong economic reform.
   - a. This is from a formal context.
   - (b.) This is from an informal context.
5. The team of graduate students were anxious to assist the poor villagers with their projects.
   - (a.) The graduate students were going to work as a unit.
   - b. Each student was going to work as an individual with the villagers.
6. The majority often demand their rights to the economic disadvantage of the minority.
   - a. The majority in this context act like individuals.
   - (b.) The majority in this context act as one large unit.

EXPANSION IDEA

Exercise F
Divide the class into pairs and have students expand on a few of the statements, using collective nouns as both singular and plural subjects.

For example:
This week the committees weren't able to reach a decision.

G There are five errors in the e-mail message below. The first one has been fixed. Find and correct the four errors that remain.

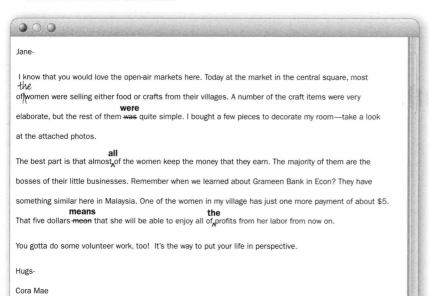

Jane-

I know that you would love the open-air markets here. Today at the market in the central square, most
~~of~~ *the* women were selling either food or crafts from their villages. A number of the craft items were very
were
elaborate, but the rest of them ~~was~~ quite simple. I bought a few pieces to decorate my room—take a look

at the attached photos.

all
The best part is that almost ^of the women keep the money that they earn. The majority of them are the

bosses of their little businesses. Remember when we learned about Grameen Bank in Econ? They have

something similar here in Malaysia. One of the women in my village has just one more payment of about $5.
means   **the**
That five dollars ~~mean~~ that she will be able to enjoy all of ^profits from her labor from now on.

You gotta do some volunteer work, too! It's the way to put your life in perspective.

Hugs-

Cora Mae

■ COMMUNICATE

H **GROUP WORK** Many people feel that Dr. Yunus
deserved the Nobel Prize for his development of
the Grameen Bank. Discuss his accomplishment
with your group. How do you compare him with
other recipients of the Nobel Prize? Many other
individuals around the world have contributed to
the welfare of the poor. How would you compare
Dr. Yunus's contribution to theirs?

Dr. Muhammed Yunus, Winner of the 2006 Nobel Prize.

■ **EXERCISE G**

1. Have students correct the errors
   in the e-mail and then check their
   work with a partner.
2. Call on volunteers to read their
   corrected e-mail aloud. Stop
   if class members disagree with
   an answer and discuss whether
   the verb in question should be
   singular or plural.

■ **COMMUNICATE**

■ **EXERCISE H**

1. Brainstorm the names of some
   Nobel Prize winners who received
   the prize for social work, such as
   Mother Teresa. Write the names
   on the board.
2. Ask students to review the
   instructions.
3. Divide the class into groups and
   have students discuss whether
   Dr. Yunus deserved the Nobel
   Prize for his development of the
   Grameen Bank.

■ **EXPANSION IDEA**

Exercise H
Ask students to write a short essay stating
their positions on the topic discussed in
Exercise H.

■ GRAMMAR AND VOCABULARY

1. Have students review the instructions and topics.
2. Answer any questions that students have about the assignment or the topics.

■ PROJECT

Review the instructions and have students conduct their interviews. Have them report back to the class at the next class meeting.

■ INTERNET

Have students conduct their searches and report back to the class.

GRAMMAR AND VOCABULARY Write a composition on one of the topics below. Use as many words as possible from the Content Vocabulary on page 73. Use quantifiers where appropriate to express your ideas, and <u>underline</u> those words and phrases.

Topic 1: What's the best way for young people to learn the value of money? Use examples from your own experience and the experience of your friends or schoolmates.

Topic 2: Many nations have special programs to assist countries in the developing world. Some of these programs send money, and others offer advice from experts. Another strategy is to send volunteers to help with various projects in villages or regions outside large cities. In your opinion, what kind of aid is the most effective? Be as specific as possible and give examples.
Answers will vary.

PROJECT Interview at least one student on your campus about credit and credit cards. Find out the student's views regarding the following information and report on it at your next class meeting.

    a. Do most students have credit cards?
    b. How do most students get a credit card? Do their parents help them?
    c. If the student that you interview has a credit card, find out what the interest rate for that card is.
    d. Do most students pay off their balance each month?

 INTERNET Go online, and use the search phrase "student credit cards." Find a website that gives information about the risks that students face when they use credit cards. Choose two important points or suggestions, and report on that information in class. **Answers will vary.**

■ EXPANSION IDEA

Project
Have students write a short essay about whether they think it is a good idea for high school students to have credit cards.

Criminal Science: Juvenile Court

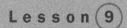

■ CONTENT VOCABULARY

Look up the words below that you do not know and enter them in your vocabulary journal. Write each word's part of speech, a definition, and an example sentence. Try to include them in your discussion and writing below.

to acknowledge	an incentive	an offense	a role model
a curfew	judicial	a prison sentence	to testify
empathy	a mentor	a procedure	testimony

■ THINK ABOUT IT

What are the roles of the people in a courtroom? What procedures are standard in a typical courtroom trial? What would you expect to see during a typical day in court? What is surprising about the people in the photo on the following page? Discuss your ideas with a classmate.

In your writing journal, write for five minutes about these questions. When you are finished, share your ideas with your classmates.   Answers will vary.

In your opinion, should courts of law treat teenagers who get in trouble with the law the same as adults? What should the police, judges, and lawyers consider when a young person commits a crime? What is the goal of the justice system when a young person commits a minor offense?

85

■ CONTENT NOTES

The topic of this lesson is Criminal Science: Juvenile Court. Students will learn vocabulary that relates to procedures in a courtroom and the sentencing of minors. Use this lesson to discuss different kinds of legal systems and make students aware of their legal rights and responsibilities while they are studying in the United States.

Lesson 9

Overview

1. Call on a few volunteers to share what they know about the North American judicial system.
2. Ask students to raise their hands if the judicial system in their country assumes that a defendant is innocent until proven guilty.
3. Have students raise their hands if the judicial system in their country treats juveniles differently than adults.

■ CONTENT VOCABULARY

Ask students to review the words in the box. Tell them to look up any unfamiliar words.

■ VOCABULARY JOURNAL

Have students add new words to their vocabulary journals and write down the parts of speech, definitions, and example sentences for each.

■ THINK ABOUT IT

1. Ask students to read the instructions.
2. Divide the class into pairs and have students discuss the roles of the people and the standard procedures in a typical courtroom trial.
3. Have students study the picture and describe what they find surprising about it.
4. Give students five minutes to write about juvenile offenders in their journals.
5. Divide the class into new pairs and have students share the ideas they wrote about in their journals.

PART ONE

Gerunds and Infinitives as Subjects

PART ONE

Gerunds and Infinitives
as Subjects

■ GRAMMAR IN CONTENT

■ GRAMMAR IN CONTENT

EXERCISE A
CD 1, Track 17

1. Play the audio and have students follow along in their books as they listen.
2. Ask a few comprehension questions, such as: *How do teenage offenders avoid a criminal record? What is the first step in the process? What is the next step? What is one of the goals of youth courts? Who are the jury members? What are some of the incentives for participating as a teen juror? What kinds of sentences do offenders receive?*

CD1,TR17

A Read and listen to the passage below. The words in bold are phrases with gerunds or infinitives as subjects.

A teenager waits to hear his sentence at a hearing.

Getting a Second Chance

Since the 1970s, teen court has provided an alternative to juvenile court for teenagers who commit certain types of crimes. Every year 110,000 to 125,000 young people go before a jury or judge in teen court, or youth court as it is known in some states. By accepting this form of trial, first-time teenage offenders can avoid a criminal record and move quickly through the legal system. **Admitting guilt** is the first step in this process. Then, **appearing before a judge and/or jury** and **answering their questions** constitutes the next step. **Fulfilling the requirements of the sentence** is the third and final step.

One of the goals of youth court is to provide positive role models. Young people on the juries in teen court serve that function. Prior to working as jurors, teenage volunteers are given lessons in asking questions and in interpreting body language. Another part of their training is to learn about the law and courtroom procedures. There are strong incentives for participating as a juror aside from putting in volunteer hours. These young people gain valuable experience in public speaking and can develop leadership and mediation skills. In fact, it becomes a goal of many of the offenders **to serve as a juror**. In recent years, almost 30% of the jurors have been former offenders.

Another primary objective is to teach teens about the consequences of their actions. As mentioned above, **acknowledging mistakes** starts the process. Offenders may be in court for their conduct at school, such as excessive tardiness or disrespectful behavior to teachers, or for committing minor crimes like theft, disorderly conduct, or possession of marijuana or alcohol. Once the jury and judge have questioned offenders, it is the duty of the court **to decide on the sentence**. **Giving offenders a voice and then making them accountable for their conduct** is the philosophy behind the decisions, not **punishing them**. The sentences may be to perform community service, to attend counseling, to give a report, or even to pay back victims for their stolen or vandalized property. The idea is to connect the offenders with the community that suffered in some way from their behavior. By interacting positively with their families, teachers, and fellow citizens, the young people can create new opportunities for themselves.

a juvenile court: a court that hears criminal cases involving minors
a criminal record: a person's permanent record of criminal behavior

aside from: excluding, except for
mediation: a process of helping two sides solve a dispute or come to an agreement
to vandalize: to destroy or damage property intentionally

■ EXPANSION IDEA

Exercise A
Divide the class into pairs and have students take turns asking and answering questions about the reading.

Gerunds and Infinitives as Subjects

Sample Sentences	Notes
Lying is never a good idea, and **lying to your family** can be even worse.	Both **gerunds** and **infinitives** can function as the subject of a verb. They are often used interchangeably.
To err is human.	
Testifying in front of other teens isn't easy.	The subject of a verb can be a simple gerund or infinitive. The subject can also be a gerund or infinitive that is part of a longer phrase.
To act defiantly doesn't sound like a good strategy in youth court.	
Listening to testimony requires a lot of attention and empathy.	Always use a singular verb with a gerund or infinitive subject.
To give young people a second chance is one goal of teen court.	Generally, use a gerund to emphasize a real action that happens regularly, and use an infinitive to express an abstract possibility or a potential, unfulfilled action.
It takes courage **to admit mistakes**.	Place an **infinitive subject** after the verb phrase and the word *it* in the subject position. This word order is preferred, but the infinitive can precede the verb, especially if the infinitive is very short.
It wasn't smart **to act belligerently** during court.	
From the beginning, it hasn't been the job of youth court **to punish offenders**.	
Admitting mistakes takes courage.	Place a **gerund subject** in regular subject position in front of the verb. There are a few exceptions in informal English where you can use *it* in subject position and the gerund after the verb phrase:
It was no use **lying to the judge**.	· *It's no use . . .*
It wouldn't be any good **blaming someone else**.	· *It's no/not any good . . .*
It was difficult **testifying before the teen jury**.	· *It's (not) easy/hard . . .*
It's unacceptable **not to be** on time for a court date.	In a negative construction, follow these patterns:
Not appearing at all is actually a crime.	· *to + not* + simple verb
	· *not + -ing* verb

B Read over your journal entry, and <u>underline</u> at least one sentence that you can revise to include a gerund or infinitive phrase used as a subject. Write your revised sentence(s) below.

   Answers will vary.

   _____

   _____

   _____

■ GRAMMAR CHART
Gerunds and Infinitives as Subjects

1. Write *gerund* and *infinitive* on the board. Ask volunteers to give examples of each.
2. Call on students to read the sample sentences and corresponding Notes.
3. Answer any questions that students have about using gerunds and infinitives as subjects.

■ EXERCISE B

Have students complete the activity and compare their sentence with a partner.

■ EXPANSION IDEA

Grammar

Divide the class into pairs. Have students talk about how to be a role model for teenagers, using gerunds and infinitives in their conversations.

■ EXERCISE C

1. Ask students to review the instructions.
2. Call on a student to read the example.
3. Have students complete the activity individually and then check their answers with a partner.
4. Call on volunteers to read their answers to the class.

■ EXERCISE D

1. Ask students to review the instructions.
2. Call on a few students to read the *Guidelines for Sentencing* aloud.
3. Call on another student to read the example.
4. Tell students to complete the activity, referring back to the reading on page 86 in the Student Book, if necessary, to help them identify the objectives of juries when they assign these actions.

C Write about the experience and emotions of an offender in youth court. Match one of the actions with an adjective, and write the sentence. Use either a gerund or an infinitive in each of your sentences. See the example.   Answers will vary.

Adjectives	Actions
difficult	answer/questions
embarrassing	admit/mistakes
frustrating	wait/sentence
intimidating	not have/criminal record
encouraging	sit/courtroom
frightening	perform/community service

1. _____ *Admitting your mistakes is very difficult.* _____
2. It must be frustrating to wait to hear your sentence.
3. Not having a criminal record is encouraging.
4. Performing community service is embarrassing.
5. It's very intimidating to answer questions from your peers.
6. Sitting in a courtroom must be frightening.

D Look at the instructions that teen jurors receive when they learn about sentences for offenders in youth court. Write down the goals or objectives of juries when they assign each of these actions.

> **Guidelines for Sentencing**
>
> Remember, connect the sentence to the offenders' behavior so that they see the consequences of their actions. You can use one or more of these sentences:
> A. paying for the damages of vandalism with money earned by the offender
> B. participating in a safe-driving program
> C. tutoring a child in reading skills
> D. writing a letter of apology
> E. touring a jail
> F. meeting with a mentor weekly
> G. having a curfew from 10 P.M.–6 A.M.

1. _____ *It's their goal to teach the offender the value of people's property.* _____
2. It is their aim to improve teenagers' defensive driving strategies.
3. It is their goal to show teenagers that they have the skills to help.
4. Their goal is to make the offender think about his/her actions.
5. Their goal is to scare teenagers into good behavior.
6. Their aim is to give teenagers an adult who will guide him or her.
7. Their goal is to get teenagers off the streets where they're likely to get into more trouble.

■ EXPANSION IDEA

Exercise D

1. Divide the class into small groups. Tell groups to decide who will be the offender and who will be the teen jurors.
2. Ask the group to decide on the offender's crime. Then have them role-play their parts, questioning him or her about the crime, and determining a sentence.
3. Encourage students to use vocabulary and grammar from the lesson.

E Read the statements, and then paraphrase the information using the phrases in parentheses. Use a variety of infinitives and gerunds.

1. Students have to work hard to get scholarships for college.

   (take hard work) _____ *It takes hard work to get a scholarship for college.*

2. Young people have to be patient and try hard if they want to be excellent in sports.

   (take patience and perseverance) **Being excellent in sports takes patience**

   and perseverence.

3. Young people have to work very hard if they want to have a part-time job and get good grades in school.

   (take a lot of effort) **It takes a lot of effort to have a part-time job and to get good grades**

   in school.

4. Teenagers need to spend many hours cooperating with other group members if they want to finish a school project well.

   (involve time and teamwork) **It involves time and teamwork to finish a school**

   project well.

5. Some families can't afford college tuition payments for their children.

   (cost too much for some families) **Paying college tuition costs too much for**

   some families.

6. Some parents encourage their children to babysit or to get summer jobs so that they can learn to be more responsible.

   (teach teenagers responsibility) **Baby-sitting or getting summer jobs teaches**

   teenagers responsibility.

7. It's hard for some young people to resist peer pressure.

   (require self-confidence) **It requires self-confidence to resist peer pressure.**

8. It is often a hard decision when teens decide that they won't use drugs.

   (take determination) **It takes determination not to use drugs.**

■ **EXERCISE E**

1. Ask students to read the instructions and the example.
2. Have students complete the activity on their own and then check their answers with a partner.
3. Call on volunteers to write their answers on the board. If any class members disagree about the answers, have them write their versions on the board. Then have the class discuss which answer is correct.

■ **EXPANSION IDEA**

Exercise E

1. Ask students to choose one of the statements from Exercise E and expand it, adding a few more sentences.
2. Call on volunteers to read their work to the class.

For example:

Resisting peer pressure is hard for some young people. Telling their friends that they don't want to smoke, drink, or use drugs is more difficult than just going along with the crowd. To take a stand against these vices takes strength of character.

■ COMMUNICATE

■ EXERCISE F

1. Have students review the instructions.
2. Call on a pair of students to read the text in the speech balloons.
3. Divide the class into pairs and have them discuss the cases and the sentences.
4. Circulate as students work and encourage them to use gerunds and infinitives in their discussion.

F **PAIR WORK** Read the case studies from teen court below, and with your partner decide on an appropriate sentence for each offender. Use infinitives and gerunds as much as possible.

> Putting Fred in jail doesn't serve any purpose. He should be given another chance.

> But it's not a good idea to let him off completely. He should have some sort of punishment.

Case 1: Fred, who lives in an inner-city neighborhood, admitted that he cut the tires of his teacher's car in the school parking lot. His teacher made him stay after school because he hadn't handed in his homework on time.

Case 2: Natasha, who lives in a middle-class neighborhood, acknowledged that she had drank at a party and then went through a red light on her way home. She is a 17-year-old high school senior and attended the party at the home of one of her classmates. Natasha had run the red light when the police stopped her around 1:00 A.M. She failed the breathalyzer test and was arrested.

PART TWO	Gerunds and Infinitives as Subject Complements; Gerunds Following a Preposition

---

PART TWO

Gerunds and Infinitives as Subject Complements; Gerunds Following a Preposition

■ GRAMMAR IN CONTENT

■ EXERCISE A

Have students complete the activity and then compare their results with a partner.

■ GRAMMAR IN CONTENT

A Reread the text at the beginning of this lesson, and (circle) the other gerunds and infinitives in the reading. Then, share your results with a partner.

Subject Complements

Sample Sentences	Notes
A common problem for youth offenders is **not having positive role models.** The point of each sentence is **to make the offender accountable for his or her actions.**	Both **gerunds** and **infinitives** can function as subject complements. Use one of the following patterns: 1. Subject + *be* + Gerund 2. Subject + *be* + Infinitive The complement explains or elaborates on the subject of the sentence.
A common problem for youth offenders is **not having a stable home environment.** A common problem for youth offenders is **not to have any positive role models.**	Use this structure to emphasize the information in the gerund or infinitive. In English, the end of a sentence is typically the **focus of new information.**

■ GRAMMAR CHART

Subject Complements

1. Write *subject complement* on the board and elicit a definition from a class member, if possible. If not, have students continue on to the chart.
2. Call on students to read the sample sentences and the corresponding Notes.
3. Call on a few volunteers to give examples of sentences with subject complements.

90 LESSON 9 | Criminal Science: Juvenile Court

■ EXPANSION IDEA

Exercise F

Ask students to write a short essay about the sentences they consider appropriate for one of the two cases described in Exercise F. Tell them to be sure to explain their goals for the offender, using infinitives and gerunds as appropriate.

Sample Sentences	Notes
First, the judge spoke with Ken **about taking** responsibility for his actions. Then, in the interest **of teaching** Ken a lesson, the judge thought **of assigning** him some hours of community service. Instead, she sentenced the young man **to writing** letters of apology to every person in his neighborhood.	Use a **gerund** after any **preposition**. This rule even applies to the preposition *to*. Use this structure to make your sentences more dynamic. Many English structures allow speakers to include more than one action in a clause. Also, see Lessons 21, 22, 25.

B Revise each sentence so that it has only one clause. Use one of the verbs from the original sentence as a gerund with a phrase in the box below.   Answers will vary.

in preparation for	with regard to	as a consequence of
~~as a result of~~	in reference to	

1. Judge Klegg has volunteered at teen court for years, so he can interpret teenagers' body language very well.

   As a result of volunteering at teen court for years, Judge Klegg can interpret teenagers' body language very well.

2. Carl talked about his participation in gang activities, and he revealed that he had also encouraged his younger brother to join.

   With regard to gang activities, Carl also revealed that he had encouraged his younger brother to join.

3. Carl was finally arrested because he and his brother stole a neighbor's car.

   Carl was finally arrested as a consequence of stealing his neighbor's car.

4. Before he heard the jury's recommendations, Judge Klegg reviewed the police report about Carl and his brother.

   In preparation for hearing the jury's recommendation, Judge Klegg reviewed the police report about Carl and his brother.

■ GRAMMAR CHART

Gerunds Following a Preposition

1. Before students review the chart, ask volunteers to give examples of sentences that have gerunds preceded by prepositions.
2. Call on students to read the sample sentences and corresponding Notes.
3. Answer any questions that students have about using gerunds preceded by prepositions.

■ EXERCISE B

1. Have students read the instructions.
2. Call on a student to read the example.
3. Have students complete the activity individually and then check their work with a partner.
4. Call on volunteers to write their answers on the board. If any class members disagree, have them write their versions on the board and have the class decide which is correct.

■ EXPANSION IDEA

Exercise B

1. Ask students to write a new sentence with gerunds and two of the five phrases from the box in Exercise B.
2. Have students compare their sentences with a partner.
3. Call on volunteers to read their sentences to the class.

EXERCISE C

1. Have students read the instructions and review the phrases in the box.
2. Call on a student to read the example.
3. Have students complete the activity on their own and then check their work with a partner. Encourage students to discuss their answers.
4. Call on volunteers to read their answers to the class.

EXERCISE D

1. Have students read the instructions.
2. Ask students to read the first question. Have them brainstorm some reasons why Carl argued with his father.
3. Have students complete the activity on their own.
4. Call on volunteers to read their answers to the class.

C Paraphrase one of the clauses with a gerund and a phrase from the box below.

be upset about	be afraid of	be guilty of
be familiar with	be used to	

1. Carl feared that he would reveal the names of other gang members.
   Carl was afraid of revealing the names of other gang members.

2. Carl tried to protect his brother during the trial.
   Carl was used to taking care of his brother and wanted to protect him.

3. Carl admitted that he had endangered his brother with his gang connections.
   Carl was guilty of endangering his brother.

4. Carl didn't like the fact that he had to spend time with younger kids.
   Carl was upset about the sentence, but he had no choice.

D How did Carl end up in teen court? What was the situation in his family? Use your imagination to answer the questions about his dysfunctional home life. **Answers will vary.**

1. What did he argue with his father about?
   He argued with his father about joining a gang.

2. What did his mother blame him for?
   His mother blamed him for getting his brother into trouble.

3. What did Carl always complain about?
   Carl always complained about looking after his brother.

4. What was his younger sister always talking about?
   His younger sister was always talking about staying away from drugs.

5. What did Carl's brother care about?
   Carl's brother cared about looking cool.

6. What did Carl feel like?
   Carl felt like getting a car to drive, so they stole one.

EXPANSION IDEA

Exercise D

1. Have students write an account of Carl's dysfunctional family situation based on their answers to Exercise D.

2. Ask volunteers to read their accounts to the class.

CD1,TR18

E Read and listen to these community leaders talk about their work with young people. Then, answer the questions that follow.

1. **Coach Tennyson:** Most kids nowadays want to be big sports stars, like Kobe Bryant or Tiger Woods, and earn millions of dollars. You know as well as I do that most of them will never be basketball or golf stars. What they have to learn is to work together and not to be selfish. When they grow up, those skills are going to help them get a job and keep it.

   According to Coach Tennyson, what's the point of team sports?
   The point is learning to work with other people and not being selfish.

2. **Ms. Davies:** Lots of people ask me why I waste my time with a bunch of teenage girls every week. For me, it's time that's well-spent. When the girls start out, all they care about is their hair, their clothes, or their cell phones. Many of them have never been outside the city. I love to see their faces when we go hiking on the weekend or when we cook over a campfire for the first time. They're just like kids again—instead of cool teenagers.

   What's the motivation of this Girl Scout leader?
   Her motivation is to improve girls as people.

3. **Mr. Henderson:** I believe that students learn history much better when they have a hands-on project. They have to negotiate among themselves and take responsibility for their part of the project. They can be creative—and see that history is much more than what's in their textbooks.

   What's Mr. Henderson's reason for assigning group projects?
   He believes they learn history better that way.

4. **Judy Callahan:** Whenever I tutor one of my classmates, I realize that I probably learn more than the other person. You know, it's really hard to explain math if the other person feels like he can't get it. When the other person finally understands, I feel happy for him, but I also feel like I passed a big test, too.

   What's Judy's motivation for doing peer tutoring?
   So that she can help and so that she can learn.

5. **Mr. Patterson:** When I was young, I was lucky to have a father who supported me and always gave me great advice. Even when I made mistakes, he stood behind me. When I graduated from college and went into business, there were other people who helped me along the way. Nowadays so many young men need that kind of positive support. I'm just following in my father's footsteps.

   What's Mr. Patterson's idea about being a mentor?
   His idea is that people need positive support to succeed.

■ **EXERCISE E**
CD 1, Track 18

1. Ask students to read the instructions.
2. Call on a student to read the example.
3. Have students complete the activity on their own and then check their work with a partner.
4. Call on volunteers to read their answers to the class. After each answer is read, ask the rest of the class whether they agree or disagree, and have students who disagree read their answers.

■ **EXPANSION IDEA**

Exercise E
1. Divide the class into pairs. Have each student choose one of the community leaders from Exercise E to role-play.
2. Have students role-play a conversation between the leaders, discussing their work with young people and why they do it.
3. Circulate as students work. Assist as needed and encourage them to use vocabulary and grammar from the lesson.

1. Review the instructions with the class and answer any questions students have about the activity.

2. Call on a student to read the example. Discuss the edited answer with the class.

3. Have students complete the activity individually and then check their work with a partner. Students should discuss any differences of opinion about whether to edit or leave the sentence in the same form.

4. Call on volunteers to read their answers to the class. Discuss any differences of opinion.

F If appropriate, edit the underlined sentence in each of the texts below so that the new information is at the end of the sentence. Explain your decision to edit or to leave the sentence in the same form.

1. Teenagers have to deal with an intimidating situation when they appear before the
   Facing a judge and jury of your peers takes a lot of courage.
   judge and jury in youth court. ~~It takes a lot of courage to face a judge and jury of your~~

   ~~peers.~~ Teenagers with that kind of courage and determination will probably benefit

   from having a second chance.

   REASON: _____*"Courage" is new information so it needs to be at the end.*_____

2. Many youths who appear in youth court made one bad decision. Making one

   wrong choice shouldn't be the reason for having a criminal record according to the

   philosophy of youth court. Instead, young people who admit their guilt and fulfill

   other requirements can avoid getting a record.

   REASON: **Philosophy is new and goes at the end. No change.**

3. Teenage jurors shoulder a lot of responsibility as they decide on sentences for
   Making good decisions about another person's life takes training.
   other teens. It takes a lot of training to make good decisions about another person's

   life. That training is an ongoing activity in teen court as judges help the jurors to

   understand their options in choosing the proper sentence.

   REASON: **Training is new information so it needs to be at the end.**

4. Communities with teen courts have demonstrated an understanding that not all

   "troublemakers" are bad kids. Some teenagers get into trouble because of peer

   pressure. Saying "No" to your friends requires a lot of self-confidence at that age.

   Adults have seen that teenagers can gain that feeling of self-worth as they fulfill the

   requirements of their youth court sentences.

   REASON: **Self-confidence is new information. No change.**

5. Some adults get involved in youth court because of their own experiences as
   Helping young people avoid such experiences is the reason they become mentors.
   teenagers. The reason that they become mentors is to help young people avoid such

   experiences. The mentors try to guide the teenagers so that they make different

   friends and better choices.

   REASON: **Mentoring is new information so it needs to be at the end.**

■ **EXPANSION IDEA**

Exercise F

Divide the class into small groups. Have students discuss with each other any work that they have done with younger people. Tell them to describe what they did and to talk about how fulfilling or frustrating the experience was.

G Find and correct the four errors in the e-mail below.

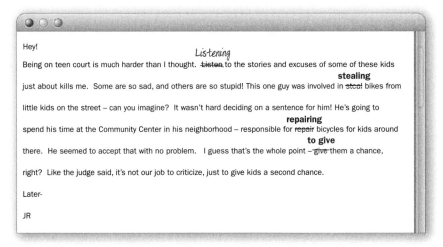

Hey!

Listening

Being on teen court is much harder than I thought. ~~Listen~~ to the stories and excuses of some of these kids

stealing

just about kills me. Some are so sad, and others are so stupid! This one guy was involved in ~~steal~~ bikes from

little kids on the street – can you imagine? It wasn't hard deciding on a sentence for him! He's going to

repairing

spend his time at the Community Center in his neighborhood – responsible for ~~repair~~ bicycles for kids around

to give

there. He seemed to accept that with no problem. I guess that's the whole point – ~~give~~ them a chance,

right? Like the judge said, it's not our job to criticize, just to give kids a second chance.

Later-

JR

■ **COMMUNICATE**

H **PAIR WORK** Brainstorm types of youth programs that teenagers can join outside of
school. Choose one of the programs and prepare a list of the goals of that organization.
Then, for each of the goals, develop a list of 2–3 actions or activities that teenagers
or their mentors do in order to implement the goals. When you are finished, share your
program description with your class.

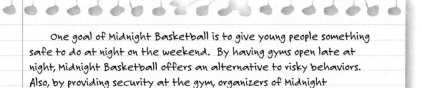

One goal of Midnight Basketball is to give young people something
safe to do at night on the weekend. By having gyms open late at
night, Midnight Basketball offers an alternative to risky behaviors.
Also, by providing security at the gym, organizers of Midnight
Basketball ensure that the environment is safe for everyone.

Answers will vary.

■ **EXERCISE G**

1. Have students find and correct
   the mistakes in the e-mail.
2. Call on volunteers to read the
   corrected e-mail aloud.

■ **COMMUNICATE**

■ **EXERCISE H**

1. Review the instructions with the
   class. Tell students that they may
   use examples of youth programs
   from their home countries if
   they are unfamiliar with those
   available in the United States.
2. Call on students to read the
   example aloud.
3. Divide the class into pairs and
   have students choose their youth
   programs and develop their lists
   of goals and activities.
4. Call on volunteers to share their
   programs with the class.

■ **EXPANSION IDEA**

Exercise H
Have students write a short essay
about the youth program they chose.
They should include any experiences
they personally have had with the
organization, using prepositions with
gerunds as often as possible.

EXERCISE I

1. Discuss the instructions with the class.
2. Call on two students to read the text in the speech balloons.
3. Have the class brainstorm some films that deal with young people who get into trouble. Write the titles on the board. Tell students they may use examples of films in their first languages as well.
4. Divide the class into groups and have students discuss the questions posed in the exercise.
5. Circulate as students work and assist as needed. Encourage them to use prepositions with gerunds as often as possible.

Connection

Putting It Together

GRAMMAR AND VOCABULARY

1. Review the instructions with the class.
2. Call on two students to read the topics aloud.
3. Tell students to choose a topic and write their compositions, using as many of the words and structures learned in the lesson as possible.

PROJECT

1. Ask students to raise their hands if they are aware of any campus judicial committees. Have them name the committees, if possible.
2. Review the instructions with the class. Tell students to conduct their interviews.
3. Call on students to share their results at the next class meeting.

INTERNET

Have students conduct their searches and share the information they find at the next class meeting.

---

1 **GROUP WORK** Talk about 2–3 films that deal with young people who get in trouble at school or with the law. What happens to the teenagers? Who are the adults that try to help them? What are the objectives of those adults? How do they mentor the young people? Use prepositions with gerunds as often as possible.

Radio was a movie about a great football coach. He gave his team a lesson **in respecting** one another.

I saw that movie, too. The coach prevented the players **from being** mean to Radio, who was mentally challenged. You could tell the coach cared **about giving** all the players an equal chance.

Connection Putting It Together

GRAMMAR AND VOCABULARY Write a composition on one of the topics below. Use as many words as possible from the Content Vocabulary on page 85. Use gerund and infinitive structures from this lesson to express your ideas, and <u>underline</u> those structures.

Topic 1: The parents of teenagers who break the law should receive a fine. If the crime is serious, the parents should also serve time in jail. Do you agree?

Topic 2: It's one of the goals of teen court to teach young people to be good citizens. Is the idea of civics, that is, lessons about good citizenship, still important in our modern world, or is it too old-fashioned?
Answers will vary.

PROJECT Interview at least one student on your campus about judicial affairs on campus. Find out the following information, and report on it at the next class meeting.

   a. Is there a judicial board or an honor board on campus?
   b. What is its purpose?
   c. What kinds of offenses does the board handle?
   d. What happens when students are guilty?

 INTERNET Go online, and use the search term "youth court" to find information on the federal youth court system in the United States. Find out the answers to the following questions and be prepared to present the information in class.

   1. Where are youth courts located? Select four states and find out how many youth courts operate there.
   2. What kinds of scholarship opportunities exist for young people who are involved in youth court?
   Answers will vary.

EXPANSION IDEA

Project
Divide the class into groups and have them role-play a student being brought before the campus judiciary board or committee. The board members should question the student, who should give his or her version of what happened. A sentence should be handed down by the committee.

Lesson (10)

Environmental Chemistry: H$_2$O

■ CONTENT VOCABULARY

Look up the words below that you do not know and enter them in your vocabulary journal. Write each word's part of speech, a definition, and an example sentence. Try to include them in your discussion and writing below.

a compound	mercury	to ascertain	to discharge
distilled water	preliminary	to contaminate	to dispose of
lead	a residue	to dilute	toxic

■ THINK ABOUT IT

How do chemicals and pollutants enter our water supply? What are the short-term and long-term dangers associated with impure water? How can we purify our sources of water and keep them clean?

In your writing journal, write for five minutes about the questions below. When you are finished, share what you wrote with the class.
Are people in your community concerned about the environment? Do they tend to pay attention to reports on air or water pollution? Are they aware of the companies or businesses that may be guilty of having contaminated the air or water in your area?
Answers will vary.

97

Lesson (10)

Overview

1. Ask students to raise their hands if they had to take chemistry in high school. Ask how many of them enjoyed the class, and have them explain why they did or did not like it.
2. Have students brainstorm some of the careers associated with chemistry. Ask whether any students in the class intend to pursue a career that requires them to continue to study chemistry.

■ CONTENT VOCABULARY

Ask students to review the words in the box. Tell them to look up any unfamiliar words.

■ VOCABULARY JOURNAL

Have students add new words to their vocabulary journals and write down the parts of speech, definitions, and example sentences for each.

■ THINK ABOUT IT

1. Ask students to read the instructions.
2. Hold a short class discussion about how chemicals and pollutants enter the public water supply and how water sources can be purified and kept clean.
3. Give students five minutes to write in their journals about community environmental awareness.
4. Ask volunteers to share what they wrote with the class.

■ CONTENT NOTES

The topic of this lesson is Environmental Chemistry: H$_2$O. Students will learn vocabulary associated with air and water pollution and will discuss how environmental pollution occurs.
Use this lesson to discuss recycling and environmentally responsible behavior with your students. You may also want to inform them about local penalties for littering and other ways in which they are expected to protect the environment while living in the United States.

PART ONE

Gerunds and Infinitives: Perfect Forms

■ GRAMMAR IN CONTENT

■ EXERCISE A
CD 1, Track 19

1. Ask students to look at the two photographs and comment on them.
2. Have students follow along in their books as they listen to the audio.
3. Ask a few comprehension questions, such as: *What kind of class is this? What kind of research project will students participate in? What is the students' goal for the semester? In what way will students perform a public service?*
4. Ask students who are familiar with the BOD and COD tests to raise their hands. If any have conducted these tests, have them discuss where and why they took them.

■ GRAMMAR IN CONTENT

A Read and listen to the passage below. The words in bold are gerunds or infinitives in the perfect form.

CD1,TR19

Chemistry 091: Chemistry for Non-Majors

Dr. N. Sato
Semester Research Project

As we examine the role chemistry plays in our lives this semester, you will participate in a research project on the safety of the waterways near campus. In the past, several local industries were guilty of **having discharged** their wastewater directly into local streams. For example, Prestige Paper routinely got rid of the chlorine that they used in paper-processing in Maple Hill Creek until the early 1970s. Although conditions have improved since the Clean Water Act of 1972, some local farmers and small business owners still tend to use local streams and creeks as a way <u>to dispose</u> of wastewater, and unintentional run-off still occurs as well.

Your goal in this project is **to have measured** the quality of water in a particular stream or creek in three ways by the end of the semester. Local officials claim **to have monitored** these same waterways since the 1990s, but citizens have often complained about unpleasant odors and a slightly metallic taste in the tap water. In light of these complaints, you will perform a public service by <u>ascertaining</u> the current quality of our tap water and by <u>following up</u> on your results with recommendations for punishing those who seem to be responsible for **having contaminated** the water.

PROCEDURES
1. You will work in teams of 4. In this way, our class will manage to investigate all of the local waterways.
2. Each team will conduct a biochemical oxygen demand (BOD) test and a chemical oxygen demand (COD) test <u>to check</u> for organic material in the water. In both tests you will determine the amount of dissolved oxygen in the water samples.
3. The second tests will focus on inorganic substances, such as rocks, minerals, and metals, in the water. These tests involve filtering the water.
4. The last set of tests will measure the level of toxic chemicals, such as chlorine, ammonia, or petroleum products, in the water samples. For these tests you will monitor small organisms, such as algae or minnows, <u>to ascertain</u> the concentration of toxic compounds.

SCHEDULE:
The BOD and COD tests are conducted over a 5-day period. You should plan **to have completed** the first set of measurements by the end of this month. The other tests will be assigned as we cover the material pertinent to the research procedures.

run-off: an overflow of liquid or rainwater
an organism: a form of life
organic: materials made of carbon, such as plants and animals

algae: aquatic, photosynthetic organisms
a minnow: a small fresh-water fish
pertinent: relevant

■ EXPANSION IDEA

Exercise A
Ask the students about a body of water (lake, river, or pond) that they are familiar with. Have them describe to the class whether the body of water is polluted and whether it can support life.

Gerunds and Infinitives: Perfect Forms

Sample Sentences	Notes
Professor Irving's achievement was **having proven** the source of mercury in the water.	Use the perfect form of a gerund or infinitive to emphasize that the action happened before the action of the main verb.
TTR Industries denied **having done** anything illegal.	A perfect gerund takes this form: *having* + **past participle**.
You can't expect them **to have admitted** dumping mercury in the water.	A perfect infinitive takes this form: *to have* + **past participle**.
As a result of **not having disposed** of the mercury properly, the company will have to pay a large fine.	Put *not* before the gerund in a negative phrase: *not having* + **past participle**.
They pretended **not to have lied** about the mercury spill.	Put *not* before an infinitive in a negative phrase: *not to have* + **past participle**.
The Water Board expects **to have measured** the level of chlorine in all local streams by the end of next month.	An **infinitive in the perfect form** may be similar in meaning to an action expressed in future perfect, especially with the main verbs *expect, hope, plan.*
It's Senator Marksbury's ambition **to have revised** the law on clean water by this summer. Senator Marksbury **will have revised** the law on clean water by this summer.	The future perfect generally expresses greater certainty than does a perfect infinitive that the action will be completed by a future date or time.

B Read over your journal entry, and <u>underline</u> at least one sentence that you can revise to include a gerund or infinitive in the perfect form. Write your revised sentence(s) below.

Answers will vary.

_____

_____

_____

■ **GRAMMAR CHART**
Gerunds and Infinitives: Perfect Forms

1. Call on a volunteer to give an example of a gerund and an infinitive.
2. Call on students to read the sample sentences and corresponding Notes.
3. Answer any questions that students have about how and when to use gerunds and infinitives in perfect forms.

■ **EXERCISE B**

Have students complete the activity and share their sentence with a partner.

■ **EXPANSION IDEA**

Grammar

1. Divide the class into small groups. Ask students to discuss environmental laws in their home countries.

2. Circulate as students work; assist as needed. Encourage them to use gerunds and infinitives in perfect forms in their discussions.

■ EXERCISE C

1. Have students read the instructions.
2. Call on a student to read the example.
3. Have students complete the activity and then check their work with a partner.
4. Call on volunteers to read the paragraph aloud. Ask for corrections if needed.

■ EXERCISE D

1. Ask students to review Professor Sato's notes.
2. Call on a student to read the example.
3. Have students complete the activity individually and then check their answers with a partner.
4. Call on volunteers to read their answers to the class.

C Complete the sentences in the text below with the appropriate perfect gerund or infinitive. Use verbs from the box below.

neutralize	pour	add	make	measure
follow	demonstrate	use	lie	start

As a result of ___*having poured*___ (1) only distilled water into a beaker, each student started last Tuesday's lab assignment with a completely neutral liquid with a pH of 7.0. Then, they were supposed to mix an equal amount of an acid and a base, but because of ___**having made**___ (2) a mistake in his measurement, Ken had an acidic mixture. When his professor Dr. Fletcher checked the pH of the liquid in his beaker, Ken denied ___**having measured**___ (3) the liquids incorrectly. As a consequence of ___**having added**___ (4) too much acid, Ken ended up with a mixture that had a pH of 3.0 instead of 7.0. Dr. Fletcher used Ken's mistake in the next step of her lesson since her goal was ___**to have demonstrated**___ (5) the process of neutralization by the end of class. She planned ___**to start**___ (6) with a strong acidic mixture in her demonstration, so it was convenient to use the liquid in his beaker. Dr. Fletcher measured and poured some of a base liquid into Ken's beaker, and as a result of ___**having neutralized**___ (7) the acid, she could prove to the students that the pH of the liquid was back to 7.0. After class, Ken apologized to Dr. Fletcher for not ___**having followed**___ (8) her directions more carefully.

D Answer the questions on the next page using information from Professor Sato's project schedule. Use the verb in parentheses with a perfect gerund or infinitive.

Second Round of Water Quality Testing

Group/Leader	Waterway	Estimated Date of Completion	Chemical Analysis	Finding? mg/L
Team 1: Nick	Wolf Stream	Week 6	copper	1.3
Team 2: Judy	Stone Creek	Week 7	sulfate	250
Team 3: Ryan	Maple Hill Creek	Week 8	lead	0.015

■ EXPANSION IDEA

Exercise C

1. Divide the class into pairs.
2. Have students decide who will be Ken and who will be Dr. Fletcher. Then have them role-play a conversation using the information in Exercise C.
3. Remind students to use the verbs in the box as perfect gerunds and infinitives.

1. According to Professor Sato's schedule, when should he receive results from the second round of testing? (anticipate)

   Professor Sato anticipates having received the results by week 8.

2. Ryan has been really busy this semester and wanted to do their experiment as soon as possible. What was his tentative schedule for Team 3's experiment? (hope)

   Ryan hoped to have finished the experiment by the end of week 8.

3. Judy's team works very well together and did a good job on the previous experiment. When does Judy think that they will be able to complete this assignment? (expect)

   She expects to have completed this assignment by week 7.

4. Professor Sato is eager to start the next round of experiments. Which week looks good for starting that lesson? (plan)

   Prof. Sato plans to have started the next round of experiments by week 9.

5. The students have a final exam in this class in Week 15. When would they prefer to finish the final set of tests for this course? (want)

   They want to have finished the tests by week 14 at the latest.

6. After each round of tests, the students report on their findings in class. When do the students think that they will present their test results? (anticipate)

   The students anticipate having presented their first results by week 9.

E Look at the chart on page 100 again. Answer the questions about Professor Sato's class using the adjectives in parentheses and the perfect form of a gerund or infinitive.

1. Professor Sato was very surprised at the finding of Team 1, which has done very careless work in the past. How does he explain their results? (likely)

   They are likely to have made a mistake in their measurement.

2. How did Team 1 feel about discovering a high level of copper in the water? (worried about)

   Team 1 was worried about having made another mistake in their measurements.

3. How did Team 3 feel about finding so much lead? (shocked at)

   Team 3 was shocked at finding so much lead.

4. Team 3 realized that their finding could have a great impact on the health of the community. How did they feel about uncovering the dangerous level of lead? (proud)

   Team 3 was proud of uncovering the dangerous level of lead.

5. Professor Sato had not anticipated Team 3's discovery of high levels of lead. How did he feel about assigning Team 3 to check lead in that particular river? (lucky)

   He felt lucky about assigning Team 3 to check lead in that particular river.

■ **EXERCISE E**

1. Have students review the instructions.
2. Call on a student to read the example.
3. Have students complete the activity individually and then check their answers with a partner.
4. Call on volunteers to read their answers to the class.

■ **EXPANSION IDEA**

Exercise E

1. Ask students to write a short composition about Professor Sato's class's findings, using *likely*, *worried about*, *shocked at*, *proud*, and *lucky* in their writing.
2. Call on a few volunteers to read their compositions to the class.

1. Ask students to review the instructions.
2. Call on a student to read the example.
3. Ask a volunteer to explain how combining the two sentences strengthens the writing.
4. Have students complete the activity individually.
5. Call on volunteers to read their revised sentences to the class. After each sentence has been read, ask the class to decide whether the meaning of the original sentences has been maintained.

■ COMMUNICATE

■ EXERCISE G

1. Review the instructions with the class.
2. Call on two students to read the text in the speech balloons.
3. Divide the class into groups and have students discuss the problems of water pollution in their local regions and what steps the government has taken to stop and/or reverse the pollution.

F Revise the sentences below. Combine them by replacing the second sentence with a perfect infinitive or gerund.

1. *The Sentinel* has accused Lycome Corporation of water pollution. According to the article, the company has been discharging ammonia into Willow River for five years.

   The Sentinel has accused Lycome Corporation of having discharged ammonia into Willow River for five years.

2. According to their spokesperson, the company planned a solution to the ammonia problem. The solution was to dilute the ammonia to an acceptable level.
   According to their spokesperson the company planned to have diluted the ammonia to an acceptable level.

3. Another article congratulated Dale Franklin for improvements at his ranch. Franklin has eliminated the run-off of his cattle waste into Sydney Stream.
   In the same issue, the article congratulated Dale Franklin of Rolling R Ranch for having completely eliminated run-off into the Sydney Stream.

4. However, some of Franklin's neighbors claim the opposite. Supposedly they found evidence of wastewater from the ranch farther down the stream.
   However, some of Franklin's neighbors claim to have found evidence of waste water from the ranch further down the stream.

5. The paper suspected a local chicken farm of similar pollution. The farm may have dumped an illegal amount of their organic material in Queensland Creek.
   Earlier this year, the paper suspected a local chicken farm of having dumped an illegal amount of organic material in Queensland Creek.

6. A nearby pet food producer was charged with the same violations. The company got rid of large amounts of waste through their sewer lines.
   About 2 years ago St. Devlin Co., a nearby pet food producer, was charged with having gotten rid of large amounts of waste through their sewer lines.

7. Employees pretended otherwise, but it was obvious that they had known about the waste in the sewer lines.

   St. Devlin employees pretended not knowing about the waste in the sewer lines.

8. The newspaper also blamed a large farm for deforestation. According to the report, the farm had cut all the trees in a local forest.
   Another time the newspaper blamed a large nursery upriver for having cut trees along the river which had minimized the effects of pollutants there.

■ COMMUNICATE

G GROUP WORK Discuss problems of water pollution in your local region. Who or what has caused the pollution? What steps has the government taken, if any?

People usually blame the mining companies for having dumped toxic chemicals in the local rivers.   Yeah, and the mining companies deny having done anything illegal.

■ EXPANSION IDEA

Exercise G

Have students research an event that caused well-documented pollution problems, such as the crash of the *Exxon Valdez* in Alaska. Have students report their findings to the class.

GRAMMAR IN CONTENT

A Reread the text at the beginning of this lesson, and <u>underline</u> the other gerunds and infinitives in the text.

Gerunds and Infinitives with Phrasal Modals

Sample Sentences	Notes
Our goal is **to be able to drink** water out of any stream in this area without ill effect.	Use *to be able to* + verb or *being able to* + verb to express ability.
I appreciate **being able to drink** water out of a river when I go hiking.	
Did the authorities acknowledge **not being able to find** the source of contamination?	Use the word *not* in front of the phrasal modal to express negation of the gerund or infinitive.
People get tired of **having to boil** their water and of **not being able to take** showers.	Use *to have to* + verb or *having to* + verb to express necessity.
We prefer **not to have to buy** bottled water, but in some places the water tastes bad.	

Gerund and Infinitive Review

Sample Sentences	Notes
The test for mercury **kept showing** a positive result.	Verbs such as *keep, fail, cause, continue, prefer, forget, remember, stop,* and *try* must be followed by a gerund or infinitive. See Appendix 1 for a complete list of these verbs.
The test **failed to show** any increase in copper.	
We should **continue monitoring/to monitor** the oxygen level daily.	For most verbs with both gerund and infinitive objects there is little difference in meaning.
Dr. Dix **forgot to get** a sample at Willow Creek, so he had to go back to get one. Maybe next time he'll **remember to go** there.	For the following verbs, however, the use of a gerund or infinitive object marks a difference in meaning: *forget, remember, stop, regret, try.*
Dr. Penn **remembered putting** the samples in the lab but completely **forgot turning** on the equipment. Luckily, Dr. Dix turned it off, and the machine **stopped filtering** the water. Dr. Penn **tried measuring** the solids on the filter and it worked.	With these verbs, remember that a gerund emphasizes a real action that occurred before the action of the preceding verb/the main verb and an infinitive expresses a possibility or a potential, unfulfilled action.

EXPANSION IDEA

Grammar

1. Ask students to write sentences using five of the verbs in the Grammar Chart. Challenge them to use more than one in a sentence.

2. Call on volunteers to read their sentences to the class.

Gerunds and Infinitives with Phrasal Modals: Review

GRAMMAR IN CONTENT

EXERCISE A

Have students complete the activity and then check it with a partner.

GRAMMAR CHART

Gerunds and Infinitives with Phrasal Modals

1. Ask volunteers to name some phrasal modals and write them on the board.
2. Call on students to read the sample sentences and corresponding Notes.
3. Answer any questions that students have about using gerunds and infinitives with phrasal modals.

GRAMMAR CHART

Gerund and Infinitive Review

1. Quickly review verbs that must be followed by a gerund or infinitive. Direct students' attention to the complete list in the appendix of their book.
2. Call on students to read the sample sentences and corresponding Notes.
3. Answer any questions that students have about verbs that require gerunds and infinitives.

1. Ask students to read the instructions.
2. Call on a student to read the example. Ask a volunteer to explain why *a* is the correct interpretation of the sentence.
3. Have students complete the activity individually and then check their answers with a partner.
4. Call on volunteers to read their answers to the class. If any students disagree, discuss the two answer choices as a class.

B Circle the letter of the correct interpretation of each sentence.

1. The water here appears to contain a lot of calcium and magnesium because we often get a white film on the faucet.
   a. The water must have calcium and magnesium in it.
   b. The water has calcium and magnesium in it.

2. Before class was over, Dr. Sato remembered to assign the second set of experiments.
   a. Dr. Sato realized that he had already assigned the experiments.
   b. Dr. Sato did not forget that he had to give the next assignment.

3. Dr. Sato's students managed to find a significant amount of lead in the river.
   a. It took a lot of effort, but the students succeeded in analyzing the lead content.
   b. The students organized themselves efficiently so that they could find the lead.

4. Students on Team 3 tried collecting their next samples from Maple Hill Creek according to Dr. Sato's instructions.
   a. The students wanted to collect the samples, but they weren't successful.
   b. The students hadn't collected samples this way before, but it worked.

5. Some people pretend to follow clean water laws.
   a. Some people say that they follow the laws, but they don't.
   b. Some people have the intention of following the laws.

6. While the students on Team 3 were testing the water for lead, they stopped to check their preliminary results.
   a. The students decided not to check their results any more.
   b. The students decided to discontinue their tests so that they could check the results.

7. After the mercury scare, Hendersonville has resumed testing its tap water regularly.
   a. The city has started testing the tap water again.
   b. The city has summarized the results of the water tests regularly.

8. Many citizens resent having to boil their tap water when the water supply is contaminated.
   a. Many citizens feel angry and irritated when they have to boil their tap water.
   b. Many citizens don't want to boil their tap water when it has been contaminated.

9. Dr. Sato regretted telling the teams about making recommendations to local officials now that they had actually found lead in the water.
   a. Dr. Sato was sorry that he had already told the students about making recommendations.
   b. Dr. Sato was sorry that he had to tell the students about the recommendations.

10. A local company neglected to neutralize the acids that it uses in one process before they discharged the wastewater from their factory.
    a. The company succeeded in neutralizing the acids.
    b. The company failed to neutralize the acids properly.

EXPANSION IDEA

Exercise B
Ask students to select one of the sentences from Exercise B and expand it by adding a few sentences that contain gerunds and/or infinitives.

For example:
After the mercury scare, Hendersonville has resumed testing its tap water regularly. Mercury failed to show up in the next two tests and scientists are able to say with some certainty that the quality of the water in Hendersonville will continue to improve.

C Complete each sentence with the appropriate phrasal modal + gerund or infinitive, using the verb in parentheses.

1. To do their experiments, Dr. Sato's students need ___*to be able to conduct*___ various types of tests. (ABILITY/conduct)

2. At the beginning of the semester, some of his students may be anxious about

   ___**having to collect**___ samples because they've never done it before. (NECESSITY/collect)

3. Dr. Sato is accustomed to ___**having to demonstrate**___ various experimental techniques before his students can begin their projects. (NECESSITY/demonstrate)

4. He expects all of them ___**to be able to filter**___ liquids because it is so similar to using a coffee filter. (ABILITY/filter)

5. Many students can't imagine ___**being able to determine**___ the amount of dissolved solids in water until they see that it just involves filtering and boiling off the water, and then weighing the residue. (ABILITY/determine)

6. When the students evaluated their water samples for toxic compounds, the

   experiments involved ___**having to place**___ organisms in the samples. (NECESSITY/place)

7. Some of the students felt uncomfortable about ___**having to endanger**___ the lives of creatures in their research. (NECESSITY/endanger)

8. Dr. Sato wanted the students ___**to be able to measure**___ the toxicity of the water so he assured them that the experiments were necessary. (ABILITY/measure)

9. A few students really resented not ___**being able to conduct**___ the research without killing the minnows that they were using. (ABILITY/conduct)

1. Have students read the instructions.
2. Call on a student to read the example.
3. Have students complete the exercise and then check their work with a partner.
4. Call on volunteers to read their answers to the class. After each sentence is read, check with the class to see if they agree that the phrasal modal has been used correctly.

■ **EXPANSION IDEA**

Exercise C
Divide the class into small groups and have students discuss how they feel about using animals in their research.

Encourage them to talk about necessity and ability.

EXERCISE D
CD 1, Track 20

1. Ask students to look at the diagram.
2. Call on a volunteer to explain osmosis, and relate the explanation to desalinization and the diagram.
3. Play the audio and have students listen for comprehension only.
4. Ask students to read through the questions. Then play the audio again, pausing frequently to give students time to write their answers. Play the audio again if necessary.
5. Call on volunteers to read their answers to the class. If there is any disagreement about answers, replay the audio.

D Listen to Dr. Sato's introduction to desalination and answer the questions below. Try to use a gerund or infinitive in your answers.

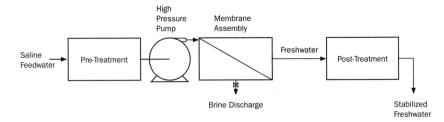

1. How do some arid regions manage to get drinking water?
   Some arid regions manage to get fresh water from salt water.

2. Why does Dr. Sato recommend using the Middle East as an example?
   They are lucky enough to have the resources to solve their water shortages.

3. What does desalination technology require?
   Desalination technology requires water treatment equipment and salt water.

4. What do they need to have done before sea water can become drinkable?
   Before sea water can become drinkable, they need to have distilled it.

5. In reverse osmosis, what are the membranes in the system effective at doing?
   The membranes are effective in filtering out salt.

6. What is involved in producing drinking water from distilled water?
   It involves mixing distilled water with other water.

7. What is a desalination plant capable of doing?
   A desalination plant is capable of producing 15–50 gallons of water from 100 gallons of sea water.

EXPANSION IDEA

Exercise D
Ask students to summarize Dr. Sato's introduction, using the information they wrote down in Exercise D.

E Find and correct the five errors in the e-mail message below.

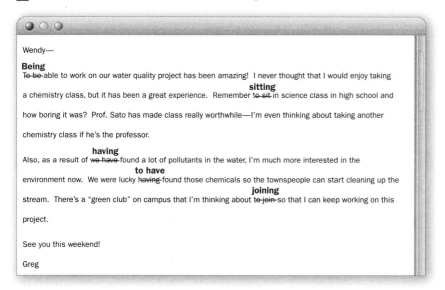

Wendy—

Being
~~To be~~ able to work on our water quality project has been amazing! I never thought that I would enjoy taking

a chemistry class, but it has been a great experience. Remember **sitting** ~~to sit~~ in science class in high school and

how boring it was? Prof. Sato has made class really worthwhile—I'm even thinking about taking another

chemistry class if he's the professor.

having
Also, as a result of ~~we have~~ found a lot of pollutants in the water, I'm much more interested in the

to have
environment now. We were lucky ~~having~~ found those chemicals so the townspeople can start cleaning up the

joining
stream. There's a "green club" on campus that I'm thinking about ~~to join~~ so that I can keep working on this

project.

See you this weekend!

Greg

■ **COMMUNICATE**

F **PAIR WORK** Dr. Sato's students have found unacceptable levels of lead and copper in sources of local drinking water, and they are going to discuss their findings with town officials tomorrow. Prepare some questions that will help students during their meeting. Use the main verbs in the box below and appropriate gerunds or infinitives.   Answers will vary.

manage	~~arrange~~	~~demand~~	resume	avoid
threaten	acknowledge	propose	expect	tolerate

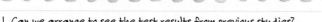

1. Can we arrange to see the test results from previous studies?
2. Should we demand to talk with the previous researchers?

G **SMALL GROUP WORK** Discuss the importance of water conservation. Put together a list of 4–5 pressing issues related to water. What is the best response to these issues? Discuss possible solutions, and then share your ideas with your classmates.   Answers will vary.

---

1. Have students correct the errors in the e-mail.
2. Call on volunteers to read the corrected e-mail aloud.

■ **COMMUNICATE**

■ **EXERCISE F**

1. Ask students to review the instructions.
2. Call on students to read the examples.
3. Divide the class into pairs and have them write their questions using the main verbs in the box and appropriate gerunds or infinitives.

■ **EXERCISE G**

1. Divide the class into small groups and have them discuss the importance of water conservation.
2. Have them list pressing issues related to water, and then call on volunteers to share their ideas.

■ **EXPANSION IDEA**

Exercise G

1. Ask the class to choose one important water issue to debate.
2. Divide the class into two groups. Have the students decide which group will support the suggested issue and which group will take the opposing view.
3. Have groups prepare a list of points to debate. Ask them to use vocabulary and grammar from the lesson whenever possible.
4. Have teams select one or two group members to debate.
5. Have students debate the topic.

Connection

Putting It Together

▣ GRAMMAR AND VOCABULARY

1. Review the instructions with the class.
2. Call on two students to read the topics aloud.
3. Tell students to choose a topic and write their compositions, using as many of the words and structures learned in the lesson as possible.

▣ PROJECT

1. Ask students to raise their hands if they have a bottle of water in their backpacks. Have them take out the bottles and set them on their desks.
2. Ask students to raise their hands if they drink at least one bottle of water a day.
3. Ask students to discuss why they drink bottled water as opposed to tap water in the United States.
4. Review the instructions with the class. Tell students to conduct their interviews.
5. Call on students to share their results at the next class meeting.

▣ INTERNET

1. Go over the instructions with the class. Write the names of a water organization in your area on the board.
2. Have students conduct their searches and share the information they find at the next class meeting.
3. Discuss with the class whether they should drink bottled water in your area.

GRAMMAR AND VOCABULARY Write a composition on one of the topics below. Use as many words as possible from the Content Vocabulary on page 97, and (circle) them in your composition. Use gerund and infinitive structures from this lesson where appropriate to express your ideas, and <u>underline</u> those verb phrases, i.e., the verbs and the gerunds or infinitives that follow them.

Topic 1: Water has shaped the culture, history, and economy of countries around the world. What kind of impact has water had on your country? Are people in some areas concerned about being able to maintain a safe water supply? How secure is the water supply as a result of having diverted water for agricultural purposes? Explain and give concrete examples.

Topic 2: Many students complain about having to take chemistry classes because they consider chemistry to be irrelevant to their lives. In the media, stories about chemists and chemistry often highlight accidents or the harmful effects of chemicals even though scientists may deny having created the problem. How has chemistry actually contributed to making all of our lives better?
Answers will vary.

PROJECT Interview at least one student on your campus about the question of drinking bottled water. Find out the following information, and report what you found out to your classmates.

1. What kind of water does the student drink?
2. Is it safe to drink the water in public places in the U.S.?
3. Why do Americans tend to drink so much bottled water?
4. What kind of water does the student recommend drinking?

 INTERNET Go online to the website of your local water authority and check the water quality in your area. Ask your instructor for the name of the organization in your area, for example, the "Sewerage and Water Board of New Orleans." If possible, check the water quality in nearby cities or counties for comparison. Bring your findings to class and discuss them. Should you drink bottled water in your area?

If you are interested in desalination, use the search phrase "desalination plant diagram" to find information about the equipment involved in this process. Print out the diagram if possible to show your classmates as you describe the system.

Review the information on the costs of desalination plants that use distillation technology and plants that use reverse osmosis. Present the information to your classmates.
Answers will vary.

▣ EXPANSION IDEA

Grammar and Vocabulary

1. Divide the class into pairs and have them edit each other's compositions. Ask them to comment on where additional gerunds and infinitives could be used.
2. Give students time to rewrite their compositions.
3. Call on volunteers to read their compositions to the class.

A (Circle) the letter of the word that correctly completes each sentence, and then write the word in the blank space.

1. Reporters have been investigating the contamination of a nearby river by local

   companies, and they _____**should**_____ release their results soon.

   a. must   (b) should   c. would

2. According to the reporters' preliminary results, Oxtle Corporation ___**must not**___ have disposed of toxic compounds in the river because the chemical analysis shows a low level of pollutants related to their business.

   a. can't   b. may not   (c) must not

3. The reporters _____**could**_____ have tried to find eyewitnesses to the contamination, but they relied on the chemical analysis of the river water instead.

   (a) could   b. might   c. can

4. Once the analysis becomes available, the reporters may reveal that **all the/all of the** companies along the river were guilty of polluting the water to some degree.

   a. all the   b. all of the   (c) either a. or b.

5. None of the companies _____**have**_____ responded to the reporters' allegations.

   a. has   (b) have   c. either a. or b.

6. The spokesperson for Oxtle Corporation has objected ___**to providing**___ chemical formulas that Oxtle has developed to outside researchers.

   (a) to providing   b. to provide   c. for providing

7. According to town officials, it is no use **to object/objecting** because the court will require companies to reveal the compounds that they produce.

   a. to object   b. objecting   (c) either a. or b.

8. After the trial began, Oxtle Corporation regretted ___**not having cooperated**___ with the reporters' investigation.

   a. not to have cooperated   b. not to cooperate   (c) not having cooperated

9. An eyewitness ___**was about to**___ testify against Oxtle when the company lawyer interrupted and asked to speak to the judge.

   a. was to   (b) was about to   c. was able to

10. The president of Oxtle was unhappy about _____**having to**_____ pay a $500,000 fine, but he preferred it to going to jail.

    (a) having to   b. to have to   c. have to

Review 6-10

Review Lessons 6–10

The purpose of this lesson is to help students review the language and concepts they have learned in the last five lessons. Encourage them to go back to the lessons and review the grammar charts to help them complete the review activities.

■ EXERCISE A

1. Ask students to review the instructions.
2. Have students complete the activity individually and then check their work in pairs.
3. Call on volunteers to read their answers to the class. Discuss any answers that class members disagree about.

■ EXPANSION IDEA

Exercise A

1. Divide the class into pairs.
2. Ask students to discuss the claims made by reporters regarding contamination of a nearby river by local companies.

For example:

Student 1: *If the companies are responsible for contaminating the river, they should have to clean it up and pay fines.*

Student 2: *First, investigations must prove which companies are guilty.*

■ **EXERCISE B**

1. Ask students to read the instructions.
2. Have students complete the activity individually and then check their work in pairs.
3. Call on volunteers to read their answers aloud.

■ **LEARNER LOG**

Have students complete the Learner Log. Suggest that they review the Grammar Charts for areas that need more practice.

B Use the correct form of the verb in parentheses. Add negation when necessary for the meaning of the sentence.

1. Our university committee on ethical research always _____**has to ascertain**_____ (ascertain) how experiments will protect the health of test subjects.

2. The number of experiments with animal test subjects _____**has decreased**_____ (decrease) since 1990.

3. Before then, there _____**must have been**_____ (must be) some problems with unethical procedures since the committee has shown much more concern about test subjects in recent years.

4. In some labs they still _____**could be using**_____ (could use) procedures that the committee has not approved, but researchers know that they should follow the guidelines.

5. They _____**are not supposed to follow**_____ (be supposed to follow) any procedures that may endanger the physical or psychological health of human subjects.

6. For the last decade, researchers _____**have had to submit**_____ (have to submit) research proposals to the committee for review.

7. It takes the committee several months _____**to review**_____ (review) each research proposal.

8. With regard to _____**approving**_____ (approve) a proposal, the committee members prefer careful consideration over speed.

9. The committee also wants to avoid any bad publicity for the university as a consequence of _____**not considering**_____ (consider) a research proposal carefully.

10. The long approval process irritates some researchers who resent _____**not being able to begin**_____ (be able to begin) their work for many months.

LEARNER LOG Check (✔) *Yes* or *I Need More Practice.* Answers will vary.

Lesson	I Can Use . . .	Yes	I Need More Practice
6	Academic Phrasal Modals and Other Modal Verbs		
7	Modal Verbs in the Past Logical Scale and Other Perfect Modals		
8	Quantifiers and Subject-Verb Agreement		
9	Gerunds and Infinitives as Subjects and Subject Complements; Gerunds Following a Preposition		
10	Gerunds and Infinitives in Perfect Forms and with Phrasal Modals		

■ **EXPANSION IDEA**

Pair students with a partner and have them brainstorm the ethical guidelines that scientific procedures and experiments should follow. Have a representative from each group write their answers on the board, and invite a class discussion about everyone's ideas.

Lesson (11)

Human Resources: The Multigenerational Workplace

■ CONTENT VOCABULARY

Look up the words and phrases below that you do not know and enter them in your vocabulary journal. Write each item's part of speech, a definition, and an example sentence. Try to include them in your discussion and writing below.

the bottom line	hands-on	savvy	a work ethic
to buy into	haphazardly	to socialize	a workforce
friction	multitasking	to take up the slack	a workload

■ THINK ABOUT IT

Look at the photo on the following page. What do you notice about the types of employees working at this particular restaurant? Would you find the same kind of staff at a similar restaurant in your neighborhood or community? Why, or why not? Discuss your ideas with a classmate.

In your writing journal, write for five minutes about the questions below. When you are finished, share what you wrote with the class.

In your experience as an employee, have you worked with people of different ages? What was your relationship with co-workers or supervisors of various ages? What kinds of problems or conflicts did your co-workers have because of age differences? If you've ever been an employee, write about a work conflict you may have seen or heard about. **Answers will vary.**

111

Overview

1. Write *multigenerational* on the board. Underline *multi* and solicit a definition of the prefix. Then call on a volunteer to explain the complete term.
2. Ask students to read the title of the lesson. Have them discuss what they imagine the composition of workers in a multigenerational workplace looks like.

■ CONTENT VOCABULARY

Ask students to review the words in the box. Tell them to look up any unfamiliar words.

■ VOCABULARY JOURNAL

Have students add new words to their vocabulary journals and write down the parts of speech, definitions, and sentences for each.

■ THINK ABOUT IT

1. Have students read the instructions.
2. Divide the class into pairs and have them discuss the questions posed in the exercise.
3. Circulate as students work and assist with vocabulary as needed.
4. Give students five minutes to write in their journals. Then call on volunteers to discuss issues in the workplace that resulted from age differences.

■ CONTENT NOTES

The topic of this lesson is Human Resources: The Multigenerational Workplace. Students will learn about how differences in the ways that generations approach life and work affect workplace relationships and management. Use this lesson to discuss how generational differences are similar and different in students' countries of origin.

PART ONE

Review of Adverbials

■ GRAMMAR IN CONTENT

■ EXERCISE A
CD 2, Track 1

1. Call on a student to read the title of the reading ask students to predict what the reading will be about.

2. Write *1965–1981* on the board and ask students to raise their hands if they know the name given to the generation born between these years. Write their suggestions on the board.

3. Play the audio and have students follow along in their books as they listen. Ask students to circle any unfamiliar words or phrases.

4. Ask students to read the words they circled. Elicit definitions from other class members if possible.

5. Check comprehension by asking questions such as the following: *What is the generation born between 1982 and 2002 known as? Who are the Baby Boomers? How do Generation X-ers tend to view authority figures? What is another name for the Traditionalist Generation? Why do many retired workers rejoin the work force?*

■ GRAMMAR IN CONTENT

CD2,TR1

A Read and listen to the passage below. The words in bold in the text are adverbials.

Working with Grandpa

Across the U.S., Americans are encountering co-workers and colleagues who are quite different in age and outlook. In fast food restaurants, home repair centers, and many other retail stores, teenagers and people the age of their grandparents are working **side by side.** Managers in such businesses have realized that their bottom line depends on a workforce that spans generations. For corporate and public sector administrators, leading **effectively** means finding ways for their employees, who may have **fundamentally** different values and expectations, to work **cooperatively.** This attitude toward leadership differs **significantly** from those held **when the workforce was predominantly made up of white men of the pre-World War II generation.** Experts in the field of human resource management have identified characteristics that help managers understand the motivations and issues important for each generation of employees in the workplace.

For the most recent generation in the workforce, known as Generation Y, technology plays a **quite** important role in their worldview. Members of Generation Y, who were born between 1982 and 2002, incorporate computers and other technology in their private and work lives **seamlessly.** The parents of these "Millennials" or "Echo Boomers" involved themselves **actively** in the lives of their children, who now interact **positively** with older co-workers and tend to prefer project-oriented work assignments.

In contrast to the Millennials, members of Generation X perform job-related tasks **more independently.** Preferring results over a cooperative work-style, Generation X-ers view authority figures **more skeptically** than their younger colleagues. Clearly, this attitude can **potentially** lead to conflict in the workplace as these adults, born between 1965 and 1981, set very clear boundaries between their work and private lives.

Members of the largest and currently the most powerful generation differ **considerably** from the younger generations. Baby Boomers, born during the years of great cultural and social change from 1946–1964, tend to view the world **optimistically.** Characterized **quite accurately** as workaholics, they desire acknowledgment of their own personal accomplishments and respect the accomplishments and power of others. For this generation, work always comes first.

Although the number of workers from the Traditionalist (or Silent) Generation, who were born from 1927 to 1945, is decreasing, these people **still** influence the workplace. Some of them continue in their jobs **long past the traditional retirement age.** Also, many retired workers have been re-joining the workforce to earn money as part-time employees or to contribute as volunteers. Employers value their loyalty and positive work ethic.

Faced with global competitive pressures, managers need to ensure that their employees perform **efficiently** so that tasks and projects are completed **on time** and products or services are delivered **properly.** Excellent managers have to build a team based on the strengths that all of these workers bring to the workplace and to build respect among the team members for smooth working relationships.

an outlook: perspective, point of view
to span: to go across, to range

predominantly: mostly
acknowledgment: recognition

■ EXPANSION IDEA

Exercise A
Divide the class into pairs. Ask pairs to look at the bolded adverbials in the reading passage and discuss which questions they answer.

Sample Sentences	Notes
The VPs **unanimously** selected Jim Green and Pam Connors to work on the Harris project.	Most adverbials answer one of these questions: · How? · Where/In which direction? · When/How often? · Why? · To what extent?
Green moved **overseas** **when he got a promotion.**	
Connors has been e-mailing Green **constantly** **because of the project deadline.**	
The deadline is **especially** important for their client.	Adverbs that answer "To what extent?" modify or intensify adjectives, for example, *very careful*, *extremely powerful.*
Ms. Carlson may send Connors **to Asia** **eventually** since she and Green have performed **so well.**	Adverbs that answer "To what extent?" can also modify other adverbs, as in *quite slowly.*
The tech team meets **every week** /**at 12:00**/ **on Wednesdays.**	Adverbials can take the form of simple words (*very*, *completely*), phrases (*every day*, *in a minute*, *at home*), and clauses (*when we arrived in Beijing*).
The newer members of the team sit in the chairs **toward the back of the room.**	Put adverbials at the end of the sentence in this order: *How? Where? When? Why?*
Some old-timers **voluntarily** sit **in the back of the room** to talk with the newer staff.	The order of adverbials that tell *How?* and *Where?* can be switched. The same is true for *When?* and *How often?* and *Where?* and *In which direction?*
In the back, staff can come and go **as they please.**	Less frequent positions for adverbials: Where? When? ⎤ in sentence-initial position Why? ⎦ How? ⊐ in the same position as frequency adverbs
During the meeting, everyone shares ideas **freely.**	
We can **usually** find an empty table in the lunchroom.	Some frequency adverbs (*always, usually, sometimes, rarely,* etc.) appear after the first auxiliary verb.
I am **always** the first person to arrive.	If there is no auxiliary verb, adverbs appear after *be* but before other verbs.

B Read over your journal entry, and <u>underline</u> at least one sentence that you can revise to include an adverbial. Write your revised sentence(s) below.

Answers will vary.

■ **GRAMMAR CHART**
Review of Adverbials

1. Call on a volunteer to define *adverbial.* Then ask students if they agree or disagree with the definition.
2. Call on several volunteers to give sentences that include adverbials. Write the sentences on the board, underlining the adverbials. Call on new volunteers to say what question the adverbials answer.
3. Call on students to read the sample sentences and accompanying Notes.
4. Answer any questions that students have about how and when to use adverbials.

■ **EXERCISE B**

Have students complete the exercise and compare their sentence with a partner.

■ **EXPANSION IDEA**

Grammar Chart

Have students write five sentences using adverbials that answer the questions posted in the first note box in the Grammar Chart (How? Where/In which direction? When/How often? Why? To what extent?)

1. Read the instructions and example.
2. Have students complete the activity. Then have them compare their work with a partner.
3. Call on volunteers to read their answers to the class, explaining their choices if challenged by classmates.
4. Answer any questions students have about adverbial placement.

C (Circle) the letter of the correct completion(s) to the sentences below.

1. As soon as he read the e-mail from his boss, Martin Cates walked
   a. purposefully toward the 3rd floor meeting room.
   b. toward the 3rd floor meeting room purposefully.
   (c.) both of the above.

2. A staff meeting had already begun when Cates entered
   (a.) the meeting room about 5 minutes late.
   b. about 5 minutes late the meeting room.
   c. both of the above.

3. Gina Tatum was explaining their new marketing strategy
   a. at the head of the table at that moment.
   b. at that moment at the head of the table.
   (c.) both of the above.

4. Gina and Martin had been working on the strategy
   (a.) to impress their boss in their spare time.
   b. in their spare time to impress their boss.
   c. both of the above.

5. Martin could tell that Gina had introduced their marketing concept
   a. before his entrance capably.
   (b.) capably before his entrance.
   c. both of the above.

6. Gina was going through their slide presentation
   (a.) with handouts instead of a projector due to a problem with the equipment.
   b. due to a problem with the equipment with handouts instead of a projector.
   c. both of the above.

7. Gina and Martin had printed the handouts
   a. the previous afternoon quickly in the company copy center.
   (b.) quickly in the company copy center the previous afternoon.
   c. both of the above.

8. Now he was very glad they had taken that precaution because the staff was responding
   (a.) so positively during her presentation.
   b. during her presentation so positively.
   c. both of the above.

■ **EXPANSION IDEAS**

Exercise C
Divide the class into pairs. Have students circle the adverbials in each sentence and identify the questions they answer.

Exercise C
1. Have students write scrambled sentences that include at least one adverbial.

For example: *Mrs./client/an/Smith/important/is/extremely.*
(Mrs. Smith is an extremely important client.)

2. Divide the class into pairs and have students unscramble each other's sentences. If there is more than one place where the adverbial can be used, have students point this out.

D Use one of the adverbs in the box below to modify an adjective or adverb in each sentence. Many of these adverbs are interchangeable, and there are more adverbs than necessary to complete the exercise.

extremely	completely	highly	fairly	appreciably	a little
~~quite~~	amazingly	perfectly	somewhat	rather	a bit

                                         quite

(1) Of all her employees, Mrs. Lawrence is ˅impressed with the newest staff member,

Karen Bunting. **(2)** Hired right out of college as an accountant, Ms. Bunting has learned the
          extremely, rather, relatively
company's system˅quickly. **(3)** Normally it takes a new accountant several months to handle
     rather, somewhat, fairly   **rather, somewhat, fairly**
the workload˅comfortably. **(4)** During Ms. Bunting's job interview, she seemed˅competent,
                                              fairly, extremely
but not as well-prepared as she appears to be. **(5)** Mrs. Lawrence feels˅confident that within

a short time Ms. Bunting will be one of her star employees.
                           a little, extremely, somewhat, fairly
(6) In contrast to Karen Bunting, Mrs. Lawrence is˅concerned about Richard Acton,

a long-time employee in the sales department. **(7)** Several co-workers have mentioned that
a bit, a little, somewhat
he seems˅depressed lately. **(8)** Recently two younger sales representatives have joined that
                extremely, highly, relatively
department and added to the˅competitive atmosphere there. **(9)** Up until now, Acton has
             completely
always met his sales goals˅satisfactorily and contributed positively to the company's bottom
             a little, a bit, appreciably, somewhat
line. **(10)** If his sales numbers get˅lower, Mrs. Lawrence may have to speak with him about

his performance.

---

1. Review the instructions.
2. Call on a student to read the example. Then give students time to complete the activity.
3. Have students compare their answers with a partner.
4. Call on volunteers to read their answers to the class, explaining them if classmates disagree.

■ **EXPANSION IDEA**

Exercise D

1. Divide the class into pairs. Tell students that one of them will play the role of Mrs. Lawrence and the other will be one of her colleagues. Have them discuss Karen Bunting and Richard Acton's performances using as many of the adverbs as possible from the box in Exercise D.

For example:

Mrs. Lawrence: *I'm really happy with Karen Bunting's performance so far.*
Colleague: *Why are you so pleased with her?*
Mrs. Lawrence: *Well, she is extremely competent and is a quick learner.*

2. Call on a few pairs of volunteers to role-play for the class.

■ EXERCISE E

1. Ask students to review the instructions and examples. Answer any questions they have about the placement of *rigidly* in the sentence.
2. Have students complete the activity.
3. Call on volunteers to read their answers to the class, explaining them if classmates disagree.

■ EXERCISE F

1. Ask students to read the instructions.
2. Call on a volunteer to read the first two sentences of the paragraph. Point out that *That week* refers to information already given in the first sentence, so it is placed in the sentence-initial position.
3. Have students complete the activity individually.
4. Ask students to check their work with a partner.

E Edit the sentences with "X" to show where the adverbial in parentheses can be added to the text.

1. Younger co-workers may criticize older employees when they ˣfollow company rules.ˣ (**rigidly**)
2. Workers in the Silent Generation have tended to remain at the same workplace.ˣ (**until retirement**)
3. It is ˣunrealistic to think that everyone born in a certain generation will have the same work ethic. (**inherently**)
4. Colleagues from different generations can ˣwork together effectively if they respect each other's strengths and weaknesses. (**eventually**)
5. A good manager will ˣpraise a Baby Boomer ˣin public while she will give a Gen X-er positive feedback in private. (**explicitly**)
6. All employees will perform their jobs in a new way ˣif their supervisor insists on it. (**temporarily**)
7. If employees are motivated to continue with new procedures, their services or products may ˣimprove. (**qualitatively**)
8. New procedures will not ˣmake services better ˣunless the employees buy into the need for change. (**automatically**)

F Edit the paragraph to improve its coherence. Place adverbials in sentence-initial position when the information is already known from the text.

Evan Gibbons started his new job at Patterson, Inc. and ran into some trouble in
the first week. *That week h* His boss assigned him to an ongoing project ~~that week~~. Most of his new
colleagues were more experienced, and they had also been working together for years. **During that time** His
colleagues had become friends ~~during that time,~~ and their families often socialized together.

Although his co-workers treated him politely, he felt isolated and wondered how to improve
Because of his negative feelings,
his situation. He finally made an appointment to talk to his supervisor ~~because of his~~
~~negative feelings.~~

■ EXPANSION IDEA

Exercise F

1. Divide the class into pairs. Have students discuss Evan Gibbons's problem, using as many adverbials as possible in their discussions. Ask them to pay attention to adverbial placement as they speak.
2. Circulate as students discuss, assisting and correcting as needed.

G **PAIR WORK** Brainstorm adverbials that can be used to describe good job performance for the tasks and behaviors listed below. Then, define "excellent" performance by adding an intensifier to the description.   Answers will vary.

- Interact ∧ with the public
  very politely
  courteously
- Respond ∧ to inquiries or requests for information
  quickly
- Fulfill one's job duties ∧
  closely
- Follow the supervisor's directions ∧
  reverently
- Respond to feedback ∧
  graciously
- Assist colleagues/co-workers ∧
  carefully
- Handle payments ∧
  efficiently
- Process paperwork ∧

H **PAIR WORK** Ms. Guzman has written a draft of a letter of recommendation for Susie Dawson. Add appropriate adverbials to make the letter even more positive. Use at least six appropriate adverbs.   Answers will vary.

To Whom It May Concern:

Ms. Susie Dawson requested that we send a letter of recommendation to you. Ms. Dawson worked as a cashier for us last summer from June 1 to August 15. When she began her job, she had no experience. Our accountant gave her a one-week training course and reported that Ms. Dawson learned our procedures. After her training, she worked in our gift shop. She performed her job, cashiering and interacting with our customers. Many customers commented to us about her work. We were sorry that she had to leave.

We recommend Ms. Dawson for the position in your company. If you have any questions about Ms. Dawson's job performance, please contact us.

Sincerely,
Elena Guzman

■ **COMMUNICATE**

■ **EXERCISE G**

1. Review the instructions with the class.
2. Divide the class into pairs and have students complete the activity. Encourage them to be creative in their choices of adverbials.
3. Call on volunteers to read their answers to the class.

■ **EXERCISE H**

1. Have students choose a new partner. Then ask them to complete the activity together.
2. Call on a few volunteers to read their letters to the class.

■ **EXPANSION IDEA**

Exercise H

1. Ask students to write a letter of recommendation for themselves. Instruct them to refer to their definitions of "excellent performance" in Exercise G, and to use as many adverbials as possible.
2. Call on volunteers to read their letters to the class.

PART TWO

Adverbs in Sentence-Initial Position

■ GRAMMAR IN CONTENT

■ EXERCISE A

Ask students to complete the activity and then check their work with a partner.

■ GRAMMAR CHART

Adverbs in Sentence-Initial Position

1. Call on students to read the sample sentences and corresponding Notes aloud.
2. Answer any questions that students have about which adverbs should be in the sentence-initial position.

■ GRAMMAR IN CONTENT

A Reread the text at the beginning of this lesson, and (circle) the example of an adverb in sentence-initial position. What is the function of this adverb?

Adverbs in Sentence-Initial Position

Sample Sentences	Notes
It will take awhile for Ms. Aguilar to understand how our company works. **Typically,** new managers need time to understand a company's culture.	Use particular adverbs in sentence-initial position to comment on or to express an attitude about the information that follows. Use a comma to separate these adverbials from the main clause.
The interns have complained about Mr. Johnson's e-mails. **Evidently,** he is having trouble communicating with some younger workers.	**Probability:** *certainly, surely*
There have been some clashes between our senior staff and the new recruits. **Regrettably,** the age difference has led to some misunderstandings.	**Frequency:** *frequently, occasionally* **Typicality:** *generally, typically*
Technically, all new employees have 10 vacation days annually, but not everyone takes them.	**Clarity/Obviousness:** *obviously, clearly, evidently* **Viewpoint:** *luckily, (un)fortunately, hopefully, regrettably*
Fortunately, their supervisors are monitoring them closely, so we can tell if anyone is getting burned out.	***Fortunately*** shows that things are more positive than expected.
Unfortunately, many talented computer techs don't stay long at one job.	***Unfortunately*** is used to show regret.
	The following adverbials don't require the use of a comma.
Perhaps they need to be encouraged to take their vacation days.	***Perhaps*** is more formal than *maybe,* and is often used to persuade the listener.
Maybe the employees don't want to appear lazy.	***Maybe*** is often used with negatives.
Of course we know that none of them is lazy because their work has been excellent so far this year.	***Of course*** is more common in speech than in writing. Its use assumes the listener has the same background information as the speaker/writer.

Other Adverbs Used in Sentence-Initial Position

frankly	naturally	possibly	actually	ultimately
superficially	technically	theoretically	strangely	(not) surprisingly

---

■ EXPANSION IDEA

Grammar

Divide the class into pairs. Have students take turns making sentences using the words in the box at the bottom of the chart.

B With a partner, comment on the job performance of Franco Drake, 25, and Sylvia Cates, 49, who are working together on an advertising project for an important client. Decide which of you will play the role of the supportive supervisor or the critical supervisor, and then take turns giving your feedback. Answers will vary. Sample answers below.

1. Franco and Sylvia are seriously behind schedule.

   Supportive: _Technically, they are behind schedule, but they have improved the original concept substantially._

   Critical: _Unfortunately, they have disagreed about every aspect of this project._

2. Franco and Sylvia often argue loudly, but then they get back to work.

   Supportive: Actually, they work well despite frequent differences in opinion.

   Critical: Frankly, their interaction skills are disturbing to the other employees.

3. Franco has much more artistic imagination even though Sylvia has a degree in design.

   Supportive: Surprisingly, Franco is quite imaginative despite a lack of degree in art design.

   Critical: Technically, Sylvia's design work should be more imaginative since she has a degree in design.

4. Sylvia's children have been sick with the flu this week, so Franco has had to take up the slack.

   Supportive: Typically, we can depend on Franco to complete projects and meet deadlines.

   Critical: Obviously, Sylvia places the well-being of her family above her work responsibilities.

5. Franco expects a bonus when the project is complete.

   Supportive: Frankly, our company benefits from employees like Franco who produce excellent work and expect adequate pay.

   Critical: Maybe Franco should be less focused on financial rewards for meeting deadlines.

6. Sylvia originally felt uncomfortable about working with such an inexperienced colleague.

   Supportive: Fortunately, Sylvia shares her feelings with her supervisor so we can deal with her questions before problems come up.

   Critical: Naturally, Sylvia dislikes having inexperienced co-workers because she doesn't want to take time to train them.

7. They have generated impressive graphics, but the message still needs to be revised considerably.

   Supportive: Of course, they always design wonderful graphics.

   Critical: Ultimately, they will have to spend much more time on the client's message so that it matches the quality of the design.

8. The clients prefer to speak with Sylvia when they contact the advertising agency.

   Supportive: Evidently, Sylvia has strong skills in pubic relations since clients always prefer to speak with her.

   Critical: Regrettably, Franco has weak "people skills"; consequently, he needs to work with a partner who communicates with clients.

■ **EXERCISE B**

1. Call on a student to read the instructions.
2. Ask a pair of students to read the example. Then have students complete the activity in pairs.
3. Call on volunteers to read their answers to the class.

■ **EXPANSION IDEA**

Exercise B

1. Tell students to write a supportive or critical paragraph of either Franco's or Sylvia's performance. Ask them to use as many adverbials that use sentence-initial position as possible.
2. Call on volunteers to read their paragraphs to the class.

CD 2, Track 2

1. Call on a student to read the instructions.
2. Play the audio and have students listen carefully.
3. Ask a student to read the example. Call on a volunteer to say which generation Don belongs to and to explain the answer.
4. Have students complete the activity and then check their answers with a partner.
5. Call on volunteers to read their answers to the class.

C Listen to the statements of various employees at Freeman Services, and comment on their attitudes or work ethic, using information in the chart below. If their dates of birth are not given, try to determine which generation they belong to based on the information given.

CD2,TR2

	Work-life vs family-life?	Approach to authority?	Optimistic?	Personal achievement?	Technological know-how?
Silent Gen. (1927–45)	separate	strong respect	so-so	obedience is more important	no
Boomers (1946–64)	workaholic	little respect	yes	yes	so-so
Gen X (1965–81)	balanced	casual	no	important outside workplace	yes
Gen Y/ Millennials (1982–present)	work-oriented	respect	yes	yes	yes

1. Don, born 1950: *Obviously, Don doesn't have very strong computer skills, as with many other Boomers.*

2. Olivia, born 1982: **Possibly Mrs. O'Connor is an authority figure that Olivia respects.**

3. LeShanda: **Clearly, LeShanda is a member of Gen X.**

4. Richard, born 1939: **Evidently, Richard is not a member of the Silent Generation.**

5. Juanita: **Perhaps Juanita is a Baby-Boomer.**

6. Will, born 1962: **Obviously, as a Baby Boomer Will has little respect for authority.**

7. Aisha: **Frankly, Aisha sounds like a Gen X-er because she is tech-savvy.**

8. Jerry, born 1985: **Interestingly, Jerry doesn't have the same tech skills that most people in Gen Y have.**

■ **EXPANSION IDEA**

Exercise C

1. Ask students to choose a family member or friend who belongs to each of the four generations. Have them consider whether the attitudes listed apply to the people they selected.

2. Divide the class into small groups. Have students discuss how accurate the information in the chart was for the people they selected.

3. Call on a member of each group to discuss his/her group's findings.

D Find and correct the five errors in the informal e-mail message below.

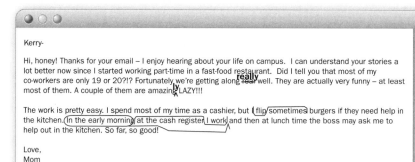

Kerry-

Hi, honey! Thanks for your email – I enjoy hearing about your life on campus. I can understand your stories a lot better now since I started working part-time in a fast-food restaurant. Did I tell you that most of my co-workers are only 19 or 20?!? Fortunately we're getting along ~~really~~ well. They are actually very funny – at least most of them. A couple of them are amazing ly LAZY!!!

The work is pretty easy. I spend most of my time as a cashier, but I flip / sometimes burgers if they need help in the kitchen. In the early morning at the cash register I work and then at lunch time the boss may ask me to help out in the kitchen. So far, so good!

Love,
Mom

■ C O M M U N I C A T E

E **SMALL GROUP WORK** Talk about your expectations of a workplace where you can perform your job comfortably and confidently. How should your employer treat you? Include the following ideas in your conversation.

   a. providing a mentor or coach
   b. giving feedback
   c. assigning projects
   d. providing technology
   e. offering flexible working hours
   f. working on a team
   g. providing training for professional development

Be prepared to share your ideas with another small group in your class.

■ **EXERCISE D**

1. Have students find and correct the errors in the e-mail.
2. Ask students to check their work with a partner.
3. Call on a volunteer to read the corrected e-mail aloud.
4. Call for corrections from volunteers as needed.

■ **COMMUNICATE**

■ **EXERCISE E**

1. Call on a volunteer to read the instructions.
2. Go over the ideas listed.
3. Call on volunteers to suggest other ideas to add to the list, and write them on the board.
3. Divide the class into small groups and have students discuss their workplace expectations.
4. If time permits, have students share their ideas with another small group.

■ **EXPANSION IDEAS**

Exercise D

1. Have students write a response to the e-mail. Tell them to use as many adverbials as possible.
2. Ask students to exchange work with a partner. Tell them to correct errors and suggest places where additional adverbials can be added.

3. Call on a few volunteers to read their e-mails to the class.

Exercise E

Ask students to write a paragraph describing their ideal workplace.

Connection

Putting It Together

GRAMMAR AND VOCABULARY

1. Ask students to read the instructions.
2. Call on two students to read the topics aloud.
3. Ask students to choose one of the two topics and give them time to write their compositions.

PROJECT

1. Ask students to review the instructions.
2. Ask students to brainstorm a few more ideas about what to ask during their interviews. Write the ideas on the board.
3. Call on students at the next class meeting to report their findings.

INTERNET

1. Call on a student to read the instructions.
2. Have students conduct their searches and then report to the class on their findings.

GRAMMAR AND VOCABULARY Write a composition on one of the topics below. Use as many words as possible from the Content Vocabulary on page 111, and ⟨circle⟩ them in your composition. Use sentences with adverbials to express some of your ideas, and <u>underline</u> those sentences.

Topic 1: New employees need orientation to the organization and job training for their specific duties. Of course supervisors can help new employees become valuable employees. The next time that you start a new job, how can your supervisor train you effectively? Would you like to read a manual, listen to explanations, do hands-on activities by yourself, or have a mentor? Explain and give concrete examples.

Topic 2: During a job interview, prospective employers often ask candidates about their strengths and weaknesses for a particular job. In preparation for such an interview, write an analysis of yourself for a job in a workplace that includes people of different generations. Select a specific job that would interest you for this composition.
Answers will vary.

PROJECT Interview at least one student on your campus who has a job. Ask him or her questions about intergenerational relations at the workplace.
Here are some ideas:

1. Where has the student worked?
2. Who else was on the staff at that workplace? Was everyone about the same age?
3. Were there ever any misunderstandings or conflicts among the staff?
4. Did the ages or values of the co-workers result in any friction?

Give a short oral report on the results of your interview to your class.

 INTERNET Go online, and use the search phrase "managing millennials." Find a website with information or tips about managing Millennials successfully. If you are a Millennial, choose 2–3 tips that would be good advice for your future boss. Share this information with your class, and tell why you chose the tips.

If you are not a Millennial, choose 2–3 tips that would be difficult for you to follow if you were the supervisor of a Millennial. Share this information with your class and tell why following the tips would be difficult for you.
Answers will vary.

■ EXPANSION IDEA

Internet
1. Have students write a short composition about "managing millennials," using the information they found through their Internet searches.

2. Ask students to exchange compositions with a partner. Have them edit each other's work.

Counseling: Rites of Passage

■ CONTENT VOCABULARY

Look up the words and phrases below that you do not know and enter them in your vocabulary journal. Write each item's part of speech, a definition, and an example sentence. Try to include them in your discussion and writing below.

endurance	an initiation	a ritual	to signify
a gang	a myth	to distance oneself from	a transition
guidance	an ordeal	to mature	a vision

■ THINK ABOUT IT

When you see younger people today, what is your impression? Do you identify with them? Why or why not? Discuss your ideas with a classmate.

In your writing journal, write for five minutes about the questions below. When you are finished, share your information with the class.

There are many ceremonies and "rites of passage" associated with the transition from adolescence to adulthood. Some of them are formal, while others are not. What are some of these rites of passage in different cultures you know?

Answers will vary.

Overview

Ask students to brainstorm about events that were milestones in their lives. Write them on the board.

■ CONTENT VOCABULARY

Ask students to review the words in the box. Tell them to look up any unfamiliar words.

■ VOCABULARY JOURNAL

Have students add new words to their vocabulary journals and write down the parts of speech, definitions, and sentences for each.

■ THINK ABOUT IT

1. Have students read the instructions.
2. Divide the class into pairs and have them discuss the questions posed in the exercise.
3. Circulate as students work and assist with vocabulary as needed.
4. Give students five minutes to write in their journals. Then call on volunteers to discuss rites of passage.

■ CONTENT NOTES

The topic of this lesson is Counseling: Rites of Passage. In this lesson, students will learn about ceremonies and traditions that mark the transition from adolescence to adulthood. This is a good time for students to discuss their cultural differences and similarities.

PART ONE   **Sequential Connectors**

■ **GRAMMAR IN CONTENT**

■ **EXERCISE A**

CD 2, Track 3

1. Call on a student to read the title of the reading. Ask students to predict what the reading will be about.

2. Ask students to name some ways in which adolescents in their countries express themselves. Ask if they dye their hair, get tattoos, or use their own kinds of slang.

3. Play the audio and have students follow along in their books as they listen. Ask students to circle any unfamiliar words or phrases.

4. Ask students to read the words they circled. Elicit definitions from other class members, if possible.

5. Check comprehension by asking questions such as the following: *Why is "outrageous" teen behavior not just a phase that teens are going through? Who guided the transition from adolescence to adulthood in traditional societies? What is a "vision quest"? What are some of the other rites of passage mentioned in the reading?*

■ **GRAMMAR IN CONTENT**

A Read and listen to the passage below. The words in bold in the text are sequential connectors.

CD2,TR3

The Journeys of Life

What's up with the green hair? Parents and teachers wonder what ever happened to that sweet child Katie, who now has a pierced navel and a tattooed ankle and a chip on her shoulder. How about Eugene, who seems to wear the colors of the local gang?

As families fret about their teenagers, counselors and anthropologists have an explanation for the weird appearance and outrageous behavior of many teenagers. It's not just "a phase" that these adolescents are going through. They are in the middle of a journey from childhood to adulthood, a journey that experts call a "rite of passage." In the modern version of this rite of passage, young people separate themselves from childhood and find their own ways toward the meaning of being an adult. Similarly, young people throughout history have made this journey, but there was an important difference. For youths from traditional cultures, the elders strictly guided their change of identity and taught them the meaning and obligations of adulthood. Their time of transition often involved special initiation rites, which involved separation from everything that they knew, tests of endurance, and sacrifice. Once the difficult passage was over, the whole community celebrated as the new adults took their places in society.

Initiation into adulthood isn't clearly defined in some cultures anymore, but some counselors advise parents and troubled teens to view the experiences of these years in terms of the traditional pathway. We can re-invent myths, those traditional stories about ancient heroes, in a way that young people can understand and incorporate in their lives. David Oldfield, a mental health professional, advocates the use of these stories so that youths have positive role models and can learn what life is really all about as they realize the steps that all people take as they mature. **First**, a youth answers a "call of adventure," which means leaving the safety of home. In most cases, the hero has no choice and must leave to handle a problem. **Second**, the young person "finds a path" while learning to be independent and developing a view of life. Another name for this step is a vision quest. **Third**, "entering the labyrinth" means that the hero has to endure some kind of testing or ordeal. Young persons overcoming such an ordeal prove themselves worthy of being an adult. **Fourth**, the hero encounters "the woods between the worlds," in which he or she must express a new vision of life to others in the community. Young adults express that vision in words, in music, or in art. **Finally**, the community celebrates the end of the journey with a ceremony. This ceremony often includes special clothing, food, decorations, gifts, and perhaps even a new name.

Teenagers are not the only members of society who experience a rite of passage. Marriage and the birth of a child mark milestones in people's lives. Modern society offers other opportunities for celebrating transitions, such as high school graduation, a new job, or retirement from the workforce. In each case, there are special rituals that we can follow to signify someone's transition from one identity to a new one. Modern sophisticates may scoff at or ridicule such ceremonies, but these celebrations link us strongly to our communities and to past generations at the same time that they recognize our progress through life.

to have a chip on your shoulder: to resent, to have a negative attitude

to fret: to worry

a milestone: a distance marker; a sign of an important event

a sophisticate: a person with experience and knowledge of the world

a labyrinth: a confusing, complex path

124   LESSON 12 | Counseling: Rites of Passage

■ **EXPANSION IDEA**

Exercise A

1. Have students write a short essay about the most common ways in which teenagers from their home countries celebrate the transition to adulthood. This may include Quinceañera parties, bar mitzvahs, or ways in which teens dress, speak, or express themselves.

2. Have students exchange essays with a partner. Ask them to edit each other's work.

3. Call on volunteers to read their essays to the class.

Sample Sentences	Notes
Rick's family made all the preparations for his marriage to Cindy. **First of all,** they found a nice restaurant for the rehearsal dinner. **Second of all,** they sent out invitations to all of the wedding party.	Use the sequential connectors below to express the order of events or ideas. • *first, second, third, last/finally* • *first, next, then, last/finally* • *firstly, secondly, lastly/finally* • *in the first place, in the second place, last/finally* • *first of all, second of all, last of all* • *after that*
Rick's father planned to make a toast at the rehearsal dinner. **After that,** he wanted to give Rick and Cindy a special gift.	Connectors may express • a real-time relationship of events • the author's order of ideas or events
There were different reasons for boys to leave home for their initiation rites. **In the first place,** they needed to make a break from their mothers and the comfort of home. **In the second place,** they had to learn about manhood from the men of the community.	The author's order may be from least to most important or from most to least important.
Cindy's parents needed several months for her wedding preparations. **First,** they had to rent a place for the reception many weeks ahead of time and send out invitations to all the guests. **Next,** they needed to order Cindy's dress. Cindy wanted a custom-made dress so they knew it would take several weeks; **then,** she had to find all of the accessories for the dress.	Connectors that express a sequence are the type of adverbials that connect two independent clauses. Follow the rules of punctuation below for connectors in this category: a. clause₁; connector, clause₂ b. clause₁. Connector, clause₂ Choose option b if you want to emphasize the connector or if the clauses are quite long.
Cindy's parents were very patient during the hectic preparations. Cindy wanted a custom-made dress **first,** and they agreed to it. She **then** saw a dress that she really liked in a magazine. **Finally,** she found one at the local mall.	English speakers sometimes use a connector from this category after the subject or at the end of the clause. Don't use a comma in these cases. **NOTE:** *At first* means "at the start of a process or situation" and *at last* means "finally after much effort, time, or worry." These phrases are not connectors.

B Read over your journal entry, and <u>underline</u> at least one sentence that you can revise to include a sequential connector. Write your revised sentence(s) below.

Answers will vary.

_____

_____

_____

■ **GRAMMAR CHART**

Sequential Connectors

1. Write on the board *First, I sit down and lock the door. Next, I fasten my seat belt. Then I check the rearview mirror. Finally, I start the ignition.* Underline *first, next, then,* and *finally.* Call on a volunteer to say what part of speech these words belong to (*adverbials*) and then ask what they do (*express the order of events*).

2. Call on students to read the sample sentences and accompanying Notes.

3. Answer any questions students have about how and when to use adverbials.

■ **EXERCISE B**

1. Have students complete the exercise.

2. Ask students to exchange work with a partner. Have partners suggest other places where sequential connectors might be added.

■ **EXPANSION IDEA**

Grammar Chart

1. Have students write the steps involved in a process, using sequential connectors.

2. Call on volunteers to read their processes to the class.

1. Ask students to read the instructions.
2. Call on a student to read the example.
3. Have students complete the activity. Then have them compare their work with a partner.
4. Call on volunteers to read their answers to the class, explaining their choices if challenged by classmates.

■ **EXERCISE D**

1. Ask students to read the instructions, then have them complete the exercise.
2. Call on students to read the order of their notes. Have them explain their order if other students disagree.

C Add two more sequential connectors to the text below, where appropriate. Add the appropriate punctuation.

Many people think that some aspects of military service are similar to traditional initiation rites of young men. Nowadays both young men and women enter military service in some countries. During "boot camp" they undergo training that can be compared to those older rites. *First of all, t*These young people go to a training base away from their homes. *Second, a*A master sergeant there takes a group of youths under his or her wing. Under this supervision, the young soldiers learn what it means to be a soldier. *Finally, b*Boot camp always involves a number of physical tests as they gain new skills. The young soldiers must demonstrate skills in handling equipment and must know how to survive under dangerous conditions.

D Imagine that you took the notes below during a class lecture. Reorganize the information into a clearer order, and write up the notes with the appropriate connectors. Be prepared to explain the order of your notes.   Answers will vary.

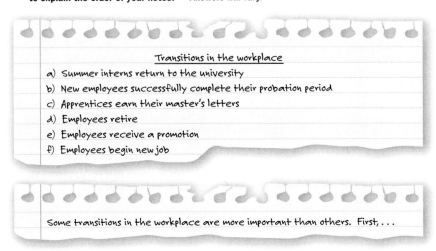

Transitions in the workplace
a) Summer interns return to the university
b) New employees successfully complete their probation period
c) Apprentices earn their master's letters
d) Employees retire
e) Employees receive a promotion
f) Employees begin new job

Some transitions in the workplace are more important than others. First, . . .

■ **EXPANSION IDEA**

Exercise D

1. Divide the class into pairs. Have students discuss transitions in school. For example, *First, kids in my country go to preschool. They usually start when they are three years old.*
2. Circulate as students work; assist as needed.

E Edit the text so that there are sequential connectors between the appropriate clauses.

When young people graduate from high school, their community celebrates this step toward adulthood. For many youths, graduation signifies the transition from being a child to becoming a contributing member of society. The school is at the center of the ceremony. ^*First of all, the staff* ~~The staff first~~ plans the location and date of the graduation ceremony ^*; then* They prepare the diplomas. The diplomas are usually printed in elegant lettering and proclaim each student's graduation in formal language ^**Next, t**~~T~~he students receive their caps and gowns, which they will wear for the ceremony, shortly before graduation day ^**Finally, p**~~P~~arents often finish the big day with a party for their graduate at home with family and friends.

■ COMMUNICATE

F **PAIR WORK** With a partner, talk about wedding preparations in your culture, from the engagement to the wedding day. Tell about the order of events for each wedding tradition.

I'm from a small town with very traditional values. The man **first** asks his girlfriend to marry him and **then** he talks to her father. **After that** they can tell other people about it.

Oh, really? The place I'm from is even more conservative. A man has to get permission from his girlfriend's father **first**. He formally asks her to marry him **after that**.

■ EXERCISE E

1. Ask students to read the instructions.
2. Have students read the first four sentences of the paragraph.
3. Call on a volunteer to explain why the sequential connector is placed at the beginning of the fourth sentence.
4. Have students complete the activity on their own and then check their work with a partner.
5. Call on a volunteer to read the paragraph aloud. If any classmates disagree with sequential connector placement, have students discuss their choices.

■ COMMUNICATE

■ EXERCISE F

1. Ask students to read the instructions.
2. Call on two volunteers to read the text in the speech balloons.
3. Divide the class into pairs, pairing students from different countries or cultures, if possible.
4. Have students discuss wedding preparations in their cultures.
5. Call on volunteers to tell the class what they learned about their partners' cultures.

■ EXPANSION IDEA

Exercise F
1. Have students write a short composition about wedding traditions in their partner's culture.

2. Have partners exchange compositions to edit and suggest changes.
3. Call on volunteers to read their compositions to the class.

PART TWO

Connectors of Equivalence

■ GRAMMAR IN CONTENT

■ EXERCISE A

1. Ask students to complete the activity and then check their work with a partner.
2. Call on volunteers to read the connectors of equivalence that they found in the reading, and write them on the board.

■ GRAMMAR CHART

Connectors of Equivalence

1. Call on students to read the sample sentences and corresponding Notes aloud.
2. Answer any questions that students have about connectors of equivalence.

■ EXERCISE B

1. Go over the instructions with the class.
2. Call on a student to read the example.
3. Have students complete the exercise. If they find it too difficult, have them work in pairs.
4. Have class members discuss their answers.

■ GRAMMAR IN CONTENT

A Reread "The Journeys of Life" at the beginning of this lesson, and <u>underline</u> the clause that is introduced with one of the connectors in italics below.

Connectors of Equivalence

Sample Sentences	Notes
In some traditional African cultures, boys receive new names as men; **similarly**, Native American youths received their adult names during their vision quest.	Use the connectors of equivalence below to highlight similar ideas or to clarify information by providing a restatement or an example.
Boys had spiritual lessons from the elders; **by the same token**, girls learned about the meaning of life from older women in the community.	For similar ideas or information, use *similarly, likewise, in the same way, by the same token.* For elaborating ideas or information, use *for example, for instance.*
Young adults showed the death of their childhood in a new appearance; **for example**, they often received new clothes.	Connectors in this category, like sequential connectors, are adverbials. Follow the rules of punctuation below: a. clause$_1$; connector, clause$_2$ b. clause$_1$. Connector, clause$_2$
Young men in traditional cultures often had a haircut as they separated from their families. **In the same way**, gang members usually have a distinctive haircut or hairstyle.	Sometimes connectors introduce identical ideas in a phrase, not a clause. See Lesson 29, Part 2.

B Using your own personal knowledge, complete the following sentences about rites of passage from around the world. If you are unfamiliar with a particular rite or culture, write what you think may be true. You can discuss your answers with your classmates. Answers will vary. Sample answers below.

1. For centuries adults had different hairstyles from those of children. For example,
   European women and girls had long hair but only girls wore their hair down.

2. After some rites of passage, adults change their names; for example,
   many American women take the family names of their husbands.

3. In some cultures, when a spouse dies, the surviving spouse may wear black for the funeral and for a time afterward. In the same way,
   German women often wear dark colors after their husbands die.

4. On her wedding day, a bride often wears a dress of a significant color. For instance,
   American brides usually wear white dresses which symbolize purity and innocence.

■ EXPANSION IDEA

Exercise B
Divide the class into small groups and have them discuss how traditions in their countries are changing as a result of technology or globalization.

5. On his wedding day, a bridegroom might wear a very formal suit; likewise,

men in my country have formal traditional wedding clothes.

6. Guests at a wedding reception often give the newlyweds advice. For example,

the best man may tell the newlyweds to work hard but make time for each other.

7. Some religions observe special rites for young people. For example,

families in my country celebrate each daughter's 16th birthday.

8. Likewise, boys used to prove themselves by hunting or fighting; in the same way,

many people expect boys to play sports to prove themselves.

C Add the correct punctuation to each sentence. If necessary, add capital letters.

1. Youths in traditional societies underwent initiation with a group of peers, similarly, many modern young people mature with their teammates in various sports.

2. In traditional societies, village elders provided instruction for teenagers, by the same token, coaches nowadays teach young athletes skills and proper behavior.

3. Parents also trusted the mentors to guide their children, for instance, modern parents rarely contradict a coach's instructions to their children.

4. Village elders had to teach that life has both light and dark sides, likewise, coaches help athletes to accept winning and losing.

5. Youths benefit from having peers in the transition to adulthood; for instance, young athletes can share their frustration and joy with teammates.

6. Adults look back often on the lessons of their initiation into adulthood; for example, they remember the praise of their mentors and try to follow their advice.

D Listen to a short lecture on an updated version of rites of passage and answer the questions below. Any or all of the following are acceptable answers.

CD2,TR4

1. Who or what is most likely to provide "rite of passage" experiences for young Americans?

a. Many teachers still guide young people to adulthood. b. Coaches provide guidance.

c. Kids learn through volunteering. d. Employers and supervisors give life lessons.

2. What example did the lecturer give for each type of "rite of passage" experience?

a. Teachers provide an encouraging atmosphere. b. Coaches teach good sportsmanship.

c. Volunteering teaches kids about life. d. Receiving feedback

■ **EXERCISE C**

1. Have students review the instructions.
2. If students are uncertain about how to punctuate sentences with connectors of equivalence, have them study the grammar chart.
3. Have students complete the activity on their own and then check their work with a partner.
4. Call on volunteers to read their answers to the class, pointing out where they put commas and semicolons.
5. Answer any questions students have about how to punctuate sentences that include connectors of equivalence.

■ **EXERCISE D**

CD 2, Track 4

1. Ask students to read the instructions and the two questions.
2. Tell students that they will hear the lecture twice. Play the audio and have students listen carefully.
3. Play the audio again. Then give students time to answer the questions.
4. Go over the answers together. If students disagree about an answer, play the audio again so that they can identify the correct interpretation.

■ **EXPANSION IDEA**

Exercise D

Have students write a summary of the lecture about an updated "rite of passage."

■ EXERCISE E

1. Ask students to read the instructions.
2. Divide the class into small groups and have students discuss films that follow the story of a rite of passage.
3. Call on a member of each group to name the movies his or her group chose. Write the titles on the board.
4. Call on a few volunteers to discuss the movies.

Connection

Putting It Together

■ GRAMMAR AND VOCABULARY

1. Ask students to read the instructions.
2. Call on two students to read the topics aloud.
3. Ask students to choose one of the two topics and give them time to write their compositions.

■ PROJECT

1. Ask students to review the instructions.
2. Answer any questions that students have about the project.
3. Call on students at the next class meeting to report their findings.

■ INTERNET

1. Call on a student to read the instructions.
2. Have students conduct their searches and then report back to the class on their findings.

E **GROUP WORK** Brainstorm a list of 3–5 movies that follow the story of a rite of passage. The character may follow the journey from childhood to adulthood or make the transition to some other phase of life. Then, describe the steps or phases that the character experiences during the film. **Answers will vary.**

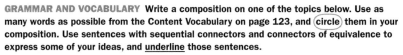

Connection | Putting It Together

GRAMMAR AND VOCABULARY Write a composition on one of the topics below. Use as many words as possible from the Content Vocabulary on page 123, and (circle) them in your composition. Use sentences with sequential connectors and connectors of equivalence to express some of your ideas, and underline those sentences.

Topic 1: Tell the story of an important mythical (or fictional) hero from your culture with David Oldfield's five steps, which were explained in "The Journeys of Life" on page 124. Use at least one example for each step on your journey.

Topic 2: How do young people in your culture prove themselves? What are the typical tests, sacrifices, and ordeals that a young person must endure before older people respect them as adults? Give specific examples.
Answers will vary.

PROJECT Interview at least one student on your campus about initiation rites for students who join clubs such as fraternities or sororities. Find out the following information, and prepare a brief oral report on your interviewee's comments.

1. What does "hazing" mean?
2. Has your interviewee heard of any hazing on campus?
3. What kinds of rituals do students on campus go through to join special clubs? to be part of the "in-crowd"? to be cool?

 INTERNET Go online and use the search phrase "name meanings." Find a website where you can find an analysis of the meanings of different names. Select 3 or 4 names and give a short oral report on those meanings in class. Also, in your report tell your classmates about the customs in your culture regarding a change of names. If people change their names, does the change usually coincide with a transition in their lives?
Answers will vary.

■ EXPANSION IDEA

Grammar and Vocabulary

1. Divide the class into pairs of students who wrote on the same topic.
2. Have students exchange compositions. Ask them to edit each other's work, suggesting places where additional sequential connectors and connectors of equivalence might be added.

Engineering: Emergency Preparation and Management

Lesson ⑬

Overview

Ask students to brainstorm about different types of natural disasters and the severity of damage they can cause. Write their ideas on the board.

■ CONTENT VOCABULARY

Look up the words below that you do not know and enter them in your vocabulary journal. Write each word's part of speech, a definition, and an example sentence. Try to include them in your discussion and writing below.

an aftermath	to comprise	to mitigate	to stock
a building code	a fault line	to precipitate	to upgrade
a buoy	imminent	to scrutinize	vulnerable

■ THINK ABOUT IT

The photo on the next page shows the impact of Hurricane Katrina on the infrastructure of the New Orleans area. What other kinds of public structures are often affected by natural disasters? Can you remember any specific examples from other natural catastrophes around the world? Discuss your ideas with a classmate.

In your writing journal, write for 5–10 minutes about the questions below. When you are finished, share what you wrote with the class.
Describe briefly what happened in a recent natural disaster. How did emergency workers respond? What were the needs of the people in the disaster, and what did various responders do to meet those needs?
Answers will vary.

■ CONTENT VOCABULARY

Ask students to review the words in the box. Tell them to look up any unfamiliar words.

■ VOCABULARY JOURNAL

Have students add new words to their vocabulary journals and write down the parts of speech, definitions, and sentences for each.

■ THINK ABOUT IT

1. Have students read the instructions.
2. Divide the class into pairs and have them discuss the questions posed in the exercise.
3. Circulate as students work; assist with vocabulary as needed.
4. Give students five minutes to write in their journals. Then call on volunteers to discuss the responses to a few recent disasters.

131

■ CONTENT NOTES

The topic of this lesson is Engineering: Emergency Preparation and Management. Students will learn about how different types of natural disasters can be managed and will acquire the vocabulary needed to discuss catastrophic events and their aftermath.

■ GRAMMAR IN CONTENT

■ EXERCISE A
CD 2, Track 5

1. Call on volunteers to read the title of the article and describe how they think it relates to the photo. Encourage them to use new content vocabulary.

2. Play the audio and have students follow along in their books as they listen. Ask students to circle any unfamiliar words or phrases.

3. Call on students to read their circled words and elicit definitions or explanations from volunteers if possible.

4. Check comprehension by asking questions such as the following: *Why don't experts think disasters are exceptional events? Why does the author state that "there is little excuse for being caught unprepared for a disaster"? What are the four stages associated with a disaster?*

5. Call on volunteers to summarize each of the paragraphs.

PART ONE   Connectors of Causality

■ GRAMMAR IN CONTENT

A Read and listen to the passage below. The words in bold in the text are connectors of causality.

CD2,TR5

Emergency Management: Planning and Responding

Current wisdom inclines toward the view that disasters are *not* exceptional events. They tend to be repetitive and to concentrate in particular places. With regard to natural catastrophes, seismic and volcanic belts, hurricane-generating areas, unstable slopes, and tornado zones are well known. Moreover, the frequency of events and **therefore** their statistical recurrence intervals are often fairly well established—at least for the smaller and more frequent occurrences—even if the short-term ability to forecast natural hazards is variable. Many technological hazards also follow more or less predictable patterns, although these may become apparent only when research reveals them. Finally, intelligence gathering, strategic studies, and policy analyses can help us to understand the pattern of emergencies resulting from conflict and insurgence. **Thus**, there is little excuse for being caught unprepared.

The main scope of emergency planning is to reduce the risk to life and limb posed by actual and potential disasters. Secondary motives involve reducing damage, ensuring public safety during the aftermath of a disaster, and caring for survivors and the disadvantaged. Inefficiencies in planning translate very easily into loss of life, injuries, or damage that could have been avoided. **Thus**, emergency planning is at least a moral, and perhaps also a legal, responsibility for all those who are involved with the safety of the public or employees. When a known significant risk exists, failure to plan can be taken as culpable negligence. Moreover, planning cannot successfully be improvised during emergencies: this represents one of the worst forms of inefficiency and most likely sources of error and confusion. Fortunately, however, 50 years of intensive research and accumulated experience have furnished an ample basis for planning.

Given that disasters tend to be repetitive events, they form a cycle that can be divided into phases of mitigation, preparedness, response, and delivery, including reconstruction. The first two stages occur before catastrophe strikes and the last two afterwards. The actions taken, and **therefore** the planning procedures that predetermine them, differ for each of the periods, as different needs are tackled. Mitigation comprises all actions designed to reduce the impact of future disasters. These usually divide into structural measures (the engineering solutions to problems of safety) and non-structural means, which include land-use planning, insurance, legislation, and evacuation planning. The term *preparedness* refers to actions taken to reduce the impact of disasters when they are forecast or imminent. They include security measures, such as the evacuation of vulnerable populations and sandbagging of river levees as floodwaters begin to rise (**thus** the *planning* of evacuation is a mitigation measure, whereas its *execution* is a form of preparedness). Response refers to emergency actions taken during both the impact of a disaster and the short-term aftermath. The principal emphasis is on saving and safeguarding human lives. Victims are rescued and the immediate needs of survivors are attended to. Recovery is the process of repairing damage, restoring services, and reconstructing facilities after disaster has struck. After major catastrophes it may take as long as 25 years, although much less time is needed in lighter impacts or disasters that strike smaller areas.

Principles of Emergency Planning and Management by David Alexander, Oxford University Press, 2002, pp 4-5. By permission of Oxford University Press, Inc.

an insurgence: a rebellion or revolt

culpable negligence: legal responsibility for a failure to prevent injury or damage

■ **EXPANSION IDEA**

Exercise A

1. Divide the class into pairs and have students take turns asking and answering questions about the reading.

2. Circulate as students work; assist as needed. Encourage them to use vocabulary from the unit.

Sample Sentences	Notes
Strong winds can lift houses off their foundations. **As a result**, the entire structure can be damaged beyond repair.	Connectors of causality introduce the result or consequence of an idea or action.
Hurricane Katrina destroyed many oil rigs in the Gulf of Mexico; **therefore**, oil production in the U.S. was significantly affected in the days after the disaster.	*Therefore* signals a result or consequence that readers/listeners could infer or predict themselves from the situation.
In 2005, hurricane winds rose above 90 mph; **consequently**, several boats from the harbor were lifted out of the water and landed on the beach highway.	*Consequently* and *as a result* signal a situation that was actually caused by previous actions or conditions, but may not be predictable.
Ocean waves that are generated by earthquakes can be detected by a network of buoys in the Indian Ocean; **thus/hence**, coastal residents may be alerted to flee to higher ground before a tsunami strikes.	*Thus* and *hence* are used primarily in formal contexts.
Preparing efficient routes away from the coast facilitates mass evacuations; **therefore**, traffic engineers should devise systems to increase the flow of vehicles. OR Preparing efficient routes away from the coast facilitates mass evacuations. **Therefore**, traffic engineers should devise systems to increase the flow of vehicles. OR Traffic engineers should, **therefore**, devise systems to increase the flow of vehicles.	Follow the rules of punctuation below for this category of adverbial connectors: a. clause$_1$; connector, clause$_2$ b. clause$_1$. Connector, clause$_2$ Connectors in this category can also be used in the middle of a result clause. In that case, two commas often separate the connector from the clause. The connector usually appears after the subject or the first auxiliary verb.

B Read over your journal entry, and <u>underline</u> at least one sentence that you can revise to include a causal connector. Write your revised sentence(s) below.

Answers will vary.

■ GRAMMAR CHART
Connectors of Causality

1. Write on the board *In a disaster electricity is often cut; therefore, you should have several flashlights.* Underline *therefore.* Call on a volunteer to explain what this connector does.
2. Call on students to read the sample sentences and accompanying Notes.
3. Answer any questions that students have about connectors of causality. Be sure that students understand the punctuation used with these connectors.

■ EXERCISE B

1. Have students complete the exercise.
2. Ask students to exchange work with a partner. Have partners suggest other places where connectors of causality might be added.

■ EXPANSION IDEA

Exercise B
1. Divide the class into small groups and have them discuss emergency planning in their home countries.

2. Circulate as students work; assist as needed. Encourage them to use connectors of causality in their conversation.

EXERCISE C

1. Have students read the instructions. Instruct them to review the rules of punctuation in the Grammar Chart if necessary.
2. Divide the class into pairs and have students check their work.
3. Call on volunteers to read their answers aloud, indicating where they have placed commas and semicolons.

The shaded area of this map is known as "Tornado Alley."

C Replace "so," which is an informal oral causal connector, with the appropriate word or phrase to connect the two clauses, and revise the punctuation. Use each connector from the chart on page 133 at least once.

1. Natural disasters affect some areas of the world more frequently than others, ~~so~~ *; therefore,* scientists closely monitor weather conditions in those areas.

2. U.S. meteorologists know "Tornado Alley" may have more than 500 tornadoes per year, ~~so~~ **as a result,** they track weather conditions that may cause these "twisters."

3. Other dangerous weather phenomena such as hurricanes and typhoons are also seasonal, ~~so~~ **Hence,** meteorologists scrutinize particular weather data during those months.

4. Rain or snowfall may precipitate avalanches or mudslides, ~~so~~ **Consequently,** meteorologists and engineers have to cooperate to assess the threat of such phenomena.

5. Extensive monitoring equipment measures the seismic activity along fault lines, ~~so~~ **Thus,** scientists can analyze the chances of an earthquake or a volcanic eruption.

6. Earthquake movement can extend to the ocean floor, ~~so~~ **As a result,** people thousands of miles away can be in as much danger as those who live near the fault line.

EXPANSION IDEA

Exercise C

1. Divide the class into small groups. Ask students to look at the map of the United States. Point out that the shaded area shows "Tornado Alley." Ask students to discuss other areas of the United States that are prone to specific kinds of disasters, such as earthquakes in California or hurricanes in Florida.
2. Call on a member of each group to point out the disaster areas his/her group identified.

D In each text below, connect two clauses with one of the causal connectors in this lesson. Follow the example.   Answers will vary.

1. One way to prepare for water-related disasters is to raise the land. For centuries
   people have built levees along ~~rivers. Water that~~ *rivers; as a result, water that* rises during heavy rains or very
   high tides remains in the river channel and does not damage property.

2. The levee system along the Sacramento River in California originally protected
   farmland from flooding. The population of Sacramento, the capital of California, has
   grown to more than 400,000 people, and approximately 2 million live in the Greater
   Sacramento area. **consequently,** Engineers are repairing parts of the levees that offer minimal
   protection to the surrounding homes.

3. Planners and residents in Sacramento are very concerned about the levee
   situation in the aftermath of Hurricane Katrina. The levees in New Orleans failed
   catastrophically due to inadequate maintenance. They were also below the height
   that experts recommended for severe local hurricane conditions. **hence,** Engineers in
   Sacramento are re-examining local needs and want to upgrade their system.

4. The Dutch also have an elaborate system of dikes, or levees. Much of the land of the
   Netherlands is below sea level. It flooded regularly until they began an ambitious
   project of raising the land above sea level. They also invested billions in the
   construction of protective walls that they close during storms and extremely high
   As a consequence,
   tides. The Dutch have almost eliminated the threat of floods.

1. Review the instructions and the example with the class.
2. Have students complete the activity individually and then check their answers with a partner.
3. Call on volunteers to read their answers to the class. You may want to call on more than one student per question.

■ **EXPANSION IDEAS**

Exercise D
Divide the class into small groups and have them discuss the ways in which communities can prepare for water-related disasters.

EXERCISE E

1. Review the instructions.
2. Call on a student to read the example aloud.
3. Have students complete the activity individually and then compare their answers with a partner.
4. Call on volunteers to read their answers to the class.

■ COMMUNICATE

EXERCISE F

1. Ask students to read the instructions.
2. Call on a volunteer to read the text in the speech balloon.
3. Tell students to make their lists.
4. Call on volunteers to read their lists to the class.

E Complete each of the sentences below with another clause. The first one has been done as an example.   Answers will vary.

1. Emergency officials need to communicate information about imminent dangers to their population. Therefore, *they should work closely with the local media./they should broadcast announcements on all radio stations.*

2. In some emergencies the population needs to collect food and other supplies before dangerous storms hit; thus, **stores ought to stock enough emergency supplies.**

3. At other times, people have to leave the area as fast as possible; consequently, **local officials should inform citizens of a mandatory evacuation as soon as possible.**

4. In some areas, there may be many foreign tourists who don't speak the local language. Therefore, **hotel employees should have emergency instructions available in multiple languages.**

5. **Some citizens may not be aware of a weather threat.** As a consequence, the police may have to drive around the area and announce the news.

6. **Natural disasters may occur when most people are sleeping.** Hence, an alarm siren may be the most suitable strategy for communicating a warning.

7. **Tornadoes can form within minutes;** consequently, all TV and radio programming should be interrupted to give important information.

■ COMMUNICATE

F **PAIR WORK** Emergency experts recommend a personal plan for everyone who has to evacuate a disaster area. Imagine evacuating for a few days and staying in a shelter. What will you take with you? Make a list of at least 7–8 items that you will need to take along. Share your list of items with the class.

> The shelter will probably have some simple meals; therefore, we need to take some fruit, sandwiches, and other snack food.

■ EXPANSION IDEA

Exercise F
Write an e-mail to a friend describing conditions in the shelter. Mention items that you wish you had brought and how the things that you did bring were or were not useful.

■ GRAMMAR IN CONTENT

A Read the text on page 132 again, and (circle) any examples of concessive connectors such as *although, whereas,* and *while*. Compare your answers with a partner.

Concessive Connectors	
Sample Sentences	**Notes**
Sometimes people have to evacuate for their own safety **although** they really don't want to go.	Concessive connectors express an unexpected contrast between two clauses. Both clauses are true, but the concessive clause highlights the importance of the main clause and de-emphasizes the information in the dependent clause, which begins with the concessive connector.
Even though evacuating can be inconvenient and costly, it is better than an injury or even death.	*Though* is more informal and *even though* is more emphatic than *although.*
Evacuees often complain about shelters though they are also thankful.	
While/Whereas emergency shelters may be uncomfortable, they protect people from threatening weather conditions.	*While* is not used as frequently as the other connectors for this meaning. *Whereas* is formal and is used less frequently than the other connectors.
To secure a structure for natural disaster, structural engineers have developed many special construction techniques. In hurricane zones, engineers recommend that home builders use special hurricane straps for roofs. **Although** the straps may add to the price of the roof, this precaution may keep the roof from blowing off.	These adverbial connectors introduce a dependent clause, which modifies the main, or independent, clause. Never use a dependent clause without an independent clause in the same sentence. Follow the rules below for adverbial connectors: 1. Main clause + *although* + dependent clause. 2. *Although* + dependent clause +□+ main clause.
The angle of a roof can protect a structure from high velocity winds. **Even though** a roof with a lower angle might seem to be safer, houses with steeper roofs have a better chance of escaping catastrophic wind damage.	Choose 1. when the information in the dependent clause is closely linked to the main clause. Choose 2. when the subordinate clause is more closely linked to previous information.
Although the wind was extremely strong, but my roof sustained very little damage.	Do not use *but* along with another connector to express a concessive relationship.
Don't think that a steep roof will protect you in every storm, **though.**	Use *though* in final position informally. Use a comma in front of *though* at the end of the sentence.

Concessive Connectors

■ GRAMMAR IN CONTENT

■ EXERCISE A

1. Ask students to complete the activity and then check their work with a partner.
2. Call on volunteers to read the concessive connectors that they found in the reading, and write them on the board.

■ GRAMMAR CHART
Concessive Connectors

1. Call on students to read the sample sentences and corresponding Notes aloud.
2. Answer any questions that students have about concessive connectors.

■ EXPANSION IDEA

Exercise A
Divide the class into pairs. Have students take turns constructing sentences using concessive connectors.

■ EXERCISE B

1. Ask students to read the instructions.
2. Call on a volunteer to read the example and explain why *a* is a better choice than *b*.
3. Have students complete the activity and then check their work with a partner.
4. Call on volunteers to read their answers aloud. Discuss any differences in opinion among class members.

B Select the clause that is more appropriate for completing each sentence below. (Circle) the letter that shows your choice. Follow the example.

1. People tend not to evacuate their homes even though
   a.) local officials may strongly recommend that they leave the area.
   b. they make their own preparations and stock emergency supplies.

2. In past hurricane seasons, some evacuations from American cities involved terrible traffic on the highways although
   a. people don't want to evacuate any more.
   b.) officials had advised voluntary evacuation in time for people to leave.

3. While _____, citizens still need to obey the order for mandatory evacuation.
   a.) an evacuation can be stressful and inconvenient
   b. they are preparing themselves for a natural disaster

4. Although _____, traffic engineers have devised new systems of "contraflow" on highways to ease traffic congestion.
   a. traffic will move at a steady, but slower pace
   b.) traffic will always be heavy during peak evacuation times

5. During "contraflow" all cars on the highway move in only one direction away from the danger even though
   a.) highways are designed for two-way travel.
   b. officials want as many cars as possible to leave the area quickly.

6. While _____, traffic engineers plan ways to direct drivers to the correct lanes.
   a.) this strategy might sound dangerous
   b. local officials are announcing the evacuation

7. Though _____, local transportation officials realize that some drivers won't know about the plan and will need their help.
   a.) a contraflow plan is always widely publicized in the local media
   b. a contraflow plan is the safest way to move more people more quickly

■ EXPANSION IDEA

Exercise B

1. Have students work in pairs. Ask them to write main clauses that make sense with the wrong answers for Exercise B.

For example:
Many people who don't evacuate during floods die even though they make their own preparations and stock emergency supplies.

2. Call on volunteers to read their answers to the class.

C Read the sentence, then look at the clause below it. Should the clause go in (a) or (b)? Decide on the appropriate location for the clause, and write X on the blank. Add commas where necessary. Then write the reason for putting the clause in that position.

1. After a natural disaster, residents of the affected area may need temporary housing.

   __X,__ the housing needs to protect people from the weather conditions _____.
   (a)   (b)

   Clause: although it is temporary

   Reason: *The word "temporary" is linked closely to the previous sentence.*

2. In some cases emergency workers face great difficulty in supplying shelter for people

   who live in remote areas. __X__ emergency agencies need to act fast _____.
   (a)   (b)

   Clause: while delivering basic shelters to outlying areas is very difficult

   Reason: "Delivering basic shelters" is linked to the previous sentence.

3. After the tsunami in 2004, people around the world donated supplies to help the

   victims. _____ the supplies took weeks to reach some of the survivors __X__.
   (a)   (b)

   Clause: although governments used high-tech equipment to deliver them

   Reason: The main clause is linked to the previous sentence, and the subordinate clause develops the idea in the main clause.

4. The situation of the earthquake survivors in the mountains of Pakistan in 2006

   touched people around the world. _____ emergency workers were able to deliver
   (a)

   only simple tents for many of the survivors __X__.
   (b)

   Clause: even though the winter weather conditions were very bitter

   Reason: See #3.

5. In the aftermath of some disasters, it is clear that rebuilding will take a very long

   time. __X__ temporary housing rarely offers the comforts of a real home _____.
   (a)   (b)

   Clause: although it provides shelter for some people for months or years

   Reason: "For months" in the clause linked to "a very long time" in the previous sentence.

6. Many residents of Kobe, Japan, lived in containers during the reconstruction of

   their city after their big earthquake. _____ the people resigned themselves to such
   (a)

   difficult living conditions and stayed in their hometown __X__.
   (b)

   Clause: although the rebuilding process took years

   Reason: See #3.

■ EXERCISE C

1. Go over the instructions with the class.
2. Call on a student to read the example. Then discuss the correct answer with the class.
3. Have students complete the activity individually and then check their answers with a partner.
4. Call on volunteers to read their answers aloud. Discuss any differences in opinion among class members.

■ EXPANSION IDEA

Exercise C

1. Have students research a natural disaster and write five sentences about it with a clause in each.
2. Put students into pairs and have them trade sentences, underlining the clause and explaining the reason why their partner put the clause in that position in the sentence.

EXERCISE D

CD 2, Track 6

1. Tell students that they will hear a lecture about the threat of natural disasters in Jamaica. Have them look at the five topics that they will be writing about.
2. Play the audio, instructing students to listen carefully.
3. Play the audio again, this time instructing students to take notes as they listen.
4. Give students time to write their answers.
5. Call on volunteers to read their answers to the class.
6. If there is any disagreement among class members about the answers, play the audio one more time.

EXERCISE E

1. Go over the instructions with the class.
2. Call on a student to read the example.
3. Give students time to complete the activity.
4. Call on volunteers to read their questions to the class.

CD2,TR6

D Take notes on the short lecture on Jamaica and the threat of natural disaster there. Then, summarize the information according to the categories below. Use concessive clauses in your summary sentences.

1. **Terrain:** _Even though Jamaica has coastal areas with beaches, it also has the tallest mountains in the Caribbean._

2. **Economy:** The Jamaican economy relies heavily on tourism although traditionally it has based its economy on agricultural products.

3. **Rural/Urban Populations:** While the majority of Jamaicans live in rural areas, an urban area along the north coast has developed with the growth of tourism.

4. **Potential Natural Disasters:** Although most people know that Jamaica may be hit by hurricanes, they don't realize that earthquakes and tsunamis are also a serious threat.

5. **Safety of Housing:** Many houses in Jamaica have not been built to withstand severe weather even though the country has a national building code.

E Complete the sentences below to create a question about the best ways to respond to natural disasters.   Answers will vary.

1. Although the victims of natural disasters need immediate help, _what can the average citizen do to help them_ ?

2. While many organizations ask people to donate money for disaster victims, how can we be sure that the money reaches the victims ?

3. Even though the Red Cross or the Red Crescent are supposed to help disaster victims, why do people criticize these organizations so much ?

4. Although millions of dollars may be collected for disaster relief, why do they always ask for more ?

5. Should we send only money even though we have clothing and supplies that disaster victims could use ?

6. Is it a good idea to travel to the affected area as a volunteer although I don't have any special skills to help in rebuilding ?

7. Does my small donation really help even though some people and governments give so much money and so many supplies ?

8. While the media often forgets about victims soon after a disaster, how can we find out more information about the recovery efforts ?

EXPANSION IDEA

Exercise E

1. Have students write answers to the questions they wrote in Exercise E.
2. Call on volunteers to read their answers to the class.

F Edit the text below to include some of the connectors in the box below. Place the appropriate connectors in the text, connecting clauses near the slash marks.

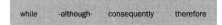

while   ~~although~~   consequently   therefore

Once a disaster has occurred, engineers assess the damage and study ways to improve

safety in future catastrophic events. / ~~They~~ *Although they* have to think in terms of costs and benefits.

~~Engineers~~ *, engineers* have to give risks to human life the highest priority. They can often design new

structural ways to control natural hazards for public safety.

Therefore
/ They are trained to find ways to strengthen buildings or to control the forces of nature. The

strategy of improving construction has proven very successful in earthquake and hurricane

; consequently,
zones. Construction can also harm the environment. / Environmental change can lead to

unforeseen dangers, such as a levee system actually causing increased flooding.

■ **COMMUNICATE**

G **SMALL GROUP WORK** Tell a chain story about the experience of a group of university-age volunteers who went to Southeast Asia to help with recovery efforts after the 2004 tsunami hit. For every sentence of your story, begin with *although* + the main clause of the previous sentence.

Although they didn't know anybody in Thailand, Victor, Jim, and Will decided to go there to help after the tsunami.

Although they decided to go there, they had no idea exactly where to go.

Although they didn't know exactly where to go, they . . .

■ **EXERCISE F**

1. Ask students to review the instructions.
2. Call on a volunteer to read the example.
3. Have students complete the activity individually and then compare their answers with a partner.
4. Call on volunteers to read their answers to the class.

■ **COMMUNICATE**

■ **EXERCISE G**

1. Ask students if they have ever participated in telling a chain story. Call on a volunteer to explain how chain stories are told.
2. Ask students to read the instructions.
3. Call on three students to read the text in the speech balloons.
4. Divide the class into small groups and have them tell their chain stories using *although* plus the main clause of the previous sentence.
5. Circulate as students work; assist as needed.

■ **EXPANSION IDEA**

Exercise G

1. Have students write a paragraph about helping with the recovery effort in Southeast Asia. Encourage them to use as many concessive connectors as possible in their writing.

2. Ask students to exchange work with a partner. Have partners suggest places where additional connectors might be added.
3. Call on a few volunteers to read their paragraphs aloud.

Connection

Putting It Together

■ GRAMMAR AND VOCABULARY

1. Ask students to read the instructions and topics.
2. Answer any questions that students have about the assignment.
3. Ask students to choose one of the two topics and give them time to write their compositions.

■ PROJECT

1. Ask students to review the instructions and questions.
2. Answer any questions that students have about the project.
3. Call on students at the next class meeting to report their findings.

■ INTERNET

1. Call on a student to read the instructions.
2. Have students conduct their searches and then compare their findings in class.

GRAMMAR AND VOCABULARY Write a composition on one of the topics below. Use as many words as possible from the Content Vocabulary on page 131. Use sentences with connectors of causality and concessive connectors to express some of your ideas, and <u>underline</u> those sentences.

Topic 1: After a natural disaster, victims need a lot of assistance; as a result, there are many opportunities for young people to play a part in the recovery. What is the best way for young adults from your country to help victims of a natural disaster? How is this different from the kind of help that you might expect from older adults in your country? Give concrete examples if you can.

Topic 2: Although many people live in areas where natural disasters may strike, most people face greater dangers in their everyday lives. The number of people who die in natural catastrophes is much lower than the number of people who die of other causes. Compare or contrast the safety of citizens in your hometown with the safety of the place where you are living right now. Give concrete examples.
Answers will vary.

PROJECT Interview at least one student on your campus about threats of natural disasters in your area. Find out the following information and give an oral report to your classmates.

1. What kind of natural disaster is the most likely in this area?
2. What should you do in case such a disaster occurs?
3. What does the student plan to do in case of such a disaster?

 INTERNET With your classmates, make a list of some colleges or universities that are located in "Tornado Alley," earthquake zones, and areas threatened by hurricanes or typhoons. Include your own school if it is affected by any of these potential threats. Select two or three of the schools, and check their websites for emergency instructions. In class, compare the information from various schools that might experience the same type of disaster. Then, decide which university seems to have the best disaster preparedness plan.
Answers will vary.

■ EXPANSION IDEA

Internet
Have students design an emergency escape plan for themselves in the case of a fire or earthquake. Suggest that they think about what they would want to grab as they were fleeing their homes.

Education: Service Learning

■ CONTENT VOCABULARY

Look up the words below that you do not know and enter them in your vocabulary journal.
Write each word's part of speech, a definition, and an example sentence. Try to include them
in your discussion and writing below.

appreciation	a food bank	literacy	to reinforce
to empower	to implement	a partnership	to revitalize
to enhance	insight	to reflect	self-motivating

■ THINK ABOUT IT

Should your grade in a high school or university class depend on your work as a volunteer in
your community? Discuss your ideas with a classmate.

In your writing journal, write for five minutes about the questions below. When you are
finished, share what you wrote with the class.
Has one of your teachers or professors ever assigned a "hands-on" project in your
community? Have you ever volunteered in your community as part of a school project? How
do people from your culture view volunteer work? If you have done this kind of work, what
have you learned from it?
Answers will vary.

■ CONTENT NOTES

The topic of this lesson is Education:
Service Learning. Students will learn
about how volunteering on a community
project can help them with their studies
and future careers. Use this lesson to
encourage students to participate in
some sort of community project in their
college communities.

Lesson (14)

Overview

1. Ask students to raise their hands
   if they have ever worked as a
   volunteer on a community service
   project.
2. Ask students to name some of
   the organizations that they have
   volunteered for in the United
   States or in their home countries.
   Write them on the board.

■ CONTENT VOCABULARY

Ask students to review the words in
the box. Tell them to look up any
unfamiliar words.

■ VOCABULARY JOURNAL

Have students add new words
to their vocabulary journals and
write down the parts of speech,
definitions, and sentences for each.

■ THINK ABOUT IT

1. Have students read the
   instructions.
2. Divide the class into pairs and
   have them discuss the question
   posed in the exercise.
3. Circulate as students work and
   assist with vocabulary as needed.
4. Give students five minutes to
   write in their journals. Then call
   on volunteers to discuss their
   answers.

■ GRAMMAR IN CONTENT

■ EXERCISE A
CD 2, Track 7

1. Call on volunteers to read the title of the passage and describe how they think it relates to the photo. Encourage them to use new content vocabulary.
2. Play the audio and have students follow along in their books as they listen. Ask students to circle any unfamiliar words or phrases.
3. Call on students to read their circled words and elicit definitions or explanations from volunteers if possible.
4. Check comprehension by asking questions such as the following: *How does volunteering help students understand economic theory and analysis? What kinds of valuable information do students gain through volunteering? In what ways does service learning empower students?*
5. Call on a volunteer to summarize the passage.

■ GRAMMAR IN CONTENT

A Read and listen to the passage below. The words in bold are phrases in which the author omitted repetitious words.

CD2,TR7

Education in the "Real World"

For students who complain that their economics courses have little to do with their lives, service learning can be a welcome relief — **something new and different** for most economics students. But by the end of the semester, students who choose the service option also are often surprised **when they look back and see** how effectively their service-learning experience increased their awareness of what economics is and how it can be used. Through their experience and through a self-reflective process by which they analyze that experience, students gain a new appreciation for how **economic theory and analysis** can help us not only understand problems but also begin to solve them. One of the reasons for this increased awareness is that while students often initially approach their service with skepticism, at some point during their service most allow their whole being to get involved—the physical and intellectual, the emotional, and often the spiritual. This total immersion experience seems to increase student learning significantly (relative to a nonservice option) while providing students with **meaningful and rewarding experiences.** Although I see **an increased awareness of** what economics is and how it can be used as service learning's most important contribution to economics classes, many other benefits are also involved. Service provides a real-world issue on which students can focus. Students gain an appreciation for how real people in the world are trying to solve concrete development problems. Agencies often invite students who provide the best service to work as paid employees. Thus, service provides students with valuable contact opportunities that may help in their future careers. A related benefit is that service often helps students learn job skills and helps prepare them for careers after college. Another benefit for students is that their service helps them retain **important concepts they learn in class.** Service also enhances personalized education for the students and teaches positive attributes, such as leadership, citizenship, and personal responsibility (students may not care about a D or an F as much as about the impression they make in the real world and the fact that they learn about local economic problems). Service learning invites students to become involved members of their communities, and students frequently **say they will continue to volunteer after the course ends.** Furthermore, service learning empowers students as learners, teachers, achievers, and leaders. Service learning also contributes to a university's collaboration and partnerships, broadening the concept of service in which faculty must be engaged, and giving faculty a service option that integrates service with teaching and reinforces both. Service learning also contributes to people in need through nonprofit agencies, nongovernmental and governmental agencies, and even some private-sector companies.

skepticism: a feeling of doubt or disbelief
relative to: compared to
to engage in: to be involved in, to be active in

■ EXPANSION IDEA

Exercise A
Divide the class into small groups and have students discuss how their experiences volunteering have helped prepare them for the real world.

Ellipsis

Sample Sentences	Notes
"Hope you're OK." "Got an umbrella?" "Catch you later." "I know ~~that~~ you'll enjoy our literacy project." The woman ~~who~~ you were talking to has been my supervisor on the project ~~for~~ 2 months. Have you ever met Ms. Dixon, ~~who is~~ the director of the literacy project? "Budget at ~~the~~ Senior Center ~~was~~ Reduced" "Senior Center ~~is~~ Anticipating ~~an~~ Increase in ~~the~~ Number of Student Volunteers" Jim is so excited about his project at the Senior Center, and I am ~~excited~~, too. Whoever wants to ~~ride in the van~~ can ride in the van to the training site.	Avoid repeating words in order to improve your English style. One way to avoid redundancy is to delete or omit words or phrases that are repetitious. Use ellipsis (or deletion) when the missing words can be understood from your speech or writing. **Ellipsis can be situational:** In conversations, we know the missing words at the beginning of common expressions and sentences. **Ellipsis can be structural:** We know the missing words from our knowledge of grammar. Headlines are good examples of this kind of ellipsis. **Ellipsis can be textual:** We know the missing words from other words in the text or conversation.
Do you know if the 4:00 van for the Senior Center is the last ~~van~~ this afternoon? One university van leaves at 4:00 and another ~~van~~ is scheduled for 4:30. I enjoy the feedback from Dr. Winters, but I don't get much out of Dr. Sun's ~~feedback~~. Dr. Winters didn't come to the last session, but he should have ~~come~~. He forgot to give us our assignments, and he's not going to ~~give us our assignments~~ until next week. Rachel got her new assignment by e-mail, but I didn't ~~get my assignment by e-mail~~.	When a noun is deleted, the modifiers of that noun remain in the sentence. Avoid repetition by substituting *one* for a noun: *Do you know if the 4:00 van for the Senior Center is the last one this afternoon?* *One university van leaves at 4:00 and another one is scheduled for 4:30.* When a verb or verb phrase is deleted, the subject and the auxiliary verb(s) remain.

B Read over your journal entry, and <u>underline</u> at least one sentence that you can revise by omitting repetitious words. Write your revised sentence(s) below.

   Answers will vary.

1. Write *ellipsis* on the board. Explain that this term refers to deleting or omitting words.
2. Call on volunteers to give examples of ellipsis. Write them on the board.
3. Call on students to read the sample sentences and accompanying Notes.
4. Answer any questions students have about ellipsis.

■ EXERCISE B

1. Have students complete the exercise.
2. Ask students to exchange work with a partner. Have partners suggest other places where repetitious words could be left out.

■ EXPANSION IDEA

Grammar Chart

1. Divide the class into pairs. Have them make up short conversations about volunteering using as much ellipsis as they can. Be sure they know that you cannot eliminate pronouns the way you can in some languages (such as, How doing? Are feeling well?).

For example:

Student 1: *Hope you're enjoying your volunteer work.*
Student 2: *It's okay. Not exactly what I expected, but okay, I guess.*

2. Circulate as students work; correct and assist.

1. Ask students to read the instructions.
2. Call on a student to read the example.
3. Have students complete the activity individually and then check their work with a partner.
4. Call on pairs of volunteers to read the conversations aloud.

■ EXERCISE D

1. Ask students to read the instructions and example.
2. Have students complete the activity individually and then check their work with a partner.
3. Call on volunteers to read their answers to the class.

C Read the informal conversations below, and underline phrases where ellipsis has occurred. Then, write the missing words above the phrase.

1. **Karen:** OK, everybody, *are you* ready to go? The van's out in front.

   Greg: Pat isn't here yet. Can we wait a few more minutes?
   Karen: *I have . . . with that* No problem. It only takes about 10 minutes to get to the Literacy Center.

2. **Karen:** OK, you guys, we'll pick you up in about 2 hours.
   Betty: *Will you pick us up . . .* Right here on the corner?

   Karen: It's probably better if we wait for you behind the Center. *Have you . . .* Got all of your equipment for today's activities?
   Greg: I think we're set. *We'll . . .* See you later.

3. **Mr. Newton:** *I'm . . .* Glad to see that you all made it today. *Did you have . . .* Any trouble finding a place to park?

   Karen: Karen just dropped us off, so we didn't have any hassle.

   Mr. Newton: OK, then, let's get down to business.
4. **Greg:** *did you . . .* Hey, Pete, bring that book that we were working on last time?

   Pete: Sure, I did all the homework that you gave me, too. *Do you . . .* See?
   Greg: *You are . . .* Looking good. I can see that you're getting more serious about reading.

D Interpret the headlines below in complete sentences. Follow the example.

1. Local Teens Donate Time at Senior Center

   Local teens have been donating their time at the Senior Center.

2. Volunteer Offers Yoga Wednesdays at Sports Complex

   A volunteer is offering Yoga instruction on Wednesdays at the Sports Complex.

3. Free Swimming Classes Open to All

   Free swimming classes are open to everyone.

4. Student Club IDs New Projects Based on Report Findings

   A student club identifies new projects based on a report's findings.

5. Air Quality Increase Due to Jackson Plant Closing

   There has been an increase in air quality because the Jackson plant closed.

■ **EXPANSION IDEA**

Exercise D

1. Divide the class into pairs. Tell students to think about recent world or local events and to write headlines for articles about two of them using ellipsis.

2. Call on volunteers to write their headlines on the board. Then call on other students to interpret the headlines in complete sentences as in Exercise D.

E Create headlines from the first sentence of these newspaper articles. There is more than one possible headline for each sentence.   Answers will vary.

1. The Houston City Council voted to cut the Arts Council budget by 15%.

   Arts Council Budget Cut by 15% ; City Council Cuts Arts Budget 15%

2. The Baltimore AIDS Taskforce is promoting more information sessions in local high schools and technical schools.

   Baltimore AIDS Taskforce Promoting Info Sessions in Schools

3. The Back Bay district has continued its revitalization efforts through university volunteers who help plan and implement changes in the neighborhood.

   Back Bay District Revitalizing Neighborhood Through Volunteers

4. Local volunteers held a book drive and other fundraising activities to raise over $300,000 for the Kerry Library.

   $300,000 raised for Kerry Library

5. For their course on public administration, Parklane University students have identified over 50 streetlights that are missing bulbs in the Highland Park area.

   PU Students Documenting Missing Bulbs

6. The proceeds from last night's benefit dinner at Clancy's will finance a new playground in Oaklawn Park.

   Benefit Proceeds Financing Playground

7. According to students at Dawson State, the parking needs at Memorial Hospital are growing annually by 3–5% as the hospital gains importance in this region.

   Growing Importance of MH Means Increasing Parking Problems

F PAIR WORK Brainstorm a list of 3–5 ways that a service-learning project could change your relationships with classmates. What benefits could you gain from such cooperative work? Then, write sentences comparing the normal type of student-student relationship with the relationships that you have brainstormed.

Normally you don't care if the other students behave responsibly, but in this type of project you have to.

■ **EXERCISE E**

1. Ask students to read the instructions.
2. Call on a volunteer to read the example aloud.
3. Ask volunteers to suggest other ways of creating headlines from the statement.
4. Have students complete the activity individually.
5. Call on several volunteers per question to read their headlines to the class.

■ **EXERCISE F**

1. Call on a student to read the instructions aloud.
2. Call on another student to read the text in the speech balloon.
3. Divide the class into pairs and have students brainstorm and write their sentences.
4. Call on volunteers to read their sentences to the class.

■ **EXPANSION IDEA**

Exercise F

1. Ask students to write a short composition using their own sentences from Exercise F as well as some of the others read aloud in class.

2. Have students exchange compositions with a partner. Ask them to read each other's work and then discuss what they wrote.

PART TWO

Parallelism

■ GRAMMAR IN CONTENT

■ EXERCISE A

1. Ask students to complete the activity and then check their work with a partner.
2. Call on volunteers to read their underlined phrases or clauses aloud.

■ GRAMMAR CHART
Parallelism

1. Write on the board *You'll enjoy helping, learning, and to make new friends too.* Call on a volunteer to explain what is wrong with this sentence.
2. Call on students to read the sample sentences and corresponding Notes aloud.
3. Answer any questions that students have about parallelism.

■ EXERCISE B

1. Go over the instructions with the class.
2. Call on a student to read the example.
3. Have students complete the exercise individually and then check their work with a partner.
4. Call on volunteers to read their answers aloud. Have class members discuss their answers.

■ GRAMMAR IN CONTENT

A Reread the text at the beginning of the lesson, and <u>underline</u> phrases or clauses that are grammatically similar within a sentence. (The first example of parallelism, or grammatical similarity, is in the second sentence.) Compare your answers with one of your classmates.

Parallelism	
Sample Sentences	**Notes**
We haven't heard **where the Center is** or **what we need to do.** **If you want to get some practical training** and **if you like to work with kids,** you should volunteer for the after-care project. Some students don't like **to write papers** or **do academic research.**	Use parallel structures to emphasize the connection of ideas. When structures are parallel, they are connected by a coordinate conjunction and are grammatically the same. Use ellipsis to avoid redundancy in sentences with parallelism.
You can hand in your project report **right now** or **anytime tomorrow.** Leave it **here** or **in my box.**	In the case of adverbials, the structure may not be structurally parallel, but the expressions of time, place, or manner should be parallel in meaning.

B Use the phrases or clauses in parentheses to complete each sentence. Edit for appropriate grammar structures, add words when necessary, and check for parallelism.

1. (select a project / establish a vision)

    To make a service-learning project effective, professors should interest their students
    in selecting a project and establishing a vision.

2. (solve interpersonal problems / interact appropriately with people in the community)
    Solving interpersonal problems among the group members and interacting appropriately with people in the community.

    can be very important lessons that students take away from their service-learning

    experience.

3. (have great success / meet all the goals)

    Professors shouldn't expect every project-team **to have great success or to meet all**

    the goals.

■ EXPANSION IDEA

Exercise B
Divide the class into small groups. Have students discuss the qualities of a good volunteer. Tell them to be sure to use parallel structures when they describe these qualities.

For example: *A good volunteer gives of his or her time freely, works hard, and makes an important contribution to the community.*

4. (write journals or reflective essays / make formal presentations)

At the end of the semester, students may have a choice of **writing journals or reflective essays or making formal presentations** about their projects.

5. (apply business analysis to real-life situations / understand social issues in the community)

An effective service-learning project for business students demands **applying business analysis to real-life situations and understanding community issues.**

6. (put a human face on a social issue / make students feel responsibility for project results)

The goal of professors that assign students service-learning projects is **to put a human face on a social issue and to make students feel responsibility for project results.**

C Read the questions below. Then, listen to a telephone conversation between Barbara Reilly, an economics professor, and Jim Brewer, the manager of the Millvale Food Bank and Community Kitchen, as they make final arrangements for Professor Reilly's service-learning project. Take notes on their conversation, and use the information to answer the questions below.

CD2,TR8

1. How will the students get to the project site?

The students will go there in Professor Reilly's car or in the university van.

2. What are Professor Reilly's goals for the project?

His goals are to show the implications of economic decisions on the under-privileged.

3. What are Mr. Brewer's concerns about the students?

Mr. Brewer is concerned about how the students will talk to the clients and what they will be wearing.

4. What will most of the students be involved in during the first weeks of the project?

Most of the students will be involved in making an inventory and helping out in the kitchen.

5. How will the students assist the staff and clients in the second part of the project?

The students will assist the other volunteers by preparing and serving the evening meal.

■ COMMUNICATE

D GROUP WORK Brainstorm a list of projects that a group of students could do in order to accomplish a goal in health care, education, journalism, or engineering. When you are finished, share your ideas with your classmates.

1. Ask students to read the instructions and the five questions.
2. Tell students that they will hear the conversation twice. Play the audio and have students listen carefully.
3. Play the audio again. Then give students time to answer the questions.
4. Go over the answers together. If students disagree about an answer, play the audio again so that they can identify the correct interpretation.

■ **COMMUNICATE**

■ **EXERCISE D**

1. Divide the class into groups and have them brainstorm a list of projects they could do to accomplish a goal in health care, education, journalism, or engineering.
2. Call on a member of each group to read the groups' lists to the class.
3. After each list is read, have class members suggest other possible projects.

■ **EXPANSION IDEA**

Exercise D
Have students write a composition about a specific goal that they would like to accomplish in one of those disciplines. Remind students to use grammar and vocabulary from the lesson whenever possible.

Connection

Putting It Together

■ GRAMMAR AND VOCABULARY

1. Ask students to read the instructions.
2. Call on two students to read the topics aloud.
3. Ask students to choose one of the two topics and give them time to write their compositions.

■ PROJECT

1. Ask students to review the instructions.
2. Answer any questions that students have about the project.
3. Call on students at the next class meeting to report their findings.

■ INTERNET

1. Call on a student to read the instructions.
2. Have students conduct their searches and then report to the class on a program that interests them.

GRAMMAR AND VOCABULARY Write a composition on one of the topics below. Use as many words as possible from the Content Vocabulary on page 143, and (circle) them in your composition. Use sentences with ellipsis and parallelism to express some of your ideas, and underline those sentences.

Topic 1: Many Americans criticize U.S. colleges and universities for preparing young people for their careers but not for citizenship. These critics feel that institutions of higher education should prepare such young adults to be sensitive to less fortunate citizens and to enhance their communities. Do people in your community share this view of the purpose of higher education? Give examples.

Topic 2: According to Herbert Spencer, an English philosopher who lived from 1820 to 1903, "The great aim of education is not knowledge, but action." Do you agree or disagree? Give examples.
Answers will vary.

PROJECT Interview at least one student on your campus about service learning. Find out the following information, and give a brief oral report on it to your classmates.

1. Is there a special office on your campus that provides information about service-learning opportunities?
2. Has the student ever participated in a service-learning project?
3. If so, what was the project and what did the student learn from the experience?
4. If the student hasn't had this kind of experience before, what does he/she think about having a service-learning option in an academic course?

INTERNET Go online and use the search phrase "National Service-Learning Clearinghouse." Find out what "Service-learning Projects" are under way in your state and/or city, and select one or two topics that you find interesting. Read about the projects and choose one to describe to your class. Report briefly on the program at your next class meeting.
Answers will vary.

■ EXPANSION IDEA

Grammar and Vocabulary

1. Ask students to exchange compositions with a partner who wrote on the same topic.
2. Have students check use of vocabulary words, parallelism, and ellipsis in their partner's work.
3. Ask students to discuss each other's ideas.

Lesson ⑮

Public Policy and Administration: NIMBY

Overview

1. Write *NIMBY* on the board. See if anyone can guess what the letters stand for (Not In My Back Yard).
2. Ask students to think about a kind of building or facility that they would apply this acronym to.
3. Call on volunteers to name the buildings or facilities. Write them on the board.

■ CONTENT VOCABULARY

Look up the words and phrases below that you do not know and enter them in your vocabulary journal. Write each item's part of speech, a definition, and an example sentence. Try to include them in your discussion and writing below.

to advocate	a controversy	ill-advised	property values
a building permit	a developer	an initiative	to sign a petition
circumstances	a group home	a phenomenon	zoning laws

■ THINK ABOUT IT

How would you feel about living near a nuclear power plant? A rehabilitation center for drug addicts? Why? How can urban and regional planners decide on the best locations for such facilities? What criteria are the most appropriate? Discuss your ideas with a classmate.

In your writing journal, write for five minutes about the questions below. When you finish your writing, share your ideas with your classmates.   Answers will vary.
Near your family's home, are there any buildings, businesses, or other facilities that are very unpopular in your neighborhood? Why do your family members or your neighbors feel unhappy about the situation? What can you do about it?

151

■ CONTENT VOCABULARY

Ask students to review the words in the box. Tell them to look up any unfamiliar words.

■ VOCABULARY JOURNAL

Have students add new words to their vocabulary journals and write down the parts of speech, definitions, and sentences for each.

■ THINK ABOUT IT

1. Have students read the instructions.
2. Give students five minutes to write in their journals. Then call on volunteers to discuss their answers.
3. Divide the class into small groups and have them discuss the question posed in the exercise.
4. Circulate as students work and assist with vocabulary as needed.

■ CONTENT NOTES

The topic of this lesson is Public Policy and Administration: NIMBY. In this lesson, students will have an opportunity to discuss the rights and responsibilities of community members with regard to the introduction of potentially controversial institutions into their neighborhoods. Use this chapter to discuss the rights of the individual versus the needs of a group or the community as a whole.

PART ONE

Fronting Negative Elements

■ GRAMMAR IN CONTENT

■ EXERCISE A

CD 2, Track 9

1. Ask students to identify the structure in the photograph.

2. Ask students to read the title of the passage. Then call on volunteers to describe how they think it relates to the photo. Encourage them to use new content vocabulary.

3. Play the audio and have students follow along in their books as they listen. Ask students to circle any unfamiliar words or phrases.

4. Call on students to read their circled words and elicit definitions or explanations from volunteers if possible.

5. Check comprehension by asking questions such as the following: *Why do residents object to the construction of a school in their neighborhood? How did members of the local school board react? Who is Valerie Newcomb? Why was she perplexed by residents' reactions to the project?*

PART ONE | **Fronting Negative Elements**

■ GRAMMAR IN CONTENT

A Read and listen to the passage below. The words in bold are negative elements.

CD2,TR9

"NIMBYism" Blocks Construction of Elementary School

WILLIAMSBURG, VA. Residents along Brickyard Road have successfully brought plans for the construction of Henry Elementary School to a halt. Their opposition to the school, a classic case of "not in my backyard" (NIMBY), has resulted in a second court case that will delay any resolution of the situation for several more months. Not only families on the road where the school is to be built but also people on nearby residential streets where the school buses will have to go are claiming that the proposed school will affect their property values and their quality of life. Meanwhile, both teachers and parents of local elementary school students strongly defend the need for another school in town.

"**Not once** did I think that the people on Brickyard Road had such an anti-education attitude," commented one of the members of the local school board. "I knew that they were concerned about the traffic, but this is really unreasonable. In fact, **seldom** have I heard such a selfish point of view when we're talking about improving our children's educational opportunities."

Valarie Newcomb, Williamsburg's city manager, was also perplexed by the reaction. "Either they haven't listened to our plans for traffic control, or they just don't understand that we have to find a solution that is fair for all members of our community. **At no time** did they come forward with their complaints before they filed the court case."

The NIMBY phenomenon is nothing new. When the atomic power facility in Surry County was built two decades ago, hundreds of citizens protested. Neither their protests nor local politicians' proposals for alternate locations had any effect on the state energy commission. State energy officials had to balance the needs of the whole region against the interests of one sparsely populated county. Such controversies arise all across the nation, and **rarely** do local politicians have it easy in pushing for development while satisfying the concerns of their constituents.

to claim: to assert, to state an opinion

perplexed: confused, at a loss

to file a court case: to register a case with the court

a constituent: a citizen, a voter

■ EXPANSION IDEA

Exercise A

1. Divide the class into pairs. Ask students to role-play a dialog between a resident and a politician regarding the construction of a nuclear power plant in a residential neighborhood. Encourage students to use new vocabulary.

2. Call on a few pairs of volunteers to role-play their dialogs for the class.

Sample Sentences	Notes
Never had the mayor heard such nonsense when it came to new school construction.	Put negative words or phrases at the beginning of the sentence (or clause) for emphasis. With this word order, invert the subject and verb, and use the auxiliary *do* if necessary.
Under no circumstances should an official ignore the strength of NIMBY attitudes.	
At no time did the opponents of the school talk to the press.	
I don't like their attitude about the school, and **neither do** a lot of residents.	
Seldom are city council meetings without controversy.	Follow the same rule for words and phrases with a negative meaning or very restrictive meaning, such as *few, little, rarely, least of all,* and *seldom.*
Little do some city planners realize how upset citizens can become about a park.	Such sentences are often very formal or literary in style.
Least of all would one expect a new park to upset local residents.	Formal constructions such as these often have a main verb in passive voice.
Few words could be spoken without upsetting the audience members further.	

B Read over your journal entry, and <u>underline</u> at least one sentence that you can revise to include one of the negative elements in the chart above in initial position. Write your revised sentence(s) below.

   Answers will vary.

_____

_____

_____

■ GRAMMAR CHART
Fronting Negative Elements

1. Write on the board *I have never been so embarrassed in my life.* Ask a volunteer to come to the board and rewrite the sentence so that it begins with *never*. If any class members disagree, have them write their versions on the board.
2. Discuss the different versions of the rewritten sentence.
3. Call on students to read the sample sentences and accompanying Notes.
4. Answer any questions students have about fronting negative elements.

■ EXERCISE B

1. Have students complete the exercise.
2. Ask students to exchange work with a partner. Have them look for additional places where sentences could be revised to use negative elements in the initial position.

■ EXPANSION IDEA

Grammar

1. Divide the class into pairs. Have students discuss an issue of mutual interest using the grammar and vocabulary introduced in the lesson.
2. Circulate as students work and assist as needed. Be sure that students are inverting the subject and verb in sentences using initial negative elements.

1. Ask students to read the instructions.
2. Call on two students to read the example.
3. Ask students to complete the activity and then correct their work with a partner.

C Rewrite the underlined text in each conversation, emphasizing the negative elements. In some cases you will have to revise the sentence considerably.

1. **Frank:** I can't believe that they are talking about building a new racetrack close to the kids' playground.

   Marcie: I can't either. It doesn't make any sense. Is the mayor out of his mind?

   Neither can I.

2. **Mayor Clark:** I'm thinking about putting our plan for a new racetrack on the agenda for the town meeting tonight.

   Mr. Dunner: Mr. Mayor, I have seldom heard you make such an ill-advised statement. You know very well that more than half the town hates that idea.

   seldom have I heard you make such an ill-advised statement.

3. **Council-member Wagner:** Mayor Clark, I wholeheartedly agree with Mr. Dunner. You cannot mention one word about the racetrack. Don't even say "horse!"

   Not one word can you mention about the racetrack.

4. **Mayor Clark:** John, what do you think? Is the time right?

   Council-member Owens: There is no way that you can mention it without causing a big uproar. The press will be all over you.

   No way can you mention it without a big uproar.

5. **Mayor Clark:** Men, I think that you are over-reacting. Ms. Yoder, what's your take on the racetrack?

   Council-member Yoder: With all due respect, Mayor, you shouldn't bring up the track under any circumstances. Our polls show that it is a political disaster waiting to happen.

   under no circumstances should you bring up the track.

6. **Mayor Clark:** Ms. Yoder, I'm really surprised at you. I would expect such advice least of all from you. Don't you own several racehorses?

   Council-member Yoder: Be that as it may, I stand by my words.

   Least of all from you would I expect such advice.

7. **Mayor Clark:** I'll bow to your expert advice. I have little hope that the racetrack will be approved without all of your support.

   Little hope do I have that the racetrack will be approved without all of your support.

■ **EXPANSION IDEA**

Exercise C

1. Divide the class into new pairs.
2. Ask students to take turns role-playing the conversations in Exercise C.
3. Circulate as students work; assist with pronunciation and intonation as needed.
4. Call on volunteers to role-play the conversations for the class.

D Choose one negative element in each of the letters to the editor below, and rewrite that sentence to emphasize it. Give your reason for emphasizing a particular negative element.

1.
> I firmly believe that our community needs at least five more group homes for our fellow-citizens with developmental disabilities. Such homes pose no danger to families and property values in the neighborhood. Research studies have shown this to be true in cities across the U.S. Our citizens need to inform themselves about the facts and not listen to false information about dangers. Families of these citizens don't want their loved ones to live far away, and I don't either. It's not fair!

Negative Statement: _No danger is posed to families in the neighborhood._

Reason: _The main argument is the lack of danger, so it should be emphasized._

2.
> Just as our citizens' committee had warned, the new motel on Jamestown Road has increased traffic in our neighborhood. I used to let my children walk to school and cross at the intersection of Jamestown and First Streets. I can no longer do that in good conscience. I can never be sure that they will cross the street without some out-of-town visitor running them over. ~~I have never before felt so betrayed by my elected officials.~~

Negative Statement: Never before have I felt so betrayed by my elected officials.

Reason: Strong, emotional conclusion to the letter

3.
> I call on the City Council to oppose the mayor's ill-advised plan to relocate the city jail to Morningside, a section of town five miles from the closest police station. I have never heard of a politician with so little concern for the welfare of taxpayers. We elected Mayor Burns for his innovative ideas on economic development, but ~~he didn't give us reason at any time during the campaign to believe that our lives would be in danger as a result of his ideas.~~

. . . but at no time during the campaign did he give us reason to believe
Negative Statement: that our lives would be in danger as a result of his ideas.

Reason: Strong emphasis on danger of his ideas

4.
> We should all be very alarmed that the Bluebird Café has applied for a liquor license. Many of us concerned neighbors don't want to see college students making noise late at night with their drunken friends. This neighborhood has never had many college students, but now they will be around at all hours of the day and night. The City Council should in no way consider this application seriously. ~~In fact, there's no way in a million years that we will put up with it.~~ I strongly urge everyone to send a letter to the City Council.

Negative Statement: In fact, no way in a million years will we put up with it.

Reason: Emotional emphasis on the person's resistance

■ **EXERCISE D**

1. Go over the instructions with the class.
2. Ask students to review the example. Answer any questions students have about the activity.
3. Have students complete the activity individually and then check their work with a partner.
4. Call on volunteers to read their answers to the class. If anyone disagrees, ask him or her to read their answers and decide on the correct one as a class.

■ **EXPANSION IDEA**

Exercise D

1. Divide the class into four small groups.
2. Write the numbers 1 through 4 on slips of paper to correspond with the four letters to the editor. Have a member of each group pick one of the slips.
3. Ask groups to formulate an answer to each of the letters.
4. Call on a member of each group to read his/her group's letter to the class.

EXERCISE E

1. Ask students to review the phrases in the box.
2. Have students identify any phrases that they don't understand. Call on volunteers to explain them, if possible.
3. Ask students to read the instructions.
4. Call on a student to read the example.
5. Have students complete the activity individually and then compare their work with a partner.
6. Call on volunteers to read their answers to the class.

E Read the following situations and make an emphatic response that expresses NIMBY. Use one of the phrases in the box below at the beginning of your sentence.

no way	never in a million years	not for all the money in the world
rarely	in no uncertain terms	not for a million dollars
not for one minute	never once	at no time

1. The City Council has introduced a plan to build a health-care clinic in the next block.

   Not for one minute will I support this plan because the traffic and parking will be terrible around my house.

2. You read in the newspaper that a local developer wants to convert an apartment building nearby to housing for poor people.

   No way will that developer be permitted to convert the building to housing for poor people.

3. A person asks you to sign a petition that supports the construction of a new soccer field across the street from your house.

   Not for a million dollars will I sign a petition that supports the construction of a soccer field across from my house.

4. You attend a City Council meeting and listen to the mayor's proposal for a waste treatment plant in your town.

   At no time has the City Council voted any support for the mayor's proposal for a waste treatment plant in our town.

5. One of your neighbors asks you to join a local planning committee. The committee advocates building a wind energy park with 25 turbines at the edge of town near your house.

   Rarely have I heard such a terrible idea as the plan to locate a wind energy park near my house.

6. On the local TV news, they have been reporting all week about the need for a new landfill in the region. It seems that your county is at the top of the list because the population is so low.

   Not for all the money in the world do I want to live next to a new landfill.

7. In the governor's campaign for reelection, she has said that the solution to traffic congestion on the highway near your town is to build more on- and off-ramps. One of the proposed exits will cut through your neighborhood.

   In no uncertain terms should we tell the governor that we strongly oppose the proposed exits through my neighborhood.

■ EXPANSION IDEA

Exercise E

1. Ask students to write a short composition that expands their answers to one of the seven situations. Encourage them to use several of the phrases in the box, if possible.

2. Have students exchange compositions with a partner. Ask them to suggest ways in which the compositions can be made more emphatic.

3. Call on a few volunteers to read their work to the class.

F **PAIR WORK** Discuss your reaction to the construction of a high school, a group home for adults with developmental disabilities, a casino, a nightclub, a 10-story hotel, and a solar power plant in your neighborhood.

> Not for a moment would I consider a nightclub being built in my neighborhood.

> Neither would I. It wouldn't be a good influence on my kids.

PART TWO	Correlative Conjunctions

■ GRAMMAR IN CONTENT

A Reread the text on page 152, and <u>underline</u> all of the sentences with one of the following pairs of connecting words: *either . . . or, neither . . . nor, both . . . and, not only . . . but also.*

Correlative Conjunctions

Sample Sentences	Notes
Either Fred **or** George will speak first at the meeting.	Connect elements in your sentences with the correlative conjunctions below.
Both Fred **and** George will support the plan.	· *Either . . . or* Only one of two items is true.
Neither Fred **nor** George can predict the results.	· *Both . . . and* Both items are valid.
Not only did Fred speak effectively, **but** he **also** won the election.	· *Neither . . . nor* Both items are false. · *Not (only) . . . but (also)* The first statement is unexpected or surprising and so is the second one.
Either George will volunteer for the recycling center, **or** he will find another project to work on.	Follow the rules of subject-verb inversion when a negative correlative element begins a clause.
	Use parallel structures after correlative elements in formal English.
Not only does George volunteer a lot, **but** he **also** donates to community projects.	Use *either . . . or* and *not (only) . . . but also* to connect clauses. Use a comma after the first clause.
Neither they **nor** Fred is surprised that the recycling center won approval.	When *neither . . . nor* or *either . . . or* connect two subjects, follow the proximity rule of subject-verb agreement: "the verb agrees with the closer subject."
Neither they **nor** he have heard any criticism of the center.	If, however, both subjects are pronouns, English speakers prefer a plural verb.
Both his co-workers **and** his wife think that Fred is going to do a great job.	Subjects connected with *both . . . and* and *not only . . . but also* always have plural subject-verb agreement.

■ **COMMUNICATE**

■ **EXERCISE F**

1. Call on a student to read the instructions aloud.
2. Call on two other students to read the text in the speech balloons.
3. Divide the class into pairs and have students discuss their reactions.

PART TWO

Correlative Conjunctions

■ **GRAMMAR IN CONTENT**

■ **EXERCISE A**

1. Ask students to complete the activity and then check their work with a partner.
2. Call on volunteers to read their underlined sentences to the class.
3. Write on the board the following:

   Either I'll go to France and I'll stay at home.
   Both Dan or I will go to Mexico.
   Neither Kate or Becca will come.
   Not only Kate but Becca will come.

   Call on volunteers to correct the sentences.

■ **GRAMMAR CHART**
Correlative Conjunctions

1. Ask students to read through the sample sentences and Notes.
2. Answer any questions that students have about how and when to use correlative conjunctions.

■ **EXPANSION IDEA**

Exercise A
1. Write on the board *Jill/the/win/John/neither/election/nor/will.* (Neither Jill nor John will win the election.)
2. Ask students to unscramble the sentence.
3. Call on a volunteer to read the unscrambled sentence aloud. Ask for corrections from the class needed.
4. Instruct students to write four scrambled sentences.
5. Have students exchange sentences with at least two partners.

1. Ask students to read the instructions.
2. Call on two students to read the first question and the example.
3. Call on a volunteer to combine the sentences in another way.
4. Have students complete the activity on their own and then compare their work with a partner.
5. Have volunteers read their answers, calling on more than one per question to show different ways in which the sentences can be combined.

B Combine the sentences below using one of the pairs of correlative conjunctions. There may be more than one way to combine the sentences.

1. When citizens protest against the construction of a group home in their neighborhood, they are concerned about falling property values. These citizens are also worried about more traffic in their neighborhood.

   Citizens that protest against the construction of a group home in their neighborhood are concerned about both falling property values and more traffic in their neighborhood.

2. Homeowners generally agree that a community needs to provide housing for people with disabilities. Politicians tend to agree that a city should provide housing for citizens who cannot care for themselves.

   Both homeowners and politicians generally agree that a community needs to provide

   housing for mentally handicapped citizens.

3. Selecting a particular street for a group home doesn't seem fair to the neighbors there. Changing the zoning laws on a particular street doesn't seem right to the local residents.

   Neither selecting a particular street for a group home nor changing zoning laws on a street

   seems fair to residents.

4. When increased traffic seems a real possibility, officials should look for a location outside a quiet residential neighborhood. When personal safety may be an issue, planners need to consider an alternative site.

   When increased traffic or personal safety may be an issue, officials look for a location

   outside a quiet area.

5. According to public policy analyses, group homes have no statistical effect on the property values in a neighborhood. The analyses also show that such homes do not have any negative impact on the character of the neighborhood.

   According to public policy analyses, group homes have neither a statistical effect on

   property values nor on the character of a neighborhood.

6. Effective city planners choose projects that will bring about the greatest benefits to the community. Good administrators also select projects that produce the least harm to society.

   Effective city planners choose projects that will both bring about the greatest benefits and

   produce the least harm to a community.

7. Being part of a group enriches the lives of people with disabilities. Living in a group setting gives them opportunities for social interaction and shared responsibilities.

   Both participating in normal community life and living independently in a group setting

   enrich the lives of mentally challenged people who are able to live in a group home.

■ EXPANSION IDEA

Exercise B

Ask students to write a short composition using the information in Exercise B. Encourage them to use vocabulary from the lesson and correlative conjunctions.

C Select the best verb from the box to fill each blank, and be sure to use the proper form of the verb for the context.

be	~~advocate~~	oppose	voice
urge	support	consult	interview

About three months ago, T-Mart announced its interest in opening a new store in the vicinity of Beaumont. In recent weeks, neither Mayor Nichol nor City Council members _____*have advocated*_____ having a T-Mart in the city limits. They support
(1)
local businesses instead. However, all this week, both the T-Mart representative and their corporate lawyers _____**have consulted**_____ with local citizens' groups who
(2)
would like to see a T-Mart store in the community. A sizeable proportion of the local population _____**opposes**_____ the initiative to build a T-Mart. The local media
(3)
_____**have been interviewing**_____ people from each side. Not only the mayor but also the
(4)
City Council _____**have urged**_____ citizens to consider the impact of T-Mart on
(5)
local small businesses very carefully. Also, they have cautioned the T-Mart supporters that either the empty field by Lafayette School or the acres of marshland by Lake Kennesaw _____**are**_____ the only available site for the giant retailer.
(6)
The mayor has already heard that neither the environmentalists nor the School Board
_____**support**_____ the use of city land for the construction of a T-Mart.
(7)

D On a separate piece of paper, write a summary of the opinion poll results below for your boss, Mayor Gregson. Use correlative conjunctions in your memo.

Survey Question: In the upcoming referendum on proposed city development, will you vote for the following projects in your neighborhood?   **Answers will vary.**

	Absolutely	Maybe	No Way
a. a police substation	25%	15%	60%
b. a drug rehabilitation center	10%	15%	75%
c. a recycling center for garden waste	25%	40%	35%
d. a children's day-care center	40%	40%	20%
e. a group home for juvenile offenders	5%	15%	80%

■ **EXERCISE C**

1. Have students read the instructions.
2. Call on a student to read the example aloud.
3. Have students complete the activity individually and then check their work with a partner.
4. Call on students to read the text aloud.

■ **EXERCISE D**

1. Go over the instructions with the students.
2. Give students time to write their summaries.
3. Have students exchange their summaries. Ask them to look for ways to include additional correlative conjunctions.

■ **EXPANSION IDEAS**

Exercise C

Divide the class into pairs. Have students discuss the information in Exercise C using appropriate vocabulary and correlative conjunctions.

For example:

Student A: *Neither Mayor Nichol nor the City Council want to have a T-Mart go in here.*

Student B: *That's what I heard. I guess both the major and the council members think it would hurt local businesses.*

Exercise D

1. Have students design their own survey that concerns a question of local interest.
2. Give students time to survey their classmates.
3. Divide the class into small groups and have students discuss the results of their surveys.

CD 2, Track 10

1. Ask students to read the instructions. Then have them look at the map to locate sites to be discussed in the audio.

2. Have students read the six questions.

3. Play the audio and have students listen for comprehension. Tell them that they will hear the recording again.

4. Play the audio again. Tell students to circle the answers as they listen.

5. Play the audio again so that students can check their answers.

6. Call on volunteers to read their answers to the class. If there is any disagreement, play the audio again.

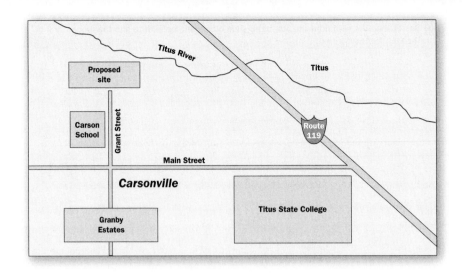

E Listen to some community leaders in Carsonville give their recommendations for the location of the new recycling center. After listening to each speaker, ⟨circle⟩ the letter of the correct interpretation.

1. a. The Green Club neither supports the construction of the center nor the mayor's recommendation for its location.
   (b.) The Green Club both supports the construction of the center and recommends a different site for its location.

2. a. The Sierra Club recommends both accepting household chemicals and locating the center in a different location.
   (b.) The Sierra Club recommends either changing the location of the center or changing the items that the center will accept.

3. a. The Carsonville School Board agrees with either the Green Club or the Sierra Club.
   (b.) The School Board is worried not only about the chemicals but also about the noise.

4. a. Titus State College supports neither the location on Grant Street nor the alternative site by Route 119.
   (b.) TSC both understands the concerns of the other speakers and suggests finding a different alternative location.

5. (a.) Jim Samuel has not only investigated sites in Carsonville but has also discussed a site near Titus.
   b. Jim Samuel recommends the site either at one end of Grant Street by the school or at the other end beyond Granby Estates.

6. a. Mr. O'Malley either wants the recycling center near the school or near the TSC campus.
   (b.) Mr. O'Malley both objects to the recycling center near his neighborhood and threatens to resist this idea strongly.

160 LESSON 15 | Public Policy and Administration: NIMBY

■ **EXPANSION IDEA**

Exercise E

1. Divide the class into pairs and have students discuss where they think the new recycling center should be located. Tell them to point out the benefits and disadvantages of the various locations.

2. Circulate as students work; assist as needed.

3. Poll the class to determine which location they consider to be the best one.

F There are four errors in the e-mail message below. Find and correct the errors.

Dear Steve,

You should have been at the meeting on the recycling center last night. It got pretty tense. There was supposed to be a time limit for each speaker. Not only ~~the~~ the mayor let them talk as long as they wanted, she **did** also asked a lot of questions. I thought that we would be there till midnight!

I guess that most of the speakers actually presented their opinions both clearly and ~~they talked politely~~. One of **have I** **neither kept** the last guys was the worst. Seldom ~~I have~~ heard such an arrogant person. It was incredible. He ~~kept neither~~ to the point nor tried to be respectful to the other groups in the meeting. We were all happy when it was over.

Now we have to make the final recommendations to the City Council. There should be some more fireworks at that meeting!

What's the latest on your end?

Lenny

■ **COMMUNICATE**

G **SMALL GROUP WORK** Prepare a short presentation to local homeowners who are very concerned about a new 100-occupant dormitory that your school wants to build in the neighborhood. The neighbors are worried about noise, traffic and parking, trash, and the general appearance of the property as well as drugs and alcohol.

 Not only will the dorm residents keep the property clean, we will also be responsible for garbage cans on garbage pick-up days.

Answers will vary.

EXERCISE F

1. Ask students to read the instructions.
2. Have students complete the activity individually and then check their work with a partner.

■ COMMUNICATE

▧ EXERCISE G

1. Call on a student to read the instructions aloud.
2. Call on another student to read the text in the speech balloon.
3. Divide the class into small groups and have them prepare their presentations.
4. Call on each group to make a presentation to the class.

▧ EXPANSION IDEA

Exercise G

Divide the class into pairs. Have one student role-play a homeowner who does not want the dormitory to be built in his/her neighborhood, and the other a representative of the school that wants to build the dorm.

Connection

Putting It Together

■ GRAMMAR AND VOCABULARY

1. Ask students to read the instructions.
2. Call on two students to read the topics aloud.
3. Ask students to choose one of the two topics and give them time to write their compositions.

■ PROJECT

1. Ask students to review the instructions.
2. Answer any questions that students have about the project.
3. Call on students at the next class meeting to give their oral reports.

■ INTERNET

1. Call on a student to read the instructions.
2. Have students conduct their searches and then report to the class on the second NIMBY issue that he/she read about.

GRAMMAR AND VOCABULARY Write a composition on one of the topics below. Use as many words as possible from the Content Vocabulary on page 151, and (circle) them in your composition. Use sentences with fronted negative elements and correlative conjunctions to express some of your ideas, and underline those sentences.

Topic 1: Changes in a neighborhood or city district concern those who live there. For example, safety issues worry not only homeowners but also renters. Residents also complain about changes that could lead to more noise, pollution, or traffic. Explain one example of the NIMBY phenomenon in your town or city in detail.

Topic 2: Not only on the local level will one find the NIMBY phenomenon. It also exists on the state and national level in the U.S. Other countries also practice NIMBY. Discuss the NIMBY phenomenon in your region or country. Give concrete examples.
Answers will vary.

PROJECT Interview at least one student on your campus to find out that person's attitudes about NIMBY. Find out the following information, and give a brief oral report at the next class meeting.

1. How would you describe your neighborhood?
2. How would you or your family feel if your town/city decided to build one of the following in your neighborhood? Why?
   a. a high school
   b. a group home for adults with developmental disabilities
   c. a nightclub
   d. a 10-story hotel
   e. a solar power plant
3. How can a community both respect families and their homes and provide important services (like schools, rehabilitation centers, housing for the poor, etc.) for everyone in the community?

 INTERNET Go online, and use the search phrase "NIMBY headlines" to find a website with current articles about NIMBY issues. Then, select and read two different articles. Write a brief summary of one of the articles, using at least one pair of correlative conjunctions. In class, tell your class about the NIMBY issue in the other article that you read.
Answers will vary.

■ EXPANSION IDEA

Internet
1. Have students write a comparison of their articles using vocabulary and grammar from the unit.
2. Ask students to exchange work with a partner. Tell them to suggest ways in which negative elements might be used in the initial position and correlative conjunctions can be added.

A Select the appropriate connector or adverbial from the box to complete the idea in each pair of sentences. Add punctuation where necessary.

thus	first of all	ultimately	while
evidently	even though	both	similarly

1. Many college students work part-time during their studies. _____**Ultimately/Thus,**_____ they probably have some experience interacting with older co-workers.

2. Many experienced employees enjoy working with young people. _____**While**_____ they listen politely to the ideas and suggestions of their younger co-workers, the employees may not accept their ideas easily.

3. New, inexperienced employees could feel frustrated for several reasons. _____**First of all,**_____ they might have the feeling that their co-workers don't take their ideas seriously. They might also feel like their supervisors are scrutinizing them.

4. A new employee may share her ideas with her supervisor. _____**Ultimately,**_____ the supervisor will decide whether to implement the new idea.

5. Residents in some towns protest changes in zoning laws to protect the value of their property. _____**Similarly**_____ homeowners in other places are against school construction close to their neighborhood.

6. In some cities, residents protest against any change. _____**Both**_____ jails and schools are particularly controversial.

7. Protesting against school construction may seem incredible. _____**Even though**_____ families benefit from having new schools, most people don't want to live near one.

8. Recently the local school board voted against building a new school in our district. _____**Evidently**_____ no one could agree on the location of the new construction.

Review 11-15

Review Lessons 11-15

The purpose of this lesson is to help students review the language and concepts they have learned in the last five lessons. Encourage them to go back to the lessons and review the grammar charts to help them complete the review activities.

■ EXERCISE A

1. Ask students to read the instructions and review the connectors and adverbials in the box.
2. Have students complete the activity individually and then check their work in pairs.
3. Call on volunteers to read their answers aloud. Discuss any differences of opinion about the answers among class members.

■ EXPANSION IDEA

Exercise A

1. Have students write a paragraph about young people interacting with older co-workers or residents in towns protesting against school construction in their neighborhoods.
2. Circulate as students work; assist as needed. Encourage them to use connectors and adverbials in their writing.
3. Divide the class into pairs and have students edit each other's work, paying particular attention to the correct use of connectors, adverbials, and punctuation.
4. Call on a few volunteers to read their paragraphs to the class.

■ EXERCISE B

1. Have students read the instructions.
2. Give students time to complete the activity on their own. Then have them check their work in pairs.
3. Call on volunteers to read their answers aloud.

■ LEARNER LOG

Have students complete the Learner Log. Suggest that they review the Grammar Charts for areas that need more practice.

B (Circle) the letter of the best completion for each sentence below.

1. _____ miss the opportunity to join a service-learning project.
   - (a.) Under no circumstances should you
   - b. Under no circumstances you should

2. During her project at the Food Bank, Tamika has not only shared her accounting experience _____
   - (a.) but also her organizational skills.
   - b. but also used her organizational skills.

3. Tamika and two classmates work _____ to fulfill a service-learning requirement for a course that they are taking.
   - a. every week there
   - (b.) there every week

4. _____ and her classmates are glad that they chose the service-learning option.
   - a. Both Tamika is enthusiastic
   - (b.) Both Tamika

5. Neither her classmates nor Tamika _____ signing up for this course option.
   - a. regrets
   - (b.) regret

6. _____ fulfill the course requirement with this project, _____ have made useful contacts in the community.
   - (a.) Not only do they . . . but they also
   - b. Not only they . . . but also they

7. Tamika hasn't decided which courses she'll take next year or _____
   - a. what to major in.
   - (b.) what she'll major in.

8. However, she is _____ that she will participate in another service project.
   - a. quitely sure
   - (b.) quite sure

LEARNER LOG Check (✔) *Yes* or *I Need More Practice*. Answers will vary.

Lesson	I Can Use . . .	Yes	I Need More Practice
11	Adverbials and Adverbs in Sentence-Initial Position		
12	Sequential Connectors and Connectors of Equivalence		
13	Connectors of Causality and Concessive Connectors		
14	Ellipsis and Parallelism		
15	Fronted Negative Elements and Correlative Conjunctions		

■ EXPANSION IDEA

Exercise B

1. Divide the class into pairs.
2. Have students discuss how Tamika felt about missing the opportunity to join a service-learning project.
3. Circulate as students work and assist as needed.

PART 1
Review of the Passive Voice

PART 2
Passive Options with Verbs
Taking Two Objects

Lesson 16

Lesson 16

Cultural Anthropology: The Gullah

■ CONTENT VOCABULARY

Look up the words below that you do not know and enter them in your vocabulary journal. Write each word's part of speech, a definition, and an example sentence. Try to include them in your discussion and writing below.

to carve	a grain	means	a practice
to commence	to investigate	norms	to transmit
to compile	to isolate	oral history	unscrupulous

■ THINK ABOUT IT

What do you know about the American South? Who settled there? What was the basis of their economy? What was the importance of these states during the 1700s and 1800s? Discuss your ideas with a classmate.

In your writing journal, write for 5–10 minutes about the questions below. When you are finished, share what you wrote with the class.

The topic of this lesson is the culture and language of a particular group of Americans who have a "rice culture." Do you belong to a rice culture? If not, what dietary culture do you belong to? What does it mean to belong to a culture that is defined by a type of food?

Answers will vary.

165

Overview

1. Write *anthropology* on the board. Call upon volunteers to tell the class what anthropologists study. Explain that the word comes from the Greek words *anthropos* ("human") and *logia* ("study").
2. Write *the Gullah* on the board. See if anyone in the class has heard of this ethnic group. Tell the class that they will be reading about the Gullah in the lesson.

■ CONTENT VOCABULARY

Ask students to review the words in the box. Tell them to look up any unfamiliar words.

■ VOCABULARY JOURNAL

Have students add new words to their vocabulary journals and write down the parts of speech, definitions, and sentences for each.

■ THINK ABOUT IT

1. Have students read the instructions.
2. Divide the class into pairs and have students discuss what they know about the American South.
3. Call on volunteers to state facts about the American South and the reasons why southern states were important in the 1700s and 1800s.
4. Have students read the journal writing instructions. Answer any questions they have about the topic. Then give them five minutes to write in their journals.

■ CONTENT NOTES

The topic of this lesson is Cultural Anthropology: The Gullah. Students will learn about this particular community and how a culture can be identified by its diet. Use this lesson to discuss how regional differences in cuisine have evolved in the United States based on the cultures of the people who settled in certain areas. Also, discuss dietary habits in your students' home countries.

■ **EXERCISE A** 🎧

CD 2, Track 11

1. Ask students to raise their hands if they have ever visited the Sea Islands of South Carolina and Georgia. If anyone has, ask him or her to describe the experience.

2. Ask students to read the title of the passage. Call on volunteers to discuss how they think cultural isolation and preservation are related.

3. Play the audio and have students follow along in their books as they listen. Ask students to circle any unfamiliar words or phrases.

4. Call on students to read their circled words and elicit definitions or explanations from volunteers if possible.

5. Check comprehension by asking questions such as the following: *Why were slaves from specific areas in West Africa sought? Which states in particular wanted these slaves? What is the most significant way in which the Gullah express their cultural identity? What are some other typical Gullah foods?*

| PART ONE | Review of the Passive Voice |

■ GRAMMAR IN CONTENT

🎧 CD2,TR11   **A** Read and listen to the passage below. The words in bold are verbs in the passive voice.

The Gullah: Cultural Isolation and Preservation

Gullah communities in the Sea Islands and neighboring mainland regions in Georgia and South Carolina provide a unique opportunity to study some of the distinctive elements of African cultural influences on African American culture in the United States. . . . One significant characteristic of these communities, for example, is that most residents are descendants of enslaved Africans who worked on these islands as early as the seventeenth century. Beginning in that period, Africans **were captured and transported** as slaves from various regions in Africa, extending from Angola to the Upper Guinea Coast region of West Africa. Between 1670 and 1800, however, Africans from rice-cultivating regions in West Africa, such as Liberia, Sierra Leone, Senegal, Gambia, and Guinea, **were sought** because of their knowledge of cultivation of rice, which was then a lucrative crop in Georgia and South Carolina. Rice planters were particularly interested in enslaving Africans from the "Rice Coast" of West Africa because the planters themselves lacked knowledge about rice cultivation under tropical conditions. . . .

Dependence on rice as a staple food is the most significant way the Gullah express cultural identity through food practices. Rice is the main food that links Gullah dietary traditions with the food traditions of West African food cultures; women play a primary role in fostering the continuance of these practices. In such cultures a person **is not considered** to have eaten a full meal unless rice **is included**.

Although most Gullah families no longer cultivate rice regularly, people are still conscious of its significance. Rice **was described** as the central part of the main family meal by at least 90% of the women I interviewed. . . .

One way of promoting [traditional values] through food practices is in the observance of strict rituals of rice preparation. In Gullah and West African rice cultures, for example, it is typical to commence the preparation of rice by picking out any dirt or dark looking grains from the rice before washing it. Then the rice **is washed** vigorously between the hands a number of times before it **is considered** clean enough for cooking. As a girl growing up in Sierra Leone, I **was taught** to cook rice in this way. I still follow this practice faithfully, even though most of the rice available for sale today in the U.S. **is labeled** as prewashed. . . .

Gullah culture **is influenced** strongly by rules and norms of West African food preparation. Many women who cook perpetuate these practices daily. One of these practices involves the selection, the amounts, and the combination of seasonings for food. These elements differentiate Gullah cooking practices from those of other cultures, according to many women I interviewed. Although the Gullah identify certain foods as their own, such as Hoppin' John (rice cooked with peas and smoked meat), red rice, rice served with a plate of shrimp and okra stew, and collard greens and cornbread, the interaction between European American, Native American, and African American food systems in the South has carried these popular Southern dishes across ethnic lines. One way in which Gullah women try to control cultural boundaries in their way of cooking these foods, as distinct from other Southern practices, is to assert that although similar foods **are eaten** by others in the South, their style of preparation and the type of seasonings they use are different.

lucrative: profitable

to foster: to promote and protect

okra: a green vegetable used in soups and stews

collard greens: kale, a green leafy vegetable

■ **EXPANSION IDEA**

Exercise A

1. Ask students to write down the food they ate at each meal on a typical day when they were children.

2. Divide the class into small groups, grouping students from different countries, if possible.

3. Ask students to discuss their lists and talk about which meal (breakfast, lunch, or dinner) is the most important meal of the day in their home country.

4. Circulate as students work; assist as needed.

Sample Sentences	Notes
Because European planters had no experience with growing rice, slaves **were put** in charge of its cultivation. Rice **was introduced** to South Carolina agriculture in the late 1600s. The name "Gullah" **might have been derived** from Angola, which was home to many slaves in South Carolina. To avoid punishment, a house slave might say, "The rice platter **was broken**" or "The dinner **was overcooked.**" Slaves also developed means of irrigating the rice fields. Elaborate systems **were dug** and **monitored** for water levels that were appropriate for cultivating rice.	Use **passive structures** to focus attention on the person or thing that experiences or receives an action, not the agent or doer of the action. Focus on the object when • the agent is obvious or very general • the agent is unknown • the agent is known, but you want to avoid naming that person or thing • the object is more important to the text than the agent. In scientific and technical texts this is common. The context of a sentence often determines whether the agent or object is the focus of attention.
In the 1780s after the Revolutionary War, slaves were transported to South Carolina **by Danish ships.** The first rice crops were ruined **by the poor farming techniques** of the white planters. The slave trade was directed **by Henry Laurens,** who was President of the Continental Congress in the 1770s.	Include the agent in the sentence if • the agent is new information • the agent is not a person (because this is unexpected) • the agent is well-known or famous
In England **they** imported tons of rice from South Carolina. The adaptable Asian white-grained species, *Oryza sativa,* **was introduced** into West African agriculture and replaced *O. glaberrima,* which had been cultivated in Senegambia since 1500 BCE.	English speakers prefer active rather than passive sentences in many instances. • In conversation, use "they" for obvious, general, or unknown agents to avoid passives. • In scientific writing, however, use passive voice to emphasize the topic of interest/focus of research.

B Read over your journal entry, and <u>underline</u> at least one sentence that you can revise to include a verb in the passive voice. Write your revised sentence(s) below.

Answers will vary.

_____

_____

_____

■ **GRAMMAR CHART**
Review of the Passive Voice

1. On the board, write *active* and *passive.* Call on a volunteer to explain the difference between these two voices.
2. On the board, write *Women always prepare the food.* Call on a volunteer to come to the board and rewrite the sentence in the passive voice.
3. Ask students to review the sample sentences and Notes.
4. Answer any questions that students have about the passive voice.

■ **EXERCISE B**

1. Have students complete the exercise.
2. Ask students to exchange work with a partner. Have them look for additional places where sentences could be revised to use a verb in the passive voice.

■ **EXPANSION IDEA**

Exercise B

1. Ask students to write six active sentences.

2. Have students exchange sentences with at least one partner. Ask them to rewrite the sentences in the passive.

1. Ask students to read the
instructions and look at the
illustrations.
2. Give students time to complete
the activity. Then have them
check their work with a partner,
making sure that the past passive
has been used in each answer.
3. Call on volunteers to read their
answers to the class. You may call
on more than one student, as
answers may vary slightly.

C Explain the steps in cultivating and harvesting rice on a South Carolina farm using the
illustrations. Use the past passive.   Answers will vary.

1. _____First, the irrigation canals and ridges were created._____

2. Second, rice seeds were planted in trenches and then covered in dirt.

3. Next, the fields were flooded with water either from the river or from the
swamp.

4. After that, the dry fields were weeded.

5. The rice was harvested, dried, tied into sheaves, and then the sheaves
were stacked.

6. The heads of the rice were separated and then the grains were winnowed.

■ **EXPANSION IDEA**

Exercise C
1. Tell students to think of a four- or
five-step process.
2. Divide the class into small groups. Tell
students to take turns naming their
process and then acting it out. The rest
of the group should say what is being
done using the past passive.

For example:
1. First, the coffee beans were
measured.
2. Then the beans were ground.

D **Underline** agents that should be omitted, and then write the reason for omitting or keeping the agent. Consider the information in previous sentences as you decide whether to omit an agent.

1. The isolation of the Gullah is mentioned <u>by researchers</u> in many academic research projects.

   Reason: _____ The context makes "researchers" obvious. _____

2. Their separation from slave owners was greater than in other regions because the planters' houses were built far away from the rice fields.

   Reason: _the agent is obvious_____

3. Many planters were infected with malaria or yellow fever <u>by the slaves</u>, so slave owners kept their distance.

   Reason: _new or unknown information_____

4. The diseases were transmitted <u>by the slaves</u> but did not affect them due to the Africans' inherited resistance to those illnesses.

   Reason: _now the information is known_____

5. Also, the planters and their families were affected <u>by the humid, semitropical climate of the coastal region</u>; consequently, they spent many months of the year farther inland.

   Reason: _new and unknown information_____

6. While the families stayed away, the plantations were managed <u>by a few European supervisors and some trusted slaves</u>.

   Reason: _new information_____

7. Finally, slaves from other American colonies or from the Caribbean weren't bought <u>by the planters</u> because only Africans from the Guinea Coast knew how to cultivate rice.

   Reason: _obvious agent_____

8. The language and customs of the slaves on coastal rice plantations were constantly renewed <u>by Africans of the same background</u> so that they were able to keep their cultural identity.

   Reason: _new information_____

■ **EXERCISE D**

1. Ask students to read the instructions.
2. Call on a student to read the example.
3. Ask a volunteer to explain the answer.
4. Have students complete the activity individually and then compare their answers with a partner.
5. Call on volunteers to read their answers to the class. Discuss any differences of opinion students have about the correct answers.

■ **EXPANSION IDEA**

Exercise D
Divide the class into pairs. Have students talk about Gullah isolation using the information provided in Exercise D. Tell them to use the past passive as often as possible.

EXERCISE E

1. Call on a volunteer to explain how changing a verb to the passive can change the focus of information in a sentence.
2. Have students read the instructions and the example. Be sure that they understand that their task is to identify the topic of the sentences and make sure that the writing focuses on it.
3. Divide the class into pairs and have students complete the activity together.
4. Circulate as students work and assist as needed.
5. Call on volunteers to read their answers aloud. If any students disagree with the answers that are read, discuss them as a class.

E Edit the following passages to adjust the focus of the information. Read the entire passage before you change any verb forms to passive. Give the reason(s) for your edits.

1. Numerous linguists have conducted research on the language of the Gullah since the 1930s. Before that, however, ~~outsiders considered the language~~ *the language was considered* a simplified, even barbaric means of communication. Plantation owners in particular thought the Gullah way of talking wasn't a "real" language.

   Reasons: *The first sentence introduces new information on the language of the Gullah. The language, not the outsiders, is the topic of the next sentence, with new information at the end of the sentence. The final sentence also continues the focus on the language.*

2. Perceptions of the language of the Gullah began to change thanks to the research of Lorenzo Turner, who was an African American linguist. He lived among the Gullah for many years, recorded their speech, and compared it to African languages. The languages of the Guinea Coast showed a number of similarities in grammar, vocabulary, and pronunciation. *Those similarities were published in his book in 1949.* ~~A company published his book on those linguistic similarities in 1949.~~

   Reasons: The previous sentence has linguistic similarities, and the book is new information.

3. In contrast to the work of some other linguists, Turner discovered thousands of words that Gullah speakers share with speakers of African languages. Some of those words were in stories, songs, and prayers that Turner learned in the Gullah community. *Also, hundreds and hundreds of other words were found.* ~~Also, he found hundreds and hundreds of other words,~~ but these words were personal names that are used only within the family. Having two kinds of names is not uncommon in traditional African societies.

   Reasons: The words were introduced in the previous sentence. Turner is not the focus of the sentences—just the Gullah words.

■ EXPANSION IDEA

Exercise E

1. Have students write a short composition that describes how modern linguists determined that Gullah is a Creole language. Encourage them to use the past passive whenever possible and appropriate.
2. Ask students to exchange work with a partner. Have them compare their compositions and suggest improvements and additional use of the past passive.
3. Call on a few volunteers to read their compositions to the class.

4. As Turner gained the trust of the Gullah, he found out about their naming practices. For example, "Joe" appears to be an English nickname, but it could also be the shortened form of "Cudjo" for a male child born on Monday. Along the Guinea Coast ~~parents often named children for the day~~ **children were often named for the day** that they were born.

   Reasons: _The agent of the action is obvious and important._

   _____

   _____

5. Modern linguists agree that Gullah is a Creole language. Such languages develop in situations where people of different cultures need to communicate. Gullah made communication possible ~~among speakers of various African languages~~ **Africans** and with the white planters and their families.

   Reasons: _Emphasizes the end results of Gullah._

   _____

   _____

■ COMMUNICATE

F **SMALL GROUP WORK** Discuss the isolation of groups in a society. Talk about any examples of an ethnic or social group that was isolated from a mainstream culture. How was the group isolated? What happened to the language or culture of that group? Can you compare that group to the Gullah in any way?

G **PAIR WORK** Discuss naming practices in your community and culture. Who is involved in selecting the name(s)? Are names chosen for particular meanings? For family reasons? Try to find some interesting similarities or differences between your cultures. Use passive constructions whenever appropriate.

> In some parts of Mexico, names **are passed down** from one generation to the next. I **was named after** my grandfather, for example.

> In Japan, we **aren't necessarily named after** our grandparents, but names are often chosen by them.

■ COMMUNICATE

■ EXERCISE F
1. Call on a student to read the instructions.
2. Divide the class into small groups and tell them to discuss any isolated groups they are familiar with.
3. Assist as needed. If groups are unable to think of any isolated populations, suggest tribes in the Amazon, New Guinea, or India.

■ EXERCISE G
1. Call on a student to read the instructions aloud.
2. Ask two other students to read the text in the speech balloons.
3. Divide the class into pairs and have them discuss naming practices in their communities and homes.
4. Call on a few volunteers who learned something surprising to share what they learned with the class.

■ EXPANSION IDEA

Exercise G
1. Have students write a short composition about naming practices in their partner's community. Remind them to use the passive when possible.

2. Call on a few volunteers to read their compositions to the class.

PART TWO

Passive Options with Verbs Taking Two Objects

■ GRAMMAR IN CONTENT

Ask students to complete the activity and then check their work with a partner.

■ GRAMMAR CHART

Passive Options with Verbs Taking Two Objects

1. Write on the board *direct object* and *indirect object*. Challenge students to write a sentence that has both a direct object and an indirect object.
2. Call on a few volunteers to write their sentences on the board.
3. Write *ergative verb* on the board. Explain that an ergative verb is a verb whose action affects the subject, rather than the object, of the verb. Write the following examples: *The ice melted.* and *She closed the window.*
4. Ask students to review the sample sentences and Notes. Answer any questions that students have about passive options.

■ GRAMMAR IN CONTENT

A Look at the passive verb forms in bold print in the text at the beginning of the lesson. Which one of those verbs can have both a direct object and an indirect object?

Passive Options with Verbs Taking Two Objects

Sample Sentences	Notes
Nowadays, **children** are read the traditional African stories of their ancestors. **The elderly** have always been shown respect in Gullah culture. Respect has always been shown **to the elderly** in Gullah culture. Special rice dishes are cooked **for children** on their birthdays.	Choose the **direct** or **indirect object** as the subject of a passive verb according to the focus of your sentence. See list of verbs on next page. Use *to* with the indirect object when the direct object is the passive subject. Passive forms of verbs with *for* + indirect object usually take only the direct object as the subject.

Did the slaves **get kidnapped** from their homes in West Africa?
 	
Sometimes African families **got separated** on their arrival in America.
 	
Gullah children didn't **get educated** with white children, so they only learned the language that their parents spoke.
 	
In the early 1900s, the Gullah **got criticized** for their language.
	Use *get* instead of *be* for a more informal passive construction. Typically this option
	  · specifies no agent
	  · has a human grammatical subject
	  · has an action verb
	
	This construction often implies that something negative happened to the grammatical subject (who may or may not have responsibility for the negative consequence). In contrast to some other languages, in English only passive sentences with this "get" structure can imply a negative consequence except with this structure.

During the hurricane one boat **was sunk** by an oar that crashed through its hull. Nearby a small rowboat **was sunk** in just a few feet of water.
 	
Several small fishing boats **sank** during the storm. Several others **capsized** but did not actually **sink**.
	Use ergative verbs in passive structures or in the middle voice. (See Lesson 4.)
	  · Choose the passive form of an ergative verb to stress that an agent of the action exists even if you do not specify the agent.
	  · Use the active form of ergative verbs in the middle voice if the agent is not relevant or if there are many possible agents.

■ EXPANSION IDEA

Grammar Chart

1. Ask students to use the verbs in the box to write two sentences that take the indirect object as the passive subject.

2. Call on a few volunteers to write their sentences on the board, and discuss the examples as a class.

Verbs Commonly Taking an Indirect Object as the Passive Subject			
bring	hand	owe	send
deny	lend	promise	show
give	offer	read	teach

B Change the focus, or topic, of the sentences below by using a passive construction.

1. Gullah women show their children the way to prepare rice in the traditional style.

   New focus: the way to prepare rice

   The way to prepare rice in the traditional style is shown to Gullah children.

2. Men taught some young boys wood-carving so that they could continue the tradition.

   New focus: some young boys

   Some young boys were taught wood-carving so that they could continue the tradition.

3. Slave traders brought South Carolina plantation owners slaves from the Guinea Coast because they needed them for cultivating rice.

   New focus: South Carolina plantation owners

   SC plantation owners were brought slaves from the Guinea Coast because they needed them for cultivating rice.

4. The plantation owners offered top dollar for slaves from Sierra Leone.

   New focus: top dollar

   Top dollar was offered to slave traders for slaves from Sierra Leone.

5. Sometimes agents bought families of slaves so they could stay together.

   New focus: families of slaves

   Sometimes families of slaves were bought so they could stay together.

6. Owners sometimes lent other planters in South Carolina their slaves.

   New focus: slaves

   Slaves were sometimes lent to other planters in South Carolina.

7. Planters in South Carolina didn't deny the slaves the chance to earn a little money.

   New focus: the slaves

   The slaves weren't always denied a little money.

8. Planters promised each slave a small piece of land for growing vegetables.

   New focus: a small piece of land

   A small piece of land for growing vegetables was promised to each individual slave.

9. Gullah speakers have taught many linguists the Gullah language in recent years.

   New focus: many linguists

   Many linguists have been taught the Gullah language in recent years.

■ **EXERCISE B**

1. Call on students to read the instructions and the example.
2. Answer any questions that students have regarding changing the focus of a sentence through the use of a passive construction.
3. Have students complete the activity on their own and then check their work in pairs.
4. Call on volunteers to read their answers to the class.

■ **EXPANSION IDEA**

Exercise B

Divide the class into small groups and have them discuss the information in the exercise, using passive constructions as often as possible.

■ EXERCISE C

1. Ask students to read the instructions.
2. Have students look over the words in the box. If they are unfamiliar with any of them, call on another student, if possible, to define the terms.
3. Call in a student to read the example.
4. Answer any questions that students have about paraphrasing the statements with passive sentences that use *get*.
5. Have students complete the activity individually and then check their work in pairs.
6. Call on volunteers to read their answers to the class. If other students have paraphrased the sentences differently, ask them to read their answers as well.

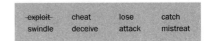

C Paraphrase the statements below with a passive sentence with *get* to make the statement less formal. Use one of the verbs in the box below as the main verb.

exploit	cheat	lose	catch
swindle	deceive	attack	mistreat

1. The Gullah, like all other enslaved Africans, felt that Europeans had taken advantage of them.

   Similar to other African slaves, the Gullah got exploited by Europeans.

2. Many planters punished slaves, including the Gullah, very severely for a variety of reasons.

   Slaves, including the Gullahs, got mistreated.

3. Although planters found many slaves who tried to escape, hundreds of Gullah escaped to Florida.

   Hundreds of Gullah didn't get caught.

4. In Florida they lived with the Indians there and fought with them when Europeans invaded their villages.

   They fought with the Indians when they got attacked by white men.

5. After people began to appreciate Gullah culture, outsiders bought their baskets and other homemade items and handicrafts at extremely low prices.

   Gullah craftspeople got cheated by outsiders.

6. Sometimes unscrupulous researchers used stories and other family information in their publications that the Gullah had shared only in private conversations.

   Sometimes the Gullah got deceived by researchers.

7. Outsiders are still coming into Gullah communities and buying beach property at extremely low prices.

   Nowadays the Gullah get swindled by people buying land.

■ EXPANSION IDEA

Exercise C
1. Tell students to write four formal statements.

For example:
A. *Young children in my country are given almost anything they want.*
B. *Sometimes children are allowed to stay up late at night.*

2. Have students exchange work with a partner. Tell them to rewrite the sentences using *get* as they did in question 1.

For example:
A. *Young children in my country get almost everything they want.*
B. *Sometimes children get to stay up late at night.*

🎧 **D** Listen to the comments of Sharon Carpenter, a visitor to the Sea Islands of South Carolina, and explain what happened to her and her friend.

CD2,TR12

1. _The bus left without her._
2. They were so interested in the demonstration and they didn't have time for the shops.
3. Her friend got injured.
4. They were interested in the delicious aroma and went into the kitchen.
5. They ate too much.
6. Her friend was too hot to continue walking.
7. They became lost, so they missed the bus.

E There are five errors in the e-mail message below. Find and correct the errors.

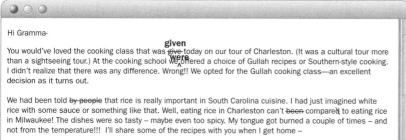

Hi Gramma-

You would've loved the cooking class that was ~~give~~ **given** today on our tour of Charleston. (It was a cultural tour more than a sightseeing tour.) At the cooking school we^**were** offered a choice of Gullah recipes or Southern-style cooking. I didn't realize that there was any difference. Wrong!! We opted for the Gullah cooking class—an excellent decision as it turns out.

We had been told ~~by people~~ that rice is really important in South Carolina cuisine. I had just imagined white rice with some sauce or something like that. Well, eating rice in Charleston can't ~~been~~ compared to eating rice in Milwaukee! The dishes were so tasty – maybe even too spicy. My tongue got burned a couple of times – and not from the temperature!!! I'll share some of the recipes with you when I get home –

Love,
Molly

■ COMMUNICATE

F **PAIR WORK** Children often learn traditional crafts, traditional ways of preparing food, and other traditional activities. Discuss what you were taught, shown, given, read, and/or offered while you were growing up. Who taught you these traditional things? How were you taught? Use passives whenever appropriate.

In my country, children **are taught** to show respect from an early age.

What's one way they do that?

For example, if you give them something, they don't just grab it. Both hands **are cupped together** to receive it.

Part Two | Passive Options with Verbs Taking Two Objects **175**

■ **EXERCISE D** 🎧
CD 2, Track 12

1. Ask students to read the instructions.
2. Tell the class to listen carefully to the audio.
3. Play the audio again, this time telling students to take notes.
4. Give students time to write a list of things that happened to Sharon and her friend.
5. Call on a few volunteers to tell the class what happened.

■ **EXERCISE E**

1. Have students complete the activity and then check their work in pairs.
2. Call on volunteers to read the corrected e-mail one paragraph at a time.

■ **COMMUNICATE**

■ **EXERCISE F**

1. Call on a student to read the instructions aloud.
2. Call on two other students to read the text in the speech balloons.
3. Divide the class into pairs and have them discuss personal experiences with traditional activities.
4. Call in a few volunteers who learned something interesting from their partners.

■ EXPANSION IDEA

Exercise E

1. Ask students to write a response to the email, using the passive voice whenever possible.
2. Have students exchange e-mails with a partner. Ask them to make corrections and suggestions about where additional use of the passive is possible.
3. Call on a few volunteers to read their e-mails to the class.

Connection

Putting It Together

■ GRAMMAR AND VOCABULARY

1. Ask students to read the instructions.
2. Call on two students to read the topics aloud.
3. Ask students to choose one of the two topics and give them time to write their compositions.

■ PROJECT

1. Ask students to review the instructions.
2. Answer any questions that students have about the project.
3. Call on students at the next class meeting to give their oral reports.

■ INTERNET

1. Call on a student to read the instructions.
2. Have students conduct their searches and then write their summaries.
3. Ask students to report to the class on the characters in the story they chose.

GRAMMAR AND VOCABULARY Write a composition on one of the topics below. Use as many words as possible from the Content Vocabulary on page 165, and (circle) them in your composition. Use sentences with verbs in the passive voice to express some of your ideas, and underline those sentences.

Topic 1: In many ethnic or cultural groups, maintaining traditional norms and practices is very difficult in our busy modern world. Some research shows that traditions are kept alive and transmitted to the younger generation by women. Why and how is this role taken on by the female members of such groups? Use concrete examples.

Topic 2: Select an ethnic or cultural group that you are familiar with and explain some of their traditions and customs. For example, what food customs were practiced by these people and have they been transmitted to younger members of the group? What kinds of occupations did members of the group have and how were their job tasks performed? Use concrete examples.
Answers will vary.

PROJECT Interview at least five students on your campus about their names. Find out the following information, and give a brief oral report on your findings at your next class meeting.

1. the students' complete names (including the spelling)
2. who named them
3. why they were named this way
4. the reason for the spelling of the name (if there is a choice of spellings)
5. family traditions for naming

 INTERNET Go online and use the search phrase "Gullah video" or "Gullah storytelling." Listen to a story in Gullah, and make notes on the basic plot of the story. Write a brief summary of the plot that you will hand in at your next class meeting. Also, be prepared to talk about the characters in the story in class.
Answers will vary.

■ EXPANSION IDEA

Internet
1. Tell students to conduct an online search using the key words "cultural" and "traditions."
2. Tell them to take notes on the cultural traditions of a group with which they are not familiar.
3. Call on volunteers to tell the class about the traditions they noted.

PART 1
Gerunds and Infinitives in the
Passive Voice

PART 2
Passive Voice in Other Complex
Sentences

Lesson 17

Industrial
Design: Modern
Wheelchairs

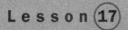

Lesson 17

Overview

1. Ask students to name some items that help disabled and elderly people live more comfortable and productive lives.
2. Have them brainstorm about how designers can make a difference in the lives of these individuals.

■ CONTENT VOCABULARY

Ask students to review the words in the box. Tell them to look up any unfamiliar words.

■ VOCABULARY JOURNAL

Have students add new words to their vocabulary journals and write down the parts of speech, definitions, and sentences for each.

■ THINK ABOUT IT

1. Have students read the instructions.
2. Divide the class into pairs and have students discuss their observations regarding the two wheelchairs.
3. Have students read the journal writing instructions. Answer any questions that they have about the topic. Then give them five minutes to write in their journals.
4. Have students share their journal entries with the class.

■ CONTENT VOCABULARY

Look up the words and phrases below that you do not know and enter them in your vocabulary journal. Write each item's part of speech, a definition, and an example sentence. Try to include them in your discussion and writing below.

access	a component	to donate	mobility
assembly	to deny	high performance	to mold
assistive technology	a disability	to maneuver	a strap

■ THINK ABOUT IT

Take a look at the two wheelchairs shown on page 180. What adjectives could you use to describe their general appearance? Have you ever seen a wheelchair similar to the one on the right? Where did you see it and what was the person in the wheelchair doing? Discuss your ideas with a classmate.

In your writing journal, write for five minutes about the questions below. When you are finished, share your information with the class.

In your opinion, what needs to be done in your hometown so that people with disabilities have easier access to public places? Is your school or place of work accessible to people with disabilities? What else needs to be done?

Answers will vary.

177

■ CONTENT NOTES

The topic of this lesson is Industrial Design: Modern Wheelchairs. Students will learn how modern wheelchair designs make it possible for individuals with disabilities to participate in every aspect of life. It also brings up the topic of the right of disabled people to have access to public places.

■ EXERCISE A

CD 2, Track 13

1. Write *high-tech* on the board.
2. Call on volunteers to say what the term means to them and give a few examples of *high-tech* items.
3. Have students read the title of the passage. Call on volunteers to discuss what they think the qualities of a high-tech wheelchair should be.
4. Play the audio and have students follow along in their books as they listen. Ask students to circle any unfamiliar words or phrases.
5. Call on students to read their circled words and elicit definitions or explanations from volunteers if possible.
6. Check comprehension by asking questions such as the following: *In which fields of science have advances made better wheelchairs possible? What are some of the advantages of high-tech wheelchairs? What does the Free Wheelchair Mission do?*

A Read and listen to the passage below. The words in bold are phrases with the passive form of the gerund or the infinitive.

CD2,TR13

High-Tech Wheelchairs

There's a revolution going on in the field of wheelchair design. People whose lives used to be severely restricted by their lack of mobility have benefited greatly from advances in materials science and in the aerospace industry. Engineers and researchers have been inspired to incorporate new lightweight materials into more user-friendly wheelchair designs. Some new wheelchairs are intended to enhance wheelchair athletes' performance, others are meant to be easier for people with severe disabilities to use, and still others are expected to be distributed to people with disabilities in developing countries.

Exotic materials **permit wheelchairs to be constructed for various functions.** The standard wheelchair, made of a common steel alloy, provides temporary mobility for people in such places as hospitals. For this traditional type of wheelchair, weight, long-term comfort, and ease of maneuvering do not concern designers. However, weight, comfort, and maneuverability acquire much greater importance when engineers design a wheelchair for an individual's long-term use. **In addition to being constructed** of high performance aluminum or titanium, lightweight or ultralight wheelchairs may also have certain components that are molded from advanced composites, such as carbon fiber, fiberglass, and Kevlar®. Wheelchair users can be assured of greater freedom of movement and will avoid repetitive stress injuries to their arms and shoulders with such wheelchairs.

Some designers specialize in chairs for wheelchair athletes, who can now participate in sports from road racing to rugby to fencing. For example, **being involved in wheelchair sports** has a special meaning at the University of Illinois in Urbana-Champaign. Since the 1940s, students in wheelchairs have participated in competitive wheelchair sports, starting with basketball. On another part of campus, students in industrial design classes have put their minds to solving mobility problems faced by the student athletes. One design team, for example, tackled the braking system for basketball players. The brakes on their chairs **needed to be applied** while they held the ball. The student engineers developed a braking system in the seatback.

Making wheelchairs available to 100–150 million needy people around the world is the mission of other designers and their nonprofit organizations. Some of these organizations have been prompted to design wheelchairs of cheap, readily available materials. The Free Wheelchair Mission, for instance, has distributed more than 175,000 of its wheelchairs in more than 60 countries since 2005. **In order to be redistributed later,** used wheelchairs are cleaned and refurbished by other organizations. They feel that wheelchairs **need to be custom fit** to the new owner and reject the "one-size-fits-all" mentality. Finally, some nonprofit organizations design new wheelchairs for the lifestyle and environment of the user and find local workers who can build and maintain the chairs. Regardless of the views of wheelchair suppliers, bringing assistive technology, like the wheelchair, to people who don't have it certainly means some kind of improvement in their lives.

---

fiberglass: a material made of fine glass fibers

Kevlar®: a strong material used for bulletproof vests and radial tires

to put one's mind to: to concentrate on

to tackle: to deal with, to work hard on

to prompt: to move into action

■ **EXPANSION IDEA**

Exercise A

1. Divide the class into small groups and have students discuss what they know about wheelchairs. If any of the students have ever been wheelchair-bound, have them describe the experience.

2. Ask students to make a list of activities that would require a specialty wheelchair.

3. Have a class discussion about what other sorts of assistive technology they believe should be developed.

Gerunds and Infinitives in the Passive Voice

Sample Sentences	Notes
Wheelchair athletes risk **being injured** just like any athlete.	Make passive gerunds and infinitives by applying the basic rules for each form to the auxiliary **be:**
Nowadays, marathon racers expect **to be included** in any marathon.	Gerund: **being** + past participle
The coach wouldn't allow the team **to be photographed** without their trophy.	Infinitive: **to be** + past participle
Being respected for your efforts makes hard work worthwhile.	Use **passive gerunds** and **infinitives** for the same functions that you use the active form of these phrases.
My goal for this year is **to be chosen** for the assistive technology research team.	
Weren't you sad about **being rejected** by that team?	
Trish denied **having been contacted** by our competitor's research team.	Use the perfect form of the passive constructions to emphasize a time that contrasts with the time of the main verb:
Ted preferred **to have been included** in the project even though he had other work to do.	Gerund: **having been** + past participle Infinitive: **to have been** + past participle
Ted didn't admit **having been offered** a higher salary by our competitors.	These forms are infrequently used.

B Read over your journal entry, and <u>underline</u> at least one sentence that you can revise to include a gerund or an infinitive in the passive voice. Write your revised sentence(s) below.

Answers will vary.

_____

_____

_____

■ GRAMMAR CHART
Gerunds and Infinitives in the Passive Voice

1. Write *gerund* and *infinitive* on the board. Call on volunteers to come to the board and write an example of each.
2. Go over each set of sample sentences and Notes with the class. Be sure that the explanations are clear before moving on to the next topic.

■ EXERCISE B

1. Have students complete the exercise.
2. Ask students to exchange work with a partner. Have them look for additional places where sentences could be revised to use a gerund or infinitive in the passive voice.

■ EXPANSION IDEA

Grammar

1. Ask students to write two sentences that use *being*, and two that use *to be*. Then have them scramble their sentences.

   For example: a/being/is/thing/doctor/most/the/life/his/in/important
   Being a doctor is the most important thing in his life.

2. Pair up students and have them unscramble each other's sentences.

1. Go over the instructions and the example with the class.
2. Have students complete the activity individually and then correct it in pairs.
3. Call on volunteers to read the corrected sentences to the class.

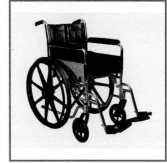

C Underline the correct form of the gerund or infinitive in each sentence.

1. Lightweight wheelchairs need (to construct / <u>to be constructed</u>) of titanium, high performance aluminum, or advanced composites.

2. (<u>Propelling</u> / Being propelled) the wheelchair by the hand rims is hard on bumpy terrain.

3. The standard wheelchair is not designed (to lift / <u>to be lifted</u>), so its weight is not that important.

4. Other kinds of wheelchairs, however, often require (lifting / <u>being lifted</u>) because they are transported in vans and car trunks.

5. Designers try to design wheelchairs so that users can avoid (treating / <u>being treated</u>) for repetitive stress injuries.

6. The goal of many wheelchair designs is for the user (to see / <u>to be seen</u>) before the chair; in other words, for the wheelchair to blend into the background.

7. In the interest of (<u>riding</u> / being ridden) more comfortably, users of ultralight wheelchairs often have specially molded seats to fit their bodies.

8. Some designs enable wheelchairs (to adjust / <u>to be adjusted</u>) manually to the widths of doors and other narrower spaces.

9. Designers also have to protect young wheelchair users from (injuring / <u>being injured</u>) if the wheelchair is not the right size for them.

■ **EXPANSION IDEA**

Exercise C
Ask students to write a short composition about modern wheelchairs using the information in Exercise C and the correct form of as many gerunds or infinitives in the passive voice as possible.

D Select a phrase in the box to complete each sentence.

~~choose for a wheelchair rugby team~~	release from the hospital	confine to a wheelchair
select for the Paralympics in the next Olympiad	~~take seriously as an athlete~~	sideline with an injury
train in wheelchair techniques	offer a rugby scholarship	equip with a safety strap
fit for an ultralight wheelchair	worry about rough play	injure on the court

1. Jamaal is interested in _____ *being chosen for a wheelchair rugby team.*

2. Since his motorcycle accident, he has wanted _*to be taken seriously as an athlete.*_

3. Before the accident, he had hoped _to be offered a rugby scholarship._

4. For a while Jamaal was very depressed about _being confined to a wheelchair._

5. To help Jamaal return to sports, his physical therapist encouraged him
   to be fitted for an ultralight wheelchair.

6. Now his goal is _to be selected for the Paralympics in the next Olympiad._

7. As he has become accustomed to his wheelchair, Jamal is putting his energy into
   training in wheelchair techniques.

8. It's hard to avoid _being injured on the court_
   because rugby is a rough sport, even in a wheelchair.

9. However, he doesn't want to risk _being sidelined with an injury_
   during the Paralympic trials, so he tries not to push too hard.

10. For that reason he admitted _to being worried about rough play_
    when he spoke with his physical therapist.

11. After that, the therapist authorized Jamaal's wheelchair _to be equipped with a_
    safety strap.

EXERCISE D

1. Ask students to review the phrases in the box.
2. Call on volunteers to explain any of the phrases that are unfamiliar to class members.
3. Call on two volunteers to read the examples. Answer any questions students have about them.
4. Have students complete the activity individually and then check their work with a partner.
5. Call on volunteers to read their answers to the class.

EXPANSION IDEA

Exercise D

1. Divide the class into pairs. Have them role-play a conversation between Jamaal and his physical therapist, using gerunds and infinitives in the passive voice.

For example:
Jamaal: *Being stuck in a wheelchair is not as bad as I thought it would be.*

Therapist: *You have to learn to be grateful for all of the things you can do.*

2. Call on a few pairs of volunteers to role-play their conversations for the class.

1. Call on students to read the instructions and the example.
2. Ask a volunteer to point out the passive gerund phrase in the example.
3. Answer any questions that students have about the activity.
4. Have students complete the exercise on their own and then check their work with a partner.
5. Call on volunteers to read their answers to the class. If other class members have different answers, ask them to read these aloud as well. Discuss the answers.

■ EXERCISE F

1. Go over the instructions and the example with the class.
2. Divide the class into pairs and have them complete the activity together.
3. Call on volunteers to read the paragraph aloud, one sentence at a time. Stop after each sentence to ask whether the rest of the class agrees. Discuss any disagreements.

E Paraphrase each of the sentences below with a sentence that includes at least one passive gerund phrase. Use the verb in parentheses as your only main verb.

1. When a wheelchair user participates in sports, he often says that he was motivated by the competition. (admit)

   A wheelchair user who participates in sports often admits being motivated by the competition.

2. When wheelchair users get an ultralight chair, they have to be measured for the seat. (involve)

   When wheelchair users get an ultralight chair, it involves being measured for the seat.

3. When wheelchair athletes participate in some sports, they have to be strapped into their chairs. (require)

   Participating in some wheelchair sports requires being strapped into the chair.

4. When the athlete returned to the locker room, he said that he was not exhausted by the game. (deny)

   When the athlete returned to the locker room, he denied being exhausted by the game.

5. One athlete was angry because a player had hit him from behind. (recall)

   One athlete was angry because he recalled being hit from behind.

6. When the player hit his opponent from behind, the referee could have ejected him from the game. (risk)

   When the player hits his opponent from behind, he risks being ejected from the game.

7. When a wheelchair is made out of titanium, it is lighter and stronger. (mean)

   When a wheelchair is made of titanium, it means being lighter and stronger.

F Read the text below and <u>underline</u> all of the gerund and infinitive phrases. Then, change the gerund or infinitive to the perfect form if appropriate.

Nathan Dearborn was proud of <u>being chosen</u> [*having been chosen*] for the wheelchair design team in his industrial design class. He recalled <u>seeing</u> [*having seen*] prototypes of several types of lightweight chairs, and Nathan was hoping <u>to be involved</u> in another groundbreaking innovation. When Professor Hadley interviewed him about his project preferences, Nathan couldn't deny <u>being</u> fascinated [*having been fascinated*] by racing wheelchairs at an early age. Seeing the Boston Marathon every spring had introduced him to marathon racers, and he had pursued that interest in <u>learning</u> more about the mechanical side of the sport. Now Professor Hadley was encouraging him to contribute his ideas to the new semester project.

■ EXPANSION IDEA

Exercise F

1. Have students write an e-mail to a friend in which they discuss a class project. Encourage them to use gerunds and infinitives in the perfect form, when appropriate.

   For example: *I was scared about having been chosen to narrate the play. I had been offered another part, but had turned that down.*

2. Have students exchange work with a partner. Tell them to make suggestions and corrections.
3. Call on a few volunteers to read their e-mails to the class.

G **PAIR WORK** Talk about different types of assistive technology that benefit people with disabilities. Use gerunds and infinitives in the passive voice whenever possible.

> How do people with a particular disability need **to be helped**?

> I think they need **to be given** more mobility and access. Too many places are hard to access by wheelchair.

PART TWO	Passive Voice in Other Complex Sentences

■ GRAMMAR IN CONTENT

A Reread the passage at the beginning of this lesson, and <u>underline</u> all other passive constructions. Then, find any examples of a passive verb that is followed by an infinitive or a *that* clause.

Passive Voice in Complex Sentences

Sample Sentences	Notes
The designers **have been authorized** to use the highest grade titanium for their projects. Barbara's design **is expected** to win a design award. She **was warned** that she might lose to Joe. Joe and Barbara **were informed** that she had won the top prize. **Was Joe told** that the award included a $1,000 prize?	Most **passive constructions** with complex complements follow one of two patterns: 1. Direct object + passive verb + infinitive 2. Indirect object + passive verb + *that* clause. In both cases, the object functions as the subject of the passive verb.
Barbara **was named** the winner of the competition. Although Barbara won, Joe **was made the** head of the research team. Barbara **wasn't elected** the team leader due to her poor leadership skills. Has a specific wheelchair design ever **been declared** the best design of that competition?	When using the passive in sentences with a direct object and an object complement, follow this pattern: Direct object + passive verb + object complement See Lessons 21, 23, and 25 for other complex passive structures. Verbs with direct objects and object complements in the passive include: *appoint, call, certify, choose, declare, elect, make, name,* and *vote*.

■ **EXPANSION IDEA**

Grammar

1. Divide the class into pairs and have them discuss something that is expected to occur, using the passive voice in complex sentences.

2. Circulate as students work and assist as needed.

■ COMMUNICATE

■ **EXERCISE G**

1. Call on a student to read the instructions aloud.
2. Call on two other students to read the text in the speech balloons.
3. Divide the class into pairs and have them discuss different sorts of assistive technology. Remind them to use gerunds and infinitives in the passive as often as possible.
4. Circulate as students work and assist as needed.

PART TWO

Passive Voice in Other Complex Sentences

■ GRAMMAR IN CONTENT

■ **EXERCISE A**

1. Ask students to complete the activity and then check their work with a partner.
2. Call on volunteers to read their underlined sentences to the class.

■ **GRAMMAR CHART**
Passive Voice in Complex Sentences

1. Ask students to read the sample sentences and Notes.
2. Go over the first section of the chart. Write on the board: *direct object + passive verb + infinitive.* Call on a volunteer to come to the board and write a sentence that follows this pattern.
3. Do the same thing with the pattern *indirect object + passive verb + that clause.*
4. Go over the second part of the chart. Write on the board *direct object + passive verb + object complement.* Call on a volunteer to come to the board and write a sentence that follows this pattern.

1. Go over the instructions and example with the class.
2. Have students complete the activity individually and then check their work with a partner.
3. Call on volunteers to read their answers to the class.

B Change the topic of the second sentence by using a passive construction.

1. Don Schoendorfer contacted his Chilean distribution agent Steve Colón about the new shipment of Free Wheelchair Mission wheelchairs. ~~Schoendorfer authorized Colón to pick up the container shipment at the warehouse.~~

   Colón was authorized to pick up the container shipment at the warehouse.

2. Schoendorfer didn't know about a problem in the shipment in Chile. ~~Colón notified Schoendorfer that some of the~~ wheelchair assembly kits were missing the instructions.

   Schoendorfer was notified that some of the . . .

3. Under normal circumstances the wheelchairs are shipped with illustrated instructions and assembly tools for local workers. ~~Schoendorfer expects the workers to assemble the wheelchairs for people.~~

   The workers are expected to assemble the wheelchairs for people.

4. The Free Wheelchair Mission depends on donations from churches and other groups. ~~Schoendorfer notified the donors that~~ the cost of each wheelchair was $44.40 including shipping.

   The donors were notified that . . .

5. Although many donors support the distribution of their wheelchairs, the Free Wheelchair Mission has many critics. ~~The availability of Schoendorfer's wheelchairs has not convinced other organizations that~~ such wheelchairs are actually good for people with disabilities.

   Other organizations have not been convinced that . . .

6. Critics agree with Schoendorfer's goal of making wheelchairs available, but they aren't sure that the chair really meets the medical needs of everyone who has one. ~~Schoendorfer's goal constrains it to be "one-size-fits-all."~~

   The chair is constrained to be "one size fits all."

7. When he travels around the world to monitor the program, people with disabilities always thank him for the dramatic change in their lives. As a result, ~~the response of wheelchair recipients has encouraged Schoendorfer to continue~~ with his mission.

   Schoendorfer has been urged to continue . . .

■ **EXPANSION IDEA**

Exercise B

1. Ask students to write a summary of the information in Exercise B, using passive constructions wherever possible.

2. Call on a few volunteers to read their summaries to the class.

CD2,TR14

C Listen to each conversation, and then (circle) the letter of the correct interpretation.

1. a. Sam persuaded Kirk to photograph the team.
   (b.) Kirk persuaded Sam to be photographed.
2. (a.) The coach allowed Kirk to interview Jeff.
   b. Jeff was allowed to be interviewed.
3. (a.) Kirk encouraged Sam to help Jeff with his equipment.
   b. Kirk was encouraged to help Jeff.
4. (a.) The coach prompted Sam to introduce Jeff to the others.
   b. Sam was prompted to be introduced to Jeff.
5. a. Sam expected Kirk to pass him the first ball of the game.
   (b.) Sam was expected to pass Kirk the first ball of the game.
6. a. Sam doesn't permit Kirk to check his wheelchair.
   (b.) Sam isn't permitted to check Kirk's wheelchair.
7. (a.) Only the coach is authorized to load the wheelchairs in the van.
   b. The coach has authorized only one person to load the wheelchairs in the van.
8. (a.) This season the coach made Kirk captain of the team.
   b. Next season Sam will be made captain.

■ **COMMUNICATE**

D **GROUP WORK** What devices have been invented or refined to increase our mobility? Discuss the design, purpose, and benefits of these inventions. Use gerunds and infinitives with passive constructions whenever possible.

Elevators **were invented** to help people get to the top of a high building.

What about escalators? They **are used** for going up just one or two levels.

Nowadays there are even moving sidewalks, especially at airports. They **might have been invented** for people who can't walk, but lots of people use them because they're tired or want to move more quickly.

■ **EXERCISE C**
CD 2, Track 14

1. Tell students that they will hear several short conversations.
2. Play the audio and have students listen for content only.
3. Play the audio again, this time pausing after each conversation so that students have time to circle the correct answers.
4. Call on volunteers to read their answers. If there is any disagreement among class members, play the audio again.

■ **COMMUNICATE**

■ **EXERCISE D**

1. Call on a student to read the instructions aloud.
2. Call on three other students to read the text in the speech balloons.
3. Divide the class into groups and have them discuss the different devices that have been developed to increase human mobility.
4. Circulate as students work and assist as needed.
5. Call on a member of each group to name the devices and write them on the board.

■ **EXPANSION IDEA**

Exercise D

1. Ask students to consider the pros and cons of having so many devices to increase our mobility.
2. Divide the class into pairs and have students discuss the positive and negative effects of these devices.

For example:
Student 1: *These devices were invented to make our lives easier.*

Student 2: *Yes, but their use is making people lazier and fatter.*

3. Hold a short class discussion about the topic.

Connection

Putting It Together

■ GRAMMAR AND VOCABULARY

1. Ask students to read the instructions.
2. Call on two students to read the topics aloud.
3. Ask students to choose one of the two topics and give them time to write their compositions. Tell them to review the Grammar Chart if they are uncertain about how to use sentences with gerunds and infinitives in the passive voice and other complex structures.

■ PROJECT

1. Ask students to review the instructions.
2. Answer any questions that students have about the project.
3. Call on students at the next class meeting to give their oral reports.

■ INTERNET

1. Call on a student to read the instructions.
2. Have students conduct their searches and then report to the class on the information they find about wheelchair sports teams.

GRAMMAR AND VOCABULARY Write a composition on one of the topics below. Use as many words as possible from the Content Vocabulary on page 177, and circle them in your composition. Use sentences with gerunds and infinitives in passive voice and other complex passive structures to express some of your ideas, and <u>underline</u> those sentences.

Topic 1: There are many people with disabilities who are not chosen to compete in the Olympic Games although they are excellent athletes. The Paralympics and Special Olympics provide an opportunity for those members of society to be selected for national teams. How do athletes with disabilities benefit from being included in world-class competition?

Topic 2: In previous generations, people with disabilities had little access to public facilities. In fact, they were not encouraged to participate in school or sports activities, and they were expected to stay home. Explain how the opportunities for people with disabilities have changed in your lifetime where you live.
Answers will vary.

PROJECT Interview at least one student on your campus about services available for students with disabilities. Find out the following information, and report on your findings at the next class meeting.

1. Are all of the buildings required to be built for wheelchair access?
2. In what other ways do students with disabilities have access to school facilities?

 INTERNET Go online to one of the university websites below and check out their wheelchair sports teams. Follow the links, and report to your class about (1) the sports that male wheelchair athletes can participate in and (2) the sports for female wheelchair athletes. Tell your classmates about other information you got from that part of the university's athletics website.

a. University of Illinois at Urbana-Champaign: www.uiuc.edu
b. University of Alabama: www.ua.edu
c. University of Texas-Arlington: www.uta.edu
d. University of Wisconsin-Whitewater: www.uww.edu
e. Edinboro University of Pennsylvania: www.edinboro.edu
f. University of Arizona: www.arizona.edu

If you prefer to investigate the world of wheelchair basketball, go to www.nwba.org, which is the website for the National Wheelchair Basketball Association. Then, give a brief oral report on the other opportunities for wheelchair basketball players.
Answers will vary.

■ EXPANSION IDEA

Internet

1. Have students perform online research on how wheelchair athletes train.

2. Divide the class into small groups and have them compare wheelchair training with typical athletic training.

PART 1
Restrictive vs. Nonrestrictive
Relative Clauses

PART 2
Reduced and Special
Nonrestrictive Relative Clauses

Lesson ⑱

History of Philosophy of Science

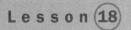

Lesson ⑱

Overview

1. Call on a volunteer to explain what a hypothesis is to the class.
2. Ask students if they are familiar with the scientific process (method). Hold a short discussion about the process, leading to proving or disproving a hypothesis.

■ CONTENT VOCABULARY

Look up the words below that you do not know and enter them in your vocabulary journal. Write each word's part of speech, a definition, and an example sentence. Try to include them in your discussion and writing below.

an artery	to determine	a hypothesis	a phenomenon
a blood vein	empiricism	to incorporate	to pursue
a breakthrough	a figure	logic	a substance

■ THINK ABOUT IT

During the 1500s and 1600s, many important inventions enabled scientists to discover and understand natural phenomena. Brainstorm 2–3 inventions from these centuries with a classmate.

In your writing journal, write for 5–10 minutes about the questions below. When you are finished, share your ideas with the class.
During the 1500s and 1600s, scientists changed the way that people understood the universe and our world. Some of these pioneers were Galileo, Isaac Newton, and Linnaeus. Do you know what any of these scientists were famous for? What were some important scientific ideas from this period?
Answers will vary.

■ CONTENT VOCABULARY

Ask students to review the words in the box. Tell them to look up any unfamiliar words.

■ VOCABULARY JOURNAL

Have students add new words to their vocabulary journals and write down the parts of speech, definitions, and sentences for each.

■ THINK ABOUT IT

1. Have students read the instructions.
2. Divide the class into pairs and have students discuss what they know about scientists of the 1500s and 1600s.
3. Call on volunteers to discuss scientific pioneers and their ideas.
4. Have students read the journal writing instructions. Answer any questions that they have about the topic. Then give them five minutes to write in their journals.
5. Have students share their journal entries with the class.

187

■ CONTENT NOTES

The topic of this lesson is History of Philosophy of Science. Students will learn about the scientific pioneers of the 1500s and 1600s and will acquire some of the vocabulary needed to discuss scientific research. Use this lesson to highlight the contributions that were made by scientists from a variety of cultures and countries.

PART ONE

Restrictive versus
Nonrestrictive Relative Clauses

■ GRAMMAR IN CONTENT

■ EXERCISE A
CD 2, Track 15

1. Ask students whether they know how the spread of Islam affected the development of science and mathematics, and where the compass, printing paper, and explosives were invented.

2. Have students read the title of the passage. Call on volunteers to suggest some ways in which the scientific revolution changed the way people analyzed the world.

3. Play the audio and have students follow along in their books as they listen. Ask students to circle any unfamiliar words or phrases.

4. Call on students to read their circled words and elicit definitions or explanations from volunteers if possible.

5. Check comprehension by asking questions such as the following: *Which centers of foreign learning were ahead of Western Europe at the end of the Middle Ages? What was science called? What did Tycho Brahe observe? What was Sir Isaac Newton's most famous experiment?*

■ GRAMMAR IN CONTENT

A   **Read and listen to the passage below. The words in bold are nonrestrictive relative clauses.**

CD2,TR15

The Scientific Revolution: New Ways to Analyze the World

During the sixteenth and seventeenth centuries, the Scientific Revolution, **which brought about a new understanding of the universe and the world of living things**, took place in Western Europe. When Europe emerged from the Middle Ages, other centers of learning in the world were far ahead. Muslim scientists and thinkers, **who had come in contact with the philosophy and science of the ancient Greeks during the expansion of Islam**, further developed many of their ideas on mathematics, astronomy, physics, alchemy, geography, astrology, and medicine. Then, during the 1300s scholars in Europe began translating the Arabic and Greek scientific writings into Latin, used exclusively for written works at European universities, to disseminate their discoveries. At approximately the same time, various Chinese inventions, such as printing, paper, explosives, and the compass, became available in Europe as a result of growing commercial contacts between Europe and Asia. The Chinese, **whose technical expertise was famous along the Silk Road**, provided the Europeans with tools and technology for their emergence from the Dark Ages.

Science, **which was called "natural philosophy" in those centuries**, expanded dramatically as men observed, measured, and experimented in new ways. For example, astronomers had begun to question the concept that Earth was the center of the universe and that the universe was finite and unchanging. The Danish astronomer Tycho Brahe, **who observed a comet beyond the moon in 1577**, demonstrated that the universe did indeed change. His precise observations of celestial, or heavenly, objects also enabled him to predict positions of the moon. Using Brahe's detailed information, Johannes Kepler determined not only that planets had elliptical orbits but also that their orbital speed depended on their distance from the sun. Other characteristics of the planets and their moons became observable with the invention of the telescope, **which Galileo used in his discoveries in the early seventeenth century**.

The study of natural philosophy became more sophisticated as researchers developed devices to measure phenomena more accurately. For instance, advances in astronomy relied heavily on improvements in the study of optics. As the quality of telescopes rose, astronomers could both see objects more clearly and measure angles in space. Another groundbreaking invention in this period was the air pump, **which resulted from the discovery that air has both weight and pressure**. With the invention of this instrument, researchers pursued the concept of a vacuum.

Finally, thanks to experimentation, scientists were able to demonstrate important properties of natural phenomena. Sir Isaac Newton, **who directed sunlight through a prism in his famous optical experiment**, was able to show that light is made up of various colors. Previously, people had believed that light was transformed into different colors. Magnetism, emerging as a completely new scientific field, resulted from William Gilbert's experiments. Thanks to his laboratory work on magnets and compass needles, new explanations of Earth's rotation and ocean tides became available.

The observations, measurements, and experiments performed by European natural philosophers paved the way for later scientists, such as Charles Coulomb, Antoine-Laurent Lavoisier, and Carl Linnaeus. Fields of study that had been born during the Scientific Revolution contributed to the birth of new sciences like chemistry or botany. With the dawning of the Age of Enlightenment, also known as the Age of Reason, in the eighteenth century, science gained an increasingly stronger impact on society, which has continued to the present day.

---

alchemy: a mystical philosophy that sought to understand how materials may be chemically combined

to disseminate: to spread, especially ideas and information

elliptical: in an oval shape

■ EXPANSION IDEA

Exercise A

Divide the class into small groups. Have students discuss what they learned from the reading. Encourage them to use vocabulary from the lesson.

Restrictive vs. Nonrestrictive Relative Clauses

Sample Sentences	Notes
The man who/that was the most famous astronomer at the beginning of the 1600s was Tycho Brahe.	Restrictive relative clauses identify and define a noun, making it more specific.
Kepler, who worked as Brahe's assistant, published a book in 1609.	Nonrestrictive clauses describe and add information about the noun. They give nonessential information about a noun that is unique or already clear from the context or situation. These nonrestrictive clauses modify proper nouns or definite proper nouns.
That book described Kepler's first important analysis, which involved the orbit of Mars.	
Kepler's work disputed the circular orbit of celestial bodies, which was the commonly held view up to this time.	
Brahe, whose data Kepler used in his analyses, did not share Kepler's views on Earth's role in the universe.	Use commas to separate any nonrestrictive clause from the main clause.
Galileo, with whom Kepler was in contact, had devised his first telescope with a concave eyepiece.	In conversation, English speakers pause slightly at the beginning and end of these clauses.
Also working in the field of optics, Kepler suggested using a convex lens in the eyepiece, which improved telescopes considerably.	Use only *who, whom, whose,* and *which* as relative pronouns in restrictive clauses.

B Read over your journal entry, and <u>underline</u> at least one sentence that you can revise to include a nonrestrictive relative clause. Write your revised sentence(s) below.

  Answers will vary.
  _____
  _____
  _____
  _____

■ GRAMMAR CHART
Restrictive versus Nonrestrictive Relative Clauses

1. Write on the board *The woman who discovered the element polonium was Marie Curie.*
2. Ask a volunteer to come to the board and underline the relative clause in the sentence.
3. Call on a volunteer to say whether the clause is *restrictive* or *nonrestrictive* and to explain why.
4. Have students review the sample sentences and Notes. Answer any questions that students have about nonrestrictive relative clauses.

■ EXERCISE B

1. Have students complete the exercise.
2. Ask students to exchange work with a partner. Have them look for additional places where sentences could be revised to include another nonrestrictive relative clause.

■ EXPANSION IDEA

Grammar

1. Tell students to write four simple sentences that contain no clauses, such as: *Maria isn't home.*
2. Have students exchange work with a partner. Then tell them to rewrite the sentence, including a nonrestrictive clause in each. They should include at least one clause that requires commas: *Maria, who is visiting from Hamburg, isn't home.*

EXERCISE C

1. Review the instructions and example with the class.
2. Have students complete the activity individually and then check their work with a partner.
3. Call on volunteers to read their answers aloud, saying *comma* when commas are needed.

C <u>Underline</u> all of the relative clauses in the sentences below, and add commas where appropriate.

1. Philosophers in ancient Greece gained their knowledge through logic, <u>which they used to understand the basic characteristics of objects</u>.

2. Natural philosophers considered the rules of correct thinking <u>which Aristotle and his followers had applied</u> to be inadequate for the complexity of natural phenomena <u>that they were discovering</u>.

3. During the Scientific Revolution researchers began to use inductive reasoning, <u>which bases hypotheses and theories on observation and experimental results</u>.

4. Francis Bacon, <u>who advocated empiricism</u>, felt that knowledge would grow the fastest if facts could be collected from observation and experiments.

5. According to Bacon, experiments <u>that show aspects of nature which we cannot observe</u> will lead to new knowledge to benefit humankind.

6. Advocates of "mechanical philosophy," <u>who believed that nature works like a machine</u>, focused their experiments on the motion of objects.

7. Having mastered the translated texts <u>which ancient Greek and Islamic mathematicians had written</u>, Europeans were able to solve problems in navigation engineering and even clock-making as they further developed mathematical analyses.

8. Europeans began to learn about the new scientific methods and knowledge in such books as John Wilkins's *A Discourse Concerning a New World & Another Planet*, <u>which was published in English in 1640</u>.

EXPANSION IDEA

Exercise C

1. Ask students to write a summary of what they learned in Exercise C. Instruct them to use as many relative clauses as possible in their writing.
2. Have students exchange work. Tell them to check for correct punctuation and suggest places where additional relative clauses might be included.
3. Call on a few volunteers to read their summaries to the class.

D (Circle) the letter of the correct interpretation of the sentences below.

1. European scientists who performed experiments on air pressure used the newly invented air pump.

    a.   All European scientists used the air pump.
    b.   Not all of the European scientists used the air pump.

2. Robert Boyle's early experiments, which focused on air pressure, led him to understand the relationship between air pressure and the volume of air.

    a.   All of Boyle's early experiments focused on air pressure.
    b.   Not all of his early experiments focused on air pressure.

3. Later scientists were influenced by Kepler's Law which explained the motions of all planets.

    a.   Kepler developed only one law.
    b.   Kepler developed more than one law.

4. In addition to his expertise in performing experiments, Robert Hooke is known for Hooke's Law, which explains the power of springs.

    a.   Hooke developed only one law.
    b.   Hooke developed more than one law.

5. Many important observations were made possible by the microscope, which was greatly improved as techniques of lens grinding were refined.

    a.   All microscopes improved in quality.
    b.   Only one particular microscope improved in quality.

6. The microscope which Robert Hooke used in his experiments had a mirror for added light.

    a.   Hooke's microscope had a mirror.
    b.   All microscopes had mirrors.

7. The Scientific Revolution came about due to the efforts of the natural philosophers, who incorporated observation, measurement, and experimentation in their work.

    a.   All natural philosophers used these methods.
    b.   Not all natural philosophers used these methods.

■ **EXERCISE D**

1. Ask students to review the instructions and example.
2. Call on a volunteer to explain why *b* is the correct answer.
3. Have students complete the activity individually and then have students correct their work in pairs.
4. Call on volunteers to read their answers. If any classmates disagree, go over the sentences. Have students read them, asking them to exaggerate a pause at the beginning and end of the relative clauses.

■ **EXPANSION IDEA**

Exercise D

1. Divide the class into pairs. Have students discuss how the sentences would have to be read and punctuated in order for the incorrect interpretations to be correct.

For example:
European scientists, who performed experiments on air pressure, used the newly invented air pump.

2. Circulate as students work; assist as needed.

1. Ask students to look at the picture and describe what they see.
2. Have students review the instructions and read the notes.
3. Call on a student to read the example.
4. Have students complete the summary sentences individually.
5. Call on volunteers to read their sentences.

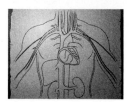

E Write a summary sentence from the class notes below about each of the men involved in the discovery of the circulation of blood in the human body. Use nonrestrictive relative clauses in your sentences.   Answers will vary.

Realdo Colombo (1510-1559): "pulmonary circulation"
   pulmonary vein: blood (not air!!!) from heart (right side) → lungs
   lungs → heart (left side) = blood is much brighter & redder

Girolami Fabrici (1533-1619): "valves in the veins"
   = blood only flows toward heart

William Harvey (1578-1657): "blood circulation"
   blood = maintains body organs, NOT for heat distribution
   heart contraction = only action: from heart → lungs → heart →
      arteries → veins → heart

Marcello Malpighi (1628-1694): saw capillaries that connect arteries and veins
   = one of most important microscope discoveries of century (= in 1661)

1. _Realdo Colombo, who did research on pulmonary circulation, discovered the purpose of the pulmonary vein._

2. Fabrici, who investigated valves in veins, discovered that blood only flows in the direction of the heart.

3. William Harvey, who lived from 1578–1657, determined that blood maintains the body's organs.

4. Marcello Malpighi, who made one of the most important microscope discoveries of the century, observed that capillaries connect arteries and veins in the human body.

■ **EXPANSION IDEA**

Exercise E

Have students use the following information to write a short composition about research into heredity. Tell them to use vocabulary and grammar from the lesson.

1745: Pierre Louis Moreau de Maupertuis → proposed an adaptationist account of organic design → assumed that animals somehow adapted to their environment

1859: Charles Darwin → published *Origin of the Species* → Maupertuis's theory was strengthened

1865: Gregory Mendel → published study about inherited traits → implied that traits are carried by distinct units, or genes

1869: Johann Friedrich Miescher → discovered DNA → suggested that it has a function in heredity

F Combine sentences (a) and (b) to create one sentence with a nonrestrictive relative clause.

1. a. European scientists experimented with material substances.
   b. They continued the work of medieval Islamic alchemists.

   European scientists, who experimented with material substances, continued the work of medieval Islamic alchemists.

2. a. Gerber was a famous eighth-century Persian alchemist.
   b. Gerber believed that matter had both visible and hidden qualities.

   Gerber, who was a famous 8th century alchemist, believed that matter had both visible and hidden qualities.

3. a. A magical "elixir" was known as "the Philosopher's Stone."
   b. This "elixir" was supposed to cure illnesses as well.

   This "elixir," which was also known as "the Philospher's Stone," was supposed to cure illnesses as well.

4. a. Paracelsus lived from 1493 to 1541.
   b. He pursued his work on chemical elements in the human body to cure illnesses.

   Paracelsus, who lived from 1493 to 1541, pursued his work on chemical elements in the human body to cure illnesses.

5. a. Alchemists believed that they could find the way to "grow" metals.
   b. They developed many alloys, or mixtures of metals, during their experiments.

   Alchemists, who believed that they could find a way to "grow" metals, developed many alloys, or mixtures of metals, during their experiments.

6. a. Isaac Newton's interest in alchemy lasted for 25 years.
   b. His work on attraction and repulsion was influenced by his work on the "active principles" of alchemy.

   Isaac Newton, whose work on attraction and repulsion was influenced by his work on the "active principles" of alchemy, remained interested in alchemy for 25 years.

7. a. Alchemy was sometimes condemned by the Catholic Church.
   b. It was encouraged by many European rulers.

   Alchemy, which was encouraged by many European rulers, was sometimes condemned by the Catholic Church.

■ **EXERCISE F**

1. Write the following on the board:
   Women were not allowed to study at universities.
   They got their educations in convents.
2. Call on a volunteer to come to the board and combine the sentences using a nonrestrictive clause.
   (Women, who were not allowed to study in universities, got their educations in convents.)
3. Have students read the instructions.
4. Call on a student to read the example.
5. Ask students to complete the activity individually.
6. Call on volunteers to read their answers aloud. If any class members combined the sentences differently, have them read their answers.

■ **EXPANSION IDEA**

Exercise F
1. Divide the class into pairs.
2. Ask students to try rewriting the work they did in Exercise F.

   For example:
   Alchemy, which was sometimes condemned by the Catholic Church, was encouraged by many European rulers.

   → *Alchemy, which was encouraged by many European rulers, was sometimes condemned by the Catholic Church.*

3. Have them take turns reading the sentences, pausing before and after each comma. Ask them to discuss if the two versions of the sentences have the same meaning.

■ EXERCISE G

1. Call on a student to read the instructions aloud.
2. Call on another student to read the text in the speech balloon.
3. Divide the class into small groups and have them discuss important scientists and other thinkers from their cultures.
4. Call on a few volunteers who learned something new and interesting to share it with the class.

PART TWO

Reduced and Special Nonrestrictive Relative Clauses

■ GRAMMAR IN CONTENT

■ EXERCISE A

1. Ask students to complete the activity and then check their work with a partner.
2. Call on volunteers to read their underlined sentences to the class.

■ GRAMMAR CHART
Nonrestrictive Relative Clauses

1. Ask students to read the sample sentences and the Notes.
2. Answer any questions that students have about word order and punctuation.

G GROUP WORK Share information about important scientists and other thinkers from your culture who have contributed to the growth of knowledge about our world. Use nonrestrictive relative clauses whenever possible.

> Al-Khwarizmi, **whose Latinized name is Alghorismus,** worked on square roots and complex fractions.

PART TWO	Reduced and Special Nonrestrictive Relative Clauses

■ GRAMMAR IN CONTENT

A Reread the text at the beginning of the lesson, and <u>underline</u> examples of phrases or clauses that have been separated from the main clause by commas. Do not underline adverbials, examples, or connectors.

Nonrestrictive Relative Clauses

Sample Sentences	Notes
Advocates of mechanical philosophy, **who believed** that the world worked like a machine, investigated motion. Advocates of mechanical philosophy, **believing** that the world worked like a machine, investigated motion. Advances in science depended to a great extent on the microscope, **which was used** to unlock many secrets of nature. Advances in science depended to a great extent on the microscope, **used** to unlock many secrets of nature.	Like restrictive relative clauses, nonrestrictive relative clauses can also be reduced. Make the following changes: • Omit the relative pronouns *who* or *which* when they function as subjects in the relative clause. • Omit any auxiliary verbs. • Use **the present participle** for active verbs and **the past participle** for passive verbs. Use commas to separate any nonrestrictive phrase from the main clause. Use the context of the sentence to understand the time of the verb in the phrase.
Natural philosophers advocated observing and experimenting, **which** was a major change in the way that people understood natural phenomena. The mathematical concept of zero was frightening to ancient people, **which** surprises many people today.	Use a nonrestrictive clause to comment on the information in the entire preceding main clause. This kind of clause • always comes at the end of the sentence • is always separated from the main clause by a comma • always begins with *which*

■ EXPANSION IDEA

Grammar
1. Ask students to write two sentences with reduced relative clauses.

2. Call on volunteers to read their sentences to the class.

B Reduce the relative clauses if possible and add commas where necessary.

1. Christiaan Huygens, ~~who worked~~ *working* on mechanics, invented the pendulum clock and then improved it in 1673.

2. In the early 1600s, telescopes, ~~which provided~~ *providing* magnification up to 15 diameters at that time, made the discovery of distant celestial bodies possible.

3. During the late 1600s, the lenses of microscopes, ~~which were~~ ground to a much finer quality than ever before, enabled scientists to examine cells in plants and animals.

4. Robert Hooke is credited with the invention of the universal joint, with which a machine can combine rotary motion and movement in different directions.

5. The air pump that von Guericke experimented with in the seventeenth century couldn't produce a total vacuum.

6. Galileo's first thermometer, ~~which dates~~ *dating* to the late 1500s, was a glass bulb with water inside.

7. The instrument ~~which was~~ invented by Islamic scientists to distill liquids is called a retort.

8. Scientists who studied electricity could store energy in Leyden jars, which consisted of a glass jar with metallic foil inside and outside and a wire which passed through the opening in contact with the inside foil.

9. Blaise Pascal's experiments on air pressure, which involved instruments with tubes of mercury, led to the invention of the barometer.

■ **EXERCISE B**

1. Ask students to read the instructions.
2. Call on a volunteer to read the example and explain what has been done to reduce the relative clause.
3. Have students complete the activity individually and then check the answers in pairs.
4. Call on volunteers to read their answers aloud.

■ **EXPANSION IDEA**

Exercise B

1. Ask students to try to reduce the relative clauses in three of the sentences in Exercise F on page 193.

2. Call on volunteers to write their answers on the board.
3. Discuss the sentences as a class.

For example:
European scientists, experimenting with material substances, continued the work of medieval Islamic alchemists.

1. Go over the instructions with the class.
2. Call on a student to read the example.
3. Have students complete the activity individually.

C Edit each text, reducing one of the nonrestrictive relative clauses in each text to a phrase. Follow the example. <u>Underline</u> any other relative clauses that you could reduce.

> 1. Learning from Greek texts, Arab mathematicians made significant progress in algebra, ~~which is~~ derived from the Arabic word *al-jaber*. The Arab world provided Europe not only with their understanding of algebra but also with Arabic numerals, ~~which are~~ used in mathematics today. However, these numbers, which took the place of Roman and Greek numerals, were not used in the first algebraic equations. Instead, Arab mathematicians wrote words, <u>which may seem surprising since they already had the numeric symbols.</u>

> 2. For ancient people, zero was a number that did not function like other numbers, <u>which put it into a troublesome category.</u> It represented emptiness, ^signifying^ ~~which signified~~ chaos and darkness to the ancients. The Greeks learned about zero from the Babylonians, whose texts show that zero had the function of a placeholder. It wasn't until the 1600s that zero was commonly used.

> 3. Warfare in the sixteenth and seventeenth centuries, which depended greatly on cannonballs and other projectiles, benefited from a better understanding of both natural and violent motion. Niccolo Tartaglia, ^experimenting^ ~~who experimented~~ with the angles of cannons and the weights of cannonballs, performed experiments on types of motion. Consequently, he was able to predict the most effective position for such armaments, <u>which led to more death and destruction.</u>

■ **EXPANSION IDEA**

Exercise C

1. Have students reduce to a phrase one more nonrestrictive relative clause in each of the texts.
2. Have students compare their work with a partner.
3. Call on volunteers to read their answers aloud. Try to cover all of the possible answers in each of the texts.

CD2, TR16

D Listen for Professor Jensen's comments about information she presents during a science class. Use the verb indicated, as in the example, to paraphrase her comments.

1. suspect: *She suspects that students will think it is strange to learn about the people behind the ideas.*

2. consider: **She considers going to prison a high price for discovering a fact.**

3. realize: **She realizes that many people get confused by the name of the Physics Dept.**

4. mention: **She mentions that many people don't think of Spain when they hear "Islamic" in this historical context.**

5. expect: **She expects the students to study for this class every day.**

E There are four errors in the e-mail message below. Find and correct all four errors. (The commas for one clause count as one error.)

Jill-

Have you ever taken a course in the History of Philosophy? Or the History of Science? The Philosophy Department, ~~that is~~ *which is* supposed to be one of the best in the country, offers an intro class, that I'm thinking about taking. Do you know anything about Professor Jensen? I heard that she's tough. My advisor who has always pushed me toward these kinds of courses, thinks that I can handle it. I really don't mind a lot of reading and I'd rather write papers than take exams, ~~what~~ *which* means that I guess I'd enjoy the class. Maybe it's a good idea to talk to Jensen before I register. Any thoughts?

N.

■ **COMMUNICATE**

F **GROUP WORK** Discuss the importance of learning about the people behind the history of science and philosophy. Should students have to learn about the people behind great scientific breakthroughs? Give some examples to support your opinion.

 When I take a math or science course, I don't see the point of learning about the people involved in those fields.

 But don't you think that it's interesting or important to know that Al-Khwarizmi, who is known as the "Father of Algebra," was Persian—or that Liu Hui, who lived in China round 300 BCE, found the approximate value of pi?

■ **EXERCISE D**
CD 2, Track 16

1. Tell students that they will hear comments about information presented during a science class.

2. Have them read the example and the words *consider, realize, mention, expect.*

3. Play the audio, telling students to listen for content only.

4. Play the audio again, this time asking students to take notes using the verbs indicated.

5. Play the audio again so that students can check their work.

6. Call on volunteers to read their answers aloud. If there is any disagreement, play the audio again so that students can determine the correct answer.

■ **EXERCISE E**

1. Tell students to find and correct the four errors in the e-mail.

2. Call on volunteers to read the e-mail, one sentence at a time, aloud.

■ **COMMUNICATE**

■ **EXERCISE F**

1. Call on a student to read the instructions aloud.

2. Call on two students to read the text in the speech balloons.

3. Divide the class into small groups and have them discuss the importance of learning about the people behind the history of science and philosophy.

4. Call on a few volunteers to give some examples of people who were behind scientific breakthroughs and whom students should have to learn about.

■ **EXPANSION IDEA**

Exercise F
Ask students to write a short composition about the importance of learning about the people behind the history of science and philosophy. Tell them to be sure to use the grammar and vocabulary learned in the lesson and to use specific examples.

Connection

Putting It Together

■ GRAMMAR AND VOCABULARY

1. Ask students to read the instructions.
2. Call on two students to read the topics aloud.
3. Ask students to choose one of the two topics and give them time to write their compositions.

■ PROJECT

1. Ask students to review the instructions.
2. Answer any questions that students have about the project.
3. Call on students at the next class meeting to give their oral reports.

■ INTERNET

1. Call on a student to read the instructions.
2. Have students conduct their searches and take a quiz.
3. Ask students to report back to the class about their quiz results.

GRAMMAR AND VOCABULARY Write a composition on one of the topics below. Use as many words as possible from the Content Vocabulary on page 187, and (circle) them in your composition. Use sentences with nonrestrictive and restrictive relative clauses to express some of your ideas, and underline those sentences.

Topic 1: Throughout the centuries scientists have made discoveries that contradict people's perceptions of the world and religious teachings. This happened during the Scientific Revolution, and it is happening today. What is the responsibility of the scientists when their work goes against society's ethical, religious, or moral values? Use concrete examples in your writing.

Topic 2: Do people respect scientists and their work? What is the perception of scientists in popular culture, for example, in movies and on TV? How do the media treat scientists in your culture? Use concrete examples in your writing.
Answers will vary.

PROJECT Interview at least one student on your campus about his or her knowledge about prominent individuals from the history of science. Find out the following information, and report on it at your next class meeting.

1. Ask your interviewee about four to five of the scientists mentioned in this lesson. Report on how much information your interviewee knew about each one.
2. Ask how important it is to know about the scientists who made significant discoveries. If your interviewee thinks that it is important, find out why.

 INTERNET Go online and use the search phrase "science quizzes" to find a website that has quizzes on various branches of science. Select at least one quiz, and take it. Report orally on your quiz results at your next class meeting.
Answers will vary.

■ EXPANSION IDEA

Project

1. Ask students to write a short report about the results of their interviews. Tell them to be sure to use the grammar and vocabulary learned in the lesson.

2. Have students exchange work with a partner. Ask them to correct errors, make suggestions, and point out where additional reduced and nonrestrictive relative clauses might be used.

Lesson 19

Marketing: Packaging Strategies

■ CONTENT VOCABULARY

Look up the words below that you do not know and enter them in your vocabulary journal. Write each word's part of speech, a definition, and an example sentence. Try to include them in your discussion and writing below.

to allot	a coupon	to launch	to reseal
to appeal to	to display	loyalty	to tamper with
a commodity	glass-blowing	perishable	a wrapper

■ THINK ABOUT IT

What products do you know that are well packaged? What are the characteristics of an effective package for any kind of product? Discuss your ideas with a classmate.

In your writing journal, write for five minutes about the questions below. When you are finished, share what you wrote with the class.
Of the items that you normally buy, which one has the most effective packaging? What do you like about the container? What kind of information do you think an effective package should include?
Answers will vary.

199

■ CONTENT NOTES

The topic of this lesson is Marketing: Packaging Strategies. Students will learn about how packaging influences purchasing. They will acquire the vocabulary needed to discuss how packaging has evolved and differs from culture to culture. You can use this lesson to encourage students to recycle by pointing out how much of North American packaging can be reused.

Lesson 19

Overview

1. Divide the class into groups and have students discuss what they look for when they select a new product. Have them make a list that is sorted in order of importance to them.
2. Call on a member of each group to read the list to the class.

■ CONTENT VOCABULARY

Ask students to review the words in the box. Tell them to look up any unfamiliar words.

■ VOCABULARY JOURNAL

Have students add new words to their vocabulary journals and write down the parts of speech, definitions, and sentences for each.

■ THINK ABOUT IT

1. Have students read the instructions.
2. Divide the class into pairs and have students discuss the characteristics of effective packaging.
3. Poll the class to see which characteristic is the most important.
4. Have students read the journal writing instructions. Answer any questions they have about the topic. Then give them five minutes to write in their journals.
5. Have students share their journal entries with the class.

■ **GRAMMAR IN CONTENT**

■ **EXERCISE A** 🎧
CD 2, Track 17

1. Ask students to read the title of the article. Call on a few volunteers to give their interpretations of the meaning of "Old Friends and New Temptations." Have them relate this to their own purchasing habits.

2. Play the audio and have students follow along in their books as they listen. Ask students to circle any unfamiliar words or phrases.

3. Call on students to read their circled words and elicit definitions or explanations from volunteers if possible.

4. Check comprehension by asking questions such as the following: *What are some of the ways in which shoppers have been prepared for the shopping experience? Why does the author say "Packaging is the temptation"? What are some of the things that a shopper considers when he or she looks at a product? Why do many people choose not to wear their glasses when they go shopping?*

■ **GRAMMAR IN CONTENT**

🎧 **A** **Read and listen to the passage below. The words in bold are relative adverbial clauses.**

CD2,TR17

Old Friends and New Temptations

For manufacturers, packaging is the crucial final payoff to a marketing campaign. Sophisticated packaging is one of the chief ways people find the confidence to buy. It can also give a powerful image to products and commodities that are in themselves characterless. In many cases, the shopper has been prepared for the shopping experience by lush, colorful print advertisements, thirty-second television mini-dramas, radio jingles, and coupon promotions. But the package makes the final sales pitch, seals the commitment, and gets itself placed in the shopping cart. Advertising leads consumers into temptation. Packaging *is* the temptation. In many cases it is **what makes the product possible**.

You put the package into your cart, or not, usually without really having focused on the particular product or its many alternatives. But sometimes you do examine the package. You read the label carefully, looking at what the product promises, what it contains, what it warns. You might even look at the package itself and judge whether it will, for example, reseal to keep a product fresh. You might consider **how a cosmetic container will look on your dressing table**, or you might think about whether someone might have tampered with it or whether it can be easily recycled. The possibility of such scrutiny is one of the things that make each detail of the package so important.

With its thousands of images and messages, the supermarket is as visually dense, if not as beautiful, as a Gothic cathedral. It is as complex and as predatory as a tropical rain forest. It is more than a person can possibly take in during an ordinary half-hour shopping trip. No wonder a significant percentage of people who need to wear eyeglasses don't wear them when they're shopping, and some researchers have spoken of the trancelike state that pushing a cart through this environment induces. The paradox here is that the visual intensity that overwhelms shoppers is precisely the thing that makes the design of packages so crucial. Just because you're not looking at a package doesn't mean you don't see it. Most of the time, you see far more than a container and a label. You see a personality, an attitude toward life, perhaps even a set of beliefs.

The shopper's encounter with the product on the shelf is, however, only the beginning of the emotional life cycle of the package. The package is very important in the moment **when the shopper recognizes it either as an old friend or a new temptation**. Once the product is brought home, the package seems to disappear, as the quality or usefulness of the product it contains becomes paramount. But in fact, many packages are still selling even at home, enticing those who have bought them to take them out of the cupboard, the closet, or the refrigerator and consume their contents. Then once the product has been used up, and the package is empty, it becomes suddenly visible once more. This time, though, it is trash that must be discarded or recycled. This instant of disposal is the time **when people are most aware of packages**. It is a negative moment, like the end of a love affair, and what's left seems to be a horrid waste.

a payoff: a reward or final result
a jingle: a short song used for advertising purposes
predatory: dangerous, threatening

a trance: a state between being asleep and being awake; being semiconscious
a paradox: a contradictory statement or situation
paramount: of great importance or concern

■ **EXPANSION IDEA**

Exercise A
Divide the class into small groups. Have students discuss how shopping in a large American grocery store is similar to or different from shopping in their home countries. Encourage them to use vocabulary from the lesson.

Relative Adverbial Clauses

Sample Sentences	Notes
Spring is the time **when some packaging changes to lighter colors.**	Adverbial clauses that specify a time, a location, or a reason usually follow one of the patterns below.
Marketers hope that their new products will be in places **where shoppers see them immediately.**	**Pattern 1:** head noun + relative adverb + rest of clause
	Generally, relative clauses of this type are restrictive, so there is no comma.
Shoppers may not be able to say the reason **why they choose a particular product** except that it looks attractive.	In formal usage, prepositional phrases are often used instead of relative adverbs: *Shoppers may not be able to say the reason **for which** they chose a product.*
I remember the time when I bought some perfume just because I liked the bottle. I can't remember the place where I bought it. Now I laugh about the reason why I bought it.	English speakers commonly delete some words in the next type of relative clause.
	Pattern 2: head noun + rest of clause
Do you know **when** that perfume first came on the market?	**Pattern 3:** relative adverb + rest of clause
Have you got any idea **where** I can get some more?	
Have you ever visited **the French factory** where that perfume is bottled?	Don't delete the head noun if it includes **important information.**
I've never thought about the way in which perfume is bottled.	The *wh-* word *how* does not function exactly like *when, where, why:* • **Pattern 1** does not apply: *how* can't modify the head noun *the way*
The way expensive perfumes are packaged adds to their value.	• **Pattern 2** applies: the way ~~in which~~ we met / the way we met
Since expensive perfumes still come in glass bottles, how they package it must be important to shoppers.	• **Pattern 3** applies: ~~the way in which~~ we met / how we met

B Read over your journal entry, and <u>underline</u> at least one sentence that you can revise to include a relative adverbial clause. Write your revised sentence(s) below.

Answers will vary.

_____

_____

_____

■ GRAMMAR CHART
Relative Adverbial Clauses
1. Write on the board *I go home when I want a good meal.*
2. Ask a volunteer to come to the board and underline the adverbial clause in the sentence.
3. Call on a volunteer to say whether the clause is *restrictive* or *nonrestrictive* and to explain why.
4. Have students review the sample sentences and Notes. Answer any questions that students have about relative adverbial clauses.

■ EXERCISE B
1. Have students complete the exercise.
2. Ask students to exchange work with a partner. Have them look for additional places where sentences could be revised to include another relative adverbial clause.

■ EXPANSION IDEA

Grammar
1. Ask students to write the beginning of five sentences.

   For example:
   Ecuador is . . .
   My father never understood . . .

2. Have students exchange sentences with a partner. Partners should finish the sentences using relative adverbial clauses.
3. Call on volunteers to read their sentences to the class.

EXERCISE C

1. Ask students to review the instructions.
2. Call on a student to read the first two sentences of question 1. Then ask the students to suggest how to change the final sentence.
3. Have students complete the activity individually and then check their work with a partner.
4. Call on volunteers to read their answers aloud.

EXERCISE D

1. Ask students to read the instructions and the example.
2. Have students complete the activity individually. Encourage students to be creative.
3. Call on a few volunteers to read their memos to the class.

C Edit the texts below so that there is a variety of relative adverbial clauses.

1. In former times glass containers were very precious, and only valuable commodities such as perfume were packaged in glass. The scarcity of glass was the reason ~~why~~ the containers were so expensive. The island of Murano near Venice is the place where glassblowers practiced their craft.
2. The way ~~that~~ Europeans produced glass in those days was not their invention, but the invention of people in the eastern Mediterranean. The extensive experience of these people with glass production explains ~~the reason~~ why the blowpipe was invented there in Sidon, Phoenicia, about 100 BCE. This is the place ~~where~~ glassmaking had started sometime before 3000 BCE.
3. Glassblowing continued in Sidon until 1200 CE, and certainly, glass containers from there came to the attention of Europeans. This is ~~the region~~ where the Europeans fought during the Crusades in the eleventh to the thirteenth centuries. Their presence in the eastern Mediterranean clarifies the way ~~that~~ they came in contact with these valuable objects.
4. Once glassworkers began producing glass in Murano, the Italians maintained a monopoly on its production. Indeed, the glassworkers were not permitted to leave ~~the island~~ where they worked. For centuries they successfully guarded the secrets of the way ~~that~~ glass was blown. However, by the sixteenth century other glassblowers were practicing their craft in France, where the demand for bottles for wine was high.

D Using the clue in parentheses, complete each sentence with a relative adverbial clause.

TO: All distributors of *Luxor*
FROM: Stephanie Dunn, Marketing Manager
RE: Marketing Campaign for *Luxor*

You can expect to receive the first shipment of *Luxor* within the next two weeks. Please let us know (time) _when it arrives_ (1), so that we can put advertisements in your local newspaper. According to our agreement, you should put 5–6 bottles (location) __where they can be seen easily__ (2) so that window-shoppers will see that the perfume is actually in stock. (manner) __How you arrange the bottles__ (3) is your decision since you have professional window-dressers on your staff. We have confidence that you will display *Luxor* as attractively as you have handled our other perfumes. When customers purchase a bottle of *Luxor*, please ask them to fill out the enclosed survey so that we can know (reason) __why they decided to try our new perfume__ (4). That information will be of great help to our Product Development team. Finally, with regard to Ms. Nicole Babineaux's visit to your boutique, we will inform you (time) __when she will come by__ (5) and expect you to publicize the event.

EXPANSION IDEA

Exercise D

1. Divide the class into pairs.
2. Tell students that they will role-play a conversation between Stephanie Dunn and a Luxor distributor. Remind them to use a variety of relative adverbial clauses in their conversations.

For example:
Ms. Dunn: *Where did you put the bottles? They aren't visible from outside.*
Distributor: *I put them next to the register, where everyone can see them.*
Ms. Dunn: *That is not the way expensive perfume should be displayed.*

2. Call on a few volunteers to role-play their conversations for the class.

E Using relative adverbial clauses, write guidelines for displaying your new perfume.

1. The large display bottle must be ___*where the light will shine directly on it.*___

2. The two enclosed photo displays should be on countertops __where customers will see them right away.__

3. Your employee who will hand out samples to customers ought to stand __where the customers enter the store.__

4. The special decorative boxes for the large-sized bottles would look especially nice __where people are standing in line to pay.__

5. The coupons for special gift sets of perfume can be __where other coupons are displayed.__

F Explain the reason for the type of packaging of the grocery items below.

1. Eggs are very fragile, and ___*that is why each egg has to be protected by the carton.*___

2. People enjoy soft drinks in many different locations and circumstances, and __that's why six-packs are so convenient.__

3. It's hard to keep coffee or other ground foods fresh, so __that's why vacuum-packed bags are so practical.__

4. Ramen noodles make a quick, easy snack, and __has thin, distinctive packaging that makes the noodles easily accessible and affordable.__

5. Toothpaste has a thick consistency, so __that's why a tube is the best kind of packaging for this kind of product.__

G Complete the sentences to explain the packaging for the items below.

1. Breakfast cereals usually come in a sealed plastic bag inside a cardboard box, and ___*that's how they stay crisp.*___

2. Most over-the-counter, or nonprescription, medicines have a safety seal around the lid because __that's how to prevent children from getting into them.__

3. Strawberries usually come in little pint cartons, and __that's usually the amount people want to buy at a time.__

4. Frozen vegetables are usually packaged in paper boxes because __that's how to keep them fresh.__

EXERCISE E

1. Have students read the instructions.
2. Call on a student to read the example. Then ask a few volunteers to supply their own relative adverbial clauses to finish the sentence.
3. Have students complete the exercise on their own. Encourage them to be creative.
4. Call on volunteers to read their answers to the class.

EXERCISE F

1. Ask students to read the instructions and the example.
2. Have students complete the exercise on their own.
3. Call on volunteers to read their answers to the class.

EXERCISE G

1. Ask students to read the instructions and the example.
2. Have students complete the exercise on their own.
3. Call on volunteers to read their answers to the class.

EXPANSION IDEA

Exercises E–G

1. Have students work with a partner.
2. Instruct them to pick a product that they will package and advertise.
3. Have them design their package and write a short advertisement using as many relative adverbial clauses as possible.
4. Call on students to present their products to the class.
5. Poll the class on which advertisement was most convincing.

■ EXERCISE H

1. Call on a student to read the instructions aloud.
2. Call on two students to read the text in the speech balloons.
3. Divide the class into pairs and have students discuss packaging and in-store locations of various items in different countries. Encourage them to use vocabulary and grammar from the lesson.
4. Call on a few volunteers who learned something new and interesting to share it with the class.

PART TWO

Noun Clauses

■ GRAMMAR IN CONTENT

■ EXERCISE A

1. Ask students to complete the activity and then check their work with a partner.
2. Call on volunteers to read their underlined sentences to the class.

■ GRAMMAR CHART

Noun Clauses with Wh- *Words*

1. Write on the board *How do they know how much to spend?*
2. Call on a volunteer to underline the noun clause.
3. Have students read the sample sentences and Notes.
4. Answer any questions students have about noun clauses with *wh-* words and *how.*

H **PAIR WORK** Share information about the packaging and store location of various items in different countries. Include relative adverbial clauses whenever possible.

> In Cameroon, where I'm from, bread is sold on the street. We buy it **the way you do in bakeries**—without any plastic wrapper.

> It's the same in Albania, but you can find bread in a grocery store, too. It's usually **where the other baked goods are.**

PART TWO	Noun Clauses

■ GRAMMAR IN CONTENT

A Reread the text at the beginning of this lesson, and <u>underline</u> clauses that are introduced by *wh-* words other than *when, where, why,* and *how.*

Noun Clauses with *Wh-* Words	
Sample Sentences	**Notes**
Producers have to consider **how much** the packaging adds to the price of the item. Managers should also check **how far** related items, such as flour and sugar, are from each other. Managers usually decide **whether** seasonal items should be displayed at the front of the store.	Like the relative adverbial clauses with *when, where, why,* and *how,* these *wh-* words introduce noun clauses: *how much/many* *how often* *how far* *how long* *how* + Adjective or Adverb *whether (or not)* *what* *which* *who*
How do they figure out **what** the customers find attractive about the products?	Only use a question mark at the end of the sentence if the main clause is in the form of a question. Noun clauses must be phrased as statements.
Whether the item appeals to teenage girls determines the colors of the packaging. Designers need to check **whether the colors on a package are appropriate in other cultures.**	These clauses function as: • **Subjects** • **Complements** • **Direct Objects** • **Objects of Prepositions**

■ EXPANSION IDEA

Grammar

1. Divide the class into pairs.
2. Tell students to role-play two commuters waiting for a train that is late.

For example:
Student 1: *Have you heard any news about why the train is late?*
Student 2: *There was an announcement a while ago, but*

I couldn't understand what the speaker was saying.

Student 1: *I really don't know how long I can wait here. I'm going to be late for an important meeting.*

3. Call on a few pairs of volunteers to role-play their dialogs for the class.

B Revise each sentence, using a noun clause in place of the underlined noun phrase.

What a container looks like

1. ~~The appearance of a container~~ can catch a customer's eye.
   ˄

   how much the luxury items cost.
2. Elegant packaging can contribute to <u>the price of luxury items.</u>

   how long perishable items stay on the shelf.
3. The appropriate packaging can affect <u>the length of time that perishable items can</u>

   <u>stay on the shelf.</u>

   whether a shopper will buy a new product.
4. An eye-catching package may influence <u>a shopper's decision on buying a</u>

   <u>new product.</u>

   which product to choose
5. When shoppers are undecided about <u>the choice between products,</u> the design of the

   label may be the deciding factor.

   who will receive gift boxes
6. Designers also have to think about <u>the recipients of gift boxes</u> when they select

   colors and sizes.

   how frequently customers use a certain product
7. Companies did research on <u>customers' frequent use of certain food items like cheese</u>

   and realized that resealable bags would make their products more convenient and,

   therefore, more attractive.

8. Snack food companies have taken advantage of Americans' diet-consciousness and

   how many cookies are in some packages

   reduced <u>the number of cookies or crackers in some packages</u> so that people wouldn't

   feel guilty about buying them.

9. When a company wants to launch a new product, they have to take into

   how loyal customers are to a competing brand.

   consideration <u>customers' loyalty to a competing brand.</u>

   What ads and pretty labels promise   **what people expect of a product.**
10. <u>The promises of advertising and pretty labels</u> play a role in <u>people's expectations of</u>

    <u>a product.</u>

■ **EXERCISE B**

1. Ask students to read the instructions.
2. Call on a student to read the example.
3. Have students complete the activity individually. Then have them check their work with a partner.
4. Call on volunteers to read their answers to the class.

■ **EXPANSION IDEA**

Exercise B

1. Write the following sentences on the board:

   I don't know who is it.
   How does she know what do they want?
   He recommended that we should to stay in the car.
   I'm not sure who are they.
   What he did say?

2. Have students correct the errors.
3. Call on volunteers to read the corrected sentences aloud.

EXERCISE C

1. Ask students to review the adjectives in the box. Call on volunteers to define any of them which are unfamiliar to any class members.

2. Call on a student to read the example. Answer any questions that students have about the exercise.

3. Have students complete the activity individually. Then have them check their work with a partner.

4. Call on volunteers to read their answers to the class.

C Complete each sentence with a noun clause using an adjective in the box below. Follow the example. Answers will vary. Note: Not all noun clauses in the box will be used.

tamper-proof	colorful	protective	rigid/flexible
shatter-proof	recyclable	stackable	aseptic
lightweight	permeable	durable	fresh

1. Package designers need to think about _how well the packaging can be recycled._

2. Superior Egg Company has been pleased with _how well their cartons protect their eggs from being broken._

3. Some items remain on the grocery shelves for months and months, so manufacturers have to think about _whether the packaging will keep their items safe._

4. Some perishable items are flown to overseas markets; consequently, producers pay close attention to _whether the packaging will protect the items during transport._

5. Containers for medicines can be difficult for some people to open, but manufacturers have to be very careful about _how easily someone can tamper with packaging._

6. Store managers are pleased with _how difficult it is to shatter some containers_ because they have fewer broken jars and bottles to clean up in the store aisles.

7. Grocery stores allot each product or food item a particular amount of space, so the actual amount of any product on a shelf depends on _how many items can be stacked on top of each other._

8. Some fruit and vegetable products are sold in transparent containers because customers like to be sure of _how fresh the items look._

EXPANSION IDEA

Exercise C

1. Divide the class into small groups. Have members of each group discuss how they answered each of the questions. Answers will vary substantially, so group members should be sure that sentences are logical and have the correct word order.

2. Circulate as students work; assist as needed.

D Listen to the press briefing by Marlene Bigelow, the spokesperson for Lambton Foods and for their product "FruityBites," and answer the comprehension questions using relative adverbial clauses or noun clauses.

CD2,TR18

1. What did parents complain about when the first snack came out?

   They complained about how much sugar the snack contained.

2. What was Lambton Foods unsure about?

   Whether parents would try their snacks again.

3. Aside from a new recipe, what other change did Lambton Foods make?

   How they packaged the snacks.

4. What does Marlene Bigelow explain to the first reporter?

   Why each snack is wrapped in plastic.

5. What does Sue Green ask about?

   Whether it's really necessary to add to our nation's garbage with more plastic.

6. What information does Marlene Bigelow give about the plastic wrappers?

   How the wrappers are made.

7. What is the last information that Bigelow gives the reporters?

   When the snacks will be available in stores.

■ C O M M U N I C A T E

E **GROUP WORK** Create a dialog between a packaging designer and the manufacturer of an innovative toothbrush. They should discuss an eye-catching design for the new product. In your dialog use as many noun clauses as possible. When all of the groups are finished, each group can perform their dialog while the other teams listen and identify all of the noun clauses.

---

1. Tell students that they will hear a press briefing about a new product.
2. Have students read through the list of questions.
3. Play the audio and have students listen for comprehension only.
4. Play the audio again, this time telling students to take notes so that they will be able to answer the questions.
5. Give students time to write their complete answers.
6. Play the audio again so they can check their answers.
7. Call on volunteers to read their answers to the class. If there is any disagreement, play the audio again.

■ **COMMUNICATE**

■ **EXERCISE E**

1. Go over the instructions with the class.
2. Divide the class into small groups and give students time to write their dialog. Remind them to use as many noun clauses as possible.
3. Call on groups to perform their dialogs for the class.

■ **EXPANSION IDEA**

Exercise D

1. Have students write a summary of the press conference, using the information they wrote down for Exercise D.
2. Divide the class into pairs and have students correct each other's work.

Tell them to check for word order and punctuation and to suggest where additional noun clauses or relative adverbial clauses might be added.

Connection

Putting It Together

■ GRAMMAR AND VOCABULARY

1. Ask students to read the instructions.
2. Call on two students to read the topics aloud.
3. Ask students to choose one of the two topics and give them time to write their compositions.

■ PROJECT

1. Ask students to review the instructions.
2. Answer any questions that students have about the project.
3. Call on students at the next class meeting to give their oral reports.

■ INTERNET

1. Call on a student to read the instructions.
2. Ask students to report back to the class about the winning packaging.

GRAMMAR AND VOCABULARY Write a composition on one of the topics below. Use as many words as possible from the Content Vocabulary on page 199, and (circle) them in your composition. Use sentences with relative adverbial clauses and noun clauses to express some of your ideas, and <u>underline</u> those sentences.

Topic 1: Describe the effective packaging of a particular item. Explain what the packaging looks like. Then, explain why the packaging is so appropriate to the product and to your lifestyle and/or culture.

Topic 2: "People in the U.S. should be more concerned about how much plastic packaging we use and how little recycling we do." Do you agree or disagree? Use concrete examples in your response.
Answers will vary.

PROJECT Interview at least one student on your campus about the packaging of popular products. Find out the following information, and present your findings orally at your next class meeting.

1. What American products are distinctive, or even famous, for the shape of their containers? (Ask your interviewee to describe the containers.)
2. Which American products have the most effective or attractive containers?
3. How important is the packaging in his/her decision to buy a new product?
4. What are five items in a grocery store that are typically not packaged in plastic?

 INTERNET Go online and use the search phrase "packaging competition" to find a website that shows winners in a recent competition for effective packaging. Such websites may represent a particular industry, such as "paperboard," or a certain company, for example, Dupont may sponsor an annual competition. Look at all of the winning packaging, and select one or two of the winners that you like. Be prepared to describe the product and its packaging and to tell your classmates why you find it effective or attractive.
Answers will vary.

■ EXPANSION IDEA

Project
1. Ask students to interview four classmates about packaging that they find unattractive or undesirable. This may refer to appearance, lack of environmental friendliness, or messiness.
2. Call on students to report their findings.
3. Vote on the least popular form of packaging.

Lesson 20

Health Sciences: Transcultural Nursing

■ CONTENT VOCABULARY

Look up the words and phrases below that you do not know and enter them in your vocabulary journal. Write each item's part of speech, a definition, and an example sentence. Try to include them in your discussion and writing below.

an assessment	physical therapy	solely	to treat
an intensive care unit	a recovery	straightforward	vital signs
the next of kin	a remedy	to take one's pulse	welfare

■ THINK ABOUT IT

Doctors and nurses treat patients from various cultures. What are some potential misunderstandings that could happen as a result of these cultural differences? Discuss your ideas with a classmate.

In your writing journal, write for five minutes about the questions below. When you have finished, share your experiences with your classmates.
Have you ever gone to the doctor's office or to the student clinic on your campus? What did you think about or worry about when you realized that you needed to see a doctor? What was strange or difficult for you when you were in the clinic or speaking with the nurse or the doctor? What procedures were different from those that you're accustomed to?
Answers will vary.

209

■ CONTENT NOTES

The topic of this lesson is Health Sciences: Transcultural Nursing. In this lesson, students will discuss the importance of good communication between patients and healthcare providers. They will also have the opportunity to talk about how cultural misunderstandings can interfere with successful treatments and outcomes. Use this lesson to inform students about the health services available to them on campus and in the community.

Lesson 20

Overview
1. Ask students to raise their hands if they had a flu shot this year.
2. Call on a few students and ask where they went to get the shot. Write the places on the board. Ask students to brainstorm other places where they can go to take care of health problems.

■ CONTENT VOCABULARY

Ask students to review the words in the box. Tell them to look up any unfamiliar words.

■ VOCABULARY JOURNAL

Have students add new words to their vocabulary journals and write down the parts of speech, definitions, and sentences for each.

■ THINK ABOUT IT

1. Have students read the instructions.
2. Divide the class into pairs and have students discuss potential misunderstandings that can occur when doctors or nurses treat patients from different cultures.
3. Have students read the journal writing instructions. Answer any questions that they have about the topic. Then give them time to write in their journals.
4. Have students share their journal entries with the class.

PART ONE

Anaphoric References

■ GRAMMAR IN CONTENT

■ EXERCISE A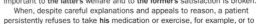
CD 2, Track 19

1. Ask students to read the title of the article.

2. Have students look at the picture and call on a volunteer to explain what is occurring in it.

3. Play the audio and have students follow along in their books as they listen. Ask students to circle any unfamiliar words or phrases.

4. Call on students to read their circled words and elicit definitions or explanations from volunteers if possible.

5. Check comprehension by asking questions such as the following: *According to the author, what is one of the most frustrating experiences in nursing? What kinds of messages do people unconsciously transmit? What are some of the methods nurses use to alter a stubborn patient's behavior? On what levels can explanations for noncompliant patients be found?*

■ GRAMMAR IN CONTENT

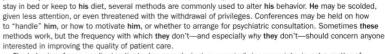

A Read and listen to the passage below. The words in bold are some examples of anaphoric references.

CD2,TR19

Misunderstandings Among Nurses and Patients

Perhaps one of the most frustrating experiences in nursing is being unable to get patients to do what one wants **them** to do even when it is for **their** own good. What appears to be a patient's outright resistance to the medical and nursing regimen designed solely for **his** well-being and, hopefully, for **his** recovery can generate in a nurse any number of negative reactions: a sense of failure, helplessness, irritation, or even anger. However rigorously **she** may have disciplined **herself** not to reveal emotional responses of **this** nature, **they** are usually communicated to **her** patient in one or several of the ways in which people unconsciously transmit messages. **Such** messages, more meaningful to patients than is generally recognized, do not ameliorate the situation; rather, **they** tend to evoke such counter responses as anxiety, withdrawal, or alienation. The resulting impairment of the therapeutic process is often compounded by negative assessments of the noncompliant patient. **He** is labeled "uncooperative," "difficult," "stubborn," "perverse," or "a problem." Once **this** occurs, the kind of relationship between nurse and patient that is so important to **the latter's** welfare and to **the former's** satisfaction is broken.

When, despite careful explanations and appeals to reason, a patient persistently refuses to take **his** medication or exercise, for example, or to stay in bed or keep to **his** diet, several methods are commonly used to alter **his** behavior. **He** may be scolded, given less attention, or even threatened with the withdrawal of privileges. Conferences may be held on how to "handle" **him**, or how to motivate **him**, or whether to arrange for psychiatric consultation. Sometimes **these** methods work, but the frequency with which **they** don't—and especially *why* **they** don't—should concern anyone interested in improving the quality of patient care.

The behavior of noncompliant patients, however deviant or seemingly inappropriate, is not a matter of mere capriciousness. There are reasons why **they** respond as they do, and, apart from reasons that are solely physiologic or organic, **explanations** may be found on other levels: psychologic, sociologic, and/or cultural.

to ameliorate: to ease, to lessen	**noncompliant:** disobedient
capriciousness: erratic or impulsive behavior	**a regimen:** a plan of treatment
an impairment: damage, obstacle	**rigorous:** strong, demanding
outright: direct	**to scold:** to tell somebody in an angry way that he or she did something wrong

■ EXPANSION IDEAS

Exercise A

1. Divide the class into pairs. Have students role-play a discussion between a nurse and a noncompliant patient. Encourage students to use vocabulary from the lesson. For example:
Student 1: *You really need to go on a rigorous diet. We can work out a regimen that you'll be able to follow.*
Student 2: *I don't think I'm fat. I just came here to get a prescription refilled, not to get scolded by you.*

2. Circulate as students work; assist as needed.

3. Call on a few volunteers to role-play their conversations for the class.

Exercise A

Put students into groups of three or four and have them discuss whether they have seen any misunderstandings in a hospital that led to noncompliant patients. If students have no examples, have them imagine ways in which a hospital could help communicate information to a patient, such as through a translator.

Sample Sentences	Notes
Nurse Dern has been concerned about **a patient** on her ward. **The patient** has **complained** about **the food** every day. **Those complaints** seem unreasonable since all of the other women in the ward like **it**.	Use various types of anaphoric references to make your speech and writing clearer and to avoid repeating words. These words and phrases refer to a noun or a whole idea that was mentioned previously in your conversation or your text.
	The article *the* and demonstratives *this, that, these,* and *those* are common referents. Pronouns and possessive determiners also function this way.
The doctor ordered a special diet on Monday. **Since then,** the patient hasn't been eating. The patient's behavior worries her because most patients like **such a** diet. To Ms. Dern, **such** behavior means something is wrong.	Some adverbs refer to times and places that were specified previously: *then, here, there, earlier, before then/this/that, since then/this/that.*
	Use *such* with nouns to signal that the noun or idea was mentioned earlier: *such a* + singular noun *such* + noncount noun/plural noun
Doctors often order diets **of this type** so that patients can regain their strength.	Other phrases also signal a previous reference: *of this type, in this style, of the same nature.*
Nurse Dern consulted Dr. Grant and Dr. Owen about her patient. **The former** suggested tests on the patient's digestive system. **The latter** preferred to wait and see.	Use special adjectives functioning as noun substitutes (*the former/the latter*) to point back to earlier information referring to the sequence as well as the antecedent.
The **physicians** finally referred **the medical case** to a specialist.	Use synonyms of nouns to avoid too much repetition and too many pronouns or to make the reference clearer for your listener or reader.

B Read over your journal entry, and <u>underline</u> at least one sentence that you can revise to include an anaphoric reference. Write your revised sentence(s) below.

Answers will vary.

_____

_____

_____

■ GRAMMAR CHART
Anaphoric References

1. Write *anaphora* on the board and ask if anyone is familiar with the term. If so, call on the person(s) to explain the concept to the class.
2. Write on the board *Rebecca needed the bag, so I ran to get it.*
3. Underline *it* and ask what the word refers to.
4. Explain that words or phrases are *anaphoric* when they refer to something that was mentioned earlier.
5. Go through the sample sentences and Notes one section at a time. Answer any questions that students have about anaphoric references before moving on to Exercise B.

■ EXERCISE B

1. Have students complete the exercise.
2. Ask students to exchange work with a partner. Have them look for additional places where sentences could be revised to include another anaphoric reference.

■ EXPANSION IDEA

Grammar

1. Divide the class into pairs.
2. Have students look for examples of anaphoric references in the passage on page 210.
3. Circulate as students work; assist as needed.

■ EXERCISE C

1. Go over the instructions and the example with the class.
2. Have students complete the activity individually and then check their work with a partner.
3. Call on volunteers to read their answers aloud.

■ EXERCISE D

1. Ask students to read the instructions.
2. Call on a student to read the first two sentences of the text.
3. Ask for volunteers to point out how to use anaphoric references to reduce repetition.
4. Have students complete the activity individually and then compare work with a partner.

C Circle the anaphoric references in the texts below and then underline and draw an arrow to the word or phrase that it refers to.

1. During the regular weekly meeting, Nurse Peter King described Dr. Upton's treatment plan for a young patient with severe allergies. She had been admitted to the hospital on Friday and had been taking various medicines since then. Such allergies demand constant attention so that the proper drugs can be administered whenever needed.

2. Nurse practitioners often staff school clinics and small walk-in ambulatory care clinics. In the former, they treat schoolchildren who develop health problems during the school day. These problems aren't usually serious, but the nurses can send the youngsters home if necessary. In much the same way, such medical professionals treat people off the street at clinics that operate in many drugstores. Anyone with a serious condition or illness is referred to a doctor's care.

D Edit the text below, adding various types of anaphoric references including synonyms.

Good medical care depends on clear communication between patients and doctors or
        such
nurses. Unfortunately, ~~clear~~ communication doesn't always take place when patients in the
                                      American
United States can't speak English well. According to the U.S. Census, about 20% of the ~~U.S.~~
population does not speak English at home. In the last 10–15 years, hospitals and clinics
                                   medical
have begun to tackle the problem of poor communication between patients and ~~doctors and~~
professionals
~~nurses.~~ Now more than 40 states have laws about language access for medical care. ~~The~~
       These laws
~~laws about language access~~ are not always enforced because it can be expensive to enforce
    them   **medical facilities**
~~the laws.~~ Also, ~~hospitals and clinics~~ often have difficulty locating translators for languages
that are less commonly spoken, such as Hmong or Mongolian.
                   this expense   **the problem of finding**
    In response to ~~the expense of enforcing the law~~ and ~~the difficulty locating~~ translators,
hospital staff and administrators
~~doctors, nurses, and hospital administrators~~ are encouraging an increase in the number of
                         programs of this type
interpreter-certification programs. Graduates of ~~interpreter-certification programs~~ can help
medical personnel
~~doctors and nurses~~ provide better medical care for patients and avoid costly mistakes.

■ EXPANSION IDEA

Exercise D

1. Divide the class into small groups.
2. Ask them to discuss whether they think non-English-speaking patients are entitled to have a translator present whenever they meet with a health-provider, and if so, how to implement this.
3. Circulate as students work. Assist as needed, encouraging them to use the vocabulary and grammar from the lesson.
4. Call on each group to present a summary of the group's discussion.

E Listen to the conversation between two nurses and then answer the questions.

CD2,TR20

1. What attention has Mr. Bratt received from his nurse?

   His nurse has been very attentive—offering water, juice, and a back-rub.

2. Which liquids are going to make him feel better sooner?

   The water and juice.

3. When did his complaints begin?

   After his surgery.

F Now listen to a follow-up conversation between one of the nurses and Mr. Bratt. Answer the questions when you have finished listening to the recording.

CD2,TR21

1. Who is "the latter" in this conversation?

   Betty, the day nurse.

2. What would be rude for Mr. Bratt?

   To accept the nurse's offers.

3. Mr. Bratt says that in Sweden people don't act "that way." What does he mean?

   Swedes don't accept an offer until people ask at least two or three times.

■ **COMMUNICATE**

G **PAIR WORK** Tell the story of Mr. Kerry, who had to see a doctor while he was on a business trip abroad and had some unexpected experiences. Take turns telling the story, with each partner adding one sentence at a time. In each sentence you should include an anaphoric reference.

Mr. Kerry had been coughing and sneezing for three days and finally went to see a doctor in Mexico City.

His hotel recommended a nearby doctor, and Kerry took a taxi to that doctor's office.

When you finish your story, tell your classmates about Mr. Kerry's surprising trip to the doctor.

■ **EXPANSION IDEA**

Communicate

1. Ask students to write a short story about Mr. Kerry's experience seeing the doctor in a foreign country. Remind them to use anaphoric references in their writing.

2. Have students exchange stories with a partner. Ask them to correct each other's work, and to point out places in which anaphoric references could be added.

3. Call on a few volunteers to read their stories aloud.

■ **EXERCISE E**
CD 2, Track 20

1. Tell students that they will hear a conversation between two nurses. Have them read through the questions.

2. Play the audio and tell students to listen for comprehension only.

3. Play the audio again, this time asking students to answer the question. You may choose to stop the audio periodically to give students time to write.

4. Call on volunteers to read their answers aloud. If any class members disagree with the answers, play the audio again.

■ **EXERCISE F**
CD 2, Track 21

1. Tell students that they will now hear a conversation between Mr. Bratt and one of the nurses. Ask students to read the three questions.

2. Play the audio and tell students to listen for comprehension only.

3. Play the audio again, this time asking students to answer the question. You may stop the audio periodically to give students time to write.

4. Call on volunteers to read their answers aloud. If any class members disagree with the answers, play the audio again.

■ **COMMUNICATE**

■ **EXERCISE G**

1. Call on a student to read the instructions aloud.

2. Call on two students to read the text in the speech balloons.

3. Divide the class into pairs and have them continue the story of Mr. Kerry's doctor's visit.

4. Circulate as students work and assist as needed.

PART TWO

Prepositions: *Against, Among, Between, Through, Toward*

■ GRAMMAR IN CONTENT

■ EXERCISE A

Ask students to complete the activity and then check their work with a partner.

■ GRAMMAR CHART

Prepositions: Against, Among, Between, Through, Toward

1. Place a book and a pencil on your desk. Say *The book is next to the pencil.*
2. Put another book on the other side of the pencil and say *The pencil is between the books.*
3. Add a third book and say *The pencil is among the books.*
4. Ask a volunteer to explain when to use *between* and when to use *among.*
5. Ask students to read the sample sentences and Notes.
6. Answer any questions that students have about using appropriate prepositions.

A Reread the text at the beginning of this lesson, and (circle) examples of any of the prepositions listed in the chart. Which of the meanings below does the preposition have?

Prepositions: *Against, Among, Between, Through, Toward*

Sample Sentences	Notes
The nurses' station is **between** Radiology and the doctors' offices on the third floor.	Use these prepositions for location and destination:
Go **through** the children's ward **toward** the elevators. Then, when you get to the emergency exit, turn left and you'll see the station **between** the women's restroom and the lounge.	*against:* touching the side surface of
	among: in an unspecified position in the middle of three or more items (which are not uniquely specified)
You'll find Dr. Huston's office **among** the other doctors' offices on the fourth floor.	*between:* in the middle of two items
Don't lean **against** the emergency door—the alarm might go off.	*through:* moving along a passage; beyond
	toward: going in the direction of a destination (which is not necessarily the final destination)
Nurse Adams has protested **against** the rule about family visits after 7 P.M. His colleagues are **against** Adams because they know that such visits comfort patients.	Other meanings for these prepositions: *against:* in opposition to; have no solidarity or sympathy for
The nurses determine the work schedule **among** themselves.	*among:* concerning more than two people
Nurses are on duty from 7 A.M. to 5 P.M., but visitors are only allowed **between** 2:00 and 4:00.	*between:* a. specifying a beginning and end point b. intervals for events or objects that repeat c. concerning two people
Between meals the patients can't have any snacks. In double rooms, patients have to share a bathroom **between** themselves.	

214 LESSON 20 | Health Sciences: Transcultural Nursing

■ EXPANSION IDEAS

Grammar

1. Divide the class into pairs.
2. Have students take turns pointing to classroom items and making sentences.

   For example: *Sarah's desk is between Frank and Mark's desks.*
   Mrs. Smith is walking towards the door.

3. Circulate as students work and assist as needed.

Grammar

1. Ask students to write sentences using two meanings of *against*, *between*, and *through*.
2. Call on volunteers to read their sentences to the class.

At least one nurse is on duty (all) **through/throughout** the night.

The lights went out (all) **through/throughout** the hospital until the generators started up.

The nurse was able to communicate with Mr. Ortiz **through** an interpreter. He needed to understand that **through** physical therapy he could improve his strength and balance.

through:
a. duration
b. pervasive quality; all over
c. by means of
d. enduring; tolerating

For a. and b., you can also use *all through* or *throughout.*

B Complete each sentence, using a preposition from the chart.

1. Mr. Davidson, a heart patient, wanted to return to work two months after surgery.
   His nurse, Ms. Granger, advised ____*against*____ such an action.

2. According to his doctor, Mr. Davidson could recover more quickly ____through____ physical therapy.

3. Whenever it's time for Mr. Davidson's medicine, the hospital pharmacist looks
   ____among____ the bottles of medicine in the drug cabinet to fill the prescription for him.

4. Mr. Davidson is still so weak that Nurse Granger has to help him out of bed. As he
   walks along, he leans ____against____ the nurse.

5. Mr. Davidson's doctor makes his morning rounds some time ____between____ 7:30 and 8:30.

6. The doctor still wants someone to monitor Mr. Davidson's vital signs ____all through____ the night.

7. ____Among____ all the nursing staff, Mr. Davidson trusts Nurse Granger the most.

8. When Nurse Granger heard an urgent page for her last night, she rushed
   ____towards____ Mr. Davidson's room.

■ **EXERCISE B**

1. Ask students to read the instructions and the example.
2. Have students complete the activity individually and then check their work in pairs.
3. Call on volunteers to read their answers aloud.

■ **EXPANSION IDEA**

Exercise B
1. Divide the class into pairs.
2. Have students role-play a conversation between Mr. Davidson's doctor and his nurse, Ms. Granger. Challenge students to use the prepositions with as many of their meanings as possible.

1. Go over the instructions and the example with the class.
2. Have students complete the activity in pairs.
3. Call on volunteers to read their answers to the class. Discuss the differences in the sentences.

C Explain the differences in meaning between the sentences below. Follow the example.

1. To get to the visitor's lounge on the third floor, go
   a. through the red double doors. ___*enter the doors*___
   b. by the red double doors. ___*go past the doors, but don't enter them*___

2. Nurse Johnson was paged as he was wheeling a patient
   a. toward the Radiology Department. __in the direction of that dept.__
   b. to the Radiology Department. __the dept. is their destination__

3. Nurse Johnson left the wheelchair in a space
   a. between the others. __there are two wheelchairs there__
   b. among the others. __there are at least three wheelchairs there__

4. When Nurse Johnson came back to get the wheelchair, it was
   a. against the wall. __part of the wheelchair was touching the wall__
   b. by the wall. __it was next to the wall__

5. By midnight it was quiet
   a. all through the Intensive Care Unit. __in every part of the ICU__
   b. in the ICU. __generally quiet in the ICU__

6. Next of kin may visit patients in the Intensive Care Unit
   a. from 10:00 A.M. to 2 P.M. daily. __They can stay the entire time if they want to.__
   b. between 10 and 2 daily. __They can come during those hours.__

7. Many patients can recover their strength
   a. through regular physical therapy. __They recover by means of physical therapy.__
   b. during regular physical therapy. __They recover in physical therapy.__

8. Family members may decide on a loved one's treatment plan
   a. between themselves. __Two family members decide.__
   b. among themselves. __Three or more family members decide.__

9. Patients should stay in their rooms
   a. between therapy sessions. __They stay there from one session to the next.__
   b. after therapy sessions. __They should stay there when the sessions are over.__

10. Once they had read the new policies about visiting hours, several nurses argued
    a. against them. __They opposed the policies.__
    b. for them. __They supported the policies.__

■ **EXPANSION IDEA**

Exercise C
1. Ask students to write six pairs of sentences similar to those in Exercise C, using the prepositions taught in the lesson.

2. Divide the class into pairs and have students discuss the meanings of their sentences.

D There are four errors in the e-mail message. Find and correct all four errors.

Hi Phil-

I have had a hectic week at the hospital. Between the paperwork and the patients' demands, I'm always on the run. How's it going with you?

Remember the patient from Thailand that I wrote you about? She's doing better. It seems that her English is better than we thought. I guess that she was just scared and nervous at the beginning and couldn't understand much. I can't imagine being in such ~~a~~ situation. ~~Among~~ **Between** you and me, I hope that I never have to go to a hospital abroad.

I can't wait to see you this weekend. Remember – when you exit I-95 at Grant Street, turn ~~to~~ **toward** the river. Then, you'll have to drive ~~between~~ **through** the tunnel. The way that you usually come is blocked right now.

Later-
Joan

■ COMMUNICATE

E **PAIR WORK** Select one of the groups of common prepositional phrases below and prepare a dialog with your partner. The subject of your conversation is cultural misunderstandings or an experience at the doctor's office. Use at least three of the prepositional phrases.

Group 1	Group 2	Group 3
between you and me	among my classmates	between each other
through thick and thin	through dumb luck	through and through
against all odds	against my better judgment	a race against time
toward downtown	toward the cafeteria	toward the airport
among friends	between ourselves	among other things

 Did you hear the news? Mr. Yamamoto recovered against all odds.

 I didn't know he was ill.

■ **EXERCISE D**

1. Have students correct the errors in the e-mail.
2. Call on volunteers to read their corrections to the class.

■ **COMMUNICATE**

■ **EXERCISE E**

1. Call on a student to read the instructions aloud.
2. Call on two students to read the text in the speech balloons.
3. Ask students to review the prepositional phrases. Point out that many of these are idiomatic and cannot be translated literally. If anyone is unsure about the meaning of the phrases, call on volunteers to explain them.
4. Divide the class into pairs and have them prepare their dialogs.
5. Circulate as students work and assist as needed.
6. Call on a few pairs to role-play their dialogs for the class.

■ **EXPANSION IDEAS**

Exercise E

1. Ask students to write sentences using the following phrases:

   against my better judgment
   through thick and thin
   against all odds
   through dumb luck
   a race against time

2. Have students exchange work with a partner. Ask them to make sure that their partner's sentences are idiomatically correct.

3. Circulate as students work and assist as needed.

Exercise E

Ask students to find three more idiomatic prepositional phrases, such as *in one ear and out the other, once in a blue moon, kill two birds with one stone.*

■ GRAMMAR AND VOCABULARY

1. Ask students to read the instructions.
2. Call on two students to read the topics aloud.
3. Ask students to choose one of the two topics and give them time to write their compositions. Tell them to use the vocabulary and grammar from the lesson.

■ PROJECT

1. Ask students to review the instructions.
2. Answer any questions that students have about the project.
3. Call on students at the next class meeting to give their oral reports.

■ INTERNET

1. Call on a student to read the instructions.
2. Have students conduct their searches and then report back to the class on the remedies that they chose to compare.

GRAMMAR AND VOCABULARY Write a composition on one of the topics below. Use as many words as possible from the Content Vocabulary on page 209, and (circle) them in your composition. Use sentences with anaphoric references and the prepositions in this lesson to express some of your ideas, and <u>underline</u> those sentences.

Topic 1: "People put too much faith in technology and the latest drugs for curing their illnesses." Do you agree or disagree?

Topic 2: Every culture has traditional beliefs about the source of some illnesses and the ways to cure them. In some places, traditional medicines and home remedies have been used for generations. In other places, dietary traditions are of great importance in explaining sicknesses. Some cultures interpret illness as a sign of spiritual confusion or problems. Describe such traditional beliefs about health and sickness in your culture. **Answers will vary.**

PROJECT Interview at least one student on your campus about the student health clinic. Find out the following information, and make a brief report on your findings at your next class meeting.

1. What kinds of services does the student clinic provide? Has the student used them? If so, what did the student think of the services?
2. What kind of care and services do the nurses at the clinic provide?
3. What procedures do students follow when they go to the clinic for the first time?
4. What is the student's attitude about nurses and their responsibilities?

 INTERNET Go online and use the search phrase "newspaper columns, herb and home remedy" to find a website with information about home and natural remedies. Find one or two remedies that are similar to remedies that your family or friends use. What are the differences and similarities? Be ready to share this information with your classmates at your next class meeting.
Answers will vary.

■ EXPANSION IDEA

Grammar and Vocabulary

1. Divide the class into pairs.
2. Have students edit each other's compositions. Ask them to suggest additional uses of anaphoric references and to check on correct preposition usage.

A (Circle) the correct word or phrase to complete the idea of the sentence.

1. The conversation (between)/ among) Mrs. Liu's doctors took a long time yesterday, but both of them finally explained their plan of treatment to her.

2. Dr. Freeman walked (toward /(through) the recovery room with Mrs. Liu so that she could see the special equipment that they needed after her surgery.

3. She trusted both Dr. Freeman and her nurses, but Mrs. Liu liked (the former)/ the latter) better because she had been kind enough to explain the equipment in the recovery room.

4. Mrs. Liu didn't understand (the way how /(the way) some of the doctors spoke, but she could understand Dr. Freeman very well.

5. During her recovery one of the nurses asked Mrs. Liu every morning what (would she like /(she would like) for lunch and dinner.

6. Now Mrs. Liu wonders ((how long)/ how much) she will have to stay in the hospital.

7. Tomorrow Mrs. Liu will finally meet ((Dr. Phyllis Klein, who)/ Dr. Phyllis Klein who) will supervise her physical therapy.

8. Dr. Klein is well-respected in her field according to Mrs. Liu's ((favorite nurse, who)/ favorite nurse who) has taken care of many of Dr. Klein's patients.

9. Mrs. Liu's other doctors also praised Dr. Klein's work, (what /(which) also reassured Mrs. Liu.

10. Many bouquets of flowers were sent ((to Mrs. Liu)/ Mrs. Liu) during her recovery.

B If you paraphrase the sentences below with the verb in the passive voice, should the agent of the action be included? Write "Yes" if the paraphrase should include a *by* phrase; write "No" if the *by* phrase should be omitted.

____No____ 1. Someone invented the air pump in the 1600s.

____Yes____ 2. The study of alchemy influenced Isaac Newton for decades.

____Yes____ 3. People in the eastern Mediterranean region developed glassmaking sometime before 3000 BCE; in addition, glassblowers from the same area invented the blowpipe around 100 BCE.

____No____ 4. Plantation owners bought slaves from the Guinea Coast for their knowledge of rice cultivation.

____Yes____ 5. The appropriate packaging can protect fragile or perishable items very well.

____No____ 6. Engineers have updated designs for wheelchairs to take advantage of new lightweight materials.

Review Lessons 16-20

The purpose of this lesson is to help students review the language and concepts they have learned in the last five lessons. Encourage them to go back to the lessons and review the grammar charts to help them complete the review activities.

■ EXERCISE A

1. Ask students to read the instructions.
2. Have students complete the activity on their own and then check their work with a partner.
3. Call on volunteers to read their answers aloud. Discuss any differences of opinion about answers among class members.

■ EXERCISE B

1. Write *agent* on the board.
2. Call on a volunteer to explain the term.
3. Have students complete the activity on their own and then check their work with a partner.
4. Call on volunteers to read their answers aloud. Discuss any differences of opinion about answers among class members.

■ EXPANSION IDEA

Exercise A
Have students write sentences using the *incorrect* words or phrases from the exercise. Make sure to emphasize that students should write grammatically correct sentences.

EXERCISE C

1. Ask students to read the instructions.
2. Ask students to answer the first question. Then call on a volunteer to read the answer aloud.
3. Answer any questions that students have about the exercise.
4. Have students complete the activity on their own and then check their work in pairs.

LEARNER LOG

Have students complete the Learner Log. Suggest that they review the Grammar Charts for areas that need more practice.

C Write the verb in parentheses in the correct tense and voice.

1. A formal gift (expect) _____is expected_____ to (wrap) _____be wrapped_____ attractively.

2. Consumers sometimes admit (influence) _____being influenced_____ by the packaging of a product when they have a choice among several brands.

3. (select) _____To be selected as_____ the winner of an award for effective packaging is the goal of leaders in that industry.

4. Some consumers are guilty of (let) _____letting_____ the packaging of a product affect their shopping.

5. For many years food items (require) _____have been required_____ to have labels that (inform) _____inform_____ consumers about the ingredients.

6. Never buy a packaged food item that seems (tamper with) _to have been tampered with._

7. Shoppers (should / warn) _____should have_____ _____been warned_____ that the food had been contaminated, but they weren't.

8. People still remember when they (used to / buy) _____used to buy_____ food that had very little packaging.

LEARNER LOG Check (✔) *Yes* or *I Need More Practice.* Answers will vary.

Lesson	I Can Use . . .	Yes	I Need More Practice
16	Verbs in the Passive Voice and Passives Taking Two Objects		
17	Gerunds and Infinitives in the Passive Voice; Passive Voice in Complex Sentences		
18	Restrictive and Nonrestrictive Relative Clauses; Reduced and Special Nonrestrictive Relative Clauses		
19	Relative Adverbial Clauses and Noun Clauses		
20	Anaphoric References and the Prepositions: *Against, Among, Between, Through, Toward*		

EXPANSION IDEA

Exercise C

1. Divide the class into pairs.
2. Ask students to discuss their expectations for service in a department store.

For example:
Salespeople should always be polite and helpful.

Physics: Golf and Tennis Balls

■ **CONTENT VOCABULARY**

Look up the words below that you do not know and enter them in your vocabulary journal. Write each word's part of speech, a definition, and an example sentence. Try to include them in your discussion and writing below.

to absorb	protocol	a reading	to spin
to generate	quantitative	to rebound	to wind
impact	a range	to release	to wobble

■ **THINK ABOUT IT**

Think about sports in which players hit, kick, or throw a ball. What forces determine how the ball flies, bounces, and rolls? Discuss your ideas with a classmate.

In your writing journal, write for 5–10 minutes about the questions below. When you are finished, share what you wrote with the class.   Answers will vary.
Have you ever played any sports that involve a ball? Of those sports, which ones did you find the most difficult? Why? How did you feel as you were trying to improve your skills in those sports?

221

Overview

1. Ask students to raise their hands if they have studied physics.
2. Ask students to raise their hands if they have ever played golf or tennis.
3. Have the class brainstorm the relationship between physics and how these two sports are played.

■ **CONTENT VOCABULARY**

Ask students to review the words in the box. Tell them to look up any unfamiliar words.

■ **VOCABULARY JOURNAL**

Have students add new words to their vocabulary journals and write down the parts of speech, definitions, and sentences for each.

■ **THINK ABOUT IT**

1. Have students read the instructions.
2. Divide the class into pairs and have students discuss the forces that determine how a ball flies, bounces, and rolls.
3. Have students read the journal writing instructions. Answer any questions that they have about the topic. Then give them time to write in their journals.
4. Call on volunteers to share their ideas with the class.

■ **CONTENT NOTES**

The topic of this lesson is Physics: Golf and Tennis Balls. Students will learn some basic facts of physics and how they affect the way in which balls bounce. They will also acquire the vocabulary needed to discuss some basic laws of physics and gain some experience in reading graphs and diagrams. Use this lesson to talk about practical applications of science and to encourage your female students to take math and science courses.

■ GRAMMAR IN CONTENT

■ EXERCISE A

CD 3, Track 1

1. Write *bounceability* on the board and ask students to think about the meaning of the word.

2. Call on a volunteer to explain what *bounceability* refers to.

3. Play the audio and have students follow along in their books as they listen. Ask students to circle any unfamiliar words or phrases.

4. Call on students to read their circled words and elicit definitions or explanations from volunteers if possible.

5. Check comprehension by asking questions such as the following: *What is the "coefficient of restitution"? Why does a bouncing ball fail to reach its original height? Explain the Latin roots of the word "coefficient." Why do athletes prefer high-compression balls?*

■ GRAMMAR IN CONTENT

A Read and listen to the passage below. The words in bold are participles that function as adjectives.

CD3,TR1

Bounceability

An important property of the balls used in different types of ball games is the amount of energy they retain after bouncing off a surface such as golf club or tennis racket. In everyday speech people talk about the "bounce of the ball." A professional golf player can sometimes be observed to check the bounce of his ball by bouncing it on a smooth surface before starting a golf game. Scientists measure the "bounceability" of a ball by means of a quantity defined as the *coefficient of restitution*.

The term *restitution* comes from two Latin roots: "re" meaning again and "stature," to make, to stand (hence the word *statue*). To make restitution then literally means to restore an object or a situation to its original condition. We all know from experience how the return height of a **bouncing** ball decays with **repeated** bounces as shown in Figure 1. The fact that the ball fails to reach its original release height is a failure of the system to achieve restitution of the original height. The coefficient of restitution is a quantitative measure of the loss in height at each bounce. When released from the same height, a ball made of material with a low coefficient of restitution would not bounce back to the height achieved by a ball with a higher coefficient of restitution.

The term *coefficient* came into use in science when scientists were measuring many properties of materials and listing these **measured** properties before theories were known. The word was coined by joining "co," which means together, and "efficient," which originally meant capable of doing something. *Efficient* came from the Latin root words *ex*, meaning "out," and *facere*, meaning "to make." Thus, if we knew the coefficient of restitution, we would know how things worked together to make the ball bounce (See Figure 1.). Scientists exploring the properties of different materials would make balls of all sorts of different materials and measure the bounce of each ball. They would then plot the coefficient of restitution against the substance in the ball. For example, when the early manufacturers of golf balls experimented with how tightly they wound the elastic thread around the central core, they found that the tighter they wound the thread, the higher the coefficient of restitution of the **bouncing** ball. These better **bouncing** balls are called *high compression balls*.

We will meet the coefficient of restitution in any game where the ball is hit with a bat or a racket or when the ball bounces off a wall or other hard surfaces (See Figure 2.). When we bounce an ordinary rubber ball off a surface, we learn through experience that if we wish to catch the ball at the same height at which we release the ball from our own hand, we must give a ball a little bit of extra energy as we throw it down on the surface. This means we release the ball from our hand traveling at the speed it would have gathered if it had been released from a greater height. Then the first bounce will reach the position of our hand.

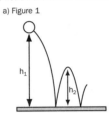

a) Figure 1

The coefficient of restitution (a) equals the square root of the rebound height (h_2) divided by the original height (h_1).

Symbolically:

$$a = \sqrt{\frac{h_2}{h_1}}$$

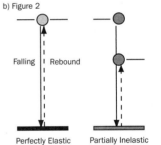

b) Figure 2

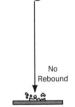

Falling | Rebound

No Rebound

Perfectly Elastic
e.g., Steel on Steel

Partially Inelastic
e.g., Rubber Ball

Completely Inelastic
e.g., Egg

■ EXPANSION IDEA

Exercise A

1. Divide the class into pairs, pairing students who are comfortable with physics with those who are not, if possible.

2. Have students reread the passage together, stopping to summarize each paragraph in their own words.

3. Circulate as students work and assist as needed.

Sample Sentences	Notes
The type of grass on a golf course can have an effect on how far a **rolling** ball will go.	An English participle can function not only as a verb form but also as an adjective.
Our newspaper ran a photo of the **smiling** winner of the local golf match.	Choose the *-ing* form of the participle if the noun that it modifies is the agent of the action or the cause of an emotion:
After the golfers asked the **whispering** spectators to keep quiet, the **surprised** onlookers left.	a rolling ball = the ball is rolling a surprising result = the result surprises you
Professional golfers throw out their **used** balls because they are **deformed**.	Use a participle if the accompanying noun is the receiver of the action or the experiencer of the emotion:
Such **deformed** balls don't fly straight when they're hit.	an **injured** person = a person who was injured a **disappointed** person = a person who felt disappointment
Physicists have studied the properties of **tightly wound** golf balls.	These participles may also be modified
Modern golf balls have 336 **symmetrically placed** holes, or dimples.	• by adverbs (an often told story, a hard-working student, a never-ending problem) • by nouns (a prize-winning team, the heart-warming story, a moth-eaten sweater)
Professional golfers are not allowed to use balls with **self-correcting** action.	

Verbs of Emotion Frequently Used as Adjectives

alarm	bewilder	disturb	frighten	overwhelm
amaze	bore	embarrass	insult	puzzle
annoy	comfort	encourage	interest	shock
astonish	convince	excite	mislead	tire

B Read over your journal entry, and <u>underline</u> at least one sentence that you can revise to include a participle that functions as an adjective. Write your revised sentence(s) below.

Answers will vary.

_____

_____

_____

_____

■ GRAMMAR CHART
Participles as Adjectives

1. Write on the board *Used balls don't bounce as high as new ones.*
2. Underline *used* and point out that it is a participle. Call on a volunteer to say how it is used in this sentence.
3. Ask students to review the sample sentences and Notes.
4. Answer any questions that students have about using participial adjectives.

■ EXERCISE B

1. Have students complete the exercise.
2. Ask students to exchange work with a partner. Have them look for additional places where sentences could be revised to include another participial adjective.

■ EXPANSION IDEA

Grammar

1. Divide the class into pairs.
2. Ask students to take turns making sentences using verbs of emotion from the Grammar Chart as adjectives.

For example:
The astonished teacher gave the student an A on his physics project.

The puzzled student didn't understand why he got such a low grade on his physics project.

3. Circulate as students work; assist as needed.

■ EXERCISE C

1. Ask students to read the instructions.
2. Call on a student to read the example.
3. Have students complete the activity individually and then check their work in pairs.
4. Call on volunteers to read their answers aloud. Call on class members who found additional ways to include participial adjectives.

■ EXERCISE D

1. Ask students to read the instructions.
2. Call on a student to read the example.
3. Ask a volunteer to explain why *amazing* is correct in the example.
4. Have students complete the activity individually and then check their answers in pairs.
5. Call on volunteers to read their answers aloud, and explain the differences in meaning in each sentence.

C Revise each of the sentences below to include at least one participial adjective.

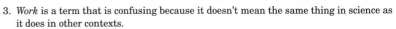

1. A golf ball that is moving has energy.
   A moving golf ball has energy.

2. If a golf ball hits another ball, it transfers energy, and in science, energy that is transferred does "work."
   A golf ball hitting another golf ball transfers energy, and in science, transferred energy does work.

3. *Work* is a term that is confusing because it doesn't mean the same thing in science as it does in other contexts.
   Work is a confusing term because it doesn't mean the same thing in science as it does in other contexts.

4. Science teachers need to explain terminology that is specialized to students who are puzzled so that they understand scientific concepts more easily.
   Science teachers need to explain specialized terminology to puzzled students so that they understand . . . .

5. For some students, terminology that is bewildering makes science too difficult.
   For some students, bewildering terminology may make science seem too difficult.

6. Scientific concepts are clear for some students, but for others the mental picture of a golf ball that is rolling or a tennis ball that is spinning can help a lot.
   Scientific concepts are clear for some students, but for others the mental picture of a rolling golf ball or a spinning tennis . . . .

7. A photo of a golf ball that has been deformed can also convince students of the effect of the high-speed impact of a golf club on the ball.
   A photo of a deformed golf ball can also convince students of the effect of a high-speed impact of a golf club on the ball.

D (Circle) the correct form of the participle in the sentences below. In some cases, both choices may be correct. If both participles can be used, explain the difference in meaning in each sentence.

1. Most people think that a rubber band is very elastic or stretchable, but it's an ((amazing) / amazed) fact that rubber is not very elastic in scientific terms.

2. (Bouncing) / Bounced) metal balls have a higher rebound than rubber balls because metal balls do not absorb energy and thus have a greater coefficient of restitution.

3. The word "elastic" is a (misleading) / misled) scientific term for many students because they don't realize it refers to energy rather than to shape.

■ EXPANSION IDEA

Exercise D

1. Divide the class into pairs.
2. Ask students to use each of the participles in a sentence.

   For example:
   1. The physicist performed an *amazing* experiment.

   2. The *amazed* physicist could not explain the results of his experiment.

3. Circulate as students work; assist as needed.

4. Thus, a scientist who describes a material with the technical term *elastic* means that the material demonstrates greater (conserving / (conserved)) energy than a material with low elasticity.

5. Professors may give ((fascinating) / fascinated) demonstrations of this concept so that their (boring / (bored)) students become more (interesting / (interested)) in lab class.

6. An ((interesting) / interested) professor can make any subject come alive.

7. If a professor uses golf balls and other examples from sports, ((struggling) / struggled) students may gain confidence in their ability to understand physics.

8. An (inspiring / (inspired)) student may decide to major in physics or chemistry and make science a career.

E (Circle) **the correct interpretation of each sentence.**

1. During class the bored lab assistant gave the students feedback on their assignments.
   - (a.) The lab assistant looked like she was sleepy or didn't care about class.
   - b. We felt sleepy because of the lab assistant's way of giving feedback.

2. The fascinating student asked the professor to explain the example in the textbook.
   - (a.) Everyone in class wanted to know and listen to the student.
   - b. The student wanted to know more and more about the example.

3. The students became quiet when they saw the disturbed look on Professor Wheeler's face.
   - (a.) The students realized that Professor Wheeler was upset about something.
   - b. The students felt upset when they saw the expression on Professor Wheeler's face.

4. An alarmed campus police officer rushed into their lab class.
   - (a.) The police officer felt anxious and afraid when she entered the classroom.
   - b. The students in the classroom felt anxious and afraid when she entered.

5. The encouraged student did much better on his second take-home exam.
   - a. The student helped to motivate his classmates to do better.
   - (b.) The student felt motivation to do better in his class.

6. An increasing number of women are studying physics and chemistry in the United States.
   - (a.) The number of women is growing.
   - b. Something caused the number of women students to grow.

■ **EXERCISE E**

1. Ask students to read the instructions.
2. Call on a student to read the example.
3. Call on a volunteer to explain why *a* is the correct interpretation of the example sentence.
4. Call on a volunteer to reword the example sentence so that *b* would be the correct answer.
5. Have students complete the activity individually and then check their work in pairs.
6. Call on volunteers to read their answers aloud.

■ **EXPANSION IDEA**

Exercise E

1. Have students rewrite each sentence so that the answer that was incorrect in Exercise E would be correct.

   For example:
   The *fascinated* student . . .

. . . the *disturbing look* on Professor Wheeler's face.

2. Call on volunteers to read their sentences aloud.

EXERCISE F

1. Go over the instructions with the class.
2. Call on a student to read the example.
3. Have students complete the activity individually and then check their work in pairs.
4. Call on volunteers to read their sentences aloud. If the answer changes the original meaning of the sentence, call on another volunteer to read his or her answer.

COMMUNICATE

EXERCISE G

Divide the class into pairs and have them work together to create a story about an embarrassing, depressing, shocking, or amusing situation.

F Rephrase the participial adjectives in the sentences with relative clauses containing verbs or predicate adjectives.

1. The lab assistant was sure that the students could handle the clearly defined experiment for that week.

   The lab assistant was sure that the students could handle the experiment, which was/had been clearly defined for that week.

2. It has always been against university policy to conduct life-threatening experiments in lab classes.

   It has always been against university policy to conduct experiments that are life-threatening in lab classes.

3. Some of the students could not read the hand-written feedback on their lab reports.

   Some of the students could not read the feedback that had been hand-written on their lab reports.

4. Although physics graduate students have to attend classes, research-related tasks take up most of their time.

   Although physics graduate students have to attend classes, most of their time is taken up with tasks that are related to research.

5. Most graduate assistants consider their poorly paid jobs a necessity if they want to become a professor later on.

   Most graduate assistants consider their jobs that pay poorly a necessity if they want to become a professor later on.

6. If grad students are especially lucky, they might have the opportunity to work on a profit generating project for the university.

   If grad students are especially lucky, they might have the opportunity to work on a project that generates profit for the university.

7. Doctoral students may even have their own university-sponsored research project.

   Doctoral students may even have their own research projects sponsored by the university.

■ COMMUNICATE

G **PAIR WORK** Work together to create a story about a situation that was embarrassing, depressing, shocking, or amusing.

EXPANSION IDEAS

Exercise F

1. Ask students to write three sentences that contain participial adjectives.
2. Have students exchange work with a partner and rephrase the sentences using relative clauses containing verbs or predicate adjectives, as in Exercise F.

   For example:
   Students may submit well-researched proposals to the committee.

   Students may submit proposals that have been well researched to the committee.

Exercise G

1. Have students work with a new partner to edit their stories.
2. Call on students to read their stories aloud.

GRAMMAR IN CONTENT

A Reread the text at the beginning of this lesson, and <u>underline</u> all of the phrases that include a subordinate conjunction such as *when* or *although* followed by a participial phrase. Compare your answers with a partner.

Participles in Reduced Adverbial Clauses

Sample Sentences	Notes
Most golfers use one or two balls **while playing a course.**	Like relative clauses, the following types of adverbial clauses can be reduced: time, conditional, and concessive.
Although appearing spherical, a used golf ball becomes deformed.	
A golf ball won't fly straight **if deformed.**	Omit the subject and revise the verb to a participial form:
When hit, a deformed ball won't "fly true" as golfers say.	subordinate conjunction + *-ing* phrase (= active verb) subordinate conjunction + *-ed/-en* phrase (= passive verb)
Until hearing this information, many players try to save money and use the same ball too many times.	NOTE: Always check that the subject of the main verb is the grammatical subject of the participial verb in the adverbial phrase.
The player decided to use a new ball, after **having made** several poor hits.	Express a time contrast to the verb in the main clause by using a <u>perfect participle</u>:
Although **having been told** that she needed to use a different club, the player hit the new ball with a driving iron.	*-ing* (= active) participle: ***having called*** *-ed* (= passive) participle: ***having been called***
The player tried his shot again, **convinced that he could do better.**	**Subordinate conjunctions** can be omitted for these types of adverbial phrases: • Time • Causal (This type is not included above!) • Conditional • Concessive
Having hit the ball correctly, the player expected to see it fly straight down the fairway. (Because he had hit . . . / After he had hit . . .)	In this case, the participial phrase may be interpreted in various ways according to the context of the sentence. If the connection of ideas in your text is very important, do not omit the conjunction.
Hit well, a golf ball should have a backspin. (If it is hit well . . ./After it is hit well . . .)	Separate the participial phrase from the main clause with a comma.

EXPANSION IDEA

Grammar

1. Divide the class into pairs.
2. Have students work together to identify the subjects of each of the reduced clauses.
3. Have students identify time contrasts and omitted subordinate conjunctions.

PART TWO

Participles in Reduced Adverbial Clauses

GRAMMAR IN CONTENT

EXERCISE A

1. Write on the board *When asked, the teacher is happy to meet with students after class.*
2. Call on a volunteer to identify the subordinate conjunction in the sentence. Underline *when.*
3. Call on another volunteer to identify the participle in the sentence and underline *asked.*
4. Have students complete the activity and then check their work with a partner.

GRAMMAR CHART
Participles in Reduced Adverbial Clauses

1. Write on the board *A golf ball won't fly straight if deformed.*
2. Call on a volunteer to identify the reduced adverbial clause.
3. Call another volunteer to the board to expand the clause (*if it is deformed*).
4. Have students review the sample sentences and Notes.
5. Answer any questions that students have about using participles in reduced adverbial clauses.

1. Ask students to read the instructions.
2. Call on a student to read the example.
3. Call on a volunteer to identify the adverbial clause in the original sentence.
4. Have students complete the activity and then check their work in pairs.

■ EXERCISE C

CD 3, Track 2

1. Tell students that they will hear a conversation between a teaching assistant and an undergraduate student.
2. Play the audio and have students listen for comprehension only.
3. Have students read through the questions.
4. Play the audio again, pausing so that students have time to write their answers.
5. Call on volunteers to read their answers aloud. If any class members disagree with what is read, play the audio again so that students can listen for the correct answers.

B Reduce an adverbial clause in each sentence below.

1. When they are bounced against a surface, all balls have a measurable coefficient of restitution.

   When bounced against a surface, all balls have a measurable coefficient of restitution.

2. Athletes have to spend a lot of extra time practicing <u>if they use a new ball with a different coefficient</u>.

   . . . if using a new ball with a different coefficient.

3. Tennis players know how balls bounce on the different surfaces <u>because they have trained on clay courts and on grass</u>.

   . . . having trained on clay courts and on grass.

4. Athletes may prefer to play on artificial turf <u>when they consider the condition of the grass in a particular stadium</u>.

   . . . when considering the condition of the grass in a particular stadium.

5. <u>When they refer to characteristics of a surface</u> that affect how a ball bounces and rolls, scientists use the term *resistance*.

   When referring to characteristics of a surface. . . .

6. <u>Although they appear more aesthetic than utilitarian</u>, the dimples on a golf ball actually help reduce air resistance.

   Although appearing more aesthetic than utilitarian. . . .

C Listen to the conversation between Larry, a teaching assistant in a physics lab, and Gina, an undergraduate. Answer a question about each part of their conversation.

CD3,TR2

1. When should Gina work on the database? *While she's waiting to take the next temperature reading, Gina should work on the database.*

2. Doesn't the equipment record the data itself?

   It's programmed to record the readings, but it's been inconsistent lately.

3. Under what circumstance will the TA tell Professor Kerry that Gina was the only person who was recording the data?

   If someone asks the TA, the TA will tell Prof. Kelly that Gina was the one recording the data.

4. When did Larry decide on Gina's role in the experiment?

   While he was planning the experimental procedure.

5. What is an important step in becoming a successful scientist?

   Mastering the techniques and protocols of lab research.

6. When did Larry visualize himself in his own lab?

   When he dreamed of being a scientist as a kid.

■ **EXPANSION IDEA**

Exercise C

1. Ask students to write a summary of the conversation between Larry and Gina, using the information in their answers to the questions in Exercise C.
2. Circulate as students write; assist as needed. Encourage students to use reduced adverbial clauses in their writing whenever possible.
3. Call on a volunteer to read his/her summary aloud.

Spin causes more air to flow over the top of the ball, which is a longer path, therefore it must move more quickly, which causes lift.

Direction of motion of the ball

D Rewrite each sentence so that the subjects of the main clause and adverbial phrases are the same.

1. When striking, a golf ball should have a backspin as it flies down the fairway.
   When struck, a golf ball should have a backspin as it flies down the fairway.

2. If served properly, a tennis player hits the ball over the net with a topspin.
   If served properly, a tennis ball is hit over the net with a topspin.

3. Good tennis players put a spin on the ball when served.
   Good tennis players put a spin on the ball when serving.

4. According to the Magnus effect, the pressure of the air molecules forces a golf ball downward when rotating with a topspin.
   According to the Magnus effect, the pressure of the air molecules forces a golf ball downward when it is rotating with a topspin.

5. A beginning golf player may not strike the ball well, although hit straight.
   Although he may hit straight, a beginning golfer may not strike the ball well.

6. Understanding the advantage of the Magnus effect, a golf ball will go much farther.
   If one understands the advantage of the Magnus effect, a golf ball will go much farther.

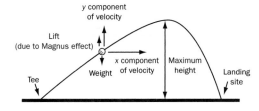

1. Ask students to study the diagram.
2. Call on a volunteer to explain the diagram.
3. Ask students to read the instructions.
4. Call on a student to read the example.
5. Ask a volunteer to explain why the original sentence is incorrect.
6. Have students complete the activity individually and then check their answers in pairs.
7. Call on volunteers to read their answers aloud.
8. Call on a volunteer to explain the graph at the bottom of the page.

■ **EXPANSION IDEA**

Exercise D

1. Divide the class into pairs.
2. Have students read each sentence in Exercise D and identify who or what the adverbial phrases refer to.

For example, in the first sentence, *When striking* refers to the golfer, not the golf ball.

3. Have them discuss why these sentences are confusing.

EXERCISE E

1. Go over the instructions with the class.
2. Ask students to read the example.
3. Answer any questions they have about the example and the activity in general.
4. Have students complete the activity with a partner. Encourage students to discuss possible answers before they write them down.
5. Call on volunteers to read their answers to the class. Discuss other options for answers.

E Paraphrase some ideas from each text with a sentence that includes an adverbial clause. Use reduced clauses, omitting any unnecessary conjunctions.

1. Ned practices his golf swing regularly. His goal is to hit balls farther and with backspin. He is taking lessons right now to improve both skills.

   While taking golf lessons, Ned has been focusing on his swing. / Hoping to hit balls farther, Ned practices his golf swing regularly. / Although practicing his swing regularly, Ned is taking lessons to improve his skills.

2. Rachel has been a long-distance runner for several years and usually runs around the track at her university. At the beginning of summer vacation, she jogged on the sidewalks in her hometown, but her knees started to hurt. Her coach told her that the hard surface of the sidewalks had caused her injury.

   Rachel's knees started to hurt because she jogged on the sidewalks in her hometown.

3. Coaches and experts in sports medicine worry about the surfaces that athletes run and jump on. Without the proper shoes for their sport, athletes can damage their knees and feet when the energy that they exert against the track "bounces back" into their bodies. Sprinters and long jump athletes take advantage of the quick rebound from the track, but long distance runners need a lower coefficient of restitution to avoid injury.

   When running or jumping on hard surfaces, athletes can damage their knees and feet.

4. Like balls, badminton birds, or shuttlecocks, can also spin, but the action is influenced by their construction. The old-fashioned type has 16 feathers, and the newer, cheaper shuttlecocks have a plastic skirt. Skilled players can cause shuttle cocks to rotate counterclockwise, but the ones with skirts rotate at half the speed of the feathered ones.

   Having a plastic skirt instead of feathers, modern shuttle cocks rotate at half the speed of the old-fashioned ones.

5. The center of gravity in a ball can be moved if the ball is damaged. Once that happens, the ball won't fly true or roll straight. Instead it wobbles. Sometimes baseball pitchers secretly "doctor" a ball, in other words put a foreign substance on the ball, so that it moves unpredictably, which makes it hard for the batter to hit.

   When doctored by a pitcher, a baseball moves unpredictably.

EXPANSION IDEA

Exercise E

1. Ask students to pick one of the five paragraphs to expand. Have them write two more sentences, each of which includes a reduced adverbial clause.

   For example:
   Although running on sidewalks is her favorite way to train, Rachel now runs on a treadmill instead. Hoping to compete in a marathon in April, she is doing everything possible to reduce strain on her knees.

2. Circulate as students work and assist as needed.
3. Have students exchange work with a partner. Tell them to check to make sure that their partner's sentences include reduced adverbial clauses.
4. Call on a few volunteers to read their work aloud.

Professor Kerry-

Just to let you know that we finished Phase 1 of the experiment this afternoon. As ~~anticipating~~ **anticipated**, the **bored**
temperature readings were all in the expected range. Although the students complained that they were ~~boring~~,
they actually did a great job. The most ~~amazed~~ **amazing** thing is that several of them came to me later and wanted to
do extra work.

Because **we're** using some different equipment for Phase 2, I'll have to close the lab for a few hours tomorrow
morning. It's a good thing that we're a little ahead of schedule.

As soon as we're ready, I'll beep you-
Larry

■ COMMUNICATE

G **PAIR WORK** Work together to prepare instructions for the steps in a process. Use as
many adverbial and adjectival participles as possible in your list of steps. When you
present your instructions to the class, one of you can demonstrate, or pantomime, as the
other gives the instructions.   **Answers will vary.**

You start with a square sheet of paper when **making** an origami crane . . .
The **finished** product can be puffed up by blowing through a hole in the bottom.

■ EXERCISE F

1. Ask students to read the instructions.
2. Have students complete the activity individually and then check their work with a partner.

■ COMMUNICATE

■ EXERCISE G

1. Go over the instructions with the class.
2. Call on a student to read the text in the speech balloon.
3. Divide the class into pairs and have them choose the process they will describe.
4. Give students time to write down the steps in their processes.
5. Circulate as students work, reminding them to use as many adverbial and adjective participles in their instructions as possible.
6. Call on volunteers to present their instructions to the class.

■ EXPANSION IDEA

Exercise F

Have students write a short e-mail from Professor Kerry to Larry. Remind them to use adverbial and adjective participles.

For example:
Larry,
I'll wait for your beep. Sorry to hear that your students said they were bored. There's *nothing worse than a classroom full of uninterested undergrads. Try to think of some new ways to present the next part of the experiment. Observing how your class reacted to Phase 1 should help you determine how to introduce Phase 2.*

Connection

Putting It Together

■ GRAMMAR AND VOCABULARY

1. Ask students to read the instructions.
2. Call on two students to read the topics aloud.
3. Ask students to choose one of the two topics and give them time to write their compositions.

■ PROJECT

1. Ask students to review the instructions.
2. Answer any questions that students have about the project.
3. Call on students at the next class meeting to give their oral reports.

■ INTERNET

1. Call on a student to read the instructions.
2. Have students conduct their searches for simplified explanations of how various machines and devices work.
3. Ask students to present their information to the class in their own words, using some reduced adverbial clauses.

GRAMMAR AND VOCABULARY Write a composition on one of the topics below. Use as many words as possible from the Content Vocabulary on page 221. Use sentences with adjectival participles and participles in reduced adverb clauses to express some of your ideas.

Topic 1: Explain the correct way to handle the ball in a sport that you enjoy playing. How do you hit, bounce, or throw it properly? How does the ball move when players handle it correctly? What do beginning players need to practice so that the ball moves efficiently?

Topic 2: All students have favorite courses and favorite teachers. In your opinion, can an interesting teacher make you like a field that you never liked before? After taking a motivating class, do you want to take more courses in that field? Can any field be fascinating and exciting with the right teacher? Give concrete examples.
Answers will vary.

PROJECT Interview at least four students on your campus about taking science courses. Find out the following information from each student, and make a brief oral report on the results of your interviews at your next class meeting.
   a. the student's major
   b. the science classes that the student took in high school and has taken in college
   c. if the student is interested in science and why
   d. what kind of classes the student finds boring

 INTERNET Go online to find simplified explanations of how various machines and devices work. Use the search term "how things work." Choose something about science or electronics, and write a summary of the explanation. Present the information in your own words, using some reduced adverbial clauses.
Answers will vary.

■ EXPANSION IDEA

Grammar and Vocabulary
1. Divide the class into pairs.
2. Have students edit each other's compositions. Ask them to suggest additional uses of participial adjectives and participles in reduced adverb clauses.

Film Studies: Documentaries

■ CONTENT VOCABULARY

Look up the words and phrases below that you do not know and enter them in your vocabulary journal. Write each word's part of speech, a definition, and an example sentence. Try to include them in your discussion and writing below.

corrupt	footage	prestigious	subject matter
to elicit	to perceive	a sequel	to survive
to excavate	to portray	the status quo	visual

■ THINK ABOUT IT

The photos on the next page surprised and delighted people in the 1880s. Before film, people had not been able to closely examine how horses galloped. What photos or films have you seen that revealed something completely new in your understanding of the world? Discuss your ideas with a classmate.

In your writing journal, write for 5–10 minutes about the questions below. When you are finished, share what you wrote with the class.
What kind of documentary films or TV programs do you enjoy watching? What do you like to see in such films and programs?
Answers will vary.

233

Overview

1. Ask students to raise their hands if they enjoy watching documentaries.
2. Call on a few volunteers to explain to the class why they like watching this type of film.

■ CONTENT VOCABULARY

Ask students to review the words in the box. Tell them to look up any unfamiliar words.

■ VOCABULARY JOURNAL

Have students add new words to their vocabulary journals and write down the parts of speech, definitions, and sentences for each.

■ THINK ABOUT IT

1. Have students read the instructions.
2. Divide the class into pairs and have students discuss the movies and photos that gave them new insights into subjects.
3. Have students read the journal writing instructions. Answer any questions that they have about the topic. Then give them time to write in their journals.
4. Call on volunteers to share their ideas with the class.

■ CONTENT NOTES

The topic of this lesson is Film Studies: Documentaries. Students will learn about early documentaries, the topics they covered, and why this sort of film appeals to audiences. They will have a chance to consider how they would present factual material to an audience and will acquire the vocabulary necessary to do so.

PART ONE | Complements of Sensory Verbs

■ GRAMMAR IN CONTENT

■ EXERCISE A
CD 3, Track 3

1. Ask students to look closely at the photo. Then call on a volunteer to describe it.
2. Write *Eadweard Muybridge* and *Robert Flaherty* on the board. Ask if anyone is familiar with the work of these early filmmakers.
3. Play the audio and have students follow along in their books as they listen. Ask students to circle any unfamiliar words or phrases.
4. Call on students to read their circled words and elicit definitions or explanations from volunteers if possible.
5. Check comprehension by asking questions such as the following: *What kinds of things in the natural world have documentaries caught on film? What did* Nanook of the North *show? Where was* Moana *filmed? What do good documentary films do beyond entertaining viewers?*

■ GRAMMAR IN CONTENT

A Read and listen to the passage below. The words in bold are clauses with participial complements.

CD3,TR3

Seeing Is Believing

During the last decade, documentaries have done very well at the box office. Films such as *Bowling for Columbine* and *March of the Penguins* have earned millions of dollars and have garnered prestigious awards in the film industry. Titles of other popular documentaries from the big screen or from TV may come to mind, but the majority of such films rarely match the drawing power of Hollywood-style movies. That is not to say, however, that documentary films lack power or influence.

Before filmmaking even began, photographs of historic events and of nature could capture the attention and imagination of the public. Through photographs, people could see what their eyes were not able to otherwise perceive. A famous example is the galloping horse of Eadweard Muybridge. By the 1880s, he was able to project photos of the horse on a screen so quickly that **viewers perceived the horse galloping**. Of course, on each frame a **viewer could only see the horse step or lift its feet**. Since those days, some documentary-makers have explored our natural world in much more detail and have caught animals hunting, protecting their territory, and taking care of their young on film.

In the 1920s, American filmmaker Robert Flaherty made the first two documentary films: *Nanook of the North* and *Moana*. Each of these films explored the lives of people in remote areas of the world. While in northeastern Canada exploring for minerals, Flaherty had come in contact with Eskimos and made friends. On film, **Nanook and other Eskimos were observed fishing, paddling their kayaks, hunting seals through the ice, and building igloos**. In the second film, Flaherty brought the world of Moana and his Polynesian family to American audiences, who **watched these islanders preparing for Moana's initiation rites**. Although these documentaries lacked story lines and portrayed real people quite different from American moviegoers, the films were very well-received.

As filmmakers in North America and Europe explored this form of visual expression, many found a new purpose for their efforts: recording their subjects to elicit reactions or actions among the viewers. From this point of view, the audience should leave the movie house thinking about their own actions or attitudes. For example, after seeing *Super Size Me*, many people have reconsidered the amount of fast food that they should eat. That 98-minute film did more to change attitudes about eating fast food than all the warnings of doctors and nutritionists!

Informative and educational, documentaries should, therefore, do more than interest and entertain us. Some of them are intended to reflect the lives of real people or other living things on our planet so that audience members can extend their horizons and develop an understanding or sympathy for foreign or exotic things. Other films function as a "call to arms," in other words, a visual stimulus to change the status quo.

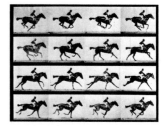

A photo-sequence by the filmmaker Eadweard Muybridge.

the box office: the place to buy tickets at a theater or stadium; the total income from ticket sales

a story line: the plot or story

to garner: to get, to win

■ EXPANSION IDEAS

Exercise A

1. Divide the class up into small groups.
2. Ask students to discuss documentaries that they've seen in English such as *Bowling for Columbine, Sicko, March of the Penguins,* and *An Inconvenient Truth.*
3. Ask them to talk about whether this type of film is commonly made in their own countries, and if so, what subjects they explore.

Exercise A

1. Ask students to write a short composition about a documentary film produced in their native language.
2. Have students exchange compositions with at least two other students.

Sample Sentences	Notes
In a film about Africa we could hear **lions roaring** close to the camp, but we didn't hear **any other animals make a noise.**	Although sensory verbs usually function as stative verbs, you can express either limited or continuing actions in their complements.
We heard **one of the hunters shoot his rifle** to scare away some hyenas. I recorded **him shooting** at least three times.	Use a **bare infinitive complement** to express a completed action: **sensory verb + direct object + bare infinitive (phrase)**
I didn't expect to see **one hyena lying** under some bushes the next morning.	Use a **complement with a present participle** to express an action in progress: **sensory verb + direct object + -ing participial phrase**
Did you spot/photograph **the other hyena hiding** in the brush?	In both cases, the direct object of the sensory verb is the agent of the action in the complement.
After the film I overheard **one moviegoer comment** on the violence to her friend.	NOTE: Do not use *perceive, photograph, smell,* and *spot* with a bare infinitive complement.
In the film *C'mon Geese,* **the pilot** is overheard **saying** "C'mon geese!" because he wants them to follow his small plane.	If **the direct object of the main clause** is the focus of attention, use a passive verb construction before the complement. • Use *hear, notice, observe, overhear, photograph, record, see, spot* in such passive constructions.
At the end of the film, **the geese** are seen **following his plane** and are heard **honking naturally** as they are in flight.	• Most passive sentences of this type have a participial complement.

Common Sensory Verbs

feel/sense	notice	overhear	photograph	see	spot
hear	observe	perceive	record	smell	watch

B Read over your journal entry, and <u>underline</u> at least one sentence that you can revise to include a clause with a sensory verb followed by a complement. Write your revised sentence(s) below.

    Answers will vary.

_____

_____

_____

_____

■ GRAMMAR CHART
Sensory Verbs

1. Ask students to brainstorm sensory verbs and write them on the board.
2. Write on the board *I noticed one small mistake on your test.* Ask students to identify the sensory verb and its voice (*stative*).
3. Add to the sentence on the board *but I didn't notice anything else wrong.* Point out that you can add limited or continuation actions in the complements of stative verbs.
4. Ask the class to read the sample sentences and Notes.
5. Answer any questions that students have about using sensory verbs.

■ EXERCISE B

1. Have students complete the exercise.
2. Ask students to exchange work with a partner. Have them look for additional places where they could include a clause with a sensory verb followed by a complement.

■ EXPANSION IDEA

Grammar

1. Ask students to write three short sentences that include sensory verbs.

   For example:
   We saw a terrible accident.

2. Have students exchange work with a partner. Have partners add complements that provide more information.

   . . . but we couldn't see whether anyone was hurt.

■ EXERCISE C

1. Ask students to brainstorm what they would expect to see or hear in an Amazon rain forest. Write their ideas on the board.
2. Have students read the instructions.
3. Call on a student to read the example and comment on whether *colorful birds hiding* and *crocodiles catching prey* are on the board. Point out that there are many possible answers.
4. Have students complete the activity individually and then compare their work in pairs.
5. Call on volunteers to read their answers aloud.

■ EXERCISE D

1. Go over the instructions with the class.
2. Have students complete the activity individually and then check their work in pairs.

C Write two sentences to describe what you expect to see or hear in each scene below.

1. (in the Amazon rain forest/see)
   a. _____ I hope to watch colorful birds hiding among the branches. _____
   b. _____ I expect to see a crocodile catch its prey in the water. _____

2. (on the ocean floor/see)
   a. I hope to see sea horses swimming around.
   b. I'd expect to observe small creatures moving around a coral reef.

3. (during a political campaign/hear)
   a. I expect to hear candidates give speeches.
   b. I hope to hear candidates, responding honestly to citizens' questions.

4. (on a trip through the Sahara Desert/observe)
   a. I expect to observe riders on camels moving along ancient routes.
   b. I'd hope to see the sun rise over the sand dunes.

5. (in the control tower of a major international airport/hear)
   a. I expect to hear controllers give orders to pilots.
   b. I hope to hear a controller talk a pilot through a difficult landing.

D Now imagine that you are part of a camera team on location. What do you expect to smell or feel in each of these situations?

1. (in a tidal pool on the coast of Australia in the summer/feel)
   a. I hope to feel a crab or other creature nibble on my toe.
   b. I expect to feel the sun beating down on my shoulders.

2. (in various coffee shops in the U.S./smell)
   a. I hope to smell something good baking in the oven.
   b. I hope to smell good coffee brewing when I open the door.

3. (in a busy subway station/feel)
   a. I expect to feel the wind rush by when a subway train passes.
   b. I hope not to feel someone push me into the subway.

4. (at a carnival or other outdoor festival/smell)
   a. I hope to smell some spicy snacks roasting.
   b. I hope to smell some hotdogs sizzling on a barbeque.

■ EXPANSION IDEA

Exercises C and D

1. Ask students to expand one of their pairs of answers into a paragraph in which they describe what they hear, see, smell, and feel. Remind them to use sensory verbs.

2. Have students exchange work with a partner. Ask partners to suggest ways to strengthen the sensory images in each other's writing.

3. Call on volunteers to read their paragraph aloud.

E The sentences below tell about a scene from a film. Use your imagination to describe something else that can be seen or heard. Follow the example. Answers will vary. Sample answers below.

1. A well-known documentary director succeeded in interviewing one of the opponents of educational reform in the United States.

   The woman is heard criticizing the importance of test scores for elementary school students.

2. One director shot two hours of film of young girls who hope to be Olympic gymnasts.

   The girls are observed practicing the same routine for hours.

3. While a director was investigating police corruption, she got footage of two police officers on their beat.

   One officer is overheard asking a shopkeeper for money.

4. A director in Milan, Italy, who is interested in the effect of the fashion world on young models, accompanied one young woman during the preparations for an important fashion show.

   She is seen putting make-up on before the show.

5. A local director was fascinated by the graffiti artists in his city.

   One artist is explaining the graffiti designs that she has developed.

6. A director has been collecting interviews with master shipbuilders, including a local man who builds canoes.

   This man is observed selecting a tree for his next canoe.

7. Another director wants to convince people that skydiving is a great sport, so she filmed a skydiving instructor.

   The instructor is heard preparing people to sky-dive for the first time.

■ EXERCISE E

1. Go over the instructions with the class.
2. Call on a student to read the example.
3. Ask the class to brainstorm more things that might be heard or seen during the interview.
4. Have students complete the activity on their own and then compare their answers in pairs.
5. Call on volunteers to read their answers aloud.

■ EXPANSION IDEA

Exercise E

1. Divide the class into groups.
2. Assign each of the groups one of the scenarios described in the seven sentences.
3. Ask students in the group to combine their answers to set up a scene.

   For example:
   Student 1: *The woman is heard criticizing the importance of test scores for elementary school students.*

   Student 2: *You can hear the sound of children playing in the background.*

   Student 3: *There is a shot of students taking a standardized test.*

4. Call on each group to describe its scene to the class.

■ EXERCISE F

1. Go over the instructions with the class.
2. Call on two students to read the text in the speech balloons.
3. Ask students to read all of the possible topics and call on volunteers to explain any that are unclear to the class.
4. Divide the class into pairs and have students choose a topic and then brainstorm the kinds of scenes their documentary should include.

PART TWO

Other Verbs with Participial Complements

■ GRAMMAR IN CONTENT

■ EXERCISE A

Have students complete the activity individually and then check their answers in pairs.

■ GRAMMAR CHART

Other Verbs with Participial Complements

1. Write on the board *It is hard to find birds building their nests.*
2. Call on a volunteer to underline the participial complement in the sentence.
3. Ask students to read the sample sentences and the Notes.
4. Answer any questions that students have about using verbs with participial complements.

F **PAIR WORK** Choose one of the topics below and brainstorm the kinds of scenes that a good documentary on this topic should include. In this documentary, you want to change people's attitudes. Describe at least five possible scenes that you want in your documentary and then share those ideas with your classmates.

- the benefits of doing yoga
- the social integration of people with disabilities
- the serious problem of bullies in schools
- the danger of driving while you talk on a cell phone
- the need to graduate from high school

Let's make a movie about bullies. I know a lot of people could relate to that. How should we start it?   The audience should see a bully starting a fight with another kid. Suddenly, we hear the bell ringing . . .

PART TWO	Other Verbs with Participial Complements

■ GRAMMAR IN CONTENT

A Reread the text at the beginning of this lesson, and <u>underline</u> *catch, discover, find,* and *leave* as main verbs. Do any of the sentences with these verbs have a participial complement? Share your answers with a partner.

Other Verbs with Participial Complements

Sample Sentences	Notes
Undercover camera operators have often **caught** corrupt officials taking bribes.	Use a present participle in the complement (after the direct object) of the following verbs: *catch, discover, find, uncover, leave.*
You don't normally **come across** a police officer accepting bribes, so hidden cameras are often the only way to film the scene.	
It's difficult to **uncover** public officials taking bribes.	The verbs **catch, find, discover,** and **uncover** all refer to a physical, not an intellectual, discovery when they are used in this construction. The prepositional verbs **come across** and **come upon** also have this meaning and the same type of complement.
In films of little known cultures, the film crew may **discover** people living in primitive conditions. They might also **find** people behaving much better than "civilized" people.	
In order to tape the day-long ceremony, the sound engineer **left** the recorder running until the last guest had left.	

■ EXPANSION IDEAS

Exercise F
Have students write a composition that describes the scenes they will include in their documentaries.

Grammar
1. Ask students to write the first half of three sentences using verbs presented in the grammar lesson.

For example: *We may never catch . . .*

2. Divide the class into pairs. Have students complete each other's sentences by adding participial complements.

   . . . these animals building their nests.

Sample Sentences	Notes
Do you **remember** the bride's father giving the groom three cows?	*Recall* and *remember* can also have a participial complement like the verbs above.
Some documentaries show the lives of homeless people in urban areas. These people **are found** living under bridges or sleeping in subway stations.	Use a passive construction if the direct object is the focus of attention. In this case, do not use either **come across** or **come upon**.

B Give suggestions for staying safe and healthy if you are shooting a film on location in an exotic or dangerous setting. Use the main verb *leave*.

1. At night, how can you avoid diseases that are carried by mosquitoes?
   You can leave the mosquito netting hanging down over your bed.

2. At night, how can you keep wild animals from entering your camp?
   You can leave a fire burning.

3. At night, how can you keep bears from entering your camp to look for food?
   You can leave the food in plastic containers hanging from a rope from a tree.

4. During the day, how can you make a quick escape in your vehicle if a lion attacks?
   You could leave the keys hanging in the ignition.

5. At night, what can alert you in case an earthquake begins so that you can escape?
   You could leave something to fall and alert you if there is an earthquake.

6. At night, what can you do in a cold climate so that your water pipes don't freeze?
   You can leave the water dripping.

7. At night, how can you keep a snake or spider from sleeping in your shoe?
   You can leave your shoes lying upside down.

■ **EXERCISE B**

1. Ask students to brainstorm some of the dangers to health and safety that are present when shooting on location. Write them on the board.
2. Have students read the instructions.
3. Call on a student to read the example.
4. Ask the class to brainstorm a few more ways of avoiding diseases that are carried by mosquitoes.
5. Have students complete the activity individually.
6. Divide the class into groups and have students compare their answers.

■ **EXPANSION IDEA**

Exercise B
Ask students to use the information from Exercise B to write a short composition about staying safe and healthy when shooting on location. Remind them to use verbs with participial complements whenever possible.

EXERCISE C

1. Ask students to look at the picture for a moment. Then have them brainstorm things that a camera might catch at this location.

2. Call on a student to read the example.

3. Have students complete the activity individually and then compare their work in pairs.

EXERCISE D

CD 3, Track 4

1. Tell students that they will hear part of a conversation between members of a film crew on location in New York's Central Park.

2. Play the audio and have students listen for comprehension only.

3. Ask students to read the questions.

4. Play the audio again, this time pausing so that students have time to write their answers.

5. Call on volunteers to read their answers aloud. If there is any disagreement about the answers, play the audio again.

C Predict three things that your camera will find or catch at each of the locations below.

1. (at a bus station)

   It'll find people rushing past each other, people standing in line to buy tickets, and people boarding buses.

2. (at the beach on a hot sunny day)

   It'll find kids playing in the sand, teenagers splashing in the water, and older people lying under umbrellas.

3. (on the banks of a river)

   It'll find an old man fishing, a deer getting a drink, and lovers holding hands.

4. (at a political rally)

   It'll find some politicians giving speeches, people wearing campaign buttons, and others protesting.

5. (at a traditional open-air market)

   It'll catch shoppers bargaining with vendors, money being exchanged, and people selling food.

6. (at a rock concert)

   It'll catch musicians using microphones, security dressed in black, and fans waving their arms.

7. (at a boxing match)

   It'll catch boxers hitting each other, the crowd cheering, and coaches calling advice.

D Listen to parts of a conversation between members of a film crew on location in New York's Central Park. Then, answer the questions, expressing your answers using the participial constructions in this lesson.

CD3,TR4

1. Where did Fred put his camera?

   Fred left the camera lying by Lou's camera.

2. What were the two strangers doing?

   They were walking around during the interview holding Fred's camera.

EXPANSION IDEA

Exercise C
Ask students to pick one of the locations from Exercise C. Tell them to write a paragraph about what they found or caught on their cameras at the location. Remind them to use verbs with participial complements.

3. What were the strangers doing when Lou saw them?

They were wandering around near the sound equipment but walked away.

4. What did the strangers say when Lou noticed them?

He didn't hear them saying anything clearly—they mumbled.

5. What did Lou hear while Fred was gone?

Lou heard someone shouting.

6. Why was Fred happy that a cop was near?

He was happy because he overheard men planning to get the camera.

7. How did Fred feel as he was waiting for the cop to come closer?

He was nervous—he could feel the sweat dripping down his face.

E Correct the five errors in the informal e-mail message below.

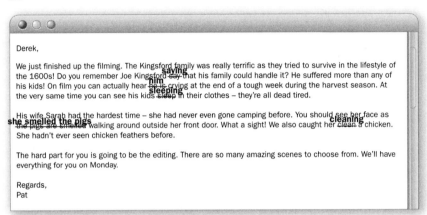

Derek,

We just finished up the filming. The Kingsford family was really terrific as they tried to survive in the lifestyle of the 1600s! Do you remember Joe Kingsford ~~say~~ **saying** that his family could handle it? He suffered more than any of his kids! On film you can actually hear ~~he is~~ **him** crying at the end of a tough week during the harvest season. At the very same time you can see his kids ~~sleep~~ **sleeping** in their clothes – they're all dead tired.

His wife Sarah had the hardest time – she had never even gone camping before. You should see her face as ~~the pigs are smelled~~ **she smelled the pigs** walking around outside her front door. What a sight! We also caught her ~~clean~~ **cleaning** a chicken. She hadn't ever seen chicken feathers before.

The hard part for you is going to be the editing. There are so many amazing scenes to choose from. We'll have everything for you on Monday.

Regards,
Pat

■ COMMUNICATE

F **GROUP WORK** Plan a documentary about your school or program. Remember that documentaries usually aren't scripted, so you need to brainstorm the kinds of scenes that an audience should see and hear to understand what it's like to be a student in your school or program. When your group is finished, share your ideas with the other groups. **Answers will vary.**

1. Ask students to find and correct the five errors in the e-mail message.
2. Have students check their work in pairs.
3. Call on three students to read the e-mail, one paragraph at a time.

■ **COMMUNICATE**

■ **EXERCISE F**

1. Go over the instructions with the class.
2. Divide the class into small groups.
3. Give students time to brainstorm the kinds of scenes they want to include in their documentaries.
4. Call on groups to share their ideas.

■ **EXPANSION IDEA**

Exercise F

1. Have groups role-play the filming of their documentary, using the scenes they brainstormed in Exercise F. They should assign a director, a camera operator, and actors.
2. Call on groups to role-play for the class.

Connection

Putting It Together

■ GRAMMAR AND VOCABULARY

1. Ask students to read the instructions.
2. Call on two students to read the topics aloud.
3. Ask students to choose one of the two topics and give them time to write their compositions.

■ PROJECT

1. Ask students to review the instructions.
2. Answer any questions students have about the project.
3. Call on students at the next class meeting to give their oral reports.

■ INTERNET

1. Call on a student to read the instructions.
2. Have students conduct their searches and choose a documentary that they would like to watch.
3. Ask students to prepare and present an oral report to the class on the documentary they chose and the reasons for their choice.

Connection | Putting It Together

GRAMMAR AND VOCABULARY Write a composition on one of the topics below. Use as many words as possible from the Content Vocabulary on page 233. Use sentences with sensory verbs and other verbs that take participial complements to express some of your ideas.

Topic 1: Documentary makers regularly discover people doing interesting activities or undertaking amazing projects. They also catch animals behaving in fascinating ways. However, documentaries are seen by fewer people and make smaller profits than feature films, like those made in Hollywood. In your opinion, what is the reason for the difference in popularity between the two types of movies? Give concrete examples.

Topic 2: Documentaries or factual programs about animals are very popular on American TV. Moviegoers around the world enjoy watching animals going about their daily lives or behaving in surprising ways. Why are viewers particularly interested in seeing and hearing wildlife living in various habitats and interacting with each other?
Answers will vary.

PROJECT Interview at least one student on your campus about documentaries. Find out the following information, and make a brief oral report on the interview at your next class meeting.

    a. What kinds of documentaries or factual programs does the student watch?
    b. Which documentaries or factual TV programs does the student recommend?
    c. What are some of the popular documentaries of the last 10 years that the student can remember?

 INTERNET Go online and use the search term "reviews of documentary films." Read the reviews or descriptions of some films that have interesting titles, and decide which movie you would like to watch. Prepare a short oral report for your class on your choice and the reasons for your choice.
Answers will vary.

242   LESSON 22 | Film Studies: Documentaries

■ EXPANSION IDEA

Internet
Have students write a review of the documentary they chose to watch. Have students compare their own reviews to those that they found on the Internet.

Grammar Connection 5 Teacher's Edition

PART 1
Reported Speech in Context

PART 2
Rules for and Exceptions to
Backshifts in Reported Speech

Lesson 23

Computer Science:
Artificial Intelligence

■ CONTENT VOCABULARY

Look up the words and phrases below that you do not know and enter them in your vocabulary journal. Write each word's part of speech, a definition, and an example sentence. Try to include them in your discussion and writing below.

to argue	to claim	to highlight	to indicate
to assume	to confirm	humanoid	a sensor
autonomous	a driverless vehicle	to imply	to state

■ THINK ABOUT IT

Look at the photo of the machine on the next page. How do you think such machines work?

In your writing journal, write for five minutes about the questions below. When you are finished, share your ideas with the class.
In your opinion, how will robots help us in our daily lives in the next 10 years? Who will benefit the most from robots?
Answers will vary.

Overview
1. Have students name some kinds of robots that are in use today.
2. Write the types of robots on the board.

■ CONTENT VOCABULARY

Ask students to review the words in the box. Tell them to look up any unfamiliar words.

■ VOCABULARY JOURNAL

Have students add new words to their vocabulary journals and write down the parts of speech, definitions, and sentences for each.

■ THINK ABOUT IT

1. Ask students to look at the photo on page 244 and think about how this kind of a machine works.
2. Call on a student to read the journal questions.
3. Give students time to write in their journals.
4. Call on volunteers to share their ideas with the class.

■ CONTENT NOTES

The topic of this lesson is Computer Science: Artificial Intelligence. Students will learn about various types of robots, their limitations, and the roles that robots can play now and in the future.

■ GRAMMAR IN CONTENT

■ EXERCISE A

CD 3, Track 5

1. Ask students to read the title of the passage.
2. Call on a volunteer to answer the question posed in the title.
3. Play the audio and have students follow along in their books as they listen. Ask students to circle any unfamiliar words or phrases.
4. Call on students to read their circled words and elicit definitions or explanations from volunteers if possible.
5. Check comprehension by asking questions such as the following: *What was DARPA interested in developing? How many teams participated in the "Great Challenge"? When did contestants get to see the route? What constraints were there on size, shape, and power source of robots competing? What was one important lesson that researchers learned from the failure of robots in the first competition? How far did the winner go? Which institution won the "Great Robot Race"? Who built "Sandstorm"?*

■ GRAMMAR IN CONTENT

A Read and listen to the passage below. The sentences in bold in the first part of the text include a *that* clause.

CD3,TR5

Who's in the Driver's Seat?

March, 2004

A remarkable race of driverless robots took place in the desert between Los Angeles and Las Vegas. The 143-mile race was the idea of DARPA, the Defense Advanced Research Projects Agency, which is interested in developing autonomous vehicles for military purposes. **They imagined that some computer scientists and software hobbyists would take the challenge to develop such vehicles,** especially with the incentive of a $1 million prize. **DARPA thought that 20 teams might participate in the "Great Challenge,"** but instead 106 teams submitted applications for the competition.

At their orientation meeting, the participants heard the requirements of the race. **They found out that they wouldn't see the route until 2 hours before the race. DARPA had already decided that only 10% of the course should be on paved roads.** Consequently, the challenge involved creating a robot to travel over desert terrain with volcanic rocks, train tracks, and rivers. In addition, the DARPA officials stated that the vehicles had to avoid contact with other robots. These were the basic rules. The officials also emphasized that there were no constraints on the robots' size, shape, or source of power.

Robot developers learned many lessons when the "winner" of the Great Challenge only made it 7 miles and most robots didn't even go 1 mile. **Researchers now know that robotic vision caused the failure of many of those vehicles. They have learned that radar, lasers, stereovision, and GPS are crucial to a robot's vision but also that effective software has to analyze the ground ahead of the robot accurately.** When that finally happens, robots will be able to maneuver more effectively and go faster.

March, 2006

Oleg: Did you see the program about the second Great Robot Race on NOVA last night?

Tish: No. How did I miss it? I have been waiting to see it since I heard that they were making a TV show about it.

Oleg: It was incredible. They said several robots actually finished the race this time. We saw the top five vehicles cross the finish line.

Tish: Who came in first?

Oleg: Do you remember the one called "Sandstorm"? It's the one built by Carnegie Mellon University.

Tish: Sure. What about it?

Oleg: They explained that it got stuck the last time. They even showed the video of it with the tires burning! They said it was one of the favorites this time, so they spent a lot of time on the Carnegie Mellon team.

Tish: So, what happened? Did they win?

Oleg: No, a guy from Stanford and his team came in first. They said that this guy'd worked at Carnegie Mellon before. I guess that the team at CMU was pretty disappointed with the results.

Tish: I'll bet that there was a big celebration at the Stanford lab after that.

Oleg: You bet! They said that the winning team would get $2 million.

paved: a hard surface that makes transport easier
terrain: land; the surface of the land

a constraint: a limit or restriction
GPS: Global Positioning System

244   LESSON 23 | Computer Science: Artificial Intelligence

■ EXPANSION IDEA

Exercise A

1. Divide the class into pairs and have students compare the "Great Challenge" with the "Great Robot Race." Remind them to use the vocabulary from the lesson whenever possible.
2. Circulate as students work and assist as needed.

Sample Sentences	Notes
Professor Chavez: "Computers will be able to think like humans by 2025."	The reporting verbs *say, tell, state, write* are neutral in meaning.
↓	
Professor Chavez **said that** computers **would be able to think** like humans by 2025.	Use other reporting verbs to express the intention of the speaker or writer. Such verbs add more meaning to statements with reported speech. See the list of some other verbs below.
↓	
Professor Chavez **asserted that** computers **would be able to** think like humans by 2025.	
Professor Chavez **said he was planning** a project with a driverless vehicle.	English speakers often omit *that* with the most frequently used reporting verbs, for example *say* and *tell*.
Professor Chavez **guaranteed that** all of his graduate students **could participate** in the project.	Include *that* in formal contexts, especially with reporting verbs that express the speaker's intention.
Professor Dern: "Future humanoid robots **will probably rely on** special 'stepper motors' for rather small adjustments in movement. We're not sure yet if other types of specialized motors can be adapted to these robotic needs."	Use **connecting words and phrases** to make the information in reported speech as clear as possible to the listener or reader.
↓	Often words are (omitted) or <u>changed</u> in reported speech, but the meaning must remain the same.
In her lecture, Professor Dern assumed that future humanoid robots would <u>depend on</u> special "stepper motors" for small adjustments in motion. Then, she <u>questioned whether</u> other types of (specialized) motors could be adapted to robotic needs.	

Reporting Verbs

admit	demand	guarantee	recommend
announce	doubt	guess	stress
complain	explain	hint	swear

B Read over your journal entry, and <u>underline</u> at least one sentence that you can revise to include reported speech using a *that* clause. Write your revised sentence(s) below.

Answers will vary.

_____

_____

_____

_____

■ GRAMMAR CHART
Reported Speech in Context

1. Write on the board *Rebecca said, "E-books will replace printed paper ones in the near future."*
2. Ask *What did Rebecca say?* Call on a volunteer to restate the sentence as reported speech.
3. Have students read the sample sentences and Notes.
4. Answer any questions students have about how to report speech in context.

■ EXERCISE B

1. Have students complete the exercise.
2. Ask students to exchange work with a partner. Have them look for additional places where they could include reported speech using a *that* clause.

■ EXPANSION IDEA

Grammar
Divide the class into pairs and have students practice reporting speech using the verbs in the box at the bottom of the chart.

1. Ask students to read the instructions and the interview notes.
2. Call on a student to read the example.
3. Answer any questions that students have about the assignment.
4. Give students time to complete the paragraph using the verbs in the box.

■ EXERCISE D

1. Ask students to read the instructions and the interview transcript.
2. Call on a student to read the example.
3. Answer any questions that students have about the assignment.
4. Give students time to summarize the report using reported speech.

C Look at the notes a journalist wrote after interviewing Hans Morasev, a well-known robotics expert. Write a short report about the interview. Use reported speech and the verbs in the box below to complete the paragraph. **Answers will vary.**

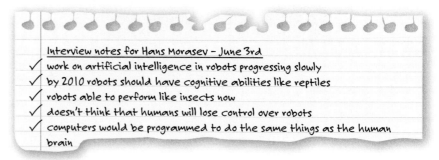

highlight   ~~confirm~~   assert   deny   imply

Interview notes for Hans Morasev – June 3rd
✓ work on artificial intelligence in robots progressing slowly
✓ by 2010 robots should have cognitive abilities like reptiles
✓ robots able to perform like insects now
✓ doesn't think that humans will lose control over robots
✓ computers would be programmed to do the same things as the human brain

Morasev confirmed that work on artificial intelligence using robots was progressing slowly.

During the interview, he highlighted that robots were able to perform like robots right now and asserted that by 2010 that they should have cognitive abilities like reptiles. He implied that computers would eventually be programmed to do the same things as the human brain. However, he denied that humans would ever lose control of robots.

D Read the following excerpt from a transcript of an interview between a reporter and Dr. Elbaz, an archaeologist. Summarize the report using reported speech. **Answers will vary.**

Chang: Good afternoon, Dr. Elbaz. This is Chang Zihong of the *New York Gazette*. What's the latest news on the robot's progress in Egypt?

Dr. Elbaz: We're all pleased with the robot's first day of work. As you know, it entered the first shaft of the Great Pyramid of Giza this morning at 6 A.M.

Chang: According to early reports, the robot got stuck down in the shaft. Is that really true?

Dr. Elbaz: No. I'm happy to report that it traveled slowly but continuously till it reached the bottom of the shaft.

Chang introduced himself as a reporter from the New York Gazette and inquired what the latest news was on the robot's progress in Egypt. Dr. Elbaz expressed approval of the robot's performance and said that it had entered the pyramid that morning. Chang asked whether reports of the robot getting stuck were true, and Elbaz denied the reports.

■ EXPANSION IDEAS

Exercise C

1. Divide the class into pairs and have students exchange paragraphs.
2. Ask them to edit each other's work and check to see whether all of the verbs in the box have been used.
3. Call on a few volunteers to read their paragraphs aloud.

Exercise D

1. Divide the class into pairs.
2. Ask student to take turns telling each other what Chang and Dr. Elbaz said, using reported speech and the verbs from Exercise C.

E Read the following newspaper article. When you are finished, complete the short summary in the space provided.

Boston- Lingua-Bots has announced the first sales of their innovative new robotic cleaning system named "BotButler." According to company spokesman B. Brummer, BotButler can understand 50 voice commands, including "load the dishwasher," "dust the furniture," and "scrub the floor." This humanoid robot stands 4 feet tall and weighs only 50 pounds. It is available online for $1,250 plus shipping and handling. Brummer stated, "BotButler is clearly superior to the first generation of cleaning bots like the Dyson vacuum cleaner and offers the latest robot technology."

The article reported that a company in Boston had announced the sales of a household robot.

Spokesman B. Brummer reported that the "BotButler" understands 50 voice commands to do

household tasks. Brummer went on to say that the robot is only 4 feet tall and weighs 50 lbs.

Brummer declares the BotButler's supremacy in household robotics. It is available for $1,250.

■ COMMUNICATE

F **PAIR WORK** On a separate sheet of paper, write your "specifications" for a new robot. The specifications can describe one of the robots shown or they can describe a robot of your own creation. Share your ideas with a partner. Make sure you understand your partner's specifications. Then, tell the class about your partner's design, using reported speech.

■ **EXERCISE E**

1. Ask students to read the instructions and the article.
2. Answer any questions that students have about the assignment.
3. Give students time to complete the summary.
4. Call on a volunteer to read his/her summary aloud.
5. Ask the class whether any information was left out of the summary, and if so, what was left out.

■ **COMMUNICATE**

■ **EXERCISE F**

1. Ask students to look at the photos and describe each one.
2. Ask students to read the instructions.
3. Give students time to write out their "specifications" for a new robot.
4. Divide the class into pairs and have them compare their specifications.
5. Call on volunteers to tell the class about their partner's robots using reported speech.

■ **EXPANSION IDEA**

Exercises E and F
1. Have students write an article about their own robots using reported speech. Ask them to model their work on the summaries they wrote for

Exercise E, using their specifications from Exercise F.
2. Call on volunteers to read their articles.

■ GRAMMAR IN CONTENT

■ EXERCISE A

Ask students to complete the activity individually and then check their work in pairs.

■ GRAMMAR CHART

Rules for and Exceptions to Backshifts in Reported Speech

1. Ask students to review the sample sentences and Notes.
2. Call on volunteers to explain using backshifts in reported speech in their own words to check for comprehension.

■ GRAMMAR IN CONTENT

A Reread the text at the beginning of the lesson, and <u>underline</u> the sentences that include reported speech or reported ideas. Which of the sentences have backshifting in the *that* clause? Review the rules of backshifting in the chart below if necessary.

Rules for and Exceptions to Backshifts in Reported Speech	
Sample Sentences	**Notes**

Dr. Clark: "Artificial brains aren't very sophisticated yet, but we have made some progress. By next year our robots will perform much more complex tasks."
 	
 Dr. Clark **explained** that artificial brains **weren't** very sophisticated yet and **asserted** that they **had made** some progress. She **predicted** that by next year their robots **would perform** much more complex tasks.
	Follow the rule of backshifts when the reporting verb is in the past tense:
	 1. Shift the tense of the main verb(s) in the *that* clause back "one step" in time.
	 2. Change modals to corresponding past forms:
	     can → *could*
	     may → *might*
	     will → *would*
	     must → *had to*

One professor **stated** that the technology **is** also available to manufacturers of industrial robots. Before the age of artificial intelligence, no one **denied** that man **is** the most intelligent being on Earth.	It isn't necessary to use backshifts in *that* clauses when the statement expresses: • an action or situation that is true and not temporary • information that people consider a general truth • an action or situation that was communicated to the speaker very shortly before the current conversation
Dr. Thurmond's students just **informed** her that their project **went** perfectly earlier that afternoon. Later, Kelly told Dr. Thurmond that the project **took** about 5 hours to finish.	English-speakers often ignore the backshift rule if: • it requires a verb in **past perfect** • the information and time context are clear without a backshift • it causes a change in meaning in modal verbs of probability
Kelly also mentioned that her team **prepared all of the materials and equipment the day before** to make it go smoothly. Kelly pointed out that they **may not have solved** all the problems in their project.	

■ EXPANSION IDEA

Grammar

Divide the class into pairs and have students discuss the "Great Challenge" (page 244). Remind students to use reported speech with backshifting whenever possible.

For example:
Student 1: *DARP officials told reporters that they'd expected only around 20 teams.*

Student 2: *Right. 106 teams entered because students thought it was an easy way to win $1,000,000. Later, though, contestants reported that the whole project was much more difficult than they'd imagined.*

B Read each situation below. Why wasn't the rule of backshifting followed? Write an explanation in the space provided. Follow the example.

1. Pat has just arrived at the computer lab late. She asked her lab partner for their latest assignment. Steve told her that they have to check the movement of the robotic arm.

   Steve probably found out right before Pat arrived that they have to check the robotic arm. There's no need to backshift because it happened so recently.

2. In response to the NASA disaster, one commentator wrote that people aren't robots and that they make mistakes.

   The commentator's remarks don't need backshifting because they express a general truth about human nature.

3. Scientists have struggled to make humanoid robots walk upright because the researchers found that maintaining balance is not an easy feat.

   People would consider that maintaining balance in humanoid robots is not easy to be a general truth, so the rule of backshifting can be ignored.

4. Competitors in the "Great Robot Race" acknowledged that they spent a lot of time on upgrading the sensors in the vehicles before the race.

   The information about the competitors was told to the speaker shortly before, so the backshifting rule can be ignored.

5. Near the end of the Great Robot Race, the MIT team didn't hear the final update. Someone among the spectators told them that the Stanford vehicle took the lead at milepost 139.

   Backshifting isn't necessary because it is clear that MIT didn't hear the final update because they knew they were going to lose the Great Robot Race.

6. Dr. Morasev confidently predicts that robots will be able to reason in our lifetimes. He has written that computers can already perform many tasks more accurately than humans.

   The backshifting rule wasn't followed here because a past perfect verb was used (has written).

7. The NASA engineers and computer scientists were extremely relieved when they saw that the Mars rover landed safely on the surface and began moving forward.

   It is clear that the action of the Mars rover already happened and is not currently taking place, so the backshifting rule can be ignored.

8. For centuries people believed that our ability to think and communicate defines us as humans. Now, however, computers are rapidly developing those same skills.

   Backshifting isn't used here because information that people consider a general truth is conveyed.

■ **EXERCISE B**

1. Ask students to read the instructions.
2. Call on a student to read the example and discuss it with the class.
3. Ask students to write their answers to the next question.
4. Call on a volunteer to read his or her answer aloud and discuss it with the class.
5. Have students complete the rest of the activity individually and then check their work in pairs.
6. Call on volunteers to read their answers aloud. If other class members disagree with the answers, discuss them as a class.

■ **EXPANSION IDEA**

Exercise B

1. Divide the class into pairs.
2. Have students take turns restating the sentences so that they include backshifts. Ask them to discuss how the contexts are different when they use backshifting.

For example:

1. *Steve told her that they had to check the movement of the robotic arm.*
2. *In response to the NASA disaster, one commentator wrote that people weren't robots and that they make mistakes.*

1. Ask students to read the instructions.
2. Play the audio, pausing after each statement so that students can mark their answers.
3. Play the audio again so that students can check their answers.
4. Call on volunteers to read their answers aloud. If class members disagree, play the audio again.

C Listen to each statement and (circle) the letter of the sentence that correctly restates the information with reported speech. It's possible that more than one paraphrase is correct. In such cases, (circle) the letter of both sentences.

CD3,TR6

The team from Stanford won the second Great Challenge.

1. (a.) He said that the team from Stanford won the second Great Challenge.
   (b.) He said that the team from Stanford had won the second Great Challenge.
2. (a.) He said that hospitals use robots to transport medical supplies and deliver meals.
   (b.) He said that hospitals used robots to transport medical supplies and deliver meals.
3. (a.) He says robots can vacuum rugs without hitting furniture.
   b. He says robots could vacuum rugs without hitting furniture.
4. (a.) She said that many movie robots had become famous.
   (b.) She said that many movie robots have become famous.
5. (a.) She stated scientists are working on robots in the shapes of animals.
   (b.) She stated scientists were working on robots in the shapes of animals.
6. a. He stated that after our disappointing results, we must think about the future of intelligent robots.
   (b.) He stated that after their disappointing results, they had to think about the future of intelligent robots.
7. (a.) They say that in a few years driverless vehicles will move more quickly over rough terrain.
   b. They say that in a few years driverless vehicles would move more quickly over rough terrain.
8. (a.) He said that some people use the word "bot" as a nickname for robots.
   (b.) He said that some people used the word "bot" as a nickname for robots.
9. (a.) Experts say that robots may change human civilization.
   b. Experts say that robots might change human civilization.

■ EXPANSION IDEA

Exercise C

1. Divide the class into pairs and have students discuss how meanings are changed in the answers in which one of the paraphrases is wrong.

2. Circulate as students work; assist as needed.

D Find and correct the four errors in the following e-mail message.

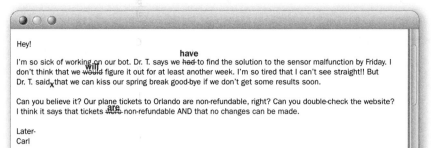

Hey!

I'm so sick of working on our bot. Dr. T. says we ~~had~~ **have** to find the solution to the sensor malfunction by Friday. I don't think that we ~~would~~ **will** figure it out for at least another week. I'm so tired that I can't see straight!! But Dr. T. said~~,~~**x** that we can kiss our spring break good-bye if we don't get some results soon.

Can you believe it? Our plane tickets to Orlando are non-refundable, right? Can you double-check the website? I think it says that tickets ~~were~~ **are** non-refundable AND that no changes can be made.

Later-
Carl

E Look at the dialog on page 244. In the spaces provided report on four statements made by Tish and/or Oleg. Follow the example.

1. *Tish said that she has been waiting to see the program since she first heard about it.*

2. Oleg said that it was incredible and that he saw the first five vehicles cross the finish line.

3. Oleg said that "Sandstorm" won and explained that they had had a difficult previous year.

4. Oleg then explained that they didn't win but a team from Stanford won.

5. Tish asserted that they must have been happy. Oleg affirmed this and said that they would get $2 million.

■ **COMMUNICATE**

F **GROUP WORK** In a group, talk about robots that you have seen in films. What were the robots' special abilities? What role did they play in the plot? When you are finished, summarize your discussion for the class.

Several people in our group said that they love the movie *Star Wars*.

Robots played a big role in that movie. Maria pointed out that R2D2 saved his robot friend C-3PO several times.

Have students complete the activity individually and then check it in pairs.

■ **EXERCISE E**

1. Ask students to read the instructions and example.
2. Answer any questions that students have about the activity.
3. Have students complete the activity individually and then check it in pairs.

■ **COMMUNICATE**

■ **EXERCISE F**

1. Ask students to read the instructions.
2. Call on two students to read the text in the speech balloons.
3. Divide the class into groups and have students talk about robots they've seen in films.
4. When they are finished, call on groups to summarize their discussion for the class.

■ **EXPANSION IDEA**

Exercise F

Ask students to select one of the robots they discussed in their groups. Ask them to write a paragraph that discusses what other group members said about the robot.

Connection

Putting It Together

■ GRAMMAR AND VOCABULARY

1. Ask students to read the instructions.
2. Call on two students to read the topics aloud.
3. Ask students to choose one of the two topics and give them time to write their compositions.

■ PROJECT

1. Ask students to review the instructions.
2. Answer any questions students have about the project.
3. Call on students at the next class meeting to give their oral reports.

■ INTERNET

1. Call on a student to read the instructions.
2. Have students conduct their searches and watch a video clip.
3. Ask students to prepare a report on three things that the speaker said.
4. Call on students to present their information at the next class, reminding them to include the name of the person and the exact title and website of the video in their reports.

GRAMMAR AND VOCABULARY Write a composition on one of the topics below. Use as many words as possible from the Content Vocabulary on page 243. Use sentences with reported speech and ideas with *that* clauses to express some of your ideas.

Topic 1: Many people adapt easily to technological change; however, others fear our growing dependence on computers and artificial intelligence in every aspect of our lives. Explain the opinions and attitudes of someone you know who criticizes this dependence. What has that person told you or expressed to you about these issues?

Topic 2: Every year new models of automobiles include more sensors and more sophisticated computers. In previous years, what did car companies claim that their cars could do? What did they announce that the new models would do? What kind of innovations do you predict the companies will produce in their vehicles in the next 15 years?
Answers will vary.

PROJECT Interview a student on your campus about robots. Find out the student's opinion regarding the following:

    a. What can robots do? Where do robots work right now?
    b. How much should we depend on robots in the future?
    c. Will robots be a danger to humans in the future?

Tell your classmates the results of your interview.

 INTERNET Go to the website www.thetech.org/robotics. Select one of the many video clips on this site. Watch the video and then prepare to report on three things that the speaker said. Be sure that you tell the name of the person and the exact title and website of the video when you present your information.
Answers will vary.

252   LESSON 23 | Computer Science: Artificial Intelligence

■ EXPANSION IDEA

Internet
Divide the class into small groups and have them discuss in greater depth what was said in their videos. Remind them to use the vocabulary and grammar from the lesson.

PART 1
Reported Speech: Paraphrases
with Infinitives and Gerunds

PART 2
Reported Speech and Thought:
Passive Forms

Lesson 24

Art History: Symbols and Allegories

■ CONTENT VOCABULARY

Look up the words below that you do not know and enter them in your vocabulary journal. Write each word's part of speech, a definition, and an example sentence. Try to include them in your discussion and writing below.

aesthetically	to commission	to disregard	perspective
affluence	to connote	an exhibit	a pigment
ambiguous	to depict	to grasp	transience

■ THINK ABOUT IT

Look at the painting on the next page and discuss its meaning with a partner. Do you like it? Do you understand it? Do any flowers have a special meaning or symbolism in your culture? Discuss your ideas with a classmate.

In your writing journal, write for five minutes about the questions below. When you are finished, share your ideas with the class.
What would you tell a foreign visitor about the art from your country or culture? How can foreign visitors understand what they see in a painting or other piece of art?
Answers will vary.

253

■ CONTENT NOTES

The topic of this lesson is Art History: Symbols and Allegories. Students will learn about the importance of recognizing symbols in works of art, and how understanding an artist's culture can help them interpret his or her work. Use this lesson to point out how much can be learned about cultures by studying their art. Point out local art museums where students can gain insight into local and international cultures through art, and encourage students to visit them.

Lesson 24

Overview

1. Write *still-life* on the board. Ask students if they are familiar with this term. Elicit a definition from a class member, if possible; if necessary, explain the term.
2. Ask students to discuss this type of art. Call on volunteers to describe the kinds of still-life paintings that are painted in their countries of origin.
3. Assemble a collection of items on your desk and ask students to discuss whether an artist could paint a great still-life of these objects.

■ CONTENT VOCABULARY

Ask students to review the words in the box. Tell them to look up any unfamiliar words.

■ VOCABULARY JOURNAL

Have students add new words to their vocabulary journals and write down the parts of speech, definitions, and sentences for each.

■ THINK ABOUT IT

1. Have students read the instructions.
2. Divide the class into pairs and have students discuss the painting on the next page and symbolism related to flowers.
3. Have students read the journal writing instructions. Answer any questions that they have about the topic. Then give them five minutes to write in their journals.
4. Call on volunteers to share their ideas with the class.

■ EXERCISE A
CD 3, Track 7

1. Ask students if they can name the flowers in the painting.
2. Write *tulip* on the board, and ask students to name the country that these flowers are generally associated with.
3. Call on volunteers to guess what tulips symbolize in Holland.
4. Play the audio and have students follow along in their books as they listen. Ask students to circle any unfamiliar words or phrases.
5. Call on students to read their circled words and elicit definitions or explanations from volunteers if possible.
6. Check comprehension by asking questions such as the following: *Where did the first tulips in Holland come from? What did tulips signify in the Middle East? What connotations did the flowers take on in Holland? Why did some people ask artists to paint tulips for them?*

A Read and listen to the passage below. The words in bold in the text are infinitive or gerund phrases used for reporting speech.

CD3,TR7

Art History and Cultural Context

To the modern eye, European paintings of tulips and other flowers of the sixteenth and seventeenth centuries may seem like pretty pictures of springtime blossoms; however, many of those flowers had a deeper significance to the viewers of those days. For example, tulips were known to symbolize a cautionary story of extravagance and foolishness to the Dutch.

Tulips arrived in Europe from Turkey in the 1500s and became popular among the rich, who could afford to have gardens. In the Middle East, especially Persia, the tulip symbolized love, but in the context of Protestant Holland the tulip gained quite different connotations. As wealthy Dutchmen developed more and more tulip varieties, the flower came to symbolize affluence. Tulip prices rose, and by the 1620s the Dutch obsession with tulips had led to an incredibly speculative market for tulip bulbs. It is said that the average annual wage in Holland at that time was 200–400 guilders, and a single *Semper augustus* tulip (with red flames on white petals) could cost 1,000 guilders. Many middle-class Dutchmen entered the tulip market, hoping to make a fortune. As the market rose, religious leaders **warned their congregations not to risk their financial and spiritual lives on a mere flower**. When the market crashed, the tulip also became a symbol of human foolishness and vanity.

Those who resisted the temptation of the tulip trade often **asked artists to create paintings of flowers** that were valued so highly at the time. During the 1500s and 1600s, the Dutch and other Europeans believed that nature taught valuable lessons about God and creation. Religious leaders **recommended reading nature as a book** filled with lessons about and from God. Therefore, naturalistic paintings of flowers could be considered not only as beautifully realistic arrangements of vivid colors and shapes, but also as a collection of lessons or reminders. Obviously, a vase of cut flowers can signify the transience of life regardless of the flower varieties in the arrangement. In those days, lilies represented purity or justice to the Dutch, and violets were known to connote sweetness and modesty.

As products of their own time and culture, painters express their ideas and emotions with images that their viewers are able to grasp and appreciate. In seventeenth-century Holland, artists created still life paintings for the enjoyment and moral education of people in their own society. Art historians **advise learning about Dutch attitudes and beliefs** if modern viewers truly wish to understand those paintings. Similarly, artists from Islamic, Buddhist, Confucian, or other religious traditions have created images based on their beliefs, histories, literature, and natural surroundings. The same holds true for artists from any other time or background. It has been said that art is a universal language, but the message can't be completely clear until we learn to interpret artists' images appropriately.

Tulips, Lilies, Irises and Roses by Anthony Claesz (1592–1635).

a cautionary story: a story with a warning

Protestant: in this context, any European Christian not belonging to the Roman Catholic Church

a speculative market: business deals in which there is a chance of great profit or loss

a congregation: people who regularly worship at a particular church or synagogue

vanity: excessive pride

naturalistic: realistic, close to nature

■ **EXPANSION IDEA**

Exercise A

1. Divide the class into small groups with students from as many different countries of origin as possible in each group.

2. Ask students to discuss flowers that have symbolic significance in their cultures.

3. Call on a member of each group to report their findings to the class.

Sample Sentences	Notes
Museum guard: "Check your bags in the coat room." The museum guard **told** the visitors **to check** their bags in the coat room.	Use infinitive complements to report: • Imperatives: *say, tell, order, command* • Invitations: *ask* + **object** + **infinitive** • Requests: *ask* + **object** + **infinitive** • Asking permission: *ask* + **infinitive**
Sean: "Would you like to come to the exhibit on Islamic art, Na Rae?" Sean **asked** Na Rae **to go** to the art exhibit.	
Na Rae: "Sean, can you save me a seat?" Na Rae **asked** Sean **to save** her a seat.	Use *order* and *command* for imperatives to emphasize the authority of the speaker. Use one of these basic patterns: • *tell* + **object** + **infinitive** • *say* + **infinitive**
Na Rae: "Sean, can I bring my cousin?" Na Rae **asked to bring** her cousin.	
Na Rae: "Pick up my cousin after work." Na Rae **said to pick up** her cousin.	
"You had better take careful notes on the lecture." Harry warned **that I should take** notes. Harry warned **me to take** careful notes.	When reporting speech, English speakers often select a main verb that expresses how they interpret the information or the speaker's intention. Use an infinitive (or in some cases a gerund) complement to paraphrase the direct speech instead of a *that* clause for variety in your English.
"Don't forget to bring the museum catalog to class." Susie reminded me **that I was supposed to bring** the catalog to class. Susie **reminded me to bring** the catalog to class.	The following verbs take an infinitive complement: *agree, claim, command, demand, order, promise, refuse, remind, say, tell, warn*.
"I swear that I didn't photograph the painting." Will **denied that he had photographed** the painting. Will **denied having photographed** the painting.	The following verbs may take a gerund complement: *advise, admit, confess, deny, mention, propose, recommend, suggest.*

B Read over your journal entry, and <u>underline</u> at least one sentence that you can revise to include a gerund or infinitive phrase used for reporting speech. Write your revised sentence(s) below.

Answers will vary.

_____

_____

_____

_____

▪ GRAMMAR CHART
Reported Speech: Paraphrases with Infinitives and Gerunds

1. Write on the board *Teacher: "Theo, please pass out the tests."*
2. Ask *What did the teacher tell Theo do to?* Call on a volunteer to restate the sentence as reported speech.
3. Have students read the sample sentences and Notes.
4. Answer any questions students have about paraphrasing with infinitives and gerunds.

▪ EXERCISE B

1. Have students complete the exercise.
2. Ask students to exchange work with a partner. Have them look for additional places where they could include a gerund or infinitive phrase for reported speech.

▪ EXPANSION IDEA

Grammar
1. Divide the class into pairs.
2. Have students take turns asking and answering questions about the text on page 254 using infinitives and gerunds in reported speech.

For example:
Student 1: *What did religious leaders tell their congregations about buying tulips?*
Student 2: *They told their congregations not to risk their financial and spiritual lives on a mere flower.*

■ EXERCISE C

1. Ask students to read the instructions and the example.
2. Have students complete the activity individually and then check their work in pairs.

■ EXERCISE D

1. Ask students to read the instructions and the words in the box.
2. Call on three students to read the example.
3. Have students complete the activity individually and then check their work in pairs.
4. Call on volunteers to read their answers to the class.

C Match the quotes to the verbs that describe your interpretation of Carla's words. Carla is speaking to Brent, her partner on a multimedia art project.

_f_	1. "Don't worry, I'll do it."	a.	confess
_d_	2. "I wouldn't do it like that if I were you."	b.	request
_g_	3. "I insist on doing it!!"	c.	agree
_i_	4. "No way am I going to do it like that."	d.	warn
_b_	5. "How about doing it this way?"	e.	claim
_a_	6. "Sorry, I did it the other way."	f.	~~promise~~
_c_	7. "Sure. No problem."	g.	demand
_j_	8. "You should do it the other way."	h.	admit
_h_	9. "I didn't do it the right way."	i.	refuse
_e_	10. "I did it better than you."	j.	recommend

D Change the quoted comments below to reported speech using a main verb that expresses your interpretation of the speaker's message. Use one of the verbs in the box below.

advise	confess	ask	mention	~~recommend~~
warn	claim	demand	remind	promise

1. **Dr. Azzam:** It would be a good idea for all of you to read about how Asian artists represented longevity and the transience of life.
   Monique: Dr. Azzam, would you mind giving us the page numbers of that section in our textbook?

   Dr. Azzam recommended reading about how Asian artists symbolized longevity and the transience of life. Then, Monique asked him to give them the page numbers of that section in their textbook.

2. **Dr. Azzam:** I am going to include European and Asian flower symbols on the next test.
   Monique: Dr. Azzam, I don't really know where to find information about symbols.
   Dr. Azzam: You should be able to get that information in the readings on reserve in the library.

   Dr. Azzam mentioned including flower symbols from European and Asian art on the next test. Monique confessed not knowing where to find information about symbols, so Dr. Azzam advised her to get the information in the reserved reading library.

■ EXPANSION IDEA

Exercise C

1. Divide the class into pairs.
2. Have students divide the words in the right column of the exercise according to their strength.

For example:

Weaker	**Stronger**
admit	confess
request	demand

3. **Monique:** I don't really have time to go to the library.
   Dr. Azzam: Don't forget that you need to do the homework reading if you want to pass.
   Monique: OK, Dr. Azzam. I'll do it this weekend.

   Monique claimed not to have time to go the library. Then Dr. Azzam reminded her to do the

   homework reading if she planned to pass the course. Monique promised to do the reading

   that weekend.

4. **Dr. Azzam:** In our next class, I'll cover mythological figures in Islamic, Asian, and European art, so all of you should have read Chapter 7 by then.

   Dr. Azzam warned them to have read Chapter 7 by the next class because he was going to

   cover mythological figures in art.

E On a separate sheet of paper, restate Professor MacDougall's instructions according to the notes below. Answers will vary. Professor MacDougall said we must write a paper comparing symbols in Islamic and Asian art. Symbols include animals, like cats and dragons, and flowers. He requires us to write 12–15 pages, and it has to be double-spaced and in Times New Roman, or a similar font. Professor MacDougall also requires us to include a bibliography with our paper, and warned us to use more than just internet resources. The paper must be delivered to the Art Department by 3:00, but he said that if we have a problem, we could turn it in by 5:00. He warned us that 5:00 was the final deadline. He requires us to turn a copy in—we cannot send it to him as an e-mail attachment.

> Due: next Friday – deliver to Art Department by 3:00 BUT if there's a problem, 5:00 is the final deadline; no email attachments
> Topic: comparison of a symbol in Islamic and Asian art -examples = animals (cats, dragon) flowers
> Length: 12-15 pages – double space, Times New Roman or similar font
> Bibliography required - not just internet resources

F Use a variety of forms of reported speech to summarize the short conversations that took place in Professor Cruz's art history class.

1. **Dr. Cruz:** Take a look at the flowers on this Japanese scroll. Can everyone see them?
   She said to take a look at the flowers on the Japanese scroll and asked if everyone could see them.

2. **Johanna:** Can you explain the meaning of the chrysanthemum on the scroll again?
   Dr. Cruz: Certainly. In Japanese art, this flower signifies sun and life.
   Johanna asked her to explain the meaning of the chrysanthemum on the scroll again.

   Dr. Cruz said that they symbolize sun and life in Japanese art.

■ **EXERCISE E**

1. Call on a student to read the instructions and answer any questions that they have about completing the activity.
2. Have students complete the activity individually and then check their answers with a partner.
3. Call on a few volunteers to read their work aloud.

■ **EXERCISE F**

1. Ask students to read the instructions.
2. Call on a volunteer to read the example.
3. Ask volunteers for other ways of summarizing the conversation, such as, "*She asked us to take a look at the flowers . . . .*"
4. Have students complete the activity individually and then check their work in pairs.
5. Call on volunteers to read their answers aloud. Ask for additional ways to restate each answer.

■ **EXPANSION IDEA**

Exercise F

1. Divide the class into pairs.
2. Ask students to role-play a conversation between students in Dr. Cruz's class. Have them discuss what went on in class using reported speech with infinitive phrases and gerunds.

For example:

Student 1: *Dr. Cruz asked the class to look at the Japanese scroll.*

Student 2: *Then Johanna asked Dr. Cruz to repeat her explanation of the meaning of the chrysanthemum on the scroll.*

EXERCISE G

1. Ask students to read the instructions.
2. Call on two students to read the text in the speech balloons.
3. Call on volunteers to share a sentence that uses the types of interaction described by each of the five bulleted words.
4. Divide the class into pairs and have them develop their mini-dramas.
5. Call on volunteers to present their mini-dramas to the class.

---

3. **Dr. Cruz:** Johanna, please don't forget to study the meanings of these flowers.
   Johanna: I'll study them again tonight.
   Dr. Cruz: Don't just memorize them. Learn them in the context of a particular piece of art. You'll remember them better that way.

   Johanna promised to study them again that night. Dr. Cruz told her not to just memorize

   them but to learn them in context.

4. **Dr. Cruz:** Who knows the meaning of the chrysanthemum in Chinese art? Philippe?
   Philippe: Sorry, Professor Cruz, I haven't read about the flower symbols yet.
   Dr. Cruz: I'm disappointed in these responses. You need to spend more time on these assignments.

   Dr. Cruz called on Philippe to answer a question about the meaning of the chrysanthemum.

   Dr. Cruz expressed disappointment about the student's lack of knowledge.

5. **Marina:** Could we have a review session on the symbols? It would be a big help.
   Dr. Cruz: We can't spend more class time on these symbols. Next week we have to move on to allegorical figures.

   Marina asked Dr. Cruz to have a review session on the symbols. Dr. Cruz said that they didn't

   have time and that they would have to move on the next week.

6. **Dr. Cruz:** I'd be willing to have an extra review class if there's interest. Would any of you come?
   Philippe: Absolutely.
   Johanna: Great.
   Marina: I'll be there.

   Dr. Cruz proposed an extra review class. Philippe, Johanna, and Marina all agreed to

   be there.

■ COMMUNICATE

G **PAIR WORK** Role-play a problem between two students who are working together on a class presentation. Choose two of the types of interactions listed below to include in your mini-drama:

- denial
- warning
- refusal
- demand
- confession

Then, perform your role-play for another pair, who will then summarize it for the class.

Did you remember to bring last week's notes so that I can copy them?

I never said that I would bring the notes. I thought *you* were going to bring the notes.

■ EXPANSION IDEA

Exercise G

1. Have students write a summary of their mini-dramas using reported speech with infinitives and gerunds.

2. Call on volunteers to read their summaries aloud.

■ GRAMMAR IN CONTENT

A Reread the text on page 254 and <u>underline</u> sentences with main verbs that express speaking or thinking. Do not underline sentences that already have words in boldface. Then, analyze the structure of the main verb and compare your analysis with a partner's.

Reported Speech and Thought: Passive Forms

Sample Sentences	Notes
It is said that Dutch tulips are even more beautiful today than they were in the 1600s.	Use a passive main verb for reporting speech or thoughts when the context is formal and the source of the information is not unknown or unimportant:
It has been suggested that the flowers in Dutch paintings don't all have symbolic meanings.	*It* + passive verb + *that* + reported information
It is reported that some tulip bulbs were worth their weight in gold; thus, it was much cheaper to commission a famous artist to paint a picture of tulips than to own the bulbs.	As in many English sentences, the new (and important) information comes at the end of the sentence. Using the word *it* as the grammatical subject is one way to allow the important information to come last.
It could be argued that American floral paintings were influenced more by Asian styles than by the Dutch.	
Birds and animals **are also known to have** different connotations; for example, the crane signifies longevity in Japanese art and vigilance in European art.	Use an infinitive complement with the verbs below when: • the main verb is in passive form • the agent or subject of the infinitive is also the subject of the main verb
The unicorn, the mythical animal with one horn, **was understood to have been** a symbol of courtly love in medieval Europe.	Subject + passive verb + infinitive complement
Impressionists **are said to have painted** their famous flower pictures without any thought of symbolism.	A perfective infinitive is used to reflect the past time of the action expressed in the infinitive.
People **say (that)** dragons connote good luck in Chinese art but may represent the devil in European art.	Since English speakers prefer active verbs, a less formal oral alternative form would begin with a phrase such as *People say (that)*.

Verbs Commonly Used in Passive Voice for Reported Speech and Thought

allege	believe	recognize	rumor	think
argue	doubt	report	say	understand
assume	hypothesize	reveal	suggest	

■ EXPANSION IDEA

Grammar Chart
1. Divide the class into pairs.
2. Have students take turns making sentences using the verbs at the bottom of the chart in the passive voice.

For example: *It is understood that a red flower symbolizes lasting love.*

■ GRAMMAR IN CONTENT

■ **EXERCISE A**

1. Ask students to name some verbs that express speaking or thinking. Write them on the board.
2. Give students time to reread the text on page 254, underlining sentences with main verbs that express speech or thought as they read. Ask them to think about the structure of the main verb in each sentence.
3. Call on a volunteer to read one of his or her underlined sentences. Analyze the structure of the main verb with the class.
4. Divide the class into pairs and have students compare their analyses.

■ **GRAMMAR CHART**
Reported Speech and Thought: Passive Forms

1. Write on the board *It is said that lavender brings good luck.*
2. Call on a volunteer to underline the passive construction in the sentence.
3. Ask students if the sentence sounds formal or informal. Ask volunteers to give some examples of when this type of speech would be used.

1. Ask students to read the instructions.
2. Call on volunteers to give examples of a few verbs that indicate uncertainty and a few that suggest certainty.
3. Call on a volunteer to read the example to the class.
4. Answer any questions that students have about the activity.
5. Have students complete the exercise on their own and then check their work in pairs.
6. Call on volunteers to read their answers aloud.

B Change the sentences below to reported speech or thought, disregarding the source of the idea. Use the passive voice, begin each sentence with *It*, and choose the main verb according to the level of certainty of the information.

1. According to experts, animals in European cave art from the Paleolithic Age (32,000 to 11,000 years ago) may have lived in that area.

   It has been suggested that animals in European cave art lived in that area.

2. Researchers are fairly sure that the art also includes imaginary animals like unicorns.

   It's generally thought that the art also includes imaginary animals.

3. There has been some discussion as to whether ambiguous symbols in the caves also represent animals.

   It has been argued that ambiguous symbols in the caves also represent animals.

4. According to one theory in the 1950s, the large number of paintings of horses and bison must have meant that these animals represented the duality of male and female.

   In the 1950's it was assumed that the large number of paintings of horses and bison meant that these animals represent male and female.

5. According to anthropologists, the red pigment found in Paleolithic cave art has been found in art from the same period around the world.

   It is known that the red pigment found in Paleolithic cave art has been found in cave art around the world.

6. According to one article, cave artists often redrew pictures on top of the old ones in order to guarantee that the animals returned the next year.

   It has been suggested that cave-artists often re-drew pictures on top of the old ones in order to guarantee the animals return that year.

7. One researcher wondered if cave artists used red pigment in the paintings because it is aesthetically pleasing.

   It has been alleged that cave artists used red pigment because it is aesthetically pleasing in paintings.

■ **EXPANSION IDEA**

Exercise B

1. Divide the class into pairs.
2. Ask students to take turns role-playing the part of a professor giving a formal lecture on Paleolithic art or another period of art with which they are very familiar. Tell them to begin as many of their sentences as possible with *it* and a main verb in the passive voice.

For example: *It has been suggested that Picasso was a modern artist. On the other hand, it is has been argued that the beginning of Impressionism is really the start of modern art.*

3. Circulate as students work; assist as needed.

Guernica symbolizes the chaos and terror of the Spanish Civil War.

C Edit one of the sentences in each of the texts below, focusing on the information rather than the source of the information. Select main verbs that express the level of certainty of the information.

1. In addition to images, colors have various connotations. In all cultures people have words for at least three colors: black, white, and red. ~~The assumption of researchers is~~ **Humans are thought to have** ~~that all humans have~~ an emotional reaction to red since it is the color of blood. It may represent life, or as the color of sunrise and sunset it may connote the East or the West.

2. Images of imaginary or mythological creatures can be found in art throughout the world. Although a creature may be frightening to people in one culture, it may be very positive in another cultural context. **For example, the bat is known to be a sign** ~~For example, people interpret the bat as a~~ ~~sign~~ of happiness in China whereas in the European tradition it is connected with darkness and black magic.

3. Groups of images and figures in some works of art may be allegories, or representations of abstract ideas. For instance, artists have often depicted "the four seasons" with four different flowers or other types of plants. **Likewise, humans are or mythological figures are understood to represent the four seasons when** ~~Likewise, viewers~~ ~~realized that human or mythological figures represented the four seasons when~~ they were shown doing seasonal tasks.

4. Pablo Picasso's black and white painting *Guernica* (1937) is a modern allegory protesting war. **The work is understood to express his** ~~One can see that the work expresses Picasso's~~ outrage at the Nazi's destruction of this Spanish town in 1937. As in a nightmare, the scene contains many images of panic and claustrophobia.

■ **EXERCISE C**
1. Ask students to read the instructions.
2. Call on a student to read the example.
3. Ask volunteers to discuss the level of certainty indicated by the main verb in the example.
4. Write *allegory* on the board, and elicit a definition of the term from a class member if possible.
5. Give students time to complete the activity. Then have them compare their work in pairs.

■ **EXPANSION IDEAS**

Exercise C
1. Divide the class into small groups.
2. Ask students to discuss examples of allegories from their cultures. Remind them to use the passive voice with words that express the correct level of certainty.

For example: *It has been suggested that the movie* Pan's Labyrinth *is an allegory of the Spanish Civil War. It appears that Captain Vidal represents Franco.*

Exercise C
Have students choose one of the four topics presented in Exercise C. Ask them to add two more sentences to the paragraph using passive and main verbs that express an appropriate level of certainty.

For example: *. . . Art historians have suggested that the screaming horse in the painting represents the human suffering that took place at Guernica. The woman and baby are thought to symbolize the suffering of innocents in war.*

EXERCISE D
CD 3, Track 8

1. Ask students to read the instructions.
2. Have them read the example and the words in the box.
3. Tell students to read the six questions.
4. Play the audio, instructing students to listen for content only.
5. Play the audio again, pausing it frequently so that students can answer the questions.
6. Give students time to write their news articles. Remind them to use the information in the answers to their questions and the passive voice.

Chinese ceramic teapot,
Kangxi Period (1662–1722).

 D Listen to a news conference about the investigation of the theft of a valuable piece of Chinese porcelain. Then, write a short news article about the theft. Use your answers to the questions and the main verbs in the box below to guide your writing.

CD3,TR8

doubt	allege	say	understand
rumor	believe	argue	suggest

1. According to experts, how many Chinese teapots of this type are in U.S. museums?
   This teapot is said to be the only one of its kind in the U.S.

2. What rumors have they heard about porcelain pieces from the Qing period?
   It has been rumored that such pieces are being quietly collected by someone on the West Coast.

3. What allegations have been made about a collector in California?
   The Californian is alleged to have stolen pieces in his/her collection.

4. What do curators agree on?
   It is understood that no one will pay a reward for these pieces.

5. What is there a controversy about?
   It is argued that not paying a reward will not recover the pieces.

6. What have museum employees discussed since the theft?
   It has been suggested that they need a new security system and better trained guards.

EXPANSION IDEA

Exercise D
1. Divide the class into pairs. Tell students to edit each other's news articles. They should check for use of reported speech and thought using passive forms, and for appropriate selection of verbs to express levels of certainty.
2. Give students time to rewrite their articles.
3. Call on a few volunteers to read their articles to the class.

E Find and correct the four errors in the e-mail message below.

Dear Mom and Dad,

You'll be happy to know that our teacher went with us today to the campus art museum. It seems pretty amazing to me that a university has its own museum. This museum ~~is~~ said that it owns several very valuable small paintings that they rarely show for security reasons.

            us

Our instructor asked to go today because they just opened a special exhibit of Native American art from

                                 that we

different parts of the U.S. Our instructor suggested ~~to~~ look at the exhibit together so that we could talk about the pieces. It was a great idea. The exhibit was fantastic, but sometimes I had no idea what the pieces really meant. According to Mr. Carson, it can be ~~argue~~ that only Native Americans can truly appreciate the spiritual

                    argued

meaning of their art. Anyway, it was a great afternoon.

Love,
Ken

■ **C O M M U N I C A T E**

F **GROUP WORK** Select four of the abstract ideas or themes below and discuss modern symbols in the context of any visual medium, including film. For example, what are some modern symbols of affluence?

- affluence
- human foolishness
- timeless beauty
- power or strength
- success
- love
- wastefulness
- hope
- friendship
- personal identity
- war and peace
- cultural traditions

When you are finished, report to your class on the results of your discussion.
Answers will vary.

■ **EXERCISE E**

1. Have students find and correct the four errors in the e-mail. Then have them correct their work in pairs.
2. Call on volunteers to read the corrected e-mail aloud.

■ **COMMUNICATE**

■ **EXERCISE F**

1. Go over the instructions with the class.
2. Ask the class to brainstorm forms of visual media, and write them on the board.
3. Elicit definitions of *affluence* and *timeless beauty* from class members, if possible.
4. Divide the class into small groups and give them time to talk about modern symbols in the context of visual medium.
5. Circulate as students work and assist as needed. Encourage students to use reported speech and the passive form of verbs as they discuss the topic.
6. Call on a member of each group to report discussion results to the class.

■ **EXPANSION IDEA**

Exercise F

Have students bring in a picture or other example of a visual medium that they think expresses one of the themes or ideas in the list. Have them explain why they think their example does so.

Connection

Putting It Together

■ GRAMMAR AND VOCABULARY

1. Ask students to read the instructions.
2. Call on two students to read the topics aloud.
3. Ask students to choose one of the two topics and give them time to write their compositions.

■ PROJECT

1. Ask students to review the instructions.
2. Answer any questions students have about the project.
3. Call on students at the next class meeting to give their oral reports.

■ INTERNET

1. Call on a student to read the instructions.
2. Have students conduct their searches.
3. At the next class meeting, call on a volunteer to define *vanitas symbols.* Discuss the term with the class.
4. Call on students to discuss the paintings they viewed and their interpretations of symbols in the paintings.

GRAMMAR AND VOCABULARY Write a composition on one of the topics below. Use as many words as possible from the Content Vocabulary on page 253. Use sentences with reported speech and thought to express some of your ideas.

Topic 1: Recall and recreate a conversation that you had with someone who spent too much money on a hobby or a fad. (A fad is a product line or activity that is extremely popular but only for a short time.) What did you recommend doing? How much did the person admit spending on the hobby or fad? What did you remind the person to do? What did that person agree to do?

Topic 2: Select a symbol that evokes a strong response from people in your country or culture. Describe the image or object, and then explain what it is believed to show or what is it said to represent. Be as specific as possible.
Answers will vary.

PROJECT Interview at least one student on your campus about visiting art museums and galleries. Find out the following information, and give a brief oral report on the information in your next class meeting.

   a. Where does your interviewee recommend going to see good art in your city or area?
   b. How often does your interviewee actually go to local galleries or museums?
   c. When your interviewee travels in the U.S. or abroad, does he or she go to art museums or galleries? Why or why not?
   d. What does your interviewee know about art in your culture?

 INTERNET Go online and use the search term "vanitas symbols in paintings." Look at two or three paintings, including a modern painting, on different websites, and make a list of different symbols that you find. Be prepared to give your interpretation of a few symbols in the paintings.
Answers will vary.

■ EXPANSION IDEA

Project and Internet

1. Tell students to go online to find art museums they would like to visit.
2. Have them make a list of works of art that they would like to view in their chosen museums.

3. Call on volunteers to report back to the class.

PART 1
Subjunctive Complements
PART 2
Causative Verbs

Lesson 25

Lesson 25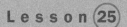

Public Health: Vaccines and Immunization

Overview

1. Write *vaccine* and *immunization* on the board. Ask students whether they are familiar with these terms. Elicit definitions from class members if possible; if necessary, explain the terms.
2. Ask students to name the diseases that people in their home countries are commonly vaccinated against. List them on the board.

■ **CONTENT VOCABULARY**

Look up the words and phrases below that you do not know and enter them in your vocabulary journal. Write each word's part of speech, a definition, and an example sentence. Try to include them in your discussion and writing below.

an antiseptic	a dose	a pandemic	to swell
a campaign/drive	infectious	a quarantine	a syringe
to dispose of	a medical practice	to sterilize	a vial

■ CONTENT VOCABULARY

Ask students to review the words in the box. Tell them to look up any unfamiliar words.

■ VOCABULARY JOURNAL

Have students add new words to their vocabulary journals and write down the parts of speech, definitions, and sentences for each.

■ **THINK ABOUT IT**

What do you know about diphtheria, polio, and hepatitis? What causes somebody to become ill with one of these diseases, and how can it be prevented? Discuss your ideas with a classmate.

In your writing journal, write for 5–10 minutes about the questions below. When you are finished, share what you wrote with the class.   Answers will vary.
What kinds of vaccinations have you had in your life? Approximately how old were you when you were vaccinated? Why did your parents think that those vaccinations were important? Have you had any vaccinations in the last few years? If so, why?

■ THINK ABOUT IT

1. Have students read the instructions.
2. Divide the class into pairs and have students discuss what they know about diphtheria, polio, and hepatitis.
3. Ask students to read the journal writing instructions. Answer any questions that they have about the topic. Then give them five minutes to write in their journals.
4. Call on volunteers to share their ideas with the class.

■ CONTENT NOTES

The topic of this lesson is Public Health: Vaccines and Immunization. Students will learn about disease prevention through immunization and will acquire some of the vocabulary needed to discuss this topic. Use this lesson to remind students that they can receive medical attention as well as vaccines and inoculations at your school's health center.

PART ONE

Subjunctive Complements

■ GRAMMAR IN CONTENT

■ EXERCISE A

CD 3, Track 9

1. Write *immunization drive* on the board. Elicit a definition of the term from a class member, or provide one if necessary. Ask students to discuss why public health offices have this kind of campaign.

2. Tell students that they will hear a message from a district supervisor to her vaccination team, giving instructions on what each team member should do.

3. Play the audio and have students follow along in their books as they listen. Ask students to circle any unfamiliar words or phrases.

4. Call on students to read their circled words and elicit definitions or explanations from volunteers if possible.

5. Check comprehension by asking questions such as the following: *What did the supervisor urge local clinics to do? What was learned on other vaccination drives? What must each team member supervise? What will the team equipment manager do? What is a challenge that team members will face? Why must team members always be close to the clinics?*

■ GRAMMAR IN CONTENT

A Read and listen to the passage below. The sentences in bold in the text include *that* clauses with subjunctive verb forms.

CD3,TR9

> **TO:** Members of the Vaccination Team
> **FROM:** Karin O'Malley, District Supervisor
> **RE:** Upcoming Vaccination Campaigns
>
> We have received confirmation from local public health officials that our immunization drive will receive widespread publicity in the weeks before your arrival. **Some weeks ago I urged that the local clinic in each region begin a word-of-mouth campaign.** Our public health colleagues will also have posters and leaflets printed so that nurses can distribute them in the clinics and in schools. As with all of our vaccination campaigns, we cannot make the people participate in the vaccinations, but we hope that they will want to bring their children to the clinics. **Also, it is crucial that local town officials be informed of our visits so that there is no unnecessary red tape.** We have learned on other vaccination drives that we have to get all local VIPs to see our program as something positive instead of as a criticism of their local health care.
>
> **It is imperative that each member of the team supervise the local health workers and not assume that the workers know the safest way to give injections.** Have one member of the team serve as the equipment manager. That person should dispose of the syringes and bottles of vaccine personally. **I highly recommend that the equipment manager check your stock of puncture-resistant boxes.** On one occasion, another team discovered that their inventory of equipment did not contain a sufficient number of boxes for the number of immunizations that they actually administered. **Remember, it is preferable that a health worker be offended by our caution and supervision** than for that person to have a needle-prick injury.
>
> You face a special challenge in keeping the vaccines cold enough. According to the manufacturer's instructions, the vaccine vials must be kept at 2–8 degrees C. Once the vials have been unloaded at the airport, **it is essential that one of you monitor the cold packs.** Local daytime temperatures range from 25–30 degrees C right now, so there is a real risk to the vaccine if you are not careful.
>
> Finally, the local clinics have agreed to let you stay in the staff dormitories. This arrangement should help you to stay on schedule. We anticipate that people will respond better to our campaign this year. Consequently, **it's quite important that you be close to the clinics** so that you can maximize the number of immunizations at each site. Also, we will have the vaccine delivered to you at some of the sites, so you need to be on hand to receive it.
>
> Best wishes.

word-of-mouth: an informal person-to-person means of communication
a leaflet: a flier of information for free distribution to the public
red tape: bureaucratic paperwork and restrictions

a VIP: a Very Important Person
to administer: to give, to dispense
to be on hand: to be available, to be on-site

■ EXPANSION IDEA

Exercise A

1. Divide the class into small groups that include students from as many different home countries as possible.

2. Ask students to talk about the kinds of vaccinations that are required of children who attend public schools in their home countries. Are there places in their countries, such as the jungle, where additional vaccines are required or recommended?

3. Have students discuss why the kind of vaccination drive described in the reading would or would not be effective in their home countries.

Sample Sentences	Notes
Dr. Larson insists that her nurse **dispose** of any used syringe immediately.	Express potential control or influence over another person's actions after these verbs:
	suggest, propose weak control
Schools in my town have always required that parents **show** their children's vaccination records before the children can start school.	*recommend*
	ask, request
	insist, urge
Why did the nurse suggest that I **lie down** before she gave me an injection?	*demand, require* strong control
	Use a *that* clause with verbs in this group. Follow special rules for the *that* clause:
I asked that my doctor **not give** me the shot in my left arm since I'm left-handed.	• Use only the base form of the verb, even for the main verb *be*.
	• Use *not* without an auxiliary to express negation before the verb.
Do doctors recommend that patients **be vaccinated** against tetanus every 5 years?	• Do not use modals.
	• Use the base form for passive constructions.
It's advisable that you **not go** to areas where you might catch yellow fever.	As a result of these rules, the verb in the *that* clause does not express singular/plural subject-verb agreement (or time).
Is it really necessary that all children **be vaccinated** against chicken pox?	Follow the same rule for subjunctive complements with certain main-clause adjectives. Like the verbs above, these adjectives express a desire to control or influence the actions in the *that* clause.
It wasn't really urgent that the child **receive** a flu shot, but it seemed like a good idea.	*advisable* weaker
	desirable, preferable
It may be desirable that everyone on campus **get** a flu shot this year.	*important*
	necessary, imperative
	urgent, essential, crucial, vital stronger

B Read over your journal entry, and <u>underline</u> at least one sentence that you can revise to include a verb or adjective listed above plus a *that* clause with a subjunctive verb form. Write your revised sentence(s) below.

Answers will vary.

_____

_____

_____

_____

■ GRAMMAR CHART
Subjunctive Verbs

1. Write *suggest, ask, urge, demand, recommend, insist, require* on the board. Ask students to arrange the words from the strongest expression of potential control or influence to the weakest. Repeat with the adjectives *advisable, preferable, important, necessary, essential, crucial.*

2. Ask students to read the sample sentences and Notes. Answer any questions they have about subjunctive verbs.

■ EXERCISE B

1. Have students complete the exercise.

2. Ask students to exchange work with a partner. Have them look for additional sentences that can be revised using a verb or adjective from the list in the Grammar Chart.

■ EXPANSION IDEA

Grammar Chart

1. Divide the class into pairs.
2. Have students role-play a conversation between a doctor and the parent of a young child.

For example:
Student 1: *Is it a school requirement that I vaccinate my child?*
Student 2: *Yes, it is. It's crucial that all children starting school have had their vaccinations.*

Student 1: *I may home-school my child in that case. I've heard that it's advisable not to inoculate young children.*
Student 2: *Whoever told you that is wrong. It is not only advisable that children be vaccinated — it's essential, if we want to avoid future epidemics.*

1. Ask students to review the instructions and the words in the box.
2. Call on a student to read the example.
3. Have students complete the activity individually and then check their work in pairs.
4. Call on volunteers to read their answers aloud.

C Paraphrase each directly quoted sentence using one of the main verbs requiring a subjunctive *that* clause.

~~ask~~	insist	recommend	require	urge
demand	propose	request	suggest	

1. **School Nurse:** "Please stand in line and don't be impatient. OK, Jeff, can you please roll up your sleeve?"

   The school nurse asked that the children stand in line and not be impatient.

   Then, she requested that Jeff roll up his sleeve.

2. **School Principal:** "Mr. Grant, you have to bring Tyree's immunization record to our office. You should consult your family doctor about Tyree's records."

   The school principal insisted that Mr. Grant bring Tyree's record to their office and consult

   Tyree's doctor.

3. **Nurse:** "Dr. Tang, it would be a lot easier if everyone with the flu sits in one section of the waiting room."

   Dr. Tang: "All right. Dr. Jackson, you need to separate the flu patients from the others."

   Dr. Jackson: "Right away."

   Nurse Hathaway proposed that everyone with the flu sit in one section of the waiting room

   so that the doctors could separate them.

4. **Emergency Room Client:** "Nurse, you need to examine my daughter right away."

   Nurse: "Sir, please don't be worried."

   A person in the emergency room demanded that the nurse see his daughter right away. The

   nurse told him not to worry.

■ **EXPANSION IDEA**

Exercise C

1. Divide the class into pairs. Have students write a mini-drama that takes place between a local public health official and a member of the vaccination team. For example:

   Student 1: *I can help you keep the vaccine cold.*

   Student 2: *I am already taking care of that. You can leave.*

   Student 1: *I'm sorry, but it's my job to stay and make sure the vials are kept at 28°C.*

2. Have two pairs work together. One pair should role-play its mini-drama. The other pair should paraphrase the dialog using main verbs requiring a subjunctive *that* clause. For example:

   1. *The volunteer suggested that she could help keep the vaccine cold.*
   2. *The public health official suggested that the volunteer leave.*
   3. *The volunteer insisted that she had to make sure the vaccine was kept cold enough.*

D Match the speakers and their messages. Then write a sentence that identifies the speaker and expresses his or her message with the appropriate main verb and a subjunctive *that* clause. Follow the example.

X. Director, World Health Organization (WHO)	X. Avian flu vaccine should be available more cheaply in the Third World.
2. Aid worker for WHO	b. Every student should leave campus.
3. Director, U.S. Centers for Disease Control (CDC)	c. Residents of Houston should be quarantined to avoid catching the bird flu.
4. CDC agent	d. Every student should get a flu shot.
5. Head of Security, Chicago's O'Hare Airport	e. Anybody with suspicious symptoms should be examined at the airport.
6. Delta Airways flight attendant	f. Everyone in the neighborhood should test the water for contamination.
7. Director of your school's student clinic	g. The last vaccine vial should be used for the children in the village.
8. Nurse in your school clinic	h. The passenger in 15D should be re-seated in an area away from the others.

1. The director of WHO has urged that avian flu vaccine be available more cheaply in the Third World.

2. The aid worker for WHO may urge that the last vial be used for the children.

3. The CDC director could require that residents of Houston be quarantined.

4. A CDC agent urged that everyone in the neighborhood test the water for contamination.

5. The O'Hare Head of Security has recommended that anybody with suspicious symptoms be examined.

6. The flight attendant insisted that the passenger in seat 15D be reseated.

7. The director of our school clinic may have to require that every student leave campus.

8. The nurse in our school clinic often suggests that every student get a flu shot.

■ **EXERCISE D**

1. Write *WHO* and *CDC* on the board and ask whether anyone can share what these acronyms stand for.

2. Briefly discuss with the class what each of these organizations does.

3. Ask students to review the instructions.

4. Call on a volunteer to explain why the director of WHO is the speaker of message *a*.

5. Have students complete the matching part of the activity in pairs. Encourage them to discuss the possible answers before they make their choices.

6. Ask students to write the sentences that identify the speakers and express their messages individually.

7. Call on volunteers to read their answers aloud.

■ **EXPANSION IDEA**

Exercise D

Tell students to pick one of the messages in Exercise D and expand it into a brief news article.

For example:

The director of WHO has urged that the avian flu vaccine be available more cheaply in the Third World. She has proposed that each drug company provide 10,000 doses at $1 per vaccine to help prevent a world epidemic. She has also suggested that the UN provide doctors and nurses to administer the vaccines.

■ EXERCISE E

1. Ask students to read the instructions.
2. Call on a few students to read the procedures. Answer any questions students have about them, eliciting explanations from class members when possible.
3. Have students complete the activity individually and then compare their work in pairs.
4. Call on volunteers to read their answers aloud. After each answer is read, poll the class to see whether other class members agree with the degree of relative importance given to each procedure.

■ COMMUNICATE

■ EXERCISE F

1. Write *measles* on the board. If any class members are unfamiliar with the term, describe the symptoms of the disease.
2. Give students time to write their lists of recommendations for preventing the spread of the disease.
3. Call on volunteers to read their lists aloud.

E Determine the relative importance of the vaccination procedures below. Use an appropriate adjective and subjunctive *that* clause to express your opinion about the degree of importance. Follow the example, and note that some procedures may be of more or less the same importance.   Answers will vary. Sample answers below.

✔	put antiseptic on injection site
_____	use cotton swab with antiseptic
_____	know patient's family medical history
_____	don't use syringe more than once
_____	dispose of syringe in safety box
_____	inform patients about possible reactions
_____	don't leave vaccine in warm place
_____	store vaccine appropriately
_____	use sterile equipment
_____	share information about low risks of vaccines

1. _It's crucial that a health worker put an antiseptic on the injection site._
2. It's advisable that a nurse use a cotton swab with antiseptic.
3. It's preferable that a doctor know a patient's family history.
4. It's vital that health workers only use a syringe once.
5. It's necessary that a nurse properly disposes of syringes.
6. It's desirable that doctors tell patients of possible side effects.
7. It's essential that a worker not leave vaccines in warm places.
8. It's imperative that they store vaccines properly.
9. It's vital that doctors use sterile equipment.
10. It's very important that health workers share information about the low risk of vaccines.

■ COMMUNICATE

F **WRITE** Imagine that doctors have confirmed that two students on your campus have the measles. What should the school do so that no one else catches this contagious disease? List five or six recommendations using subjunctive verbs, and then share your ideas with the class.

■ EXPANSION IDEA

Exercise F

1. Write *cholera* on the board. Elicit a description of the disease. Ask students who come from countries where cholera is prevalent to describe the effects of a cholera epidemic.
2. Divide the class into small groups.
3. Tell students to imagine that they are members of a WHO committee assigned with the task of preventing the spread of cholera in a small village. Have them role-play a conversation in which they develop a

list of procedures using appropriate adjectives and subjunctive *that* clauses.

For example:
Student 1: *It is absolutely imperative that we prevent this disease from spreading.*
Student 2: *A clean source of water must be available to everyone in the village.*
Student 3: *Right. Everyone needs to be informed about the risk of drinking contaminated water.*

4. Call on a few groups to role-play for the class.

■ GRAMMAR IN CONTENT

A Reread the memo at the beginning of this lesson, and <u>underline</u> all of the clauses with the main verbs *cause, make, have, let, get,* or *help.* Compare your answers with a partner.

Causative Verbs	
Sample Sentences	**Notes**
Don't **let** the syringe **touch** anything!	Use *cause, get, make, have, let,* and *help* with **infinitive complements** to express causation. In this construction, the direct object is an agent or doer of the action expressed by the infinitive.
A flu shot may **cause** your **upper arm to be** sore for a few days. How did you **get** Billy **to stop** crying after his immunizations this afternoon? I should **get** my daughter **vaccinated** before school starts.	*Cause* and *get* take a **direct object** followed by an **infinitive phrase.** With *get,* the main subject encounters difficulty and must convince or force the subject of the infinitive. When using a **passive complement** with *get,* omit *to* and the passive auxiliary *be.* In such sentences, the agent of the action is often unstated or implied.
The U.S. Food and Drug Administration **makes drug manufacturers do** extensive testing on vaccines. **Health authorities** can **make citizens** with a dangerous infectious disease **stay** in restricted areas.	*Make, have,* and *let* take a **direct object** followed by a **bare infinitive phrase.** With *make,* the main subject has some kind of power over the **subject** of the **infinitive.** Coercion or the potential use of force is implied.
The doctor **had me roll up** my sleeve before she gave me the shot. Dr. Hearn **has children weighed** before he sees them.	With *have,* the **main subject** has some kind of authority or power over the **direct object** of the verb. Use passive complements with *have* following the same rules as with *get.* Use **passive complements** for *have* and *get* when the participle is preceded by a **direct object.**
Could you **help** the **nurse (to) give** some shots?	*Help* takes a **direct object** followed by an **infinitive phrase** or a **bare infinitive.**

■ EXPANSION IDEA

Grammar Chart

1. Divide the class into pairs.
2. Ask students to discuss what occurred the last time they visited the doctor. Remind them to use causative verbs as often as possible.

For example:

Student 1: *First the doctor's nurse had me fill out a short medical history.*

Student 2: *I had to do that, too. Then she had me undress and put on a short robe.*

PART TWO

Causative Verbs

■ GRAMMAR IN CONTENT

■ EXERCISE A

1. Have students review the instructions.
2. Ask students to complete the activity individually and then check their work in pairs.

■ GRAMMAR CHART
Causative Verbs

1. Write *causative verb* on the board. Ask students to infer what these verbs do. If necessary, explain that causative verbs show that somebody/something other than the subject of the sentence is indirectly responsible for an action.
2. Ask students to brainstorm verbs that they think may be used to express causation, and write them on the board. Discuss their suggestions.
3. Have students review the sample sentences and Notes.
4. Answer any questions that students have about causative verbs.

■ EXERCISE B

1. Write *made* and *had* on the board.
2. Briefly discuss the difference between these two words with the class. Call on a few volunteers to give examples of sentences in which each verb is the appropriate choice.
3. Ask students to read the instructions.
4. Call on a student to read the example.
5. Have students complete the activity individually and then compare their answers in pairs.
6. Call on volunteers to read their answers aloud. After each answer is read, poll the class to see whether other class members agree. Discuss any differences of opinion.

B **Circle** the causative verb appropriate to the context and give the reason for your choice. Both options may be appropriate in some contexts.

1. An experienced health worker ((had)/ made) the mother hold her son for his injection.

   REASON: *A health worker doesn't have the power to force a mother to hold her son. She can ask, but she can't make her do it.*

2. One of the nurses (had /(made)) the unruly children stand in line.

   REASON: **A nurse has power over patients, especially children.**

3. Dr. Dayton usually ((has)/ makes) his nurses prepare 100 doses of vaccine at a time.

   REASON: **A doctor has power over employees but can't force them to do anything.**

4. One mother ((had)/(made)) her oldest child watch several other children so that she could sleep for a little while.

   REASON: **A mother has power and authority.**

5. Has Dr. Dayton ever (had /(made)) the people in line wait while he eats lunch?

   REASON: **In this situation the doctor is in the power position.**

6. Parents don't (have /(make)) their children keep quiet while they are waiting in line.

   REASON: **In this context the parents may have to use their power.**

7. The health organization ((has)/ makes) the staff keep strict records of the vaccines because they need to have up-to-date information on their inventory of medicines.

   REASON: **An employer has the authority to enforce this policy but can't make his employees follow.**

8. The team supervisor ((has)/ makes) the local workers dispose of used syringes according to strict guidelines.

   REASON: **Like #3 and #7 a supervisor has authority but cannot force adults to follow guidelines.**

■ EXPANSION IDEA

Exercise B

1. Ask students to write a short essay about the things they did in order to meet your school's health requirements prior to enrolling, using *had* and *made*, as in Exercise B.

   For example:
   I had to ask my doctor to fill out a health form for me. He had his nurse check my health record and she checked off the vaccines that I had had. There were two missing, so the doctor had her give me two shots. I didn't want to let her, but the doctor made me. He reminded me that without them, I wouldn't be able to enroll in classes. The shots made me sick for two days.

C Paraphrase each of the sentences with one of the causative verbs in this lesson. Follow the example.

1. My last flu shot brought about swelling in my arm.

   My last flu shot caused my arm to swell./My last flu shot made my arm swell.

2. Nurse Flint didn't allow the student nurse to give any injections.

   Nurse Flint didn't let the student nurse give any injections.

3. Nurse Villalobos told little Vicki to swallow the sugar cube with the polio vaccine.

   Nurse Villalobos had little Vicki swallow the sugar cube with the polio vaccine.

4. After many attempts, Dr. Quiller finally persuaded little Nick to sit quietly for his shot.

   After many attempts, Dr. Quiller got little Nick to sit quietly for his shot.

5. When it's time for their flu shots, Mrs. Upton usually forces her son to go first so that he doesn't get too scared.

   When it's time for their flu shots, Mrs. Upton makes her son go first so that he doesn't get too scared.

6. Has your doctor ever told you to sign a form before you got a shot?

   Has your doctor ever had you sign a form before you got a shot?

7. The injection couldn't have resulted in the swelling because my arm was sore before I went to the doctor's.

   The injection couldn't have caused the swelling because my arm was sore before I went to the doctor's.

8. Dr. Thomason asked her nurse to call Clark Jones because she was worried about a possible allergic reaction.

   Dr. Thomason had her nurse call Clark Jones because she was afraid of a possible allergic reaction.

9. Nurse Higgins sometimes gives children a piece of candy after a shot because it causes them to feel better.

   Nurse Higgins sometimes gives children a piece of candy after a shot because it makes them feel better.

10. Nurse Higgins finally convinced the people in the waiting room to stop complaining after she told them that the doctor had left for an emergency.

    Nurse Higgins finally got the people in the waiting room to stop complaining after she told them that the doctor had left.

11. Dr. Franklin has always paid the DisposMed Company to pick up the medical waste from his medical practice daily.

    Dr. Franklin has always had the DisposMed Co. pick up the medical waste from his medical practice daily.

■ **EXERCISE C**
1. Ask students to read the instructions.
2. Have students complete the activity on their own and then check their work in pairs.
3. Call on volunteers to read their answers aloud.

■ **EXPANSION IDEA**

Exercise C

1. Tell students to write a paragraph about a nurse who has to give a child a shot. Remind them to use causative verbs from the lesson in their writing.

   For example:
   Nurse Bhatt couldn't get the child to sit still. She let him play with some toys she kept in the office, but he wouldn't sit down. Finally, she had his mother hold him down. The small boy screamed, but he let her give him the injection.

■ EXERCISE D

1. Call on a student to read the instructions.
2. Call on a volunteer to explain what a *passive complement* is. If necessary, have students refer to the Grammar Chart on page 271.
3. Call on a student to read the example. Discuss the reason with the class.
4. Have students complete the activity with a partner.
5. Call on volunteers to read their answers and reasons aloud. Discuss any answers that students disagree on or have difficulty understanding.

D <u>Underline</u> the five sentences that can be edited to include a passive complement for the main verb *have* or *get*. Make the changes, and explain why the change is appropriate. The first sentence has been underlined and corrected for you.

<u>WHO may have field workers vaccinate hundreds of people in one day.</u> First, some <u>health workers get all of the people to sign their health forms.</u> When that formality is finished, the team usually wants to have everyone sit down in the shade. While the crowd is sitting, someone gets the field supervisor to make an announcement about their procedures and instructions. At this point, they have a local person translate the instructions to the crowd. When the team is ready, <u>they get some people to carry elderly patients into the clinic first.</u> Meanwhile, local nurses get the little children to play together in a shady area.

At the end of the day, <u>the field supervisor has someone put the vaccines back in the coolers</u> and sterilize the equipment for the next day. <u>The next day the staff will have someone explain the procedures again before they start.</u>

1. _WHO may have hundreds of people vaccinated in one day._

   REASON: _There are two direct objects, and the agent of "vaccinate" is obvious._

2. Health workers get all of the people's health forms signed.

   REASON: The agent is clear from the context.

3. They get some elderly patients carried into the clinic first.

   REASON: Infinitive phrase includes direct object.

4. The field supervisor has the vaccines put back in the coolers.

   REASON: The agent is obvious from the context.

5. The next day the staff will have the procedures explained again before they start.

   REASON: Infinitive phrase includes a direct object.

274   LESSON 25 | Public Health: Vaccines and Immunization

■ EXPANSION IDEA

Exercise D

1. Have students rewrite the first paragraph using the passive complements they added for the exercise.

2. Call on a volunteer to read his/her work aloud.

E Listen to the health team as they plan to set up their immunization clinic. Tell the actions of the people in parentheses in sentences with causal verbs.

1. (Maria, Jim) _Maria had Jim carry the five coolers into the clinic._

2. (Maria, Larry) _Larry gets Maria to agree to check the vaccine._

3. (Maria, Barbara) _Barbara has Maria supervise the local workers again._

4. (Larry, Jim) _Larry lets Jim help him with the vials._

5. (Barbara, Jim) _Barbara has Jim watch Maria and the local nurses._

6. (Jim, Larry, Maria) _Jim gets Maria to bring in the sterilizing equipment and Larry to get the extra box of syringes._

F Find and correct the four errors in the e-mail message below.

Hi Judy-

Your e-mail made me ~~to~~ laugh so hard. Your stories about life as a WHO nurse bring tears – sometimes of laughter and sometimes of sadness. How do you keep your sense of humor?

I still can't believe that some little kids die of diseases that kids here never even catch. You should have one of your co-workers ~~taken~~ take a few photos of you and some of those kids. Then, you could send them to some nonprofit organizations and maybe get some more money for medicines. (I'd suggest that you ~~do~~ not send one of those to your mother. She would be so upset. She would worry about you even more than she does now!)

By the way, be sure that you keep e-mailing her, too. It's pretty important that she receive**s** an e-mail from you regularly. If not, she calls me and asks what's going on.

Cheers!
Lynell

■ COMMUNICATE

G **PAIR WORK** Public health officials are very concerned about the possible outbreak of a flu pandemic. In such circumstances what power and authority do health officials have? What can they have us do to prevent a pandemic? What can they make us do in case a pandemic breaks out? Brainstorm answers to these questions with your partner and then share them with your classmates.

 Officials would probably have us store food and other supplies, don't you think?

 I would hope so. They might even make schools close.

Part Two | Causative Verbs **275**

■ **EXERCISE E**

CD 3, Track 10

1. Tell students that they will hear a conversation among members of a health team as they plan to set up their immunization clinic.

2. Play the audio, asking students to listen for comprehension only.

3. Tell students that you will play the audio again. This time they must listen for the actions of specific people.

4. Play the audio, pausing it frequently so that students can write their answers.

5. Play the audio once more so that students can check their answers.

6. Call on volunteers to read their answers aloud. If there is any disagreement among class members, play the audio again.

■ **EXERCISE F**

1. Have students find and correct the four errors in the e-mail message.

2. Call on volunteers to read the corrected e-mail one paragraph at a time.

■ **COMMUNICATE**

■ **EXERCISE G**

1. Call on a student to read the instructions aloud.

2. Call on two students to read the text in the speech balloons.

3. Divide the class into pairs. Have students discuss the topic using the grammar and vocabulary from the lesson.

4. Circulate as students work; assist as needed.

■ **EXPANSION IDEA**

Exercise G

1. Have students write a short essay about how they would prevent a pandemic and what they would do in case one broke out. Remind them to use causative verbs.

2. Circulate as students work and assist as needed.

3. Have students exchange work with a partner. Tell them to correct each other's essays and suggest places where causative verbs could be added.

4. Call on a few volunteers to read their essays to the class.

Lesson 25 **275**

Connection

Putting It Together

▦ GRAMMAR AND VOCABULARY

1. Ask students to read the instructions.
2. Call on two students to read the topics aloud.
3. Ask students to choose one of the two topics and give them time to write their compositions.

▦ PROJECT

1. Ask students to review the instructions. Be sure that students are familiar with each of the three childhood diseases mentioned.
2. Answer any questions that students have about the project.
3. Call on students at the next class meeting to give their oral reports.

▦ INTERNET

1. Call on a student to read the instructions.
2. Have students conduct their searches.
3. At the next class meeting, call on a volunteer to report their findings to the class.

GRAMMAR AND VOCABULARY Write a composition on one of the topics below. Use as many words as possible from the Content Vocabulary on page 265. Use sentences with subjunctive complements and causative verbs to express some of your ideas.

Topic 1: What do you recommend that school authorities do if many students at your school got an infectious disease? What should they have the students and their families do? What is essential that every student do? Give your proposals and recommendations.

Topic 2: When an outbreak of any serious infectious disease occurs, the risk to people in other parts of the world is much greater than it used to be. The ease of international travel and the interaction of people from around the globe make the spread of disease more likely. What can we do to prevent a pandemic? What should the authorities make citizens do? What is advisable and crucial in the first days and weeks? What can the authorities insist that every traveler do?
Answers will vary.

PROJECT Interview at least two students on your campus about childhood diseases. Find out the following information, and give a brief oral report on the responses at your next class meeting.

    a. Which childhood diseases (measles, mumps, chickenpox) did your interviewee have?
    b. What did your interviewees' parents insist that they do?
    c. What did your interviewees' parents have them eat?

 INTERNET Go online to the website http://wwwn.cdc.gov/travel/contentVaccinations.aspx. Choose one part of the world and check the immunizations that the U.S. Centers for Disease Control recommend for travelers. Report on the recommendations in class, and be ready to describe briefly any disease that may be a threat to travelers in that area.
Answers will vary.

▦ EXPANSION IDEA

Project and Internet

1. Have students search online for home remedies. Tell them to find four treatments for the common cold.
2. Divide the class into small groups and have students compare and discuss their findings.

3. Call on a member of each group to report to the class.

A Change each of the quotes to reported speech in sentence a. Then, paraphrase the quote with a complement following the main verb provided in sentence b.

1. "Bob, you have to practice serving the ball."

   a. Bob's tennis coach warned him _that he had to practice serving the ball._

   b. Bob's coach insisted _he practice serving the ball._

2. "Your foot touches the line every time you serve."

   a. His coach stated _she had noticed that his foot touched the line almost every time he served._

   b. His coach has observed _his foot touching the line almost every time he served._

3. "I videotaped you when you were playing doubles with Nick."

   a. The coach told Bob _she had videotaped him when he was playing._

   b. The coach taped Bob _playing doubles with Nick._

4. "I was able to see clearly how you put a top spin on many of your balls."

   a. The coach commented _that she could see how he put a top spin on his balls._

   b. On the videotape, the coach caught Bob _putting a top spin on his balls._

5. "I'll try harder to control the spin that I put on the balls."

   a. Bob said _that he would try harder to control the spin that he put on his balls._

   b. Bob promised _to try harder to control the spin he put on his balls._

6. "You should practice at least 3 hours every day."

   a. The coach warned him _that he should be practicing for three hours every day._

   b. According to the coach, it is essential _to practice three hours a day._

7. "Nick, can you show Bob how you serve the ball?"

   a. The coach asked Nick _to show Bob how to serve the ball._

   b. The coach had Nick _show Bob how to serve the ball._

Review Lessons 21-25

The purpose of this lesson is to help students review the language and concepts they have learned in the last five lessons. Encourage them to go back to the lessons and review the grammar charts to help them complete the review activities.

■ EXERCISE A

1. Ask students to review the instructions.
2. Call on a student to read the example; answer any questions that students have about the answer.
3. Have students complete the activity individually and then check their work in pairs.
4. Call on volunteers to read their answers to the class.

■ EXPANSION IDEA

Exercise A

1. Have students write five quotes modeled on those in Exercise A.
2. Divide the class into pairs and have students exchange quotes. Tell them to paraphrase the quotes with a complement. They may choose their own main verbs.

For example:

Student 1: *Theo's doctor: "Theo, you have to take care of that leg!"*

Student 2: *Theo's doctor told him he had to take care of his leg.*

■ EXERCISE B

1. Ask students to review the instructions.

2. Have students complete the exercise and then check their work in pairs.

3. Call on volunteers to read their answers aloud.

■ LEARNER LOG

Have students complete the Learner Log. Suggest that they review the Grammar Charts for areas that need more practice.

B (Circle) the correct form of the adjective.

1. We listened to a (**fascinating**/ fascinated) lecture on documentaries produced in various countries.

2. The lecturer showed some (**amazing**/ amazed) scenes from films made on location in remote areas of the world.

3. I'll always remember the (amazing /**amazed**) expressions on peoples' faces when they saw themselves on these films. They couldn't believe their eyes!

4. In one (**frightening**/ frightened) scene, some children were being chased by a wild dog.

5. Luckily, an adult shouted quite loudly at the dog, and the (scaring /**scared**) dog ran away.

6. In another scene, an (exciting /**excited**) person ran to the filmmakers and led them to a small hut where a baby had just been born.

7. Some of the people inside the hut were (annoying /**annoyed**) because they didn't think that the outsiders should be there.

8. The (interesting /**interested**) filmmakers wanted to continue filming but decided it would be better to leave.

LEARNER LOG Check (✔) *Yes* or *I Need More Practice.*   Answers will vary.

Lesson	I Can Use . . .	Yes	I Need More Practice
21	Participles as Adjectives; Participles in Reduced Adverbial Clauses		
22	Complements of Sensory Verbs; Other Verbs with Participial Complements		
23	Reported Speech and Exceptions to Backshifts in Reported Speech		
24	Reported Speech in Paraphrases with Infinitives and Gerunds; Reported Speech with Passive Forms		
25	Subjunctive Complements and Causative Verbs		

■ EXPANSION IDEA

Exercise B

1. Write *fascinated, terrifying, interesting,* and *amazed* on the board.

2. Ask students to write sentences using the adjectives correctly.

3. Have students check each other's work in pairs.

4. Call on a few volunteers to read their sentences aloud.

PART 1
It Clefts
PART 2
It in Subject Position with
Adjective Complements

Lesson ㉖

Biology: Stress and the Immune System

■ CONTENT VOCABULARY

Look up the words and phrases below that you do not know and enter them in your vocabulary journal. Write each word's part of speech, a definition, and an example sentence. Try to include them in your discussion and writing below.

an antibody	to debilitate	physiological	to suppress
to compromise	a gland	to resist against	to thrive on
to cope with	an immune system	to stimulate	whereas

■ THINK ABOUT IT

Do you know what organs are involved in our bodies' immune systems? Take a look at the illustration on the next page and talk about the function of the organs with a partner. Why are our immune systems important? What can compromise human immune systems? Discuss your ideas with a classmate.

In your writing journal, write for 5–10 minutes about the questions below. When you are finished, share what you wrote with the class.
How does your body react to stress? What stresses you out, and how do you feel when you are in a stressful situation? Does stress ever motivate you?
Answers will vary.

279

Overview

1. Write *stress* on the board and elicit a few definitions from volunteers.
2. Divide the class into small groups and have students discuss the kinds of things that cause stress in their lives.

■ CONTENT VOCABULARY

Ask students to review the words in the box. Tell them to look up any unfamiliar words.

■ VOCABULARY JOURNAL

Have students add new words to their vocabulary journals and write down the parts of speech, definitions, and sentences for each.

■ THINK ABOUT IT

1. Have students read the instructions.
2. Divide the class into pairs and have students discuss the function of various organs shown in the illustration and the human immune system.
3. Have students read the journal writing instructions. Answer any questions that they have about the topic. Then give them five to ten minutes to write in their journals.
4. Call on volunteers to share their ideas with the class.

■ CONTENT NOTES

The topic of this lesson is Biology: Stress and the Immune System. Students will learn facts and terminology related to the human immune system and how stress can have a negative effect on their health. Use this lesson as an opportunity to remind students of the importance of finding ways to relieve the stress in their lives. Suggest that they look into some of the clubs and sports activities at your school or that they seek advice in the health center if they feel they need help dealing with stress.

PART ONE

It Clefts

■ GRAMMAR IN CONTENT

■ EXERCISE A 🎧
CD 3, Track 11

1. Ask students to read the title of the reading.

2. Call on volunteers to suggest ways in which stress can help and hurt an individual. Write their ideas on the board. As they speak, encourage students to use new content vocabulary.

3. Play the audio and have students follow along in their books as they listen. Ask students to circle any unfamiliar words or phrases.

4. Call on students to read their circled words and elicit definitions or explanations from volunteers if possible.

5. Check comprehension by asking questions such as the following: *What does the immune system do? Where are T cells produced? What are B cells? In addition to T and B cells, what system does the human immune system rely heavily upon? What happens if the T and B cells are damaged? What do researchers in the field of psychoneuroimmunology study?*

6. Call on a volunteer to summarize the information in the passage.

■ GRAMMAR IN CONTENT

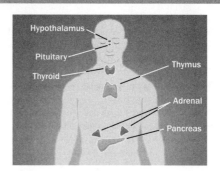

🎧 **A** **Read and listen to the passage below. The sentences in bold in the text are sentences with *it* clefts.**
CD3,TR11

Stress Can Help or Hurt You

While some people seem to thrive on stress, others of us are less productive and even get sick when we are under stress. Both kinds of reactions come from the sophisticated functioning of our immune systems. **It is this system that helps our bodies resist disease, infections, and toxic substances. However, it is also this system that can weaken or debilitate us so that we have lower resistance to the common cold or even cancer.**

Although most people have some inherited immunity against bacteria and viral infections, several glands provide us with additional resistance to disease. T cells, for example, are produced by the thymus gland, which is behind the breastbone. B cells from bone marrow are another important component of the immune system. Together these cells form a potent defense for the body. It has been shown that T cells fight off bacteria, some viral infections, fungi, and cells from transplanted organs, whereas B cells produce antibodies, which are able to fight against foreign substances.

In addition to those two specialized cells, the human immune system relies heavily on the hypothalamic-pituitary-adrenal system. The hypothalamus, located above the roof of the mouth, not only connects to the pituitary gland at the base of the brain but also interacts with most other areas of the brain. **It is from the hypothalamus that the body monitors the concentrations of hormones in the blood.** Certain concentrations of hormones from the pituitary gland can start the body's defense reactions, increase resistance, and speed recovery from infection or injury. For example, the hormone epinephrine, or adrenaline, raises the heart rate and blood pressure and helps to increase the effect of other hormones that are released during a stressful or dangerous situation. However, it is interesting to note that the same hormones that defend the body from attack can also suppress the immune system when they are released in extreme amounts. As a result, the T and B cells may be damaged, for instance, and the body's resistance will be reduced.

Researchers in the field of psychoneuroimmunology seek to understand the sensitive relationship between our immune system and sources of stress in our lives. Some studies have shown that stress can actually enhance our immune systems. **It is not the stress but its nature or duration that determines its negative effect on the immune system.** In other words, an intensely stressful situation or a stressful situation that lasts for a long time will probably have a negative impact on the immune system. It takes more than the typical stresses and strains of modern life for most healthy people to suffer long-term problems.

sophisticated: complicated, complex

a fungus; fungi (pl.): a type of organism. Mushrooms are an example of fungi.

a hormone: a substance created by one organ that affects another organ physiologically

bone marrow: the tissue in bones that produces red blood cells

---

■ EXPANSION IDEA

Exercise A
Divide the class into pairs and have students take turns asking and answering questions about the text.

It Clefts

Sample Sentences	Notes
It is our weekly deadline **that** stresses me out. **It's** my boss **who** thrives on stress.	Use *it* clefts to stress or correct one piece of information in the sentence.
Could it be your hectic lifestyle **that** you need to change?	Put the emphasized noun or noun phrase after *it* + *BE*, and explain the noun phrase further with a relative clause: *It* + *is/was* + Noun Phrase + *who/that/Ø* …
He said that **it was** the coffee **that** made him so nervous.	Follow these restrictions for *it* clefts: • use only the simple tenses of *BE* • use only *who, that,* or *Ø* in the relative clause
It may have been because of the new deadline **that** he was feeling so stressed. **Was it** during the exam **that** he got so nervous? **It was** because he worked under such stress **that** he got sick.	Emphasize or clarify information in structures other than noun phrases in the same way: *It* + *is/was* + Prepositional Phrase + *that* … *It* + *is/was* + Clause + *that* …
It's drinking too much coffee—**not** staying up late—that really affects me. It was **because he worked under such stress** that he got sick, **not** because he caught his son's cold. **It isn't the stress but my co-workers** that make me unhappy.	Clarify or correct information by: • giving **the accurate information** and introducing the wrong information with *not.* Use a comma before *not,* or enclose the negative phrase within two dashes. • negating the **mistaken information** and introducing the accurate information with *but.*
In 1932, Walter Cannon, a Harvard University physiologist, introduced stress vocabulary to the scientific world. ↓ **It was Walter Cannon** who introduced stress vocabulary to the scientific world.	You can emphasize your ideas in two ways: • with unusual word order • with a relative clause at the end of the sentence where new or important information is explained These sentences are effective because they are unusual. Use *it* clefts sparingly when writing.

B Read over your journal entry, and <u>underline</u> at least one sentence that you can revise to include an *It* cleft. Write your revised sentence(s) below.

Answers will vary.

_____

_____

_____

■ GRAMMAR CHART
It *Clefts*

1. Ask students to review the sample sentences and Notes.
2. Call on volunteers to give examples of different uses of *it* clefts. Ask them to explain the function of the *it* cleft in their sentences.

■ EXERCISE B

1. Have students complete the exercise.
2. Ask students to exchange work with a partner. Have them look for additional sentences that could be revised to include *it* clefts.

■ EXPANSION IDEA

Grammar Chart
1. Divide the class into pairs.
2. Working together, have students look for sentences in the passage on page 280 that can be revised to include *it* clefts.

For example:
It has been shown in some studies that stress can actually enhance our immune systems.

1. Ask students to read the instructions.
2. Call on a student to read the example.
3. Have students complete the activity individually and then compare work in pairs.
4. Call on volunteers to read their answers aloud.

■ **EXERCISE D**

1. Ask students to read the study notes on page 282.
2. Call on a student to read the example.
3. Have students complete the activity on their own and then check their work in pairs.
4. Call on volunteers to read their answers aloud.

C Complete the sentences below; then, use an *it* cleft to emphasize the information that you added to each sentence.   Answers will vary.

1. Stress sometimes affects ___my stomach___. (part of your body)
   _____It's my stomach that stress sometimes affects._____

2. I don't enjoy ___giving presentations___ (activity), and sometimes it really stresses me out.
   It's giving a presentation that sometimes really stresses me out.

3. I feel the most stress ___at my part-time job___. (location of an activity)
   It's at my part-time job that I feel the most stress.

4. This class sometimes stresses me out ___because I don't like one of my classmates___. (reason)
   It's because I don't like one of my classmates that this class stresses me out.

5. I get almost sick from stress ___on the day before a big exam___. (time/duration)
   It's on the day before a big exam that I get almost sick from stress.

6. I feel a lot of stress ___when the teacher calls on me in grammar class___. (time clause)
   It's when the teacher calls on me in grammar class that I feel the most stress.

7. I think ___my roommate___ (person) is very stressed out right now.
   I think it's my roommate who's very stressed right now.

D Correct the students' statements on the next page using the study notes below.

Name of Gland	Location	Function
pituitary	attached to floor of brain by thin stalk	growth of bone & muscle; stimulates other glands; affects general metabolism
thyroid	2 lobes; along side of trachea	regulates metabolic rate
parathyroid	4 glands; on thyroid lobes near the trachea	metabolism of calcium & phosphorus → bones
pancreas	near liver	produces insulin → carbohydrate, fat & protein metabolism
adrenal	near kidneys	produces steroids & epinephrine (increases blood sugar)

282 LESSON 26 | Biology: Stress and the Immune System

■ **EXPANSION IDEA**

Exercise C

1. Ask students to write five statements that include the word *stress*, modeled on those in Exercise C.
2. Divide the class into pairs and have students exchange statements. Tell them to rewrite the sentences with *it* clefts.

For example:
Student 1: *Taking exams is the most stressful part of school.*
Student 2: *It's taking exams that's the most stressful part of school.*

1. **Instructor:** Kim, where are the parathyroid glands located?
   Kim: The parathyroid glands are located alongside the trachea.
   Instructor: Juan?

   Juan: *It's the thyroid, not the parathyroid, that is located alongside the trachea.*

2. **Instructor:** What does epinephrine affect?
   Justin: Epinephrine affects carbohydrate metabolism.
   Instructor: Akiko?

   Akiko: It's not carbohydrate metabolism but blood sugar levels that epinephrine affects.

3. **Instructor:** Which gland produces insulin?
   Marcus: The adrenal gland does.
   Instructor: Benjamin?

   Benjamin: It's the pancreas, not the adrenal gland, that produces insulin.

4. **Instructor:** How many lobes does the thyroid consist of?
   Alicia: The thyroid consists of 4 lobes.
   Instructor: Mona?

   Mona: It's two lobes not four that the thyroid consists of.

5. **Instructor:** OK, Evan, what does the thyroid regulate?
   Evan: It regulates blood pressure.
   Instructor: Orlando, is that correct?

   Orlando: No, it's metabolic rate, not blood pressure, that the thyroid regulates.

6. **Instructor:** According to your reading, what does the parathyroid regulate?
   Fatima: From what I remember, the parathyroid regulates the metabolism of calcium and iron.
   Instructor: Gil, do you agree with that?
   Gil: No, it's metabolism of calcium and phosphorous, not calcium and iron, that the parathyroid regulates.

7. **Instructor:** Sandra, where is the parathyroid located in relation to the thyroid?
   Sandra: The parathyroid is located inside the thyroid gland.
   Instructor: Does everyone agree with that?

   Tran: No, it's inside the trachea, not in the thyroid gland, where the parathyroid is located.

8. **Instructor:** Last question. Why is the pancreas important?
   Irena: The pancreas is important for stimulating other glands.
   Instructor: Sorry, Irena. Who can tell her the reason that the pancreas is important?
   Lamar: It's for producing insulin, not for stimulating other glands that the pancreas is important.

■ **EXPANSION IDEA**

Exercise D
1. Divide the class into pairs.
2. Tell students to take turns scrambling information for the study notes on page 282 and correcting the information.

For example:
Student 1: *The pituitary gland has two lobes, and is along side of the trachea.*
Student 2: *No, it's the thyroid gland that has two lobes and is next to the trachea.*

1. Go over the instructions with the class.
2. Call on a student to read the example.
3. Have students complete the activity individually and then check their work in pairs.
4. Call on volunteers to read their answers to the class. Check after each statement is read to see whether the rest of the class agrees with the answer, and discuss any differences of opinion.

E (Circle) information in each sentence that you want to emphasize. Use the circled word, phrase, or clause in an *it* cleft structure.

1. Stress can affect (people with asthma,) not those with hay fever.
   It's people with asthma that stress can affect, not those with hay fever.

2. According to research, stress affects the (severity of an asthma attack,) not the onset of an attack.
   According to research, it's the severity of an attack, not the onset of an attack that stress affects.

3. Many stress sufferers develop (hives.)
   It's hives that many stress sufferers develop.

4. Stress can cause (heart damage) because stress-anxiety reactions raise blood pressure.
   It's heart-damage that stress can cause because of stress reactions raising blood pressure.

5. Researchers point to (stress-induced hormone production) as another cause of damage to the arteries.
   It's stress-induced hormone producers that researchers point to as another cause of damage to the arteries.

6. Blood pressure is also related to (caffeine consumption.)
   It's caffeine consumption that blood pressure is also related to.

7. Some people suffer from (stomach ulcers, not from heart problems,) when they are under severe stress.
   It's from stomach ulcers, not from heart problems that some people suffer when they are under severe stress.

8. The stomach produces (too much acid,) and that leads to an irritated stomach lining.
   It's too much acid that the stomach produces and that leads to an irritated stomach lining.

9. You feel dizzy, have shortness of breath, and your heart pounds when you have (an attack of anxiety hyperventilation.)
   It's when you have an attack of anxiety hyperventilation that you feel dizzy, have shortness of breath and your heart pounds.

10. Long-term stress affects (the physical health of many people.)
    It's the physical health of many people that long-term stress affects.

■ EXPANSION IDEA

Exercise E

1. Divide the class into pairs and have them role-play a discussion between a physician and a patient using the information in Exercise E.

For example:

Student 1: *In your case, it's heart damage I'm worried about, not ulcers.*

Student 2: *Why? I don't have high blood pressure and it's a raise in blood pressure that causes heart damage, isn't it?*

F Identify information that you want to emphasize in each text below. <u>Underline</u> the information, and rewrite the sentence with an *it*-cleft structure.

1. Some of the reactions that people have to stress may also be caused by other factors. <u>Some coffee drinkers experience a rise in blood pressure or more acid in their stomachs due to caffeine.</u> Other people, for example, may have heart trouble because their cholesterol level is too high.

   It's due to caffeine that some coffee drinkers experience a rise in blood pressure or . . .

2. Humans and most animals have an automatic physiological response to danger that stimulates the body functions into hyperactivity. <u>People refer to the "fight or flight" response when they describe the changes that occur in our bodies.</u> Although it helps us to react to danger, this "red alert" condition only lasts a short time.
   <u>It's the "fight or flight" response that some people respond to when they describe the changes in our bodies.</u>

3. The body works efficiently to get more oxygen in the blood. For instance, breathing becomes quicker. <u>Then, the heart pumps the blood more rapidly as the blood pressure rises.</u> Extra red blood cells come from the spleen in order to absorb more oxygen.
   <u>It's the heart that pumps the blood more rapidly as blood pressure rises.</u>

4. The body needs glucose in addition to oxygen for energy. <u>The liver changes sugar, which is stored there as glycogen, into glucose.</u> The glucose enters the bloodstream and flows throughout the body for quick energy.
   <u>It's sugar, which is stored in the liver as glycogen, that the liver changes into glucose.</u>

5. As the blood and glucose circulate, our bodies' senses change in intensity. Our hearing becomes more acute. <u>Our vision becomes more sensitive because our pupils dilate.</u> On the other hand, our brains decrease the feeling of pain.
   <u>It's because our pupils dilate that our vision becomes more sensitive.</u>

■ COMMUNICATE

G **PAIR WORK** With a partner, talk about things that stress you out. Emphasize differences between yourself and your partner by using *it* clefts.

Giving a presentation makes me really uptight and nervous. I'd rather write a paper.

For me it's the exact opposite. It's not talking in class but **writing** that stresses me out.

---

1. Ask students to read the instructions.
2. Call on a student to read the example.
3. Call on a volunteer to rewrite the sentence, emphasizing *cholesterol* instead of *caffeine.*
4. Ask students to complete the activity individually.
5. Divide the class into pairs and have students compare their answers.

■ **COMMUNICATE**

■ **EXERCISE G**

1. Ask students to review the instructions.
2. Call on two students to read the text in the speech balloons.
3. Divide the class into pairs and have them discuss the things that cause them stress.
4. Circulate as students work and assist as needed. Encourage them to use *it* clefts as often as possible.

■ **EXPANSION IDEA**

Exercise G

1. Have students write a summary of their discussions, comparing and contrasting what causes them stress with what stresses out their partner.

Remind them to use *it* clefts in their writing.
2. Call on a few volunteers to read their summaries aloud.

PART TWO

It in Subject Position with
Adjective Complements

■ GRAMMAR IN CONTENT

■ EXERCISE A

1. Have students review the instructions.
2. Ask students to complete the activity individually and then check their work in pairs.

■ GRAMMAR CHART

Review: It *in Subject Position with Adjective Complements*

1. Write on the board *It's clear that good health is important.*
2. Call on a volunteer to underline the subject of the sentence. Ask another volunteer to point out the adjective complement.
3. Call on volunteers to explain how *it* functions in the sentence.
4. Have students review the sample sentences and Notes. Then answer any questions they have about using *it* in the subject position.

■ GRAMMAR IN CONTENT

A Reread the text at the beginning of this lesson, and <u>underline</u> any clause with *it* in subject position, except for the boldfaced *it*-cleft sentences.

Review: *It* **in Subject Position with Adjective Complements**

Sample Sentences	Notes
It's obvious that stress can harm you. **It** must have been annoying that people were talking during the exam. **It** was silly of you to oversleep on the day of your job interview. **It** wasn't easy for us to relax before the exam.	*It* often takes the position of grammatical subjects in English because: • English speakers prefer long or "heavy" grammatical subjects at the end of a sentence • new information typically appears at the end of a sentence Use *it* in subject position in sentences with different types of adjective complements.
It is sad that so many people suffer from stress-related health problems. **Is it** really **true that** a little stress is a good thing?	Adjectives with *that* clauses include adjectives of emotion and adjectives of truth.
It was wrong of you to procrastinate. ↓ You were wrong to procrastinate.	Adjective that describes a person's behavior + (*of* + PERSON) + infinitive phrase. As an alternative, use the PERSON as the subject of the sentence and omit *it*.
It hasn't been easy for Kim to finish **the project**. ↓ **The project** hasn't been easy for Kim to finish.	Adjective that describes an experience + (*for* + PERSON) + infinitive phrase.
It's irritating to work with **Judy**. **Karen** is annoying to work with, too.	As an alternative, use the **direct object** or **object of the preposition** in the infinitive phrase as the subject and omit *it*. Adjectives that describe an experience include *convenient, difficult, disappointing, easy, embarrassing, fun, (im)possible, interesting,* and *surprising.* See Appendix 2 for a list of adjectives that describe emotion, truth, behavior, and experience.

■ EXPANSION IDEA

Grammar Chart

1. Divide the class into pairs and have them discuss ways to relieve stress using *it* in the subject position with adjective complements.

For example:
Student 1: *It isn't easy to relax when you're worried about a lot of things.*

Student 2: *It sounds silly, but laughing relieves stress.*

2. Circulate as students work and assist as needed.

B Use *it* in subject position to paraphrase the sentences below.

1. Rob was careless to leave the headlights on because now the car battery is dead.

   It was careless of Rob to leave the headlights on because now the battery is dead.

2. The mid-term test results were embarrassing for us to look at.

   It was embarrassing for us to look at the mid-term test results.

3. Two exams in one week are not easy to study for.

   It's not easy to study for two exams in one week.

4. Patricia may have been unwise to take 16 credits this semester.

   It may have been unwise of Patricia to take 16 credits this semester.

5. Twins or triplets are probably pretty hard for even the best parents to handle.

   It's probably pretty hard for even the best parents to handle twins or triplets.

6. My roommate was very generous to offer Evan a place to stay, but we don't have much space in our room.

   It was very generous of my roommate to offer Evan a place to stay, but we don't have much room in our place.

7. The project deadline has been alarming for us to think about ever since our boss assigned it.

   It has been alarming for us to think of the project deadline ever since our boss assigned it.

8. Wasn't Terry crazy to invite his whole soccer team for dinner this Saturday?

   Wasn't it crazy for Terry to invite his whole soccer team for dinner this Saturday?

9. Why is Terry's wife wrong to worry about Saturday's dinner?

   Why is it wrong for Terry's wife to worry about Saturday's dinner?

10. Why are the guests going to inconvenience her?

    Why is it going to be inconvenient for her to deal with the guests?

■ **EXERCISE B**

1. Ask students to review the instructions.
2. Call on a student to read the example.
3. Ask students to complete the activity individually and then correct it in pairs.

■ **EXPANSION IDEA**

Exercise B

1. Divide the class into pairs.
2. Have students take turns asking and answering questions about the statements in Exercise B. Tell them to use their imaginations.

For example:

Student 1: *Is studying for two exams in one week hard for you?*

Student 2: *Yes. It's not easy to study for two exams in one week, especially when one of them is a history exam.*

■ EXERCISE C

1. Ask students to read the instructions.
2. Call on a student to read the example.
3. Answer any questions that students may have about the difference in meaning in the two sentences of the example.
4. Have students complete the activity in pairs, discussing the possible meanings of the sentences before they write their answers.
5. Call on volunteers to read their answers aloud. Discuss any disagreements among class members.

C What's the difference in meaning between the sentences? In some cases there may be no difference in meaning.

1. a. It was awkward that Terry invited his team for dinner.
   b. It was awkward of Terry to invite his team for dinner.

   DIFFERENCE: _In a. the situation is awkward. In b. Terry's behavior is awkward or it's his fault that the situation is awkward._

2. a. It wasn't fair that Jim's boss gave him another project this week.
   b. It wasn't fair to give him another project this week.

   DIFFERENCE: _a. has more information than b.—we do not know who the "giver" is._

3. a. It's not possible that Jim can deal with any more work.
   b. It's not possible for Jim to deal with any more work.

   DIFFERENCE: _no appreciable difference_

4. a. It may have been disappointing to Jim that his boss was so inconsiderate.
   b. It may have been disappointing of Jim's boss to be so inconsiderate.

   DIFFERENCE: _In a. only Jim is disappointed, whereas in b. others are disappointed._

5. a. It seems very inconvenient that so many projects are due this week.
   b. It seems very inconvenient of Jim's boss to make so many projects due this week.

   DIFFERENCE: _a. the situation is generally inconvenient but b. only refer's to Jim's boss._

6. a. It is silly that Jim's boss assigned him to two important projects.
   b. It was silly of Jim's boss to assign him to two important projects.

   DIFFERENCE: _a. the situation is silly, but in b., Jim's boss is silly._

7. a. It seems surprising that Jim hasn't complained about his workload.
   b. It seems surprising of Jim not to complain about his workload.

   DIFFERENCE: _a. the situation is surprising but in b. Jim's behavior is surprising._

■ EXPANSION IDEA

Exercise C
1. Divide the class into pairs. Have students write three sets of sentences modeled on those in Exercise C.
2. Have pairs exchange work and ask them to discuss the sentences to determine whether there is a difference in their meanings.
3. Ask the two pairs to discuss the twelve sentences.

D Comment on the behavior of the person in each situation below. Select an adjective from the box for your comment. Use each adjective only once. Answers will vary. Sample answers below. Note: students will have to use two adjectives in multiple sentences in order for all words in the box to be used.

crazy	unwise	foolish	inconsiderate	careless
generous	silly	foolhardy	perceptive	wrong

1. Ray didn't study for his final in biology until the night before the exam.

   It was unwise of Ray to wait until the last minute to study for his exam.

2. Lynn drank so much coffee that she couldn't sleep well before her exam the next day.
   Lynn was foolish to drink so much coffee that she didn't sleep well before her exam the next day.

3. Lucy volunteered to help her roommate Cathy with a project for biology so that Cathy could finish it on time.
   It was generous of Lucy to help her roommate Cathy with a project for biology so that Cathy could finish it on time.

4. After a long weekend, Charlie drove back to campus through a big snowstorm even though his exam wasn't until the next afternoon.
   After a long weekend, it was silly of Charlie to drive back to campus in a big snowstorm even though his exam was the next day.

5. Drew lost part of his team's biology project as he biked to campus.

   It was careless of Drew to lose part of his biology team's project as he biked to class.

6. Students in the library all around Barbara were chatting while she was trying to study for her biochemistry mid-term.
   It was inconsiderate of students in the library around Barbara to chat while she was trying to study for her mid-term.

7. Professor Lopez realized that the students in his physiology class hadn't had enough time to prepare for the mid-term, so he postponed the exam for two days.
   It was perceptive of Prof. Lopez to realize that the students hadn't had enough time to study and to postpone the exam.

8. Sally was short on time, so she decided to give her three-minute speech in Public Speaking class without any preparation.
   It was crazy of Sally to give her three-minute speech in Public Speaking class without any preparation.

■ **COMMUNICATE**

E WRITE Make a list of guidelines or tips for preventing stress. Present your ideas to your classmates.

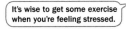 It's wise to get some exercise when you're feeling stressed.

■ **EXERCISE D**

1. Ask students to read the instructions and the words in the box.
2. Call on a student to read the example. Remind students that they may use each word only once.
3. Have students complete the activity individually and then discuss their answers with a partner.
4. Call on volunteers to read their answers aloud.

■ **COMMUNICATE**

■ **EXERCISE E**

1. Ask students to read the instructions.
2. Call on a student to read the text in the speech balloon.
3. Give students time to make their list of guidelines or tips.
4. Discuss the topic, calling on volunteers to present their ideas to the class.

■ **EXPANSION IDEA**

Exercise E

1. Have students develop their lists into a short essay. They may also want to include suggestions made by other students during the class discussion. Encourage students to use *it* in the subject position as often as possible.

2. Divide the class into pairs and have students edit each other's work. Ask them to suggest additional places where *it* could be used in the subject position.

3. Call on volunteers to read their essays aloud.

■ GRAMMAR AND VOCABULARY

1. Ask students to read the instructions.
2. Call on two students to read the topics aloud.
3. Ask students to choose one of the two topics and give them time to write their compositions.

■ PROJECT

1. Ask students to review the instructions.
2. Answer any questions that students have about the project.
3. Call on students at the next class meeting to give their oral reports.

■ INTERNET

1. Call on a student to read the instructions.
2. Have students conduct their searches.
3. At the next class meeting, ask students to discuss how they feel about counseling, and whether they think counselors should protect students' privacy.

GRAMMAR AND VOCABULARY Write a composition on one of the topics below. Use as many words as possible from the Content Vocabulary on page 279. Use sentences with *it* clefts and adjective complements to express some of your ideas.

Topic 1: We admire people for various reasons: their skills, their accomplishments, their personalities. It may be the way in which they have handled a difficult or stressful situation that makes us admire them. Describe someone that you admire for this reason. Use as much detail as possible.

Topic 2: Some people thrive on stress. It's energizing, not debilitating, for them. Would your friends or family members describe you in this way? Is it true or untrue that you respond favorably when you work or interact in a stressful environment? Explain and give concrete examples.
Answers will vary.

PROJECT Interview at least one student on your campus about his or her attitude toward counseling. Find out the following information, and give a brief oral report on your findings at your next class meeting.

1. Does your interviewee think that it is important for students at your school to have access to counseling services?
2. What is your interviewee's attitude about going to a counselor?
3. According to your interviewee, what's the most important counseling option available to students at your school?
4. According to your interviewee, is it embarrassing to go to a counselor? Why, or why not?

 INTERNET Go to your school's website (or the website of a nearby school) and find out what kind of counseling is available for students who need some kind of help. Be ready to discuss (1) all of the counseling options that are available and (2) the counseling options that you think are the most important. In your opinion, should the counseling options be confidential; in other words, should the counselors protect the privacy of students who use the counseling options?
Answers will vary.

290 LESSON 26 | Biology: Stress and the Immune System

■ EXPANSION IDEA

Grammar and Vocabulary

1. Divide the class into pairs. Try to pair students who wrote about different topics.
2. Ask students to read each other's essays and then discuss the topic.

Encourage them use vocabulary and grammar from the lesson whenever possible.

Lesson (27)

Criminal Justice:
Identification Documents
and Technology

Overview

1. Ask students to raise their hands if they have a U.S. driver's license. Then ask them to raise their hands if the have a driver's license from another country.
2. Hold a brief discussion about who generally has a driver's license in the countries represented in your class and how difficult it is to obtain one.

■ **CONTENT VOCABULARY**

Look up the words below that you do not know and enter them in your vocabulary journal. Write each word's part of speech, a definition, and an example sentence. Try to include them in your discussion and writing below.

to avert	to compromise	to counterfeit	rigorous
biometric data	to confiscate	fake	to verify
to breach	counterfactual	a fingerprint	widespread

■ **THINK ABOUT IT**

Look at the driver's license on the next page. What kind of information is usually included on a driver's license? Does your driver's license have any information on a computer chip inside it? Do people where you live use their driver's licenses as national IDs? Discuss your responses with a classmate.

In your writing journal, write for five minutes about the questions below. When you are finished, share what you wrote with the class.   Answers will vary.
What kind of ID do you carry with you every day? What kind of information is contained on that ID? Is that information different from the information on a passport? If you had lost your passport on your trip to another country, what would you have done?

■ **CONTENT VOCABULARY**

Ask students to review the words in the box. Tell them to look up any unfamiliar words.

■ **VOCABULARY JOURNAL**

Have students add new words to their vocabulary journals and write down the parts of speech, definitions, and sentences for each.

■ **THINK ABOUT IT**

1. Have students read the instructions.
2. Divide the class into pairs and have them compare the information shown and the technology used for United States licenses and on licenses from their home countries.
3. Have students read the journal writing instructions. Answer any questions that they have about the topic. Then give them five minutes to write in their journals.
4. Call on volunteers to share their ideas with the class.

291

■ **CONTENT NOTES**

The topic of this lesson is Criminal Justice: Identification Documents and Technology. Students will learn about and acquire some vocabulary needed to discuss how security concerns in a post-9/11 world have led to changes in different forms of identification documents. Use this lesson to discuss students' concerns about their own international documents. If your school has an office that deals with international students, direct students with visa problems to it, or suggest that they contact their consulates.

PART ONE

Conditional Clauses: Past Counterfactuals

■ GRAMMAR IN CONTENT

■ EXERCISE A

CD 3, Track 12

1. Ask students to read the title of the passage.

2. Have students brainstorm what might make an ID "high-tech." Write their ideas on the board.

3. Play the audio and have students follow along in their books as they listen. Ask students to circle any unfamiliar words or phrases.

4. Call on students to read their circled words and elicit definitions or explanations from volunteers if possible.

5. Check comprehension by asking questions such as the following: *What made U.S. officials look for new ways to ensure the security of U.S. identification documents? Why were government agencies able to develop new versions of driver's licenses and passports so quickly? What is a "Smart Card"? What does the acronym "RFID" stand for? What do critics of the new ID technologies fear?*

PART ONE   Conditional Clauses: Past Counterfactuals

■ GRAMMAR IN CONTENT

CD3,TR12

A Read and listen to the passage below. The sentences in bold in the text are sentences with *if* clauses that express an unreal, or counterfactual, condition in the past.

High-Tech ID

When Maureen Patterson and her business partner Brenda O'Neill used to head for the airport, they would check to be sure that their tickets and passports were readily available. Even though they only traveled to Montreal to meet with clients, the women knew that after 9/11, American passengers with passports generally re-entered the U.S. more easily than those with only their driver's licenses. They had learned the hard way: one time Ms. O'Neill had actually missed their return flight to Chicago because of the delays in her line at the security checkpoint. **If she had taken her passport along, she could probably have avoided that inconvenience.** Later, the laws were changed, making passports obligatory for U.S. air travelers to Canada. Now the women always travel with proper ID.

Since 9/11, officials have been searching for ways to ensure the security of U.S. identification documents. **If the 9/11 terrorists hadn't obtained fake IDs, they wouldn't have been able to enter the United States and the attack could have been averted.** At least that is the rationale for law enforcement and security officials at the state and federal levels who have been adapting various technologies to protect citizens' identities. **The appropriate government agencies wouldn't have developed new versions of drivers' licenses and passports so quickly if the technology hadn't existed in other forms before this need arose.**

In contrast to older forms of ID, new cards or documents have to be machine readable. Most driver's licenses, for example, have had bar codes or magnetic strips for some time. With either, the license meets the new, more rigorous standard for IDs. The computer chips that are embedded in these "smart cards" have to make contact with a scanning device to make the encoded information accessible. A more controversial method of adding "machine-readability" is to incorporate radio frequency ID (RFID) in a license or passport. This technology has been used for years in stickers that commuters have on their windshields to pass through highway tollbooths without stopping to pay. Since the sticker, or in this case a passport or license, can be read from a distance, the identification of vehicles or passengers can be confirmed speedily, and foot or vehicular traffic flows more smoothly. **Had this technology been available in 2001, airport security officers could have spotted some problems with the biometric data in the IDs of the terrorists and would have used additional methods to verify their identities or their status.**

Critics of the new ID technologies fear that anyone with such RFID cards or documents will be in greater danger of identity theft. If hackers manage to compromise the system, they could have access not only to a person's passport number and date of birth, but other private information as well.

a rationale: a reason, a justification

a bar code: a series of vertical lines on many products that can be read by a scanner

to embed: to place within, to enclose

to encode: to put information in a code or in a different set of symbols

---

■ EXPANSION IDEA

Exercise A

1. Divide the class into small groups.

2. Ask students to discuss whether they feel safer as a result of increased security measures. Do they fear that their personal data is at risk or that the government might use it against them?

3. Have a member of each group report back to the class.

Sample Sentences	Notes
If I had forgotten my passport last week, they never would have let me on the airplane to Moscow.	Express actions or situations that never happened or were impossible in the past in conditional sentences.
If my passport had been stolen, I would have been forced to stay in Moscow longer.	**Main Clause** [= result clause]: SUBJECT + *would* + *have* + PAST PARTICIPLE
Of course, if I had been on an all-expense-paid vacation, I would have enjoyed staying in Moscow longer.	**Passive Main Clause:** SUBJECT + *would have been* + PAST PARTICIPLE
I wouldn't have felt comfortable if I had left my passport in my hotel room.	**Dependent *if* Clause** [= conditional clause]: *If* + SUBJECT + PAST PERFECT
If your passport had been stolen, would your embassy in Moscow have helped you?	**Passive *if* Clause:** *If* + SUBJECT + *had been* + PAST PARTICIPLE
Would you have locked your passport in the hotel safe if you had been in my shoes?	Begin a sentence with the *if* clause in most cases. Place the main clause at the beginning if: • the conditional clause is long and "heavy" or • the main clause contains a strong or interesting topic you want to stress or the *if* clause is an afterthought
Would you have had a hard time if you had had to get a new passport overseas?	Remember that the verb tenses in these sentences express a counterfactual condition in the past time.
If you had had to travel alone to Moscow, what would you have done?	When the *if* clause begins the sentence, separate it from the main clause with a comma.
I probably could have gotten some photos in Moscow if I had actually needed them. If I hadn't put my passport inside my pocket, a pickpocket might have stolen it.	*Would* is the most frequently used modal in past counterfactual conditional sentences. Use *could* or *might* to express: • a past opportunity or ability (= *could*) • a past possibility (= *might*) In both examples, the past action or situation in the result clause did not take place.

B Read over your journal entry, and <u>underline</u> at least one sentence that you can revise to include an *if* clause that expresses an unreal, or counterfactual, condition. Write your revised sentence(s) below.

Answers will vary.

_____

_____

_____

■ GRAMMAR CHART
Conditional Clauses: Past Counterfactuals

1. Write *counterfactual* on the board.
2. Call on a volunteer to use the two roots in the sentence to define the term.
3. Ask students to read the sample sentences and Notes.
4. Answer any questions that students have about conditional clauses with past counterfactuals.

■ EXERCISE B

1. Have students complete the exercise.
2. Ask students to exchange work with a partner. Have them look for additional places where conditional clauses with past counterfactuals could be added.

■ EXPANSION IDEA

Grammar Chart

1. Divide the class into pairs.
2. Have students look for places where sentences can be rewritten to include conditional clauses with counterfactuals.

For example:
If she had taken along the proper documents, she wouldn't have missed her flight.

1. Ask students to read the instructions.

2. Call on a student to read the example.

3. Have students complete the activity individually and then check their work in pairs.

4. Call on volunteers to read their answers to the class.

C Complete the sentences below for DeShawn Williams, who imagines how her trip to China could have been ruined.   Answers will vary.

1. If my roommate Angela and I had waited until the last minute to apply for passports, *we wouldn't have received them in time.*

2. If we hadn't applied for a visa to China, **we would have been turned away in Beijing.**

3. If I had packed my passport in my suitcase, **I would have caused a scene at** **the airport.**

4. We wouldn't have gotten through the security checkpoint in Seattle **if we had left** **our documents at home.**

5. If the Chinese immigration officials had confiscated my passport, **I would have been** **trapped inside China.**

6. We wouldn't have been able to fly from Shanghai to Beijing **if we hadn't shown** **our visas.**

7. If Angela and I had switched passports by mistake, **the officials would have given us** **a hard time.**

8. We would have been questioned for a long time on our return to Seattle **if we had** **arrived without our passports.**

■ EXPANSION IDEA

Exercise C

1. Divide the class into pairs.

2. Ask students to develop a travel situation in which an oversight causes problems.

For example:
Three friends plan a trip to Europe. They have bought a student train pass, but forget to take their student IDs.

3. Ask students to write a series of statements describing what occurs as a result of the mistake. Tell them to use conditional clauses with past counterfactuals in their writing.

For example:
If we had remembered to bring along our student IDs, none of the problems that we had would have occurred.

D In each situation below, there was a problem of identification that prevented the crime from being solved. How could law enforcement officials have solved these crimes? Work in small groups to brainstorm solutions.   Answers will vary.

1. Unfortunately, the surveillance camera at the First National Bank wasn't operating when the bank was robbed.

   If the camera had been operating, they could have identified the robbers.

2. The crime scene investigators dusted Danson's Custom Jewelry Store for fingerprints, but none of the prints were usable.

   If the fingerprints had been complete, they could have traced them through a database.

3. The thief was able to use Bert's driver's license because he resembled Bert.

   If the store clerk had checked the photo better, he could have alerted the police.

4. Intruders were able to breach security at TechSure Corporation because they forced the CEO to put her finger on the scanner near the office entrance.

   If the company had used a security camera too, they could have identified the thieves.

5. Although the kidnappers had spent several days at their "safe house," the crime scene investigators could not find any DNA samples.

   The investigators may have been able to identify the kidnappers if they had spent more time looking for DNA evidence.

6. A spy was able to enter the United States in 2000 with a counterfeit passport because it was the old-fashioned kind without any encoded biometric information.

   Officials wouldn't have permitted the spy to enter if they had insisted on seeing a passport with biometric information.

7. A thief broke into the high tech company two weeks before their retinal scanner was installed.

   If they had used other surveillance means, the company would have had some kind of ID on the thief.

8. The kidnapper disguised his voice when he called the family to make his demands.

   If the FBI had high-tech audio equipment, they could have identified his voice.

■ **EXERCISE D**

1. Go over the instructions with the class and answer any questions students may have about the activity.
2. Divide the class into small groups.
3. Give students time to answer the questions.
4. Call on members of each group to state how law enforcement officials could have solved the crimes.

■ **EXPANSION IDEA**

Exercise D

1. Divide the class into pairs.
2. Ask pairs to choose one of the eight situations from Exercise D to expand into a short dialog using conditional clauses with past counterfactuals.

For example:
Student 1: *If the kidnappers hadn't been so careful, the investigators might have found some DNA.*

Student 2: *Right. If they hadn't worn gloves, or had left behind a strand of hair, DNA could have been recovered.*

3. Call on volunteers to role-play for the class.

EXERCISE E

1. Ask students to read the instructions.
2. Have students complete the activity in pairs, discussing which word to choose as they work.
3. Call on volunteers to read their answers to the class. Discuss any differences in opinion.

E Use the appropriate conditional verb forms in the conversation below. Be careful of the time of each action. Insert the subject whenever necessary.

1. **Ed Higgins:** Meredith, did you put the passports in our suitcase?

   Meredith Higgins: Why ____*would I have done*____ (do) such a thing?

   Ed: I can't find them anywhere.

2. **Meredith:** I ____*'d look*____ (look) in the carry-on bag again if I

   ____*were*____ (be) you.

   Ed: I've looked in it five times.

   Meredith: Here, let me look.

3. **Meredith:** Did you look in the outside pockets?

   Ed: Of course I did.

   Meredith: Well, the passports are right here. If they ____*were*____

   (be) any closer, they ____*would have bitten*____ (bite) you!

   Ed: You know, that is really a ridiculous saying.

4. **Meredith:** Whatever. The main thing is that we have the passports.

   Ed: You're right.

   Meredith: If I ____*were*____ (be) you, I

   ____*would calm down*____ (calm down). The security official might think that

   you are acting strangely.

5. **Ed:** That's the last thing that we need.

   Meredith: You know, if you ____*had helped*____ (help) me pack last night,

   you ____*would have known*____ (know) that the passports weren't in the suitcases.

   Ed: All right, all right. Can we drop this subject?

6. **Meredith:** Sure. I'm a little worried about getting through this security line.

   Ed: We still have 30 minutes. Don't worry.

   Meredith: It ____*would have been*____ (be) better if we

   ____*had left*____ (leave) the house earlier. You know how the traffic can

   be this time of the day.

   Ed: Now you are worrying too much. Even if we ____*were*____ (be)

   20 feet back in line, we still ____*would have*____ (have) enough time to get

   through security.

EXPANSION IDEA

Exercise E

1. Divide the class into pairs.
2. Have them add two more exchanges between Ed and Meredith.

For example:

Meredith: *If we had already gotten through this line, we would be shopping in the duty-free store right now.*

Ed: *True, but if we had had time to do that, we would have had to carry a lot of extra bags on board.*

F **PAIR WORK** Imagine that you and your partner volunteered to check IDs for a concert that your student club sponsored. Now the other students are upset at you because many people entered who shouldn't have. Because the concert was on campus, the rules said "No one under 18" and "No alcohol permitted." Practice asking and answering questions about the problems that occurred.

What **would** you **have done** if a professor **had brought** his 15-year-old son?

I **would have told** them that nobody under 18 was allowed. Then I **would have told** the professor's son about another upcoming event he could attend.

PART TWO	Conditional Clauses: Word Order

■ GRAMMAR IN CONTENT

A Reread the text at the beginning of this lesson, and find another sentence that expresses a counterfactual situation. How is that sentence different from the boldfaced sentences in the text? Compare your answer with a partner.

Conditional Clauses: Word Order

Sample Sentences	Notes
Had I known about the new ID regulations, I would have brought my passport. The security lines would have moved faster **had the travelers followed** the new rules.	In formal English, *if* can be omitted in certain cases. This rule applies to *if* clauses with: • *had* (in past counterfactual conditions) • *should* (meaning "happen to")
Should you find someone's ID, check for a phone number so that you can contact the person. Contact the embassy **should you need** more pages in your passport.	*If* is omitted less frequently in conditional clauses with *were* (in present hypothetical or counterfactual conditions). In this case, the conditional clause appears in the initial position.
Were passports unnecessary, travel would be considerably more convenient. **Were the radio frequency ID** absolutely secure, no one would worry about identity theft.	Change the word order at the beginning of the clause: *Had* *Should* — + SUBJECT *Were*

■ **COMMUNICATE**

■ **EXERCISE F**

1. Call on a student to read the instructions out loud.
2. Ask two students to read the text in the speech balloons.
3. Answer any questions that students have about the activity.
4. Divide the class into pairs and have them practice asking and answering questions about the problems that occurred.
5. Circulate as students work and assist as needed. Remind them to use conditional clauses in their questions and answers.

PART TWO

Conditional Clauses: Word Order

■ **GRAMMAR IN CONTENT**

■ **EXERCISE A**

1. Ask students to read the instructions.
2. Give them time to find the sentence that includes a counterfactual situation, and decide how it is different from the boldfaced sentences in the text.
3. Have students compare their answers in pairs.
4. Discuss the answers as a class.

■ **GRAMMAR CHART**
Conditional Clauses: Word Order

1. Ask students to review the sample sentences and Notes.
2. Answer any questions that students have about correct word order in formal English sentences with conditional clauses.

■ **EXPANSION IDEA**

Grammar Chart
1. Have students rewrite bolded sentences in the text on page 292, omitting *if*.

   For example:
   Had she taken her passport along, she would have avoided that inconvenience.

2. Divide the class into pairs and have students check their work.

■ EXERCISE B

1. Have students review the instructions.
2. Call on a volunteer to read the example aloud.
3. Have students complete the activity individually and then check their work in pairs.
4. Call on volunteers to read their answers aloud.

B Rewrite each sentence by omitting the *if* clause and then putting the conditional clause at the beginning of the sentence.

1. I would have applied for a passport sooner if I had known about the new rules.

   Had I known about the new rules, I would have applied for a passport sooner.

2. If the passport biometric coding were easy to decode, they wouldn't have decided to use it.

   Were the passport biometric coding easy to decode, they wouldn't have decided to use it.

3. If you were to burn the tip of your right index finger, would that fingerprint be the same after your finger healed?

   Were you to burn the tip of your right index finger, would the fingerprint be the same after it had healed?

4. If they should smudge a fingerprint during the investigation, could crime scene investigators identify the fingerprint?

   Should crime scene investigators smudge a fingerprint during the investigation, could they identify it?

5. If a criminal had left any fingerprints at the scene of the crime, could a fingerprint expert have known that she was a smoker?

   Had she left any fingerprints at the scene of the crime, could a fingerprint expert have known if she was a smoker?

6. If someone should steal your biometric data, you might not be able to use it for the rest of your life.

   Should someone steal your biometric data, you might not be able to use it for the rest of your life.

■ EXPANSION IDEA

Exercise B

1. Ask students to write four sentences, modeling them on the ones in Exercise B.

   For example:
   If someone stole your identity, your credit rating might be ruined for years.

2. Divide the class into pairs and have students rewrite each other's sentences by omitting the *if* clause and then putting the conditional clause at the beginning of the sentence.

C Make a conditional sentence that expresses how you will or would deal with the situation differently. Omit *if* in your sentence. Be aware of the timeframe in each situation.

1. When the police officer stopped my car and asked to see my driver's license, I realized that it had expired.

   Had I taken it out of my wallet recently, I would have remembered the expiration date.

2. When I go to the ATM, other people seem to watch me type my PIN number.

   Should other people seem to watch what I type at the ATM, I'll move my body to block the view.

3. I was in such a hurry to pack that I put my passport and airline ticket in my suitcase with my travel books.

   Had I paid more attention, I wouldn't have put the travel documents in there.

4. At the mall yesterday I didn't have a photo ID so I couldn't use my credit card at Dunbar's.

   Had I only put my driver's license in my pocket, I wouldn't have had any trouble.

5. I can never remember my different passwords on different Internet sites.

   Should I forget them again, I'll write them down in some secret place.

6. I didn't realize that I needed passport photos for my visa, so I couldn't send the paperwork to the embassy until yesterday.

   Had I realized that I needed passport photos for my visa, I could have sent everything earlier.

7. I haven't kept my passport up to date; therefore, I'll have to get a new, more expensive one before my trip.

   Should I have to travel overseas again, I'll have to pay more attention to my passport.

8. I didn't have enough money to rent a car, so I had to use public transportation.

   Should I go overseas again, I'll be sure to rent one.

■ **EXERCISE C**

1. Call on a student to read the instructions aloud.
2. Ask a student to read the example aloud.
3. Call on a volunteer to identify the time frame in the example.
4. Ask volunteers to explain why it is important to be aware of the time frame in the exercise.
5. Have students complete the exercise individually and then compare their work in pairs.
6. Call on volunteers to read their answers aloud and identify the time frame in each.

■ **EXPANSION IDEA**

Exercise C

1. Ask students to write a few more conditional sentences expressing what will or would happen in one of the situations in Exercise C.

   For example:
   Had I realized that my license was about to expire, I would have renewed it. Had I renewed it, I wouldn't have gotten a ticket when the police officer stopped my car. Had I not received a ticket and a $100 fine, I would have had enough money to buy a ticket for the concert.

2. Circulate as students work and assist as needed.
3. Call on volunteers to read their work aloud.

■ EXERCISE D

CD 3, Track 13

1. Ask students to read the instructions.
2. Call on a student to read the text in the speech balloon.
3. Call on a volunteer to read the example.
4. Discuss the answer to the example.
5. Play the audio, pausing after each statement to give students time to circle their answers.
6. Play the audio again so that students can check their answers.
7. Call on volunteers to read their answers aloud. If there are any disagreements among class members, play the audio again.

D Listen to each statement in the recording and (circle) the letter of the correct interpretation.

CD3,TR13

> Mr. Richards, if you had brought all the necessary documents, you would have received your passport last week.

1. (a.) Mr. Richards submitted all the necessary documents.
   b. Mr. Richards didn't receive his passport last week.
2. a. Mr. Richards didn't need his passport right away.
   (b.) Mr. Richards didn't submit his passport application at the Post Office.
3. a. The photo was the wrong size.
   (b.) The photo is the wrong size.
4. a. They don't have all of the paperwork.
   (b.) They didn't have all of the paperwork.
5. (a.) He included his birth certificate.
   b. He didn't include his birth certificate.
6. (a.) They didn't send it by express mail.
   b. He included extra postage.
7. (a.) The ATM machine rejected her bank card.
   b. Miss Sanders typed in the correct PIN number.
8. a. The ATM machine recognized her card.
   (b.) She didn't type in the correct number the second time.
9. (a.) Her PIN number isn't valid.
   b. Her PIN number wasn't valid.
10. (a.) The ATM machine kept her card.
    b. She typed in the correct number.

■ EXPANSION IDEA

Exercise D

1. Divide the class into pairs.
2. Have students write statements that would make the interpretations that were incorrect in Exercise D correct.

   For example:
   If you had sent your application last month, you would have received your passport last week.

3. Call on volunteers to read their answers aloud.

E Find and correct the four errors in the e-mail message below.

○ ○ ○

Dad-
        had
If I ~~would have~~ listened to you, I could have saved myself a lot of trouble. Yesterday morning I lost my passport downtown. It's a good thing that my advisor made a photocopy of it during orientation. I went to the office right
        had
away and told them about it. If they ~~have~~ not helped me, I don't know what I would have done. First, we had to call the police and make a report. Then, I had to call the consulate and tell them. If there weren't a consulate
        had
here¸I might have⁄to fly to Washington to get a new passport. Luckily, I can pick up my new one in 5 days.

Don't tell Mom!
Jackie

■ COMMUNICATE

F **GROUP WORK** Many people are critical of modern airports and the security procedures that passengers have to go through. Have you been to an airport recently? How could the airport have been set up better for passengers? If you haven't been to an airport recently, have you gone through a security check somewhere else? How could the security area have been set up better? Share your thoughts and experiences in a group discussion.

> When I arrived in Miami, the baggage and immigration were too close together. If they had located the immigration area farther from the baggage claim, it wouldn't have been so confusing.

■ **EXERCISE E**

1. Have students correct the four errors in the e-mail message.
2. Have students check their work in pairs.
3. Call on volunteers to read the corrected sentences.

■ **COMMUNICATE**

■ **EXERCISE F**

1. Ask students to read the instructions.
2. Call on a student to read the text in the speech balloon.
3. Divide the class into small groups and have students discuss their experiences with airport security.
4. Circulate as students work and assist as needed.
5. Call on a member of each group to summarize his or her group's discussion.

■ **EXPANSION IDEAS**

Exercise E

Have students write a response to Jackie's e-mail.

For example:
You're right. If you hadn't made a photocopy of your passport, you would have had an even bigger problem.

Exercise F

Ask students to write a summary of their group's discussion.

For example:
Samir pointed out that if immigration officials had looked at his passport more carefully, they wouldn't have sent him to be interrogated and he wouldn't have missed his flight to Boston.

■ GRAMMAR AND VOCABULARY

1. Ask students to read the instructions.
2. Call on two students to read the topics aloud.
3. Ask students to choose one of the two topics and give them time to write their compositions.

■ PROJECT

1. Ask students to review the instructions.
2. Answer any questions that students have about the project. Suggest that they interview students who are not from their own countries of origin.
3. Call on students at the next class meeting to give their oral reports.

■ INTERNET

1. Call on a student to read the instructions.
2. Have students conduct their searches.
3. Ask students to take their fingerprints using an ink pad and divide the class into groups to compare fingerprints.

GRAMMAR AND VOCABULARY Write a composition on one of the topics below. Use as many words as possible from the Content Vocabulary on page 291. Use sentences with conditional structures to express some of your ideas.

Topic 1: People often respond to extreme or dangerous situations by making changes in laws or procedures so that the danger can be avoided in the future. For example, if 9/11 hadn't happened, forms of ID wouldn't have changed so quickly in the United States. Describe another example of a change in a law or an attitude in the United States or another country that was a response to something dangerous or frightening that happened.

Topic 2: Describe an incident in which you or someone that you know had to show some ID. Why did that person have to show the ID? What would have happened if the person had not been able to show a form of ID? According to that person, could the situation have been handled more appropriately? How?
Answers will vary.

PROJECT Interview at least one student on your campus about IDs. Find out the following information:

1. What kind of ID does your interviewee carry every day?
2. How often has your interviewee had to show the ID recently? To whom?
3. Does your interviewee have a passport? Why or why not?
4. Would your interviewee mind being fingerprinted when he/she visits another country?

 INTERNET Go online and do a search using the key word "fingerprints." Find out about the history, use, and classification of fingerprints. You and your classmates may even want to take your own fingerprints (using ink pads) and then try to sort or classify them using the information you learned online.
Answers will vary.

■ EXPANSION IDEA

Internet
1. Write *biometric authentication technology* on the board.
2. Ask students to do a search using these keywords and to take notes on how this technology differs from fingerprints.
3. Call on volunteers to report their findings to the class.
4. Have students discuss the type of identification method that they prefer.

Lesson 28

Astrobiology and Marine Sciences: Exploration

Lesson 28

Overview

1. Ask students to raise their hands if they have ever gone scuba diving.
2. Call on volunteers to describe the strangest plants and animals they have encountered underwater.
3. Ask students if they think many undiscovered life forms exist underwater.

■ CONTENT VOCABULARY

Look up the words and phrases below that you do not know and enter them in your vocabulary journal. Write each word's part of speech, a definition, and an example sentence. Try to include them in your discussion and writing below.

in close quarters	extraterrestrial	a specimen
a creature	hypothetical	a submersible
an expedition	a space capsule	symbiotic

■ THINK ABOUT IT

Look at the photos on the next page of some creatures that live in the oceans. Have you seen any of them before? Could these creatures tell us about life forms in outer space? How might they give scientists insights into conditions that are suitable for life? Discuss your ideas with a classmate.

In your writing journal, write for five minutes about the questions below. When you are finished, share your opinions with the class.　Answers will vary.
In your opinion, does life exist beyond Earth? Should we try to find new life forms? What might happen if we did? Do you know what scientists are doing now to find extraterrestrial life?

■ CONTENT VOCABULARY

Ask students to review the words in the box. Tell them to look up any unfamiliar words.

■ VOCABULARY JOURNAL

Have students add new words to their vocabulary journals and write down the parts of speech, definitions, and sentences for each.

■ THINK ABOUT IT

1. Have students read the instructions.
2. Divide the class into pairs and have students discuss their ideas about the creatures on page 304.
3. Have students read the journal writing instructions. Answer any questions that they have about the topic. Then give them five minutes to write in their journals.
4. Call on volunteers to share their ideas with the class.

303

▨ CONTENT NOTES

The topic of this lesson is Astrobiology and Marine Sciences: Exploration. Students will learn about and acquire some of the vocabulary needed to discuss the search for new life forms deep in the sea and in outer space.

PART ONE

Conditionals: Conjunctions

■ GRAMMAR IN CONTENT

■ EXERCISE A

CD 3, Track 14

1. Write *astrobiology* on the board.

2. Call on a volunteer to define the term using the roots *astro* and *bio*.

3. Play the audio and have students follow along in their books as they listen. Ask students to circle any unfamiliar words or phrases.

4. Call on students to read their circled words and elicit definitions or explanations from volunteers if possible.

5. Check comprehension by asking questions such as the following: *What usually motivates explorers? What is the focus of contemporary adventurers? What do astrobiologists search for? What is the "Habitable Zone"? Which conditions are needed to support life?*

■ GRAMMAR IN CONTENT

CD3,TR14

A Read and listen to the passage below. The words in bold in the text are clauses that are introduced by a conditional conjunction.

Exploring Our World and Beyond

Throughout human history we have explored. In ancient times, adventurers set sail **even if they feared** that they might drop off the end of the world. Others left home for months or years to satisfy their curiosity about other lands and people. Still others stared into the evening skies, saying to themselves, "**If only I could travel to the ends of the universe.**" Although these explorers were often motivated by curiosity and restlessness, others represented commercial interests that hoped to benefit from the precious metals, exotic furs, or agricultural products that foreign places and people might have to offer. Times have changed, but the attractions and benefits of exploration remain.

This other-worldly looking fish lives near the ocean floor.

Contemporary adventurers focus on the exploration of our universe and Earth's underwater world. As technology has enabled marine biologists to venture into extremely deep regions of the ocean, they have discovered incredible life forms. Similarly, geologists and oceanographers who have been searching the ocean floors for new sources of minerals, such as manganese, nickel, and gold, have discovered not only rich seafloor mining possibilities, but also unexpected life forms. For example, snails the size of baseballs were found near a submarine hot spring at a temperature of 280 degrees Celsius. If these researchers had not seen such life forms, no one would suspect that life could survive in such extreme conditions. Since then, biologists have been uncovering other unexpected conditions in which life can thrive, including extremes of temperature, salinity, pH, and atmospheric pressure.

Our search for life in space has benefited greatly from such findings. Astrobiology, a branch of biology that studies life forms we may encounter in outer space, has guided the search for extraterrestrial life. **Unless we actually find life in the universe or it finds us,** scientists have to be content with looking for secondary evidence that life exists or existed. In other words, they have to analyze debris from asteroids or comets and rock samples from our visits to the moon and Mars in order to check for evidence of life. Scientists may wish that they had other means of collecting data, but current technology limits our ability to go out and search for ourselves as we used to do. Computer models of the "Habitable Zone," a term that defines the set of conditions that support life on Earth, allow researchers to search beyond our solar system to identify other similar planets. These conditions include an atmosphere with oxygen, the stable presence of water, and gravity, among others. **Only if these conditions are met** do researchers believe that there is hope for finding another planet that supports life. Even though a number of similar planets are known to exist outside our solar system, scientists have already determined that none of them matches Earth's characteristics. Naturally, the search goes on.

a commercial interest: a group of businesspeople or companies that work together

salinity: the amount of salt in a liquid or solid

debris: the leftover pieces of something broken or destroyed

secondary: not original or direct

to thrive: to live or grow well

■ EXPANSION IDEA

Exercise A

1. Divide the class into pairs and have students take turns asking and answering questions using conditional sentences with conjunctions *even, unless, if only, only if.*

2. Circulate as students work and assist as needed.

Sample Sentences	Notes
Life forms may be too simple to communicate with us **even if** we find them.	Select one of the phrases below to modify the meaning of *if* in conditional clauses.
Even if we wanted to communicate with beings in far away galaxies, our level of technology wouldn't allow us to do so.	• *Even if* emphasizes an unexpected or surprising connection or relationship.
In the early years of space exploration, people were chosen to be astronauts **only if** they were men.	• *Only if* expresses a single or unique condition. Use negative fronting (see Lesson 15) when *only if* begins the sentence.
If only we had been able to build a space station on Mars years ago, astronauts could have gathered more data about the planet.	• *If only* expresses regret. *If only* + clause can be used without a main clause to comment on an unfortunate action or situation.
If only the Mars rovers were able to move over more of the surface of Mars!	
They'll launch the satellite tonight **unless** there's a thunderstorm. (**Explanation:** They'll launch it only if it doesn't storm.)	Introduce an exceptional or unique hypothetical condition with *unless:*
The astronauts will check the exterior cameras soon **unless** they haven't finished another task. (**Explanation:** They'll check the cameras only if they've finished their other work.)	• *Unless* implies a negative condition. Essentially, *unless* introduces a condition that is opposite to the condition introduced by *only if.* • When a clause with *unless* contains a negative, the paraphrase is affirmative with *only if.* • When an *unless*-clause is affirmative, the paraphrase with *only if* contains a negative.
They can't continue checking the equipment **unless** they get some rest. (**Explanation:** They can continue only if they can rest.)	
The old equipment doesn't work properly **unless** they monitor it regularly. (**Explanation:** The equipment works properly only if they monitor it regularly.)	The changes in affirmative or negative form can occur in the main or the conditional clause. Check the meaning of the sentence to decide the appropriate position for the negation.
Technicians didn't call for help **unless** the equipment shut down completely. (**Explanation:** Technicians called for help only if the equipment shut down completely.)	Avoid using negation in both clauses for clearer communication of your ideas.

B Read over your journal entry, and <u>underline</u> at least one sentence that you can revise to include a clause introduced by one of the conditional conjunctions listed above. Write your revised sentence(s) below.

Answers will vary.

_____

_____

_____

GRAMMAR CHART
Conditional Sentences: Conjunctions

1. Ask students to read the sample sentences and Notes.
2. Call on a few volunteers to make up conditional sentences using *even if, only if, unless.*
3. Answer any questions students have about conditional sentences with conjunctions.

EXERCISE B

1. Have students complete the exercise.
2. Ask students to exchange work with a partner. Have them look for additional places where sentences could be revised to include a clause introduced by a conditional conjunction.

EXPANSION IDEA

Grammar Chart

1. Ask students to expand one of the questions that they answered in their journals into a short essay.
2. Divide the class into pairs and have students read each other's essays and then discuss them.
3. Circulate as students discuss and assist as needed. Remind them to use clauses introduced by conditional conjunctions whenever possible.

■ EXERCISE C

1. Ask students to read the instructions.
2. Call on a student to read the example.
3. Have students complete the exercise individually and then check their work in pairs.
4. Call on volunteers to read their answers aloud.

C Edit the conjunctions in the sentences about historic explorers, adding *even* or *only* as appropriate. Follow the example.

Christopher Columbus

1. A man of modest means, Columbus could afford
   only
   to set sail for the New World ˄if Queen Isabella
   financed his voyage.

   Even
2. ˄If Charles Darwin hadn't developed his theory
   of evolution while sailing on the *Beagle,* he
   still would have been famous for his extensive
   collections of animal and plant life from this
   voyage.

3. Leif Erickson would have been credited with
   only
   discovering America if˄enough Scandinavians had
   settled in the New World.

4. Captain James Cook would have been famous for his three voyages of discovery in
   even
   the Pacific Ocean˄if the Cook Islands hadn't been named for him.

   Only
5. ˄If you read about the arduous expedition of Meriwether Lewis and William Clark
   across the land of the Louisiana Purchase to the Pacific Ocean, can you understand
   the important contribution of the Native American woman Sacagawea.

6. The admiration and respect of South Americans for the German naturalist Alexander
   only
   von Humboldt can be fully appreciated˄if you know how many things—from schools
   to an ocean current—have been named after him.

   Even
7. ˄If the British team of Stanley and Livingston had never found the source of the Nile
   River, they would still be famous.

■ EXPANSION IDEA

Exercise C

1. Ask students to write a sentence that includes a clause introduced by *even* and one with a clause introduced by *only if.*

   For example:
   You can call yourself an explorer only if you discover something new.

2. Have students scramble their sentences.

For example:
new/can/explorer/if/yourself/discover/only/call/you/an/something/you

3. Divide the class into pairs and have students unscramble each other's sentences.

D Read each sentence and look at the two sentences that follow. Which one correctly paraphrases the first sentence? (Circle) the letter of the best choice.

1. Unless scientists find other intelligent life in the universe, people won't care too much about space exploration.
   a. People will care about space exploration only if scientists find other intelligent life in the universe.
   b. People won't care about space exploration only if scientists find other intelligent life in the universe.

2. If only we could prove that life exists on other planets.
   a. The speaker means that we can't prove that life exists there.
   b. The speaker expresses regret that we haven't been able to prove that life exists there.

3. Americans would be more enthusiastic about space exploration if only the *Challenger* hadn't exploded.
   a. The speaker emphasizes that the unfortunate *Challenger* explosion caused Americans to lose their enthusiasm for space exploration.
   b. The speaker means that the *Challenger* explosion caused Americans to lose their enthusiasm for space exploration.

4. The government will reduce its spending on space exploration unless citizens communicate their support of it.
   a. The government will reduce its spending only if citizens do not communicate their support of the space program.
   b. The government will reduce its spending only if citizens communicate their support of the space program.

5. Astrobiologists wouldn't have assumed that life forms live in extreme conditions unless they had seen such specimens on Earth.
   a. Astrobiologists have assumed that life forms can live in extreme conditions only because they have seen such specimens on Earth.
   b. Astrobiologists haven't assumed that life forms can live in extreme conditions only because they haven't seen such specimens on Earth.

6. Even if we find extraterrestrial life forms in the universe, they may not be complex life forms like us.
   a. The speaker implies that we can't expect to find complex life forms.
   b. The speaker implies that we have the remote possibility of finding complex life forms.

7. According to some scientists, we should search for extraterrestrial life only if we also want to be found by other life forms.
   a. We shouldn't search for extraterrestrial life unless we want to be found.
   b. We should search for extraterrestrial life because we want to be found.

■ **EXERCISE D**

1. Call on a student to read the instructions.
2. Ask a student to read the example.
3. Call on a volunteer to explain why *a* is the correct paraphrase.
4. Have students complete the activity individually and then check their work in pairs. Encourage students to discuss the two paraphrases.
5. Call on volunteers to read their answers aloud.

■ **EXPANSION IDEA**

Exercise D
1. Divide the class into pairs.
2. Have students choose four of the questions in Exercise D. Ask them to rewrite the sentences so that the paraphrase that was originally incorrect is now correct.

For example:
Even if astrobiologists devote all of their time to searching for life on other planets, they will never prove that it exists.

EXERCISE E

1. Go over the instructions with the class.
2. Call on a student to read the example.
3. Ask a few volunteers for alternative ways of finishing the first sentence.
4. Have students complete the activity on their own. Encourage them to use their imaginations as they finish the statements.

Using your own words and ideas, complete the conditional clause in each sentence below.

1. A person can't travel into space unless _she undergoes training as an astronaut._

2. In the old days, sea captains couldn't begin long exploratory voyages unless _they had enough supplies to last months._

3. Columbus wouldn't have been able to set sail unless _he had received financing from Queen Isabella._

4. Even though Columbus set sail to find a new route to India, _he ended up finding America instead._

5. Even if Columbus had landed on Cuba instead of Hispaniola, _he would have arrived at the wrong place._

6. Unless _they had enough pack animals,_ an overland expedition was able to move only a few miles per day.

7. Unless _they had special tires or other equipment,_ a caravan of vehicles would have difficulty crossing rough terrain.

8. Many European explorers wouldn't have reached their destinations in America unless _they had loaded enough supplies and had good weather._

9. There are many stories of Native Americans helping European explorers even though _the Indians were suspicious of the Europeans' motives._

10. Even if _they heard about dangerous terrain and fierce Indians,_ Europeans continued to explore the American West.

EXPANSION IDEA

Exercise E

1. Divide the class into small groups.
2. Have students take turns reading their answers.
3. Ask volunteers to read their answers, calling on two or three per question, as time allows.

"Rare Earth" Hypothesis – Ward and Brownlee

our planet = unusual → little chance of other life forms in universe

a) our unique position in relation to sun	→ liquid H$_2$O is stable
b) stable relationship to great planets	→ their powerful gravity protects us from asteroids and comets, e.g. Jupiter
c) our large moon	→ decreases gravitational pull of Sun and Jupiter, so Earth has stable orbit & rotation → stable seasons
d) our atmosphere	→ protects life from solar radiation → keeps heat near Earth
e) our magnetic field	→ protects us from solar wind (=deflects wind)
f) plate tectonics	→ maintains carbon balance in atmosphere → continues building mountains so that erosion doesn't result in completely flat land

F With a partner, explain some conditions necessary for life based on the notes from Astrobiology 101 shown above. Use *unless, only if,* or *even if.*

1. There is little chance of life as we know it unless there is a planet similar to Earth.

2. Only if a planet rotates in the same unique position in relation to a star will water be stable.

3. Unless a planet has a stable relationship with other planets, it won't be protected from comets and asteroids.

4. Even if a planet has a moon, it has to be stable enough to permit seasons.

5. Only if a planet has an atmosphere similar to ours can heat be kept near the surface and life be protected.

6. Even if a planet has a similar atmosphere, it also needs a magnetic field which helps to deflect solar winds.

7. Unless there is a mechanism like plate techtonics to move the ground, erosion will cause the land to become completely flat.

1. Ask students to read through the handwritten notes.
2. If students do not understand any of the terms used in the notes, call on class members to explain them.
3. Have students read the instructions.
4. Call on two students to read the examples.
5. Divide the class into pairs and have students complete the activity.
6. Circulate as they work; assist as needed.

■ **EXPANSION IDEA**

Exercise F

1. Ask students to write a short essay about why Ward and Brownlee believe there is little chance of other life forms existing in the universe, using the information in Exercise F.
2. Circulate as students work and assist as needed. Remind them to use *unless, only,* and *even if* in their writing.
3. Divide the class into pairs and have students edit each other's essays.
4. Call on a few volunteers to read their essays to the class.

■ EXERCISE G

1. Ask students to read the instructions.
2. Call on a student to read the text in the speech balloon.
3. Divide the class into pairs and have students discuss the type of exploration that attracts them, the kind of fieldwork they would undertake, and the kind of information they would focus on.

PART TWO

Conditional Sentences: Verbs + *That* Clauses; Mixed Conditions

■ GRAMMAR IN CONTENT

■ EXERCISE A

Have students complete the activity and check their work with a partner.

■ GRAMMAR CHART
Conditional Sentences: Mixed Conditions and That *Clauses*

1. Have students review the sample sentences and Notes.
2. Answer any questions that students have about conditional sentences containing verbs + *that* clauses and mixed conditionals.

G PAIR WORK Discuss the type of exploration that would attract you to study a particular field. If you had the training and the financial backing for an exploratory trip, what kind of fieldwork would you undertake? What kind of new information about our world or universe would be the focus of your exploration?

I would be interested in doing research on life forms at the South Pole, but only if I were part of a team. It'd be too dangerous by myself.

PART TWO	Conditional Sentences: Verbs + *That* Clauses; Mixed Conditions

■ GRAMMAR IN CONTENT

A Reread the text at the beginning of the lesson, and <u>underline</u> any other clauses that include conditional forms of verbs.

Conditional Sentences: Mixed Conditions and *That* Clauses

Sample Sentences	Notes
People with boring jobs might wish **that they had explored** other job options earlier in life.	Use verbs of wishing or imagining to introduce *that* clauses that express counterfactual conditions.
Children sometimes wish that a spaceship **would take** them on an adventure.	*Wish* introduces: • **present counterfactual** conditions • **past counterfactual** conditions • **future hypothetical** conditions
Pretend that you **were living** in a lab deep under the ocean. What would you do to relax? Suppose that Alan Shepard **hadn't been chosen** as an astronaut. Who would have been the first American in space?	*Imagine, pretend,* and *suppose* introduce: • **present counterfactual** conditions • **past counterfactual** conditions • **future hypothetical** conditions These three verbs are commonly used in the imperative form with this structure.
If we had already discovered a planet with life on it, **researchers would receive** more money for research. If people hadn't told so many unbelievable stories about extraterrestrials, **we might take** the evidence more seriously.	Use a combination of conditional verb forms to express the hypothetical or nonfactual impact of a past action on a present situation: *If* + PAST PERFECT, would / might / could + BASE FORM

■ EXPANSION IDEA

Exercise G
Ask students to write a short essay about the exploratory trip they discussed in Exercise G. Remind them to use grammar and vocabulary from the lesson.

B Complete the part of the conversations below with a *that* clause and a question.

1. **Barbara:** I'm really getting burned out. In fact, sometimes I regret getting a PhD in biology because I have to spend so much time in the lab.

   Shelley: Suppose *that you get training to be a wildlife biologist. Would you feel better about spending time outside doing research?*

2. **Cindy:** Dad, can we go back to the planetarium again next weekend?

   Eric: Let's wait till they have a different star show, honey. I'm glad that you liked it so much.

   Cindy: I hope someday that I can go into outer space.

   Eric: Pretend __that you were an astronaut. Where would you like to go?__

3. **Justin:** Why in the world do you believe in UFOs and space aliens?

   Lenny: How can you not believe? There's a lot of evidence.

   Justin: Evidence? I won't believe it until I see some hard evidence.

   Lenny: Suppose __that I showed you photos with suspicious aircraft in them. Would that satisfy you?__

4. **Ms. Brinkley:** I understand that you need another $5 million for the seafloor mining operation. Why should we spend that kind of money on exploration that has little chance of becoming profitable?

   Dr. Forester: Our competitors are having considerable success with similar seafloor exploration. Imagine __that we found a new source of gold. Would that make it worthwhile?__

   Ms. Brinkley: That kind of result would certainly impress me.

5. **Gina:** What could we do to get on TV? I think that it's our turn for "15 minutes of fame," don't you?

   Jackie: That's one of the silliest things that I have ever heard you say.

   Gina: No, I'm serious. What about extraterrestrials? There haven't been any stories about them in a while. OK, let's pretend __that aliens visited us last night. Would that attract media attention?__

6. **Dr. Klinger:** OK, class, today we're going to talk more about the possibility of finding life elsewhere in the universe. You'll remember that life on Earth survives and even thrives in some unlikely environments. So let's suppose __that were were climbing up Mt. Everest. What kinds of life forms would we find?__

■ **EXERCISE B**

1. Ask students to read the instructions.
2. Call on a student to read the example.
3. Give students time to complete the activity.
4. Circulate as students work and assist as needed. Remind them to use a *that* clause and a question.

■ **EXPANSION IDEA**

Exercise B

1. Divide the class into small groups.
2. Have students take turns reading their questions aloud.
3. Ask group members to make suggestions and corrections as appropriate.

EXERCISE C

1. Go over the instructions with the class.
2. Call on a student to read the example.
3. Have a few volunteers comment on their own feelings about participating in a trip to the Space Station.
4. Give students time to complete the activity.
5. Divide the class into pairs and have students compare their answers.
6. Call on volunteers to read their answers aloud.

C Comment on your interest in participating in each of the exploratory missions below with a conditional sentence.

The International Space Station

1. Astronauts who carry out experiments on the Space Station have to spend up to six months there.

   I wish that I could visit the Space Station, but I wouldn't want to stay there that long.

2. The submersible *Clelia* regularly transports three researchers and/or observers on short research missions in shallow water, during which they collect samples and photograph or videotape plant and animal life. On occasion, their missions include investigating archaeological sites and sunken ships.

   Going on a research mission in shallow water sounds really interesting only if we don't have to stay underwater for too long.

3. In 1845, Sir John Franklin and his crew sailed in two ships from England to North America to find the Northwest Passage. (In those days, people thought that a waterway existed between the North Atlantic and the North Pacific.)

   I wouldn't have gone on that voyage even if you had paid me a million dollars.

4. Since 2001, archaeologists have been exploring the area once occupied by the Fremont, a group of Native Americans who lived in a mountainous area in Utah. So far, they have discovered many simple structures and artifacts in remote areas.

   Exploring ruins in Utah sounds like a great adventure unless we had to do it in the heat of summer.

5. Meteorologists regularly explore storm phenomena by flying into hurricanes or by following tornadoes in vehicles to collect data.

   I'm interested in learning about storm phenomenon only if I don't have to put myself in danger.

6. Since 1960, cavers of various nationalities have been exploring Krubera Cave in Abkhazia on the Black Sea. In 2004, a Moscow-based team made it to 1,775 meters below the surface, and Ukrainians reached 2,080 meters. There are still more areas to explore.

   I wish I could go into caves, but I can't.

■ EXPANSION IDEA

Exercise C

1. Have students pick one of the exploratory missions described in the exercise. Ask them to develop their answer into a paragraph, using conditional sentences.

   For example:
   If it were possible to make a short trip, I would definitely go. I would be happy to spend two weeks at the Station, if that were an option.

2. Have students exchange work with a partner. Ask them to edit each other's paragraphs, suggesting ways of including more conditional sentences.

3. Call on volunteers to read their paragraphs to the class.

D Listen to the interview with Dr. Isadora Vincenzi and answer the questions below.

CD3,TR15

1. Who expected to see creatures living near a hydrothermal vent?

   In the past, no one expected to see them.

2. Did biologists discover the creatures?
   No, some researchers looking for a hydrothermic vent found them.

3. Did staff members of the Woods Hole Oceanographic Institution see the creatures first?

   No, it was the researchers.

4. Is Dr. Vincenzi a chemist?

   No, a deep-sea biologist.

5. When does Dr. Vincenzi do fieldwork near a black smoker?

   Only if there's evidence of a new life form.

6. Did Dr. Vincenzi discover the symbiotic relationship between two life forms?

   Yes, between bacteria and clams.

7. Who else discovered this particular relationship?

   No one else, but they would have if Vincenzi hadn't.

■ COMMUNICATE

E GROUP WORK Brainstorm five questions that will elicit speculation about how our world or universe would or might be different. Base each question on a past situation or event, and imagine that it didn't actually take place or that it occurred differently. When you are finished, share your questions with the class.

What if the Japanese had settled America before the Europeans? What would North America be like today?

■ EXERCISE D
CD 3, Track 15

1. Ask students to read the instructions.
2. Call on students to read the questions aloud.
3. Play the audio, instructing students to listen for content only.
4. Play the audio again, this time pausing it frequently to give students time to answer the questions.
5. Play the audio again so that students can check their answers.
6. Call on volunteers to read their answers aloud. If any class members disagree, play the audio again.

■ COMMUNICATE

■ EXERCISE E

1. Call on a student to read the instructions aloud. Answer any questions that students may have about them.
2. Ask a student to read the text in the speech balloon.
3. Discuss the question as a class for a few minutes.
4. Divide the class into small groups and have them brainstorm their questions.
5. Call on groups to read their questions aloud.

■ EXPANSION IDEA

Exercise E
1. Ask students to choose one of the questions posed by their own or one of the other groups. Tell them to write a short essay in answer to the question.
2. Divide the class into pairs and have students read and discuss each other's essays.
3. Call on a few volunteers to read their essays aloud. Have the class discuss their ideas, if time allows.

Lesson 28   **313**

Connection

Putting It Together

GRAMMAR AND VOCABULARY

1. Ask students to read the instructions.
2. Call on two students to read the topics aloud.
3. Ask students to choose one of the two topics and give them time to write their compositions.

PROJECT

1. Ask students to review the instructions.
2. Answer any questions that students have about the project.
3. Call on students at the next class meeting to give their oral reports.

INTERNET

1. Call on a student to read the instructions.
2. Have students conduct their searches and prepare their summaries, and comment on the information using *wish*, *imagine*, or *suppose*.

GRAMMAR AND VOCABULARY Write a composition on one of the topics below. Use as many words as possible from the Content Vocabulary on page 303. Use sentences with conditional structures or conjunctions to express some of your ideas.

Topic 1: "Exploring" can mean discovering new ideas and ways of thinking. As you think about your education so far, what regrets and wishes do you have about the kinds of classes that you have and have not taken or opportunities that you have or have not taken advantage of ? Explain and give concrete examples.

Topic 2: People who choose to explore often have to subject themselves to difficult conditions during their journeys. Sailing ships and caravans were certainly uncomfortable means of travel. Nowadays, explorers may have to spend long stretches of time in a space station, a submersible like *Alvin*, or another restrictive and potentially dangerous place. Under what circumstances would you consider undertaking such research and exploration? **Answers will vary.**

PROJECT Interview at least one student on your campus about extraterrestrial life. Find out the following information, and make a brief oral report of your findings at your next class meeting.

1. Does the person you interviewed believe that there is extraterrestrial life?
2. How much effort should people put into finding extraterrestrial life?
3. What is the opinion of the person you interviewed regarding the current space program, including the Space Station?

 INTERNET Visit a website related to space exploration, or go directly to the website www.discoverynow.us and click on one of the audio selections. (These audio selections have also been played on the radio.) Prepare a short summary of the report, and comment on the information with a sentence using *wish*, *imagine*, or *suppose*. **Answers will vary.**

EXPANSION IDEA

Internet
1. Ask students to visit a few websites related to UFOs.
2. Have them decide whether there is compelling evidence that UFOs exist.
3. Ask them to present their findings to the class.

Sociology of Sports

■ CONTENT VOCABULARY

Look up the words and phrases below that you do not know and enter them in your vocabulary journal. Write each word's part of speech, a definition, and an example sentence. Try to include them in your discussion and writing below.

an assumption	to disprove	to hustle	to sacrifice
a cliché	folk wisdom	a rationale	a sphere
to compete	gender	to resort to	underlying

■ THINK ABOUT IT

Read over the sports clichés below and talk over their meanings with a partner. Be prepared to paraphrase them.

He has all the moves.
He's a natural hitter.
She turned the game around.

We stayed too long with our game plan.
They have a killer instinct.
It was a team effort.

In your writing journal, write for five minutes about the questions below. When you are finished, share your ideas with the class.   Answers will vary.
What do young people learn when they participate in sports during their school years? In your opinion, what are the positive and negative lessons that young people may learn from their physical education classes or from competing in sports?

315

■ CONTENT NOTES

The topic of this lesson is Sociology of Sports. Students will discuss some of the assumptions made about athletes and will relate them to some common clichés.

They will also discuss stereotypes and how many folk beliefs are not founded in facts.

Overview

1. Ask students to raise their hands if they have ever participated in a team sport.
2. Call on volunteers to describe the experience of being a member of a team.
3. Have students discuss briefly how important it was for their team to win.

■ CONTENT VOCABULARY

Ask students to review the words in the box. Tell them to look up any unfamiliar words.

■ VOCABULARY JOURNAL

Have students add new words to their vocabulary journals and write down the parts of speech, definitions, and sentences for each.

■ THINK ABOUT IT

1. Have students read the instructions.
2. Elicit a definition of the term *cliché* from a class member, if possible.
3. Divide the class into pairs and have students talk about the meanings of the sports clichés listed below the instructions.
4. Call on volunteers to paraphrase the meaning of each of the clichés. Assist as needed.
5. Have students read the journal writing instructions. Answer any questions they have about the topic. Then give them five minutes to write in their journals.
6. Call on volunteers to share their ideas with the class.

PART ONE

Noun Complements

■ **GRAMMAR IN CONTENT**

■ **EXERCISE A**

CD 3, Track 16

1. Write *sociology* on the board.

2. Ask class members to brainstorm the types of things sociologists study, and how these might relate to sports.

3. Play the audio and have students follow along in their books as they listen. Ask students to circle any unfamiliar words or phrases.

4. Call on students to read their circled words and elicit definitions or explanations from volunteers if possible.

5. Play the audio again.

6. Check comprehension by asking questions such as the following: *In the past, why was sports not approached as a legitimate area of study by social scientists? What are Dunning's reasons for claiming that sports and games are "real"? What does Zijderveld mean when he says that our society is "clichégenic"? According to the author, is it true that "sport provides a model of racial equality"?*

■ **GRAMMAR IN CONTENT**

A   **Read and listen to the passage below. The words in bold in the text are complements of the preceding noun.**

CD3,TR16

Truth or Just Clichés?

Because sport is a major phenomenon in modern society, one might speculate as to why it has only recently been approached as a legitimate area to study by social scientists. Perhaps one answer to this question lies in the assumption **that sport was primarily meant to be physical rather than social interaction and was thus devoid of interest to social scientists.** In an insightful essay entitled "The Interdependency of Sport and Culture," Gunther Lüschen points out that even the most simple physical activities, such as walking, are social in nature. In a like manner, the more complex physical activities that are classified as sport involve greater suffusion from the social and cultural milieus. Another explanation for the late entry of social scientists into the analysis of sport may be that the world of sport is often perceived in terms of illusion and fantasy, as a sphere apart from the "real world."

The 2006 Asian Games.

Eric Dunning, an expert on the sociological aspect of sports, has argued that sociologists who define play and sport in terms of fantasy, and who are thus ambivalent about seriously studying the topic, may be reflecting a Protestant Ethic orientation that considers the study of play, games, sport, and leisure as frivolous and unbecoming of a "serious scientist." In response to these sentiments, Dunning emphasizes that "sports and games are 'real' in the sense they are observable, whether directly through overt behavior of people or indirectly through the reports which players and spectators give of what they think and feel while playing and 'spectating.'"

There is an increasing realization **that sport permeates and articulates with many other social institutions.** Furthermore, sport is an important ingredient in people's lives. In the absence of scientific investigation, folk wisdom and assumptions have prevailed as "facts." These include ready-made words, statements, phrases, and slogans that trigger speech and behavior in a kind of stimulus-response fashion and thus bypass cognitive thought and reflection. Because sport has become so much a part of our everyday life, this segment of social life is especially vulnerable given the clichés and assumptions. Furthermore, as we noted previously, these assumptions are easily transferred as metaphors to other spheres of social life. In a sense, a double falsehood may be perpetrated if a falsehood as it applied to the sport world is transferred as "fact" to other spheres of behavior. Anton C. Zijderveld, a sociologist, argues that modern society is filled with conflicting norms and values, vagueness, and emotional and moral instability. Thus, our society is clichégenic in the sense that it promotes clichés that provide ready-made but artificial clarity, stability, and certainty.

In the world of sport these clichés are readily apparent; for example, one of the most frequently cited functions of sport is that it "builds character." This common assumption has been the theme of many speakers at athletic banquets. On closer investigation, we find that this "truth" is probably more accurately described as a half-truth. Another commonly held assumption is that athletic pursuits detract from academic concerns (resulting in the "dumb jock" stereotype). Research findings are also providing important qualifications to this assumption. The belief **that sport provides a model of racial equality and a means for many blacks to become professional athletes** is another unfounded assumption. Considerable data have been accumulated that, likewise, raise serious questions about this folk belief. Another commonly held stereotype is that female athletes are physical "Amazons" who tend to be more masculine than most females and are thus likely to suffer from a confusion of sex roles and self-concept. Once again, recent research has refuted these assumptions. Additional questions might be raised regarding the validity of other assumptions such as the following: Sport is a preparation for life; sports are a way to get ahead; the will to win is the will to work. Recent research has begun to raise questions about these assumptions. Scientific investigation moves beyond conjecture to test assumptions in a disciplined manner. New observations and findings about the world of sport frequently demonstrate that previously held perspectives of social reality were distorted.

frivolous: silly, not serious
unbecoming: inappropriate

an Amazon: a tall, aggressive woman; in mythology, Amazons were women warriors

---

■ **EXPANSION IDEA**

Exercise A

1. Divide the class into pairs.

2. Have students reread the passage, stopping after each paragraph to paraphrase the information.

3. Circulate as students work and assist as needed. Encourage students to read for general comprehension, as this is a difficult passage.

4. Call on volunteers to paraphrase each paragraph for the class. Call for additions and corrections as needed.

Noun Complements

Sample Sentences	Notes
The belief **that effort and persistence will result in victory** motivates many young athletes.	Explain the meaning of some abstract nouns with a complement clause (see the list below). Such clauses: • begin with *that* • are always directly after an abstract noun
Do you have the impression **that the coach pushes the team too hard?**	
Everyone is talking about the news **that the women's soccer team beat the men's team.**	These clauses differ from relative clauses because they actually explain what the noun means:
How can their coach accept the excuse **that the team lost their momentum** in the second half?	Their idea **that sport is a preparation for life** can't be proven.
How can their coach accept the excuse **that the players gave** about their poor playing?	Their idea is **that sport is a preparation for life,** and this idea can't be proven.
Coach Rogerson's **recommendation that Pat play** defense more aggressively was the right one.	Use a subjunctive verb form in the complement (see Lesson 21) after nouns that are related to the verbs that require this kind of verb form, for example: *demand, order, recommendation.*
The coach was angry about Pat's **demand that he be paid** more than the other players.	
As a result, Coach Rogerson has **given the order that Pat not play** for the next three games.	

Abstract Nouns That Often Have a Noun Complement

assumption	excuse	news	recommendation
belief	fact	order	reply
claim	idea	possibility	report
demand	message	proposal	suggestion

B Read over your journal entry, and <u>underline</u> at least one sentence that you can revise to include a noun complement. Write your revised sentence(s) below.

Answers will vary.

_____

_____

_____

_____

1. Ask students to review the words in bold in the text on page 316.
2. Write *noun complement* on the board and call on a volunteer to explain the term. Discuss the meaning with the class.
3. Ask students to review the sample sentences and Notes. Answer any questions that they have about noun complements.
4. Call on a volunteer to explain the difference between a *noun complement* and a *relative clause* in his or her own words.
5. Ask students to review the list of abstract nouns that often have a noun complement.

■ EXERCISE B

1. Have students complete the exercise.
2. Ask students to exchange work with a partner. Have them look for additional places where sentences could be revised to include noun complements.

■ EXPANSION IDEA

Grammar Chart

1. Ask students to write two sentences that include an abstract noun from the list in the Grammar Chart.

For example:
The assumption was accepted by most of the team members.

2. Divide the class into pairs. Have students add a noun complement to each of their partner's sentences.

For example:
The assumption that a team can only have one star player was accepted by most of the team members.

■ EXERCISE C

1. Ask students to read the instructions.
2. Call on a student to read the example.
3. Ask a volunteer to identify the noun complement in example *a*.
4. Have students complete the activity on their own and then check their work in pairs.

1. __X__ a. Can you support the assumption that women are too weak to compete in boxing?

   _____ b. Can you support the assumption that the Boxing Federation expressed in the media?

2. __X__ a. Have you read the report that women at universities still receive fewer athletic scholarships than men do?

   _____ b. Have you read the report that our university published about athletic scholarships for women?

Naoko Takahashi set a world record of 2:19:45 when she won the Berlin Marathon on September 30, 2001.

3. _____ a. A report that the Athletics Department distributed will be unpopular.

   __X__ b. A report that some men's sports will be cut is going to be unpopular.

4. __X__ a. The claim that women weren't really interested in sports used to be a rationale for keeping women out of some sports.

   _____ b. The claim that people made about women's lack of interest in sports was a rationale for keeping women out of some sports.

5. __X__ a. For centuries people had the impression that sports could be physically harmful to girls.

   _____ b. For centuries the impression that people had about women's sports was unquestioned.

6. _____ a. The idea that society had about "ladylike" sports hasn't disappeared yet.

   __X__ b. The idea that girls should only play "ladylike" sports is still strong in some places.

7. __X__ a. Those old-fashioned ideas sent a message that sports are not appropriate for girls.

   _____ b. Those old-fashioned ideas sent a message that is inappropriate in today's society.

■ EXPANSION IDEA

Exercise C

1. Ask students to add a noun complement to each of the sentences in Exercise C that don't have one.

   For example:
   Can you support the Boxing Federation's assumption that boxing is a men's sport?

2. Have students compare work with a partner.
3. Call on volunteers to read their answers to the class.

D Use the notes below from a lecture on American cultural values in sports and comment on the similarity or difference between your values and those in American sports.

```
Playing sports = learning to play the game of life
US cultural values:
1.  personal character: be honest, be loyal to your team, be a leader, don't be
selfish, sacrifice for the team, be a good sport
2.  discipline: accept the rules and live by them, learn self-control
3.  competition: always hustle, be persistent, losers lack motivation, winning isn't
everything, teamwork means social responsibility
4.  fitness: keep physically fit, "clean living," be mentally alert, continue
education
```

1. *I don't believe the idea that an athlete should not be selfish is part of American culture.*

2. We also learn the message that athletes learn self-control in school.

3. Our belief that students learn persistence from sports is also very strong.

4. We share the attitude that it is necessary to be a good sport.

5. The idea that winning isn't everything doesn't seem like an American value, but many people in my country have this value.

6. We believe that good efforts in sports are most important.

7. Our coaches also have the assumption that athletes should sacrifice for their teams.

1. Go over the instructions with the class.
2. Call on a few students to read the notes about American cultural values in sports.
3. Call on a student to read the example.
4. Give students time to complete the activity.
5. Have students compare their answers with a partner.

■ **EXPANSION IDEA**

Exercise D

Have students develop an essay about the differences between their values and those in U.S. sports using their answers from Exercise D.

EXERCISE E

1. Ask students to raise their hands if they can give an example of violence in sports.
2. Call on a few students to give their examples.
3. Have students read the instructions.
4. Call on a student to read the example aloud.
5. Ask a volunteer to identify the noun complement in the example.
6. Have students complete the activity on their own and then compare their answers in pairs.
7. Call on volunteers to read their answers to the class.

■ COMMUNICATE

■ EXERCISE F

1. Ask students to read the instructions.
2. Call on four students to read the questions.
3. Give students time to write their answers.
4. Divide the class into pairs and have students share what they wrote.

E Complete each sentence with a noun complement on the topic of violence in sports.

1. Some people avoid large sporting events because they have the belief
   that they might get hurt if some of the fans get violent.

2. Some spectators leave before the end of a big soccer match because of the possibility
   that violence might break out at the end of the match.

3. Organizers of championship games pay great attention to the claim
   that violence among fans occurs when officials appear biased so they hire referees who have
   reputations as fair and impartial.

4. When police have to break up fights among fans, they aren't interested in hearing the
   excuse **that they are just doing what the players do on the field.**

5. Beer companies ask for proof of the assumption **that alcohol is the major cause of violence.**

6. The fact **that there is violence so often after games** makes many people avoid
   the area around a soccer stadium after an important game.

7. Coaches and referees break up fights among athletes as quickly as possible because
   of their belief **that professional athletes should be role models for young people.**

■ COMMUNICATE

F **PAIR WORK** Talk over the questions about sports for young people with your partner and
then write your answers. Then, share the answers with your classmates.

1. What sports did you play in elementary school?
2. How much importance was placed on sports in elementary and high school?
3. Which sports did girls play, and which did boys play?
4. What underlying messages about sports did you receive through your teachers and
   parents?

■ EXPANSION IDEA

Exercise F

1. Divide the class into small groups. Be sure partners from Exercise F do not work together.
2. Have students discuss the questions from Exercise F and then discuss whether there was sexism in the sports programs at their elementary and high schools. Ask them if it was "cooler" to be athletic or smart when they were in school.
3. Circulate as students work, and remind them to use noun complements in their discussions.
4. Call on a member of each group to report to the class.

■ GRAMMAR IN CONTENT

A Reread the first three paragraphs of the text on page 316, and <u>underline</u> each phrase that is a restatement of the preceding noun.

Appositives

Women competed in tennis and golf in Paris, ~~which was~~ the site of the 1900 Olympics.	Like relative clauses, an appositive describes, restates, or elaborates the noun phrase it follows. However, the appositive is a shortened form of a relative clause in which *who is/was* or *which is/was* has been deleted.
Martina Navratilova, ~~who was~~ the incredible tennis star, won her record ninth singles title at Wimbledon in 1990.	
Thousands of girls benefit from Title IX, ~~which is~~ the law that gave female students access to school-sponsored sports.	
Have you heard of Wilma Rudolph, ~~who was~~ the winner of three Olympic gold medals?	
The tennis player **Althea Gibson** was the first African American woman to win a title at Wimbledon. (restrictive)	Appositives can be **restrictive** or **nonrestrictive**.
	No commas are used with a restrictive appositive. The nonrestrictive appositive provides nonessential information about the preceding noun phrase, so commas are used.
Any professional player wants to compete at Wimbledon, **the most famous tennis tournament in the world.** (nonrestrictive)	
The first woman to run the Boston Marathon, **namely** Katherine Switzer, was disguised as a man.	Use an adverbial connector with the appositive:
Now girls can participate in male-dominated sports, **such as soccer.**	• to make it explicit • to express that the appositive is an example of the other noun phrase • to express the appositive in a particular or special example
These sports, **especially contact sports,** used to be considered too rough for women.	

Other Adverbials Used to Introduce Appositives

chiefly	for example	in particular	particularly
especially	for instance	notable	primarily
e.g. (= *for example*)	i.e. (= *that is*)		

■ GRAMMAR IN CONTENT

■ EXERCISE A

Have students complete the activity and check their work with a partner.

■ GRAMMAR CHART
Appositives

1. Write *appositive* on the board and elicit a definition and example from a volunteer, if possible.
2. Ask students to review the sample sentences and Notes.
3. Answer any questions that students may have about identifying and using appositives.
4. Have students review the box "Other Adverbials Used to Introduce Appositives."

■ EXPANSION IDEA

Grammar Chart

1. Divide the class into pairs.
2. Have students take turns using the adverbials in the box to introduce appositives about sports.

   For example:
   Women athletes, particularly those in colleges and universities, had to beg for funds to support their teams.

3. Circulate as students work and assist as needed.

1. Ask students to review the instructions.
2. Call on a student to read the first sentence.
3. Ask a volunteer to provide punctuation for the underlined appositive phrase.
4. Call on a volunteer to come to the board and write the second sentence, underlining the appositive phrase and punctuating the sentence.
5. Have students complete the activity individually and check it in pairs.

B <u>Underline</u> the appositive phrases in the texts below. Then, add commas where necessary. Each text may have more than one appositive.

1. Beginning with Title IX, <u>the law that opened educational activities to any student regardless of gender</u>, female students gained the opportunity to participate in many more sports at school. In addition, they became eligible for athletic scholarships, <u>the ticket to higher education for many students.</u>

Louisiana plays against Arizona during the Women's NCAA Mideast Regional Games in 2001.

2. Club sports, <u>the only opportunity open to female athletes before 1972</u>, received no funding from schools. Female participants had to buy their own uniforms and play with used equipment, <u>the "hand-me-downs" from the men's teams.</u>

3. Before Title IX, female teams had to pay their own way to sporting events. If they couldn't afford it, the team might resort to a bake sale, <u>a typical female strategy to raise money from friends and neighbors.</u>

4. Distributing funds among various collegiate sports programs is the responsibility of the athletic director, <u>the administrator for all university team sports</u>. Female coaches, <u>traditionally the coaches with the least influence on financial decisions on campus</u>, still have to fight for support for some of their sports. Title IX does not guarantee that an equal amount of money is spent on each sport or on each individual student athlete.

5. The primary athletic organization for colleges and universities, <u>the NCAA</u>, now sponsors championships for over 30 sports for female athletes. Basketball, <u>the number one competitive sport for women in the U.S.</u>, is increasingly popular among fans, and the NCAA "Final Four" for the women's teams always has high TV ratings.

■ **EXPANSION IDEA**

Exercise B

1. Ask students to add two sentences to one of the topics in the exercise.

   For example:
   Female activists, who recognized the injustice of this situation, took the matter in their own hands. They worked with their coaches, who were also fed up with having no funds, to pressure Congress to pass Title IX.

C Listen to the speakers from the Gators basketball team and answer the questions about their conversation.

CD3,TR17

1. What assumption does Coach Lyons express?

   That the team isn't trying hard enough.

2. What belief does Rina express?

   That the other team was covering her so that she couldn't shoot.

3. What impression does Vanessa express?

   That the other team had been guarding Rina more than the others.

4. What message does Coach Lyons express?

   That they better try harder or that other players will replace them.

5. What recommendation did Coach Lyons express?

   That the team follow the game plan.

■ **COMMUNICATE**

D **GROUP WORK** Discuss the image of athletes in your cultures. Do star athletes serve as role models for young people? What lessons should young people learn from them? Talk about the image of female and male athletes in the media. Then, share your ideas and beliefs with your classmates.

■ **EXERCISE C**

CD 3, Track 17

1. Write *Gators* on the board and see if anyone in the class can identify what city this team plays for.
2. Have students read the instructions.
3. Play the audio, asking students to listen for comprehension only.
4. Call on five students to read the questions aloud.
5. Play the audio again, this time stopping to give students time to answer the questions.
6. Play the audio again so that students can check their answers.
7. Call on volunteers to read their answers aloud. If there is any disagreement among class members, play the appropriate section of the audio.

■ **COMMUNICATE**

■ **EXERCISE D**

1. Call on a student or two to read the instructions aloud.
2. Divide the class into groups of students from as many different cultures as possible.
3. Give students time to discuss the questions. Remind them to use appositives whenever possible.

■ **EXPANSION IDEA**

Exercise D
1. Have students write a summary of their group discussions.
2. Circulate as students write and assist as needed. Encourage them to use vocabulary and grammar from the lesson, particularly appositives.

Connection

Putting It Together

▆ GRAMMAR AND VOCABULARY

1. Ask students to read the instructions.
2. Call on two students to read the topics aloud.
3. Ask students to choose one of the two topics and give them time to write their compositions.

▆ PROJECT

1. Ask students to review the instructions.
2. Answer any questions that students have about the project.
3. Call on students at the next class meeting to give their oral reports.

▆ INTERNET

1. Call on a student to read the instructions.
2. Have students conduct their searches and prepare their summaries, and compare the photos of male and female athletes.
3. Call on students to report to the class.

GRAMMAR AND VOCABULARY Write a composition on one of the topics below. Use as many words as possible from the Content Vocabulary on page 315. Use sentences with noun complements and appositives to express some of your ideas.

Topic 1: Do people in your culture share the assumption that participating in sports is a crucial part of growing up? Use two or three sayings, proverbs, or clichés from your language to explain the beliefs, ideas, and messages about participation in sports.

Topic 2: Many Americans share the belief that young people should participate in sports to prepare them for "the game of life." Do you agree with the assumption that young people learn important values for their future when they participate in sports at school or in sports clubs? Give concrete examples to support your opinion.
Answers will vary.

PROJECT Interview at least two female students on your campus about their participation in sports. Ask about the following information, and make a brief oral report on the information in your next class meeting.

1. what sports each of them participated in during their school years
2. whether they participated on a varsity or a school team
3. whether they know any women students who have athletic scholarships
4. how much support women's teams have on your campus or in your area

 INTERNET Go online to sports websites, such as www.espn.com, www.sportsillustrated.cnn.com, or www.msn.foxsports.com, or check the website of your local newspaper for the sports report. Compare the photos of male and female athletes. Try to find photos of men and women who compete in the same sport. Do the photos demonstrate that the gender of the athlete is important for the style of photo on the website? Prepare a short oral report on your research.
Answers will vary.

▆ EXPANSION IDEA

Internet
1. Ask students to check a website for information on Title IX. Ask them to take notes.

2. Divide the class into small groups and have students share their information about Title IX and how it changed the face of U.S. college sports.

Political Science: Political Parties

■ CONTENT VOCABULARY

Look up the words and phrases below that you do not know and enter them in your vocabulary journal. Write each word's part of speech, a definition, and an example sentence. Try to include them in your discussion and writing below.

an adherent	a campaign	to downgrade	to oust
to advocate	a catch-all	an elite	to overgeneralize
autonomous	a constituent	partisan politics	

■ THINK ABOUT IT

In the United States, people often avoid talking about politics and religion with people that they do not know very well. Do your family members or people that you know also avoid these topics under similar circumstances? Why, or why not? Discuss your ideas with a classmate.

In your writing journal, write for five minutes about the questions below. When you are finished, share your ideas with the class.
In your opinion, are young people in your country interested in politics? Who has more interest in politics—older people or younger people? Why?
Answers will vary.

■ CONTENT NOTES

The topic of this lesson is Political Science: Political Parties. Students will learn about and acquire the vocabulary needed to discuss political parties and how they relate to geography, economic interests, and ideology. Use this lesson to talk about the history of the U.S. political system and to compare and contrast it with the political systems of other countries.

Lesson 30

Overview

1. Ask students to raise their hands if they belong to a political party in the United States or in another country.
2. Call on volunteers to explain what it means to belong to a party.
3. Have students discuss briefly how important it is for citizens of a country to actively participate in politics.

■ CONTENT VOCABULARY

Ask students to review the words in the box. Tell them to look up any unfamiliar words.

■ VOCABULARY JOURNAL

Have students add new words to their vocabulary journals and write down the parts of speech, definitions, and sentences for each.

■ THINK ABOUT IT

1. Have students read the instructions.
2. Give students a few moments to think about the questions.
3. Divide the class into pairs and have students talk about whether their family members or acquaintances generally avoid talking about politics and religion with people they don't know well.
4. Ask them to discuss some of the reasons why many people avoid these topics.
5. Have students read the journal writing instructions. Answer any questions they have about the topic. Then give them five minutes to write in their journals.
6. Call on volunteers to share their ideas with the class.

■ **GRAMMAR IN CONTENT**

■ **EXERCISE A**
CD 3, Track 18

1. Write *Democratic Party* and *Republican Party* on the board.

2. Ask volunteers to discuss what they know about these two U.S. parties. Ask them which party is generally considered to be the more liberal of the two.

3. Call on volunteers to name U.S. presidents and identify them as Democrats or Republicans.

4. Play the audio and have students follow along in their books as they listen. Ask students to circle any unfamiliar words or phrases.

5. Call on students to read their circled words and elicit definitions or explanations from volunteers if possible.

6. Play the audio again.

7. Check comprehension by asking questions such as the following: *In broad terms, how are political parties organized? Which group dominated the Democratic Party in the 1850s? What did members of the Free Soil Party oppose? Why? How did parties that evolved at the state level affect the outcome of national elections?*

■ **GRAMMAR IN CONTENT**

A Read and listen to the passage below. The words in bold in the text are logical connectors.

CD3,TR18

Who Do American Political Parties Really Represent?

In broad terms, political parties are organized in three ways: by geography, by economic interests, and by ideology. These divisions are by no means mutually exclusive; **to the contrary**, geography and economic interests often coincide, only to be divided by ideology.

For example, in the 1850s, the Democratic Party was dominated by the southern farmers who owned large cotton and tobacco plantations worked by slaves. To keep the loyalty of this key constituency, the Democratic Party supported slavery, which was an economic issue in the South but an ideological and moral issue in the North. Opposition to slavery on principle became the preserve of the Liberty Party (1840–48) and eventually of the Republican Party. For the Free Soil Party (1848–54), also, the issue of slavery was economic, but from a different viewpoint. The Free Soil Party did not challenge slavery in the South, **but** it did oppose the spread of slavery into western territories in order to prevent slave labor from competing with free white settlers.

For over a century, the Republican Party managed to capture the White House and a majority in Congress without carrying a single state of the former Confederate States of America.

Some parties have evolved on the state level, such as the Law and Order Party (1841–51) in Rhode Island, the Farmer-Labor Party (1918–44) in Minnesota, and the Liberal Party (1944–) in New York. These state parties succeeded in gaining power within a single state, but never spread elsewhere. They nevertheless had the potential of playing a national role by affecting the electoral college vote in presidential elections and by influencing policies of national parties seeking to capture the loyalty of their adherents.

It is tempting, and not entirely misleading, to see broad economic issues at the heart of the differences between the major parties, with Democrats broadly presenting themselves as representatives of working people and Republicans as representatives of the business sector. But that division ignores important sets of issues that are not economic in nature. Social issues have long played an important part in party loyalty. Such issues range from political rights for minorities to women's rights to abortion to government regulation of individual behavior, the use of drugs, for example. Social issues often cut across economic or class lines and across regional lines, serving to unite voters whose economic interests might be widely divergent or even antithetical. When these issues involve deeply held religious beliefs, as they often have, they can be compelling to some voters. Examples of religion playing a key role range from the anti-Catholic, anti-immigrant sentiments of the Know-Nothing Party (1849–57) to arguments over reciting prayers or including religious symbols in public buildings and public schools.

Given that such a wide variety of topics and issues become embroiled in the process of choosing a government, it is no wonder that the beliefs and actions of political parties fail to fit into neat, consistent categories of ideology, geography, or economics. They are, **rather**, part of the complex swirl of human affairs known as politics.

mutually exclusive: things that cannot occur at the same time or under the same conditions

the preserve: an exclusive area of influence or power

the electoral college: the group of elected representatives that officially elects the U.S. president

an adherent: a supporter

antithetical: directly opposite

a sentiment: a thought, viewpoint

given that: acknowledged, assumed

a swirl: a twisting motion or that figure created by such a motion

■ **EXPANSION IDEA**

Exercise A

1. Divide the class into small groups.

2. Ask students to discuss if they believe that the Democratic party in the United States represents the working people, while the Republican party represents the business sector.

3. Have students discuss current U.S. politicians in terms of their ideologies and party affiliations.

4. Call on a member of each group to report back to the class.

Sample Sentences	Notes
Some political parties don't have many members, **so** they can't get their ideas put into policy. (= *informal*) Some political parties have very few members; **therefore**, they have little chance of changing government policy. (= *more formal*)	Use various types of connectors to make your ideas clearer and your English more sophisticated. You should learn the differences among connectors grouped by meaning to express yourself more effectively. The differences can be in style and/or in meaning.
Political parties used to represent particular social classes or elites, **but** now major parties try to attract big segments of the population. American voters in one region often agree on economic issues, **yet** their religious values may separate them. **While** the British Labour Party started as a party supported by trade unions, nowadays many businesspeople support it. Many political scientists have predicted that political parties would die by now; **nonetheless**, parties in many countries continue to attract new supporters. Many political scientists predicted that political parties would die by now; **instead**, parties have adapted to new technologies and people's concern about social issues.	EXPRESSING CONTRAST: • Coordinating conjunction: *but* • Subordinating conjunctions: *while, whereas* (= more formal) • Logical connectors: *however, in contrast, nevertheless, on the other hand, nonetheless* CONTRADICTING AN EXPECTATION: • Coordinating conjunction: *yet* • Logical connectors: *rather, instead, to/on the contrary* Follow the rules of punctuation for each type of connector. See Lessons 12 and 13. Other *connectors* include therefore, thus, furthermore, and consequently.

B Read over your journal entry, and <u>underline</u> at least one sentence that you can revise to include a logical connector from the chart above. Write your revised sentence(s) below.

Answers will vary.

_____

_____

_____

■ GRAMMAR CHART
Connecting Clauses: Review of Connectors

1. Write *expressing contrast* and *contradicting an expectation* on the board and call on a few volunteers to give an example of a coordinating conjunction for each of these.
2. Ask students to review the sample sentences and Notes.
3. Answer any questions that students have about connectors.
4. Write *but*, *while*, *however*, *rather* on the board. Call on volunteers to use the coordinating conjunctions in sentences.

■ EXERCISE B

1. Have students complete the exercise.
2. Ask students to exchange work with a partner. Have them look for additional places where sentences could be revised to include a logical connector from the Grammar Chart.

■ EXPANSION IDEA

Grammar Chart

1. Divide the class into pairs.
2. Ask students to take turns asking and answering questions about the text on page 326, using connectors as often as possible.

For example:
Student 1: *Did members of the Free Soil Party support slavery?*

Student 2: *The Free Soil Party members didn't object to slavery in the South, but they didn't want it to spread into western territories.*

3. Circulate as students work; assist as needed.

■ EXERCISE C

1. Tell students to review the instructions. If they are insecure about the rules of punctuation, ask them to refer to Lessons 12 and 13.
2. Call on a student to read the first question. Ask volunteers to point out any errors in punctuation and capitalization.
3. Have students complete the activity individually and then check their work in pairs.
4. Call on volunteers to read their answers, including where they corrected punctuation and capitalization.

■ EXERCISE D

1. Call on a student to read the instructions.
2. Have students answer the questions.
3. Call on volunteers to read their answers aloud.
4. Elicit answers from class members for any questions students continue to have about using connectors.

C Edit the texts to add correct punctuation and capital letters. In some cases, there may be more than one possible solution.

1. Before World War II, political parties in Europe and the U.S. represented various segments of society such as the working class. ~~during~~ *During* and after the war, thousands of women joined the labor force, yet the political importance of the working class decreased as more and more people became part of the middle class; while women didn't earn high wages, they contributed significantly to their family income.

2. After World War II most major political parties became "catch-all" parties; according to Kirchheimer, who coined this terminology, catch-all parties try to appeal to the general population by becoming less ideological; such parties downgrade issues and interests; nevertheless, these parties can usually be defined as leaning more to the right or to the left.

3. Despite their left-wing/right-wing division, catch-all parties focus on shifting the voters in the center of the political spectrum to their side; they tend to "sell" their issues and solutions to the voting public; in contrast, smaller special interest groups advocate specific views on a particular issue to the general population.

4. It is often difficult to explain the differences between catch-all parties because they often sell their image more strongly than their issues or solutions to social or economic problems; party officials feel that such marketing strategies will lead to victory on election day; on the contrary, many voters, especially young ones, are alienated from politics by such strategies.

D Reread the text at the beginning of the lesson, and (circle) the other examples of connectors from this lesson. Then, answer the questions below on a separate piece of paper.
Answers will vary.

1. Do all of the examples in the text follow the punctuation rules for these connectors? What are the "mistakes"?
2. Which connector(s) did the author use most frequently?
3. Which connector(s) did you find in the middle of a clause? What kind of punctuation did the author use? Why?
4. Use a different connector to revise clauses connected with the coordinating conjunction *but*.

■ EXPANSION IDEA

Exercise D

1. Ask students to write two sentences that include connectors.

   For example:
   It is difficult to understand how members of the Free Soil Party supported slavery in the South, yet opposed it in the West.

2. Ask students to scramble their sentences, leaving out capital letters and punctuation.
3. Divide the class into pairs and have students unscramble each other's sentences, providing punctuation where needed.

E Select the correct connector, and state the reason for your choice.

1. The way that reporters use the terms "red state" or "blue state" gives the impression that these names are well-established. The major TV networks only started using "red" for Republican and "blue" for Democratic consistently in 2000.

   (a.) however   b. on the contrary   c. either a or b

   Reason: _The second sentence expresses a correction of the first sentence, but it isn't a contradiction of expectation._

2. Residents of major cities in agricultural regions may well support the philosophy of one American political party. Farm- and ranch-owners often consider their interests better represented by the other major party.

   a. while   b. whereas   (c.) either a or b

   Reason: They have the same meaning; the context is formal enough for "whereas."

3. Virginia is traditionally a Republican state. A popular former governor was a Democrat.

   a. but   (b.) yet   c. either a or b

   Reason: The second clause includes unanticipated information, so "yet" is appropriate.

4. The major political parties count on continuing support from Americans who become members. To get their candidates elected, each party also has to attract independent voters during the campaign season.

   (a.) on the other hand   b. instead   c. either a or b

   Reason: The information is a contrast but not a contradiction of information.

5. Before the age of catch-all parties, families tended to support the same party from generation to generation. Contemporary catch-all parties risk losing such loyal members because the parties don't seem to represent strong positions anymore.

   a. however   b. but   (c.) either a or b

   Reason: Both are appropriate for simple contrast here.

6. Being independent appeals to many younger citizens. American college campuses still have clubs for students who strongly support the Republican Party or the Democratic Party.

   a. instead   (b.) nevertheless   c. either a or b

   Reason: The connection is a contrast but not a contradiction.

7. Many people think that there are only a few political parties in the United States because they usually hear only about Democrats and Republicans. American voters have a wide range of choices, from the Communist Party USA to the Green Party.

   (a.) on the contrary   b. but   c. either a or b

   Reason: The second sentence is an unexpected contradiction to the expectation in the first sentence.

1. Have students read the instructions.
2. Call on a student to read the example.
3. Discuss the reason given in the example with the class.
4. Have students complete the activity on their own and then check their work in pairs.
5. Call on volunteers to read their answers and reasons aloud. Discuss any differences of opinion among class members.

■ **EXPANSION IDEA**

Exercise E
1. Divide the class into pairs.
2. Have pairs pick alternate connectors that could be used in each of the seven sentences in the exercise.

For example: *Nonetheless* could be used in place of *however* in sentence 1.

3. Call on volunteers to read their answers to the class.

■ EXERCISE F

1. Go over the instructions with the class.
2. Call on two students to read the example.
3. Discuss with the class possible ways of finishing Tyrell's sentence.
4. Divide the class into pairs and have students complete the activity together.
5. Circulate as students work; assist as needed. Encourage students to discuss various possible connectors and appropriate punctuation.

F Complete the sentences in the different conversations below with a clause, and add the correct punctuation.

Tyrell: No political party seems to speak to me. How can I get excited about participating in the political process?

Takashi: Maybe you don't care right now; nevertheless ___, the decisions that politicians make can impact your future! , it's your duty, __(1)__ isn't it? Don't you worry about that?

Tyrell: Of course, I think about the future; however, polliticians don't seem to care much about people my age. __(2)__

Dave: What do you think of the political parties back in your home country?

Maria: To tell you the truth, I can't really see any difference among the largest ones. Last year the majority in our Parliament changed. The opposition party has been in power since then, yet they haven't made any big changes. __(3)__

Omar: Maria, you're so negative. Haven't you been following the debates? The new majority leader has proposed an educational reform, and they are discussing new environmental laws whereas the previous Parliament never talked about these issues. __(4)__

Maria: Yeah, they're always talking and discussing; instead, they should be taking some action. __(5)__

Susan: I don't know very much about the political parties in your country. Do university students pay much attention to politics?

Jeung Ae: Some students are very active in politics and often demonstrate in the streets about different issues; on the other hand, many students don't care much one way or the other. __(6)__

Susan: It sounds like you aren't very concerned about the effect of politicians and their policies on your life or on the future.

Jeung Ae: On the contrary, I often join in the protests. __(7)__

■ EXPANSION IDEA

Exercise F

1. Have pairs that worked together in Exercise F practice role-playing the conversations.

2. Call on pairs to role-play conversations for the class.

G On a separate piece of paper, write a paragraph about the differences between the Libertarian Party and the Green Party.   Answers will vary.

Issue/Viewpoint	Libertarian Party (1971- present)	Green Party (1989-present)
primary emphasis	reduce the size and role of government	limit the powers of corporations
taxes	opposes all taxes	opposes unfair taxes
education	no compulsory education; no tax money for education	more tax money should go to schools in poor areas
foreign policy	cut defense spending; quit the United Nations	cut defense spending and give more money to social welfare
health care	no tax money for any social welfare program	national health insurance for all

Candidates from smaller, more issue-oriented political parties like the Libertarian and Green parties also participate in the U.S. political process. Whereas the Green Party seeks to limit the role of corporations in American life, the Libertarian Party advocates reducing the role of government.

■ **COMMUNICATE**

H **PAIR WORK** Make a list of the issues that are important to citizens in your community. Compare and contrast these ideas with a partner.

While some people oppose the public display of religious symbols, this is not an issue where I come from.

■ **EXERCISE G**

1. Have students read the instructions and the handwritten notes.
2. Call on a student to read the example.
3. Give students time to write their paragraphs.
4. Circulate as students work; assist as needed. Remind them to use connectors with appropriate punctuation.

■ **COMMUNICATE**

■ **EXERCISE H**

1. Go over the instructions with the class.
2. Call on a student to read the text in the speech balloon.
3. Give students time to write lists of the issues that are important to members of their communities.
4. Divide the class into pairs.
5. Have students compare and contrast the issues on their lists.

■ **EXPANSION IDEAS**

Exercise G
1. Divide the class into pairs.
2. Have students exchange the paragraphs they wrote for Exercise G. Ask them to edit each other's work, paying special attention to the use of connectors and punctuation.

Exercise H
Ask students to write a paragraph about the issues that are important to their partner's community. Remind them to use vocabulary and grammar from the lesson.

■ GRAMMAR IN CONTENT

■ EXERCISE A

Have students complete the activity and check their work with a partner.

■ GRAMMAR CHART
Complex Sentences: Review

1. Write *simple sentence* and *complex sentence* on the board.
2. Call on volunteers to give examples of each type of sentence.
3. Ask students to read the sample sentences and Notes.
4. If students have any questions about gerunds or infinitive complements, elicit explanations from other class members.

■ EXERCISE B

1. Ask students to read the instructions.
2. Call on a student to read the example.
3. Call on a volunteer to revise the sentence in another way.
4. Have students complete the activity on their own and then compare their work in pairs.
5. Call on volunteers to read their answers aloud.

■ GRAMMAR IN CONTENT

A Reread the text at the beginning of this lesson, and <u>underline</u> five sentences that have just one clause with more than two verb forms in them.

Complex Sentences: Review	
Sample Sentences	**Notes**
Analysts advised that party leaders reveal the truth about their financial situation. ↓ *Analysts advised them to reveal . . .* *Analysts advised revealing the . . .* Some single-issue parties are quite popular in certain regions, yet they never win in a general election. ↓ *Despite being quite popular in certain regions, some single-issue parties . . .* There are many laws against accepting large sums of money for political campaigns. ↓ *Political campaigns are not supposed to accept large sums of money . . .* A political party that takes a firm stand on an issue may not have widespread support in the general population. ↓ *A political party taking a firm stand . . .*	In addition to using a variety of connectors between clauses, you can express your ideas by using different types of sentences, both simple and complex. Make your writing more complex and dynamic by incorporating various verb structures in your main clauses. Do this by: • using more gerund or infinitive complements • using more gerunds as objects of prepositions • expressing your attitudes and interpretations more effectively with modals • using more participial and reduced forms

B Revise the sentences below and on the next page so that they have only one clause.

1. In each House of Congress, the leaders of the major and minority parties may propose ~~that they suspend~~ *suspending* partisan politics during times of crisis.

2. The majority leader in the U.S. Senate functions as a senator from his or her home state; in addition, ~~the majority leader takes~~ *to taking* responsibility for expressing the party's position on important issues.

3. Sometimes the minority leader in the Senate has to acknowledge ~~that they don't have~~ *not having* enough votes to block the passage of a law.

■ EXPANSION IDEA

Grammar Chart

1. Ask students to write three sentences that contain two clauses.
2. Divide the class into pairs.
3. Have students exchange work and revise sentences so that they contain only one clause.

4. Despite ~~the fact that the U.S. vice president acts as~~ **acting as** the presiding officer of the U.S. Senate, the vice president has little real power in the Senate.

5. In the House of Representatives the rules ~~require that members of the majority party~~ **require members of the majority to** elect a leader who is called the Speaker of the House.

6. ~~A speaker usually has~~ **As a result of having** a moderate political ideology and strong parliamentary skills; ~~as a result,~~ the speaker will be able to guide legislation through the House.

7. An effective Speaker of the House must often persuade ~~members of Congress that they should support~~ **members of Congress to support** legislation that is preferred by the majority party.

CD3,TR19

C Listen to each part of the interview of Senator Maura Koloski and answer each comprehension question using a single clause with a modal.

1. How does Senator Koloski interpret the low attendance at her speech?

   Students may/might/could consider listening to a speech a waste of time.

2. What is Senator Koloski's alternative to making a speech to young people?

   Her alternative is writing her ideas on a blog.

3. What part of her message does the senator predict that students will care about?

   The Senator expects students to talk about their rising tuition costs.

4. What does Senator Koloski assume that students worry about?

   Students worry about paying back their loans and having credit problems later.

5. According to the senator, what is the duty of elected officials?

   Making education affordable is the duty of elected officials.

6. What position does the senator consider a necessity in order to control tuition costs?

   We have to spend more tax dollars on education to keep tuition costs from rising.

■ **COMMUNICATE**

D GROUP WORK Think of an issue that can serve as the basis for a new political party. (For example, the environment is the main issue behind "Green" parties.) Then, brainstorm strategies that this party should use to attract young voters. Write a brief, dynamic memo with your strategies to the party leadership.

■ **EXPANSION IDEA**

Exercise D

Ask students to write a paragraph about their group's discussion. Have them describe how they chose their issue, and strategies discussed that may not have been mentioned in the memo.

■ **EXERCISE C**
CD 3, Track 19

1. Ask students to read the instructions.
2. Play the audio, asking students to listen for comprehension only.
3. Call on a student to read the example aloud.
4. Call on five more students to read the rest of the questions aloud.
5. Play the audio again, this time pausing frequently to give students time to write their answers.
6. Play the audio again so that students can check their answers.
7. Call on volunteers to read their answers aloud. Replay the audio if there is any disagreement about an answer.

■ **COMMUNICATE**

■ **EXERCISE D**

1. Call on a student to read the instructions aloud.
2. Write *dynamic* on the board and ask volunteers to suggest how to make a piece of writing energetic and vibrant.
3. Answer any questions that students have about the activity.
4. Divide the class into small groups.
5. Have groups select their issue, brainstorm strategies for attracting young voters, and write their memo.
6. Call on a member of each group to read the memo to the class.
7. Have the class discuss all of the strategies presented, if time permits.

Connection

Putting It Together

■ GRAMMAR AND VOCABULARY

1. Ask students to read the instructions.
2. Call on two students to read the topics aloud.
3. Ask students to choose one of the two topics and give them time to write their compositions.

■ PROJECT

1. Ask students to review the instructions.
2. Answer any questions that students have about the project.
3. Call on students at the next class meeting to give their oral reports.

■ INTERNET

1. Call on a student to read the instructions.
2. Have students conduct their searches and prepare their oral reports on a Canadian political party.
3. Call on students to present their oral reports to the class.

GRAMMAR AND VOCABULARY Write a composition on one of the topics below. Use as many words as possible from the Content Vocabulary on page 325. Use various types of complex sentences and connectors to express your ideas.

Topic 1: Contrast the attitudes toward politics and political parties of people of your generation with those of the older generation in your country or culture. Use concrete examples.

Topic 2: In his book *Politics,* the Greek philosopher Aristotle (384–322 BCE) wrote "Man is by nature a political animal." Do you agree or disagree? Give concrete examples to support your opinion.
Answers will vary.

PROJECT Interview at least one student on your campus about national political parties. Find out the following information, and make a brief oral report on your findings at your next class meeting.

1. What are the main parties?
2. What are the main differences between the parties?
3. What are the most important political issues for college students?
4. Who are the most effective political leaders today?

 INTERNET Go online to the website www.elections.ca to find out some information about political parties in Canada. On the website, under Information for You, select "Political Parties" / "List of Registered Political Parties and Parties Eligible for Registration." On this webpage, select one of the parties and read their website. Make a short oral report on one or two issues that the party presents on its website.
Answers will vary.

■ EXPANSION IDEA

Internet
Have students expand their oral reports into essays, using vocabulary and grammar from the lesson.

A Complete the conditional sentences, using the words in parentheses in the appropriate forms to complete the ideas in the sentences. Add *not* where necessary.

1. If Megan's immune system _____**hadn't been compromised**_____

    (compromise) by her stressful lifestyle, she

    _____**would have recovered**_____ (recover) from surgery more quickly

    last month.

2. Some people think that Megan _____**might have recuperated**_____

    (recuperate) by now if she _____**hadn't weakened**_____ (weaken)

    her immune system by sleeping too little and eating an unhealthy diet.

3. _____**Had she realized**_____ (she/realize)

    the effect of her lifestyle on her health, obviously, she

    _____**would have modified**_____ (modify) her behavior to strengthen

    her body.

4. If she _____**had known**_____ (known) then what

    she _____**knows**_____ (know) now, she

    _____**would have been**_____ (be) more careful.

5. Megan _____**would be able**_____ (be able)

    to participate in her normal activities right now if she

    _____**had taken care**_____ (take care) of herself before.

6. Even if she _____**changed**_____ (change) her lifestyle,

    it _____**would take**_____ (take) some months to see the

    positive effects.

7. If only she _____**had listened**_____ (listen) to the advice of

    her friends and family a long time ago!

8. Unless she _____**makes**_____ (make)

    up her mind to live a less stressful life, Megan's general health

    _____**won't improve**_____ (improve) very much.

REVIEW | Lessons 26-30 **335**

Review Lessons 26–30

The purpose of this lesson is to help students review the language and concepts they have learned in the last five lessons. Encourage them to go back to the lessons and review the grammar charts to help them complete the review activities.

▉ EXERCISE A

1. Ask students to read the instructions.
2. Answer any questions that students have about the activity.
3. Call on a volunteer to complete the first sentence. Review the use of conditionals before students continue.
4. Have students complete the activity on their own and then check their work in pairs.
5. Call on volunteers to read their answers aloud.

▉ EXPANSION IDEA

Exercise A

1. Divide the class into pairs.
2. Ask students to take turns making comments about the consequences of stress on Megan's life.

For example:
Student 1: *Megan would have gotten better a lot faster if she had had a stronger immune system.*

Student 2: *If she had had a more relaxed lifestyle, she probably wouldn't have spent more than a few days in the hospital.*

1. Write *which* and *that* on the board.

2. Call on a volunteer to explain when to use each of these to complete an idea.

3. Ask students to read the instructions.

4. Have students answer the first question.

5. Call on a volunteer to argue why he or she chose *which/that* is correct. If there is any disagreement among class members, review the use of these words.

6. Have students complete the activity individually and then correct their work in pairs.

7. Call on volunteers to read their answers aloud. Discuss any differences of opinion among class members.

■ LEARNER LOG

Have students complete the Learner Log. Suggest that they review the Grammar Charts for areas that need more practice.

B **Circle** the words that correctly complete the idea of the sentence.

1. Many astrobiologists share the belief (which /**that**) life forms in the universe may have similar properties to some creatures on Earth.

2. How many researchers support the recommendation that their submersible (**return** / returns) to the black hole to gather new data?

3. Marine biologists, (**notably** / i.e.) astrobiologists, have made a number of interesting claims about life forms in outer space based on their research on underwater creatures.

4. The (**geologist John Edmond** / geologist, John Edmond,) was one of the people who discovered the first hydrothermal vents deep on the ocean floor near the Galapagos Islands.

5. It was the variety of life forms at the black smoker (**that** / which) surprised John Edmond and the other geologists on the research team.

6. It wasn't the variety of the life forms (**but** / rather) the size of the life forms that impressed the geologists.

7. It was perceptive (for / **of**) the geologists to call marine biologists about their discovery immediately upon their return from the Galapagos Islands.

8. At the beginning of the research about black smokers it was risky (**for** / of) the biologists to spend too much time at such ocean depths.

9. Research on life forms around black smokers may seem to be relevant to life on planets with water; (on the other hand, / **on the contrary,**) the research demonstrates that life forms can flourish in conditions previously considered too hostile for life.

10. Astrobiologists have found other life forms in extremely hostile environments; (while, / **nevertheless,**) creatures near black smokers continue to be the focus of their research.

LEARNER LOG Check (✔) *Yes* or *I Need More Practice.*   Answers will vary.

Lesson	I Can Use . . .	Yes	I Need More Practice
26	*It* Clefts and *It* in Subject Position with Adjective Complements		
27	Past Counterfactuals and Inverted Word Order in Conditional Clauses		
28	Conditional Conjunctions, Conditional Verbs with *That* Clauses, and Mixed Times in Conditional Sentences		
29	Noun Complements and Appositives		
30	Logical Connectors and Complex Sentences		

■ EXPANSION IDEA

Learner Log

1. Divide the class into pairs.

2. Ask students to go through each of the items in the log, and define the terms in the *I Can Use . . .* column.

3. Circulate as students work; assist as needed. Remind them that all of the grammar presented can be found in the chapters under review.

Verbs Followed by Gerunds and Infinitives (See Lesson 10)

Verbs Followed by Gerunds				
admit	defend	finish	postpone	resent
anticipate	delay	give up	practice	resist
appreciate	deny	go on	put off	resume
avoid	detest	imagine	quit	risk
complete	discuss	involve	recall	stop
consider	dislike	keep	recollect	suggest
can't help	enjoy	miss	recommend	take up
can't see	escape	not mind	report	tolerate

Verbs Followed by Infinitives				
agree	claim	hesitate	offer	resolve
appear	consent	hope	plan	seem
ask	decide	intend	prepare	strive
be able	demand	learn	pretend	struggle
beg	deserve	manage	promise	tend
care	fail	mean	refuse	threaten
cause	have to	need	regret	

Verbs Followed by Either an Infinitive or Gerund				
afford	can't stand	dread	love	remember*
attempt*	cease	forget*	prefer	start
begin	commence	hate	propose	stop*
can't bear	continue	like	regret*	try*

*Infinitive and gerund objects differ in meaning.

Adjectives of Emotion

afraid	glad	proud	sad	thankful
angry	grateful	resentful	sorry	

Adjectives That Describe Behavior

arrogant	courageous	greedy	silly	wrong
brave	crazy	impetuous	stingy	
careful/careless	foolish	nice	sweet	
considerate/inconsiderate	generous	perceptive	wise/unwise	

Adjectives Related to Truth and Understanding

apparent	clear	likely/unlikely	plain	true
certain	evident	obvious	possible/impossible	well-known

Adjectives That Describe or Evaluate an Experience

admirable	dangerous	embarrassing	interesting	shocking
amusing	deplorable	entertaining	odd	simple
annoying	difficult	fortunate/unfortunate	peculiar	surprising
awkward	disappointing	fun	remarkable	tough
commendable	disturbing	hard	risky	understandable
convenient/inconvenient	easy	inconceivable	safe	upsetting

- **Adjective** An adjective describes a noun. Example: *That's a **small** desk.*

- **Adverb** An adverb describes the verb of a sentence or an adjective. Examples: *He is **very** smart. I run **quickly**.*

- **Adverb of Frequency** An adverb of frequency tells how often an action happens. Example: *I **always** go to the library after class.*

- **Affirmative** An affirmative means *yes*.

- **Article** An article (*a, an,* and *the*) comes before a noun. Example: *I have **a** book and **an** eraser.*

- **Base Form** The base form of a verb has no tense. It has no ending (*-s* or *-ed*). Examples: ***be, go, eat, take, write***

- **Clause** A clause is a group of words that has a subject and a verb. Example: ***Harry likes** college.*

- **Comparative Form** A comparative form of an adjective or adverb is used to compare two things. Example: *I am **taller** than you.*

- **Consonant** The following letters are consonants: ***b, c, d, f, g, h, j, k, l, m, n, p, q, r, s, t, v, w, x, y, z.***

- **Contraction** A contraction is made up of two words put together with an apostrophe. Example: ***She's** my friend.* (She is = she's)

- **Count Noun** Count nouns are nouns that we can count. They have a singular and a plural form. Examples: ***book – books, nurse – nurses***

- **Frequency Expressions** Frequency expressions answer *How often* questions. Examples: ***once a week, three times a week, every day***

- **Imperative** An imperative sentence gives a command or instructions. An imperative sentence usually omits the word *you*. Example: ***Open** the door.*

- **Information Questions** Questions that ask *what, when, who, how,* or *which*.

- **Intransitive** Intransitive verbs do not have an object.

- **Irregular Verbs** See Appendix 3.

- **Linking Verb** A linking verb connects the subject of a sentence to a noun, adjective, or prepositional phrase.

- **Modal** Some examples of modal verbs are ***can, could, should, will, would, must.***

- **Negative** Means *no*.

- **Noncount Noun** A noncount noun is a noun that we don't count. It has no plural form. Examples: ***water, money, rice***

- **Noun** A noun is a word for a person, a place, or a thing. Nouns can be singular (only one) or plural (more than one).

- **Object** The object of the sentence follows the verb. It receives the action of the verb. Example: *Kat wrote a **paragraph.***

- **Object Pronoun** Use object pronouns (*me, you, him, her, it, us, them*) after the verb or preposition. Example: *Kat wore **it.***

- **Phrasal Verb** A verb followed by a particle, such as *point out, think over,* and *turn in.*

- **Plural** Plural means more than one. A plural noun usually ends with *-s* or *-es.* Examples: *The books are heavy. The buses are not running.*

- **Possessive Form** The possessive form of a noun has an apostrophe: *the teacher's class, Jupiter's moons.* Possessive pronouns *(my, mine, our, ours, his, her, hers, their, theirs, its, your, yours)* do not use an apostrophe.

- **Preposition** A preposition is a short, connecting word. Examples: *about, above, across, after, around, as, at, away, before, behind, below, by, down, for, from, in, into, like, of, on, out, over, to, under, up, with*

- **Punctuation (. , ' ?)** Punctuation marks are used to make writing clear (for example: periods, commas, apostrophes, question marks).

- **Regular Verb** A regular verb forms its past tense with *-d* or *-ed.* Example: *He lived in Mexico.*

- **Sentence** A sentence is a group of words that contains a subject and a verb and expresses a complete thought.

- **Singular** Means one.

- **Stative Verb** Stative verbs have no action. They do not often take the progressive form. Examples: *love, like, think, own, understand, want*

- **Subject** The subject of the sentence tells who or what the sentence is about. Example: *The water does not taste good.*

- **Subject Pronoun** Use subject pronouns (*I, you, he, she, it, we, they*) in place of a subject noun. Example: *They (= the books) are on the desk.*

- **Tense** A verb has tense. Tense shows when the action of the sentence happened.

  Simple Present: *She occasionally reads before bed.*

  Present Progressive: *He is thinking about it now.*

  Simple Past: *I talked to him yesterday.*

- **Transitive** Transitive verbs have an object.

- **Verb** Verbs are words of action or state. Example: *I go to work every day. Joe stays at home.*

- **Verb of Perception** Verbs related to the senses, such as *look, see, watch, hear, listen, taste, smell,* and *feel.*

- **Yes/No Questions** *Yes/No* questions ask for a *yes* or *no* answer. Example: *Is she from Mexico? Yes, she is.*

APPENDIX 4 Common Irregular Verbs

The following chart gives the past and past participles of some common verbs. You must memorize these forms, because they are irregular.

Base Form	Past Tense	Past Participle
be	was, were	been
begin	began	begun
bite	bit	bitten
break	broke	broken
bring	brought	brought
build	built	built
buy	bought	bought
catch	caught	caught
choose	chose	chosen
come	came	come
cost	cost	cost
cut	cut	cut
do	did	done
draw	drew	drawn
drink	drank	drunk
eat	ate	eaten
feel	felt	felt
find	found	found
give	gave	given
go	went	gone
grow	grew	grown
hide	hid	hidden
have	had	had
hear	heard	heard
keep	kept	kept
know	knew	known
make	made	made
pay	paid	paid
read	read	read
say	said	said
see	saw	seen
speak	spoke	spoken
take	took	taken
teach	taught	taught
tell	told	told
think	thought	thought
write	wrote	written

Review: Lessons 1–5
(pages 49–50)

A.

1. The
2. has exceeded
3. had planted
4. the
5. germinated
6. have been harvesting/
   have harvested
7. Ø
8. appears
9. the
10. observed
11. Ø
12. Ø
13. grow
14. am going to develop
15. will send/am going to
    send
16. the
17. Ø
18. the
19. burned down
20. struck/had struck
21. are going to build
22. returns

B.

1. have posed
2. plant
3. cotton
4. the soybean
5. walk
6. had brought; grew
7. for us
8. the barn
9. will have completed
10. have considered

Review: Lessons 6–10
(pages 109–110)

A.

1. b
2. b
3. a
4. c
5. a
6. a
7. b
8. c
9. b
10. a

B.

1. ascertains
2. has decreased
3. must have been
4. could use
5. aren't supposed to
   follow
6. have had to submit
7. to review
8. approving
9. not having considered/
   not considering
10. not being able to begin

Review: Lessons 11–15
(pages 163–164)

A.

1. Thus,
2. While
3. Firstly,
4. Ultimately,
5. Similarly,
6. Both
7. Even though
8. Evidently,

B.

1. a
2. b
3. b
4. b
5. a
6. a
7. b
8. b

Review: Lessons 16–20
(pages 219–220)

A.

1. between
2. through
3. the former
4. the way
5. she would like
6. how long
7. Dr. Phyllis Klein, who
8. favorite nurse, who
9. which
10. to Mrs. Liu

B.

1. No
2. Yes
3. Yes
4. No
5. Yes
6. No

C.

1. is expected/to be
   wrapped
2. being influenced
3. to be selected
4. letting
5. have been required
6. to have been tampered
   with
7. should have been
   warned
8. used to buy

Review: Lessons 21–25 (pages 277–278)

A.

1. (a) that he had to practice serving the ball.
   (b) that he practice serving the ball.
2. (a) (that) she had noticed that his foot touched the line almost every time he served.
   (b) his foot touching the line almost every time he served.
3. (a) that she (had) videotaped him when he had been playing/ was playing doubles with Nick.
   (b) playing doubles with Nick.
4. (a) that she had been able/was able to see clearly how he put a top spin on many of his balls.
   (b) putting a top spin on many of his balls.
5. (a) that he would try harder to control the spin that he put on the balls.
   (b) to try harder to control the spin that he puts on the balls.
6. (a) that he should put in at least 3 hours of practice every day.
   (b) that he put in at least 3 hours of practice every day.
7. (a) if he could show Bob how he served the ball/to show Bob how he serves the ball.
   (b) show Bob how he serves the ball.

B.

1. fascinating
2. amazing
3. amazed
4. frightening
5. scared
6. excited
7. annoyed
8. interested

Review: Lessons 26–30 (pages 335–336)

A.

1. hadn't been compromised; would have recovered
2. could/might have recuperated; hadn't weakened
3. had she realized; would have modified
4. had known; knows; would have been
5. would be able; had taken care
6. changed; would take
7. had listened
8. makes; won't improve

B.

1. that
2. return
3. notably
4. geologist John Edmond
5. that
6. but
7. of
8. for
9. on the contrary,
10. nevertheless,

Words in blue are part of the Content Vocabulary section at the start of each lesson.
Words in black are words glossed with the readings in each lesson.
Words in **bold** are words from the Academic Word List.

phenomenon 151, 187
physical therapy 209
physiological 279
pigment 253
pinnace 14
portray 233
postulate 63
practice 165
precipitate 131
predatory 200
predominantly 112
preliminary 97
preserve 326
prestige 13
prestigious 233
presumably 51
procedure 85
professional organization 64
profusion 14
prompt 178
property values 151
Protestant 254
protocol 221
purpose 64
pursue 187
put one's mind to 178
quantitative 221
quarantine 265
range 221
rationale 292, 315
reaction 13
reading 221
reap 23
reasonable 51
rebound 221
recovery 209
red tape 266
reflect 143
reform 51
regimen 210
reinforce 143
relative to 144
release 221
remedy 209
repertoire 41
reseal 199
residue 97
resist against 279
resistant 23
resort to 315
revitalize 143
rigorous 210, 291
ritual 123
role model 85
route 41
run-off 98
sacrifice 315

sales 233
salinity 304
savvy 111
scenario 13
scold 210
scrutinize 131
secondary 304
seismic 132
self-motivating 143
sensor 243
sentence 85
sentiment 326
sequel 233
settler 13
shelter 31
shortcut 51
signal 1
signify 123
skepticism 144
slope 132
socialize 111
solely 209
sophisticate 124
sophisticated 280
space capsule 303
span 112
specimen 303
speculative market 254
sphere 315
spin 221
state 243
status quo 233
sterilize 265
stimulate 279
stimulus 73
stock 131
story line 234
straightforward 209
strap 177
subject matter 233
subject to 63
submersible 303
substance 187
substantially 32
suppress 279
survive 233
suspicious 13
swell 265
swirl 326
syllable 51
symbiotic 303
syringe 265
tackle 178
take one's pulse 209
take up the slack 111
tamper with 199
target market 2

technique 41
terrain 244
test subject 63
testify 85
testimony 85
thrive on 279, 304
toxic 97
track record 2
trance 200
transience 253
transition 123
transmit 165
treat 209
ultimately 13
unbecoming 316
underlying 315
undermine 1
undertake 1
UNESCO 74
unforeseen 23
unique 41
unscrupulous 165
upgrade 131
vandalize 86
vanity 254
vendible 14
verify 291
vessel 14
viable 74
vial 265
VIP 266
Virginia Company 14
vis-à-vis 31
vision 123
visual 233
vital signs 209
vulnerable 131
weapon 13
welfare 209
whereas 279
widespread 41, 291
widower 14
willingness 63
wind 221
wobble 221
word-of-mouth 266
work ethic 111
workforce 111
workload 111
wrapper 199
zoning laws 151

Credits

Text Credits

"Survival in Virginia," from *Jamestown 1544–1699,* © 1980, Carl Bridenbaugh, pp. 34–35. By permission of Oxford University Press, Inc.

"If u thnk txt-spk is the deth o nglsh, thnk agin," Allen Grove, *Daily Press,* Feb. 4, 2007, pp. H1, H4.

Principles of Emergency Planning and Management by David Alexander, Oxford University Press, 2002, pp. 4–5. By permission of Oxford University Press, Inc.

"Education in the 'Real World'," from "What's Love Got to Do with It? Making Economics Relevant in Courses on Economic Development," by Janet M. Tanski, in *Putting the Invisible Hand to Work,* eds. KimMarie McGoldrick & Andrea L. Ziegert, U. of Michigan Press, 2002, pp. 254–55.

"The Gullah: Cultural Isolation and Preservation," from Josephine Beoku-Betts, "We Got Our Way of Cooking Things: Women, Food and Preservation of Cultural Identity," *Gender & Society,* Vol. 9, No. 5, October 1995, Clarity Press, Inc. 1998. Reprinted by Permission of SAGE Publications, Inc.

"Old Friends and New Temptations," from *The Total Package* by Thomas Hine, © 1995 by Thomas Hine. By permission of Little Brown & Company.

"Misunderstandings Among Nurses and Patients," by Frances C. MacGregor, from "Uncooperative Patients: Some Cultural Interpretations," January 1967, *The American Journal of Nursing,* Vol. 67, No. 1 (1967): 88–91.

"Bounceability," by Brian H. Kaye, *Golf Balls, Boomerangs and Asteroids,* pp. 8–9. 1996. Copyright Wiley-VCH Verlag GmbH & Co. KGaA. Reproduced with permission.

"Truth or Just Clichés?" from pp. 6–8 of *Social Aspects of Sport, 3rd ed.* by Eldon E. Snyder. Copyright © 1989 by Simon & Schuster. Reprinted by permission of Pearson Education, Inc.

"Who Do American Political Parties Really Represent?" from *Flash Focus: Political Parties,* 2005, Scholastic Library Publishing, pp. 4–5.

Illustrators

InContext Publishing Partners: p. 7 (bottom)

Precision Graphics: pp. 4, 7 (top), 10–11, 13, 21, 26–27, 29, 34, 37–39, 42, 46, 56, 61, 70, 76–78, 83, 88, 95, 100, 107, 117, 121, 126, 134, 152, 155, 160–161, 175, 192 (bottom), 197, 202, 217, 222, 229, 231, 241, 246–247, 250–251, 257, 263, 266, 275, 282, 301, 309, 319, 326, 331

David Preiss/Munro Campagna.com: pp. 14, 60, 168, 190–191, 192 (top), 280

Photo Credits

Page 2: © Stock Connection Blue/Alamy Page 18: © Chip Somodevilla/Getty Images Page 24: © Nick Hanna/Alamy Page 32: © Sean Gallup/Getty Images Page 51: © Steve Hamblin / Alamy/RF Page 64: © wsr/Alamy Page 67: © Photos.com/RF Page 74: © imagebroker/Alamy Page 83: © AP Photo/Bikas Da Page 86: © AP Photo/Al Schell, Pool Page 98: (All photos) © Photos.com/RF Page 112: © JUPITERIMAGES/Comstock Images/Alamy/RF Page 124: © PYMCA/Alamy Page 126: © Scott Olson/Getty Images Page 127: © Andrew Fox/Alamy Page 132: © AP Photo/Don Ryan Page 135: © AP Photo/Rich Pedroncelli Page 144: © Jim West/Alamy Page 152: © Bridget Webber/Stone/Getty Images Page 161: © Shutterstock/RF Page 166: © AP Photo/Charlotte Observer, Layne Bailey Page 180: (Left) © Photos.com/RF, (Right) © Tetra Images/Getty Images/RF Page 200: © kolvenbach / Alamy/RF Page 206: © wsr/Alamy Page 207: © Shutterstock/RF Page 210: © Peter Arnold, Inc. / Alamy Page 224: © Andrew Barker/Shutterstock/RF Page 234: © Eadweard Muybridge/Time Life Pictures/Getty Images Page 236: © Steve Cukrov/Shutterstock/RF Page 239: © Susan Meiselas / Magnum Page 240: © James Quine / Alamy Page 244: © AP Photo/Damian Dovarganes Page 247: (Left) © Paul Nicklen/National Geographic/Getty Images (Right) © Vladimir Pcholkin/Taxi/Getty Images Page 254: © Christie's Images/The Bridgeman Art Library Page 260: © Ralph Morse/Time Life Pictures/Getty Images Page 261: © 2008 Estate of Pablo Picasso/Artists Rights Society (ARS), New York Page 262: © Oriental Museum, Durham University, UK/The Bridgeman Art Library Page 266: © Chris Hondros/Getty Images Page 268: © Michael Malyszko/Taxi/Getty Images Page 274: © John Vink / Magnum Page 292: © AP Photo/Louis Lanzano Page 301: © ShutterStock/RF Page 304: © Peter David/Taxi/Getty Images Page 306: © Sebastiano del Piombo/The Bridgeman Art Library/Getty Images Page 312: © Time Life Pictures/NASA/Time Life Pictures/Getty Images Page 313: © EMORY KRISTOF AND ALVIN CHANDLER/National Geographic Page 316: © AP Photo/Hamid Jalaludin Page 318: © AP Photo/str Page 322: © AP Photo/Michael Conroy

Present Time: Contrasting Present and Past;
Present Time: Shifting to Future

Part One Present Time: Contrasting Present and Past

Exercise A, *Page 1*

1. **enjoyed**	8. hope
2. requested	9. contains
3. have been	10. desire / desired
4. met	11. are
5. rented	12. think
6. moved	13. is
7. opened	14. look

Exercise B, *Page 1*

1. **'re**	8. know
2. don't know	9. Have you done /
3. have been	Did you do
4. guess	10. finished
5. 's / is	11. did you find
6. have not started	12. has
7. is	13. got

Part Two Present Time: Shifting to Future

Exercise A, *Page 2*

1. **When are you going to open your store?**
2. What will you be selling?
3. What will your hours be?
4. Will you be open on Sundays? / Won't you be open on Sundays?
5. Will you carry the latest cell phones?
6. How many salespeople are you going to hire?
7. Are you going to offer extended service plans?
8. Are you going to have a Web site?
9. Will people be able to buy your products online?

Exercise B, *Page 3*

1. **'re going to take**
2. 's going to be / 'll be
3. going to cover
4. 're going to look / 'll look
5. 'll include / 's going to include
6. 're going to learn / 'll learn
7. 're not going to focus / won't focus
8. will we study / are we going to study
9. Will we have / Are we going to have
10. 're going to write
11. 'll be / 's going to be
12. 'll be / 's going to be

Putting It Together: Grammar

Exercise A, *Page 4*

Answers may vary.

1. **Halima started her business three years ago.**
2. First she wrote a business plan.
3. Then she got funding.
4. The business has grown every year since then.
5. Sales increased 70 percent in the second year.
6. This year she will hire/is going to hire/hired more staff.
7. She's going to/will open a second office next December.
8. According to the sales projections, the company will/is going to double its earnings in the next two years.
9. Halima wants to open a second business in three years.
10. That business will probably be a great success, too!

Exercise B, *Page 5*

1. **was**	6. has
2. began	7. receive
3. grew	8. 're
4. will remove /	9. expects
removes	10. will earn
5. wants	

Putting It Together: Vocabulary

Page 6

1. crucial	7. persevere
2. commitment	8. inadequate
3. innovative	9. undermine
4. bankrupt	10. initiative
5. franchise	11. undertake
6. signal	12. line of credit

Past Time: Simple Past and Past Perfect; Past Time: Shifting to Present

Part One Past Time: Simple Past and Past Perfect

Exercise A, *Page 7*

1. came
2. had died
3. planted, had brought
4. had been grown, was not
5. was
6. married, had saved
7. had, traveled
8. had heard, met
9. told, had accomplished

Exercise B, *Page 8*

1. **was**
2. was
3. met
4. had been
5. captured
6. brought
7. welcomed
8. offered
9. had not been
10. grabbed
11. stretched
12. stood
13. rushed
14. laid
15. declared
16. were

Part Two Past Time: Shifting to Present

Exercise A, *Page 8*

Our boat finally ~~had arrived~~ *arrived* in Jamestown three days ago. It had been a very long trip, and we ~~had been~~ *were* exhausted. There ~~had been~~ *were* 90 of us, all single women, who were to become the wives of the settlers in Jamestown. Until then, there ~~are~~ *had been / were* no single women in the colonies.

As I lay down to sleep, I ~~think~~ *thought*: Finally I ~~was~~ *am* in the New World! What a beautiful place this is! When I ~~am~~ *was* in England, I had imagined what the New World would look like—but this ~~was~~ *is* so different! Everywhere I look, I ~~saw~~ *see* lovely flowers and trees that we do not have in England.

Exercise B, *Page 9*

Last week a small group of us decided to explore the mainland near Jamestown. We had just entered the forest when we heard a noise. There, on our left, ~~was~~ *is* an enormous black bear with two cubs! She ~~growled~~ *growls* a low, soft growl and ~~walked~~ *walks* toward us. I ~~knew~~ *know* that mother bears with cubs ~~were~~ *are* very dangerous. Cubs ~~made~~ *make* a mother bear protective, and they ~~were~~ *are* much more likely to attack people when they ~~had~~ *have* cubs.

Thankfully, we had not gone far. We walked backwards until we reached the shoreline. The bear did not follow us. We jumped in our boats and rowed back to Jamestown. The wilderness ~~was~~ *is* a dangerous place!

Putting It Together: Grammar

Exercise A, *Page 9*

1. **knew**
2. moved
3. is
4. had studied
5. was
6. understood
7. said
8. had not learned
9. was
10. did not understand
11. don't stand
12. is
13. comment
14. is
15. think
16. is

Exercise B, *Page 10*

1. **work**
2. know
3. had been
4. had been
5. built
6. was not

7. began
8. is
9. had uncovered
10. wonder
11. was
12. change
13. don't have
14. enjoyed
15. did not know

Putting It Together: Vocabulary
Page 11

LESSON 3

Future Time; Review of Progressive Aspect

Part One Future Time

Exercise A, *Page 12*

1. **is going to host / will host**
2. are going to address / will address
3. is going to be / will be, are going to talk / will talk
4. are going to discuss / will discuss
5. is going to speak / will speak
6. are going to examine / will examine
7. are going to debate / will debate
8. aren't going to discuss / won't discuss
9. are going to gather / will gather
10. will have learned

Exercise B, *Page 13*

1. **will happen, are going to affect / will affect**
2. is going to continue / will continue, is going to necessitate / will necessitate
3. is going to be / will be
4. are going to continue / will continue
5. is going to become / will become
6. is going to decrease / will decrease
7. is going to determine / will determine
8. will have been / will be

Part Two Review of Progressive Aspect

Exercise A, *Page 13*

1. **are escaping**
2. have been developing
3. have been placing
4. is producing
5. have been adopting
6. are doing
7. have been questioning
8. are escaping
9. are contaminating
10. 're disrupting
11. 're using

Exercise B, *Page 14*

1. **'re you doing**
2. 's going on
3. 'm taking
4. is
5. 're learning
6. are
7. feel
8. 're always saying
9. have been developing
10. 're engineering
11. Have they been testing
12. are they imagining
13. are reviewing /
    have been reviewing
14. have been banning

Putting It Together: Grammar

Exercise A, *Page 15*

1. **will be**
2. expect / are expecting
3. will produce
4. will be
5. continues
6. need

Exercise B, *Page 16*

1. **are moving**
2. 're moving / 're going to move
3. have been wanting
4. 's going to be / 'll be
5. are they going
6. 's
7. are they going to do
8. 're going to have
9. have been eating
10. is / is going to be / will be
11. 're looking
12. are

Putting It Together: Vocabulary

Page 17

1. reap
2. genetic engineering
3. allergic reaction
4. manipulation
5. field test
6. resistant
7. unforeseen
8. acid
9. ethical
10. aware
11. base
12. germinate

Review of Verb Types; Verbs with Indirect Objects

Part One Review of Verb Types

Exercise A, *Page 18*

1. I
2. T
3. I
4. I
5. T
6. T
7. I
8. I
9. I
10. T

Exercise B, *Page 18*

1. **cleared up the case**
2. figure it out
3. had carried out the plot
4. thought it up
5. brought up a good point
6. rule that out
7. get away with it
8. get it across

Part Two Verbs with Indirect Objects

Exercise A, *Page 19*

1. **The government is sending supplies to the hurricane victims.**
2. Volunteers are bringing food and water to community shelters.
3. Others are taking medical supplies to local clinics.
4. Thousands of people have sent donations to rescue organizations.
5. Local churches are offering meals to displaced families.
6. More than 10,000 people have written letters to government officials.
7. Many local banks are lending money to affected businesses.
8. The city government will grant additional funds to all rescue efforts.

Exercise B, *Page 20*

1. **The Senate passed legislation Friday to increase federal grants for low-income students.**
2. New funds will be available to students to help them pay for college.
3. Legislators hope this will make a college education much more affordable for students.
4. Some senators also wanted to offer lower interest rates on loans to students.
5. The government will also provide loan forgiveness for those graduates who go into public-service professions.
6. The goal is to make it affordable for everyone to go to college.
7. The bill will limit payments for students to a percentage of their income.
8. A report explaining the details will be released to the public on Friday.

Putting It Together: Grammar

Exercise A, *Page 20*

Hi—

Did you read the article today about the new athletic center? They're going to start building ~~to~~ it in the next six months. A university spokeswoman showed a diagram of the building ~~for~~ *to* reporters. She pointed *out* to them ~~out~~ that it will include two pools and three gyms. She also told ~~to~~ reporters that the center will have two dressing rooms ~~to~~ *for* men and three ~~to~~ *for* women.

One reporter asked ~~for~~ her about the possibility of a gourmet restaurant in the center. "We haven't ruled ~~out it~~ *it out* yet," she replied.

Talk ~~for~~ *to* you soon!
Erin

Exercise B, *Page 21*

1. **circle: the Sampson trial; underline:** TV
2. **circle:** an alibi; **underline:** judge
3. **circle:** jail; **underline:** he
4. **circle:** attorney; **underline:** the case
5. **circle:** the maximum penalty; **underline:** Sampson.
6. **circle:** instructions; **underline:** the jury
7. **circle:** hours; **underline:** the case
8. **circle:** they; **underline:** courtroom
9. **circle:** verdict; **underline:** they
10. **circle:** prison; **underline:** the man

Putting It Together: Vocabulary

Page 22

1. NE|WS|A|NC|HO|R
2. BR|IE|FI|NG
3. DE|CL|IN|E
4. EV|AC|UE|E
5. DE|TA|CH
6. OV|ER|VI|EW
7. FI|GU|RE
8. F|A|R|E
9. D|E|A|L
10. SH|EL|TE|R
11. VI|S-|À-|VI|S
12. BR|OA|DC|AS|T

LESSON 5

Articles to Express a Generic Reference; *The* for Unique Reference: Definite Reference

Part One Articles to Express a Generic Reference

Exercise A, *Page 23*

1. **the**
2. Ø
3. Ø
4. The
5. a
6. a
7. Ø
8. the
9. Ø
10. an

Exercise B, *Page 23*

1. Although **the** economic significance of ~~a~~ *the* Silk Road was limited, ~~a~~ *the* cultural significance of the route was great.
2. Travelers along *the* road brought with them ~~the~~ new goods and ideas.
3. For example, in *the* late second century AD, the Chinese people were exposed to *a* new religion, Buddhism.
4. Buddhism did not influence only ~~a~~ *the* spiritual views of *the* Chinese.
5. It also influenced ~~a~~ *the* Chinese diet, ~~an~~ *the* arts, and *the* economic structure of their society.

Part Two *The* for Unique Reference: Definite Reference

Exercise A, *Page 24*

1. **the,** the
2. the
3. the, the
4. the, the
5. the
6. the
7. the

Exercise B, *Page 24*

1. **the**
2. the
3. the
4. the
5. the
6. Ø
7. the
8. the
9. the
10. Ø
11. the
12. the
13. the
14. the
15. the
16. the
17. The
18. the

Putting It Together: Grammar

Exercise A, *Page 25*

1. **the**
2. the
3. Ø
4. the
5. the
6. Ø
7. a / the
8. the
9. a
10. the
11. Ø
12. the
13. Ø
14. Ø
15. the

Exercise B, *Page 25*

1. **the**
2. the
3. The
4. The
5. Ø
6. Ø
7. Ø
8. a
9. the
10. the

Putting It Together: Vocabulary

Page 26

1. commodity
2. repertoire
3. goods
4. originate
5. technique
6. unique
7. fabric
8. cast iron
9. device
10. widespread
11. fiddle
12. route

LESSON 6

Academic Phrasal Modal Verbs; Modal Verb Review: Troubleshooting

Part One Academic Phrasal Modal Verbs

Exercise A, *Page 27*

1. **was about to**
2. were to
3. should
4. 've got to
5. have to
6. 're supposed to
7. ought to
8. is about to
9. 're supposed to
10. shouldn't

Exercise B, *Page 27*

1. **Should, are supposed to**
2. Should we, are to
3. have to, ought to
4. Should, shouldn't
5. is it supposed to, should not

Part Two Modal Verb Review: Troubleshooting

Exercise A, *Page 28*

1. **used to**
2. would
3. would
4. would
5. used to
6. Would
7. wouldn't
8. used to
9. Would
10. would
11. used to

Exercise B, *Page 29*

1. **must**
2. must
3. should
4. shouldn't
5. should
6. must
7. shouldn't
8. must
9. should
10. should

Putting It Together: Grammar

Exercise A, *Page 29*

1. ~~were to~~   **had to**
2. ~~ought to~~   had to
3. ~~was not supposed to~~ was supposed to
4. ~~had got to~~   had to
5. ~~used to~~   had to
6. ~~ought to~~   would
7. ~~had to~~   would

Exercise B, *Page 30*

1. **'m not supposed to**
2. used to
3. got to
4. would
5. was I supposed to
6. used to
7. had to
8. ought to
9. don't have to
10. must / have to
11. have to

Putting It Together: Vocabulary

Page 31

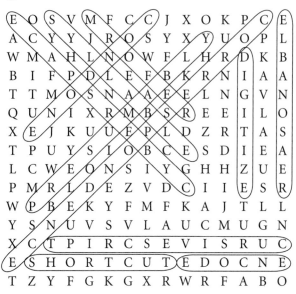

LESSON 7

Modal Verbs: Past Logical Scale; Modal Verbs: Other Perfect Meanings

Part One Modal Verbs: Past Logical Scale

Exercise A, *Page 32*

1. **could**
2. must
3. might
4. might
5. must not
6. must
7. couldn't
8. could

Exercise B, *Page 32*

1. **must have known**, couldn't have known
2. must have acted, may have acted
3. should have stopped, couldn't stop

Part Two Modal Verbs: Other Perfect Meanings

Exercise A, *Page 33*

1. **should not have asked**
2. should have recruited
3. should not have conducted
4. should not have taken
5. should not have informed
6. should not have laughed
7. should have been
8. should have had

Exercise B, *Page 34*

1. **can**
2. couldn't
3. could
4. couldn't
5. May / Can
6. Could / Can
7. could have
8. can / could
9. couldn't
10. could

Putting It Together: Grammar

Exercise A, *Page 34*
Answers may vary.

1. ~~should~~   could
2. ~~should~~   could
3. ~~must~~   might
4. ~~must~~   may
5. ~~could~~   may
6. ~~must~~   may
7. ~~may~~   might
8. ~~could~~   might
9. ~~must~~   might

Exercise B, *Page 35*

1. **must have gone**
2. may have lasted
3. can
4. might have run
5. might have taken
6. couldn't have gotten
7. could
8. may have gone out with
9. can't
10. could

Putting It Together: Vocabulary

Page 36

1. BYSTANDER
2. TEST SUBJECT
3. WILLINGNESS
4. ELECTRIC SHOCK
5. ADMINISTER
6. GUIDELINES
7. CONDUCT
8. SUBJECT TO
9. GROUND-BREAKING
10. MAZE
11. DECEPTIVE
12. POSTULATE

LESSON 8

Quantifiers with *Of*; Subject-Verb Agreement

Part One   Quantifiers with *Of*

Exercise A, *Page 37*

1. **Many *of the* people in the village wanted to start their own businesses.**
2. Very few *of the* businesses could get loans from banks.
3. Some *of the* banks thought giving business loans was too risky.
4. However, one *of them* took a chance and gave a loan to a group of women who make sweaters.
5. Some *of the* women in the group raise sheep for wool and others knit the sweaters.
6. The group divided the funds between all *of the* members.
7. Some *of the* funds went to purchasing more sheep.
8. A few *of the* women bought new machines to spin the yarn.
9. Within two years, all *of the* members doubled their income.
10. Now many *of the* banks in the village are willing to loan new businesses money.

Exercise B, *Page 37*

1. of people
2. one of the
3. half of the
4. Most of those
5. a few of them
6. many of their
7. much of the
8. some of the
9. hundreds of
10. group of
11. a portion of

Part Two   Subject-Verb Agreement

Exercise A, *Page 38*

1. is
2. have
3. consist
4. reviews
5. evaluates
6. has
7. are
8. receive
9. has
10. hopes

Exercise B, *Page 39*

1. <u>works</u>, work
2. <u>is</u>, are
3. <u>thinks</u>, think
4. <u>offers</u>, offer
5. <u>knows</u>, know
6. <u>does</u>, do
7. <u>charges</u>, charge
8. <u>is</u>, are
9. <u>costs</u>, cost
10. <u>is</u>, are

Putting It Together: Grammar

Exercise A, *Page 40*

1. A team of financial experts ~~have~~ *has* recently released a report on a number *of the* microfinance programs in rural areas of this country.
2. They ~~has~~ *have* found that the majority of these programs ~~is~~ *are* very effective in reducing poverty in those areas.
3. Almost three-quarters of the businesses that ~~receives~~ *receive* loans ~~is~~ *are* able to repay them within five years.
4. The minimum amount for loans ~~are~~ *is* usually one hundred dollars.
5. A number of *the* microfinance programs ~~is~~ *are* now accepting loans for the next fiscal year.
6. The number of funded businesses owned by women ~~were~~ *was* very small last year.
7. Next year, many of *the* funds will go to small businesses owned by women.
8. All of *the* businesses that ~~wishes~~ *wish* to apply for a loan must do so by Jan. 1.

Exercise B, *Page 40*

1. **a lot of**
2. half of the
3. Both of my
4. have
5. Many of the
6. are
7. one of the
8. was
9. none of the
10. the rest of

Putting It Together: Vocabulary

Page 42

1. default
2. comprise
3. entrepreneur
4. encounter
5. collateral
6. liable
7. stimulus
8. guarantee
9. considerable

LESSON 9

Gerunds and Infinitives as Subjects; Gerunds and Infinitives as Subject Complements; Gerunds Following a Preposition

Part One Gerunds and Infinitives as Subjects

Exercise A, *Page 43*

1. **Hearing**
2. Committing
3. Cutting, running
4. Protecting
5. Removing
6. Ordering
7. Terminating
8. Confining
9. Meeting
10. Consulting

Exercise B, *Page 44*

Answers may vary.

1. **It is the aim of juvenile court to rehabilitate offenders, not to punish them.**
2. It is a goal of the court to tailor a sentence to meet the needs of the juvenile.
3. It is another objective of the court to protect the privacy of the juvenile.
4. It is a minor offense to purchase tobacco.
5. It is an offense to fail to attend school in many states.
6. It is a serious offense to assault a person.
7. It is not uncommon to file a motion to try the offender as an adult when serious crimes have been committed.
8. It is up to the judge to decide whether to try a juvenile as an adult.
9. It is a harsh punishment to sentence a juvenile as an adult.
10. It is usually the responsibility of the Probation Office to conduct pre-trial investigations.

Part Two Gerunds and Infinitives as Subject Complements; Gerunds Following a Preposition

Exercise A, *Page 45*

1. **playing**
2. is making / to make
3. destroying / to destroy
4. Yelling, kicking, hitting
5. maintaining / to maintain
6. stopping / to stop
7. keeping / to keep
8. preventing
9. making / to make
10. having / to have

Exercise B, *Page 45*

1. **volunteering**
2. doing
3. working
4. developing
5. having
6. talking
7. communicating
8. working
9. talking
10. signing up

Putting It Together: Grammar

Exercise A, *Page 46*

1. **Having**
2. raising
3. talking
4. Working
5. preparing
6. to dress
7. dressing
8. putting
9. to admit
10. to try
11. to answer
12. having

Putting It Together: Vocabulary

Page 48

Curfew, judicial, procedure, mentor, incentive, empathy, offense, testify.

"It is important for judicial offenders to have role models."

LESSON 10

Gerunds and Infinitives: Perfect Forms; Gerunds and Infinitives with Phrasal Modals: Review

Part One Gerunds and Infinitives: Perfect Forms

Exercise A, *Page 49*

1. **having discovered**
2. Having evaluated
3. having denied
4. having accused
5. not having instituted
6. not having disposed
7. not having trained
8. not having begun
9. having concluded
10. not having had

Exercise B, *Page 50*

1. **to have purified**
2. to have completed
3. to have installed
4. to have discovered
5. to have used
6. to have reviewed
7. Not to have alerted
8. not to have ascertained
9. to have paid
10. to have hired

Part Two Gerunds and Infinitives with Phrasal Modals: Review

Exercise A, *Page 50*

1. **not being able to get**
2. having to buy
3. Having to boil
4. having to drill
5. having to pay
6. not to have to move
7. having to look for
8. to be able to have
9. having to buy
10. not to have to dispose of

Exercise B, *Page 51*

1. P
2. R
3. R
4. R
5. R
6. R
7. P
8. R
9. P
10. P

Putting It Together: Grammar

Exercise A, *Page 52*

1. **Having studied**
2. having been depleted
3. depositing / to deposit
4. dropping
5. to grow
6. to survive
7. to prove
8. monitoring / to monitor
9. to identify
10. using
11. to take

Exercise B, *Page 53*

Alan: So how's that environmental chemistry class going?

Carlos: Oh, OK, I guess. My problem is that I keep forgetting ~~doing~~ *to do* the assignments until the last minute. And trying ~~to have gotten~~ *to get* all that work done in a few hours is really hard!

Alan: You never fail ~~amazing~~ *to amaze* me! Why don't you try ~~keep~~ *to keep* a calendar?

Carlos: Well, ~~to have kept~~ *having kept* calendars in the past, I can tell you that that's not the solution.

Alan: Uh—why?

Carlos: Because I can never remember ~~to writing~~ *to write* things down in them!

Alan: Hmm. Not *being* able to remember things could be a real problem. But you want to be able to ~~getting~~ *get* into grad school, right?

Carlos: Absolutely! And having ~~achieve~~ *achieved* a 3.8 grade average, I think I'll be able to get into a lot of schools.

Alan: Well, but if you continue ~~to have handed in~~ *handing in / to hand in* poor quality work, your grades are going to suffer.

Carlos: I know, I know.

Putting It Together: Vocabulary

Page 54

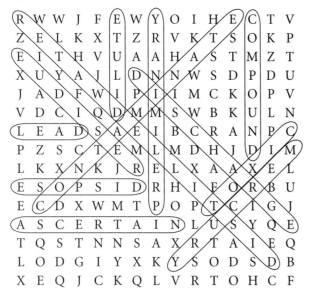

Part One Review of Adverbials

Exercise A, *Page 59*

1. **at home, Where?**
2. occasionally, When?
3. by logging on, How?
4. by e-mail, How?
5. within an hour, When?
6. Sometimes, When?
7. electronically, How?
8. at the bottom of the document's pages, Where?
9. more efficiently, How?
10. usually, When?

Exercise B, *Page 59*

Answers may vary.

1. **The workforce is *constantly* changing in many countries.**
2. Thirty years ago, most people **usually** retired by the age of 65.
3. Today, people **often** work until age 70 or 75.
4. This is **profoundly** affecting the economies in many countries (**profoundly**).
5. Some younger workers are **very** concerned about the competition from older adults.
6. They **frequently** worry that they may not have the experience to compete.
7. **Conversely,** some older people worry that they may not have the energy of younger workers.
8. Some older people who work **for large corporations** choose an early retirement package.
9. Working **from home** is becoming a popular option for all ages.
10. One thing is certain: there will **always** be change.

Part Two Adverbs in Sentence-Initial Position

Exercise A, *Page 60*

1. **Typically**
2. Understandably
3. Technically
4. Generally
5. Fortunately
6. Unfortunately
7. Not surprisingly
8. Understandably
9. Naturally
10. Of course

Exercise B, *Page 61*

1. **Frankly**
2. Typically
3. maybe
4. Actually
5. Evidently
6. superficially
7. Surely
8. Strangely
9. Fortunately
10. Of course

Putting It Together: Grammar

Page 62

Answers may vary.

1. ~~successful~~	successfully
2. ~~seem radically to differ~~	seem to differ radically / seem to radically differ
3. ~~The difference is greatest typically~~	Typically, the difference is greatest / The difference is typically greatest
4. ~~hard working~~	working hard
5. ~~actively are embracing~~	are actively embracing
6. ~~at home can work~~	can work at home
7. ~~who have worked in an office always~~	who have always worked in an office
8. ~~very are unwilling~~	are very unwilling
9. ~~feel they are most productive understandably~~	Understandably, they feel they are most productive / They understandably feel they are most productive
10. ~~actively are addressing these issues~~	are actively addressing these issues / are addressing these issues actively

Putting It Together: Vocabulary

Page 64

1. bottom line
2. hands-on
3. buy into
4. work ethic
5. friction
6. multi-tasking
7. socialize
8. workforce
9. haphazardly
10. savvy
11. take up the slack
12. workload

LESSON 12

Sequential Connectors; Connectors of Equivalence

Part One Sequential Connectors

Exercise A, *Page 65*

1. **Third**
2. First
3. Last
4. Second
5. Fourth

Exercise B, *Page 65*

1. **First**
2. Fifth
3. Fourth
4. Third
5. Second
6. Last

Exercise C, *Page 66*

Answers may vary.

1. *In the first place,* they mark the end of one phase of life, such as high school.
2. **In the second place,** they mark the beginning of a new phase.
3. **To begin,** the graduation ceremony for college students is often quite elaborate.

4. **At first,** the family and friends of the graduating students are seated before a stage.
5. **After,** there are usually performances by the school band.
6. **Next,** there are usually several speakers.
7. **Later,** the students walk across the stage and receive their diplomas.
8. **Lastly,** when the ceremonies finish, there is usually a big party for the graduates and their families.

Part Two Connectors of Equivalence

Exercise A, *Page 66*

1. **Similarly**
2. Likewise
3. For example
4. For instance
5. Similarly
6. For example
7. Similarly
8. For instance
9. For example
10. By the same token

Exercise B, *Page 67*

1. f
2. h
3. a
4. c
5. e
6. g
7. b
8. d

Putting It Together: Grammar

Page 68

Answers may vary.

1. **To begin**
2. Next
3. then
4. first of all
5. secondly
6. for example
7. After
8. next
9. for instance
10. Similarly
11. After
12. then
13. Finally

Putting It Together: Vocabulary

Page 70

LESSON 13

Connectors of Causality; Concessive Connectors

Part One Connectors of Causality

Exercise A, *Page 71*

1. c.
2. e.
3. g.
4. a.
5. b.

6. i.
7. f.
8. h.
9. d.

Exercise B, *Page 72*

Answers may vary.

1. **Therefore**
2. therefore
3. Therefore
4. therefore
5. Therefore

6. consequently
7. Therefore
8. consequently
9. Consequently
10. therefore

Part Two Concessive Connectors

Exercise A, *Page 73*

1. a.
2. b.
3. b.
4. a.

5. a.
6. b.
7. a.

Exercise B, *Page 74*

Answers may vary.

1. *Even though they* **had heard the hurricane warnings, the boys still went swimming in the ocean.**
2. Although the waves were very high, they did not reach the homes.
3. Although the bridge could not support heavy trucks, it could support cars.
4. Although it is known that hurricanes occur every year in that area, it is not known exactly where they will come onto land.
5. The kids went skiing in the mountains, even though they knew there were avalanches there.
6. Though everyone wanted some rain, they did not want the severe storms and flooding that occurred.
7. The builders did not reinforce the bridge's beams, although these reinforcements are often critical.
8. They built their house close to the volcano, even though it had erupted just a year ago.

Putting It Together: Grammar

Page 75

1. even though
2. though
3. Even though
4. Although
5. Whereas
6. Therefore

7. consequently
8. Although
9. Hence
10. though
11. even though

Putting It Together: Vocabulary

Page 76

LESSON 14

Ellipsis; Parallelism

Part One Ellipsis

Exercise A, *Page 77*

1. c.
2. g.
3. a.
4. j.
5. i.

6. d.
7. b.
8. e.
9. f.
10. h.

Exercise B, *Page 78*

Answers may vary.

1. **Volunteers Building New Homes for Katrina Victims**
2. Lakeville Youth Group Painting Senior Center
3. Fifth Graders Create Community Garden
4. Operation Home Again Served 8921 Meals in 2010
5. Southland School Students Raising Funds for Community Center
6. Morris High Volunteers Assisting Elderly
7. 2011 Budget to be Reduced 25%
8. AIDS Patients Receiving Free Medication
9. Clean Streets Members Recognized for Community Work

Part Two Parallelism

Exercise A, *Page 79*

1. **Many service-learning projects involve applying classroom learning and working with the community.**

2. The Literacy Project is an excellent choice for students who like to teach and read.

3. There are always opportunities to help others and to learn new things.

4. In this course, you will learn about why people are suffering from malnutrition and how to combat it.

5. If you like working outside and dealing with the public, you'd probably enjoy the Parks Project.

Exercise B, *Page 80*

1. **She enjoys gathering data, analyzing a problem, and solving the problem.**

2. The leader told the group they should eat a good dinner, not watch TV, and go to bed early.

3. The goal of this project is to identify the families that need help, provide the resources they need, and document the results.

4. Reading a sentence and writing one are very different skills.

5. The course looks at how service-learning projects are designed, how they are carried out, and how they help others.

6. Many people believe that learning about a problem in class, working on that problem in the community, and then discussing that experience is the best possible learning situation.

7. Most students felt that the program was run well and effectively.

8. To learn about water quality and to do something to improve it are two of Sundar's goals.

Putting It Together: Grammar
Page 81

1. **how they win**	6. their
2. the Internet	7. vote
3. substantial	8. one
4. get to	9. the election
5. do not drive	10. compiling

Putting It Together: Vocabulary
Page 82

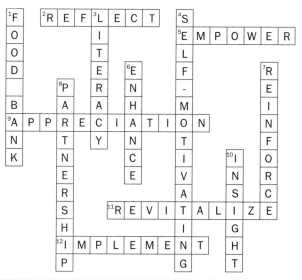

Part One Fronting Negative Elements
Exercise A, *Page 83*

1. **At no time did we consider the developer's proposal for a casino.**

2. Few people would tolerate having a casino next door.

3. There is no way we would change the zoning laws.

4. Rarely do casinos improve property values in a community.

5. Not once did the developer mention the effect of a casino on our children's lives.

6. No sooner had we voted on the issue than another developer proposed building an airport in town.

7. Under no circumstances do we want a noisy airport.

Exercise B, *Page 84*

1. **At no time did the neighbors want low-income housing in their neighborhood.**

2. Few were interested in hearing about the initiative.

3. Rarely did developers propose such housing.

4. Never had a building permit for such housing been granted.

5. Not in a million years would the mayor advocate building affordable housing.

6. Never once was there real controversy about the issue.

7. Little did people worry about housing the poor.

8. Least of all could they be expected to vote for low-income housing.

Part Two Correlative Conjunctions
Exercise A, *Page 84*

1. **nor**	6. but
2. and	7. are
3. Not only	8. are
4. Either	9. does not
5. Neither	10. but

Exercise B, *Page 85*
Answers may vary.

1. **Neither Amal nor Rani want a cell phone tower in the neighborhood.**

2. Not only would a cell phone tower provide better reception, but it would bring in revenue to the city.

3. Both the city and the state governments are in favor of the tower.

4. The tower would be built next to either the school or the mall.

5. Neither the first nor the second location is ideal.

6. Both the school board and the owners of the mall oppose the tower.

7. Not only will the cell tower be enormous, but also it will be ugly.

8. Both the mayor and the town clerk think the proposal will be defeated.

Putting It Together: Grammar

Page 86

1. **neither**
2. nor
3. are
4. have they
5. has there been
6. either
7. or
8. not only
9. but also
10. will they get
11. have
12. is that
13. have said

Putting It Together: Vocabulary

Page 88

1. CIRCUMSTANCES
2. CONTROVERSY
3. COMPRISE
4. INITIATIVE
5. PHENOMENON
6. ADVOCATE
7. ILL-ADVISED
8. ZONING LAWS
9. PROPERTY VALUES
10. DEVELOPER
11. GROUP HOME
12. BUILDING PERMIT

LESSON 16

Review of the Passive Voice; Passive Options with Verbs Taking Two Objects

Part One Review of the Passive Voice

Exercise A, *Page 89*

1. **was settled**
2. was discovered
3. was based
4. were paid
5. was proven
6. was considered
7. was known
8. were sought
9. were charged
10. were brought

Exercise B, *Page 89*

1. **The rice crops were tended by the slaves.**
2. The rice was crushed in large wooden mortars and pestles [by the women].
3. Large baskets were used [by the women] to separate the grain from the outer coverings, or chaff.
4. Elaborate irrigation systems were built by the slaves.
5. Banks and ditches were constructed to irrigate the crops.
6. The farms were abandoned [by the owners] during the rainy months.
7. Each plantation was run by a few white managers.
8. By 1708, whites were outnumbered by blacks in South Carolina.
9. A variety of African tribes were represented by the Gullahs.
10. By 1900, most rice plantations had been abandoned [by owners].

Part Two Passive Options with Verbs Taking Two Objects

Exercise A, *Page 90*

1. **American farmers were taught how to grow rice by slaves from Sierra Leone.**

2. Community life was always valued by the Gullah.
3. African folktales are still told by the Gullah.
4. Many expressions from Sierra Leone are still used by the Gullah.
5. Names from Sierra Leone are still used by the Gullah.
6. After the Revolutionary War in America, goods from British merchants were not purchased by Americans.
7. During this period, slaves were delivered to South Carolina by Danish ships.
8. Tropical diseases were brought to America by some slaves.
9. Immunity to these diseases had not been developed by most whites.
10. The Gullah were forced to live in isolation by many plantation owners.

Exercise B, *Page 91*

Answers may vary.

1. **The plantation owners were sold slaves by the British.**
2. The Gullah were promised freedom by some plantation owners.
3. The owners were taught how to cultivate rice by the Gullah.
4. The farmers were shown irrigation techniques by the slaves.
5. The neighbors were lent tools by the farmers.
6. The slaves were given houses by the farmers.
7. The right to vote was denied the Gullah for many years.
8. The British slave traders were owed money by some plantation owners.

Putting It Together: Grammar

Page 92

Answers may vary.

1. were brought
2. were captured
3. were preserved / have been preserved
4. were carried
5. were killed
6. were housed
7. were taught
8. were valued
9. were paid
10. were maintained / have been maintained
11. were kept / have been kept

Putting It Together: Vocabulary

Page 93

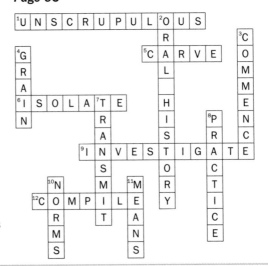

LESSON 17

Gerunds and Infinitives in the Passive Voice; Passive Voice in Other Complex Sentences

Part One Gerunds and Infinitives in the Passive Voice

Exercise A, Page 94

Answers may vary.

1. **being designed**
2. to be released
3. being changed
4. to be seen
5. being tested
6. being corrected
7. to be made
8. being developed
9. to be reduced
10. to be cut

Exercise B, Page 94

1. **Being confined**
2. being addressed
3. being featured
4. being helped
5. being made
6. to not be supported
7. being refined
8. being used
9. being designed
10. to be included

Part Two Passive Voice in Other Complex Sentences

Exercise A, Page 95

1. c.
2. f.
3. a.
4. b.
5. h.
6. d.
7. i.
8. e.
9. g.

Exercise B, Page 96

1. ~~make~~ made
2. ~~being~~ been
3. ~~been~~ being
4. ~~is~~ are
5. ~~ask~~ asked
6. ~~has~~ have
7. ~~being~~ been

Putting It Together: Grammar

Exercise A, Page 97

1. are being held
2. has been declared
3. has been told
4. was sent
5. was voted
6. is expected
7. have been purchased
8. are going to be used
9. might have bought
10. has been made

Exercise B, Page 98

Answers may vary.

Putting It Together: Vocabulary

Page 98

LESSON 18

Restrictive vs. Nonrestrictive Relative Clauses; Reduced and Special Nonrestrictive Relative Clauses

Part One Restrictive vs. Nonrestrictive Relative Clauses

Exercise A, Page 99

Objective observation, which is one of the cornerstones of modern science, depends heavily upon standardized measurements. Standardized measurements enable human perception, which can vary greatly from person to person, to be quantified. For many years, people did not have tools and units of measurement that were widely accepted.

The ability to prove a hypothesis, which is an unproved assumption, is dependent upon quantifying variables. Empiricism, which is the use of observation and experimentation of natural phemomena, requires that results be reproducible.

Several years ago, for example, NASA began measuring "far-infared" radiation, which is the invisible radiation emitted by Earth. To do so, they used new tools that can measure far-infared wavelengths that are 4/10000ths of an inch in length. Such sensitive tools were not available until recently, which made accurate measurements of the far-infared radiation impossible.

The importance of taking accurate measurements is well known to students in the United States, many of whom participate in science fairs. Students design and conduct experiments for these fairs, which are often held in the spring. They must state and then prove a hypothesis. This, of course, means that they must be able to reproduce the desired results exactly. The judges, who are often local science teachers, closely examine the students' methods and measurements. The winners of these science fairs always get a prize, which can vary from a ribbon or medal to fairly large amounts of cash.

Exercise B, *Page 100*

1. **Isaac Newton, who was born in England in 1643, is famous for his theory of gravity.**
2. Newton, who was a scholar in many areas, described universal gravitation and the three laws of motion.
3. Newton developed his theory of color, which is based on observing light through a prism, fairly early in his career.
4. Newton wrote about the three universal laws of motion in his book *Principia*, which was published in 1687.
5. Newton's one romance was with a girl named Anne Storer, who was the daughter of a local druggist.
6. From the ages of twelve to seventeen, Newton attended the Kings School in England, where his signature remains on a windowsill in the library.
7. His mother, who was widowed a second time, urged Newton to become a farmer.
8. Newton attended Trinity College in Cambridge, England, where the curriculum was based on the works of Aristotle.

Part Two Reduced and Special Nonrestrictive Relative Clauses

Exercise A, *Page 101*

1. **b.**	5. a.
2. a.	6. a.
3. a.	7. b.
4. b.	

Exercise B, *Page 102*

1. **Many important new ideas are considered part of the scientific revolution, which began around 1543.**
2. The scientific revolution was based on knowledge developed by the ancient Greeks, which had been further refined by Roman, Islamic, and European medieval scholars.
3. Experimentation and verifiable results were hallmarks of empiricism, which was developed during the sixteenth century.
4. In the sixteenth and seventeenth centuries, European scientists began describing phenomena in terms of quantitative measurement, which had been used long before by Islamic scientists.
5. During the sixteenth and seventeenth centuries, chemists talked about the active powers of matter, which alchemists referred to as "spirits."

6. It is critical to use standardized units of measurement, which include inches, meters, pounds, and kilograms.
7. Today, many measurements are taken using computers, which reduce the likelihood of human error.

Putting It Together: Grammar
Page 104

David Hume, who lived in Scotland in the 1700s, is considered to be one of the greatest philosophers and historians of his time. His philosophy, which is also called a naturalistic philosophy, held that humans beings have reason and insight into reality, which is God's creation.

Hume, who was born "David Home," changed his name to "Hume" when he was 23 because the English, who pronounced the letter "o" differently than the Scottish, were unable to correctly pronounce "Home."

Hume was sent to the University of Edinburgh at the age of twelve, ~~which was~~ an unusually young age. He did not show great respect for his teachers, whom he thought were, at best, substitutes for great books.

In 1734 Hume went to the Collège Royal Henry-Le-Grand in France, ~~which was~~ where Descartes had been educated. During that time he completed his *Treatise*, ~~which is~~ considered one of his most important works.

The critics in Great Britain declared that the *Treatise*, ~~which is~~ now considered Hume's most important publication, was "abstract." Hume, ~~who was~~ not to be outdone by the critics, retired to the country to write *The Abstract*, which was very well received.

Putting It Together: Vocabulary
Page 105

1. PHENOMENON	7. BREAKTHROUGH
2. DETERMINE	8. EMPIRICISM
3. LOGIC	9. INCORPORATE
4. FIGURE	10. PURSUE
5. SUBSTANCE	11. HYPOTHESIS
6. BLOOD VEIN	

LESSON 19

Relative Adverbial Clauses; Noun Clauses

Part One Relative Adverbial Clauses
Exercise A, *Page 106*

1. **where**	7. where
2. how	8. how
3. when	9. where
4. why	10. when
5. when	11. how
6. why	12. when

Exercise B, *Page 107*

Ming: Hey, Nora—remember that time ~~when~~ you bought all those fancy new teas?

Nora: Uh, yeah…

Ming: Do you remember the name of the store ~~where~~ you got them in?

Nora: It's that place ~~where~~ I got those beautiful jars of spices. I don't know the reason ~~why~~ I can't remember the name.

Ming: Well, maybe the reason ~~why~~ is because they were so expensive!

Nora: Oh, wait. It's right next door to that restaurant ~~where~~ Jake and Suri always go to.

Ming: Tea World! OK, do you know the days ~~when~~ they're open late?

Nora: Yeah. Mondays and Thursdays.

Ming: Thanks!

Part Two Noun Clauses

Exercise A, *Page 107*

Answers may vary.

1. **whether**
2. How many
3. How often
4. Which
5. How long
6. How often
7. Who
8. How much
9. Which
10. What
11. How many
12. Which

Exercise B, *Page 108*

1. **Marketers need to identify where people go to buy their products.**
2. They need to determine how package design affects sales.
3. They must be aware of which designs attract the most attention.
4. They should pay attention to how their products are displayed in the stores.
5. They should track how many items are sold each week in a particular store.
6. If possible, they should find out how often consumers switch brands.
7. They need to know how long it takes to move a product off the shelves in a store.
8. They should analyze why people are buying the leading brand.

Putting It Together: Grammar
Page 109

1. whether
2. what
3. why
4. where
5. that
6. that
7. how long
8. how often
9. why
10. who
11. how

Putting It Together: Vocabulary
Page 110

1. a wrapper
2. to display
3. a commodity
4. to appeal to
5. loyalty
6. to reseal
7. glass-blowing
8. to tamper with
9. a coupon
10. perishable
11. to launch
12. to allot

LESSON 20

Anaphoric References; Prepositions: *Against, Among, Between, Through, Toward*

Part One Anaphoric References

Exercise A, *Page 111*

1. **her**
2. She
3. They
4. her
5. her
6. it
7. She
8. them
9. they
10. her
11. she

Exercise B, *Page 111*

1. **Since then**
2. This
3. Such
4. Then
5. Such
6. That
7. Before then
8. Such
9. Such a
10. This

Part Two Prepositions: *Against, Among, Between, Through, Toward*

Exercise A, *Page 112*

1. **against**
2. between
3. through
4. among
5. toward
6. against
7. toward
8. through
9. against
10. between

Exercise B, *Page 113*

1. **through**
2. between
3. among
4. between
5. through
6. against
7. between
8. through
9. among

Putting It Together: Grammar
Page 113

Answers may vary.

1. **such a**
2. between
3. that
4. their
5. my
6. That
7. such
8. they
9. through
10. her
11. she
12. between
13. such
14. through

Putting It Together: Vocabulary

Page 115

1. VITAL SIGNS
2. SOLELY
3. PHYSICAL THERAPY
4. RECOVERY
5. REMEDY
6. ASSESSMENT
7. NEXT OF KIN
8. TREAT
9. WELFARE
10. TAKE ONE'S PULSE
11. STRAIGHTFORWARD
12. INTENSIVE CARE UNIT

LESSON 21

Participles as Adjectives; Participles in Reduced Adverbial Clauses

Part One Participles as Adjectives

Exercise A, *Page 119*

1. amazing
2. insulting
3. deranged
4. embarrassing
5. bored
6. shocking
7. shouting
8. screaming
9. tired
10. Overwhelming

Exercise B, *Page 120*

1. j.
2. d.
3. h.
4. f.
5. i.
6. g.
7. e.
8. a.
9. c.
10. b.

Part Two Participles in Reduced Adverbial Clauses

Exercise A, *Page 120*

Answers may vary.

1. **When colliding on the field, two football players produce enough energy to lift 23 tons of concrete one inch into the air.**
2. When thrown with a spin,
3. Although appearing effortless,
4. Until mastering his swing,
5. if damaged
6. while on the mound
7. After experimenting with several different balls,
8. If hit correctly,
9. convinced he would be a great ball player one day

Exercise B, *Page 121*

1. Some pitchers put a backward spin on a ball when^ ~~thrown.~~ **they throw it.**
2. When a basketball is not properly inflated, ^ ~~a player~~ will not handle well. it
3. After landing a slam-dunk, the ^ball ~~passed to the center.~~ center passed the
4. Thrown sideways, a football ~~player~~ moves slowly through the air.

swung

5. When ^ ~~swinging,~~ the head of a golf club travels faster than any sports car.

All balls are blocked by a

6. ^A good goalie ~~blocks all balls,~~ arriving at a great speed.

Putting It Together: Grammar

Page 122

1. flying
2. rolling
3. bouncing
4. tightly
5. loosely
6. deformed
7. shaped
8. thrown
9. deflated
10. bounced
11. speeding
12. flowing

Putting It Together: Vocabulary

Page 123

```
Q  A  E  T  O  N  O  L  T  B  I
U  D  M  G  P  P  N  R  A  O  C
A  A  I  S  E  D  L  W  N  W  A
N  W  R  R  A  N  G  E  S  I  P
T  E  I  R  R  W  S  P  I  N  R
I  V  E  L  E  O  A  I  M  D  O
T  D  I  E  B  B  A  I  P  W  T
A  O  M  A  O  B  S  E  A  L  O
T  I  E  S  U  L  O  R  C  S  C
I  O  G  E  N  E  R  A  T  E  O
V  W  I  N  D  L  B  I  S  L  L
E  C  L  T  N  R  B  D  E  A  N
```

LESSON 22

Complements of Sensory Verbs; Other Verbs with Participial Complements

Part One Complements of Sensory Verbs

Exercise A, *Page 124*

1. are seen arriving
2. eroding
3. standing
4. mounting
5. firing
6. burning
7. being built
8. discussing
9. living, working
10. rising

Exercise B, *Page 125*

1. **In the film, we see hundreds of penguins walking across the frozen landscape.**
2. We can hear them chattering among themselves at the mating grounds.
3. We view them sliding on the ice and hunting underwater.
4. We observe them choosing a mate.
5. The film shows the mother penguins leaving their eggs and returning to the ocean.
6. We watch the male penguins huddling in a group for warmth.

7. We can practically feel the cold winds blowing.
8. We witness the eggs hatching in the spring.
9. The director shows us a penguin regurgitating food for its young.
10. We watch the father penguins diving into the ocean for food.

Part Two Other Verbs with Participial Complements

Exercise A, *Page 126*

1. **d.**	4. b.
2. c.	5. f.
3. a.	6. e.

Exercise B, *Page 126*

1. In *An Inconvenient Truth*, the director captures Al Gore **waging**
   ^~~wage~~ war on global warming.
2. We hear Gore ~~he is~~ talking about ^~~disturb~~ **disturbing** changes in the environment.
3. In this Academy Award–^~~win~~ **winning** film, Gore shows us ^~~retreat~~ **retreating** **concentrated** glaciers and ^~~concentrate~~ carbon dioxide deposits at the South Pole.
4. He gives many ^~~interest~~ **interesting** facts about this human-^~~engineer~~ **engineered** crisis.
5. Not all scientists agree that the recent ^~~warmed~~ **warming** trends indicate long-term changes.
6. At the end of the film, we are left ^ the question ~~asking~~ **asking**: What can we ^~~done~~ **do** to prevent this?

Putting It Together: Grammar
Page 127

1. **amazing**	6. barking
2. boring	7. Fascinating
3. going	8. kayaking
4. waking up	9. disappearing
5. eating	10. steering

Putting It Together: Vocabulary
Page 128

1. TO SURVIVE	7. FOOTAGE
2. THE STATUS QUO	8. TO PORTRAY
3. TO PERCEIVE	9. TO EXCAVATE
4. CORRUPT	10. TO ELICIT
5. A SEQUEL	11. VISUAL
6. PRESTIGIOUS	12. SUBJECT MATTER

Reported Speech in Context; Rules for and Exceptions to Backshifts in Reported Speech

Part One Reported Speech in Context
Exercise A, *Page 129*
Answers may vary.

1. **Dr. Davis announced that robot soccer is hot.**
2. Dr. Bergen explained that robot soccer players act just like human players.
3. Dr. Davis added that the robots fall down, get up, and score goals on their own.
4. Dr. Bergen pointed out that the robots contain camera systems that function in real time.
5. Dr. Davis stressed that they process data and choose game strategies, just like humans.
6. Dr. Bergen declared that the robots could cover 2 meters per second.
7. Dr. Davis asserted that robot soccer has inspired a lot of very useful research.
8. Dr. Bergen claimed that many innovations that appear in robot soccer are later used to help people.

Exercise B, *Page 130*

1. **emphasized**	5. conceded, because
2. pointed out	6. However, added
3. added	7. Furthermore, stressed
4. emphasized, specifically	8. asserted, in conclusion

Part Two Rules for and Exceptions to Backshifts in Reported Speech
Exercise A, *Page 130*
Answers may vary.

1. **Dr. Chavez announced that they had developed a very exciting new robot.**
2. He / Dr. Chavez explained that this robot would combine two different types of intelligence systems.
3. He / Dr. Chavez stated that it would be able to learn new behaviors.
4. He / Dr. Chavez stressed that the human operator could only tell the robot whether an action is successful or not.
5. He commented that it was a lot like training a puppy.
6. He said that it might take a robot repeated tries, but eventually it would achieve success.
7. He stated that they were finalizing their designs now, and would release the first prototype in January.
8. He asserted that it would be years before we had a truly intelligent robot.

Exercise B, *Page 131*

1. **True and not temporary; Communicated recently**
2. True and not temporary; Communicated recently
3. True and not temporary; Communicated recently
4. True and not temporary; Communicated recently
5. Verb backshifted
6. True and not temporary; Communicated recently

Putting It Together: Grammar

Page 132

1. **Ari stated that there are more than a million quadriplegics—people who are paralyzed from the neck down—in the world.**
2. Tara said that these people are confined to wheelchairs.
3. Ari announced that they had developed a new brain-computer interface to help them.
4. Tara explained that they attached electrodes to a person's scalp that could detect electrical signals from the brain.
5. Ari added that these electrodes would then send wireless signals to a computer-assisted device, such as a wheelchair.
6. Tara said that their subjects had been able to make a wheelchair turn left or right just by thinking about it.
7. Ari explained that the wheelchairs they had used also had embedded sensors that would automatically avoid obstacles.
8. Tara concluded that, though testing would continue for another year, they were very excited by the results so far.

Putting It Together: Vocabulary

Page 134

1. ARGUE
2. DRIVERLESS VEHICLE
3. CLAIM
4. HIGHLIGHT
5. CONFIRM
6. HUMANOID
7. SENSOR
8. AUTONOMOUS
9. IMPLY
10. INDICATE
11. STATE
12. ASSUME

LESSON 24

Reported Speech: Paraphrases with Infinitives and Gerunds; Reported Speech and Thought: Passive Forms

Part One Reported Speech: Paraphrases with Infinitives and Gerunds

Exercise A, *Page 135*

1. **to work**
2. to list
3. to having ignored
4. to having studied
5. to explain
6. to think
7. to laugh
8. to worry

Exercise B, *Page 135*

Answers may vary.

1. **Dr. Dupont asked Lisa to identify four symbols she saw in the painting.**
2. Stella asked Sam to point to one symbol as an example.
3. Harold asked Kiku to explain (to him) what flames signify there.
4. Leela asked Deepak to hand her her glasses.
5. Professor Chander asked the class to think about what the color black symbolizes.
6. Greta ordered Ernst and Kirsten not to touch the jar of paint.
7. Seth asked Margo to go to the East Street Gallery with him on Friday.
8. Mrs. Klein told the children to put all the art supplies back on the shelves when they were done.
9. Saul asked Ajay to stand in line while he parked the car.
10. Hannah asked her mother to drive her to the art museum on Saturday.

Part Two Reported Speech and Thought: Passive Forms

Exercise A, *Page 136*

1. **It is said that the symbolism in some modern art is difficult to grasp.**
2. It has been suggested that the wolf in the painting symbolizes wildness.
3. It could be argued that the tree represented the tree of life.
4. It was said that the lotus flower connotes purity and salvation.
5. It was noted that the two golden fish are symbols for Buddha's eyes.
6. It was assumed that the eagle symbolized victory.
7. It is believed that the color yellow connotes happiness.
8. It has been reported that the paintings sold for $3 million.
9. It is rumored that the painting will be renovated next year.

Exercise B, *Page 137*

1. **a.**
2. b.
3. a.
4. b.
5. a.
6. a.
7. b.

Putting It Together: Grammar

Page 138

Answers may vary.

1. **Rosie asked Uma to come with her to the exhibit at the Getty this weekend.**
2. Uma asked her to call her in another day or two.
3. Rosie suggested that she call her tomorrow and let her know.
4. Uma agreed to call her by noon tomorrow.
5. Rosie asked her to call her on her cell.
6. Uma asked Rosie to tell her what the reviewers were saying about the show.
7. Rosie told her to remind her to read her the reviews when she called.
8. Uma asked her to say what Dormand had written.
9. Rosie asked Uma to give her twenty minutes to find the article.
10. Uma suggested she call when she found it.

Putting It Together: Vocabulary
Page 139

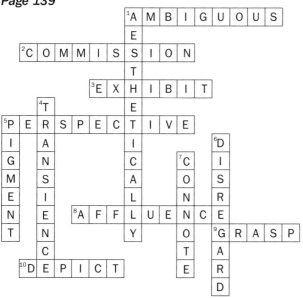

LESSON 25

Subjunctive Complements; Causative Verbs

Part One Subjunctive Complements

Exercise A, *Page 140*

1. **recommends,**
   be vaccinated
2. insists, receive
3. urges, be seen
4. requests, bring
5. insists, be immunized
6. suggests, vaccinate
7. demands, be given
8. suggests, not give

Exercise B, *Page 141*

1. **mandatory, be vaccinated**
2. imperative, have
3. recommended, receive
4. advisable, have
5. important, get
6. essential, be immunized
7. crucial, be protected
8. desirable, be vaccinated

Part Two Causative Verbs

Exercise A, *Page 142*

1. **subject: vaccine**
   verbs: (has) made, become
   direct object: polio
2. subject: incidence
   verbs: (has) caused, to doubt
   direct object: people
3. subject: schools
   verbs: make, get
   direct object: students
4. subject: clinics
   verbs: help, understand
   direct object: parents, benefits
5. subject: vaccine
   verbs: causes, to produce
   direct object: body
6. subject: body
   verbs: recognize, combat
   direct object: disease

Exercise B, *Page 142*

1. **The doctor had me make a fist.**
2. The shot caused my arm to be sore.
3. The doctor let me rest for another hour.
4. My wife made me call the doctor.
5. The nurse had me weigh myself.
6. I got Margot to clean the spot with antiseptic.
7. They let us sleep for an hour or so.
8. We helped them store all the syringes in the refrigerator.
9. She made us write the dose on the vial.
10. The doctor had them fast the night before they were immunized.

Putting It Together: Grammar
Page 143

Sade: The school recommends that all kids ^~~are~~ **be** vaccinated against polio this year.

Matt: Well, that makes sense. I mean, I think it's important that we ~~to~~ protect the kids, don't you?

Sade: Of course. It's just that they're demanding that the kids ^~~be getting~~ **get** other shots, too. I'm not so sure it's necessary for them to^ **be** immunized against hepatitis and pneumonia, for example.

Matt: Well, but if they're demanding that everyone ^~~gets~~ **get** certain shots, there's not much we can do.

Sade: I know, I know. They say it's preferable that everyone ^~~are protect~~ **be protected** against all the major diseases. And they're having us ~~to~~ send in proof of vaccination.

Matt: Why don't you just have the doctor's office ^~~faxing~~ **fax** the records to them?

Sade: Oh—I guess I could ask them ^ **to** do that. It's essential that the school ^~~receiving~~ **receive** the records by August 15.

Matt: So, call the doctor's office, then call the school and let them know ^ **to** look for the fax.

Sade: OK. Good suggestion. And I think I'll suggest they ~~will~~ notify us of next year's vaccine requirements a little earlier.

Matt: I'm sure you could get them ^~~doing~~ **to do** that.

Putting It Together: Vocabulary
Page 145

1. ANTISEPTIC
2. CAMPAIGN
3. DISPOSE OF
4. DOSE
5. DRIVE
6. INFECTIOUS
7. MEDICAL PRACTICE
8. PANDEMIC
9. QUARANTINE
10. STERILIZE
11. SWELL
12. SYRINGE
13. VIAL

LESSON 26

It Clefts; *It* in Subject Position with Adjective Complements

Part One *It* Clefts

Exercise A, *Page 146*

1. **It's giving a speech that stresses me out.**
2. It's watching "Animal Planet" that makes Lisa happy.
3. It's yoga that relaxes Kim.
4. It's eating regular meals that stabilizes Sandeep's blood sugar levels.
5. It's taking a few short breaks that makes Sundar feel much more energized.
6. It's sleeping through the night that is a problem for Dinali.
7. It's talking to her boss that is stressful for Carmen.
8. It's swimming that Bindi finds invigorating.
9. It was when Shen's mother died that he experienced chest pains.
10. It's the barrage of everyday irritants that causes headaches.

Exercise B, *Page 147*

1. **It is the quality of the sleep you get, not the number of hours you sleep, that determines how rested you feel the next day.**
2. It is excessive, not moderate exercise, that can help you to achieve your target heart rate.
3. It is laughing, not crying, that reduces the release of stress hormones.
4. It was losing her best friend, not her cat, that caused Emma to have an asthma attack.
5. It is waiting to perform, not going onstage, that makes him feel nauseous.
6. It's driving in rush hour traffic, not driving on quiet streets, that bothers her.
7. It was when he hit the brakes, not when he saw the car swerving toward him, that the adrenaline in his body was released.
8. It was when the bear ran toward them, not when they first saw the bear, that they experienced the "fight or flight" response.
9. It was the daily stress of the weeks before, not that one tragedy, that depleted her.
10. It was the threat of being laid off, not the stress of her workload, that caused her heart failure.

Part Two *It* in Subject Position with Adjective Complements

Exercise A, *Page 148*

Answers may vary.

1. It is relaxing for Selma to just think about the ocean.
2. It is exhausting to worry about things you can't change.
3. It is beneficial to your health to laugh.
4. It is essential in any stress-reduction program to exercise daily.
5. It is breathing deeply that helps your heart.

6. It causes stress to be in a bad financial situation.
7. It is a bad idea to abandon healthy habits during times of stress.
8. It can be rejuvenating to take even one day off.
9. It can be very stressful at times to raise a family.
10. It is often very depressing to be alone during holidays.

Exercise B, *Page 149*

Answers may vary.

1. It has been difficult for Alfred to lose weight.
2. It is stressful for Briana to work at that company.
3. It was surprising for us to learn the fat content of ice cream.
4. It was impossible for Fadi to regulate his breathing.
5. It was disappointing for Mika to be unable to stop smoking.
6. It was interesting for us to learn that genes play a part in reaction to stress.
7. It was notable for researchers to find that very emotional people have lower pain thresholds.
8. It had been impossible for the doctors to diagnose the problem.
9. It was embarrassing for Mona to take the personality test.

Putting It Together: Grammar

Page 150

Answers may vary.

1. **It's drinking so much coffee that stresses Sam out.**
2. It was the cats that made Sara have an asthma attack.
3. It was enjoyable for Akiro to go to the gym after work.
4. It was surprising for Jim to hear the results of his test.
5. It is sleeping too many hours that can be exhausting.
6. It was silly for you to worry.
7. It is eating good food that promotes good health.
8. It was unwise for Laila to skip breakfast.
9. It was very stressful for Ajay to start a new job.
10. It was lying on the beach that really rejuvenated them.

Putting It Together: Vocabulary

Page 151

Across / Down crossword solution:

- 1. RESIST AGAINST
- 4. WHEREAS
- 6. STIMULATE
- 9. PHYSIOLOGICAL
- 11. GLAND
- 12. SUPPRESS

Down entries: IMMUNE, DB, COMPUTE, STALTE, COPEWITH, CYSTEM, PROMIS, NTITIBOD, THRIVEON

LESSON 27

Conditional Clauses: Past Counterfactuals; Conditional Clauses: Word Order

Part One Conditional Clauses: Past Counterfactuals

Exercise A, *Page 152*

Answers may vary.

1. **If I had lost my passport, I would have been unable to fly home.**
2. If you had had no photo ID, you wouldn't have been allowed to vote in some states.
3. If she had left her student ID at home, she would have been denied access to the library.
4. If he had forgotten to update driver's license, he would have gotten a ticket.
5. If his dog had eaten his library card, the librarian would have issued him a new one.
6. If you hadn't had a photo ID, you would not have been allowed to cash checks.
7. If she hadn't had a certified birth certificate, she would not have obtained a driver's license.
8. If they had had their press IDs, they would have gained entrance to the press room.
9. If she had had a permanent resident ID, she would have been able to register for classes.
10. If we had remembered to bring our employee IDs, we would have visited our offices on Sunday.

Exercise B, *Page 153*

1. **had known**
2. **would have brought**
3. had asked
4. would have told
5. could have registered
6. had had
7. would have said
8. had known
9. had read
10. would have forgotten
11. hadn't had
12. would not have gotten

Part Two Conditional Clauses: Word Order

Exercise A, *Page 153*

Answers may vary.

1. **Had you not lost your passport, we wouldn't be in this mess.**
2. Well, had you not been rushing me, I might not have left it at the hotel!
3. Yes—and had I not been asking you to hurry up, we would have missed our flight for sure!
4. No, what I think you mean to say is: Had you not been yelling at me, I might have been able to think clearly.
5. Oh, right. Just think of our last trip. Had I not made us leave two hours early for the airport, we would never have left Chicago.
6. I don't think so! And, anyhow, had I not made the reservations two months in advance, we would never have gone to Costa Rica.

7. And how is that? Had I not suggested we go to Costa Rica, the thought never would have occurred to you!
8. Maybe not. But had I been the one to choose where we went, we probably would have gone to somewhere even nicer.
9. Me neither. I know. Had I remembered my passport, we would not have had this argument. Sorry.

Exercise B, *Page 154*

Computer Theft at Grayson Lab

                              issued

"Had the school ∧issue our new IDs last week, this never

       have happened   Had

would ∧**happen**," commented one student. "∧W̶e̶r̶e̶ the

criminals used those new IDs, the system would have b̶e̶e̶n̶

captured all kinds of data about them."

    Another student concurred. "They probably never

        have tried

would ∧t̶r̶y̶ to break in had they been b̶e̶i̶n̶g̶ forced to use the

new IDs," he said.

                                  installed

    Campus security thinks that, had they ∧i̶n̶s̶t̶a̶l̶l̶ the new

                        have

video surveillance system, they would ∧h̶a̶d̶ been able to

                  would

identify the thieves. They ∧have had photo and voice records

              had

of the break in ∧w̶e̶r̶e̶ the system been in place.

               have

    Should anyone ∧b̶e̶ ̶h̶a̶v̶i̶n̶g̶ any information about

the criminals, contact the campus security hotline:

                            find

1-800-555-9999. Should anyone ∧h̶a̶v̶e̶ ̶f̶o̶u̶n̶d̶ a student ID,

please turn it in to the security office in Baylor Hall.

Putting It Together: Grammar

Page 155

1. **hadn't walked**
2. **might have been**
3. would have done
4. had I found
5. were
6. would not be
7. had heard
8. would have called
9. could have gotten
10. had not recognized
11. had installed
12. would have happened

Putting It Together: Vocabulary
Page 157

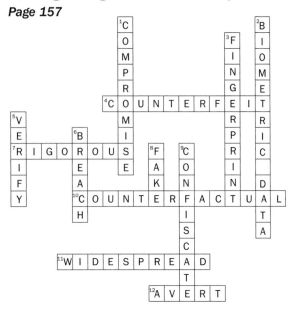

LESSON 28

Conditionals: Conjunctions; Conditional Sentences: Verbs + *That* Clauses; Mixed Conditions

Part One Conditionals: Conjunctions
Exercise A, *Page 158*

1. **even if**
2. If only
3. only if
4. only if
5. If only
6. Even if
7. If only
8. If only
9. even if
10. only if

Exercise B, *Page 159*
Answers may vary.

1. **The divers will explore the ocean floor only if the weather improves.**
2. Only if a planet had oxygen would life probably exist there.
3. Life on earth will not be finite only if the sun's rays decrease in intensity.
4. Only if there are single-cell bacteria can intelligent life forms develop.
5. Astronauts will be able to spend long periods in space only if we develop means of protecting them from radiation.
6. Only if we stop the loss of deep sea creatures will the future of our oceans not be threatened.
7. Fish populations will survive only if the deep sea life forms continue to multiply.
8. Swordfish populations will not become extinct only if people stop depleting them.
9. Only if we learn more about deep sea creatures will we understand their role in the environment.
10. We will know the effects of high temperatures on life only if we gather more data.

Part Two Conditional Sentences: Verbs + *That* Clauses; Mixed Conditions
Exercise A, *Page 160*

1. **could explore**
2. were
3. were swimming
4. would have been
5. were hovering
6. were waiting
7. would have screamed
8. could live
9. had
10. spent
11. would not have been

Exercise B, *Page 160*

1. **If we had explored the ocean years ago, we might know more about marine life.**
2. He wished that he could capture some of the deep sea creatures.
3. They imagined that there were other life forms on other planets.
4. People would be ecstatic if they had discovered gold on the ocean floor.
5. Had they not developed deep sea vessels, they would not have been able to explore the ocean floor.
6. Suppose that life had been found on Mars.
7. We used to pretend that we were living on another planet.

Putting It Together: Grammar
Page 161

1. **Even if**
2. knew
3. would not be able
4. had received
5. would be able
6. unless
7. had
8. even if
9. could analyze
10. only if
11. had
12. had not taken

Putting It Together: Vocabulary
Page 162

1. SPECIMEN
2. CREATURE
3. EXPEDITION
4. CLOSE QUARTERS
5. SUBMERSIBLE
6. HYPOTHETICAL
7. SYMBIOTIC
8. SPACE CAPSULE
9. EXTRATERRESTRIAL

LESSON 29

Noun Complements; Appositives

Part One Noun Complements
Exercise A, *Page 163*

1. **b.**
2. a.
3. b.
4. a.
5. b.
6. a.
7. b.
8. a.

Exercise B, *Page 164*

1. **We heard the news that people were protesting the Olympic Games being held in Beijing.**
2. A panel discussed the protesters' claim that China does not respect human rights.

3. It is a central belief / of the Olympics that the practice of sport is a human right.

4. There is a possibility that the torch relay will be stopped.

5. They discussed China's claim that the Dalai Lama incited violent protests.

6. The Olympic officials' suggestion that the global torch relay be discontinued forever seems extreme.

7. One commentator emphasized the fact that the protests are worldwide.

8. The panel discussed the protestors' demand that Tibet be granted freedom.

Part Two Appositives
Exercise A, *Page 165*

1. Carlton Morris, **a Special Olympics gymnast,** was inducted into the North Carolina Gymnastics Hall of Fame recently.

2. Morris, 29, is the first Special Olympics athlete to receive such an honor.

3. Morris, winner of four gold medals in the 2006 Special Olympics, has been competing for twenty years.

4. He has participated in other sports, such as basketball and cycling, during his career.

5. Jim Shaw, Morris' coach, and several members of the Hall of Fame were there to welcome Morris.

6. no corrections

7. no corrections

8. Several of Morris' family members, in particular his mother, were beaming with pride.

9. Morris had to overcome some serious obstacles, such as his fear of heights, in order to compete as a gymnast.

10. no corrections

Exercise B, *Page 166*

1. The first studies of the sociology of sports, which is also called sports sociology, were published in the 1920s.

2. The International Committee for the Sociology of Sport (ICSS) in Geneva, which was founded in 1964, attracted scholars from the fields of sociology and physical education.

3. Such well-known figures as Harry Edwards, who was a professor at the University of California, joined the organization.

4. (no corrections)

5. The study of sports subcultures, which is one of the specialties, has become very popular.

6. Sports sociologists, who are usually university graduates, are being hired by many different types of organizations.

7. Brooker and Macdonald, who are frequent contributors to sports journals, point out that sports reflect a society's values.

8. Rees and Edwards, who are authors of a well-respected sports sociology text, argue that sports sociology, which is still very new, needs more time to develop as a discipline.

9. North American Society for the Sociology of Sport (NASSS), which was organized in 1978, is one of the premier sports sociology organizations in North America.

Putting It Together: Grammar
Page 167

Kids and Sports

Some people still hold the belief is that sports, in particularly team sports, are fun, but not that beneficial to kids. Recent

        that

research ∧which was conducted at Ohio University proves otherwise.

"Sports encourage healthy development in kids," commented Dr. Taylor, who is a professor of sports psychology at OU. "Through playing team sports, such as notable baseball or soccer, kids get the message that is cooperation and fair play are important values."

                    that

The OU team made the recommendation ∧which is children begin playing sports in the first grade. "Some educators make the claim being that first graders are too young to play on teams," Taylor said. "They point to is the

            that

fact ∧which kids at that age do not have fine motor skills. We think that the fact is that their bodies are developing is all the

                    especially

more reason to participate in sports, ∧especial team sports."

"In many areas soccer, that is one of the most popular games in the U.S, is taught to kids as young as five years old," Taylor, who is an avid soccer player himself, pointed out. "We at OU have made the proposal in that kids should be allowed to play sports with adult supervision as early as they show an interest."

Putting It Together: Vocabulary
Page 169

1. ASSUMPTION	7. DISPROVE
2. CLICHE	8. COMPETE
3. SACRIFICE	9. RATIONALE
4. FOLK WISDOM	10. GENDER
5. RESORT TO	11. SPHERE
6. UNDERLYING	12. HUSTLE

LESSON 30

Logical Connectors: Contrast and Review; Complex Sentences: Review

Part One Logical Connectors: Contrast and Review
Exercise A, *Page 170*

1. **Although**	6. Whereas
2. on the other hand	7. Although
3. Nonetheless	8. however
4. Consequently	9. on the contrary
5. but	

Exercise B, *Page 171*

Answers may vary.

1. **Metz wants to increase the police force by 20%, whereas Sanchez wants to organize neighborhood watch groups.**
2. Metz wants to limit funds for ESL classes; in contrast, Sanchez wants to increase them.
3. Sanchez wants to make Sundays a "ride free" day on subways, while Metz wants to lower subway fares by 10%.
4. Metz wants to train police and fire personnel in disaster procedures; on the other hand, Sanchez wants to demand that the federal government provide troops.
5. Metz wants to give free inoculations; however, Sanchez wants to establish a health care hotline.
6. Sanchez wants to renovate all existing low-income housing units within two years, but Metz wants to build 300 new units within two years.
7. Metz wants to build two new parks; Sanchez wants to build new playgrounds in all the parks, instead.

Part Two Complex Sentences: Review

Exercise A, *Page 172*

1. **Whereas Senator Canton may not have a real chance at the nomination, she continues campaigning vigorously.**
2. She said that a candidate wanting to serve this country must persevere.
3. Some feel she might be better off persevering in other areas.
4. Some feel that a candidate trailing so far behind in the polls should step down.
5. On the other hand, those supporting Canton emphasize her continuing popularity with women voters nationwide.
6. They point to her ability to mobilize voters concerned with health care issues.
7. Her insistence on bringing home our troops appeals to many voters.
8. Although sometimes called a quitter, Sen. Canton is proving herself to be quite the opposite.

Exercise B, *Page 173*

Answers may vary.

1. **Many people support restricting campaign financing.**
2. Some have made the suggestion that candidates only use public funds.
3. Candidates receiving funds from lobbyists must declare those contributions.
4. It might help to pass new laws against huge contributions by one donor.
5. Party leaders have advised candidates to reveal all funding sources.
6. Politicians are not supposed to use campaign funds for private business.
7. It might be a good idea to outlaw contributions from companies that work for the government.

Putting It Together: Grammar

Page 174

    Whereas   emphasize

∧~~On the contrary~~ the candidates like to ∧~~emphasizing~~ their differences, in many ways they are very similar. They both ~~to~~ support sweeping reforms in health care. They have both

                     that

made the proposal ∧we bring the troops home within a year or two. They both claim the current administration has ruined

             yet

the economy—∧~~rather~~ neither one has said how they might fix it.

    The candidates ~~that~~ are not highlighting these similarities. On the contrary,   offer

∧~~On the other hand,~~ they act as though they∧ ~~offering~~ very

            to

different solutions. We would like ∧see more choices. We

      that

cherish the idea ∧democracy encourages many different views.

Putting It Together: Vocabulary

Page 175

```
P  T  O  U  D  E  C  A  M  P  A  I  G  N  T
A  A  U  T  O  N  O  M  O  U  S  T  E  H  D
R  D  D  S  W  S  N  M  I  R  O  T  V  E  I
T  V  C  E  N  M  S  N  D  W  S  C  C  C  C
I  O  A  I  G  R  T  M  T  T  O  L  O  T  T
S  C  D  C  R  R  I  W  S  N  I  H  S  C  A
A  A  H  I  A  V  T  R  C  T  D  A  G  L  R
N  T  E  O  D  U  O  C  R  R  G  R  T  S
P  E  R  I  E  R  E  R  C  I  C  S  R  A  D
O  V  E  R  G  E  N  E  R  A  L  I  Z  E  I
L  R  N  V  R  L  T  E  D  L  A  E  G  A  C
I  A  T  T  N  I  T  S  N  R  P  E  A  A  G
T  M  N  I  D  T  R  O  D  T  P  A  A  A  T
I  L  N  E  G  E  N  V  T  L  C  N  V  K  M
C  A  T  C  H  A  L  L  F  N  P  C  O  X  N
S  A  A  P  O  I  S  S  V  N  I  O  O  C  R
```

CD1

Track 6. Page 29, Lesson 3, Part 2, Exercise D

Interviewer: Patrick Sanderson and Holly Lavender are sophomores at Yale. They and hundreds of other Yale students appreciate the university's efforts to offer "sustainable" food in campus cafeterias. Patrick, what exactly does "sustainable" mean, and why is this policy so popular on campus?

Patrick: I think that most of us are trying to be responsible consumers. I have been eating organic foods for years. My parents were always shopping at co-ops and buying fruit and vegetables in the organic section of the grocery store. When I came to school, I expected to be able to eat the same quality of food. Once I got here, I got involved in an action-group that works on sustainable food. It's more than just eating organic food. It's caring about the environment—keeping it safe while growing food that's safe for us.

Interviewer: How have you been putting that philosophy into action?

Holly: We are pushing for more food that farmers in our area grow. Since last year students have been meeting with cafeteria managers regularly. Already the university is spending much more money in our region and the farmers are raising more crops that are environmentally safe.

Interviewer: But how can students influence farmers?

Patrick: It's not just students. Professors and other staff go with us to visit local farms. We have been monitoring the farmers' methods and encouraging them to avoid pesticides, for example. At first, some of them weren't very open to our ideas, but now they have been trying out new crops and alternative ways of dealing with insects and other pests.

Interviewer: How else has Yale been expanding the organic food options?

Holly: We even have a minifarm on campus—just for organic vegetables. Most of the work is done by student volunteers. I have become much more aware of my diet since I started volunteering there.

Interviewer: But how do you interest the typical student in trying organic dishes—you know, the kids who are happy to eat microwaved noodles or burritos?

Patrick: Of course, some kids could care less. Others are more and more willing to try. We have weekly ads in the student newspaper which highlight new dishes. Some volunteers have been sitting at a booth outside the cafeteria with leaflets about our mini-farm at the beginning of each semester. Soon we'll have special links on the Food Services web-page to provide information about sustainable food.

Interviewer: Patrick, let's say a student decides to try one of these dishes, how does he or she know if the cafeteria is really using these sustainable food items?

Patrick: Special labels. They are using a special logo for everything that's organic. They have been experimenting with new recipes—like for pizza and burritos—and usually those dishes are gone really fast.

Interviewer: Holly and Patrick, I know that you're off to class now. Thanks for speaking with us today.

Track 8. Page 37, Lesson 4, Part 2, Exercise C

1. I was waiting to hear about their son and daughter, but Jay didn't bring'm up.
2. The bookstore ordered us copies of the journalism textbook.
3. Mr. Edwards couldn't find the mistake, so his supervisor pointed it out.
4. George got me a newspaper on his way home from work.
5. I'll send'm an e-mail about his new deadline.
6. My editor looked'm over and then approved my articles.
7. One of my colleagues left me a message. I can't find it anywhere in my office.
8. I need to ask'm some more questions before I can finish his interview.

Track 10. Page 47, Lesson 5, Part 2, Exercise E

1. **Prof. Taylor:** Now let's listen to a song that was recorded in Iran. This particular song is a folk song from the Northwest. You'll hear the *kemancheh* clearly in the first section.
2. **Prof. Taylor:** In the next recording we're going to listen to some religious music from this area. The *ney* is one of the most commonly used instruments in this context. It is a type of flute.
3. **Prof. Taylor:** What is interesting about the *ney* is the unusual technique that players use to create music. The player has to blow across the top of the *ney* while it is against his teeth in the side of the mouth. That means that the player shapes the sound with the teeth and the tongue.
4. **Prof. Taylor:** As you'll see in the photo, the *ney* on this recording is made of bamboo, but wood, brass and copper are other materials that are typically used.
5. **Prof. Taylor:** You'll remember that the Japanese flute called *shakuhachi* is also made of bamboo. The *shakuhachi* player that we listened to yesterday produced quite strong tones which imitated the sound of birds and then softer ones to suggest wind and water.
6. **Prof. Taylor:** Like the *shakuhachi*, the *ney* is often played to create an environment that is good for meditation. The Zen Buddhists in Japan meditate to the music of the *shakuhachi* and the Sufis, followers of a mystical type of Islam, listen to heavenly sounds of the *ney*.

Track 12. Page 60, Lesson 6, Part 2, Exercise E

Prof. Wilkes: Let's turn to the article by Dr. Bosworth about globalization and technology. What is the link to our class topic today?

Orlando: Bosworth talks about Chinese and Arabic as alternative computer platforms and operating systems.

Prof. Wilkes: OK, let's take them one at a time. What are the Chinese doing?

Paula: They're creating systems that don't interface with English. Instead, they are basing their work on Chinese ideograms. Because of the close relationship between the image and the meaning of Chinese characters, they work more effectively in virtual reality than an alphabetic system like English.

Orlando: Another thing that the article said was that Chinese characters also stimulate the right-side of the brain because of their visual nature whereas research shows that alphabets and syllable-based writing systems stimulate the analytical left-side of the brain.

Prof. Wilkes: Why is that important in this situation?

Orlando: According to Bosworth, if the right-hemisphere is stimulated it could lead to a more creative and interactive relationship between people and computers.

Prof. Wilkes: What could be the impact of a Chinese writing system in the digital world?

Zhihua: This would be very attractive for millions of Japanese as well as for the Chinese, especially with China's increasing role in the world economy.

Prof. Wilkes: Then, what about Arabic?

Paula: In the Middle East the Arabic alphabet is actually replacing the Roman alphabet in computer and internet media. It's also important that with the growing Arabic immigrant population, more and more Arabic speakers can be found outside the Middle East.

Prof. Wilkes: Don't you think that most computer-literate Arabic speakers can read English, too?

Zhihua: Sure, but I also think that reading in your native language is always better.

Prof. Wilkes: What does Bosworth conclude from these developments?

Orlando: That there is some evolution taking place in cyberspace. Also, that the writing systems that are gaining importance tell us something about the direction of globalization.

Prof. Wilkes: Ok, now let's compare Bosworth's perspective with…

Track 14. Page 71, Lesson 7, Part 2, Exercise D

Prof. Dixon: OK, who can summarize Jane Elliott's experiment for us?

Dan: In 1968 Elliott conducted an exercise about discrimination with her 3rd grade class in Riceville, Iowa, on the day after Martin Luther King, Jr. was killed. First, she separated the brown-eyed children from the blue-eyed children, and then she told them that the brown-eyed children were better, cleaner and smarter. The blue-eyed kids also had to wear green armbands and follow other special rules.

Prof. Dixon: OK that sets the stage. Now Linda, how did the children react during that day?

Linda: The brown-eyed kids gained confidence and found new reasons why the blue-eyed students were inferior. Meanwhile, even the smartest blue-eyed kids began to lose their confidence and made more mistakes in their lessons. By the end of the day they were very upset, and many went home crying.

Prof. Dixon: What happened the next day?

Dan: Ms. Elliott reversed the exercise and told the blue-eyed children that they were smarter and that the brown-eyed kids were lazy. But this time, the blue-eyed children were not as mean as the brown-eyed children had been.

Prof. Dixon: How did Elliott finish the exercise?

Dan: The third day she asked them to write down what they had learned from the exercise. Most of the children wrote about their emotions when they could discriminate against the other group and when they were discriminated against. They liked the feeling of power, but they got angry or very upset when the other group discriminated against them.

Prof. Dixon: As you can imagine, parents in Riceville were very concerned about Elliott's exercise. The experiment was reported in the town newspaper and then the national media found out. Elliott was invited on TV talk shows and people around the country heard about it.

Linda: What was the national reaction?

Prof. Dixon: Elliott received a lot of criticism from around the country, and people in Riceville became even angrier with her.

Dan: But what about the children?

Prof. Dixon: Interestingly enough, many of them now give Elliott credit for an important lesson. They admit that it was tough, but that it made them more aware, and this has helped them in their lives.

Track 16. Page 82, Lesson 8, Part 2, Exercise E

Max: Professor Browning, it seems that Dr. Yunus and his Grameen Bank invented the phenomenon of microfinance, but have other countries copied the same method of giving the poor access to credit?

Browning: Not at all. Grameen Bank is just one kind of microfinance institution—we call them MFIs. For example, in Central America the majority of MFIs is controlled by non-governmental organizations. You've all heard of NGOs, right? NGOs and some private organizations supply most of their funding. Although this region has among the oldest MFIs, none of them have as many borrowers or services as the MFIs in Asia.

Karen: What kind of impact do all of these organizations have on opportunities for poor people to borrow money?

Browning: As you know from the example of Grameen Bank, a number of MFIs in Asia have low loan balances, but in Central America the balances are generally higher. Thus, we can assume that the number of extremely poor borrowers in this region is quite low. However, the data shows that women still constitute a high percentage of borrowers.

Karen: Given the various histories of countries in Central America, is it fair to say that the situation varies significantly from country to country?

Browning: Absolutely. For example, the highest number of borrowers lives in Honduras and Nicaragua, where the formal banking systems have the least to offer such people. Also, in the case of Honduras, a majority of the MFIs works with solidarity groups and village-level banks—a system that should remind you somewhat of Grameen Bank. The same cannot be said for Costa Rica, where the banking system developed quite differently.

Track 20. Page 106, Lesson 10, Part 2, Exercise D

Dr. Sato: Now that we have completed the tests of local water quality, we're going to turn our attention to the problem of the water supply in arid regions. Where would you expect such problems to exist?

Maria: In parts of Africa?

Dr. Sato: Absolutely correct. Where else?

Ryan: The Middle East?

Dr. Sato: Right, again. Even the U.S. has some areas where water is becoming scarcer, so we'll need to guarantee new sources of water for the future, too. Ryan, you mentioned the Middle East, and that is the best place to study the process of desalination because more than 60% of the world's desalination plants are located there. And that's important because changing salt water into fresh water involves having to use technology that takes a lot of energy. People in several Middle Eastern countries are lucky to be able to use their energy resources in solving their water problems.

Maria: But how does it work?

Dr. Sato: By distilling the salt water—the same way that you conducted your second test. Do you remember boiling the water until you only had residue? Well, the same thing happens on a much larger scale. This time the residue has a high concentration of salts and, of course, other compounds. As you well know, distilled water is purer than typical drinking water.

Ryan: Those people are lucky to be able to drink such pure water.

Dr. Sato: Actually, Ryan, that water is mixed with other water both for drinking and for irrigation. {Pause} There is another method of converting water that's called reverse osmosis. This kind of plant doesn't use so much energy to heat the water and instead pumps the water at high pressure through a type of filter or membrane. The salts remain on the membrane, and the water is drinkable.
I hope that you haven't forgotten doing a similar procedure in your experiments. Just to give you an idea of what these plants are capable of doing, for every 100 gallons of seawater, 15 to 50 gallons of pure water can be produced, depending on the location.

CD2

Track 2. Page 120, Lesson 11, Part 2, Exercise C

1. **Male Voice:** I appreciate the company sending me to professional workshops to improve my computer skills.
2. **Female Voice:** I really enjoy working with Mrs. O'Connor. She's been training me to respond to e-mail inquiries about the company services.
3. **Female Voice:** When it's 5:00, I'm out of here. They don't pay me to work extra hours, and I'd rather spend time at the gym with my friends or doing something else.
4. **Male Voice:** The kids that I work with at McDonald's can't believe that I know how to text-message and that I listen to my iPod while I'm flipping burgers.
5. **Female Voice:** I felt really proud when I won the 'Employee of the Month" award. It really motivated me to work harder even though some of the other employees made fun of it.
6. **Male Voice:** I'll be glad when the boss finally retires. This company just isn't doing as well as it could.
7. **Female Voice:** Sometimes my job's a little boring. I'm used to multi-tasking—you know, checking my e-mail, listening to my iPod, checking out websites. My supervisor doesn't like it because she thinks that it's distracting, but those things don't really affect my work.
8. **Male Voice:** I feel at a disadvantage. I was never interested in computers except to get my e-mail. Now I have to work on-line much of the day. Of course, the company provided training for me, but sometimes my co-workers think that I know a lot more than I really do.

Track 4. Page 129, Lesson 12, Part 2, Exercise D

Many social commentators have pointed out lately that Americans don't have any initiation rites any more. We use the term "a rite of passage" for things that are trivial when we should really save this term for experiences that are deeply moving. In fact, many critics blame this lack of ritual for the general confusion and outrageous behavior of today's teenagers. However, it's not the fault of today's youth that the adults in our society dislike imposing their values on others. Many teenagers are left alone to find their own ways to grow into adulthood, and gangs are certainly one example of initiation rites that have gone in a new and wrong direction.

When you look into the lives of many, many teenagers today, you can still find ways that adults are leading them responsibly toward adulthood. First, there are still remarkable teachers across the U.S. who provide guidance for those young people who receive little help at home. Such gifted teachers create a safe and encouraging atmosphere so that students enjoy learning. If teenagers can see the relevance of education, they will gain the tools they need to be productive members of society.

Next, sports are often seen as the ticket out of desperate home situations for minority teens. Coaches rule the time that teenagers spend together on the court or the field. As the athletes work hard on their athletic skills, a true coach also gives lessons on the right way to handle disappointment and on the right way to treat people that you beat.

No matter where we live, young people have more and more opportunities to separate themselves from their comfort zone. Third, community service activities and volunteerism bring adolescents in contact with other adults who can show them what life is really like. For example, reading about environmentalism in school is much different from working to clean the local river of garbage. Or spending time at the local food bank is an eye-opening lesson about the lives of many fellow citizens.

Finally, what about the American tradition of the summer job? Plenty of teenagers still learn important, life-changing lessons as they flip burgers or cut lawns. Sometimes the lessons come from thoughtful supervisors who take time to train the youths properly and then give feedback—either positive or negative. Adult customers add to the on-the-job education as they interact with the young person. We learn that the customer is always right, but that doesn't mean that the customer always treats you right. When teenagers enter the workforce full-time, they will be well served by the lessons they have learned in dealing with the public.

Track 6. Page 140, Lesson 13, Part 2, Exercise D

Jamaica, the third largest island in the Caribbean, has a variety of terrain that is the basis of its economy. The interior is mountainous with the highest mountains in the Caribbean while the coastline has beaches, swamps and cliffs. The island's economy has depended on its agricultural products throughout most of its history. The major export crops have traditionally been sugarcane, bananas, citrus fruit, cocoa and coffee. In recent years tourism has become more and more important to the economy, and many resorts have been built, especially along the north coast. As a result, this part of the country has a larger urban population and a higher standard of living. The majority of the population live in smaller towns and villages, often in remote areas.

Jamaica is vulnerable to a number of natural disasters. Perhaps the most obvious kind is hurricanes since the island is located in the center of the path of Caribbean hurricanes and tropical storms. Earthquakes are another serious threat since Jamaica is only 90 miles from the Caymon fault. In fact, large earthquakes hit the island in 1692 and 1907. Landslides and tsunamis have also been recorded, especially along the north coast. In addition to such threats, the island has experienced extensive areas of soil erosion. With these sources of potential disaster, most of the Jamaican population lives in areas where their lives can be in danger.

The typical housing in Jamaica poses a risk to many of the people. First, thousands of people live on terrain that can be affected by storms and earthquakes. Second, many houses have been built with very simple materials, usually wood structures with some kind of metal roofing. Jamaica has a national building code, which specifies the ways to reinforce houses to withstand dangerous conditions. Unfortunately, many houses are constructed by unskilled workers, and many structures do not meet the standards of the building codes.

Track 8. Page 149, Lesson 14, Part 2, Exercise C

Reilly: Hi, Jim, I just want to touch base with you to be sure that we're set for next week.

Brewer: Barbara, we're anxious to get started. Will you be coming with the students for their orientation session?

Reilly: Yes, I'm going to bring some of them in my car, and the others will come in the university van with DeWayne, my grad assistant.

Brewer: Great. It'll be good for you to be here during the orientation. I want you to hear what I have to say to them. I'm a little concerned that these students have never had hands-on experience with the type of folks that come to our program. The way the students talk to our clients and the kind of clothes or jewelry that they wear here can really affect our work.

Reilly: Jim, I think that you'll find that these students are pretty sensitive to those issues. After all, that's the whole point of this project. Seeing the impact of economic decisions on less fortunate people in our community means gaining some insight to your own good fortune and behavior, too.

Brewer: It sounds like we're on the same wave-length. That's good. I'm going to hand out the first assignments, too. As we discussed, one team will handle the inventory in the food bank—we need to have an up-to-date list of our supplies. The other kids will help prepare the meal in the community kitchen, and everyone will then probably help to serve the evening meal. That way they'll have some contact with our other volunteers and our clients right away.

Reilly: It sounds fine. When will the other part of the project start?

Brewer: If it still fits your course schedule alright, I'd like to start in 3 weeks. The students more interested in policy issues can show my staff how to do some basic economic forecasting. Those that would rather work on social issues can help our clients during the workshops that we offer on basic family budgeting.

Reilly: Jim, that's exactly what I expected. If anything changes, just let me know.

Brewer: Fine. Then, we'll see you next week.

Track 10. Page 160, Lesson 15, Part 2, Exercise E

1. I'm Vera Upton of the Green Club. We unanimously support the construction of a new recycling center for our area. However, we can not support the mayor's recommendation that the center be located at the north end of Grant Street. Nor can we even support the idea that the center should be located inside the city limits. Our recommendation is that the center be located by route 119 near the TSC campus.

2. My name is Henry Vernon, representing the local chapter of the Sierra Club. We are very concerned about the proposed Grant Street location of the recycling center. We understand that the center will accept household chemicals and paints on a limited basis. The Titus River flows within ½ mile of that location and research shows that pollutants can enter the groundwater within that range. Since the Titus River supplies part of our county's water, we urge great caution. Instead of risking groundwater contamination, it would be wiser either to locate the center elsewhere or not to accept hazardous chemicals.

3. Hello, I'm Janet Thomas, a member of the Carsonville School Board. As you know, we have been voicing our opposition to the Grant Street location of the recycling center for weeks. First, we are concerned about the proximity of Carson School to those hazardous chemicals that Mr. Vernon just alluded to. Second, we and the teachers feel that the noise of recycling trucks driving up and down the street in front of Carson School will be very disruptive. Our position, like the Green Club, is that the land by Route 119 across from campus would be more appropriate.

4. I'm Kristie Dawson, college attorney at TSC. Although we have great sympathy for the concerns of the previous speakers, under no circumstances can the college support the location of the recycling center across from our campus. As the largest employer in this area, TSC needs to be sure that students continue to attend college on our campus. How would it look (and smell) to prospective students and their parents if a big recycling center welcomed them to our city and college? It would be the first thing that they see when they exit Route 119. Certainly, there must be some other site that we should be considering.

5. Jim Samuel, Director of the Carsonville Recycling Center. Folks, thanks for your comments. We appreciate that not one of you has questioned the need for a new recycling center. Also, I understand your concern about the hazardous chemicals that we will start accepting once the center has been built. Ms. Dawson brought up the idea of other sites, and I'd just like to you know that we have considered others. There's the field at the other end of Grant Street beyond Granby Estates as well an area on the other side of Route 119—we've been discussing that option with Mayor Taylor over in Titus.

6. I'm Richard O'Malley, president of the homeowners association in Granby Estates. Mr. Samuel, we were afraid that you might mention the Grant Street location near Granby Estates. We have stated repeatedly that this location is out of the question. We don't want recycling trucks from all over town driving through our neighborhood. Ours is a quiet part of town. It's one thing for noisy trucks to drive past a school or campus, but it's quite different when they rumble through a residential area. You haven't heard the last of this if anyone seriously pursues the idea of a recycling center near us!

Track 12. Page 175, Lesson 16, Part 2, Exercise D

1. We took a tour bus from Charleston over to the Sea Islands for the afternoon. We wanted to walk around and check out the shops. I had read about the fantastic baskets that the Gullah are still making today. I lost track of time while I was shopping and got left behind! Can you believe it?

2. In one shop the women who weave the baskets were giving a demonstration. It was fascinating. They even gather the grasses themselves. We got involved in the demonstration and never had time to visit all of the other shops.

3. It was also a bit hard to get around. I was OK, but my friend got hurt as she was stepping out of the bus, so she was limping pretty badly. We had to take our time.

4. After we had watched the basket demo for such a long time, we wanted to check out the wood carving, too. As we were strolling along, we got side-tracked by a delicious aroma. We couldn't resist stopping for a bite of lunch to try Hoppin' John at a little café.

5. The café was terrific. Even though it was on a main street, it seemed to have authentic food. I had heard about so many dishes before my trip, and this place had most of them on the menu. My friend Judy and I couldn't say "No." We had to try about three different dishes. We got stuffed and could hardly move.

6. By this time it was the middle of the afternoon. You know how humid it gets in July. We tried to keep going, but it was tough. Thank Goodness most of the shops had awnings so that we could walk in the shade. Still my friend felt like she was getting overheated so we had to stop in another café.

7. It's really no wonder that we missed the bus. We knew that the departure time was approaching, but we just couldn't hurry. In addition, we were quite a distance from the parking lot and as we were walking, we got turned around and ended up at the other side of town. It was quite a day.

Track 14. Page 185, Lesson 17, Part 2, Exercise C

1. **Sam:** There's a photographer outside who wants to take a picture of us.
   Kirk: I don't want my picture in the newspaper.
   Sam: Why not? Publicity is good for the team.
   Kirk: OK, then why don't you let him take your photo? You're our big star.
   Sam: OK, but don't say that you didn't have a chance.

2. **Sam:** Coach, this is my friend Jeff. He'd like to join our team.
   Coach: Hi, Jeff. I'm afraid that I don't have time to talk to you right now. Kirk, why don't you talk to Jeff and you can fill me in later.
   Kirk: Sure, coach, no problem. Hey, Jeff, how're you doing?]

3. **Kirk:** Sam, I'm done talking to Jeff. He's going to join us for practice today.
   Sam: Great. I thought that he would be a good addition to our team.
   Kirk: I have to go tell the coach. Would you mind helping Jeff take his stuff to the locker room?
   Sam: No problem.

4. **Coach:** Listen up, fellas. You know how we have needed another player. It looks like we may have found somebody. Sam, he's your friend—you do the honors.
   Sam: I'd be happy to.

5. **Coach:** What are you guys doing? You need to follow the game plan!
   Sam: Sorry, Coach, I wanted to give Jeff a chance to play so I decided to pass the ball to him right away.
   Coach: You can't just decide to change the plan for your friend. Kirk should get the first ball just as we practiced before.

6. **Kirk:** Hey, Sam, what are you doing now?
   Sam: It looked to me like your brakes were a little loose.
   Kirk: You know that I don't want you or anybody else to check my chair.
   Sam: Why are you so touchy about that?
   Kirk: Let's just say that I've had some bad experiences.

7. **Coach:** Jeff, you don't need to load your chair into the van yourself.
   Jeff: That's OK, Coach.
   Coach: When we're at a game, I'm the only one who loads and unloads the chairs. That's one of the team rules.
   Jeff: Sorry, Coach, I didn't know.

8. **Coach:** It's time to choose the captain for this year. This season we have a lot of veteran players on the team, so the choice is not an easy one.
   Sam: Are we going to elect someone captain?
   Coach: Maybe next year, Sam. This year Kirk is going to be our captain.

Track 16. Page 197, Lesson 18, Part 2, Exercise D

1. This semester we're going to examine the key philosophies that helped bring about the Scientific Revolution. As we learn about these key ideas, we also need to learn about the men involved with the development of the ideas, which might strike you as an odd thing to do in a science course.

2. We'll take a look at the society in which these scientists lived because they faced many pressures as their discoveries come in conflict with accepted beliefs. In fact, some scientists were even put to death for their theories. Others spent years in prison, which is a high price to pay for discoveries we consider facts today.

3. As you know, our department has the name "Natural Philosophy," which confuses many people. By the end of this course, I hope that you will appreciate the reason for this rather old-fashioned name. We take pride in following in the tradition of the first natural philosophers.

4. If you scan the course syllabus, you'll see that we're going to spend the first few lectures reviewing ancient Greek philosophy and the progress that Islamic thinkers made during the Middle Ages in Europe. When we talk about the Islamic thinkers and mathematicians, we are talking about men not only in the area we know as the Middle East but also in the area of Spain under the control of the Moors, which many people forget when they hear the word "Islamic."

5. By mid-term, we'll have covered approximately the first half of the Scientific Revolution. I expect that you will have completed the reading assignments and that you'll be able to tell me the topic of your research paper at that time. Keeping up with the reading and deciding on your topic are crucial, which means spending time on this class almost every day. If you have trouble handling the work, I expect to see you during my office hours.

Track 18. Page 207, Lesson 19, Part 2, Exercise D

Bigelow: Thank you all for coming today. I'd like to present the newest product in our line of healthy snack foods. Then, I'd be happy to take your questions…As you know, Lambton Foods brought out our first fruit snack last year, and there were many complaints from parents who were concerned about the amount of sugar in each serving. At that time, we decided to take the snack off the market and make extensive changes. We knew that we needed to develop a completely new product because we weren't sure that parents would try our snacks again. That's why we have a new sugar-free recipe and totally different packaging for this product. You may recall that our previous snack was packaged for vending machines in schools. We realized that parents want to know more about their kids' diets and want to pack nutritious lunches. Therefore, FruityBites come 24 to a package in resealable plastic bags which are convenient for parents and kids to use at home. OK, now let me open this up for a few questions.

Sam Loew: Marlene, you didn't mention the individual wrappers on the FruityBites. Isn't it true that each snack is wrapped in plastic, too?

Bigelow: That's correct. The FruityBites are a little sticky, so it's more convenient if each piece has a wrapper.

Sue Green: But, Marlene, doesn't that mean that Lambton Foods is adding more plastic to our nation's garbage than is really necessary? I thought that Lambton Foods had promised to reduce its use of plastic.

Bigelow: Sue, you are absolutely right about our commitment to reducing the amount of plastic in our country's landfills. We know that consumers are very concerned about this. That's why we have produced the wrappers and the resealable bag with plastic made of corn.

Sam Loew: Is that the same material that some other large companies are using for packaging some of their fruits and vegetables?

Bigelow: Right, Sam. This type of plastic is more biodegradable than other commonly used plastics, so we decided to launch our new snack to appeal to parents who want healthier snacks for their kids in a package that is healthier for our environment.

By the way, we have some sample packages for you today, but we also hope that your readers will go to their grocery stores to start buying FruityBites on the first of next month. That is the kick-off date for the FruityBites campaign.

Track 20. Page 213, Lesson 20, Part 1, Exercise E

Nurse A (Anne): Bill, can you believe that Mr. Bratt, the Swedish patient, complained to his wife about his care here?

Nurse B (Bill): What's that all about? He seems so nice and polite. Every time I go into his room I offer him water or juice—sometimes even a back rub. And every time he refuses. You'd think that he would appreciate such attention, not complain about it.

Nurse A: Those liquids are going to help him feel better sooner, too. I don't understand the problem. His English is fluent—it can't be a language barrier.

Nurse B: According to his wife, he was happy enough with his surgery. From what you're saying, Anne, it sounds like he's been very dissatisfied since.

Track 21. Page 213, Lesson 20, Part 1, Exercise F

Nurse A: Mr. Bratt, I have to apologize to you. We heard that you haven't been happy with your care, and I think that we finally found the answer.

Mr. Bratt: What are you talking about?

Nurse A: Bill told me that he always offers you water or juice and sometimes even a back rub. Tina, the night nurse, told me the same thing. The former told me that you always refuse his offers.

Mr. Bratt: They're right. I can't just say "yes"—that would be so rude.

Nurse A: But, you see, that is exactly the problem. If you say "no," we believe you. We expect you to tell us in a straightforward way if you want something.

Mr. Bratt: In Sweden we don't act that way. We have to wait for people to offer at least two or three times.

Nurse A: From now on, could you please help us and let us know more directly?

Mr. Bratt: I'll try, but I can't promise. You know, old habits die hard.

CD3

Track 2. Page 228, Lesson 21, Part 2, Exercise C

1. **TA:** Be sure that you check the temperatures at least every 2 minutes. While waiting to take the next temperature reading, you'll need to add the new info to the database.

   Gina: Will I really have time to do both?

   TA: No problem, you'll see.

2. **Gina:** How long will I have to monitor the readings?

   TA: Each part of the experiment lasts at least 10 minutes.

   Gina: Doesn't the equipment record the temperatures itself? I thought we're using high tech tools here. This sounds pretty boring.

   TA: Although programmed to record the readings, it's been inconsistent lately and we can't afford to lose the data.

3. **Gina:** OK, but I hope that one of the other students can take a turn.

   TA: I guess that's OK, but you have to be sure that we don't lose any data. Professor Kerry is counting on it.

   Gina: Don't worry. I'll ask Marty or Alice to help out.

   TA: Whatever. Just remember, if asked, I'm going to tell Kerry that you were doing this part of the database.

4. **Gina:** That's not fair. You're in charge of the lab. I'm just a student.

   TA: Planning this whole experimental procedure, I decided that you should take the readings because I know that you are very careful. And I know how important the results are for Prof. Kerry. If you're going to ignore me, I'm not going to take the blame.

   Gina: I appreciate your confidence in me, but I still think it sounds boring.

5. **TA:** Working in the lab means that you often have to do routine tasks. You can't expect to work on your own projects when you're still learning the proper experimental protocols.

   Gina: I know that you're right, but it's hard to be excited about physics when all you do is check the temperature every 2 minutes.

   TA: Unless mastered, these techniques and protocols will keep you from being a successful scientist. It's part of our job training, so to say.

6. **Gina:** Do you still have to do this kind of work, too?

   TA: Not like what you are doing, but I still have to help Professor Kerry with her projects. Dreaming of being a research scientist as a kid, I visualized myself in my own lab by now, not working for a professor.

   Gina: I guess that I shouldn't complain.

Track 4. Page 240, Lesson 22, Part 2, Exercise D

1. **Fred:** Lou, have you seen my camera anywhere?

   Lou: No, what are you talking about?

   Fred: I left it lying right over there by yours. Now it's gone.

   Lou: The last time I saw it, you were filming Pete's interview.

2. **Lou:** Wait a minute. I remember somebody holding it.

   Fred: Are you sure? I haven't seen anybody else around here.

   Lou: Didn't you see the two guys walking around during the interview?

   Fred: Are you kidding? I was busy recording the audio for the interview. I wasn't paying any attention to anything else.

3. **Lou:** The way that I remember it, I came across the guys wandering around near the sound equipment. As soon as I paid attention to them, they walked away.

   Fred: What did these guys look like anyway?

   Lou: One is kind of short and the other guy was average height but a little heavy. The second one had on a leather jacket.

4. **Fred:** I think that I'll look around for them.

   Lou: I heard them talking softly, but there was no reason to pay attention.

   Fred: That's OK. I may be able to spot them walking around.

5. **Fred:** Lou, I found them sitting on a bench on the other side of those trees.

   Lou: Did I just hear you shouting at them?

   Fred: No, that wasn't me. I don't know what that was all about.

6. **Fred:** Anyway, I saw them sitting there, so I walked up behind them and hid behind a tree.

   Lou: Are you crazy? This is Central Park! Somebody might have called a cop on you!

   Fred: Luckily, one of those cops on horseback was actually coming along the path because I overheard them deciding where to sell the camera. It was under the guy's leather jacket.

7. **Lou:** What did you do?

   Fred: I didn't want to call the cop until he was really close so that he could catch the guys carrying the camera.

   Lou: That was taking a big chance!

   Fred: I could feel the sweat dripping down my face as I waited for the cop.

   Lou: You'd better not tell the boss what you did!

Track 6. Page 250, Lesson 23, Part 2, Exercise C

1. The team from Stanford won the second Great Challenge.
2. Hospitals use robots to transport medical supplies and deliver meals.
3. Robots can vacuum rugs without hitting furniture.
4. Many movie robots have become famous.
5. Scientists are working on robots in the shapes of animals.
6. After our disappointing results, we must think about the future of intelligent robots.
7. In a few years driverless vehicles will move more quickly over rough terrain.
8. Some people use the word "bot" as a nickname for robot.
9. Robots may change human civilization.

Track 8. Page 262, Lesson 24, Part 2, Exercise D

Capt. Shea: Ladies and Gentleman, let me introduce Dr. Evans, the curator of the Montgomery Museum. We'd like to update you on the status of our investigation into yesterday's theft of "The Three Friends of Winter."

Dr. Evans: As you know, this extremely rare piece of Chinese porcelain disappeared from the museum sometime yesterday afternoon. According to our research, this teapot is the only one of its kind in a U.S. collection. The title of the piece refers to the three plants which decorate the teapot: bamboo, pine and prunus. These symbols of winter are quite common in Chinese art, but this teapot is reported to be from the emperor's court during the Qing period.

Capt. Shea: We have heard stories that a private collector on the West Coast has quietly been acquiring pieces from the same period.

Dr. Evans: That's right. Several pieces have disappeared from other smaller museums around the country, and they all come from the Qing period. Detectives who specialize in art thefts are saying that a person in the Los Angeles area may be behind these thefts.

Capt Shea: We've spoken with the other curators whose Chinese porcelain pieces were stolen because we want to make sure that everyone handles the investigation in the same way.

Dr. Evans: There's general agreement among the curators that no reward for the pieces will be paid, for example. We don't want to encourage any potential thieves.

Capt. Shea: Obviously, some people may disagree with that because we might never get the porcelain back. However, we believe that this policy is the best way to handle the situation.

Dr. Evans: As you can imagine, my staff and I have discussed ways to avoid such thefts in the future. At this point we are considering adding a new security system to the museum as well as a new training program for the guards.

Capt. Shea: That's it for today. We'll be available for an update again tomorrow afternoon.

Track 10. Page 275, Lesson 25, Part 2, Exercise E

1. **Maria:** Jim, the coolers with the vaccines are heavier than I thought. Would you mind carrying them into the clinic?

   Jim: No problem. I only saw 4 of them when we were packing the van.

   Maria: Actually I think that there are 5 of them. One's under a dark bag.

   Jim: Sure, it won't take long.

2. **Larry:** Maria, I know that you are really busy, but we really need to double check the vaccine.

   Maria: You're right, Larry. But it takes so much time to unpack the vials and count them.

   Larry: I guess that we could do it tomorrow morning, but you know that it will be so hectic and I hate to keep the people waiting.

   Maria: Oh, all right. I'd rather do it now than tomorrow. If we do it together it shouldn't take that long.

   Larry: OK, I'll get the coolers.

3. **Barbara:** Before you start counting the vials with Larry, I need to talk to you.

   Maria: What's up, boss?

   Barbara: I was unhappy with the disposal of used syringes at our clinic yesterday.

   Maria: The local nurses just didn't follow my directions. When I was watching them, they did what they were supposed to do. But if I wasn't watching, they'd be very careless.

   Barbara: I don't really care how it happened. I only care that there aren't any mistakes tomorrow. That's why you have to supervise the local workers again tomorrow.

   Maria: Do I have to? It's Larry's turn.

   Barbara: I don't care whose turn it is, I want you to do it right.

   Maria: All right.

4. **Jim:** Larry, do you need a hand with the vials? I know that Maria was going to help you, but it looks like she and Barbara are having a big conversation. I'm not doing anything right now.

   Larry: Hey, Jim, thanks, I'd appreciate it.

5. **Barbara:** Jim, thanks for helping Larry with that. When you guys are done, can you help me?

   Jim: Sure, no problem….OK

   Barbara: Jim, I know that it's not your job to supervise anyone on the team, but I'd feel better if you could watch Maria and the local nurses. I won't have time tomorrow, and you're usually near the local nurses, too. Just be sure that everyone follows the safety rules, that's all.

   Jim: I'm not crazy about it, but if you think it's really necessary, I'll do it.

6. **Jim:** OK, it seems that we're done with everything for now. I'll just look over the check-list. Uh-oh, there's still a few things that we can take care of today.

   Maria: What?

   Jim: Maria, you bring in the sterilizing equipment from the van. Larry, you get the extra box of syringes, and I'll grab the bags of extra gauze.

   Maria: Hey, who made you the boss?

   Larry: Maria, who cares? Let's just finish up so we can relax a little.

Track 13. Page 300, Lesson 27, Part 2, Exercise D

1. Mr. Richards, if you had brought all the necessary documents, you would have received your passport last week.
2. Mr. Richards, you could have submitted your passport application at the Post Office if you hadn't needed your passport right away.
3. If your photo were the right size, we could process the paperwork right away.
4. Your passport would have been ready earlier if we'd had all of the paperwork.
5. We couldn't have processed your paperwork if you hadn't included your birth certificate.
6. Had you included extra postage, we would have sent your passport by express mail.
7. Miss Sanders, if you had typed in the correct pin number, the ATM machine wouldn't have rejected your bank card.
8. Miss Sanders, had you typed in the correct number the second time, the ATM machine would have recognized your card.
9. Were your PIN number valid, you could withdraw money from your account.
10. If you hadn't typed in the wrong number a third time, the ATM machine wouldn't have locked out your card.

Track 15. Page 313, Lesson 28, Part 2, Exercise D

Interviewer: Dr. Vincenzi, your work with creatures that live in extreme conditions has caught the media's attention in the last few weeks. How did you become involved in marine science?

Vincenzi: I suppose that everyone has heard the story of the researchers on the submersible the *Alvin*—the men who were looking for a hydrothermal vent near the Galapagos Islands and found all of the fish, mussels, clams and crabs at 8,200 feet below the surface.

Interviewer: Evidently they were quite astonished by the sight.

Vincenzi: Who would've expected such a sight? Anyway, when they returned, they call the Wood Hole Oceanographic Institution to tell the exciting news. If they'd been biologists, it would've been more believable. I suppose that the staff at Wood Hole wished that they had seen the creatures first. This happened back in 1977 when I was in high school.

Interviewer: How did you get interested in deep sea creatures in high school?

Vincenzi: If it hadn't been for my teacher Mr. Hughes, I'd be a chemist today! He urged all of us to keep up with scientific news to plan a career for the future. By the time I got to graduate school, there was already extensive research on these life forms. Luckily for me, there are still many questions to be answered.

Interviewer: Do you actually go down to the black smokers as they're called to do your research?

Vincenzi: Unless there's evidence of a new life form near the black smoker, I leave the fieldwork to my research assistants. I feel that my time is better spent in the lab with my staff.

Interviewer: Suppose that you hadn't discovered the symbiotic relationship between bacteria and clams from the black smoker in the Gulf of Mexico?

Vincenzi: Actually, there are several labs studying these symbiotic relationships, so someone would have found these particular results if I hadn't.

Track 17. Page 323, Lesson 29, Part 2, Exercise C

1. **Coach Bella Lyons:** We're never going to win if you don't hustle a little more. I don't see any one of you out there trying to get the ball. Are you just going to let them beat us without putting up a fight?

2. **Coach Lyons:** Rina, are you here to play today or are you just going to let everyone else run with the ball?

   Rina: I was trying, Coach, but the other team has me covered all of the time. They know that I'm the best shooter, and they won't let me close to the basket. They put their best players on me.

   Coach Lyons: That's funny, I didn't see you put much effort into breaking away from them.

3. **Vanessa:** Coach, that's not fair. It seems to me that they have been guarding Rina much more than the rest of us. Every time I try to pass the ball to her, there are two players right there. I was afraid that they'd steal the ball.

4. **Coach Lyons:** Well, ladies, the clock is ticking and they're ahead by 20 points. What do you think is going to happen if you don't start making some baskets soon? I'm thinking about replacing all of you with the other players on the bench. Maybe they will show a little more hustle than all of you.

5. **Rina:** Coach, don't do that. We worked too hard for this. Give us another chance!

   Vanessa: Rina's right, Coach. We can do it.

   Coach Lyons: Right now they seem to want this game more than you do. It's time to stop making excuses for yourselves. Right now they are in charge of the game and they know it. Go out there and follow our game plan. It's worked before and it'll work again.

Track 19. Page 333, Lesson 30, Part 2, Exercise C

1. **Interviewer:** Senator Koloski, in your recent speech at State University there were relatively few students in the audience. Does the students' apparent lack of interest in your party's position on higher education concern you?

   Senator K: Of course, I was disappointed in the low attendance, but it is possible that students think that listening to a politician's speech is a waste of time.

2. **Interviewer:** How could it be a waste of time since you were talking about issues related to students' own interests?

   Senator K: I mean that it's quite likely that young people would appreciate it if they could read my ideas on a blog, for example.

3. **Interviewer:** What part of your message would probably appeal to students the most?

   Senator K: I expect that most college students care about how they will pay their rising tuition costs in the next few years.

4. **Senator K:** I also strongly suspect that students these days worry that they won't be able to pay back their college loans and that they will have credit problems later.

5. **Interviewer:** What is your party's position on college tuition and access to higher education?

   Senator K: Access to a college education brings benefits to students and to our economy. Elected officials have the responsibility of making education affordable.

6. **Interviewer:** But how can you keep costs down? It seems like tuition costs rise every year.

   Senator K: As elected officials, it is absolutely necessary for us to propose that we spend more tax dollars on education so that we can keep tuition costs from rising so quickly.